The Whispering Giant: The Story of the
Bristol Britannia

Aircraft of Distinction

SCOVAL
PUBLISHING LTD

Written by Frank McKim and Scott Henderson

British Library Cataloguing in Publication Data
A catalogue record for this book is available from the British Library

ISBN: 1 902236 08 4

Published by:
SCOVAL Publishing Ltd
PO BOX 36
Ponteland
Newcastle-upon-Tyne
NE20 9WE
England
Tel: (01661) 820 838
Fax: (01661) 822 911
email: scovalpublishing@tiscali.co.uk

Printed by Kyodo Printing Co (S'Pore) Pte Ltd
Singapore

Edited by S Henderson, C Hymers and R James
Produced and typeset in 11pt on 13pt Quorum by J.R. Taylor
Designed by Scott Henderson, for SCOVAL Publishing Ltd

CONTENTS

ACKNOWLEDGMENTS

In seeking out information to make the writing of this book possible, I have repeatedly been made aware that my research has taken me back halfway to the beginning of aviation history. Many of the people who I would like to have talked to are, alas, no longer with us. Consequently I have from time to time had to make guesses in the absence of definite memories from people who were 'there'. I hope that I have not therefore done less than justice to various parts of the story.

In particular I am most grateful for help from the following people — Chief Test Pilot Walter Gibb, Sqd Ldr Tony Davies, Pilots John (Bill) Hickox and Dan Taylor, Flt Lts Alex Balfour, Flight Engineers Gary Mc Intosh and Arthur Mitchell, also Arthur Brown and people from the Rolls-Royce Heritage Trust including Peter Pavey, Alan Baxter, Ernie Brook and John Detheridge, also Roger Carvell and various people from the Britannia Aircraft Preservation Trust including Roger Hargreaves and Ian Lansdown. I was also able to talk to some people who flew in Britannias as passengers, in various capacities, among them Lady Pamela Barnett, wife of the late Air Marshal Sir Denis Barnett, and to the then young National Service men, Alan Clegg and Graham Davies, and to Bob Rham who flew out to the Far East as a young businessman. I am also very grateful to Scoval Publishing in general and Scott Henderson in particular for their enthusiastic support and help, and special thanks to Nick Webb for the Britannia colour drawings and Roy James for checking and verifying information.

An invaluable source of information has been the various previously published books and articles, and I am very grateful to those people who have allowed me to use data which they have assembled. The material which I found useful includes;

'A span of wings' by Sir Archibald Russell, 'Not much of an engineer' by Sir Stanley Hooker, 'Sent flying' by Bill Pegg, 'Both feet in the air' by A S Jackson, 'A history of the Bristol Britannia' by David Littlefield, 'The Whispering Giant in Uniform' and 'Tales from the Crewroom' by Sqd Ldr David Berry, 'Airlines & Airliners, No. 4, Bristol Britannia' Editor Phil Lo Bao, Many articles in 'Propliner', in 'Flight' and in 'Bristol Quarterly'. I hope that readers will feel that I have done justice to the history of this remarkable aircraft. What I have written is, of course, my responsibility, but I would be very grateful for any contact from those who can point out errors which I may have inadvertently made.

FOREWORD

The author has written a very interesting and comprehensive book, giving an insight into the development of the Britannia aircraft, the first civil aeroplane to cross the Atlantic both ways non-stop.

The British Aircraft Industry spent all of World War II producing only fighters and bombers. But in 1943 the Prime Minister set up a committee with Lord Brabazon as chairman, to come forward with recommendations for the types of civil aircraft to be produced for use after the end of hostilities. Uppermost in their minds was one to be able to cross the Atlantic from East to West. Hence their first recommendation was for the giant Brabazon I, with an all-up weight of 330,000lb, a wing span of 230ft, powered by eight Proteus prop-jet engines geared together in pairs. As the engines were still under development, it was agreed to build a prototype powered by eight Bristol Centaurus piston engines.

It was a wonderful achievement by the Bristol Aeroplane Company to get this giant aircraft flying in 1949. It was a fine aeroplane to fly and met the specification. But it did not go into production because the specification proved to be wrong for the time. However the 390 hours of flying development which we did, of which I was privileged to do half, was not wasted as it gave the company valuable data on large aircraft and their complicated systems.

Following the Brabazon, the Company gained a contract to build an aircraft to fly the Empire routes, previously carried out by flying boats. Originally the aircraft was to be powered by Centaurus engines with direct fuel injection. When the work was well advanced, it was requested that the design should change, with the engines now being Proteus prop-jets. So the Britannia was born. Twelve of these were made, then it was decided to extend the aircraft in size and range, to fly the Atlantic route.

The Company was faced with producing a new aircraft that was growing like 'Topsy', with new engines which needed a great deal of development, new control systems, new electrical systems, a pressurisation and air conditioning system, electric throttles and above all it was to operate in an altitude band between 25,000 and 35,000ft which hitherto civil aircraft had not flown in for any length of time. All this development took much longer than anticipated and sadly involved two crashes.

Finally, when the Britannia had obtained its certificate of airworthiness, the customer (BOAC) began route proving. It was then found that the engines misbehaved in clouds at cruising altitude in the tropics. This caused further delay but like many things, once we had found the cause, the remedy was quite simple; 'B' skin jets were fitted in the bend in the engine air intake. This cured the problem.

At long last the Britannia went into service, the most tested civil aircraft of its time. It proved very popular with passengers and air crew, economical and quiet which earned it the name 'Whispering Giant'. Its service life, because of the delays, was not as long as had been hoped for, as it was overtaken by the jet aircraft.

However, the Bristol factories can be proud of their record, as of the four transatlantic airliners made in Britain since World War II, three of these and their engines came from these factories, namely the Brabazon, Britannia and Concorde.

Walter F Gibb, D.S.O., D.F.C., J.P.
Last Chief Test Pilot of Bristol Aeroplane Company

FROM THE BRABAZON COMMITTEE TO THE BRISTOL BRITANNIA

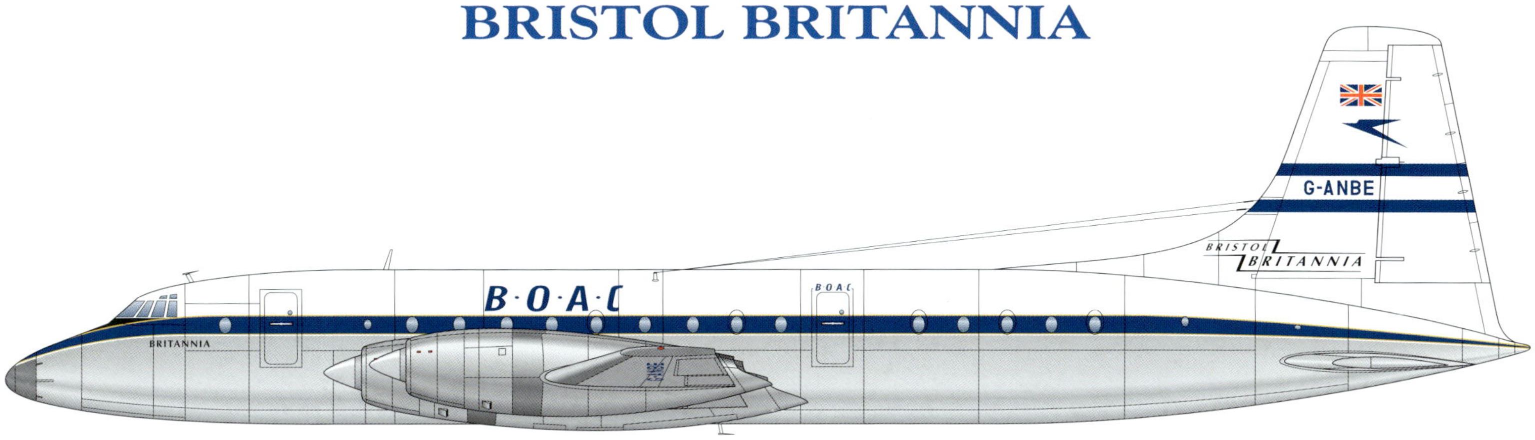

The origin of the Bristol Britannia can be traced to the recommendations of the Brabazon Committee, set up by the British Government during World War II to consider the post-war requirements of British civil aviation. In 1943 the Committee suggested that various different types of aircraft should be developed, one of which, termed the Brabazon III, was a long-range passenger transport with an all-up weight of about 100,000lb, to carry 32 passengers at a speed of 300mph with stage lengths of 2,500miles and therefore able to fly BOAC's post-war Empire routes.

An initial proposal to meet this requirement was produced by Avro, but this was withdrawn in 1947. By then the American Lockheed Constellation had become established as an efficient and economical airliner, so BOAC ordered Lockheed Constellations, with the intention of operating these until a suitable British aircraft was produced.

BOAC's updated requirements, set out in Specification 2/47 in early 1947, called for a new design. The first Bristol Aeroplane Company submission for this specification involved

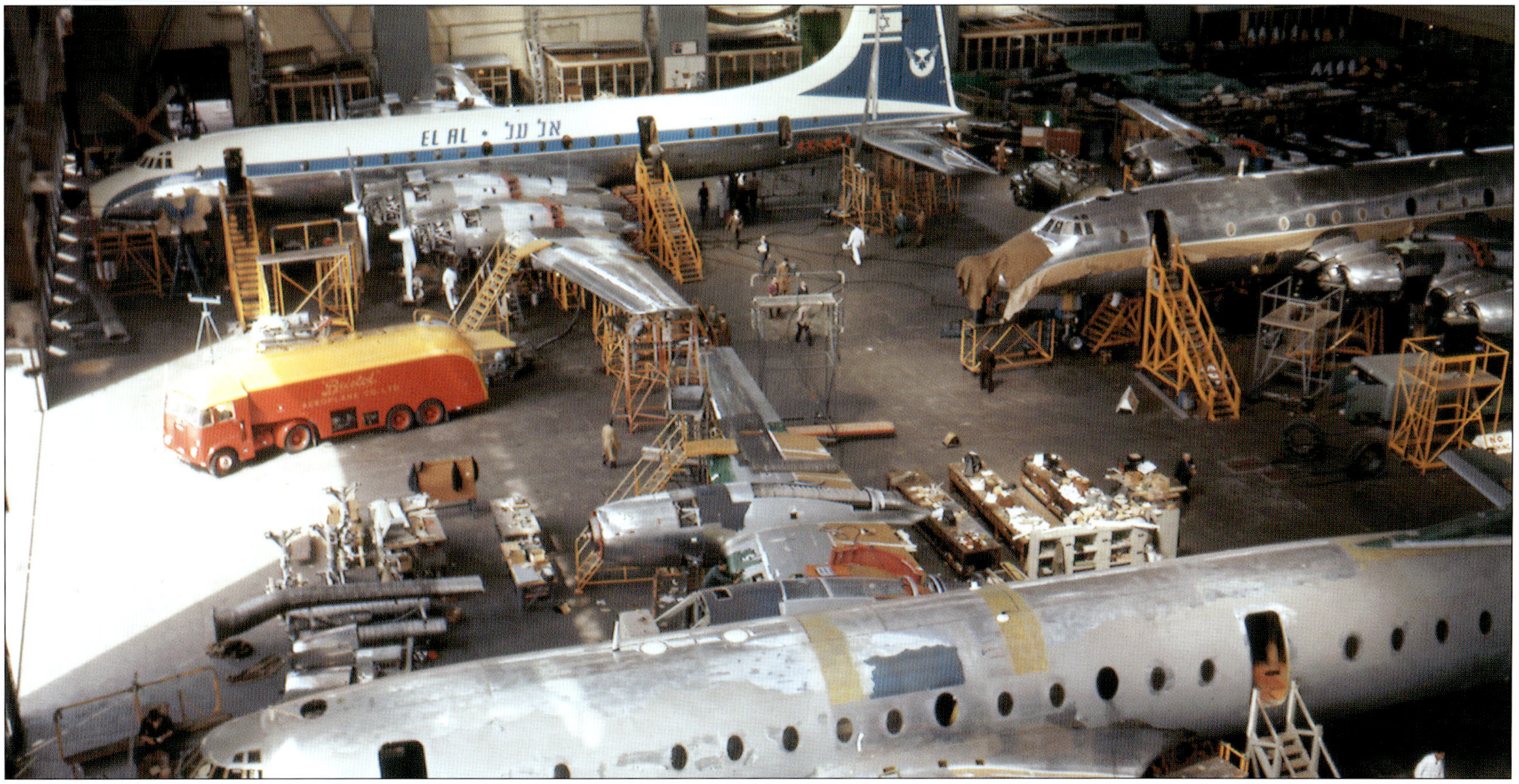

Three aircraft take shape inside the Brabazon hanger in 1956, including the ill fated 4X-AGA which crashed with the loss of 126 lives in April 1964 at Nicosia, Cyprus, when in the service of Globe Air.

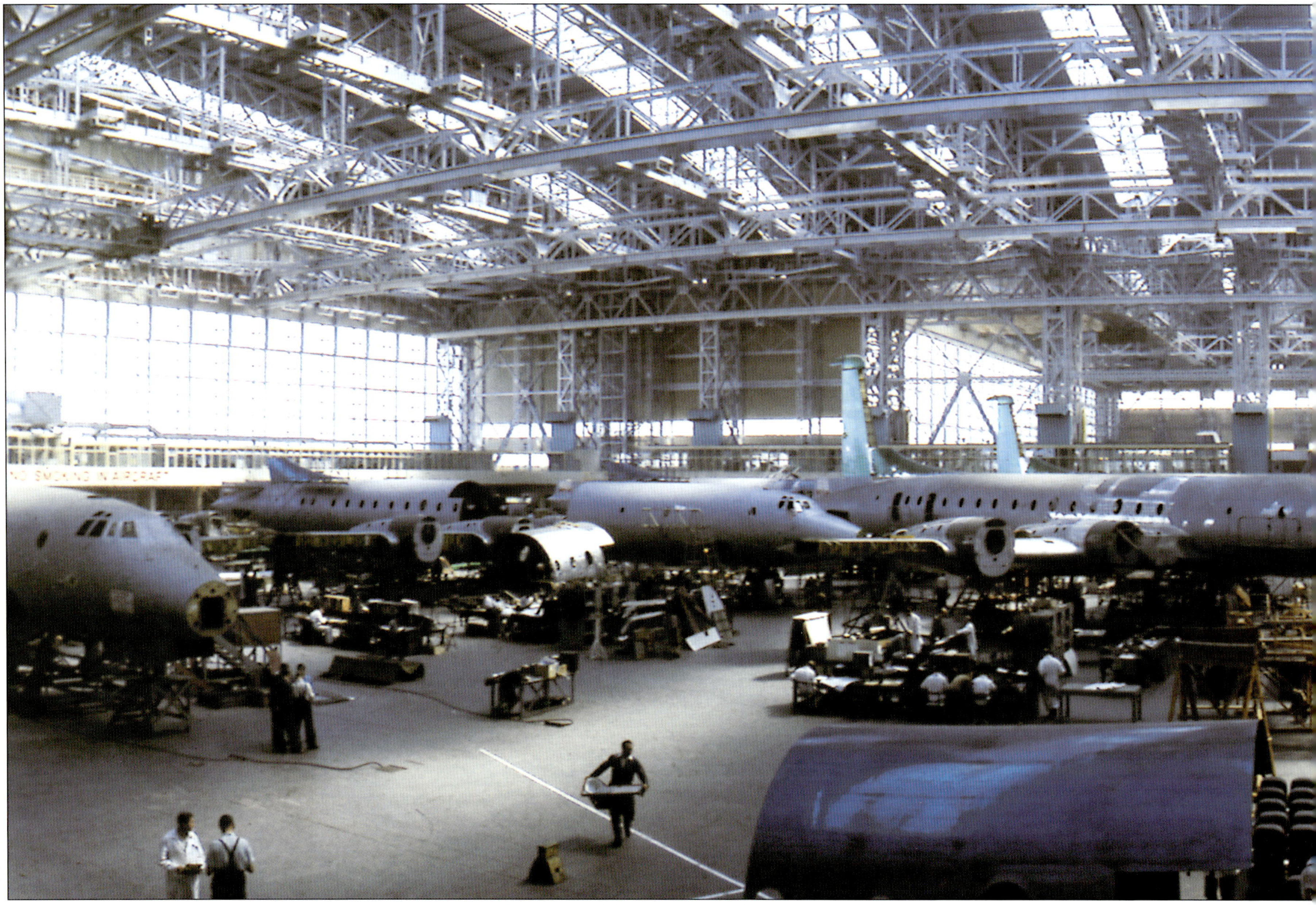

A spectacular view across the central bay of the assembly hanger at Bristol showing the enormous span of producton, used to build Concorde, convert civil Vickers VC10s to air-to-air tankers for the Royal Air Force,

using a slightly strengthened Lockheed Constellation airframe with four British-made Bristol Centaurus piston engines, built as a joint Anglo-American project. This project was vetoed by the British Government because of its dollar component.

Various firms submitted further proposals but the most promising was thought to be the Bristol Type 175, later to be named the Britannia. In October 1947 a joint working party of BOAC and Bristol personnel met to discuss the detailed size of the proposed aircraft. The initial Bristol proposal was for an aircraft of an all-up weight of 94,000lb, for 32-36 passengers, with a wing span of 120ft, wing area 1620sq.ft and powered by four Centaurus 662 radial piston engines.

The final working party proposal was for an aircraft with an all-up weight of 103,000lb, for 42-48 passengers, with a wing span 130ft and wing area 1,775sq.ft. The payload was to be carried at 310mph from Johannesburg to Nairobi against the maximum likely headwind, and the engines were to be four Centaurus radials. However, a new engine, the Proteus turbo-prop, was being developed by Bristol and it was suggested that this might be a more attractive power plant, although its performance was not guaranteed at that stage (October 1947).

In February 1948 the British Government's Ministry of Supply agreed to order several prototypes of Type 175, provided that BOAC order at least 25 production aircraft (and this even before the maiden flight of the prototype). BOAC found the risk of this too great to accept, and in July 1948 the Ministry decided to order three prototypes without waiting for the order from BOAC.

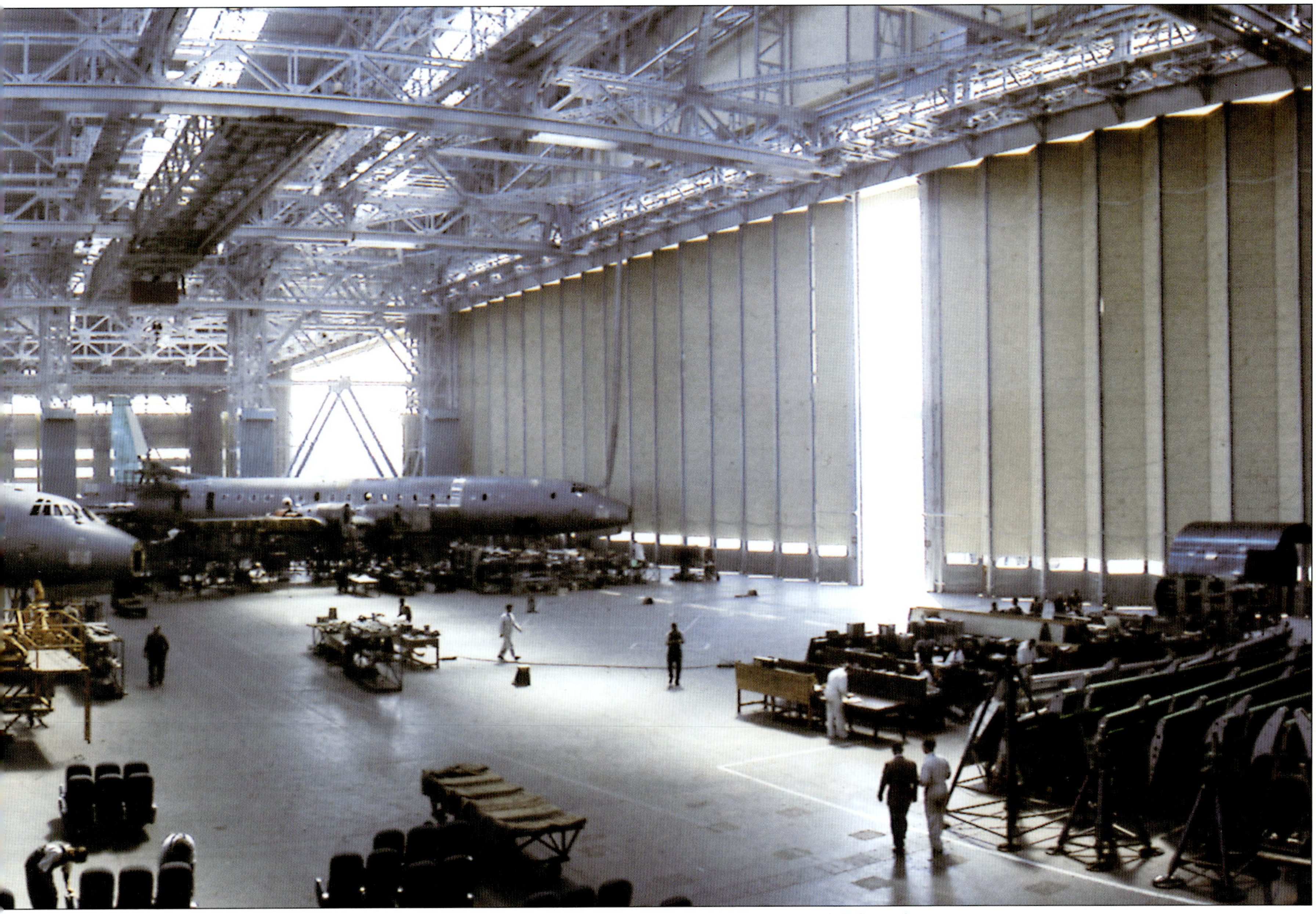

e building first constructed to house the ill fated Bristol Brabazon then later, after the end of Britannia
nd which today both services and converts Airbus A300 aircraft from passenger airliners to freighters.

In October 1948 BOAC decided to take an interest in the use of the new Proteus engine. Further discussions between BOAC and Bristol resulted in an updated version of the aircraft, with a wing span of 140ft, wing area of 2,055sq.ft and an all-up weight of 118,000lb with Centaurus engines or 119,000lb with Proteus engines. The interior layout would accommodate up to 64 day passengers or 38 sleeping berths.

In November 1948 BOAC agreed to order 25 of these aircraft, designed to take Proteus engines but initially to be fitted with Centaurus (the actual contract was not signed until July 1949). The plan was to use them on the routes to India, Pakistan and beyond.

During the intervening months, Bristol considered the possibility of getting the Type 175 powered by Proteus engines to cross the North Atlantic. With an all-up weight of 130,000lb, with fuel tankage increased to 5,790 Imperial gallons, they concluded that it would be possible to take a payload of 23,000lb across the North Atlantic, allowing for up to 83 passengers. This slightly greater size and weight required a four-wheeled bogie instead of twin wheels for each main undercarriage unit, and each unit had to retract backwards rather than sideways because of the engine tail-pipes. But in other respects the overall design remained the same, although the interior layout of the passenger space had to be altered.

Furthermore, during 1950 an uprated Proteus engine was being very successfully developed so, in December, BOAC asked for all its ordered aircraft to be delivered with Proteus engines. They also asked for the option to reduce their order

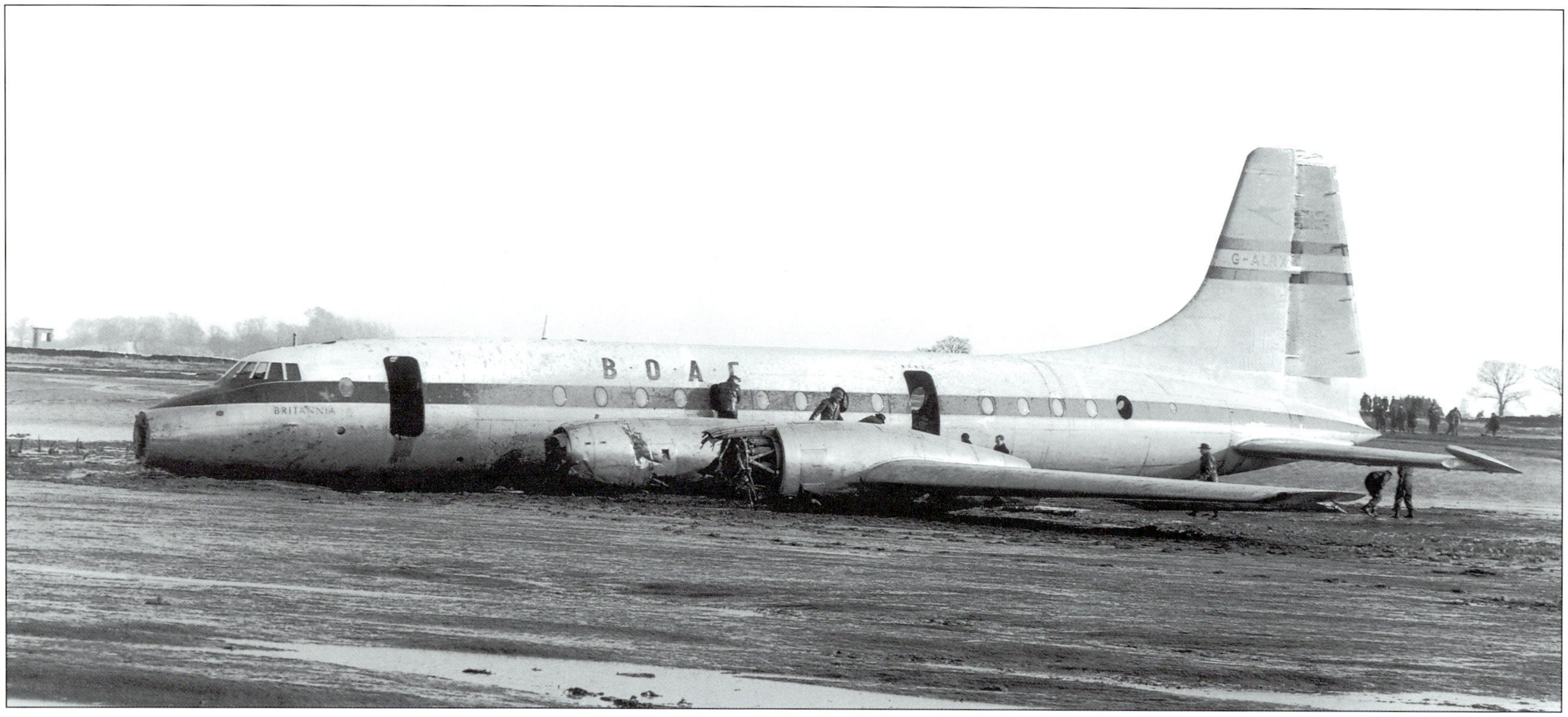

G-ALRX sits on the River Severn mud after the unfortunate crash landing on the morning of 4th February 1954. Luckily all thirteen people aboard survived.

from 25 to fifteen aircraft. The deletion of the option of Centaurus engines allowed a reduction in the frontal area of the nacelles and, at the same time, the wing flaps were changed from the Fowler type to the more efficient double-slotted design.

The first aircraft to be completed incorporating these various changes was registered as G-ALBO in July 1952 and painted in BOAC colours. It was fitted with Proteus 625 engines and its maiden flight was on the 16th August 1952, with Bristol's chief test pilot Bill Pegg in charge.

Fig. 1

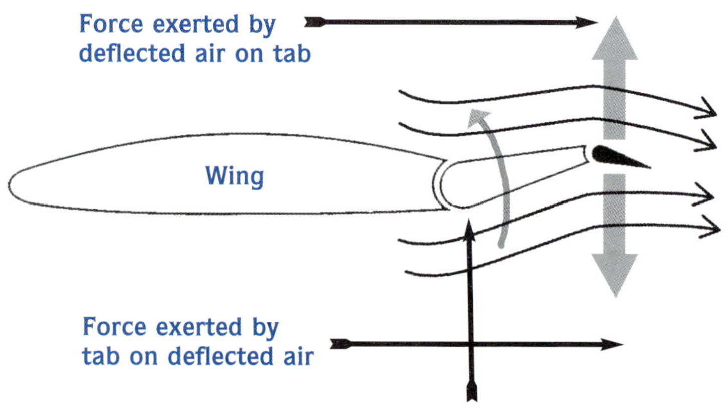

The force exerted by the deflected air on the tab causes the whole control surface to rotate as shown by the curved grey arrow. The force needed to operate the tab is considerably less than that needed to operate the whole control surface directly.

From this point onwards the development story can be divided into two parts; matters concerning the engines and matters concerning the airframe. Engine problems were substantial and are dealt with in the next chapter. Airframe problems were less severe and are dealt with here.

Immediately on take-off on the maiden flight, it was clear that the aircraft had a handling problem. It was very sensitive to movement of the elevators - small movements of the control column made the whole plane climb steeply or dive downwards. The reason for this was associated with the means of control of moveable control surfaces in an aircraft the size of the Britannia. In a small single seater aircraft, there can be a direct mechanical linkage between the pilot's control column and the control surfaces on the wing or tail plane of the aircraft. But in the Britannia, and even more in larger aircraft like the Boeing 747 jumbo-jet, the control surfaces are so large that they would require a super-human force on the control column to move them enough.

One way round this problem is to fit so-called tabs onto the trailing edge of the surfaces to be moved. The principle is indicated in Figure 1. If the small tab on the trailing edge of, say, the rudder is moved as shown, caused by the action of the pilot on his control column, then the aerodynamic force on the tab will cause the main surface to rotate in the opposite direction. The movement of the main surface is what produces the change in direction of the whole aircraft, but this is achieved by the pilot exerting a relatively small force on the small tab at the rear end of the main control surface.

On the maiden flight on 16th August 1952, the size and shape of the tabs were such that the pilot could get no 'feel' of what he was doing to the control surfaces when moving the control column. However, it was comparatively easy to adjust the tabs so that some 'feel' could be re-introduced to the flight deck, and this was done for all subsequent flights.

The maiden flight also showed up a problem with the locking mechanism on the main undercarriage. After heavy braking, the main wheels could overheat and subsequently cause bearings to seize up, so that the undercarriage would not lock down. Therefore the bearing dimensions had to be altered slightly. There was also a separate problem with the locking of the nose-wheel, caused by the small doors used to shut off the nose-wheel mechanism being unable to open unless the aircraft speed was just above the touch-down speed. A simple adjustment put that system right.

These modifications were quickly put in hand and four days later the aircraft flew again, successfully. The following month (September 1952), the Britannia made its first public appearance at the SBAC (Farnborough) Air Show.

During the next few months of test flying, some slight modifications to the airframe were introduced. The engine nacelle shapes were improved, and the wing tips were slightly extended and turned up to improve the lateral stability of the aircraft. Controls to the ailerons, elevators and inboard aileron servo-tabs were also adjusted to improve the handling of the aircraft during the approach to landing. The most important development, however, was the installation of the new Proteus 705 engines in August 1953. G-ALBO flew with these engines at the SBAC Show in September 1953.

The second prototype, registered as G-ALRX, first flew on 23rd December 1953 but it had a short life. On 4th February 1954, on a routine test flight, it suffered a failure in one engine (see next chapter) as a result of which it had to crash land in mud on the edge of the River Severn and a rising tide caused it to be damaged beyond repair.

This loss severely restricted the flight test and development programme as it left only one aircraft airworthy, G-ALBO, which was modified up to the newer 140,000lb all-up weight standard which G-ALRX had. After modifications, G-ALBO resumed test flying in March 1954 but even this did not last long. In May, during a stalling test, the flaps on one side of the aircraft would not retract due to the failure of the torque tube controlling them. This caused the aircraft to go into a rapid roll, only checked by the quick action of the test pilot, Walter Gibb. Nonetheless, the airframe had been subjected to considerable stress as a result and the aircraft had to be grounded while repairs were carried out.

The reason for the torque tube failure was established. There were two torque tubes on each wing, the inner one controlling the inner flap and the outer mechanism, and the outer one turned by the inner tube controlling just the outer flap. Both tubes looked the same but the inner tube was thicker and stronger, and at some stage two outer tubes had been fitted to the same wing by mistake. The outer tube in the inner position was the one which failed. From then on, the inner and outer tubes were made with the same external and internal diameters as each other, and of course with the stronger dimension, so that the same mistake could never occur again.

But these mishaps were beginning to cause serious delays to the introduction of the aircraft for commercial use. BOAC had originally planned to start carrying fare-paying passengers in

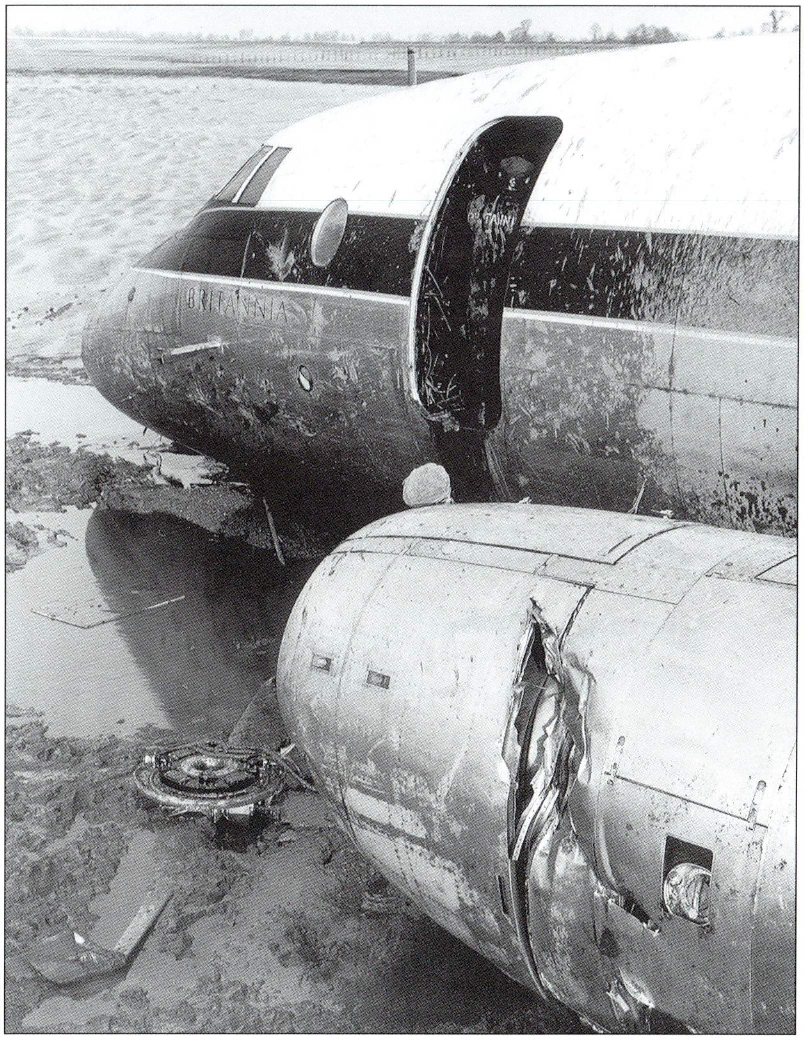

An alternative view of G-ALRX shows the damage caused to the aircraft during the crash landing

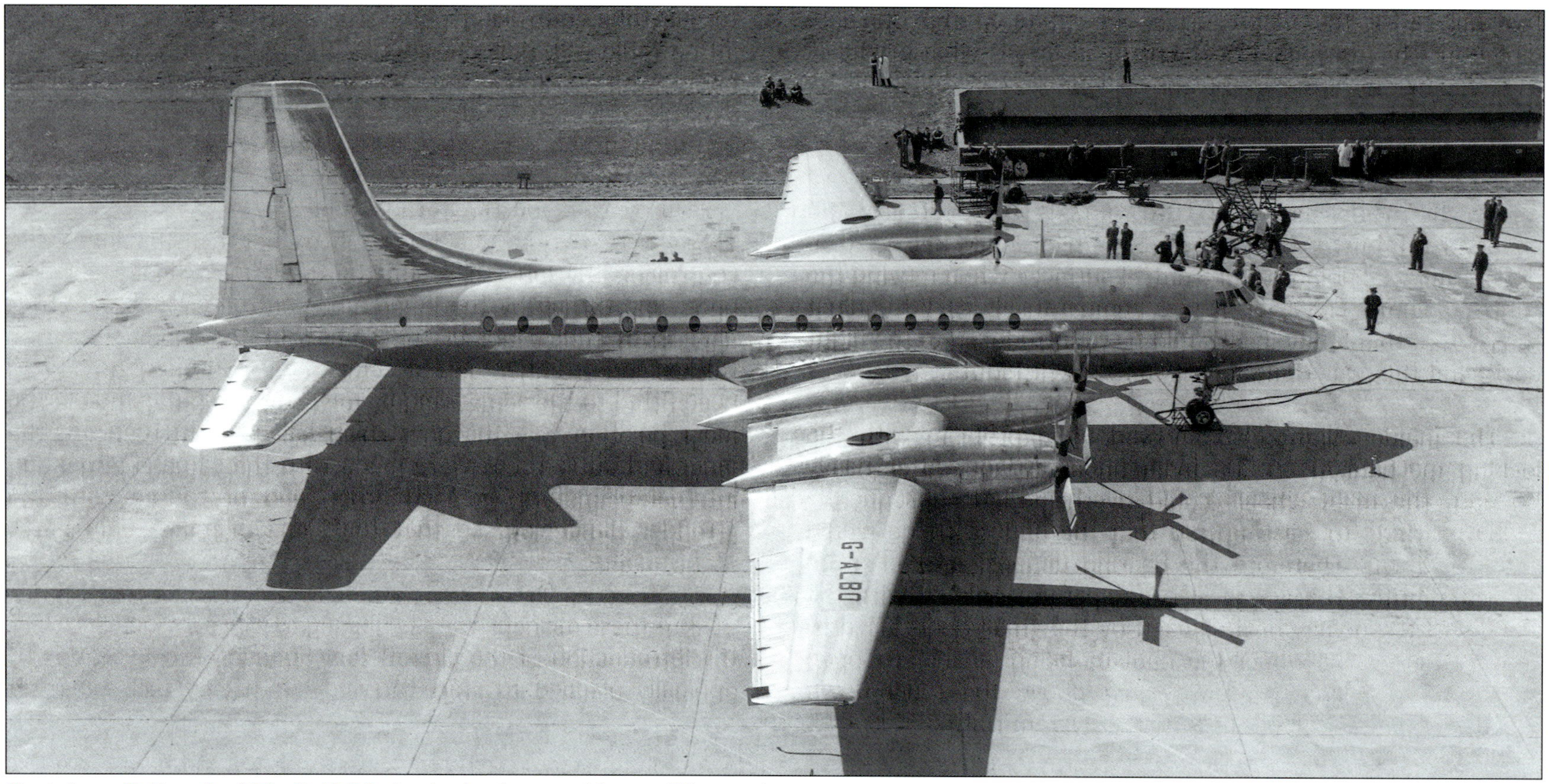

Prototype Britannia 100, G-ALBO, basks in the sunshine at Filton prior to the application of BOAC livery which it was to carry throughout certification trials. Note the early engine exhaust location on top of the engine nacelle.

May 1954, which was obviously now impossible. And there was a further complication when, in April 1954, all Comet I aircraft were grounded because of two unexplained crashes. Subsequent investigation showed the cause as an explosive decompression of the fuselage following a metal fatigue rupture. BOAC therefore demanded an especially rigorous testing of the Britannia airframe to ensure that it was completely safe, and this testing of prototype fuselages under pressure cycles in a water tank further lengthened the test procedure.

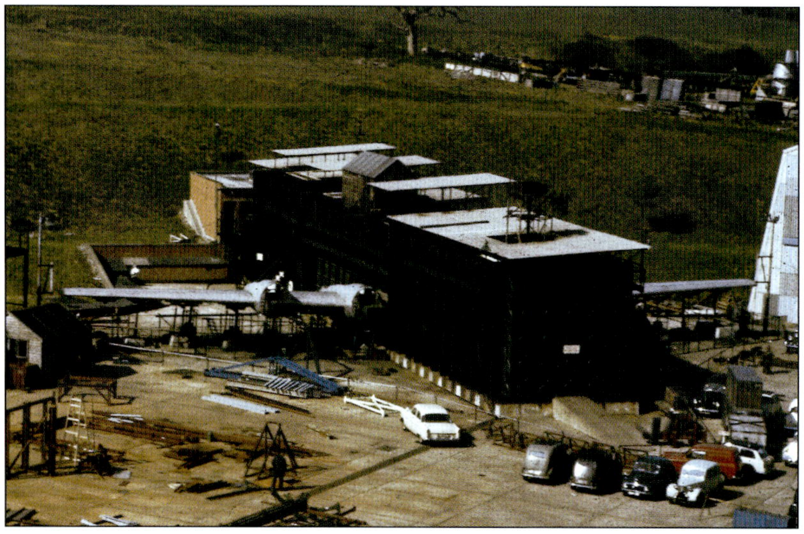

A Britannia airframe undergoing pressure testing in the water tank especially constructed for the purpose at Farnborough.

The test principle was to immerse the whole fuselage in a water tank, flooded with water inside and out. If the pressure of the water inside the fuselage is increased while that outside stays the same, the pressure difference produces an effect on the fuselage structure as if the air pressure inside a flying fuselage had stayed the same while the air pressure outside was reduced. But it is much easier to vary the water pressure on a fuselage in a tank than it would be to vary the air pressure outside a fuselage, even if the fuselage remained in a test laboratory rather than be part of a flying aircraft.

The test procedure subjects the fuselage to cycles of water pressure inside the fuselage, keeping the pressure outside constant, so as to establish how many pressure cycles the fuselage can withstand without any metal failure. This test was carried out on a Britannia fuselage.

The testing programme speeded up on the 5th September 1954 when the first production Britannia, G-ANBA, had its maiden flight, and more so with the addition of G-ANBB and G-ANBC during the first half of 1955. With the four aircraft (including G-ALBO) available, rapid progress was made.

The usual range of hot and cold trials were carried out, the hot ones in Africa and the cold ones in Canada. In addition,

G-ANBC was used by BOAC for route-proving and publicity flights over the intended routes to Africa and Asia. With all the flight trials successfully completed, the Britannia was given a full Certificate of Airworthiness on 30th December 1955. Immediately after that, at a ceremony at London (Heathrow), two Britannias, G-ANBC and G-ANBD, were handed over by Bristol to BOAC.

There then followed an intensive crew training programme over the next four months, but during this time a minor problem occurred involving condensation freezing in an engine gear box. It was easily cured, albeit causing a delay of two weeks in the programme, but on 4th April 1956 a much more serious incident occurred when all four engines on a Britannia, flying near Salisbury (Harare), suffered 'flame out'. There was obviously something seriously wrong with the Proteus engines. Finding out what it was and correcting this took many months, and is told in the next chapter. It was probably the main reason for the limited sales success of the Britannia aircraft in the world's markets.

There was another event which occurred during the flight testing of the first Series 300 aircraft. On 6th November 1957 the aircraft G-ANCA had been on a test flight lasting 1hr 40min with no evidence of malfunction when, just as she was to turn to port in order to land at Filton, she banked steeply to starboard. In spite of the efforts of the two pilots, she could not be brought under control again and crashed into a wood at Downend Bristol. Tragically all fifteen people on board were killed.

The official investigation into the accident centred on the autopilot/flight control system. There was no evidence of failure before the crash in the airframe, main flying controls, engines or propellers, but there was some evidence to suggest that the pilots had been trying to override the autopilot's instructions to the control surfaces. Whilst the investigation was proceeding, other incidents were reported (although none involved crashes) which suggested a similar cause. On 10th January 1958, on the maiden flight of Series 312, G-AOVG, the pilot ran into serious problems in controlling the aircraft and control was only re-established after cutting off the electrical supply to the autopilot.

A subsequent investigation of G-AOVG found a design fault in the electrical circuitry of the autopilot/flight system which, when corrected, enabled normal operation of the flight system to take place. The same design fault was present in G-ANCA.

A similar problem was experienced on Series 302 Britannia, XA-MEC, on a flight from Mexico City to Brownsville, Texas on 31st January 1958. There is also an unconfirmed report of a similar incident on a Series 302 Britannia which went out of control at 12,000ft when being

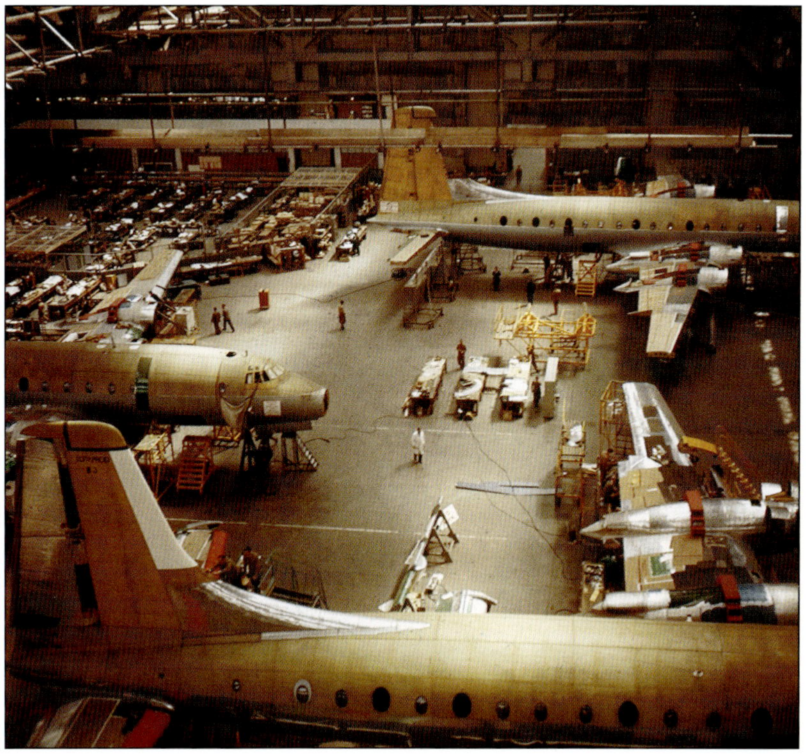

Above: A view of aircraft under construction taken from the roof of the Brabazon hanger.
Below: Britannia 102 aircraft for BOAC about to emerge from the hanger prior to flight trials.

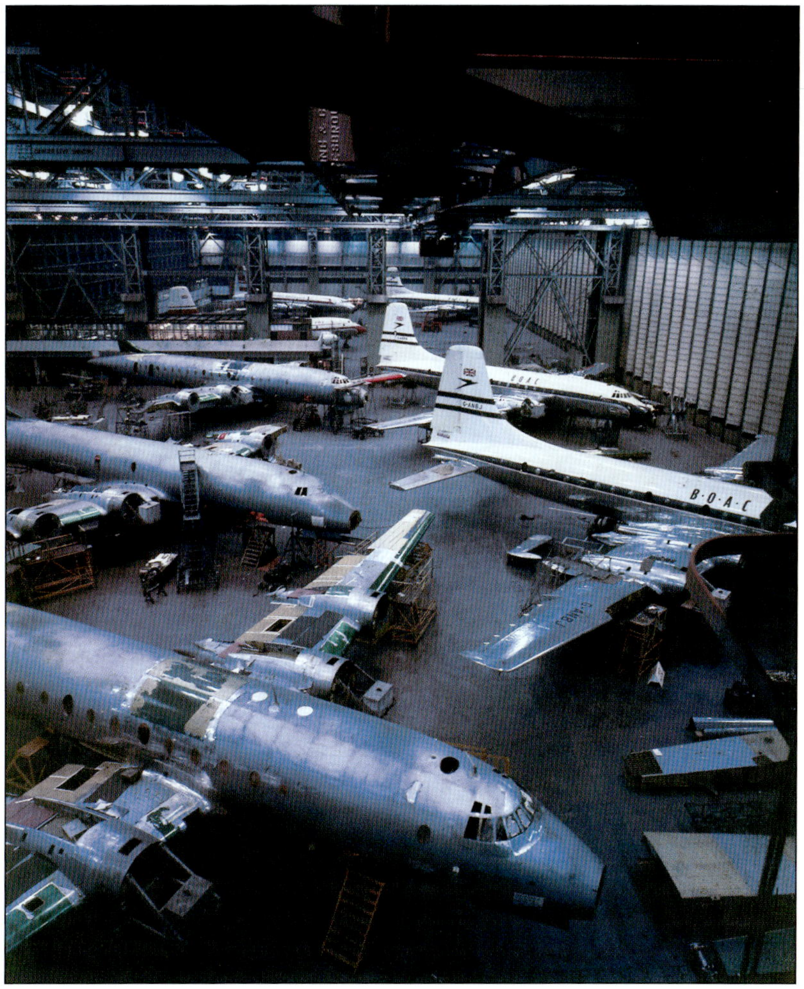

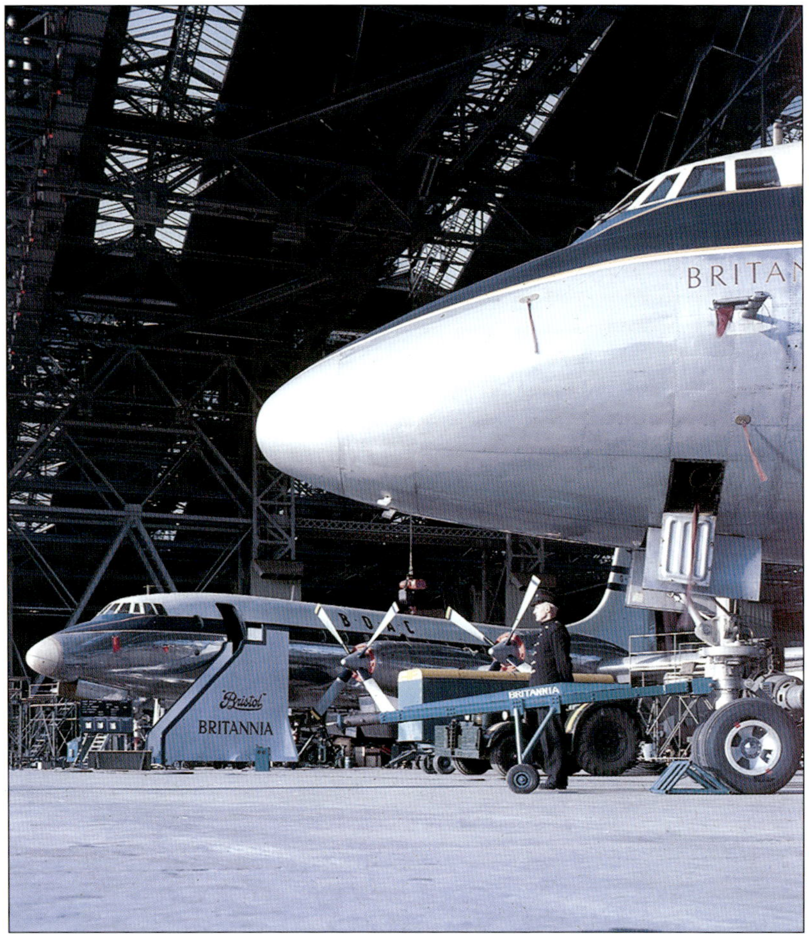

Second prototype Series 101 Britannia G-ALRX nears completion in the Brabazon hanger, in company with the first prototype aircraft G-ALBO.

flown out of Filton by Captain Griffiths. It was said that the plane descended to below 10,000ft before control was re-established and Captain Griffiths reported an autopilot/aileron problem when he landed, although subsequent ground inspection found no fault.

The autopilot manufacturers conducted their own tests and concluded that the autopilot could not have caused the aircraft to behave as she did, and therefore accepted no responsibility for the crash of G-ANCA at Downend, Bristol. Nevertheless, the final report into the crash concluded "The accident was the result of the aircraft developing a very steep descending turn to the right which the pilot was unable to control. The reason for this could not be determined but the possibility that it occurred as a result of malfunctioning of the autopilot cannot be dismissed." Before the official investigation report was published, however, the manufacturers had modified the system fitted to Britannias, as indicated after the investigation of G-AOVG, and no further control irregularities were reported thereafter.

It should be noted that this incident made no difference to the Certificate of Airworthiness which had been granted to the Britannia aircraft. It had been deemed airworthy and continued to be regarded so.

One further point should be made about the Britannia. When it first appeared, various people commented on how complex it was electrically and in other respects. Some flight engineers referred to it not as 'The Whispering Giant' but as 'The Rumbling Rectifier'. A joke about it was that it was an aircraft in which the pilot had no direct contact with the control surfaces, and in which the engine had no direct connection to the propellers.

It certainly represented a large step forward compared with other aircraft of comparable size available at the time. However, once the engine problems had been overcome and once the pilots, flight engineers, ground service personnel and others had got used to how it was built, they found it more than acceptable. One of the experienced pilots I talked to said it was 'a superb aircraft'.

By comparison with the present-day aircraft, it seems very 'low-tech' which just shows how we all find change difficult to accept. Changes are not always for the better, but often they are and we find these take some time to adjust to. In the case of the Britannia aircraft, the changes compared with what had gone before were considerable, but they were changes which pointed the way forward and more recent aircraft have moved much further in the same direction.

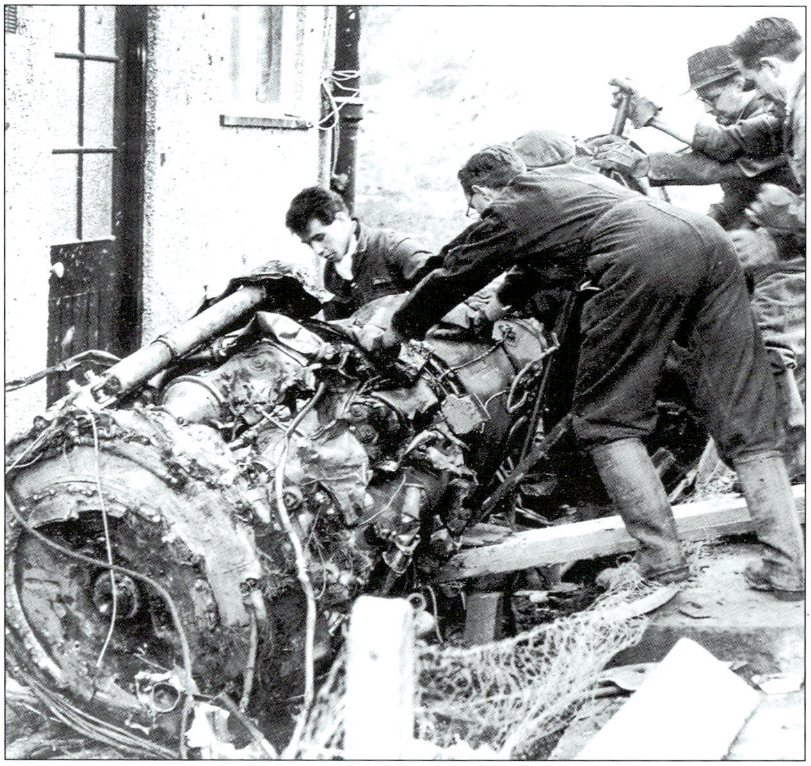

Bristol engineers struggle to recover the remains of the engine nacelle of G-ANCA, the first Series 300 built, following the tragic crash of the aircraft at Downend Bristol on 6th November 1957.

THE BRITANNIA ENGINES

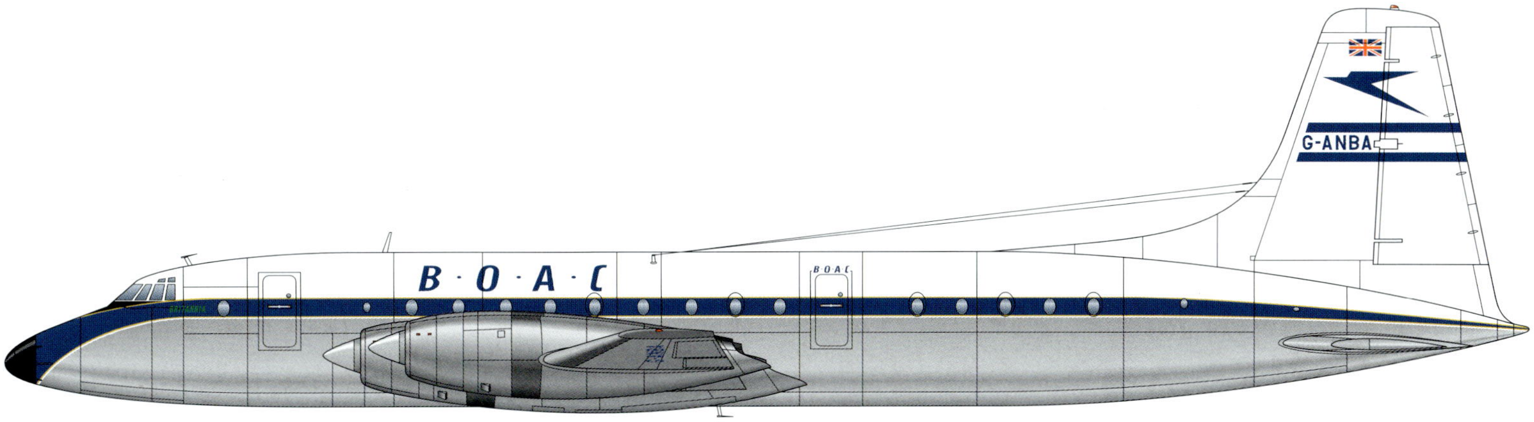

It has been said that the heart of an aircraft is its engines. Indeed 50% of the cost of developing a new aircraft can be the cost of developing its engines. It is therefore obvious that development will be made easier, quicker and perhaps cheaper if the aircraft can incorporate an engine which already exists. This is what happened in the development of the Bristol Britannia as there already existed a turbo-prop engine, the Bristol Proteus, which was deemed suitable.

The Proteus had been designed as an engine for two large aircraft which were being developed in the late 1940s; the Bristol Brabazon and the Saunders-Roe Princess. Because of this, the engine had an unusual characteristic. Both the Brabazon and the Princess had very thick wings by modern standards, and the engines were buried in the wings. There were air in-take holes in the wing leading edges, so the Proteus engine was designed with a reversed-flow layout, the air being ducted to inlets near the rear of the engine, then made to travel forward through the compressors, back through a cluster of combustion chambers and out through the turbines (Figure 2). This double reversed air flow reduced the overall length of the engine (although by only about 10cm

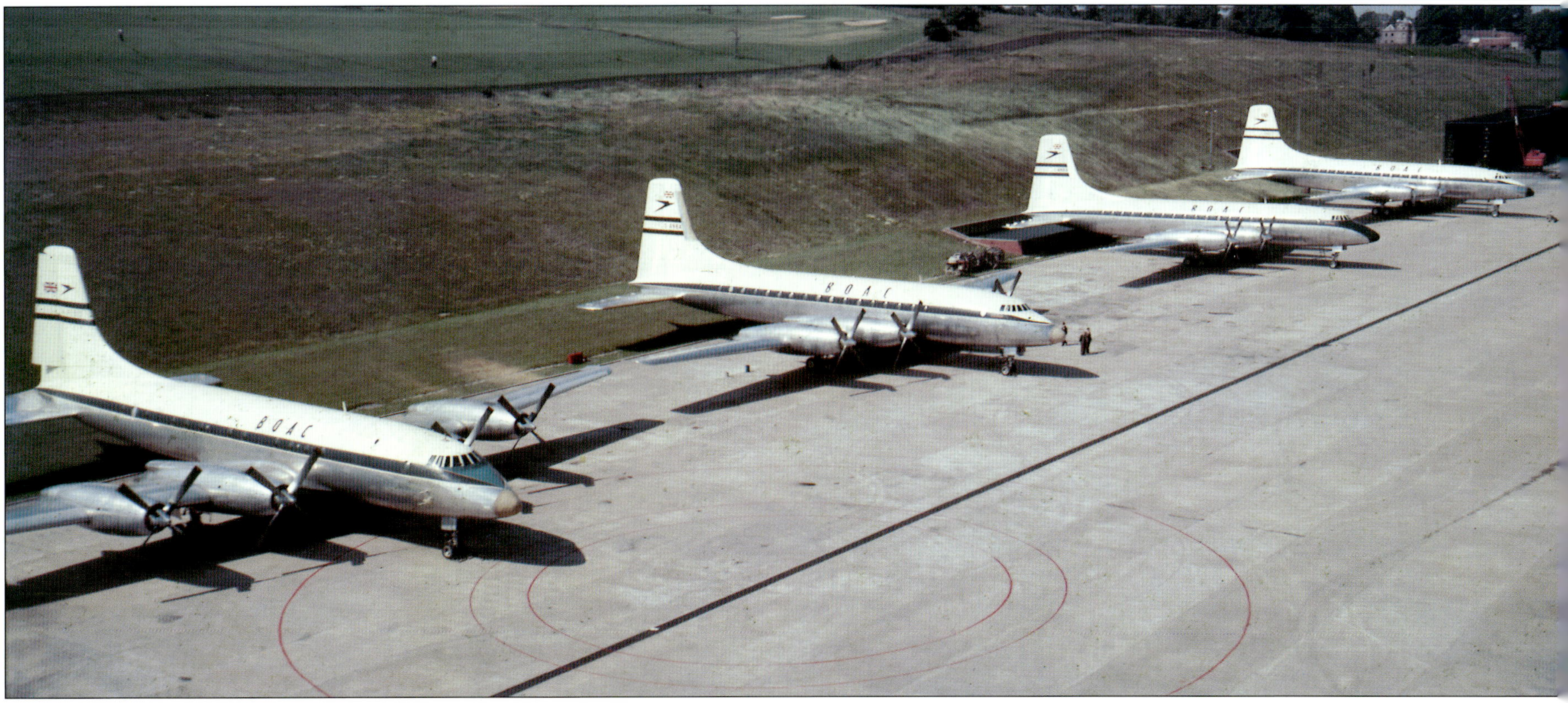

An interesting line up at Filton outside the Brabazon hanger of, from left to right respectively: The first prototype G-ALBO, and the first, second and third production Series 102 Britannias, G-ANBA, G-ANBB and G-ANBC.

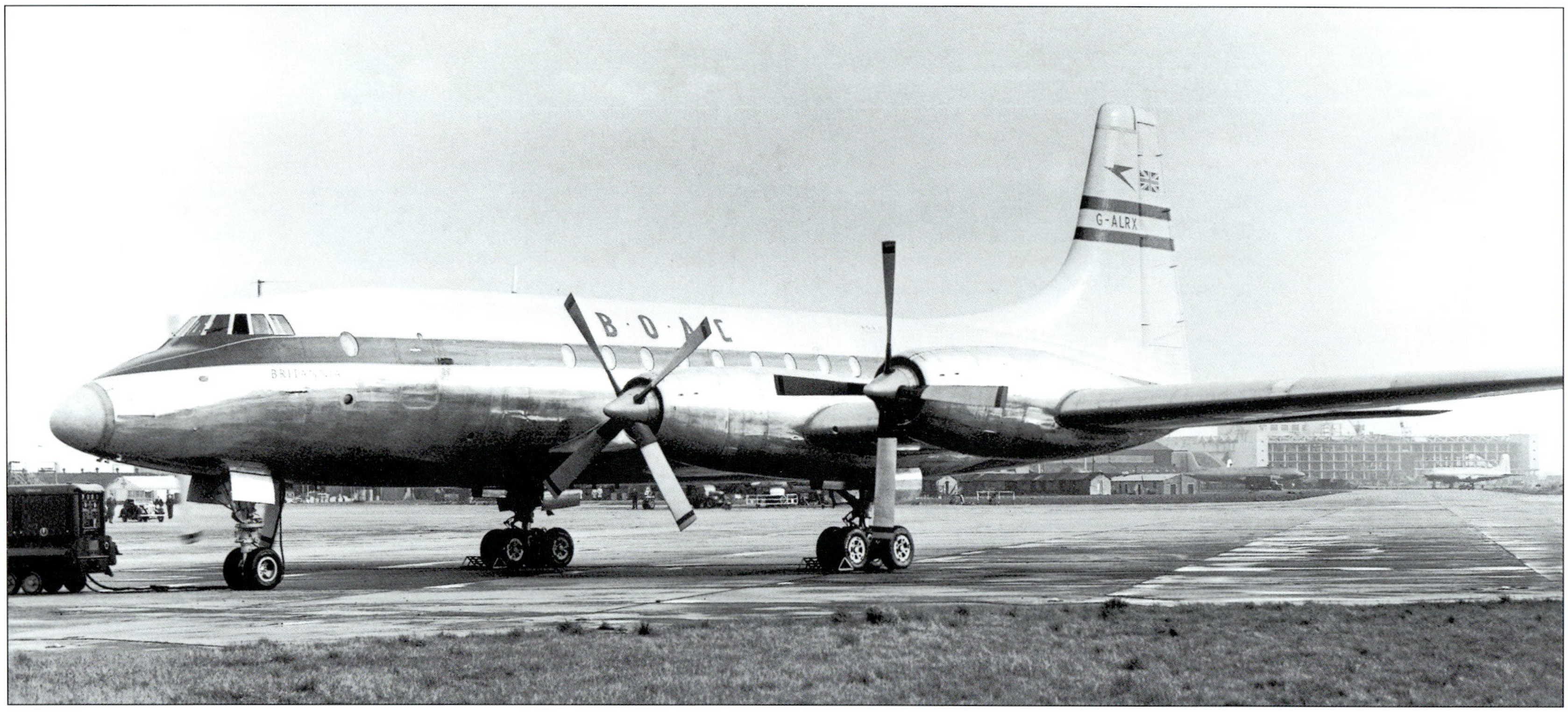

The second prototype Britannia G-ALRX resting at London's Heathrow airport during the first visit of the type, just prior to the tragic crash of 4th February 1954 on the mudflats of the River Severn.

eventually), and increased its thermal efficiency. It introduced complications, however, which took many months to overcome when in use in the Britannia aircraft.

Firstly, it was soon realised that an engine buried in a wing is difficult to service or change and this kind of engine mounting has therefore gone out of fashion. Furthermore, a thick wing inevitably produces more drag when the aircraft is flying; it is preferable to have a wing as thin as possible while still being adequately strong. But there was a very serious and unforeseen icing problem which caused a great deal of trouble throughout the life of the Proteus engine.

When Dr Stanley Hooker joined Bristol in 1949, he said he was horrified by the complexity, overall weight and performance of the engine. Once he was appointed chief-designer some eighteen months later, he set about redesigning the engine. Unfortunately, because development of the Brabazon and Princess was still continuing, the new engine had to retain the air reverse-flow layout of its predecessor and

Figure 2

Gas flow diagram of the Proteus 705 propeller turbine

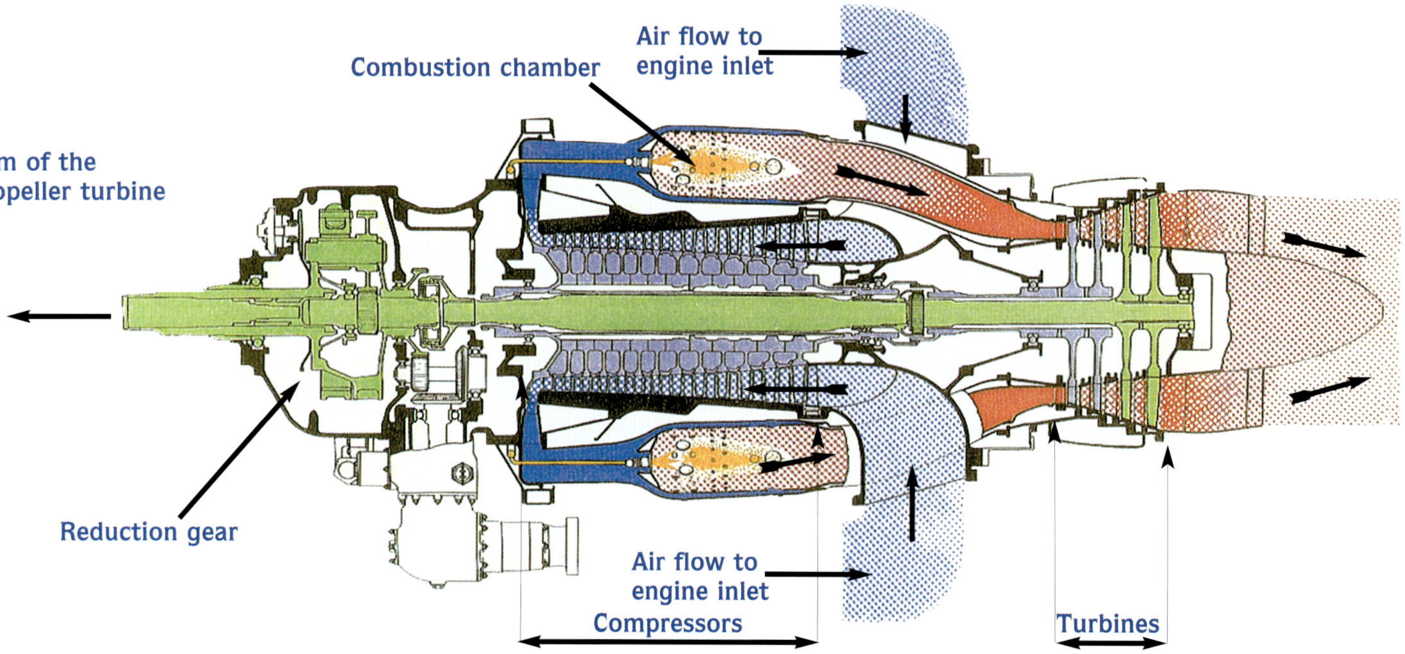

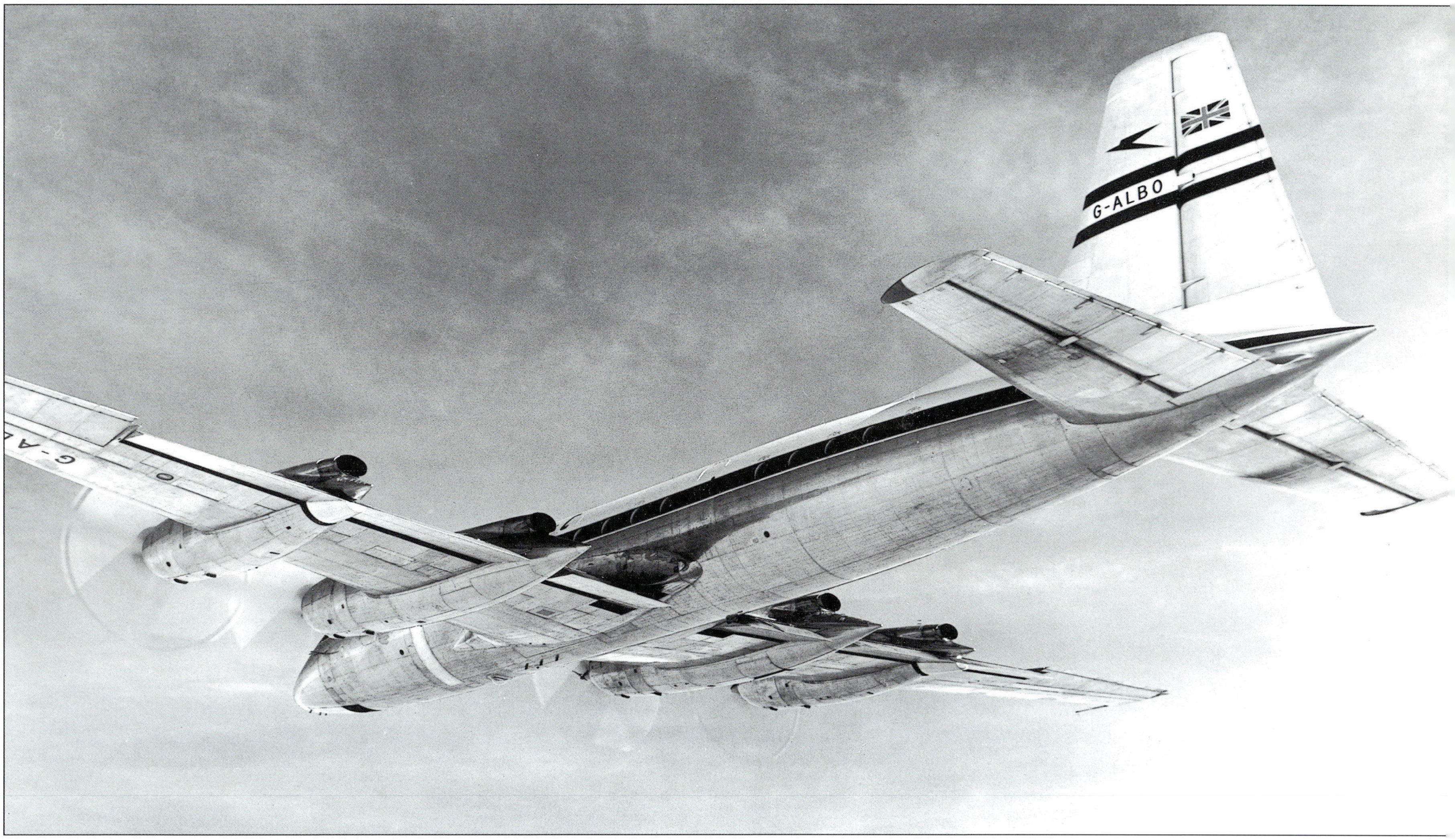

A dramatic view of G-ALBO, taken during one of the many test flights undertaken by the Britannia.

the Proteus 3, which first ran in May 1952, appeared much like the old engines although it was shorter, lighter and produced more thrust.

The irony of the situation is that the Brabazon and Princess were cancelled shortly after this. Had Hooker known that this would happen, he would have removed the reverse-flow layout in the Proteus engine, putting the air inlet ducts at the front of the engine. As it was, the reverse-flow layout in the Proteus engine was to cause many months of trouble during the Britannia development.

The first Britannia prototype, G-ALBO, made its maiden flight on 16th August 1952 piloted by A J Pegg. The engines used were Proteus 625s, the first version with only three-quarters of the power developed by the newer Proteus 705s (the Proteus 3). This maiden flight revealed minor problems with the elevator controls and undercarriage locking, as recorded in the previous chapter, but the engines were trouble free. The aircraft was soon able to fly again and appeared at the SBAC Display in September 1952.

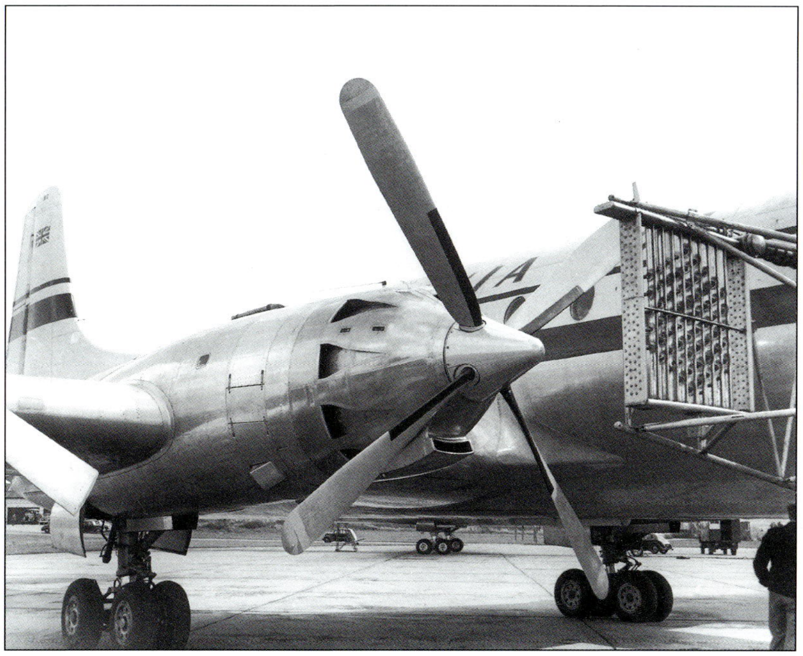

An early design study for an alternative layout to the engine air intake for the Proteus engine, with a water spray rig arranged in front, prior to de-icing tests.

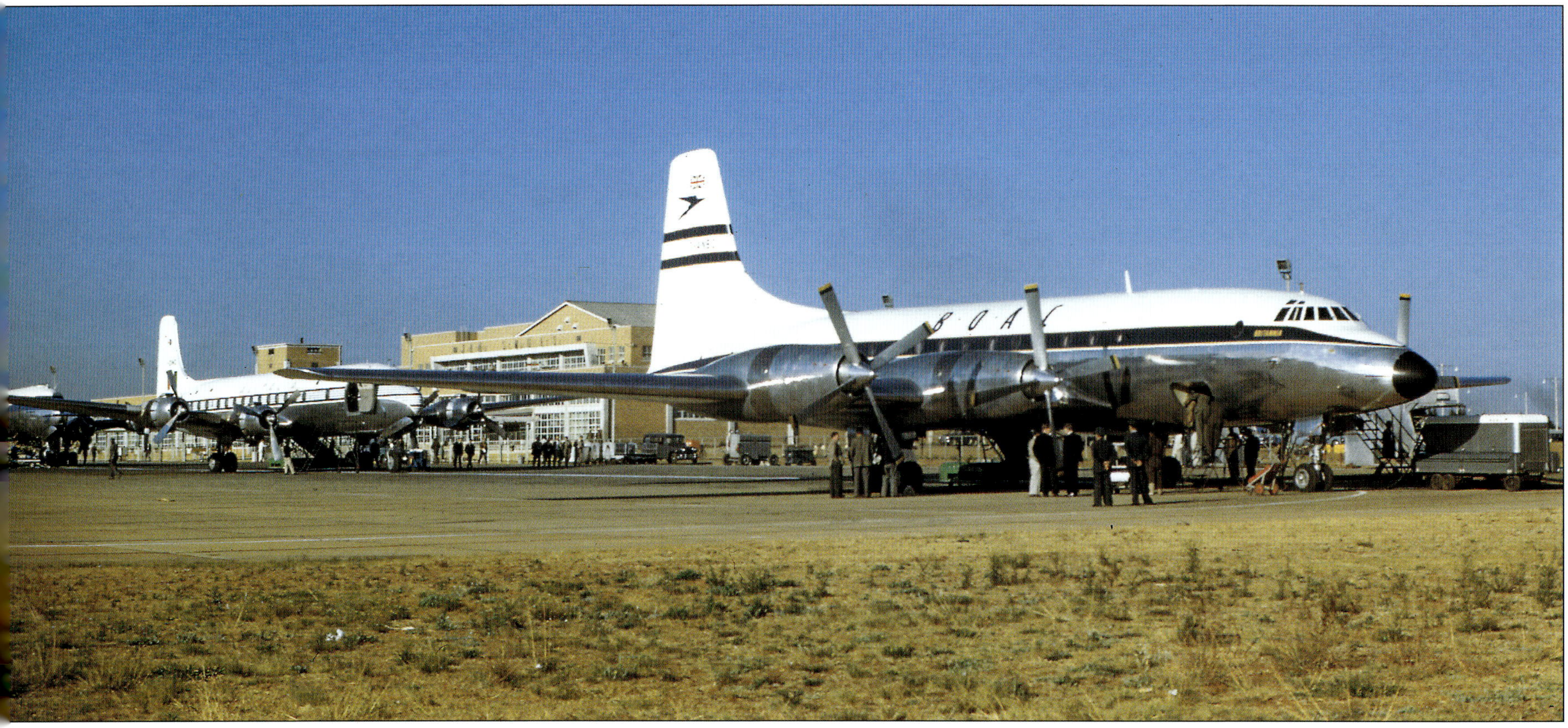

The third production Series 102 Britannia G-ANBC is serviced at Jan Smuts Airport, Johannesburg, South Africa, on the first visit of the type on 10th September 1955, during route-proving trials.

The newer engines, Proteus 705s, were installed in the prototype in August 1953 in time for the SBAC Display in September 1953.

On 23rd December 1953 the second prototype, G-ALRX, flew for the first time but, on 4th February 1954 on a test flight, there was a failure of its starboard inner engine. The reduction gear between the compressor turbine and the propeller shaft failed which allowed the compressor turbine on this engine to overspeed and explode, causing a fire so severe that the pilot (A J Pegg) decided on a forced landing on the mud of the Severn estuary. Subsequent investigation of the engine identified the cause in the reduction gear, between turbine and propeller. A new set of helical gears was produced and installed in all subsequent Proteus engines, thereby solving the problem. An additional quick-acting fuel cut-off system, to operate if the turbine speed became excessive, was installed but never activated in many millions of hours of subsequent flying. The aircraft was, however, damaged by salt water beyond repair and there was a further set-back to development in May 1954. During a stalling test on G-ALBO, a flap-torque tube failed, causing the aircraft to do a rapid roll, as explained in the previous chapter. This resulted in the aircraft being grounded for examination and repair.

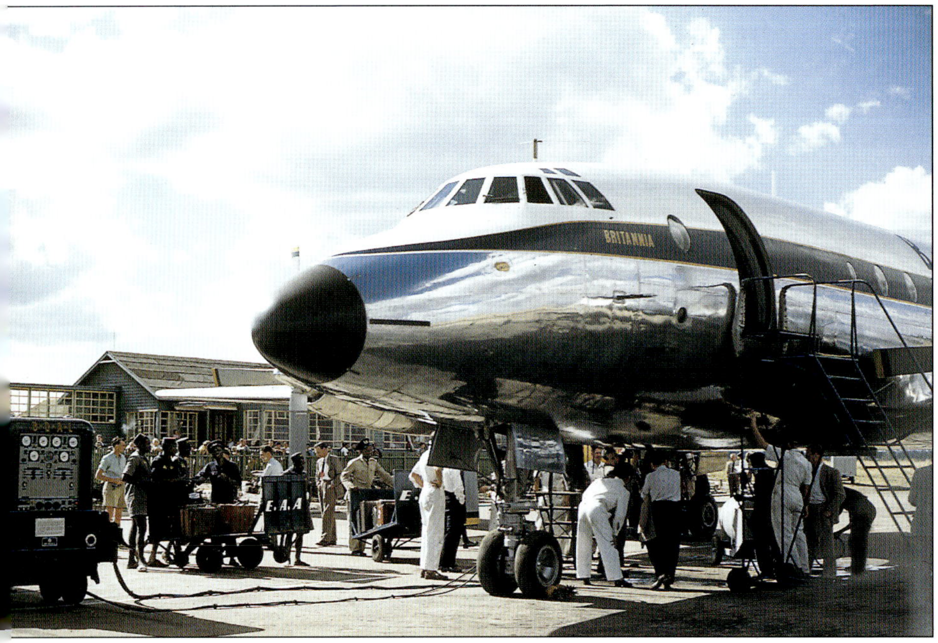

Ground staff load luggage onto G-ANBC at Khartoum during the route-proving trials in 1955.

Further test flying had to wait until the completion of the next aircraft, the first production Britannia, G-ANBA. Its maiden flight was on 5th September 1954, and this and the next three aircraft took part in the testing and route-proving, using crews formed from Bristol and BOAC personnel.

This stage of testing involved tropical trials using airports in Africa, at Idris airfield, Tripoli, (previously Castel Benito),

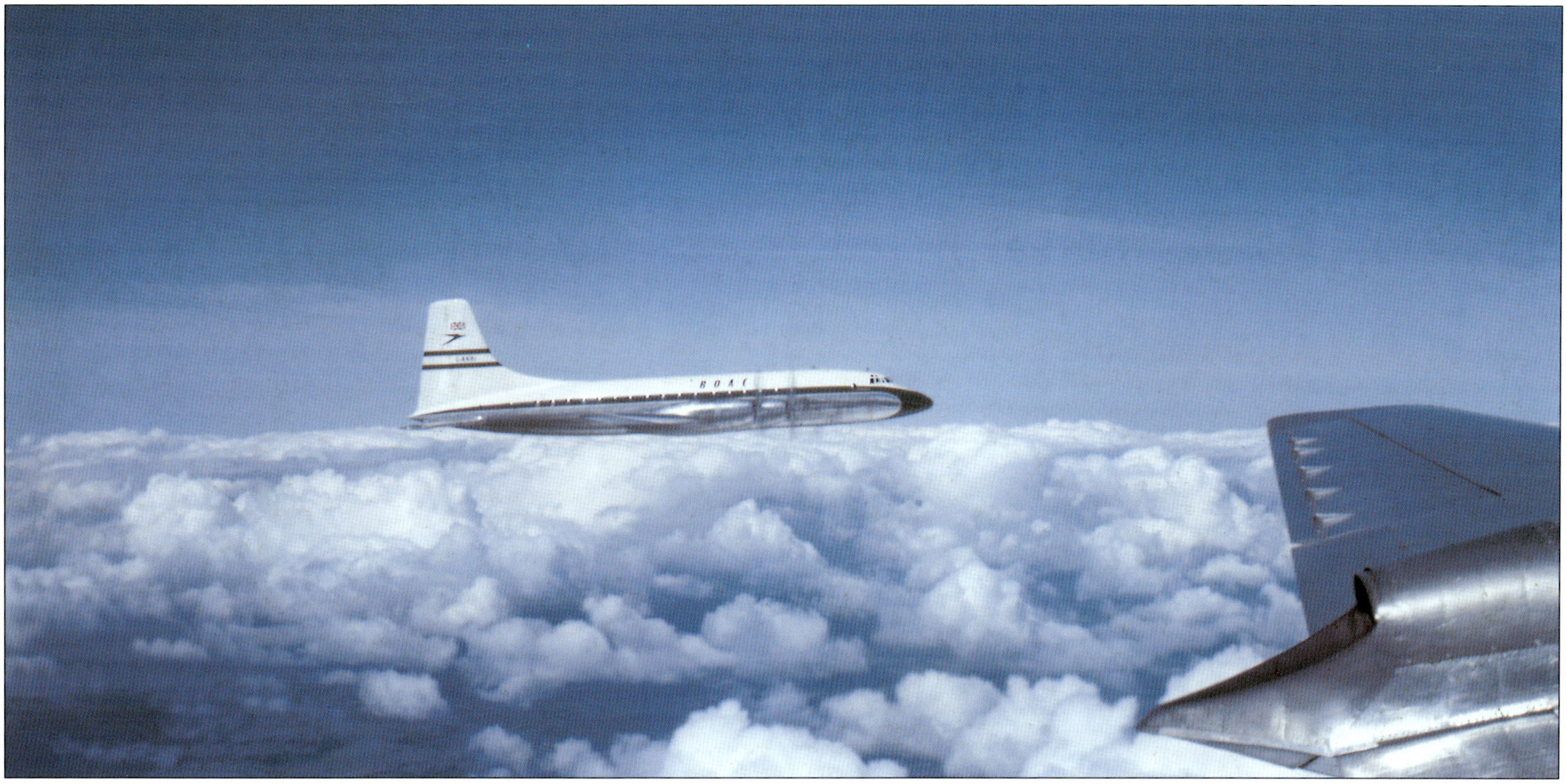

A dramatic view taken from a sister Britannia aircraft of G-ANBI flying over the Bristol Channel during flight trials in May 1956. This aircraft was destined to fly the first scheduled service to Johannesburg from London, on 1st February 1957.

Johannesburg and Khartoum. As a result of this testing the first two production aircraft, G-ANBA and G-ANBB, were granted a Certificate of Airworthiness in December 1955 and handed over to BOAC. A route familiarisation programme of about fifteen flights was then planned beginning in March 1956.

By this time the Britannia's quiet performance in flight had caused it to be termed the 'Whispering Giant'. This label seems to have first been used by a Johannesburg newspaper when describing the arrival of the first Britannia on a test flight, and official noise-level tests carried out in Stockholm confirmed the reporter's impression. Unfortunately the official report of the tests seems to have been destroyed, but memories of those who were there indicate that the Britannia's take-off run caused a sound level recorded as 81 decibels, at least twenty decibels less than the noise from any other four-engined aircraft at the time.

On 4th April 1956, one of these flights, returning from Johannesburg, was near Salisbury (Harare) when all four engines started "bumping" and then four flame-outs occurred within five minutes. This was the first demonstration that the Proteus engines had a major problem which took months to identify and rectify.

It was noted that the problem occurred while the aircraft was flying in cumulo-nimbus clouds associated with inter-tropical fronts, at very low temperatures at heights above 16,000ft. This suggested that there was some kind of icing

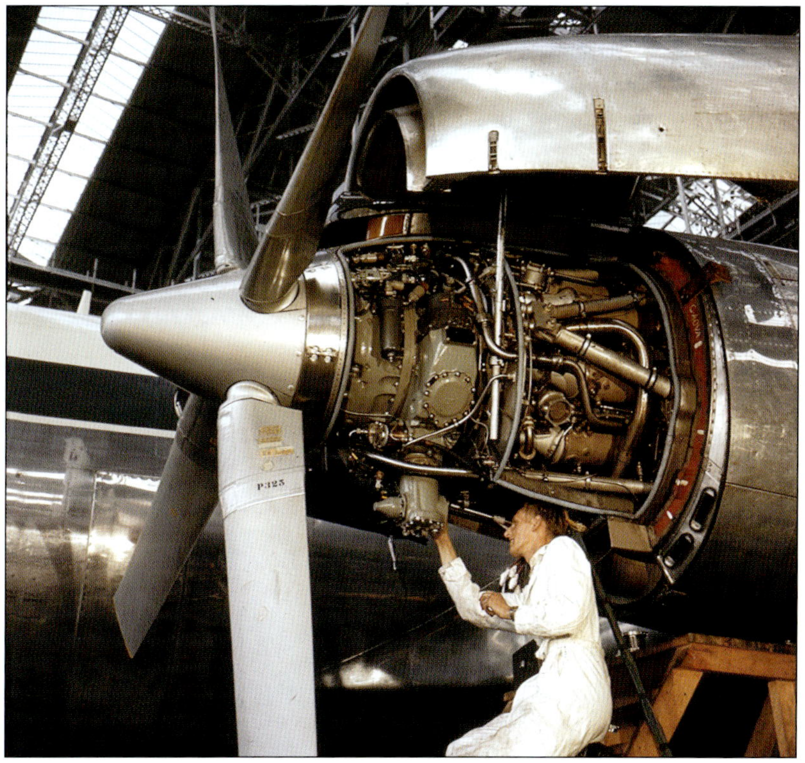

A Proteus engine is serviced in the Brabazon hanger during flight trials in 1955.

problem in the engine, although this was surprising because the engine had been subjected to rigorous icing trials in Canada and, on the basis of its behaviour, had been cleared for unlimited military and civil operations in all icing conditions then known.

The problems with the Proteus engines were almost entirely associated with the reversed air flow within the engine air intake. Other engines were like this at the time of the initial Proteus design, but what was different was the length of time that the Proteus engines in a Britannia could cruise at 20,000ft or more, and the places where it did so, particularly in tropical regions. The inherent trouble with the reversed flow design only showed up under these conditions. Once the problem had been identified and its solution published, similar problems in other manufacturers' engines were avoided.

Air supply to the manifold stops ice building at the first corner

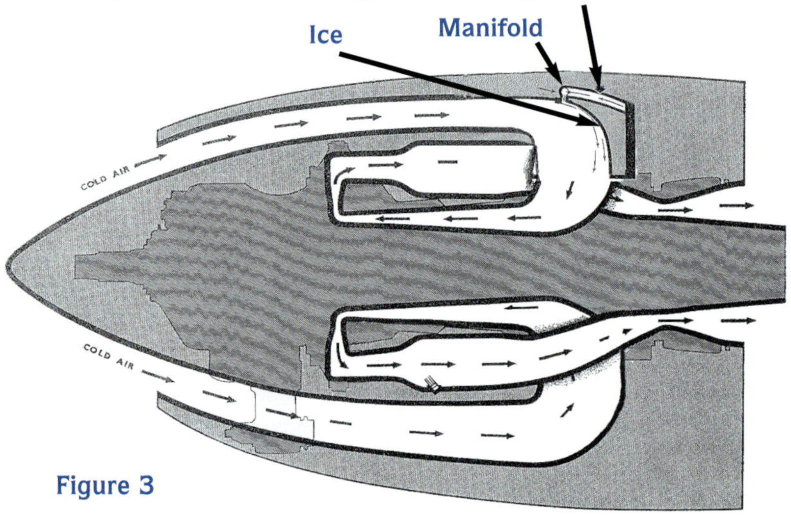

Figure 3

Bristol flew several missions with Britannias into tropical Africa, with the engines fitted with complicated extra instrumentation, including TV cameras, at various places within the engines. As a result of this it was clear that when flying through particular cumulo-nimbus clouds, conditions allowed large amounts of ice and slush to build up in the first bend of each reverse-flow air inlet pipe. When the ice broke away it went on along the pipe, through the compressor and into the combustion chamber and put the flame out.

The problem was tackled in two parts. If an engine flames out it needs to be quickly relit and this was achieved by fitting glow-plugs to four of the eight combustion chambers in each engine. Each glow-plug was a platinum alloy rod about the size and proportion of a cigarette. When the engine is running normally, the end of the plug glows white hot. A flame-out occurs when the airflow is cut, even for only a short fraction of a second. When the airflow returns, the plug is still glowing and the mixture immediately relights. This glow-plug was a near perfect addition - it had no moving parts, no electrical connections, required no maintenance and had a life time longer than that of the combustion chambers to which it was fitted. When it was fitted, the engines were found to relight quickly and smoothly. Although the glow-plug overcame the result of the flame-out, it did not eliminate its cause, which was the build up of ice in the inlet pipes. The need therefore was to eliminate this build up of ice.

The first modification made was to smooth out the inlet tubes as much as possible, giving the ice crystals no surfaces on to which they could stick. The next was to keep the intake air/ice crystal mixture as cool as possible during its first 180° turn in the inlet pipes, so that the ice crystals remained dry. This was achieved by putting a metal sleeve over each flame tube where it crossed the intake, the outer temperature of a sleeve being less hot than that of the flame tube which it enclosed.

However there were atmospheric conditions, e.g. in the monsoon over India, where stronger measures were needed. The most effective method used was to tap some air from each engine compressor and send jets of this air into the intake pipes, just before the first bend where ice tended to build up (Figure 3). These jets accelerated the movement of the boundary layer in the intake and prevented ice crystals from lodging on the walls of the intake. The extra air jets were known as B-skin jets. (A-skin is the outer cowling of the engine, B-skin the next layer into the engine, followed by C-skin and D-skin) The B-skin jets were very effective although they came with a penalty; some engine power was needed to supply the compressed air to the inlet jets. However the amount was small and it was well worth ensuring the continued functioning of the engines.

In monsoon air with the highest water content, yet more was done. A system known as cowl heating could be turned on. Some exhaust gas could be taken from the engine, aft of the combustion chambers and turbine blades (and therefore at high temperature), mixed with some intake air taken before the first intake bend, and fed into a chamber, the cowl, between the A and B skins, so as to heat up the B-skin walls. This raised the B-skin wall temperature and partially melted any ice or snow adhering to it.

Another engine problem showed up in September 1957 when a BOAC Britannia, flying in the southern USA, experienced a double engine failure. It was caused by a change in the stator material used in the intake compressor, which led to rubbing and then seizure of the compressor blades when suddenly sprayed with slush in the air intake. This problem was completely eliminated by a slight reduction in the length of the compressor blades, by approximately ten-thousandths of an inch.

The result of all this testing and modification eventually

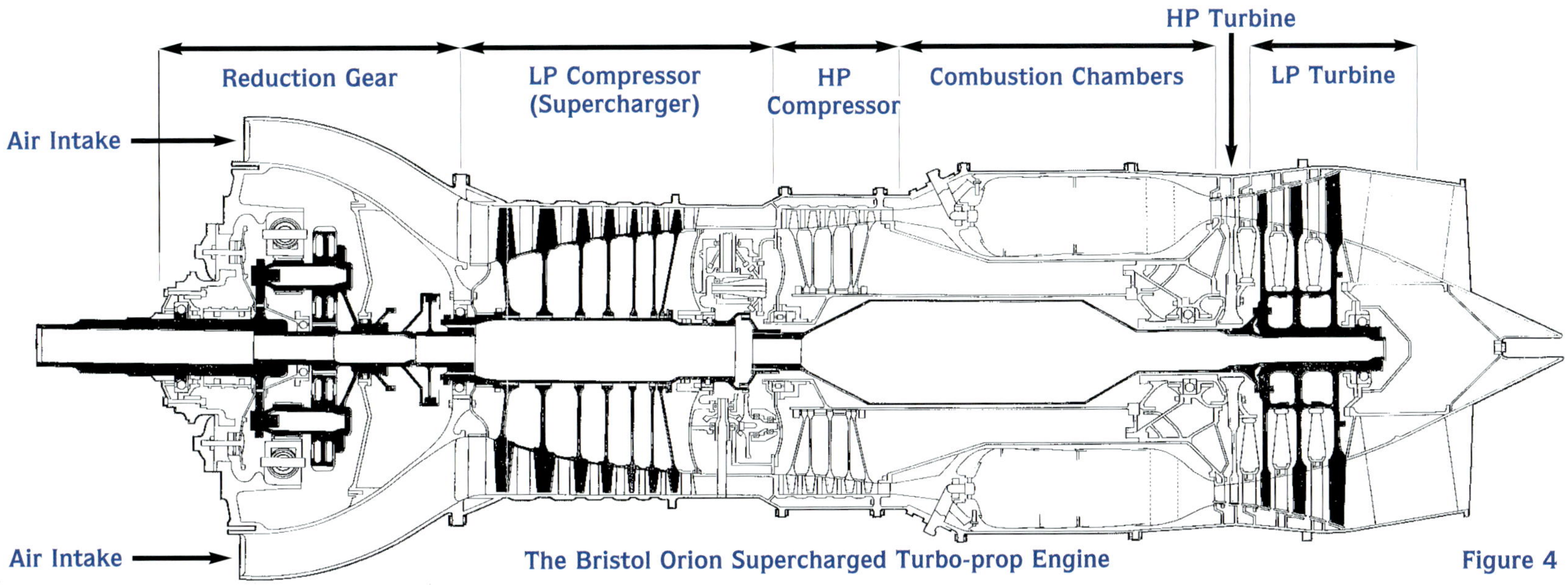

The Bristol Orion Supercharged Turbo-prop Engine

Figure 4

produced a much more reliable engine, the Proteus 755, but it is interesting to hear the opinions now of those who flew Britannias. All engines were fitted with glow-plugs, but the civil aircraft (initially with BOAC) in general had engines fitted with the B-skin jets whereas the RAF aircraft had engines fitted with cowl heating. During the service span of aircraft and air crew, some people have flown in aircraft of both types and opinions differ as to which system was the best at avoiding icing troubles. What is clear is that the Proteus engines were always a bit tricky. Wherever possible, pilots had to avoid flying through cumulo-nimbus, particularly in tropical regions, but if they could not, the engines could be made to operate satisfactorily using the various systems outlined. Although this was not an ideal situation, it is worth noting that there was

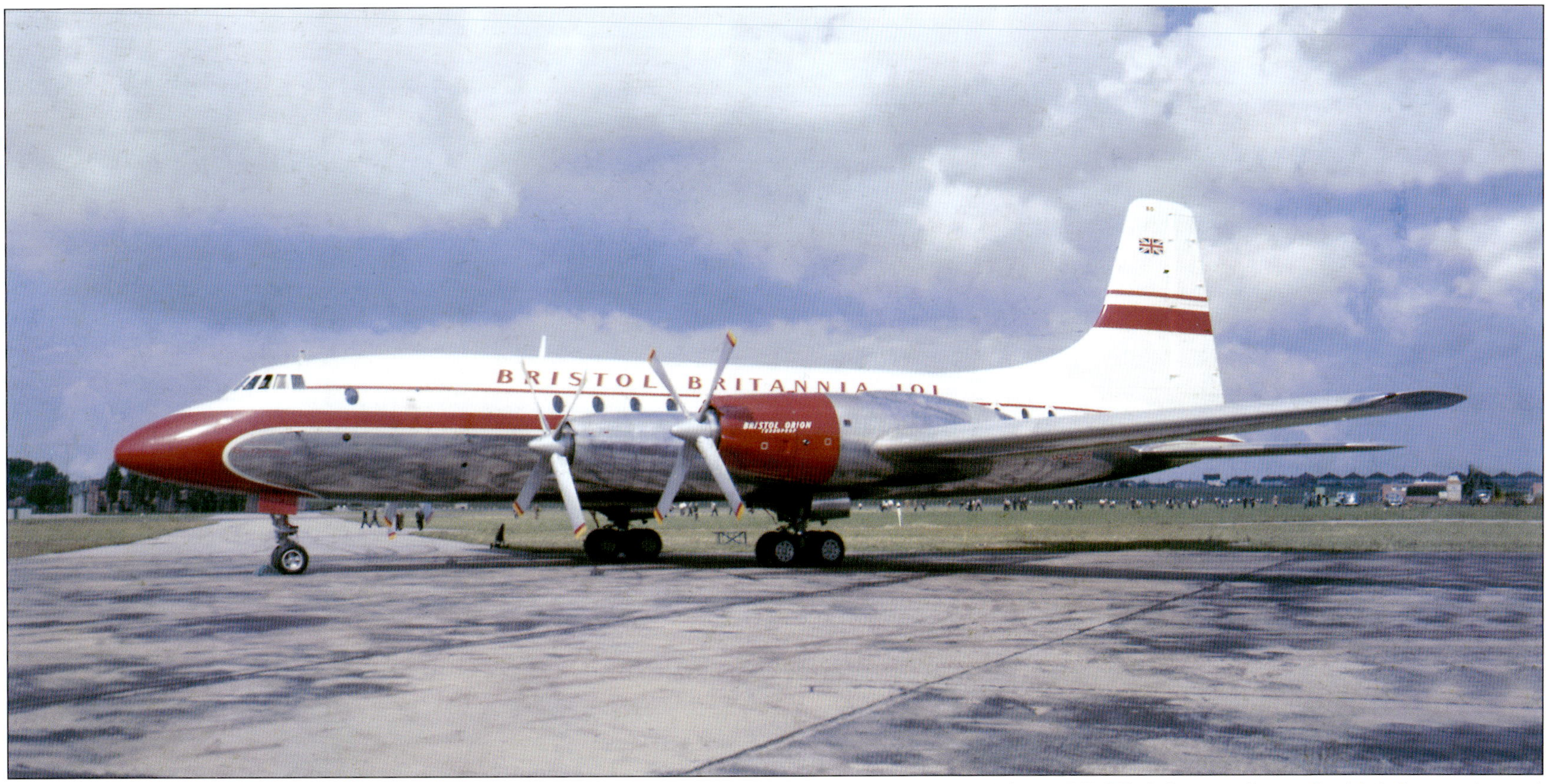

A fine shot of G-ALBO which was used for trials of the Bristol BE.25 Orion engine, of which it was hoped to fit in later versions of the Britannia. Unfortunately this was the only aircraft which actually flew with the engine and even then with only one engine fitted, the nearest in the photograph.

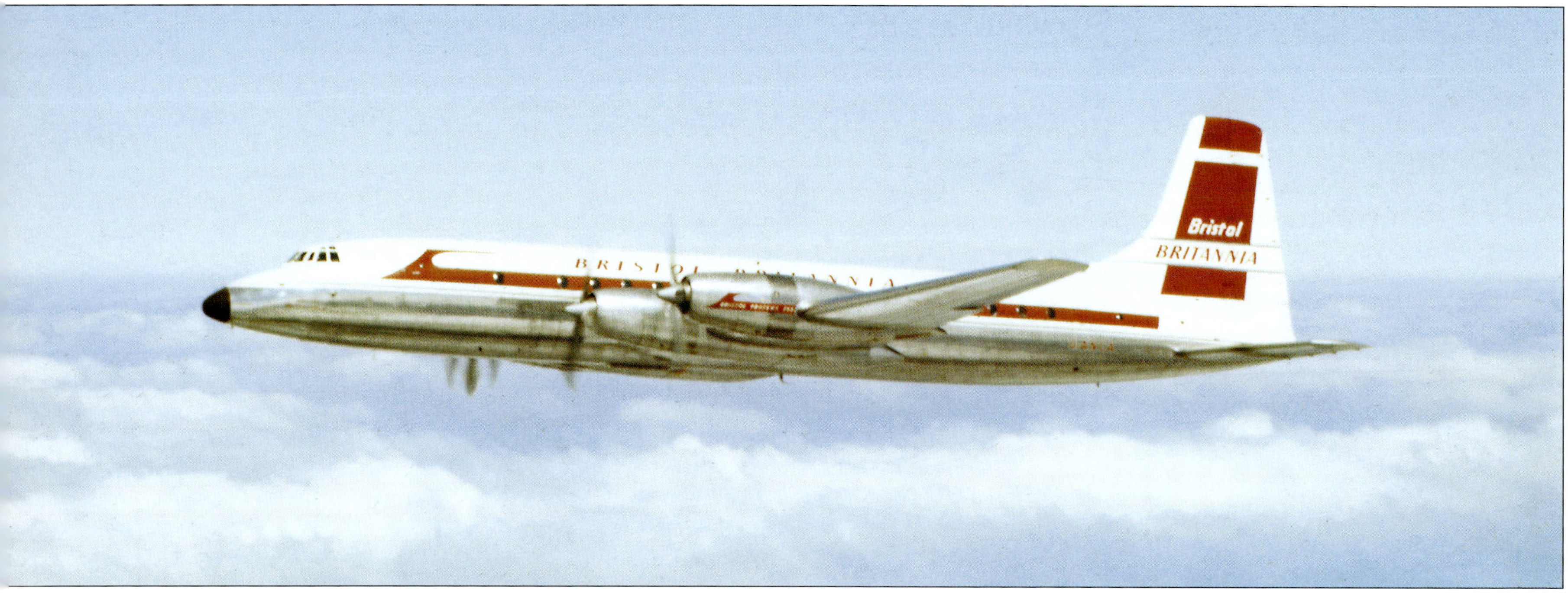

G-ANCA the first Series 300 Britannia in Bristol colours with Bristol Britannia 301 titles on the upper fuselage.

never a crash of a Britannia because of engine icing problems.

In 1956, Dr Hooker's Bristol team produced a new turbo-prop engine, the Orion (Figure 4), which avoided the reverse-flow air intake layout and gave still better fuel efficiency and thrust for less weight. Comparable figures were 5,500ehp for the Orion and 4,400ehp for the Proteus 765. One of the Orion engines began flight testing in August 1956 in G-ALBO and Bristol planned a Britannia Series 400 around this engine type. Unfortunately the British Government said it would only support the development of one turbo-prop engine of this size and chose the rival Rolls-Royce Tyne engine. The Orion was therefore cancelled in 1958.

The engine work involved in the development from the original Proteus 625 to the Proteus 755 and the Orion overcame the problems which the earlier engines had, as subsequent flying experience showed. But during this development period, the world's major airlines became more interested in the faster jet-propelled aircraft such as the Boeing 707 and the Douglas DC-8.

Had there been no problem with the Proteus engine in its early stages, the Bristol Britannia would have gone into service at least two years earlier, and there seems little doubt that it would have been much more widely adopted.

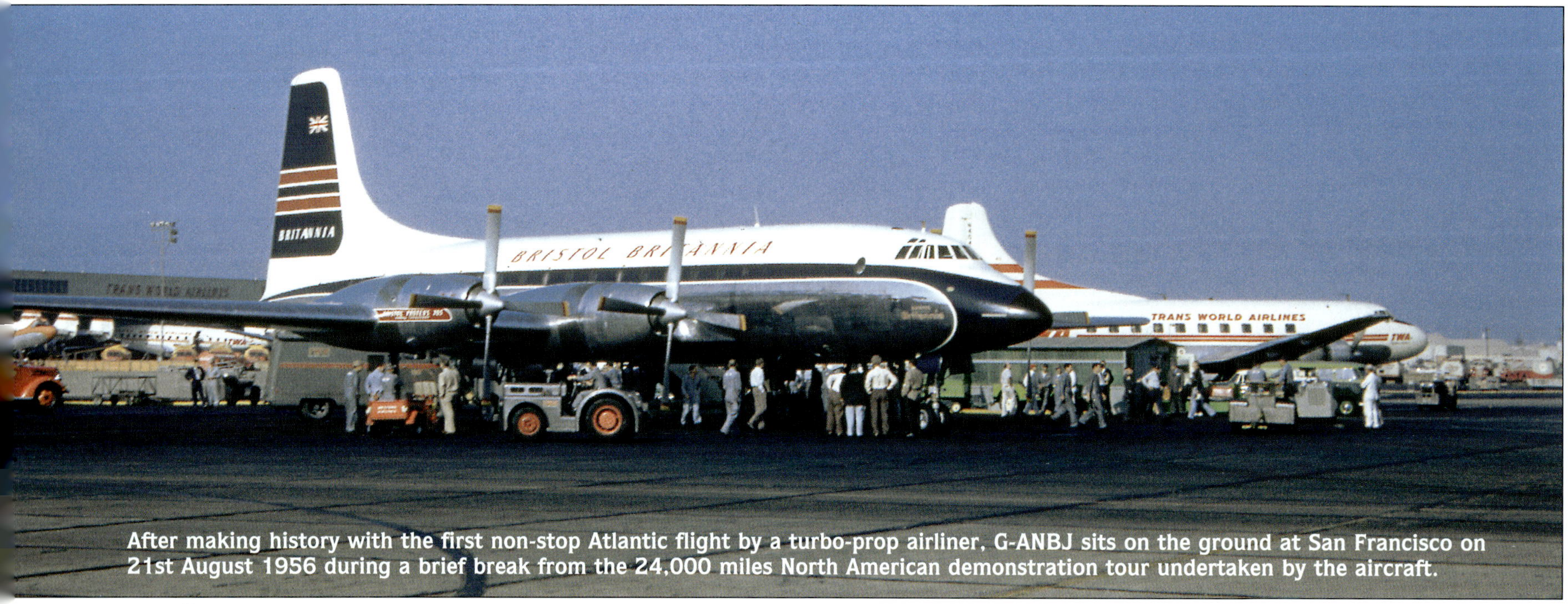

After making history with the first non-stop Atlantic flight by a turbo-prop airliner, G-ANBJ sits on the ground at San Francisco on 21st August 1956 during a brief break from the 24,000 miles North American demonstration tour undertaken by the aircraft.

INTEREST BUT NO SALES

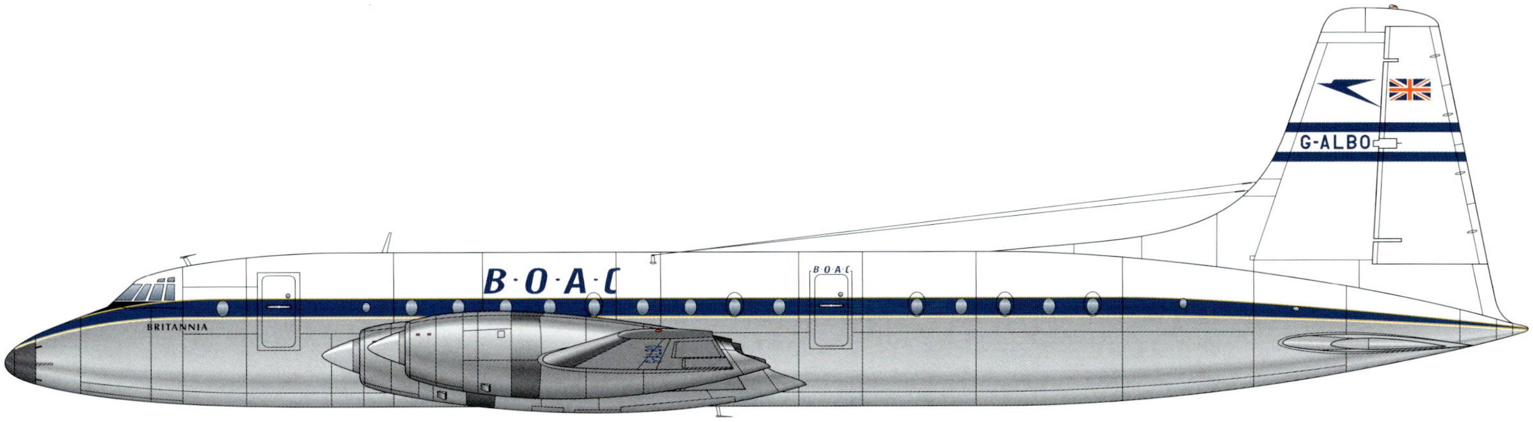

There were various airlines which expressed interest in the Britannia aircraft but who, for various reasons, did not actually buy any.

At an early stage in the Britannia's development, before its maiden flight, the Australian airline Qantas said it was interested in buying some of the aircraft. After a visit to Bristol by a Qantas representative and a presentation to officials in Australia, an order was received for six Britannias. However there was no follow-up to this and no Britannias were bought by Qantas, nor by any other Australian airline. It was rumoured that the expressed interest came because of pressure from Government to Government, and not because of economic considerations by the airline.

The situation was different with the Dutch airline KLM which was interested in using Britannias on their route to the Dutch East Indies. Bristol gave a technical presentation to the full KLM Board, and it was subsequently arranged that the chief pilot and Assistant Vice-President of KLM should go on a demonstration flight. Unfortunately the flight from Filton, by G-ALRX on 4th February 1954, ended after an engine fire with a crash landing on the mud flats of the River Severn. The KLM representatives and all others on board emerged unhurt onto the Severn mud but, perhaps not surprisingly, no orders were received from KLM to buy Britannias.

The next airline to express interest was TWA in the shape of its multi-millionaire grand patron, Howard Hughes. Contact was made when Bristol took the tenth Britannia (102 Series) to North America on a publicity tour in 1956, and had reached Montreal. In characteristically eccentric fashion, Hughes

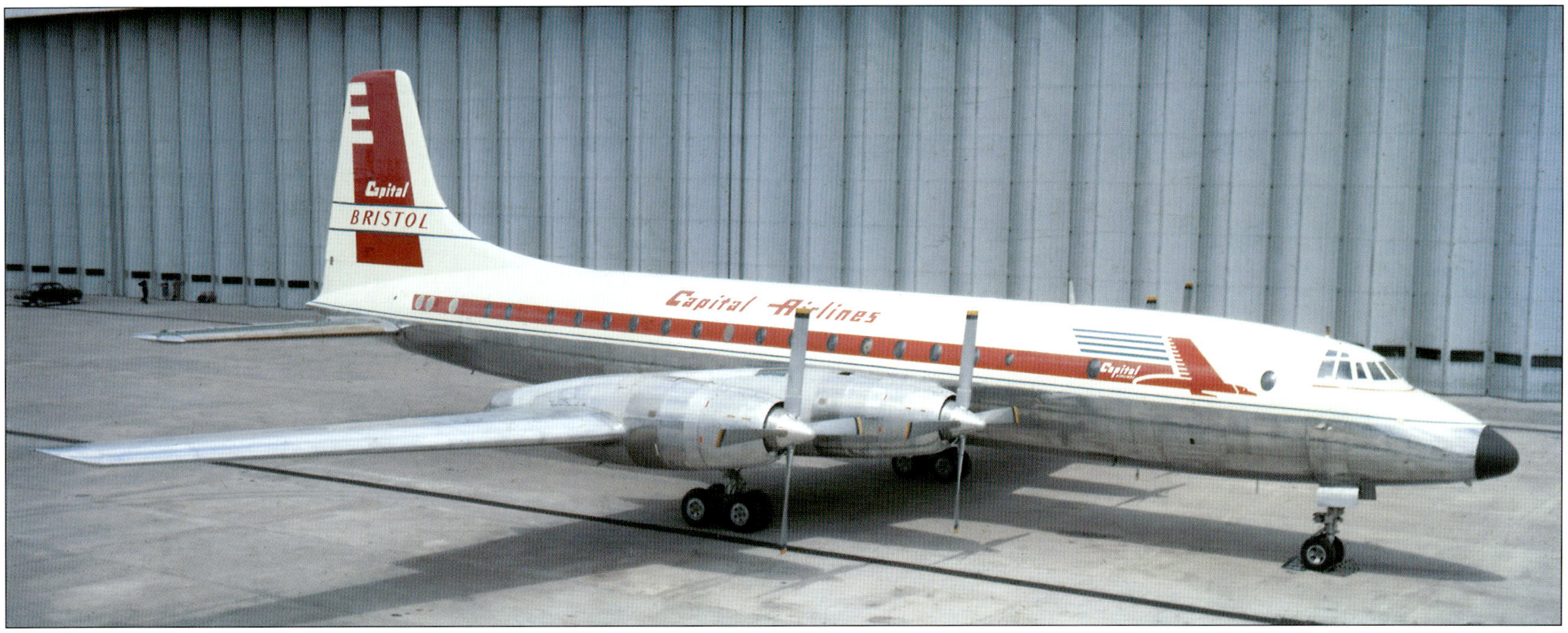

Two days prior to her first flight on 31st July 1956, G-ANCA is seen wearing the livery of Capital Airlines in front of the Brabazon hanger.

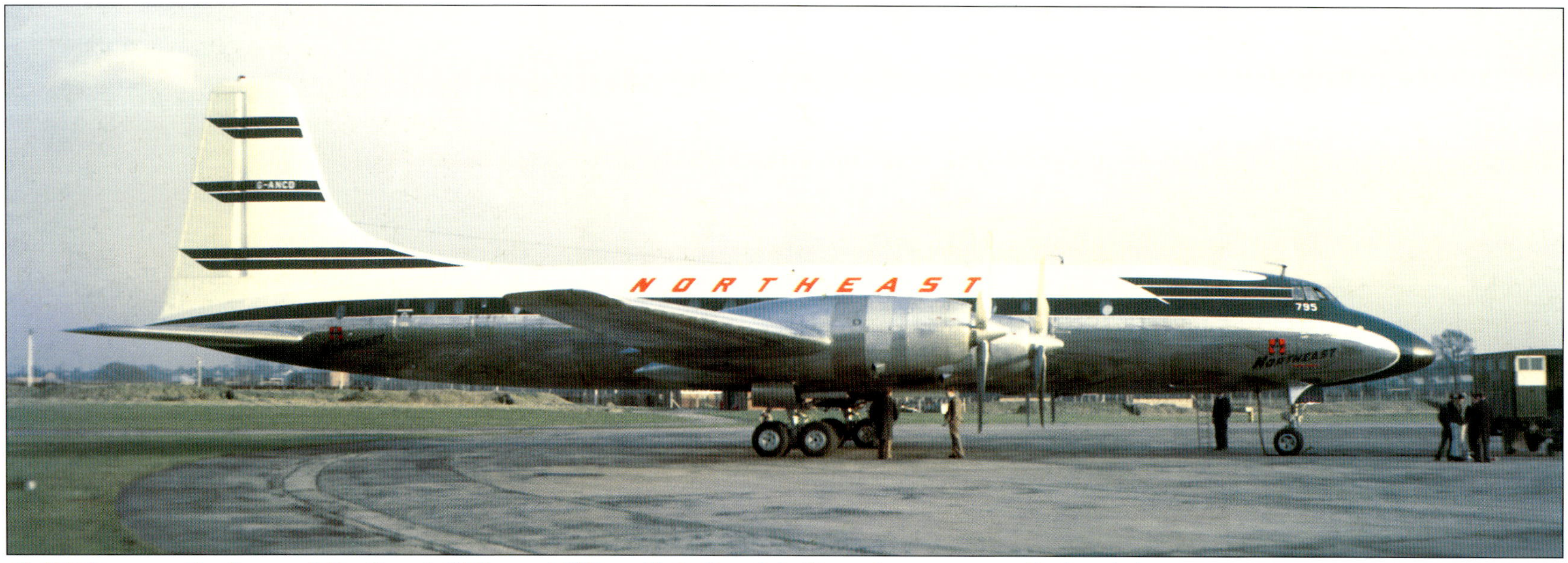

G-ANCD wears the livery of Northeast Airlines at Filton. Unfortunately the order was cancelled and the type was never used by the airline.

requested to talk to the boss - no one else would do. Sir Reginald Verdon-Smith, the then Managing Director of Bristol Aircraft, therefore made himself available and the instruction came that he was to wait at a certain street corner at midnight. This he did and eventually a man in bare feet (Howard Hughes) appeared. Hughes and Verdon-Smith proceeded to walk round the block and Hughes gave precise instructions.

He wanted no contact with any of Bristol's Britannia pilots. He wanted the key to the aeroplane (then in Montreal) and a copy of the book of Pilot's Notes. He took the Notes and studied them for two days on his own. He then returned to the aircraft and sat in the Captain's seat and instructed Chief Test Pilot Walter Gibb to sit in the co-pilot's seat. He had obviously read the Notes carefully and asked a series of perceptive questions about the flight deck layout and controls. He then

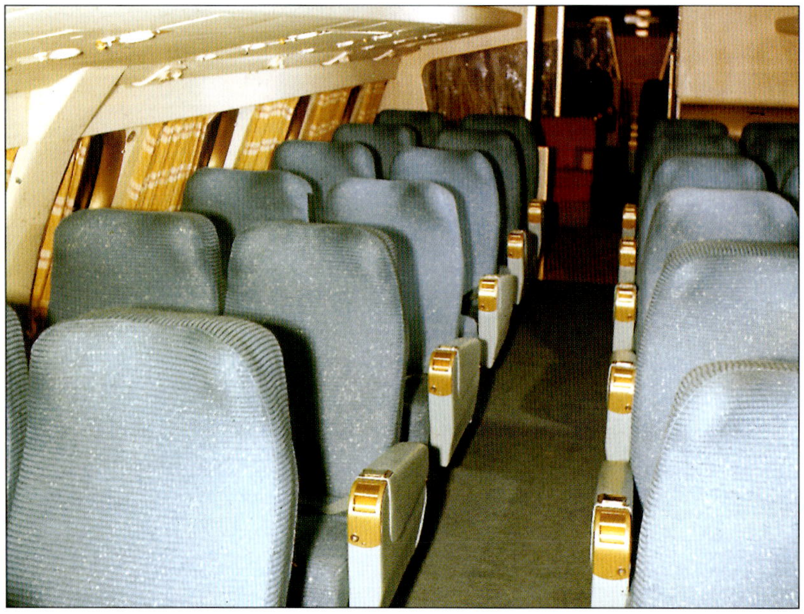

An interior view of G-ANCD fitted out to Northeast specification.

asked Walter Gibb to start the engines and take-off. Hughes then took over the controls, put the Britannia through various manoeuvres and finally took her down to land, 'very competently' according to the Chief Test Pilot! They did several more circuits in a similar manner.

Subsequently, on another midnight walk, he said that he wanted to buy 25 Britannias for TWA, specifying delivery dates which Bristol could not possibly meet. So the interest of Howard Hughes and TWA ended there, without any sales.

At about the same time another American airline, Capital Airlines, expressed an interest in the Britannia, particularly the Series 305 version, which they planned to use on their longer range North American routes. There were detailed discussions between the airline and Bristol, and the suggestion was that they would order five aircraft with the possibility of extending this to a further ten at a later date. However this potential order fell through because the airline failed to raise the necessary finance. It was suspected that the Americans were unwilling to produce support for the purchase of a British aircraft.

The failure to achieve this order was somewhat off-set by the order from El Al for three Series 313 Britannias in 1955, later increased to four. This was the first foreign sale of Britannias, which El Al used for a number of years with great success on the North Atlantic (New York-Tel Aviv) route.

In 1958 another American airline, Northeast Airlines, placed an order for the five Series 305 Britannias originally ordered by Capital Airlines and now under construction. Again this order was cancelled because of lack of US financial support. These five aircraft were completed and all sold to other airlines, but no Britannias were sold to any US airline.

IN SERVICE WITH BOAC

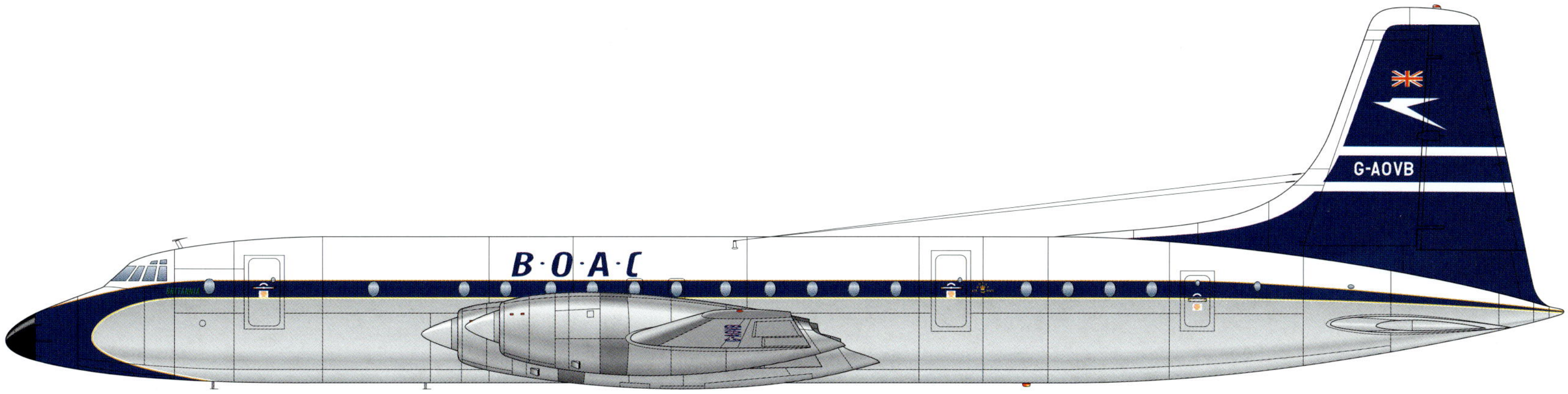

By the time that BOAC's Britannia, G-ANBI, left Heathrow for Johannesburg on 1st February 1957 to inaugurate this passenger-carrying service, over eight years had elapsed since the airline originally expressed an interest in buying the aircraft (in November 1948).

BOAC personnel gradually became increasingly involved in the Britannia development programme. They took part in the early test flying of the prototype, G-ALBO, and some of their pilots did proving and test flights of the production 102 Series aircraft.

In addition, some BOAC personnel were involved in using Britannia aircraft in special troop transport flights to Cyprus at the time of the Suez crisis and in Hungarian refugee relief flights from Vienna to London during 1956.

The result was that by the time of the inaugural

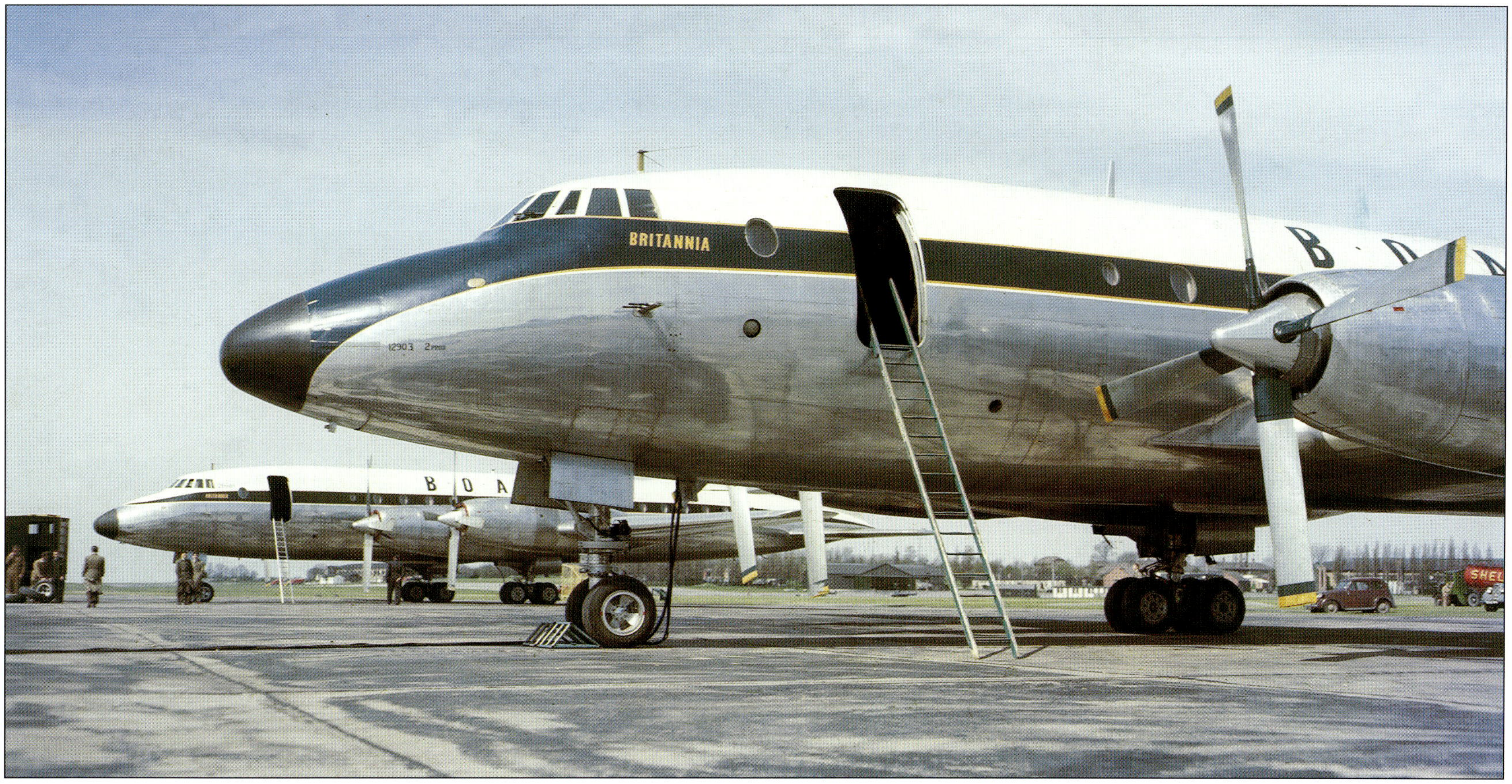

A pleasing view of two Series 102 aircraft taken during a short break early in the flight test program at Filton.

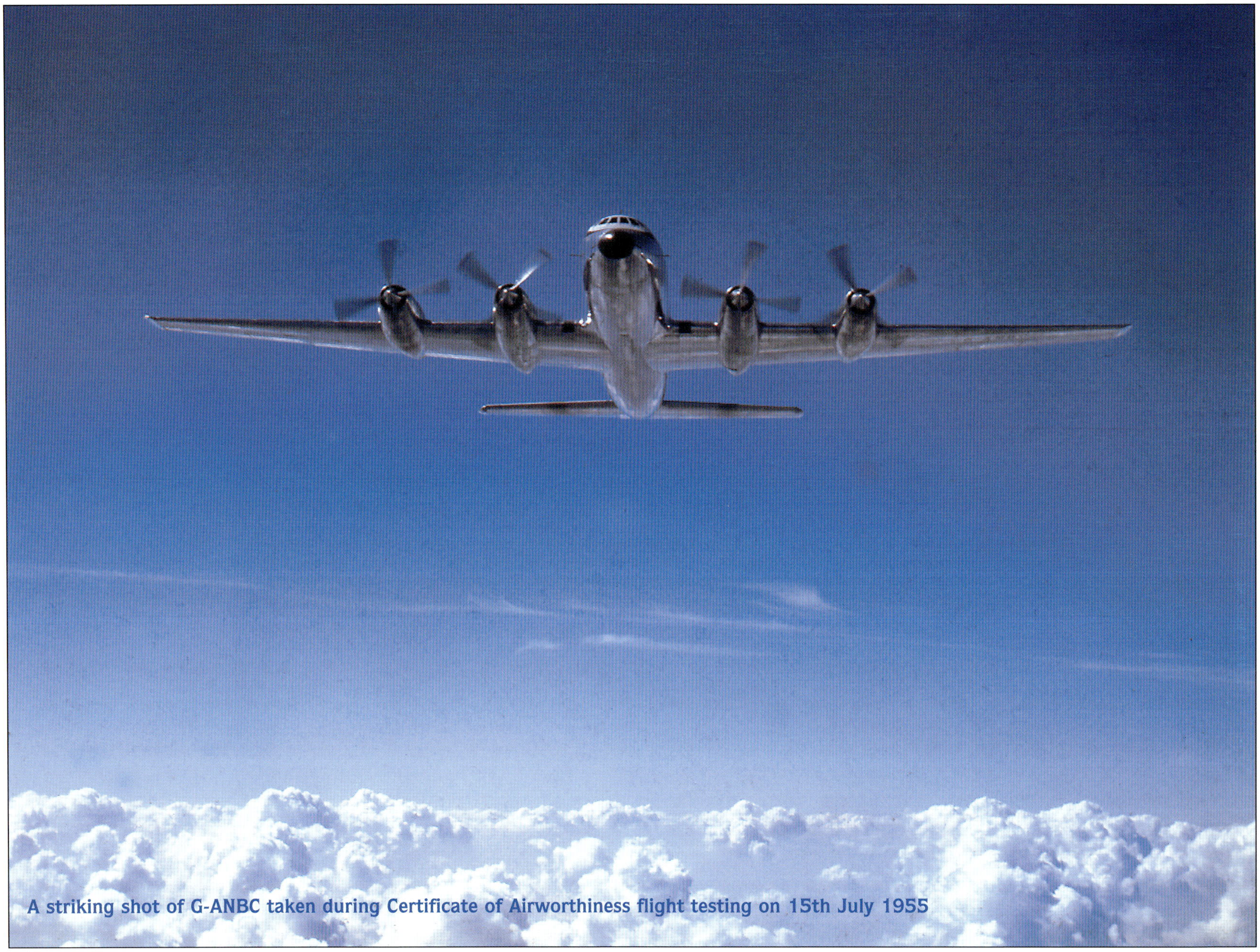

A striking shot of G-ANBC taken during Certificate of Airworthiness flight testing on 15th July 1955

passenger-carrying flights in February 1957, the Britannia was a familiar aircraft to many crews, some of whom had by then been working with it for over three years. That three years had been a time of hard, frustrating work for all concerned, associated particularly with problems in the development of the Proteus engines. BOAC had originally intended to introduce the Britannia to commercial operation in May 1954 but its plans had to be revised continually from then on.

But frustrations were not just those of BOAC because of the time it took for Bristol to eliminate the faults in the Proteus engines. Bristol were frustrated because BOAC kept changing its corporate mind about how many Britannias and of what kind it wanted. This resulted in Bristol being left with Britannias which had been ordered, but subsequently cancelled. Although there were financial penalties which BOAC incurred because of cancelled or modified orders, the economic consequences to Bristol were worse and, at one stage, there was even the possibility of Bristol going bankrupt because of them.

However the frustrations and delays seemed to be at an end when the inaugural commercial flight was fixed for 1st February 1957, but even then there was nearly a last-minute delay. BOAC had originally stated that they wished the flight deck to be arranged for operation by a Captain and First Officer but no Flight Engineer, and Bristol had designed it accordingly. BOAC revised their statement in September 1953, and then changed it again in October 1956 when they decided that they would have a Flight Engineer after all, but that he would sit in the 'jump' seat, between and somewhat behind the two Pilots. The Union representing the Flight Engineers threatened industrial action because of this

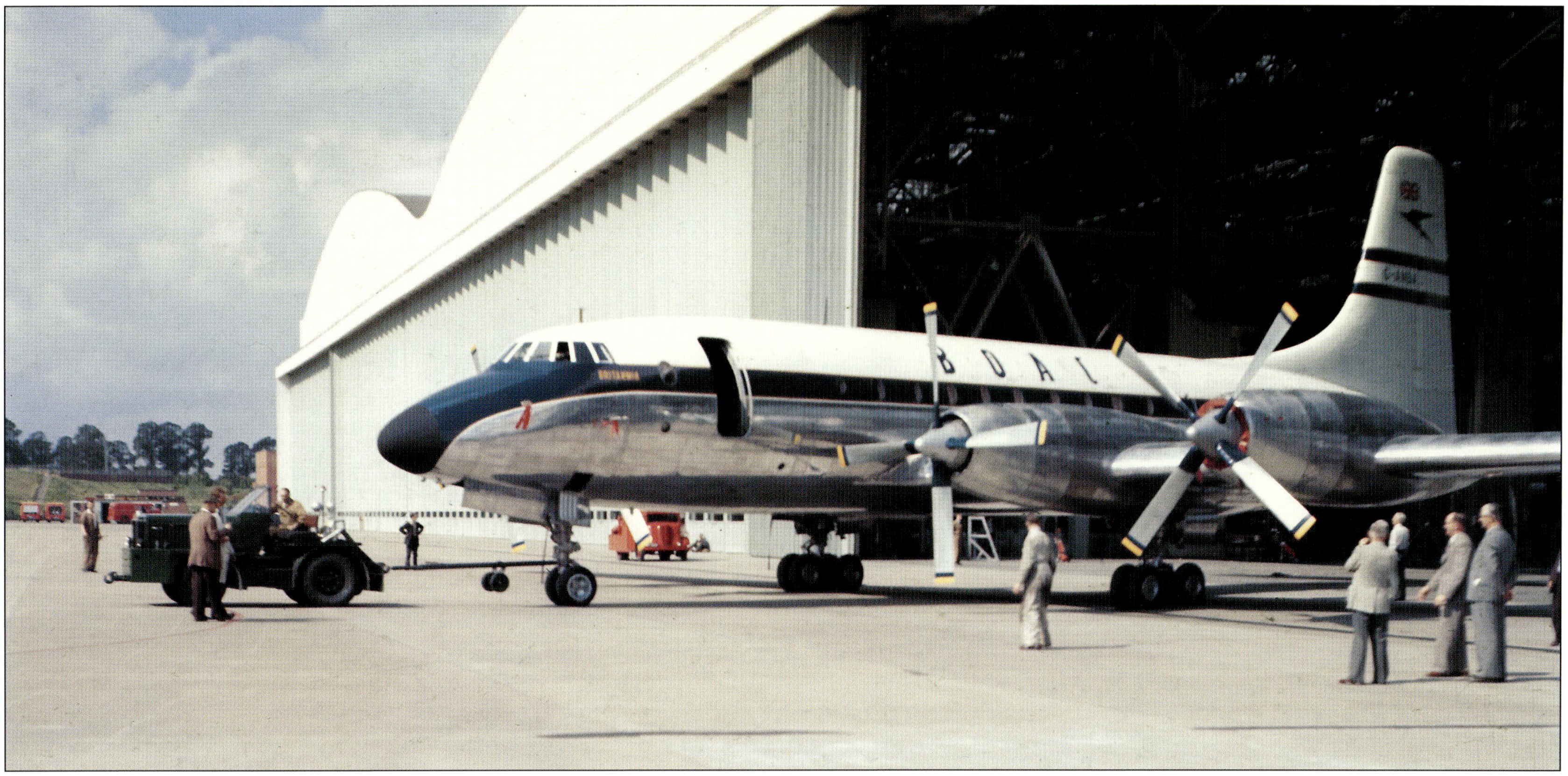

G-ANBA, the first production Britannia Series 102 for British Overseas Airways Corporation, is towed from the Brabazon hanger, prior to its first flight in September 1954.

arrangement and only lengthy discussions produced a (temporary) settlement so that the inaugural flight could go ahead on schedule. But the issue was only finally sorted out later.

Once the BOAC route to Johannesburg was introduced, the Corporation also put Britannias onto the London-Sydney route. The service ran three times per week, starting on 2nd March 1957, with stops en-route at Zurich, Istanbul, Karachi, Calcutta, Singapore, Jakarta and Darwin. The scheduled time for the whole trip was 47 hours, in contrast to the 75 hours then taken by the Constellation aircraft.

The Britannias quickly became popular aircraft with passengers on the South African and Australian routes although they were not yet very reliable. In their first 32 weeks of service there were 49 unscheduled engine changes, sixteen of them due to icing damage as well as a very high number of electrical failures. The Johannesburg service was not too bad but the Sydney one was very poor. Between 3rd March and 20th July, 7% of all London to Sydney flights were more than 24 hours delayed and a further 3% were over 48 hours late. From Sydney to London, 25% were more than 24 hours late and a further 12% over 48 hours late. BOAC and Bristol had to work hard to improve on this record.

On 30th September 1957 a new engine problem arose. Aircraft G-AOVB was on its first route-proving flight when two of its engines failed so that it had to make an unscheduled stop at Miami. The reason was found to be that the compressor blades had rubbed against the engine casings, a situation made possible because of new material used in the casings. To resolve this problem, the length of the compressor blades was

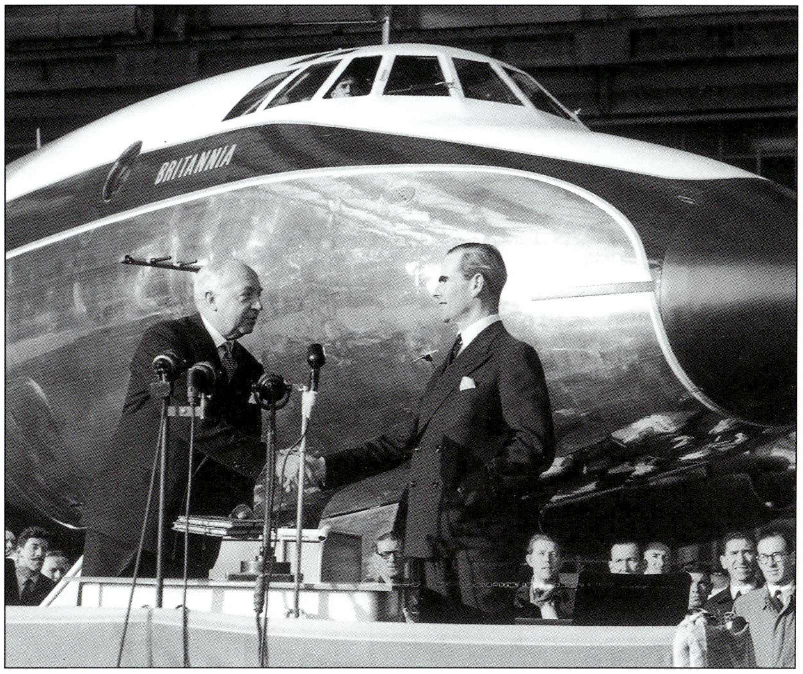

The Chairman of BOAC, Sir Miles Thomas, receives the log books of the first two Britannia aircraft G-ANBC and G-ANBD, delivered to the airline from the Chairman of Bristol, Sir Reginald Verdon Smith at Heathrow Airport on 30th December 1955.

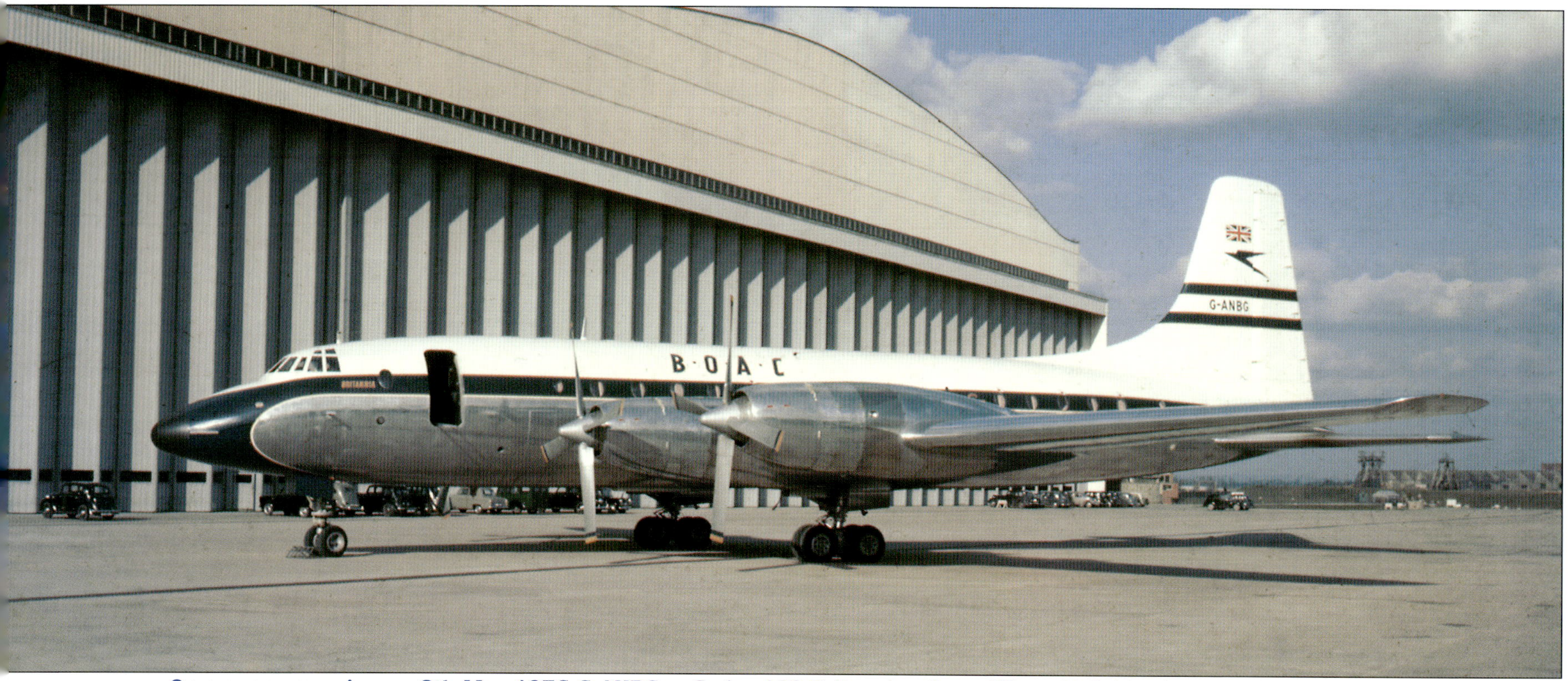

On a sunny morning on 8th May 1956 G-ANBG, a Series 102 Britannia, sits at Filton Airfield prior to delivery to BOAC later that day.

reduced by a small amount, and all Proteus engines were then modified accordingly.

By August 1958, the fifteen Britannia 102s were averaging 10.1 flying hours per day which is a very respectable utilisation. By comparison, the BOAC VC10s achieved 10.3 hours per day after about the same amount of experience.

As more of the ordered Britannias were delivered, BOAC extended the Britannia network; to Tokyo starting on 16th July 1957, to Aden (via Rome and Khartoum) on 22nd August, to Colombo (via Frankfurt, Beirut and Bombay) on 23rd August, to Hong Kong on 17th September and to Singapore on 18th September.

During 1957, Britannias also began to be used by distinguished passengers. The first member of the British Royal Family to fly by Britannia was Her Majesty Queen Elizabeth the Queen Mother. On 1st July 1957, she flew from Heathrow to Salisbury, Rhodesia aboard G-ANBF, taking off at 1845 and after a re-fuelling stop at Kano, Nigeria landing at Salisbury at 1400 on 2nd July, exactly on schedule. Captains Frank Walton and A S M Rendall were jointly in command as they were for the return trip, completed on 17th July.

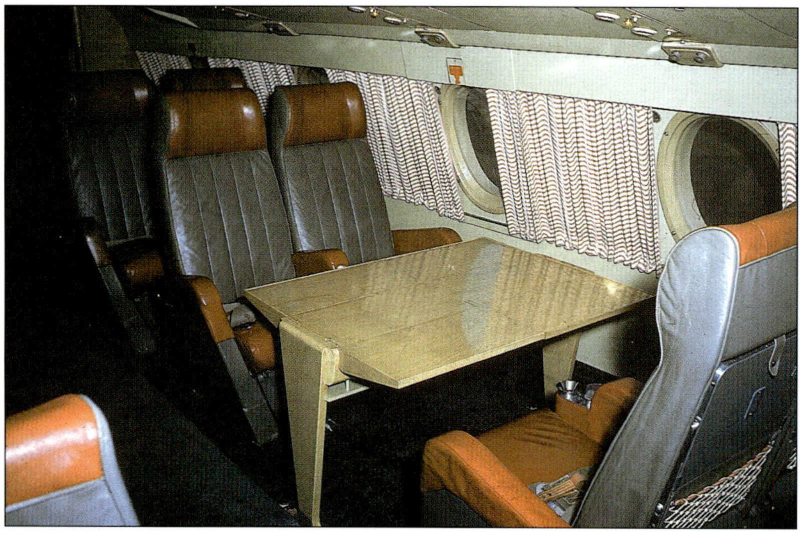

The First Class compartment in the cabin of a BOAC Series 102 Britannia with two by two seating.

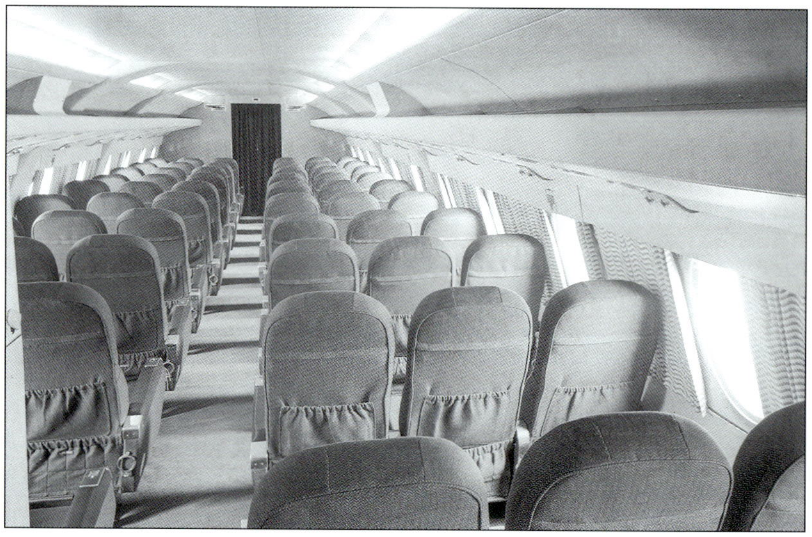

A view looking forward in the economy cabin of a BOAC Series 102 Britannia.

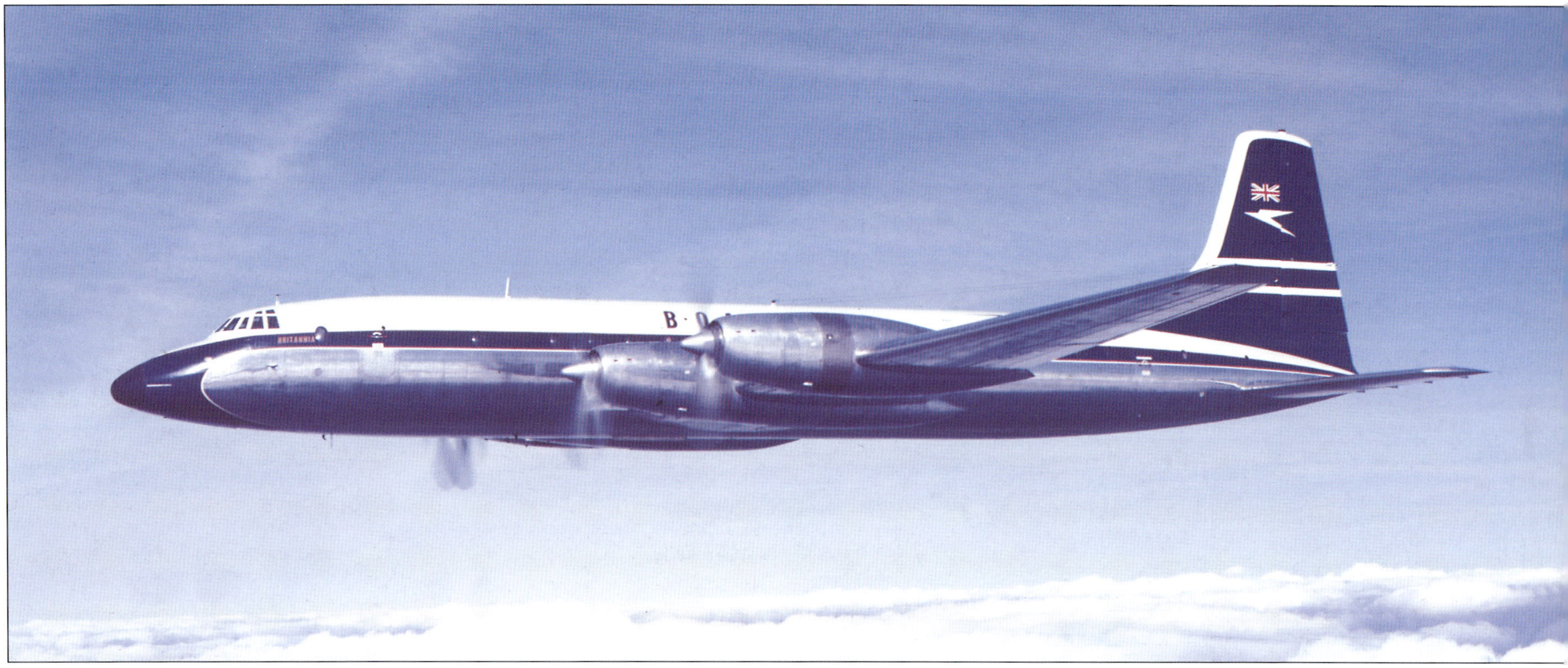

A delightful air-to-air study of Series 312 Britannia G-AOVG wearing the revised livery of BOAC in March 1958.

Another distinguished passenger at that time was the then Prime Minister Harold Macmillan who flew, with his party, on a goodwill tour to the Far East. They left Heathrow aboard G-ANBG on 7th January 1958, the Britannia fuselage having been fitted out for VIP usage, with sleeping accommodation, a dining area big enough for eight people, a lounge area and a bar. In five weeks the Britannia flew to India, Pakistan, Ceylon, Singapore, Australia and New Zealand. During this tour, the same Britannia carried the Queen Mother from Fiji to Auckland and Sydney between 28th January and 1st February. The Prime Minister's party finally returned to London on 14th February, the plane having covered almost 31,000 miles.

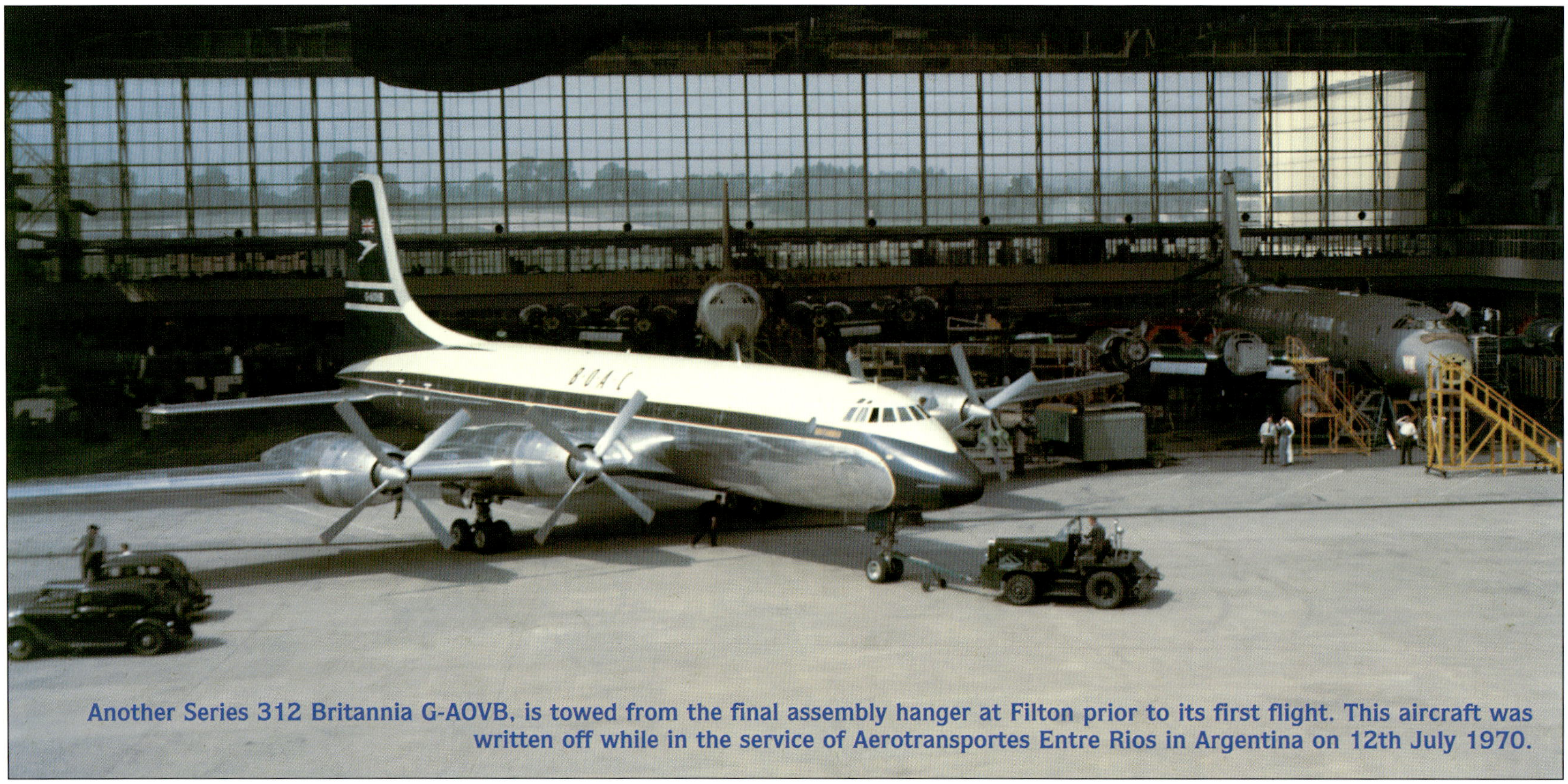

Another Series 312 Britannia G-AOVB, is towed from the final assembly hanger at Filton prior to its first flight. This aircraft was written off while in the service of Aerotransportes Entre Rios in Argentina on 12th July 1970.

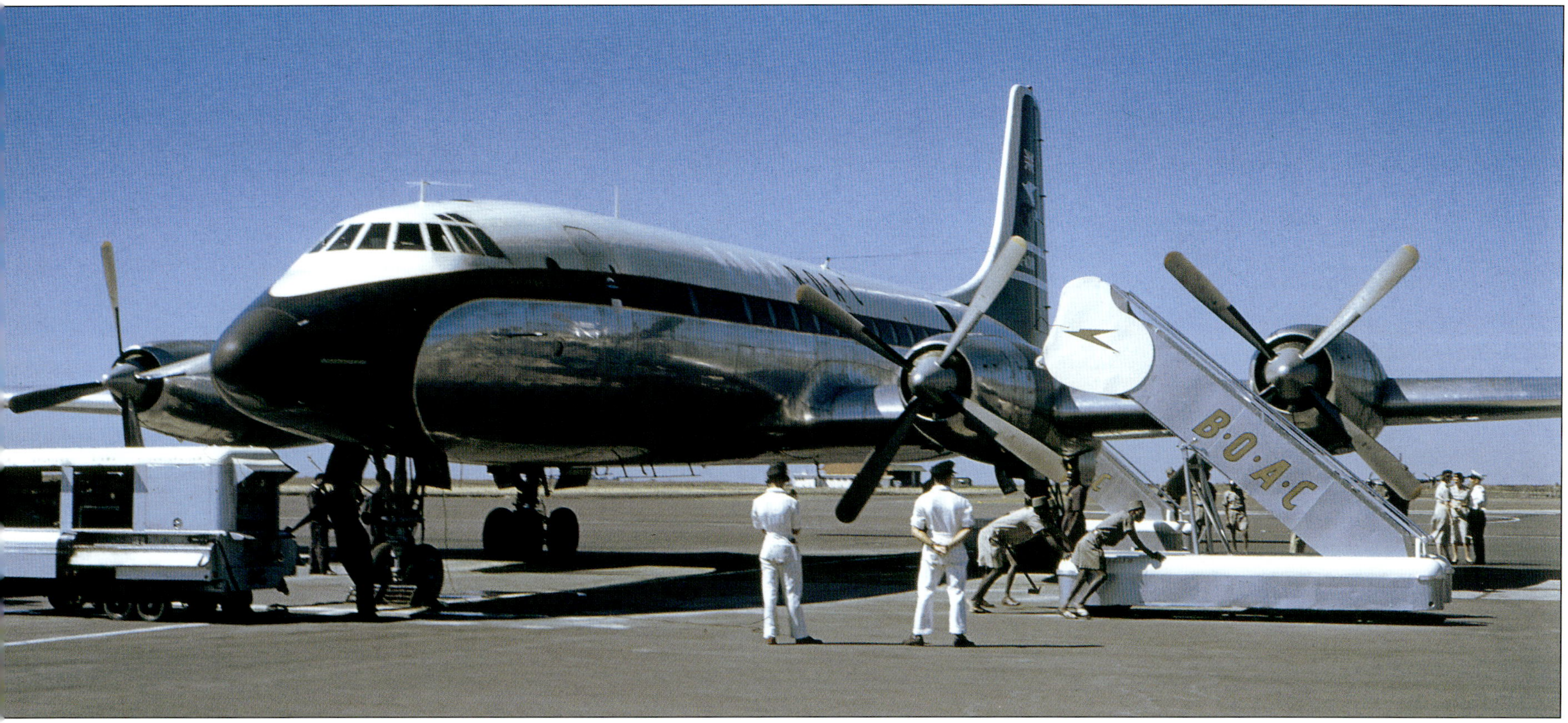

BOAC Britannia G-AOVK prepares to leave Nairobi Airport Kenya, on another stage of the journey home to Heathrow.

The growing reputation of the Britannia resulted in other special duties. At about this time, one of the City of London liveried guilds chartered a Britannia to fly a party from London to Venice. Their importance was such that on reaching Venice, they were met by limousines which took them straight to their hotel without the usual tedious formalities such as Customs inspections.

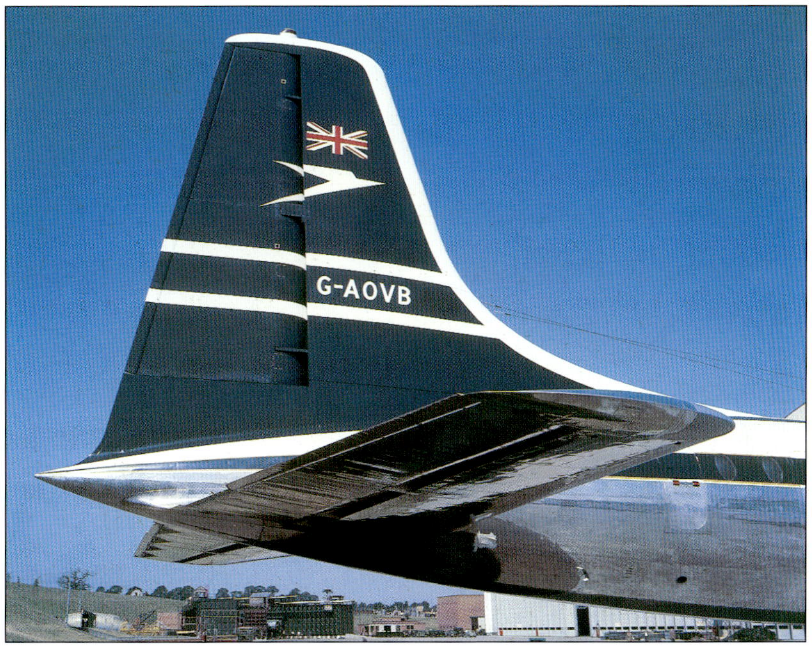

A close-up of the final tail colours carried by the Britannia in BOAC service.

All had gone well. The plane had arrived in Venice on time and the passengers had disembarked, the crew had lunch and then flew the empty plane back to London as arranged. However, as the Captain walked down the steps to the waiting crew bus at Heathrow, he was appalled to see that the ground staff had just opened the rear hold door only to reveal a full load of expensive looking suitcases inside. The ground staff at Venice, unfamiliar with the Britannia, had overlooked the existence of the rear hold. The result of this caused considerable rumbles within BOAC and BEA who had handled arrangements at Venice. The missing baggage was flown out as soon as possible by a BEA Viscount, whilst the two airlines were left to agree who would pay for the extra flight caused by this oversight.

By March 1958, Britannia 102s were operating all BOAC services to South Africa, the Far East and Australia. The London-Johannesburg route operated three times a week, departing on Tuesdays, Fridays and Saturdays. The weekday services were via Rome, Khartoum, Nairobi and Salisbury, departing at 1200 and arriving next day at 1250 local time - an elapsed time of 22hrs 50mins. The South African Airways flight, using a Douglas DC-7B aircraft, left London at 1600 arriving in Johannesburg at 1640 next day, via Amsterdam and Kano, with an elapsed time of 22hrs 40mins (10mins shorter than the Britannia, but with two rather than three stops).

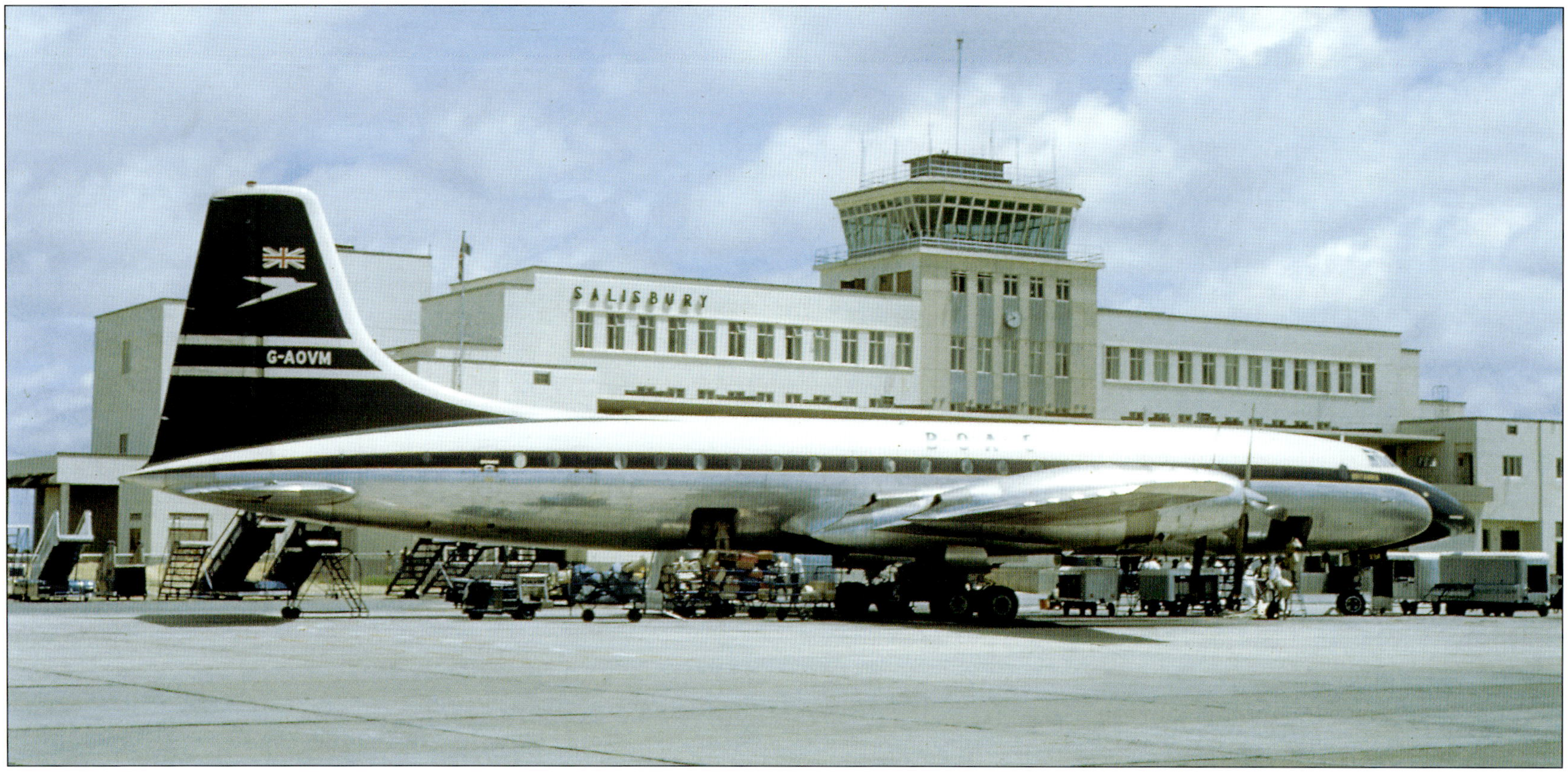

On 26th March 1964, Britannia Series 312 G-AOVM is serviced at Salisbury, Rhodesia (now Harare, Zimbabwe) in preparation for her final flight with BOAC to Heathrow Airport, London.

BOAC was also taking delivery of the new long-range Britannia 312s at this time. These had been designed to fly on the North Atlantic routes and the first such flight was on 19th December 1957, with aircraft G-AOVC. It inaugurated the BOAC London-New York service, having 26 sleeper seats, and 26 standard first-class seats, and the plan was that a high percentage of these flights should be from London to New York non-stop. Many were, but unfavourable head winds sometimes caused the early flights to have to re-fuel, for example in Newfoundland. The initial scheduled time for London to New York was twelve hours, but with operating techniques improving and as more experience was gained, direct flights became more reliable and their number increased. The scheduling also became more ambitious and, on 17th April 1958, a new transatlantic service was introduced, London-Montreal-Detroit-Chicago, the inaugural flight being by G-AOVH.

By the summer of 1958, the Britannia 312s were well established on the London-New York service and, on 6th May that year, a further schedule was introduced, London-San Francisco, with one re-fuelling stop at New York and a total flight time of 18hrs 30mins. During that summer, passengers had a choice of a daily flight on the route London-Montreal-Detroit-Chicago or a twice weekly flight London-New York-San Francisco.

The first accident to a BOAC Britannia occurred on 8th September 1958. G-ANBC was operating the Tokyo-London flight and made a scheduled landing at Rangoon, but it ran off the end of the runway in drizzle and the nose wheel collapsed in soft ground, being pushed up through the fuselage skin. All 42 people on board escaped injury but the nose area of the aircraft was badly damaged. It was decided that temporary repairs could be carried out at Rangoon and the aircraft then flown back to Filton for permanent repairs.

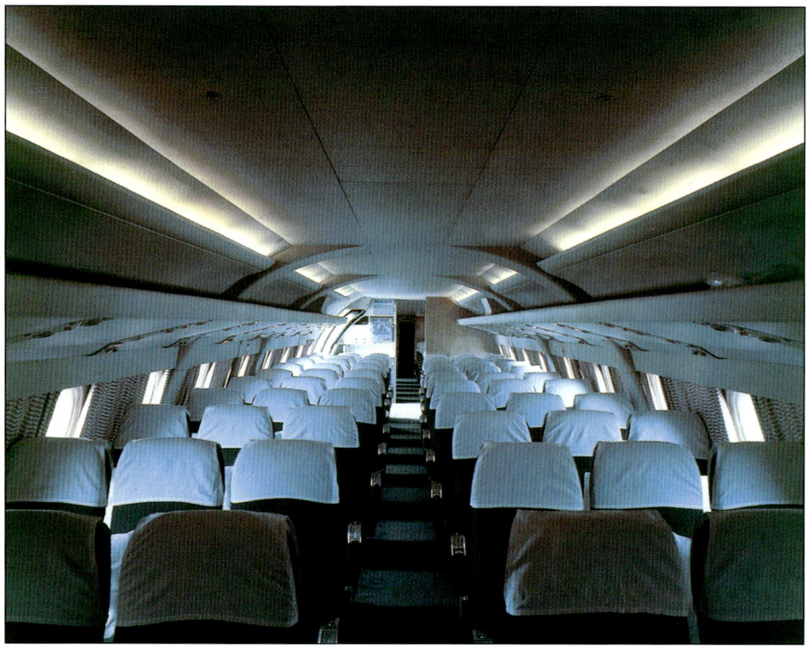

An interior view of the economy section of G-AOVM displaying the high standard of comfort in the BOAC Britannia.

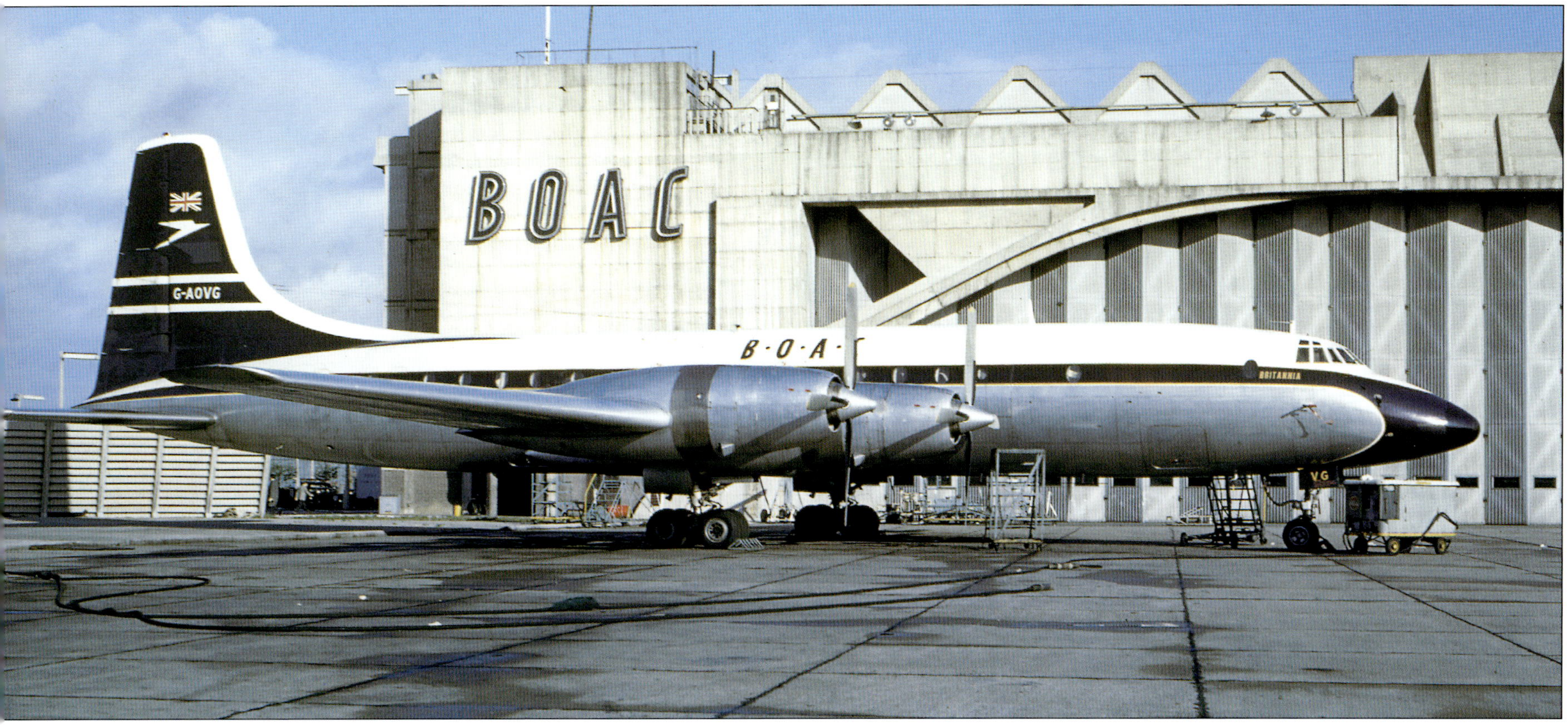

G-AOVG is seen at rest outside 'the Kremlin,' BOAC's headquarters at Heathrow Airport.

The temporary repairs began on 9th January 1959 and were completed and the aircraft test flown on 27th March. The next day she departed for the UK, with the undercarriage locked down and the whole fuselage unpressurised. She arrived at Filton on 1st April and had a whole new nose cone section fitted. This was completed and she returned to BOAC on 20th August. Two days later, she was back in service.

Alas, she lasted for just over another year. Flying out to Africa on 11th November 1960, she was approaching Khartoum in order to land when the undercarriage failed to lock down. The crew therefore decided to make an emergency landing on the grass beside the runway, fearing that the undercarriage would collapse on touch-down, which is exactly what happened. Again there were no injuries to those on board but the damage to G-ANBC was considerable and she was scrapped at the airport. This was the first Britannia to be lost in airline service.

In 1959 the 312s' route network was further extended to Tokyo with the first service, flown by G-AOVT via the USA, taking place on 1st April 1959. The first leg was delayed because of fog in the New York area, requiring a diversion to Boston, and the next leg to San Francisco was delayed because of strong headwinds. From San Francisco onwards there were some minor technical problems, and eventually the flight arrived in Tokyo some twelve hours late.

However there were more basic problems with the US Civil Aviation Board. When BOAC initially announced its intention to fly from San Francisco to Tokyo and applied to the CAB for permission to do so, Northwest Airlines objected, stating that their objection was because the British authorities were refusing to allow Northwest to open a service to Hong Kong.

For the inaugural flight, BOAC overcame the lack of permission for commercial flying between San Francisco and Tokyo by flying the passengers free of charge over that sector. They then suspended operations until official permission was granted, which occurred on 7th August 1959, and BOAC introduced a proper commercial service on 22nd August.

During the period of BOAC's operations with Britannia aircraft from 1957 to 1959, other developments were taking place in the aviation industry. An indication of these was a world tour by the BOAC chairman, Basil Smallpiece, in January 1958 during which he visited Boeing to assess the progress with the building of the 707 jet aircraft which BOAC had ordered for passenger use.

1960 was the high point for BOAC Britannia operations. All the Series 102 and 312 aircraft were kept busy and their reliability was, by then, over 90% and the frustrations associated with overcoming the development faults were gone.

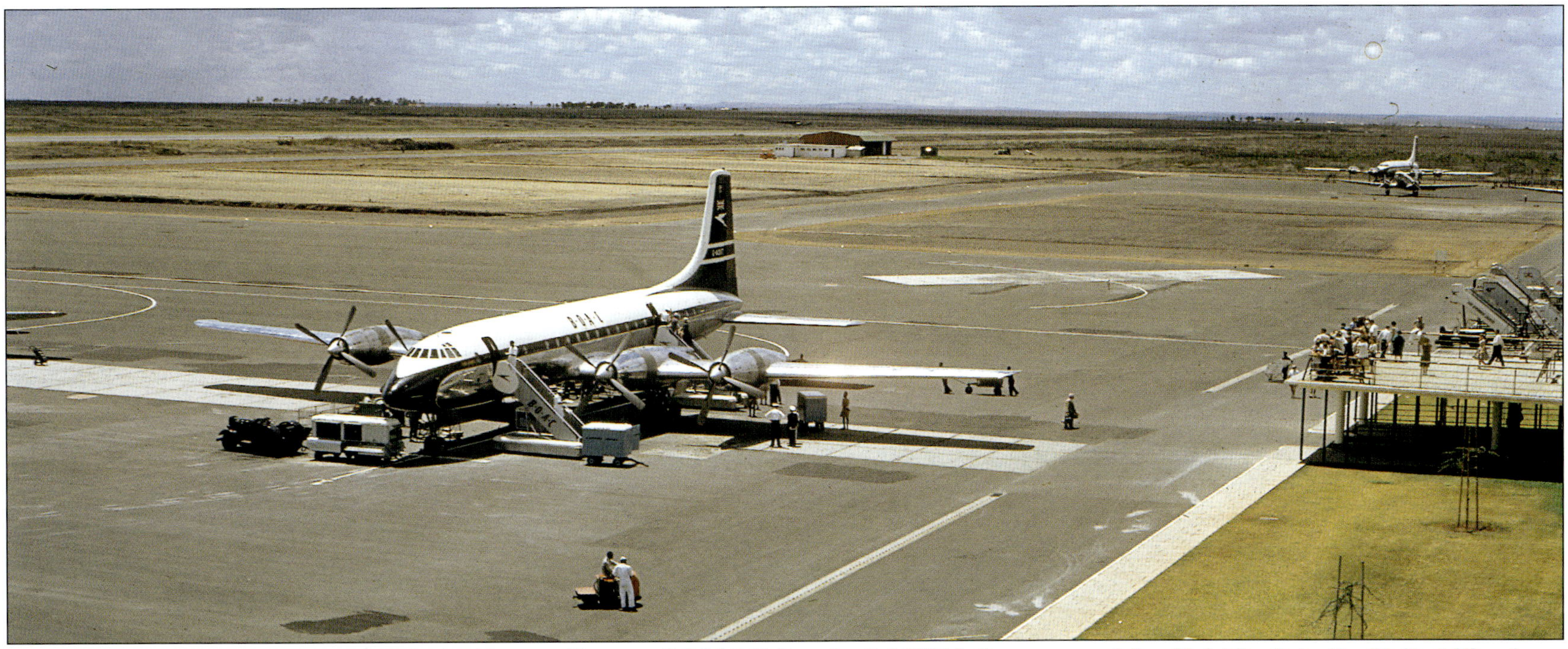

A view from the roof terrace at Nairobi Airport, Kenya, of BOAC Britannia G-AOVT being prepared for flight back to the United Kingdom. This aircraft was finally retired to Duxford Airfield, Cambridgeshire, in the colours of its last operator Monarch Airlines in June 1975.

The extent of Britannia coverage of BOAC services by this time was impressive. Britannia 312s flew London-New York twice per week (other flights by now having been taken over by Comets), London-New York-San Francisco-Honolulu-Wake Island-Tokyo-Hong Kong twice, London-Boston-New York once, London-Manchester-Prestwick-New York four times, London-Prestwick-Montreal-Detroit-Chicago twice, London-Shannon-Montreal-Detroit-Chicago twice, London-Prestwick-Montreal-Toronto twice and London-Manchester-Prestwick-Montreal once per week.

312s also flew to the Caribbean, with London-Bermuda-Barbados-Port of Spain-Caracas served once per week, London-Bermuda-Port of Spain-Caracas-Bogota once, London-New York-Nassau-Montego Bay-Kingston three times, and less than once a week Montreal to Nassau-Montego Bay-Kingston-Bermuda. The Caribbean services were helped by the leasing to British West Indian Airways (BWIA) of three 312s in succession between 1958 and 1961, in order G-AOVL, G-AOVB and G–AOVJ.

102s flew London-Karachi twice per week, London-Bahrain twice, London-Aden once, London-Nairobi three times, London-Lagos four times and London-Accra twice per week. The London-Tehran route was flown, usually by a 312, less frequently than once per week.

In a pattern to be followed elsewhere, three African routes were flown by BOAC Britannia 102s leased to other airlines; London to Dar-es-Salaam once per week by East African Airways, London-Accra twice per week by Ghana Airways and London-Lagos three times per week by Nigeria Airways.

By this time, however, the popularity of the turbo-prop driven aircraft was falling.

Wherever passengers had the choice, they chose to fly by the newer jet aircraft which were so much quicker than any propeller-driven craft. Figures for scheduled flight timings on the London-New York route make the difference clear. Before the Britannia, the fastest scheduled time e.g. by Super Constellation, was 13hrs 35mins. By Britannia, it was 10hrs 50mins, but by Boeing 707 it was down to 7hrs 40mins. Even in 1959, the sale of seats on the Britannia 312s was only 55%, whereas on the Comet 4s it was over 90%. So the introduction by BOAC of the 707 service on the North Atlantic route on 27th May 1960 made it clear that the role of the Britannias on the major routes operated by BOAC was coming to an end.

One of the consequences of this was that BOAC was prepared to lease some of its Britannias to other airlines to cover short-term problems. Cathay Pacific Airways leased three of the Series 102 variants in the period between 12th December 1960 and 31st January 1961; G-ANBB for three weeks, G-ANBO for five weeks and G-ANBL for six weeks. A similar arrangement was made with British European Airways (BEA) who leased three Series 312 variants, G-AOVG, G-AOVP and G-AOVT, to cover a short-term hiatus in aircraft on their European routes in April and May 1961.

The last scheduled flight of a Series 102 Britannia for BOAC

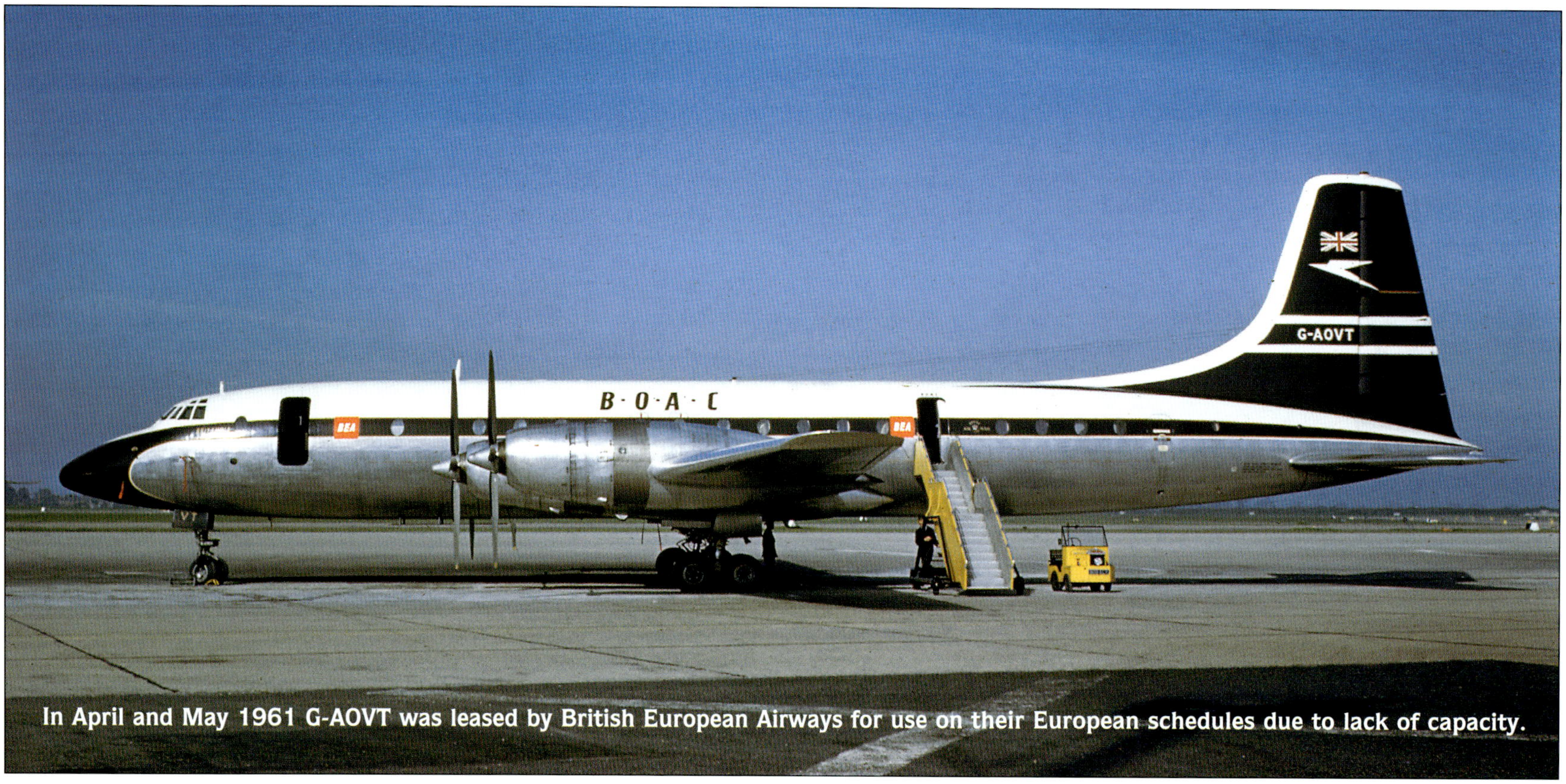

In April and May 1961 G-AOVT was leased by British European Airways for use on their European schedules due to lack of capacity.

was on 22nd November 1961 when G-ANBF flew from Hong Kong to London, although leased Britannias continued to fly for Malayan Airways on the Kuala Lumpur to London schedule until March 1963. The final scheduled flight for a Series 312 Britannia for BOAC was on 26th April 1965 when G-AOVL flew from New York to Bermuda. But this was by no means the end of the Britannia story, for while BOAC phased them out for its own use on scheduled flights, many other airlines were still keen to use them and when they became available on the open market, the Britannias were soon bought up.

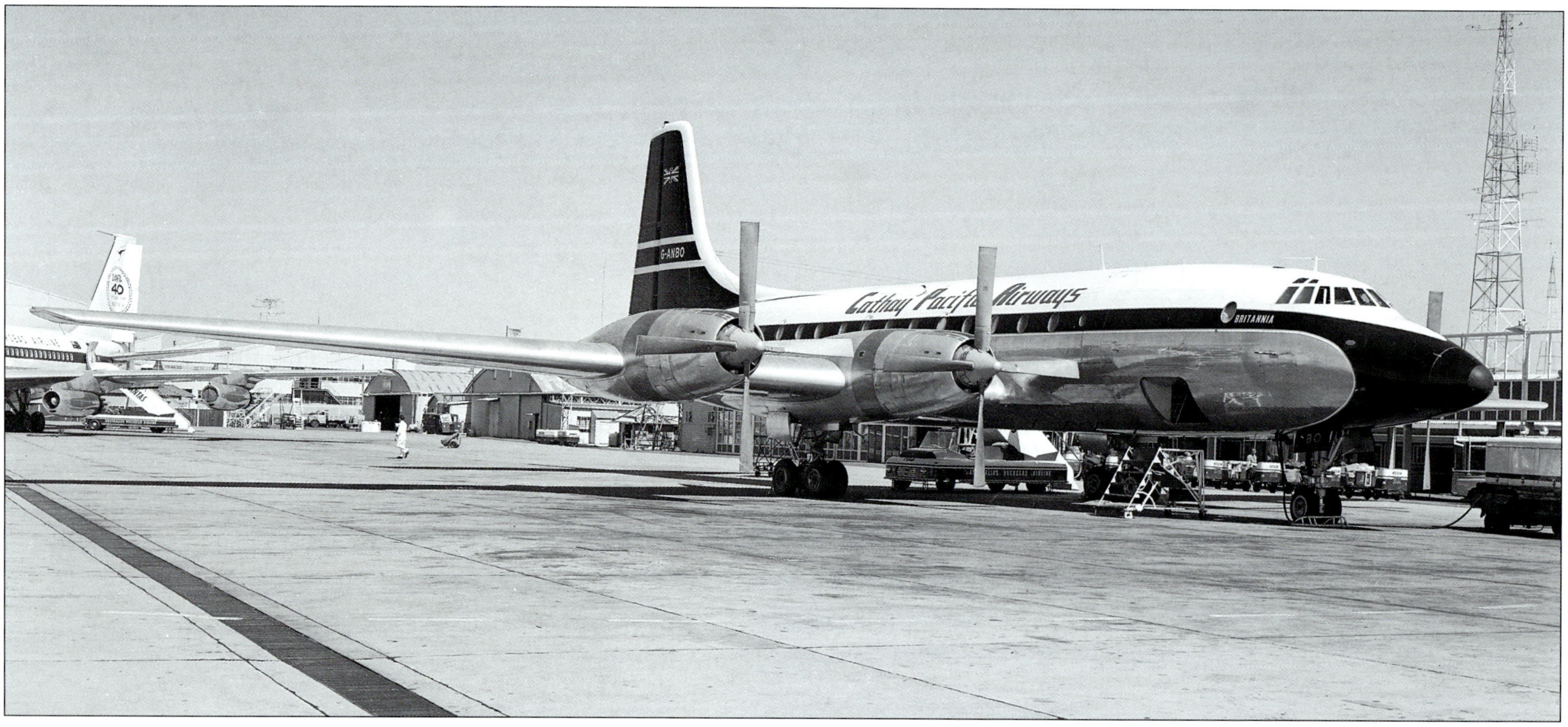

G-ANBO, the last of the Series 102 Britannias built, stands at Hong Kong in late December 1960 in the livery of Cathay Pacific Airways who leased the aircraft from BOAC from December 1960 to January 1961, whilst their Lockheed Electra aircraft were being modified.

IN SERVICE WITH RAF TRANSPORT COMMAND

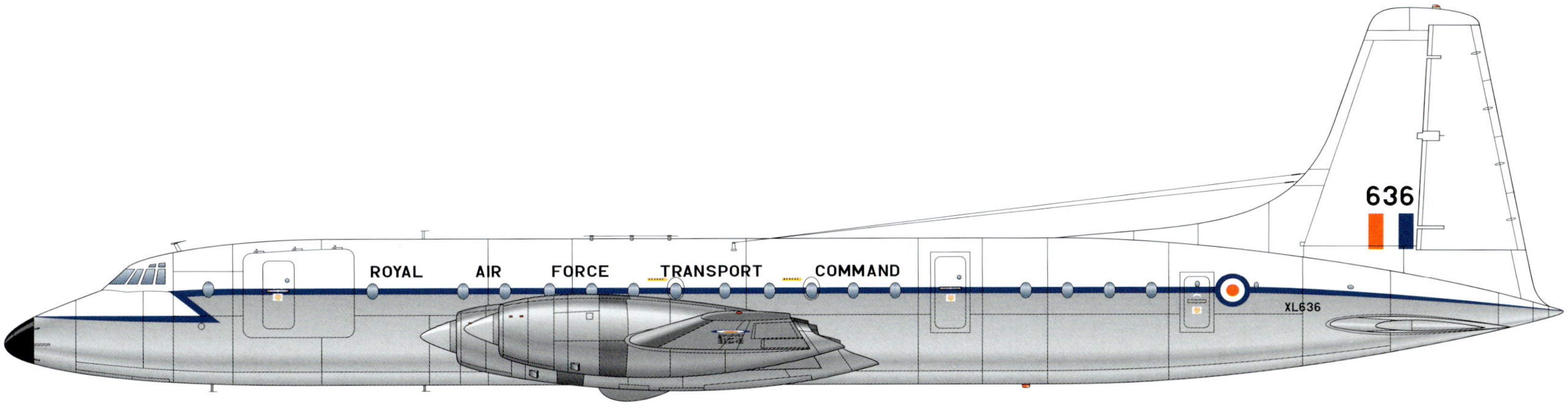

After BOAC, the next most important customer for the Britannia was RAF Transport Command. Twenty-three of the 250 Series (three as the 252 variant and twenty as the 253 variant) were supplied by Bristol in the period between April 1959 and December 1960. The 250 Series, modified specifically to RAF requirements, had a large forward freight loading door and a strengthened front region fuselage floor to enable it to carry particularly bulky loads. The fuselage could also be arranged either for normal troop carrying (with rear facing seats) or for carrying stretcher cases.

Until the introduction of Britannias to the RAF, it was normal for all new aircraft to be sent to Boscombe Down for full flight testing by RAF pilots. For the Britannia this practice was almost entirely eliminated as it was, for the first time, assumed that the civil test results could be accepted and need not be repeated.

In 1956 a committee had been set up under Rear Admiral A N C Bingley to make recommendations on the inter-service requirements of the future air transport force. The Committee's analysis of possible British commitments around the world led them to conclude that, for example, to move an Army Brigade with light equipment and some specialist reinforcements would require 54 Britannia sorties for a move to Singapore; for the Navy, a modest reinforcement of officers and ratings in the Far East would require twelve Britannia sorties; for the RAF, equipment and technical personnel to

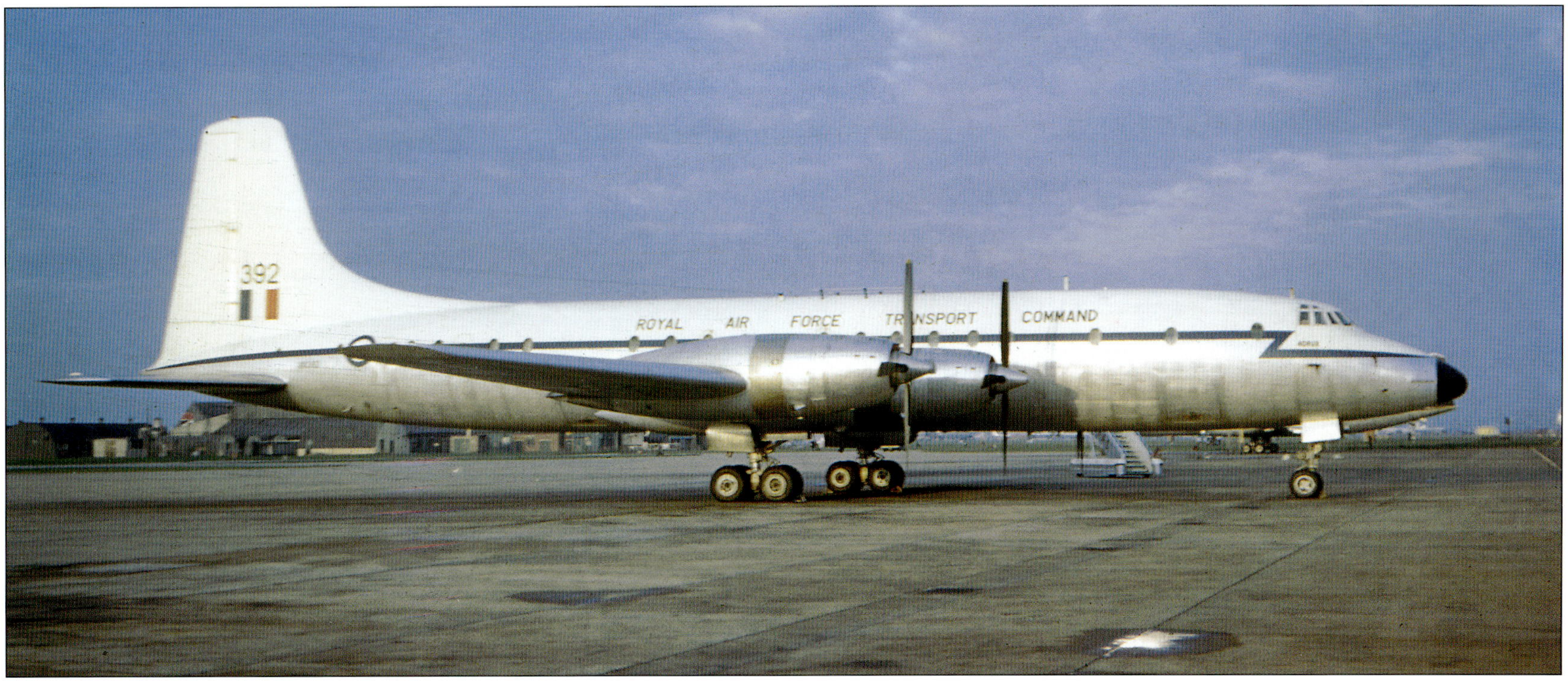

RAF Series 252C Mk 2 XN392 'Acrux' at rest at London's Heathrow Airport on 11th April 1962, displaying its early natural metal livery.

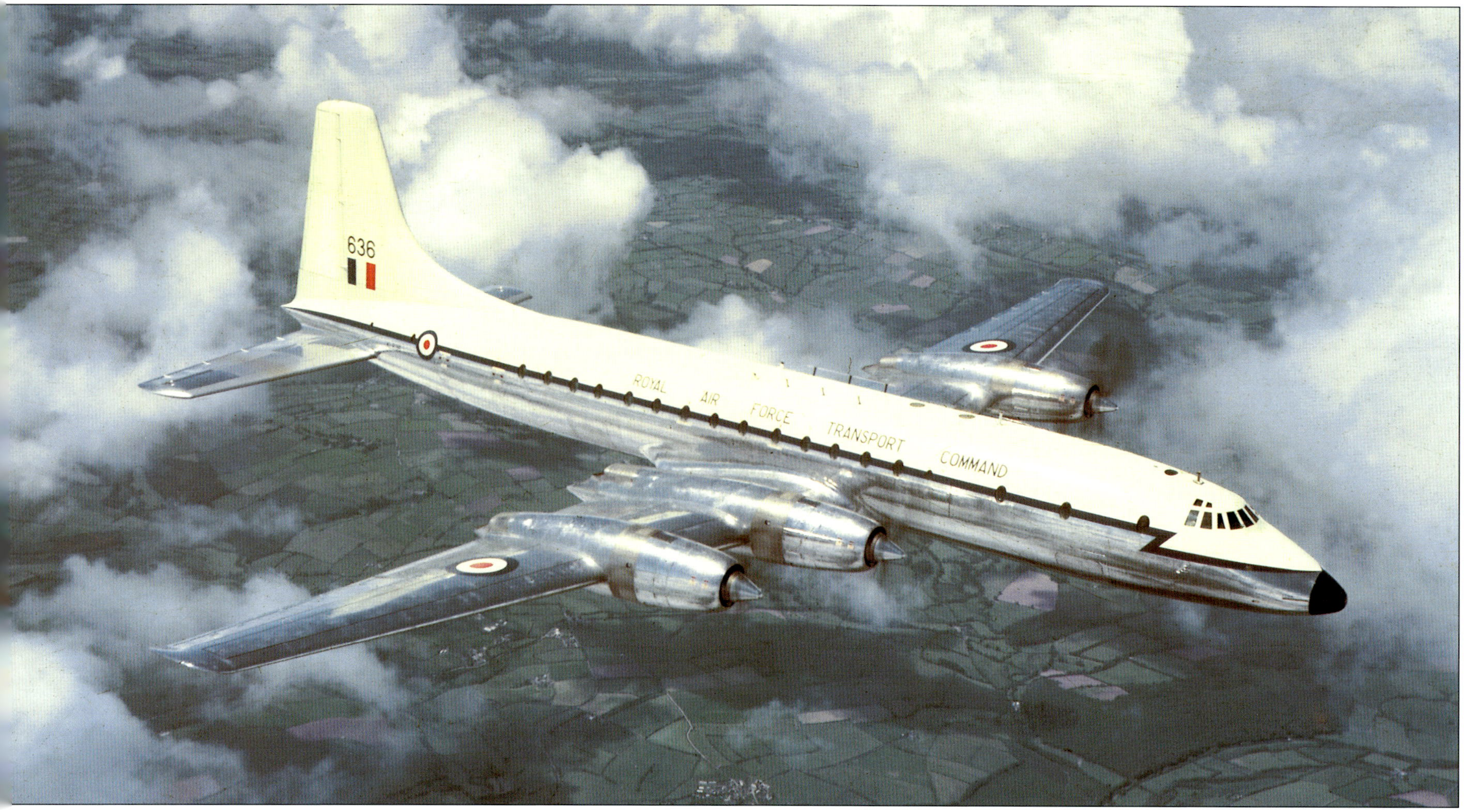

A superb shot of XL636, a Series 253C Mk 1, taken on her first flight on 23rd April 1959.

support the move of four V-Bomber (nuclear carrying) squadrons would require 34 Britannia sorties.

The size of this commitment made the Committee think that if the transport work was to be undertaken solely by RAF planes, the cost would be far too great (and the necessary aircraft might be sitting idle and not used for most of their life). So the idea was then considered that only some of the required aircraft would be RAF owned, the rest being operated by a civil consortium. The civil aircraft were to be used for the majority of routine troop movements by air, leaving the RAF aircraft to meet requirements in case of war. This was the thinking which led to the plan implied above, to order a total of twenty Britannias (of the 253 variant), together with the three Ministry of Supply aircraft (252 variant).

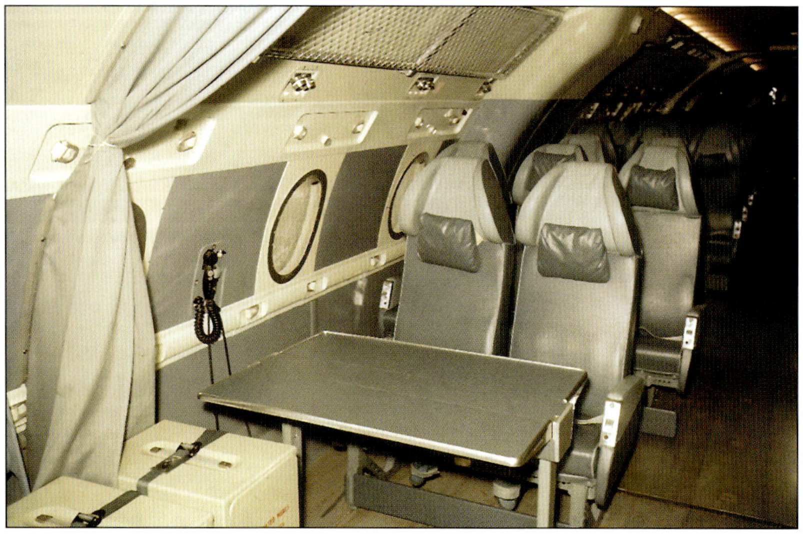

As can be seen in this interior shot of the passenger cabin of an RAF Britannia, the aircraft seating was upholstered in grey leather.

The first Britannia, XN 398, landed at Lyneham on 19th March 1959. This was the beginning of the Britannia's RAF history which spanned nearly fifteen years, ending in January 1976, although one military Britannia remained at Boscombe Down until February 1984.

The arrival of the Britannias was not without incident. On one of the early flights into Lyneham, the ground staff were somewhat disorganised. The aircraft came to a halt at the designated spot but there were no steps ready to be brought up to the fuselage door. The Captain became increasingly impatient during the ensuing wait and eventually decided to make his own emergency exit.

Just by the forward port door there was a special locker containing a rope which could be lowered so that crew members could slide down it to the ground. The Captain grabbed this and launched off but unfortunately the top end of the rope had not been attached to the aircraft and he reached the ground rather faster than he expected. Fortunately he was not badly hurt.

The arrangement on the flight deck for landing was that the Captain (in the left hand seat) or First Officer (in the right hand seat) had charge of the flying controls. The Flight Engineer sat in the seat between and somewhat behind the pilots. His function was to adjust the engine throttles, as ordered by the Captain.

On one early landing at Lyneham, all went according to plan until touch-down when, at that moment, the Engineer's seat collapsed and he landed on the floor. The Captain produced the memorable order, "When you've finished grovelling, I'll have (engines) idle." The Engineer quickly picked himself up and complied with the order.

The arrival of the Britannias resulted in the immediate reconsideration of patterns of long-range operations. For example, the aircraft could fly non-stop from Lyneham to Aden or Nairobi and next day on to Singapore, rather than have to fly to Malta or El Adem, North Africa on day one, then to Aden on day two and perhaps Karachi on day three. Such long-range flights required navigational accuracy which made an auto-pilot essential, but it greatly increased the speed of troop movements.

All the Britannias were allocated to two squadrons - numbers 99 and 511. They were originally based at RAF Lyneham but subsequently transferred to RAF Brize Norton in January 1970 when Lyneham became the base for the Lockheed C130 Hercules aircraft.

The two squadrons did not operate independently for long. By the autumn of 1960 it was realised that it was more efficient to have one centrally serviced Britannia fleet. Aircraft were placed in a central store and serviced when appropriate, and each squadron then drew aircraft from the store as it had need of them.

Over their seventeen years of service with the RAF, the Britannias were used extensively, ferrying troops and cargo throughout the world. In the early days a Britannia's carrying

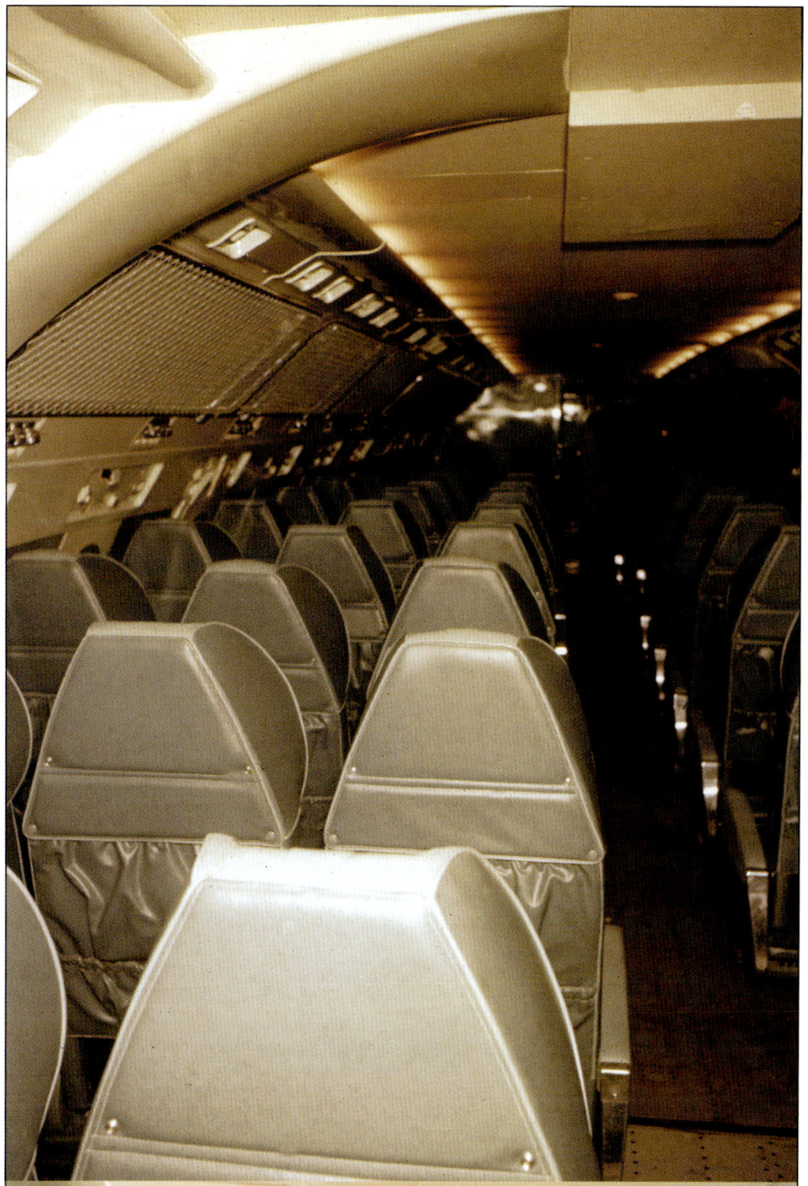

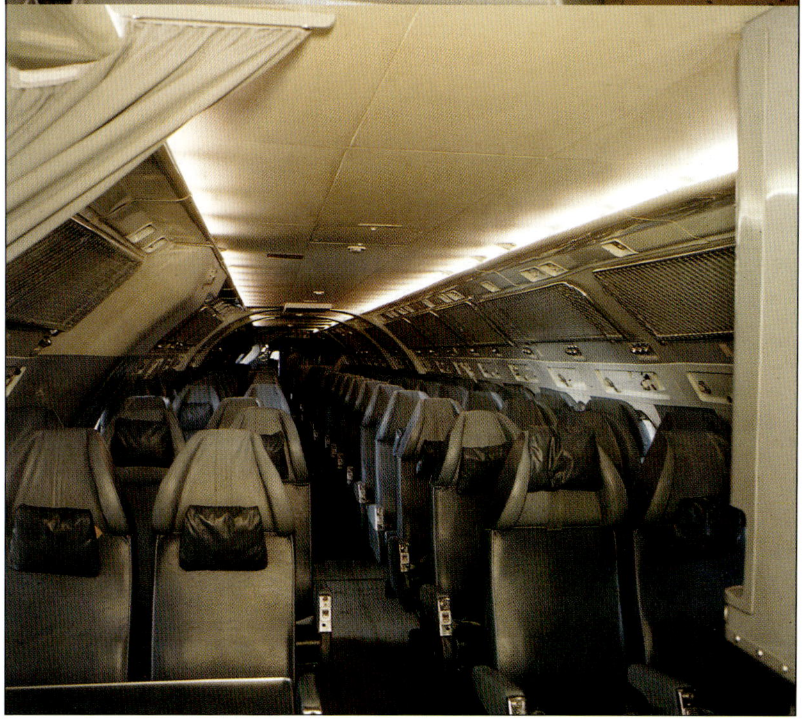

Two more illustrations of the interior of RAF Britannias give an idea of the comfort and space provided for the passengers. The aircraft were routinely used on long distance flights to the Far East and Australia so high standards of passenger satisfaction were required.

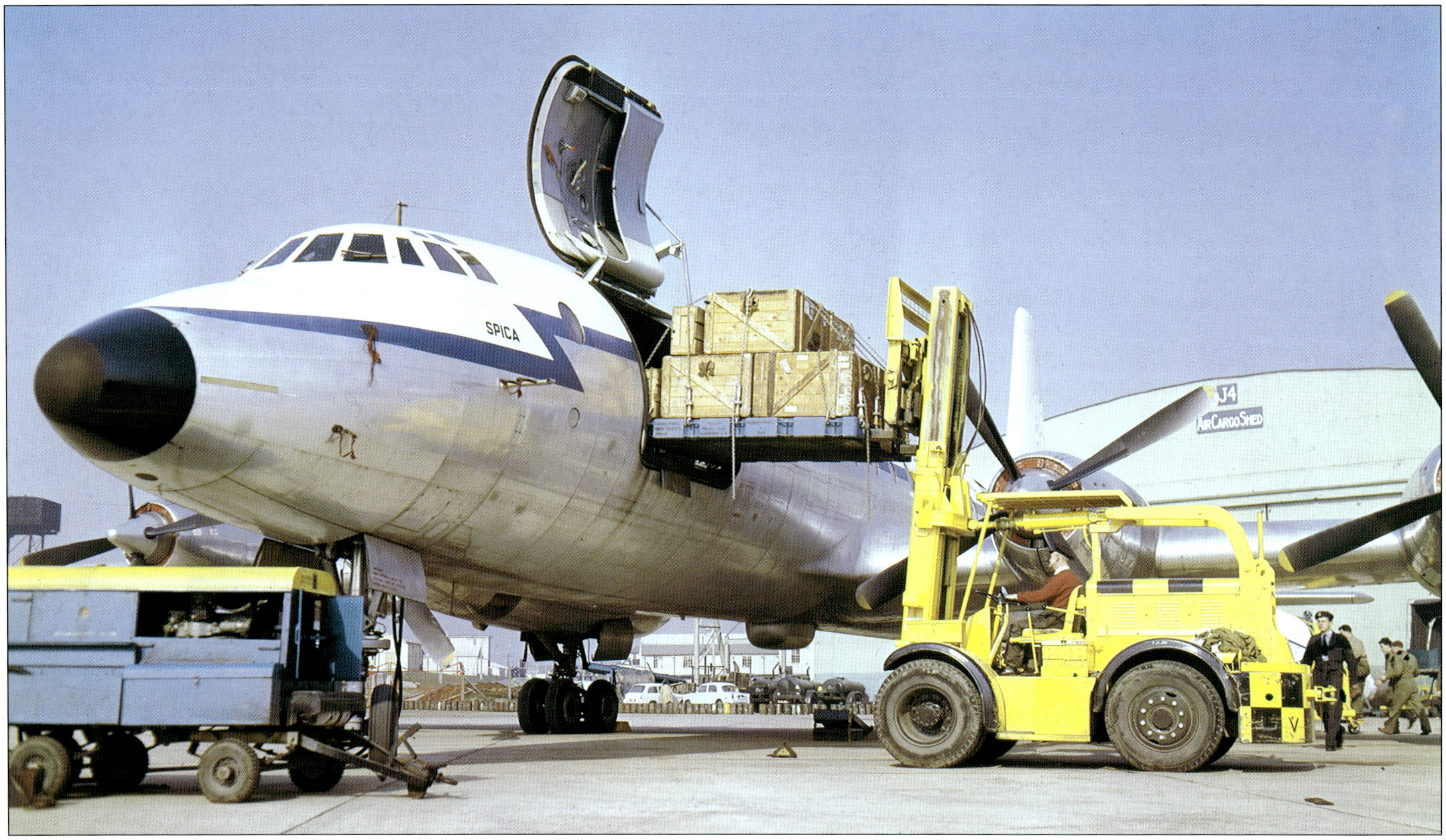

RAF Britannias were fitted with a forward fuselage cargo door for the easy loading and transport of freight.

capacity became newsworthy. The Lyneham newspaper recorded that "during the period 8th to 14th December 1959, a Britannia captained by Flying Officer Whiteight and Pilot Officer Haley transported 1231 passengers between Lyneham-Luqa-Idris-El Adem-Alconbury. 1,179 of those passengers were moved in eleven flights." This gives an average of over 107 passengers per flight, and the aircraft was designed to take 108 passengers at 39 inch seat pitch or 113 troops at 36 inch pitch, so the operation involved near maximum loads.

Another 'first' which attracted notice was a round-the-world trip in eight days. Flight Lieutenants 'Rip' Kerbey and Tom Goddard took XL 638 from Lyneham on 16th December via Nicosia, Karachi, Changi, Darwin, Christmas Island, Vancouver, Montreal and back to Lyneham on 23rd December. The trip received considerable press and TV coverage.

However not all the publicity-seeking ventures went according to plan. In one of these, a group of students from the RAF College at Cranwell were to visit their American fellow students at the USAF Academy at Colorado Springs. They were to fly in a Britannia, and given a relatively light payload and a very unusual meteorological feature, an easterly jet stream across the North Atlantic, the crew decided to try to fly from Cranwell to Colorado direct!

Alas, when the aircraft was about halfway across the Atlantic, the jet stream winds turned through 180 degrees, back to their normal westerly direction. The crew reluctantly decided to land at Montreal where the plane had to stay overnight as the crew had run out of duty time. The next day the remainder of the flight to Colorado Springs was uneventful and created no records.

In March 1960, the load carrying capacity of the Britannias was tested in what was the largest RAF/Army exercise ever to take place outside the UK. Called Exercise 'Starlight' it involved the transport of troops, equipment and vehicles to North Africa. Four Britannias from 99 Squadron and seventeen Hastings from 24, 36 and 114 Squadrons operated a shuttle service between Lyneham and El Adem, Tobruk starting on 10th March. Every day until 20th March, three Britannias each carrying 110 men and two Hastings loaded with vehicles touched down in North Africa.

For the return, the Britannias flew 39 sorties in less than five days with only ten aircraft and twelve crew (needed so as to slip crews, so that an aircraft could fly off again with a fresh crew while the previous duty crew rested). 4,000 troops were moved with one flight every eight hours.

Over the years, Britannias were called on to help in various trouble spots around the world. In 1960 a Comet from 216 Squadron, two Vulcans from 101 Squadron and a Britannia from 99 Squadron flew to Argentina for their 150th Anniversary Celebration of Argentine Independence. Just before the celebrations began however, Chile suffered a devastating earthquake and the Britannia in Argentina, XL 659, carried out two flights taking clothing, medicines and food to Santiago before re-joining the Anniversary ceremonies.

After the Congo gained independence in June 1960, there was an Army mutiny, with rioting and looting and a request for UN help to restore order. Two Britannias, XL 491 and XL 518, were involved in flying European civilians out of Leopoldville and transferring UN troops in.

In July 1961 the Iraqis made the first statement that Kuwait belonged to them and started to move forces towards the border. This caused Operation 'Vantage' to be launched, which involved moving troops, tanks and armoured cars into Kuwait to secure the airfield. Britannias were used for the long-range troop movements from the UK, Cyprus, Aden and Kenya. The result was that there was no invasion of Kuwait by Iraq as the ground force was installed in time to deter any potential invaders. From 20th July onwards, the forces were gradually withdrawn, leaving just a stand-by presence in Cyprus and Bahrain.

There was another demonstration of the long-range of a Britannia on 6th November 1961 when a lightly loaded Britannia, having flown out to Kingston, Jamaica with emergency supplies for hurricane-devastated Belize, took off at 1300 (local time) and completed 4,100 nautical miles in 12hrs 40mins. It was a record breaking non-stop flight but unfortunately it did not end at Lyneham as that airfield was fog bound and the aircraft had to be diverted to St Mawgan, Cornwall.

The role of the Transport Force of Britannias, in being able to move men and supplies quickly around the world, continued to be of great importance. In July 1963, there was trouble in British Guiana (now Guyana) where, after a long general strike, riots broke out. Operation 'Pedal' was declared and 500 men, being the 2nd Battalion, The Green Jackets and support staff, were quickly flown out from the UK.

A similar transporting challenge, but this time not an emergency, occurred in November 1963 with the longest military airlift undertaken up to that time. Seven Britannias flew the 1st Battalion, Royal Ulster Rifles the 12,000 miles from the UK to Australia for a joint exercise with the Australian Army.

Another notable exercise took place the same year. As part of Exercise Barfrost II, a fleet of Britannias carried No. 43 Commando, 640 personnel, fifteen Land Rovers, fifteen half-

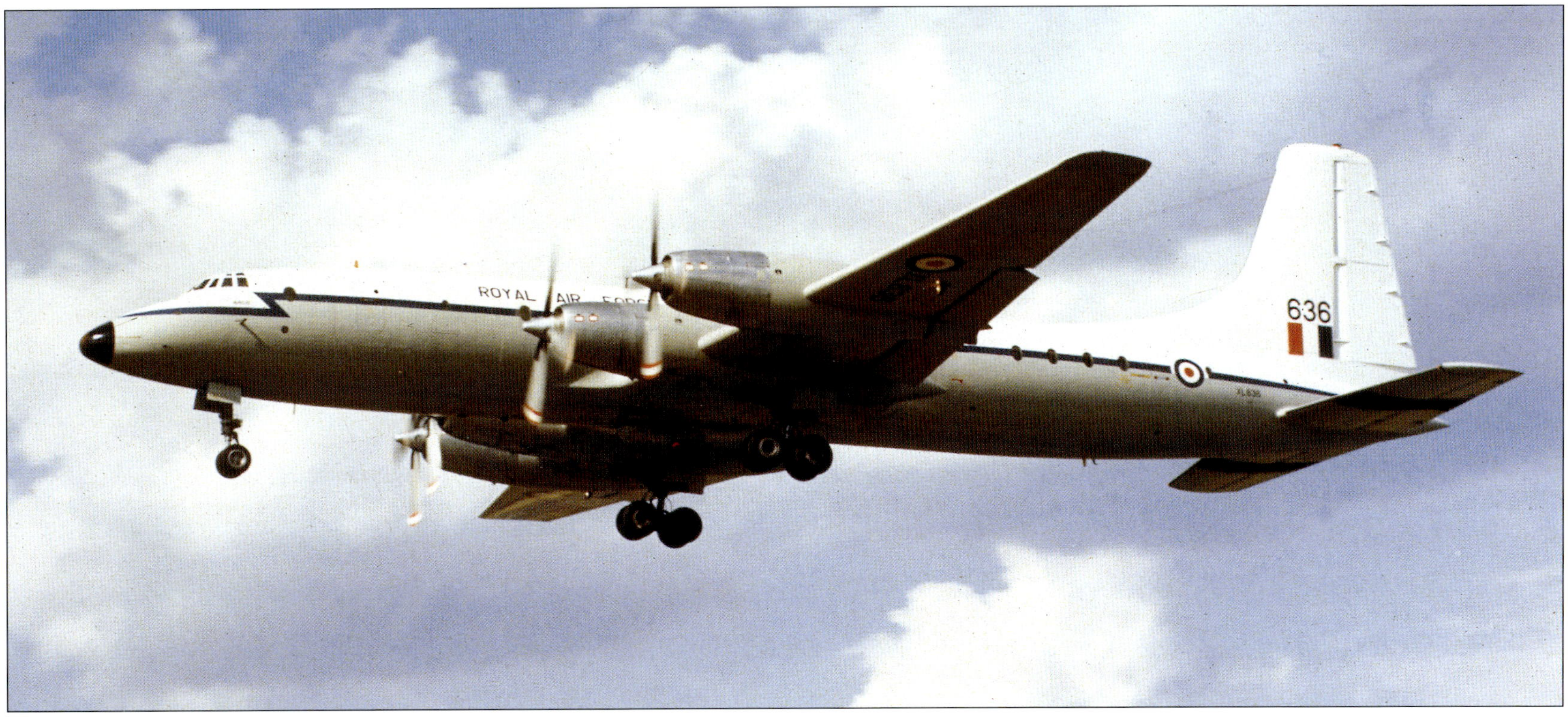

XL636 on approach to Brize Norton wearing the final livery carried by RAF Britannias of white top and grey wings and fuselage.

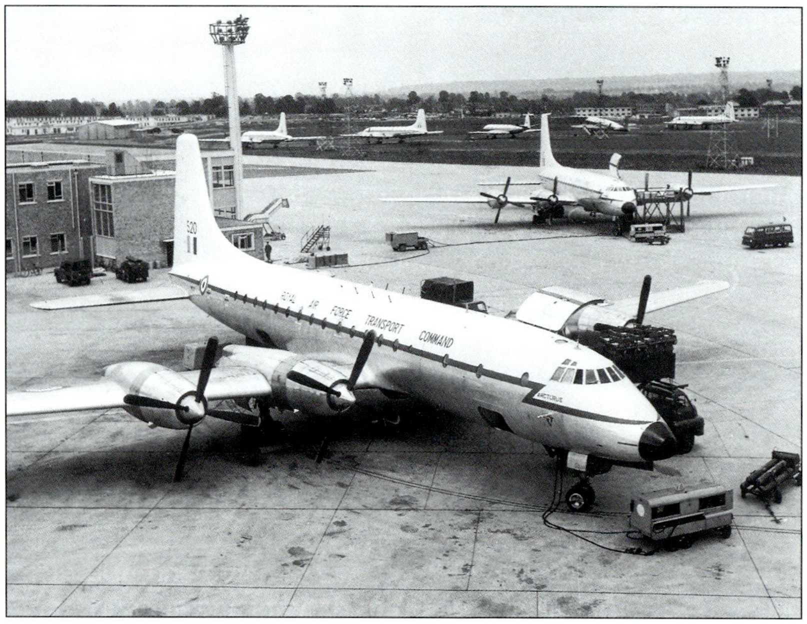

Five Britannias, a Comet and a Hastings aircraft are seen here at RAF Lyneham Airfield, Wiltshire.

ton trailers and 30,000 lbs of freight from Lyneham to Bardufoss in Northern Norway, a remote airfield well inside the Arctic Circle. Luckily the timing was in the northern summer, but it helped that the ferrying schedule required a quick off-load and take-off again, and the whole exercise went off smoothly.

In September 1964, there was unrest in Malaysia which had been formed the previous year by merging Malaya, Singapore, Sarawak and North Borneo. The Indonesian President Sukarno declared a 'crush Malaysia' policy, and there followed harassment with guerilla raids, first in Sarawak and Sabah and then landings in Malaya. So there was an urgent and large reinforcement of the British Forces in Malaysia, involving large numbers of Britannia sorties between the UK and the Far East.

Shortly after this, in October 1964, an assignment of Britannias began conveying troops and their families to and from Malta and Cyprus with regular flights three times per week. This provided a role for the three Ministry of Supply Britannias, XN 392, XN 398 and XN 404, which were variant 252s. They had a large portside forward freight door but a wooden floor for forward freight stowage and with some toilets and the galley amidships. They were not as versatile for freight transport as the variant 253s, which all the other RAF Britannias were, but for the regular shuttle movement of families between Lyneham and the Eastern Mediterranean, they were ideal and much used.

The use of the Britannias for medical flights, either to carry stretcher patients or even at times to give emergency treatment in flight, for which purpose part of the passenger cabin could be fitted out as an operating theatre, was very valuable. All overseas bases needed from time to time to return patients to the UK for specialist treatment. For example, aeromedical flights from Bahrain via Cyprus to Lyneham took place every other Monday in the 1960s. Sergeant Mike Sims from the RAF Medical Branch commented subsequently:-"The patients liked the Britannia. It was a long flight (from Bahrain to the UK) but the comfort and care they received compensated for this. After the departure of the Britannias from the Service, I felt that a large gap was left in the aeromed world and a lot of atmosphere lost that could not be found in the later aircraft used."

The only time when Her Majesty The Queen flew in an RAF Britannia was on 1st May 1962. XN 404 conveyed Her Majesty together with HRH Princess Marina and Princess Alexandra to Amsterdam to attend the Silver Wedding of Queen Juliana of the Netherlands and Prince Bernhardt. HRH Prince Philip joined the party for the return. An aeronautical footnote is that the aircraft suffered complete radio failure shortly after take-off in the London Control Zone!

In the same year, Their Royal Highnesses The Duke and Duchess of Kent flew by Britannia to Kampala for the Uganda Independence celebrations.

For any VIP flight, timing is a matter of pride for the crew involved in order to arrive and open the aircraft door at the precisely specified moment, and a great deal of

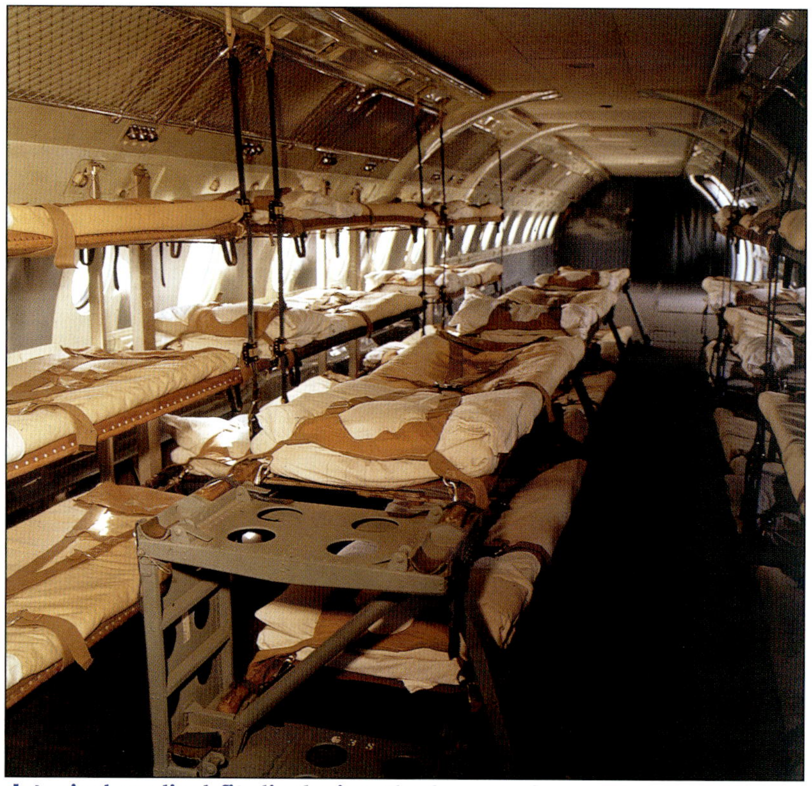

A typical medical fit displaying the layout of stretcher carriers inside an RAF Britannia.

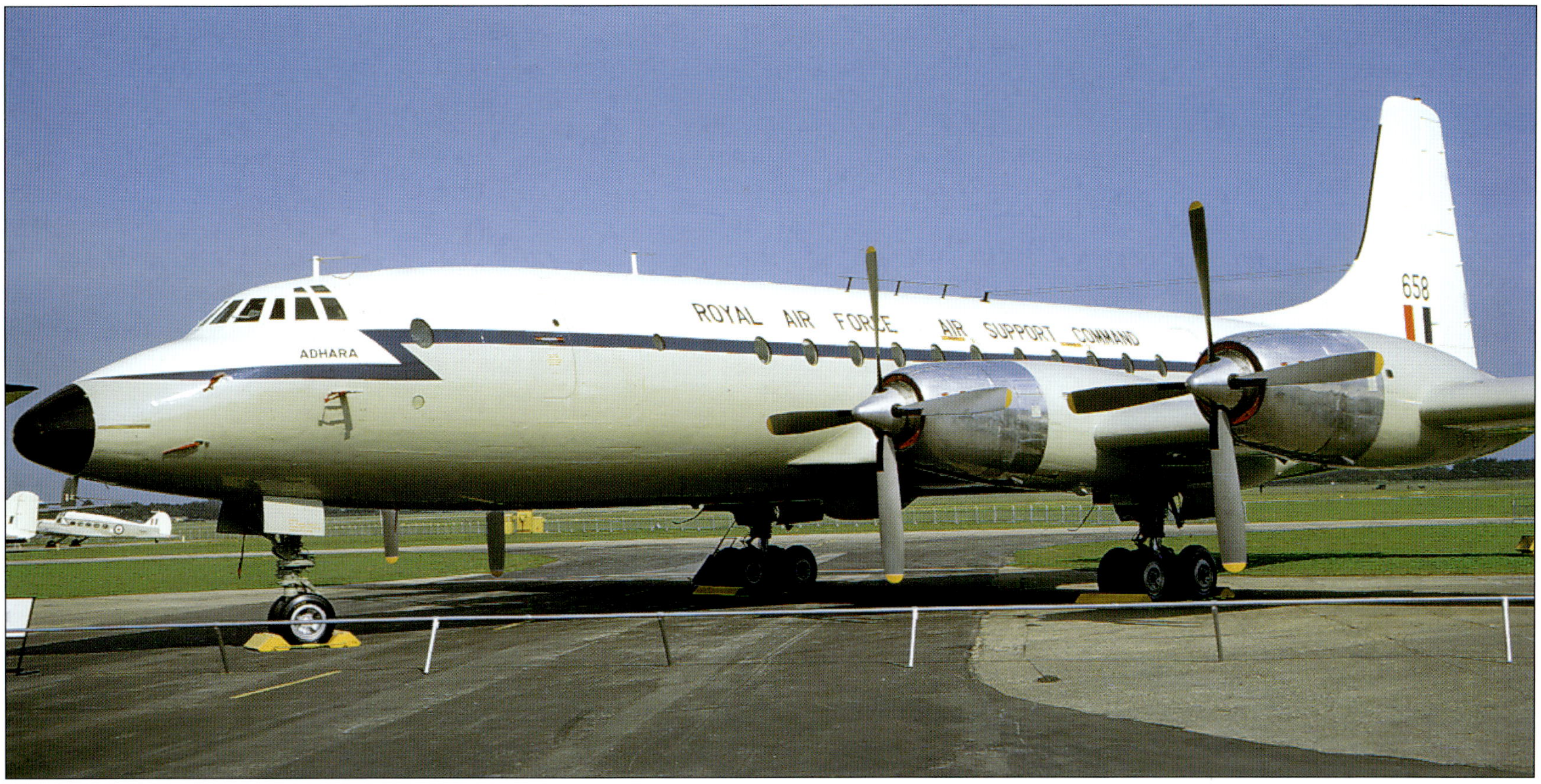

XL658 'Adhara' displays the typical immaculate condition of RAF Britannias in service. Unfortunately she was to end her life in an accident while landing at Shannon Airport in the service of Interconair in September 1977.

organisation may be involved. In April 1962, for example, a group of staff and students from the NATO Defence College were taken on a tour of Southern Europe. XM 398 with 72 students from fourteen nations took off from Le Bourget as VIP Flight 1051 for Lisbon, Malta, Istanbul, Ankara, Izmir, Athens, Naples, Rome, Turin and back to Paris. A subsequent press comment said "The whole tour was completed on schedule. Everywhere it went the aircraft left an excellent impression".

Later, in August/September 1962, fourteen staff and students from the Imperial Defence College visited fourteen major cities in East and West Pakistan (now Bangladesh and Pakistan). With this small party the fuselage of XN 392 was divided up into a standard VIP arrangement, with a sitting room, a dining room and a cocktail area. In this way the flying created a welcome breathing space between busy schedules on the ground.

With any type of aircraft there are a series of incidents in which some degree of trouble is experienced. In any article as complex as a modern aircraft, there are always minor (and sometimes major) things which go wrong, and here are some examples from the RAF Britannia fleet.

In the autumn of 1962, Britannia XL 636 was flying from the Mediterranean area back to the UK. When it was about 100 miles north of Rome, there was a sudden fire alarm and a warning light showed it to be in the forward freight bay, below the fuselage floor.

The appropriate action was taken and the Co-Pilot, Flt Lt Roy Johnson, took charge of flying the aircraft and proceeded to divert to Rome whilst the Captain, Norman Rose, organised the crew's response to the emergency. Signs of smoke were now evident on the flight deck so all donned oxygen masks. All non-essential electrical and radio equipment was switched off in order to try and isolate the cause of the fire, which was suspected to be due to some electrical circuit overheating. The Flight Engineer, Bob Anstee, climbed down into the freight bay to investigate the source of the fire and if possible to extinguish it.

In the bay there was a great deal of smoke, very little space amongst the cargo, and the Engineer was a large man. He had to hack his way through some cargo netting with an axe, but then found that the tube joining his oxygen mask to the supply was too short to enable him to move far enough into the bay. So he had to give this up and survive by taking deep breaths of air in the flight deck before diving down again into the smoke.

On further investigation, he suspected that the source of the smoke was the so-called feel simulator, the device which

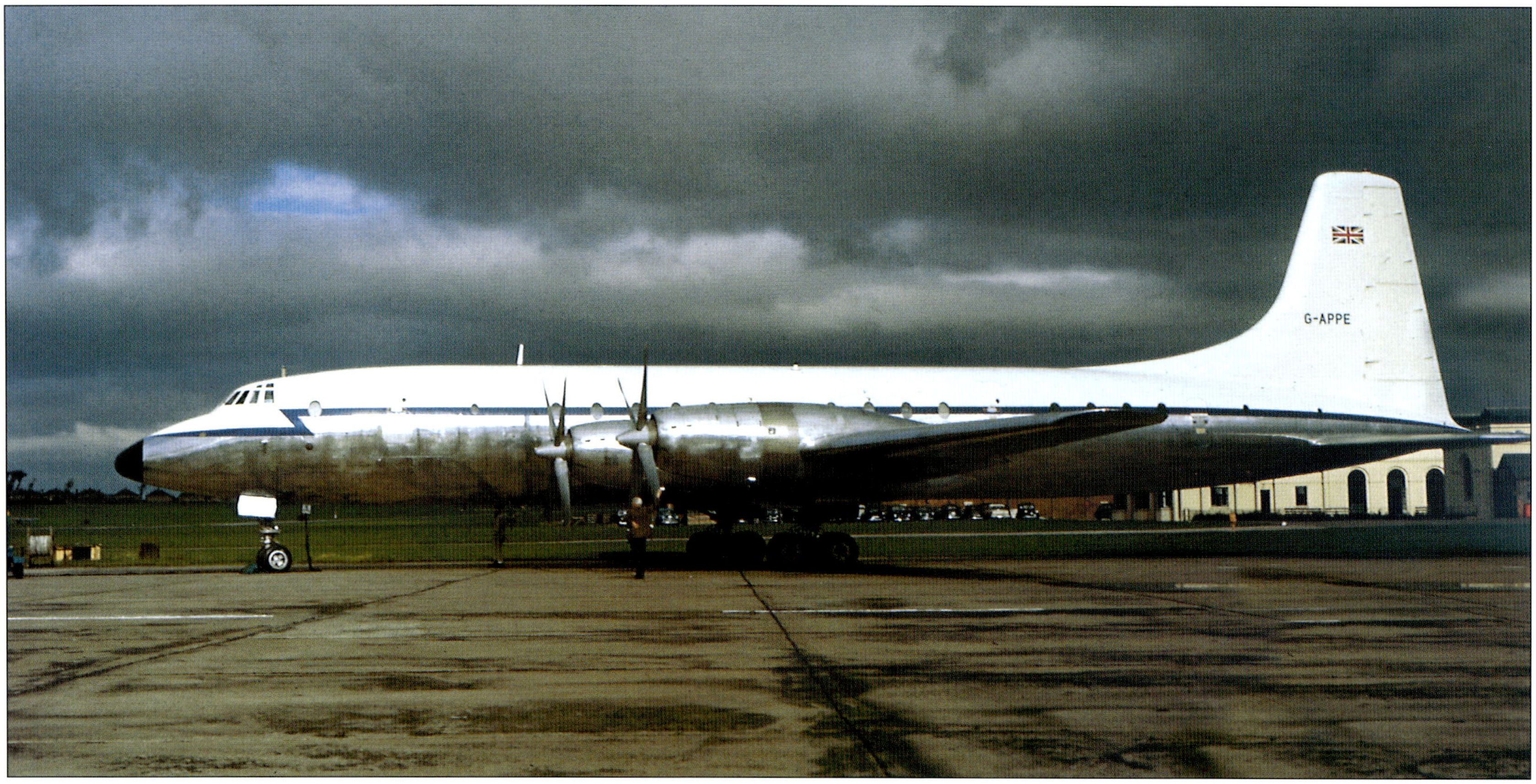

G-APPE, built to a special order for the Ministry of Supply, was one of three RAF Britannias to wear a civil registration before the application of RAF colours, and is seen at Filton Airfield prior to delivery.

enables the pilot to sense what the flying controls are doing in flight. He attacked this with a carbon dioxide extinguisher and indeed, the smoke began to disperse and things returned to normal. The diversion to Rome was cancelled and the flight resumed to the UK with all electrical equipment switched back on except for the feel simulator.

In 1966 an emergency arose in Zambia in which Britannias were heavily involved. For some time there had been trouble in an uneasy federation between Northern Rhodesia (Zambia), Southern Rhodesia (Zimbabwe) and Nyasaland (Malawi). The federation broke up in 1963 and the Rhodesian Prime Minister Ian Smith broke off discussions in 1965 and declared independence. UN sanctions were then imposed, including an oil embargo.

Land-locked Zambia was badly affected by this, for its only reasonable link with the outside world apart from through Rhodesia was by air. It was therefore decided to mount an Oil Lift into the Zambian airports at Lusaka and Ndola. Six Britannias and twelve crew formed the air side of the Oil Lift Detachment and there were also some 50 ground technicians and staff. A further oil lift was organised by the Royal Canadian Air Force and by civilian contractors.

The oil lift went on throughout 1966 until its official end on 31st October. Zambia was kept supplied with oil, and during the ten months of the emergency the RAF Britannias flew in 3.5 million gallons of oil in large drums.

Britannias continued to be used in any large scale troop movements in other parts of the world. One of these was during the autumn of 1967 with the evacuation and final close-down of the British base in Aden. Some 6,000 people, civilian families and military personnel, had to be moved, together with equipment, and the whole base then handed over to the local authorities.

Fourteen Britannias were involved, together with VC10s, Comets and the newly acquired Hercules fleet. It was the biggest operation since the Berlin airlift of 1948-9 and was completed on time but at a sad cost.

As part of the operation, at about 2300hrs on 8th October, Britannia XL 638 when landing at Aden (Khormaksar) ran off the end of the runway and ended in shallow muddy sea water. It was fairly badly damaged before it stopped, but worse was to follow. The very high Britannia tail fin had to be blown off by explosives so that the runway could continue to be used for further evacuation without delay.

But why had the aircraft overshot? It had made a perfect touch-down on the runway, before something went wrong.

The normal sequence of events for a Britannia after touch-down was for all four throttle levers to be pulled back to idle. A (side) lever on the left of the throttles was then pulled to the rear which lifted a flap at the base of the throttle levers so that they could go into the 'reverse power' range. It also activated a microswitch which turned the propeller blades into the reverse (negative) pitch. The next stage was for the Flight Engineer to lift the throttle levers over a gate and wait until four green lights confirmed that all propeller blades were reversed before speeding up the engines to give full reversed thrust.

In this case, it seems that there was an electrical fault and the side lever by the throttles did not switch on the reversed thrust circuits. The green lights never came on and the propellers never produced reversed thrust, so the aircraft ran out of runway and overshot into the water.

Subsequent checking on other Britannias at Lyneham showed that they had a potentially similar condition. After more than ten years of use, the side lever mechanism became worn so that under conditions of severe vibration, e.g. when landing, the lever could jump back and the reversed thrust circuits be switched off. As is often the case after an accident, maintenance was tightened up and crew awareness increased.

There continued to be events where people needed rescuing from difficult situations. In June 1970 a Britannia flew from Cyprus to Beirut to pick up refugees from Amman. The following month there was a special aeromedical flight from Cyprus to Brize Norton when, following a coup in Muscat and Oman, the Sultan who had been shot required medical treatment in the UK. Later, after an earthquake in Peru, there was a mercy flight of medical supplies and blankets taken by Britannia from Lima.

In 1971 there was another emergency involving British Nationals when disturbances in Dacca, East Pakistan, resulted in 100 people being evacuated by a Britannia flight. In 1973 the situation worsened and eventually East Pakistan was re-named Bangladesh and completed the split from (West) Pakistan. The result was that there were some 160,000 POWs and refugees in the wrong country so Operation 'Lucan' was launched to assist the UN repatriation activities. Two Britannias and four crews were established at Karachi and flew two round trips per day to Dacca. By the end of February 1974, over 16,000 people had been moved from Pakistan to Bangladesh and nearly 14,000 the other way. Some of the passengers were in an appalling physical state, and terrified by their first ever sight of an aircraft, let alone a first flight in rough monsoon conditions. The success of the Operation is a tribute to the refugees' resilience and to the crews' dedication.

From the story told here it is clear that the Britannias were

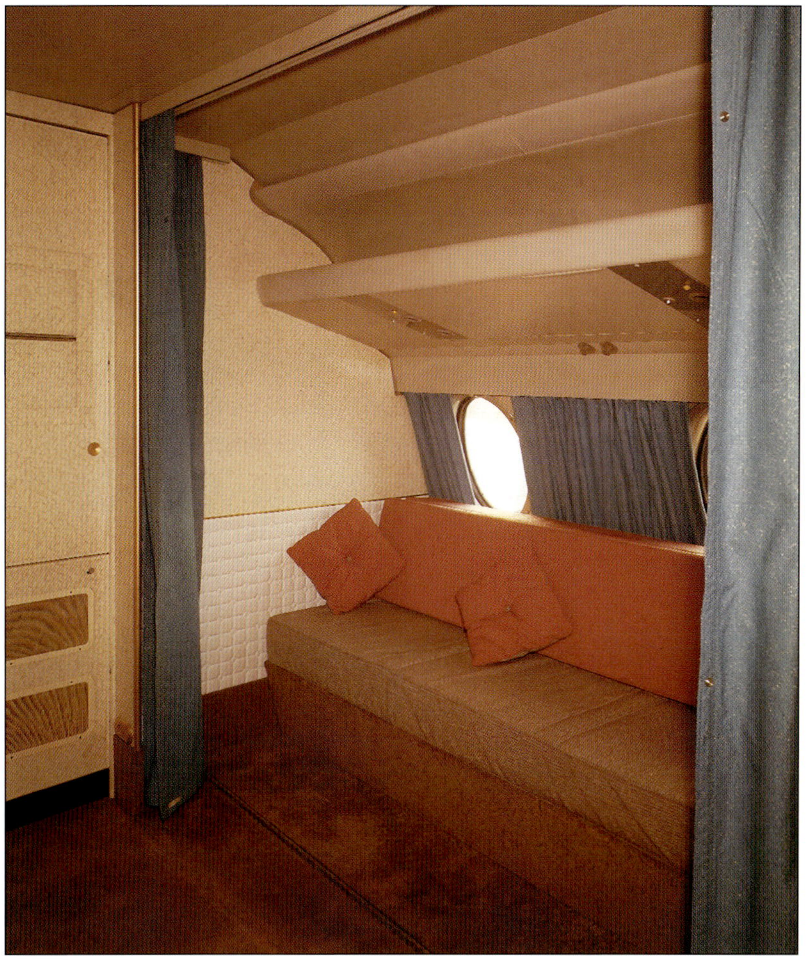

Two interior shots of G-APPE display the totally different design of the interior of the aircraft compared to the standard RAF Britannia as demonstrated on pages 34 and 35.

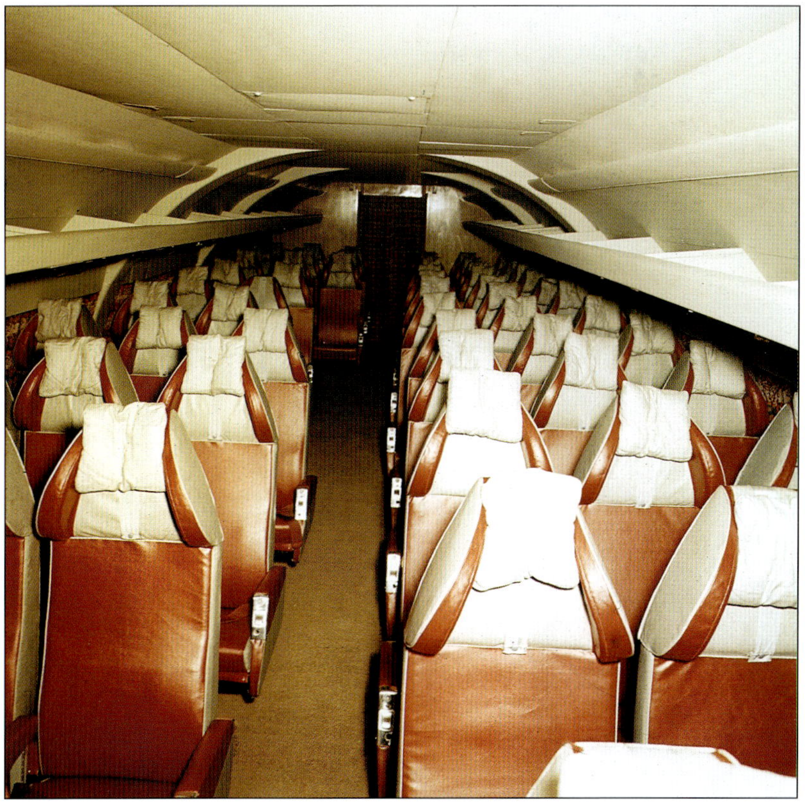

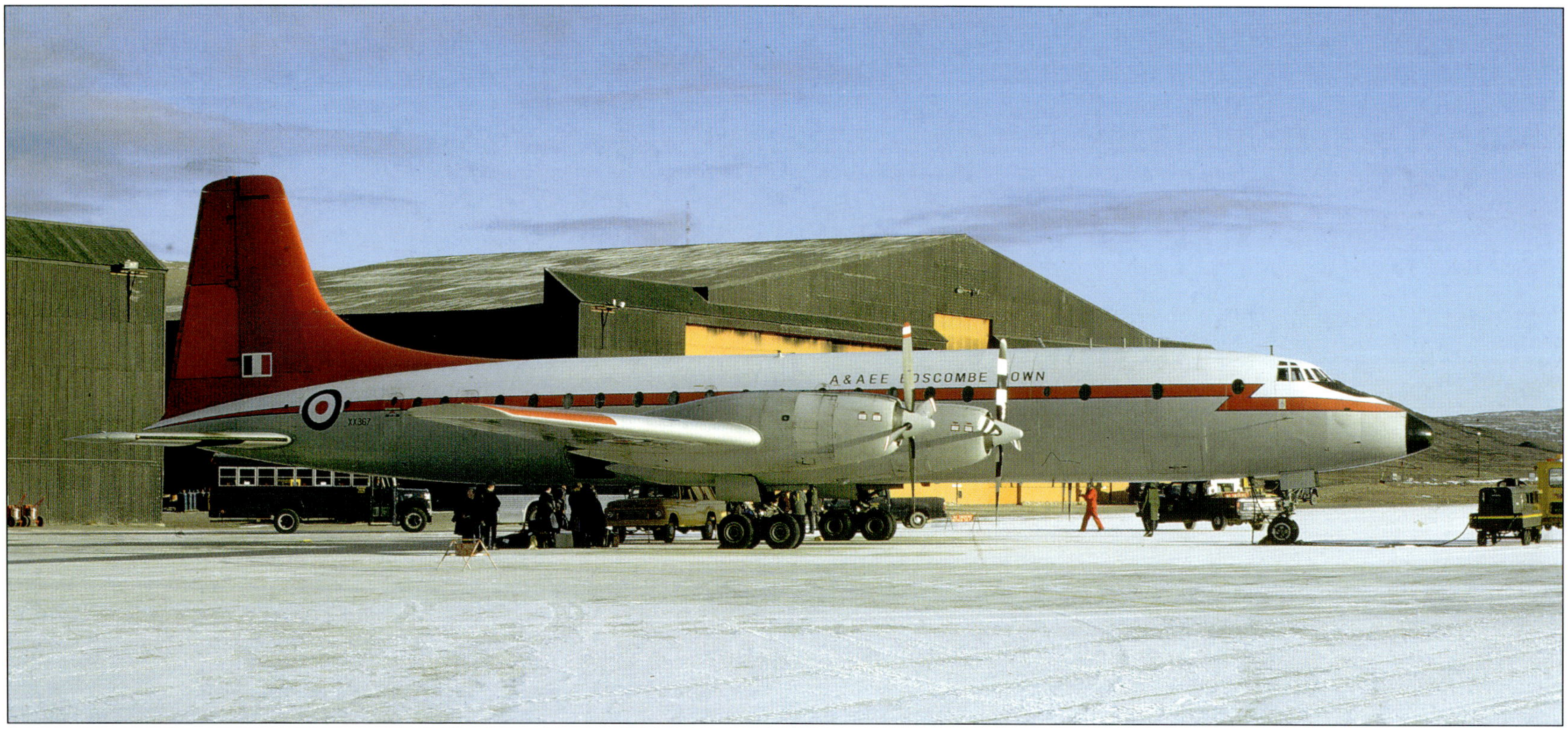

Having been bought by the UK Ministry of Defence in November 1971, XX367 is prepared for flight at Thule, Greenland before returning to her new base at Boscombe Down.

widely used by the RAF for the movement of troops and cargo round the world, and for various humanitarian missions during the 1960s and early '70s. But during the '70s there was a reducing need for airlift capability. The British Government began to make defence cuts and it was decided to disband the Britannia fleet. This was partly because they were not as convenient, as cargo planes, to load and unload as the newer Hercules (with a fuselage much nearer gound level). Also, as troop transporters, they were not as quick as the jet aircraft like the Comet or VC10 so the decision was made for the RAF to sell them. All the aircraft had relatively low flying hours compared with aircraft flying passengers commercially, and they therefore represented a good buy for interested companies.

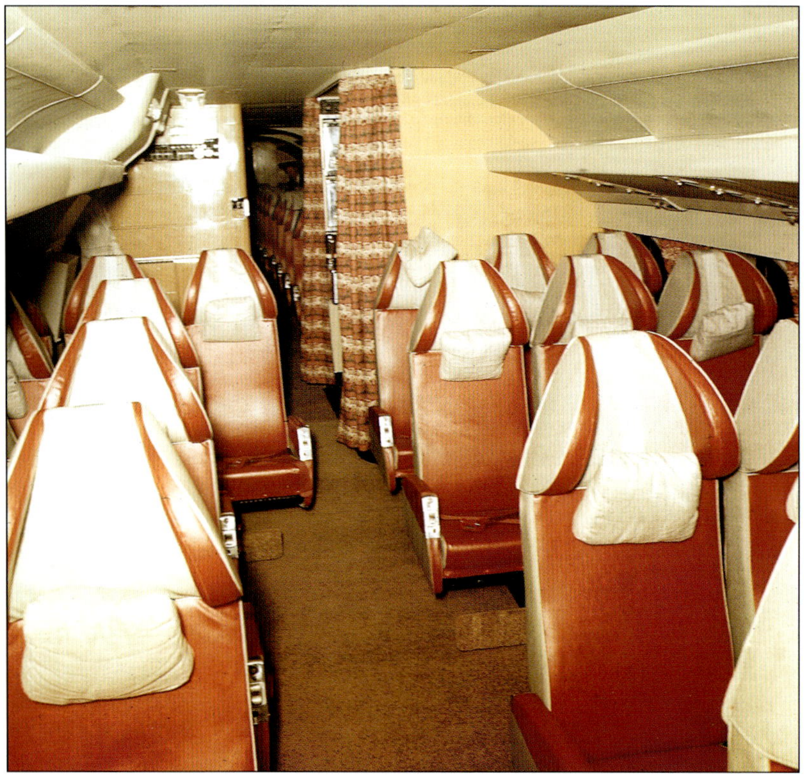

A further interior shot of Britannia G-APPE.

The fleet of 23 aircraft was offered for sale in September 1975 and by 26th May 1976 they had all been sold. So ended the service life of Britannias with the RAF.

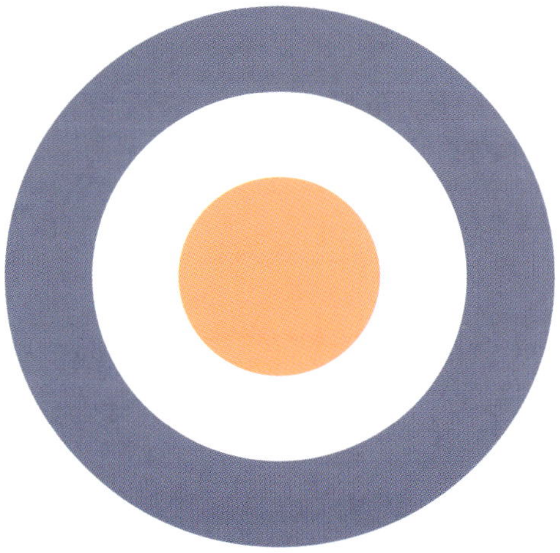

IN SERVICE WITH EL AL

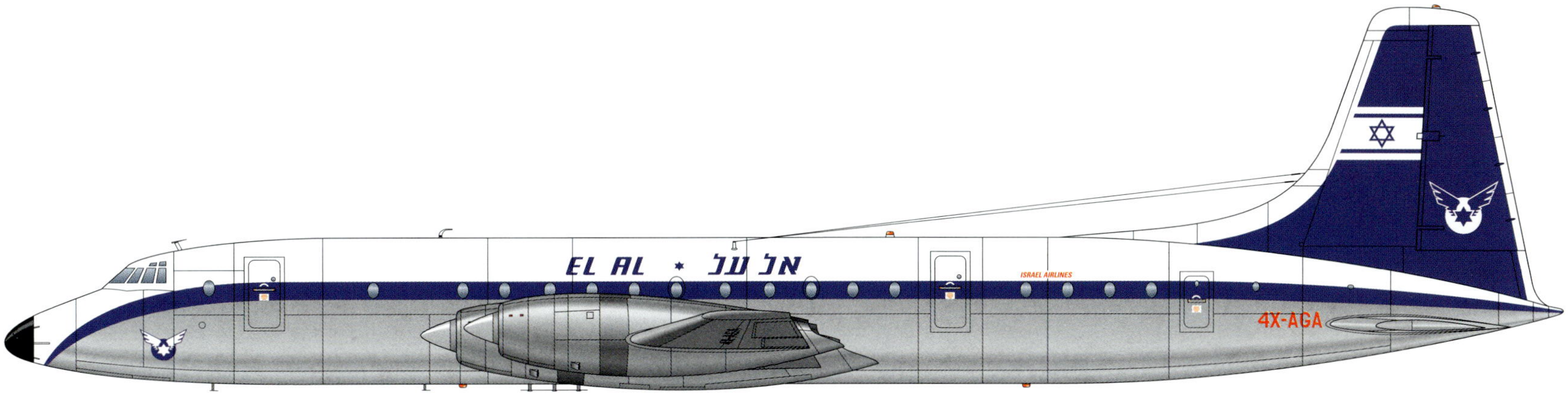

The Israeli airline, El Al, was formed in 1948 and quickly developed international schedules from Israel to New York and Johannesburg. Initially the airline used Constellations, but became very interested in Britannias following a demonstration while the Britannia tropical trials were being conducted in Africa.

A firm order for three of the Series 313 Britannias was placed in June 1955 (the first firm order from an overseas airline), to be increased to four in 1957. There was a considerable amount of advanced publicity before the introduction of Britannias to scheduled flying for El Al. On 9th July 1957 the long-range prototype G-AOVA flew to Tel Aviv on a demonstration, returning to Filton the next day. The first Britannia supplied to El Al, registered as 4X-AGA, made its maiden flight from Filton on 28th July 1957 and was formally handed over on 5th September. During the weeks leading up to the delivery date, every item of mail or document originating in the El Al offices was stamped in red ink "For your information, it's X days to the Britannia delivery date". After the handover, 4X-AGA remained at Filton for a week before flying to Tel Aviv on 12th September. That flight, of 2,400 miles, was completed non-stop in 5hrs 59mins at an average speed of 401mph and

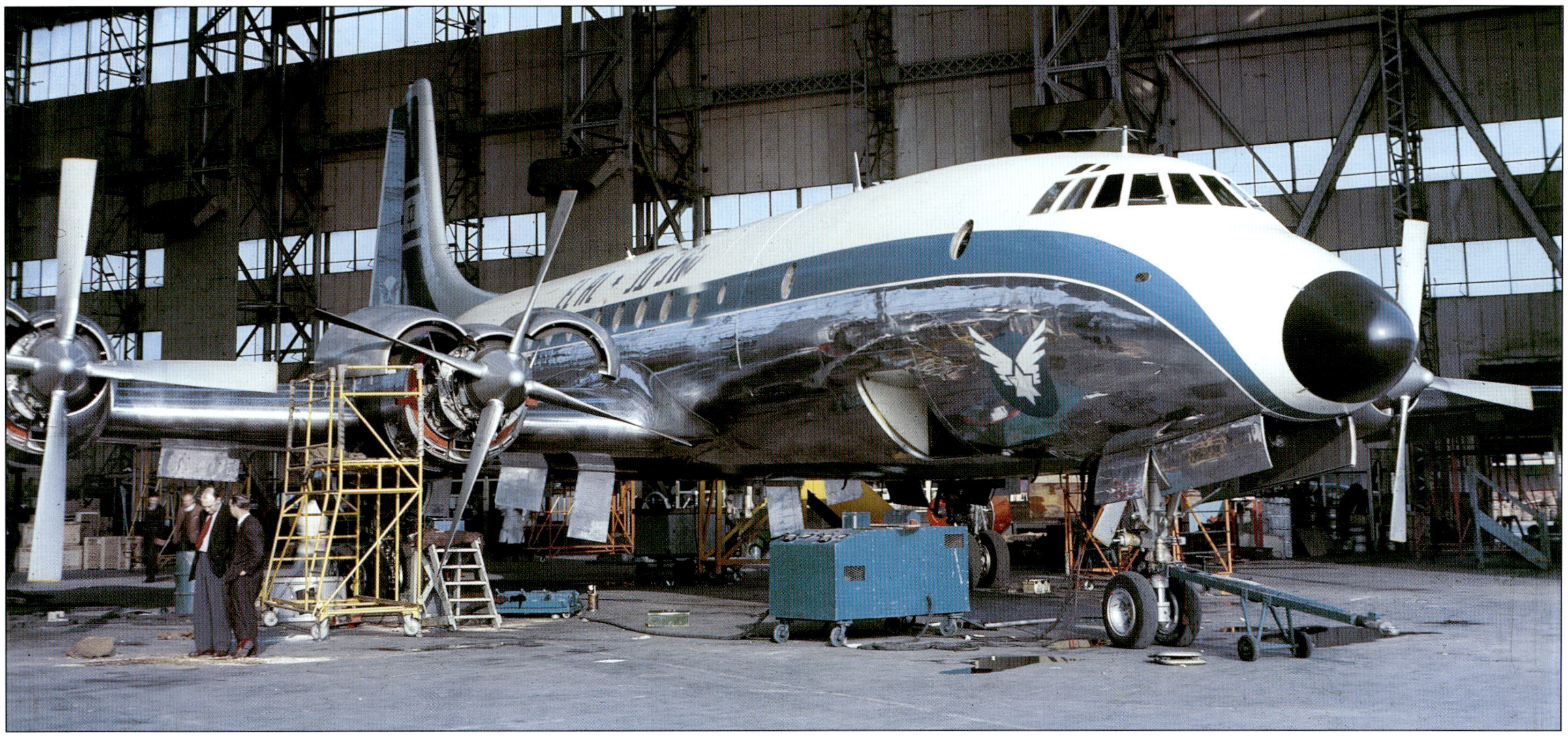

4X-AGA, the first Series 313 Britannia for El Al Israeli Airlines, is prepared for its first flight at Filton in July 1957.

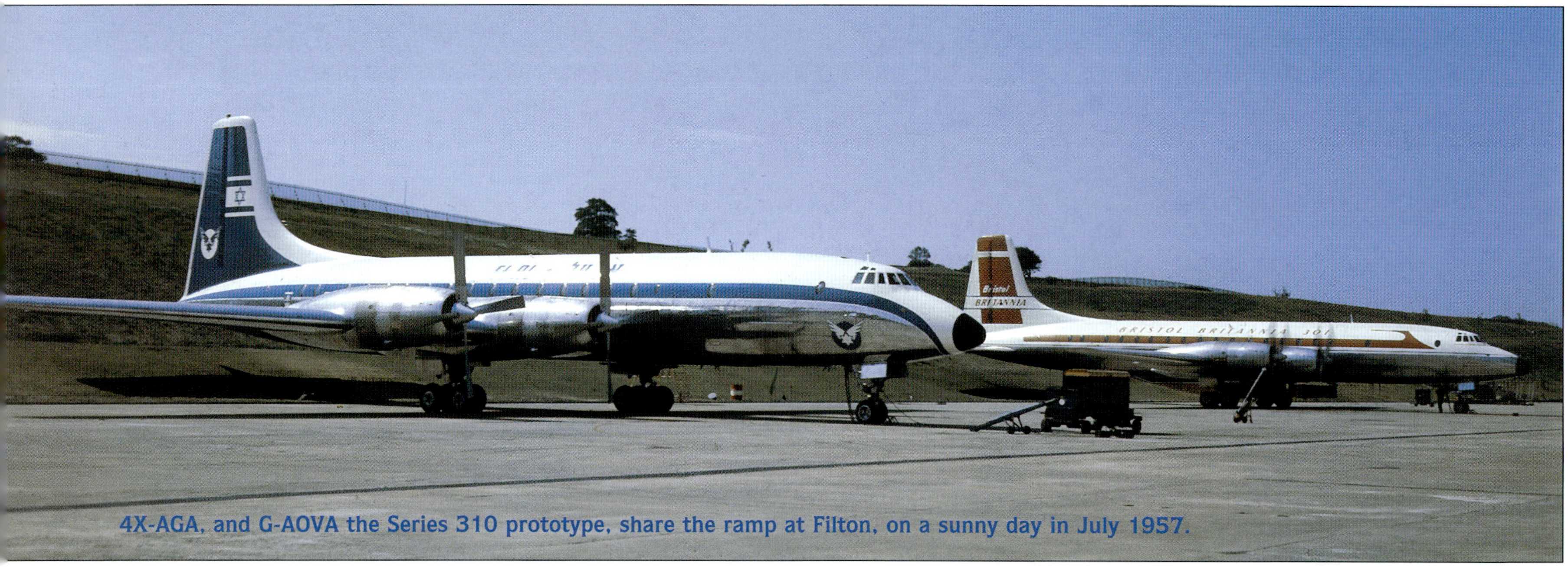

4X-AGA, and G-AOVA the Series 310 prototype, share the ramp at Filton, on a sunny day in July 1957.

many of the airline's employees turned out to greet the Britannia's arrival at Tel Aviv.

There then began an active period of crew training and route-proving, made more intense by the delivery of the second Britannia, 4X-AGB, in October and the third, 4X-AGC, in November. During this training and once scheduled flying began on 22nd December 1957, various records were broken. Early in November, 4X-AGB set the pattern with a proving flight from New York to London Heathrow in 9hrs and from Heathrow to Tel Aviv in 6hrs 50mins. On 29th November, 4X-AGC flew from Heathrow to Tel Aviv on its delivery flight in 6hrs 7mins and, on 8th of December, an El Al Britannia on a proving flight flew the 3,520 miles from New York to London in 8hrs 3mins. This record lasted for only a few weeks as, on 6th January, a BOAC Britannia 312 flew the same route in 7 hours 57mins. Then, two days later, El Al lowered the record again, to 7hrs 44mins. Perhaps the most remarkable flight was by 4X-AGC which flew non-stop from New York to Tel Aviv on 18th/19th December 1957 piloted by Captain Tohar. It covered the 6,100 miles in 14hrs 46mins at an average speed of 401mph (helped by a favourable tail wind). It was the longest non-stop flight ever made by a commercial aircraft up to that time.

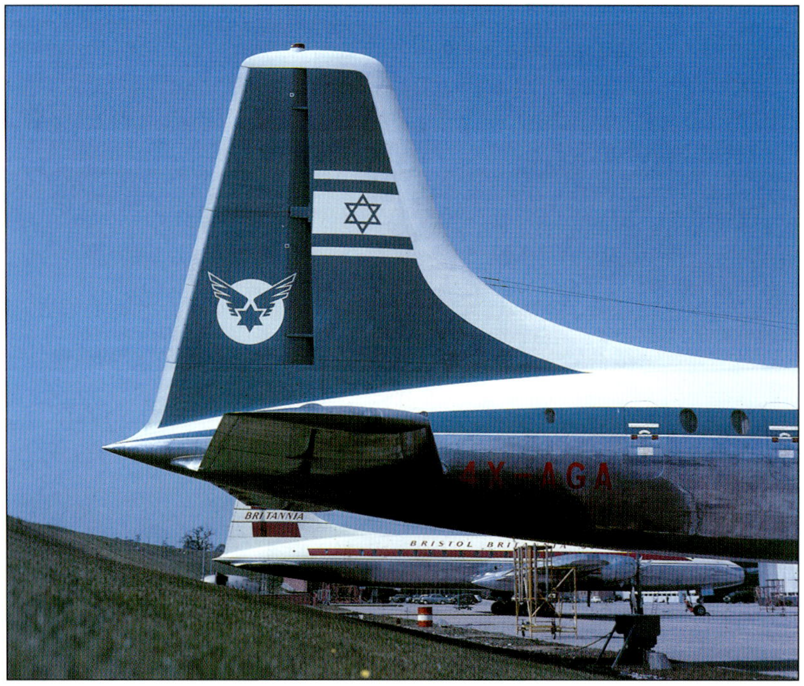

A close-up study of the tail of 4X-AGA displays the fine detail of the El Al livery applied to their Britannias.

But the development which was more significant then record breaking flights was the introduction of scheduled services. For El Al, the service Tel Aviv-Heathrow-New York began on 22nd December 1957, flown by 4X-AGB, and was flown once per week in each direction. It left Tel Aviv on Sunday afternoon and after re-fuelling in London left there at 2340 hours, arriving in New York (Idlewild) at 0530 local time on Monday morning. The return journey left New York on Wednesday evening at 1900 hours, and arrived in Tel Aviv late on Thursday afternoon.

El Al's Britannias were fitted out with 72 tourist-class seats and eighteen first-class passenger seats, four of these being special sleeperette seats. With some flair for public relations, the airline promoted the London-New York service with the slogan "No more Goose, no more Gander", emphasising the point that with the long-range Britannias it was no longer necessary to have refuelling stops at Goose Bay or in Canada.

In fact the El Al crews built up an impressive amount of expertise in operating Britannias across the North Atlantic, becoming particularly skilled at interpreting the meteorological data so that they could fly at the best altitudes. During the first six months of El Al transatlantic flights (190 in all), only four had to make intermediate stops and three of these were because of bad weather conditions over New York.

An example of the expertise of El Al crews was given in a lecture to an audience of the Royal Aeronautical Society on 4th December 1958 by Captain J Williams, El Al's Manager of Technical Planning and Development. At some unspecified date, two Britannias had taken off from New York for London, the El Al one eight minutes after the other. Both flew on the same flight paths, but each according to its own airline's procedures. The El Al aircraft was safely parked on the Heathrow apron by the time the other aircraft landed.

Scheduled flight times from London to New York were 10hrs 50mins and in the reverse direction 8hrs 30mins. These were less than the BOAC timings because the El Al pilots reckoned that they could find more favourable air space in which to fly. (In fact on 11th March 1958 an El Al Britannia flew from London to New York in 9hrs 22mins, about 1.5hrs less than the scheduled time). The high level of reliability and good schedules were reflected in passenger figures and, in the first four months of operation over the North Atlantic, El Al had higher passenger load figures than any other operator, with a load factor of almost 70% by the end of April 1958.

Inevitably there were some unplanned incidents during the operations. On 24th April 1958 during the take-off run at Tel Aviv, a Britannia burst two tyres causing damage to the undercarriage, resulting in a quick 'go-round' and landing but no further problem.

A more unusual problem occurred on 4th May. When taking off from Heathrow for New York, 4X-AGC lost the inner forward wheel on the portside undercarriage bogie. The Captain and crew were unaware of this and the alert was raised by an air traffic controller who happened to be walking near the runway at about 1000hrs and found the wheel lying on the grass. Some rapid detective work established that the wheel came from a Britannia. BOAC had had no Britannias leave London during the previous night but El Al had. 4X-AGC had taken off at 0230 hours for New York and was therefore within two to three hours of landing. Bristol Aircraft at Filton identified the serial number on the wheel as belonging to 4X-AGC, so London Control alerted Idlewild who advised the El Al Captain (Tohar) to land at Idlewild which had better emergency facilities - rather than to Boston to which he had just been diverted. The plane made a perfect landing at Idlewild and Captain Tohar subsequently commented "I noticed nothing on take-off or landing". But he certainly would have been on the lookout when landing!

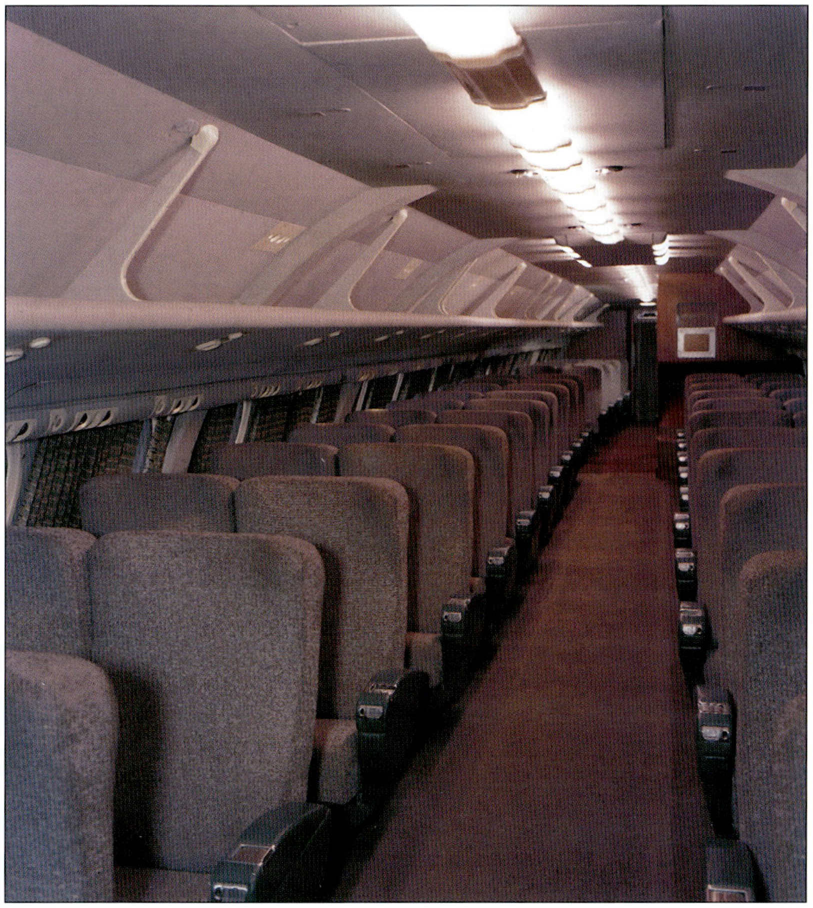

As can be seen from this photograph of 4X-AGA the interior of the aircraft was furnished in an unusual mauve colour.

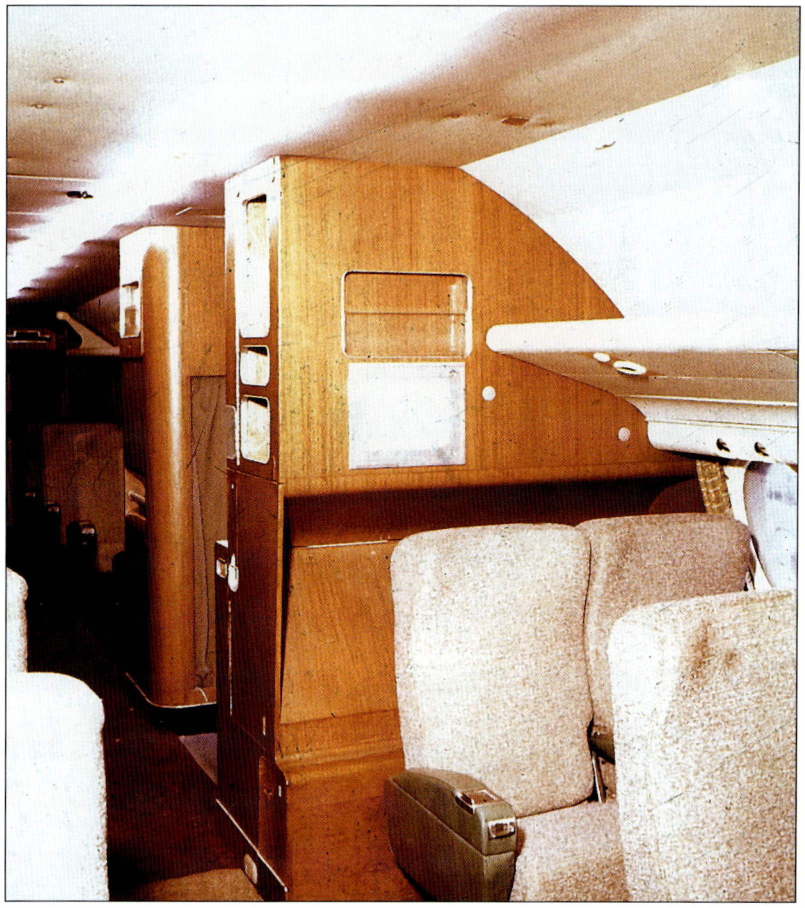

An alternative view of the interior of 4X-AGA, this time taken in the First Class compartment.

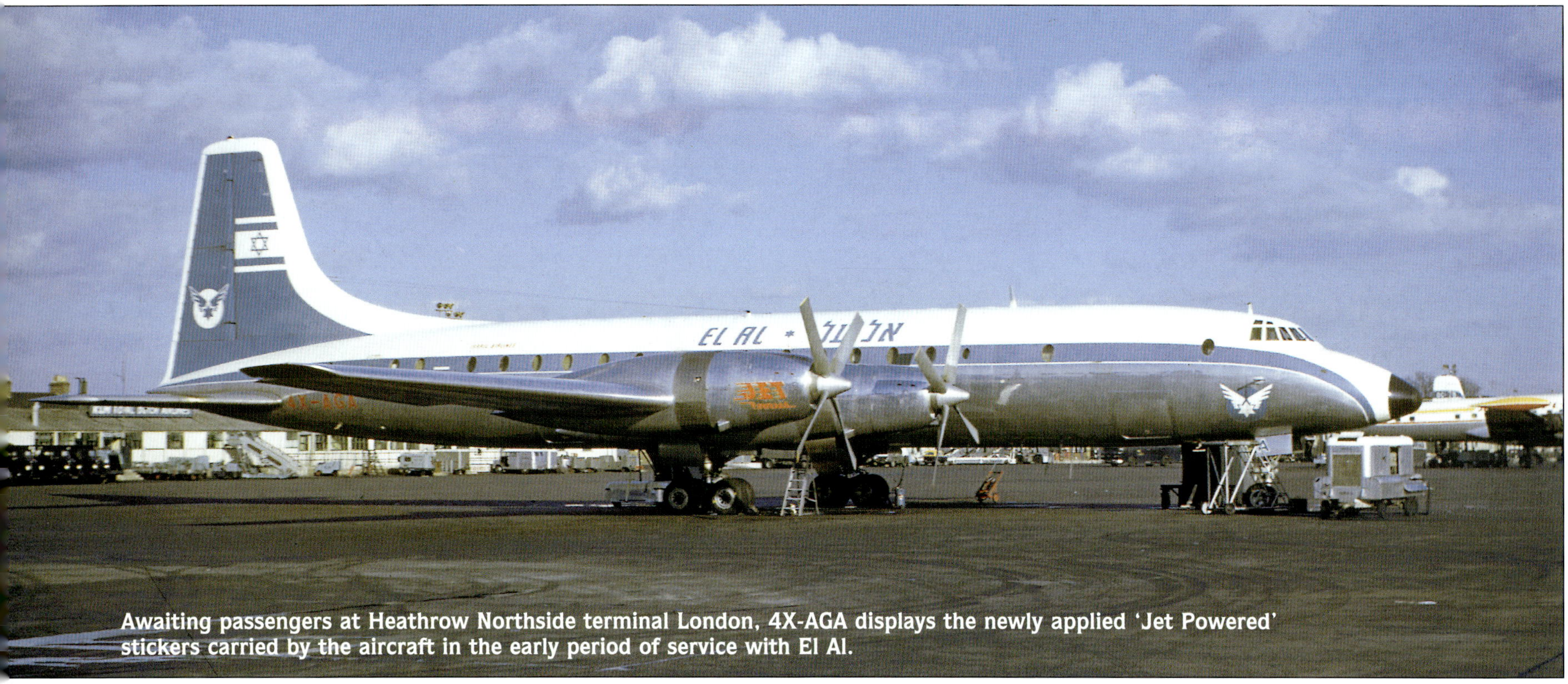

Awaiting passengers at Heathrow Northside terminal London, 4X-AGA displays the newly applied 'Jet Powered' stickers carried by the aircraft in the early period of service with El Al.

During the summer of 1958, El Al's three Britannias were kept busy on the Tel Aviv-New York run, with departure from Tel Aviv scheduled for 1700 hours on Sundays, Mondays, Tuesdays, Thursdays and Fridays. Three of these services stopped at Paris (Orly); one then went on direct to New York, while the other two went on via Heathrow. Eastwards the frequency was the same but the departure times from New York varied between 1800 hours on Mondays to 2300 hours on Saturdays. In order to cope with this demand, El Al leased a Britannia Series 306, registered as 4X-AGE, from 8th July 1958 until 6th March 1959, until their fourth Series 313 Britannia, 4X-AGD, was delivered. With the fourth (leased) Britannia, an extra service was opened, Tel Aviv-Rome-Paris-London. Britannias had now taken over all El Al transatlantic services, with the older slower Constellations still operating the majority of services from Tel-Aviv to continental European cities. This pattern of North Atlantic schedules remained for the next three years, until 1961 when jet aircraft began to be introduced.

In 1959 and 1960, while the North Atlantic operations remained unchanged, the Britannias gradually took over the services from Tel Aviv to European destinations such as Amsterdam, Athens, Brussels, Paris, Rome, Vienna and Zurich. They also flew a weekly service to Tehran and to Istanbul and Nicosia.

In 1961, however, El Al began to take delivery of its Rolls Royce powered Boeing 707s and these gradually took pride of place over the Britannias. The general public opted for a shorter length of flight time over all other considerations.

The history of the four El Al Britannias is somewhat checkered from this time onwards. 4X-AGB and 4X-AGC were leased to British United Airways and re-registered respectively as G-ARWZ and G-ARXA in February and March 1962. They were allocated to a role with the RAF as Troop transporters between Stansted and the Middle and Far East.

4X-AGA and 4X-AGD continued on European operations with El Al except for a period when El Al staff went on strike over the length of flying hours. During the strike, from 18th March until the 8th April 1963, both aircraft were leased to British United Airways and re-registered respectively as G-ASFV and G-ASFU. BUA flew these aircraft on behalf of El Al until the strike was resolved and they were then returned to El Al.

In March 1964, El Al sold 4X-AGA to Globe Air (where it was re-registered as HB-ITB), reducing the El Al Britannia fleet to one, 4X-AGD. This aircraft continued on El Al's European scheduled network, but also undertook an increasing number of charter flights taking tourists to Israel. Included among these was a service between Tel Aviv and Sofia, Bulgaria which, in July 1964, was the first service from El Al to an Eastern European country.

The three other El Al Britannias, 4X-AGB, 4X-AGC and 4X-AGD, were nonetheless gradually phased out over the next three years. BUA returned their two leased aircraft; 4X-AGC in October 1964 and 4X-AGB in March 1965. El Al sold 4X-AGD to Globe Air in March 1965, while the two remaining ex-BUA leased aircraft continued scheduled and charter flying in1965.

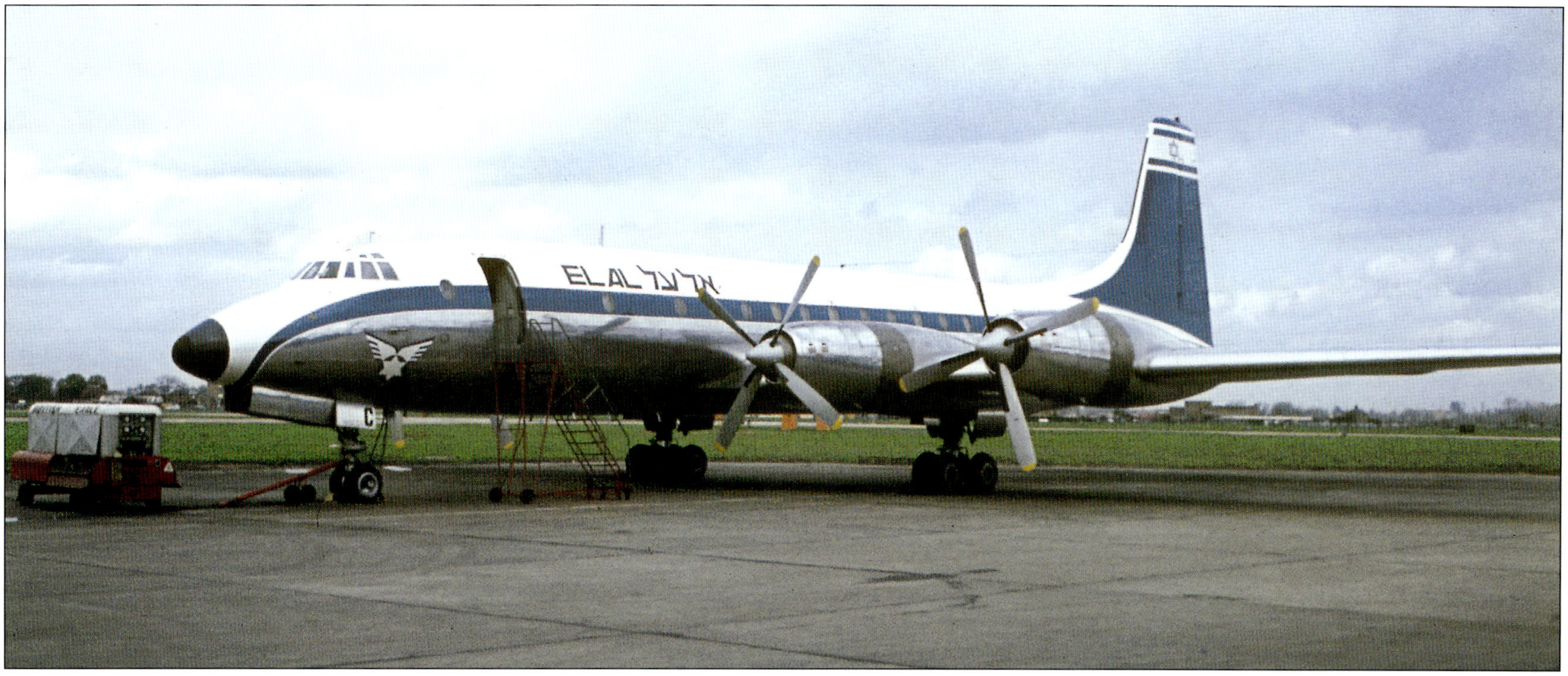

At Heathrow Airport, 4X-AGC displays the revised livery of El Al carried in the final year of service with the airline.

In April 1966 El Al sold 4X-AGC to British Eagle and finally, in March 1967, 4X-AGB to Air Spain. The final flight of a Britannia in El Al livery was the flight by 4X-AGB from Tel Aviv to Heathrow on 7th March 1967, although she did already have some of the Air Spain livery on, and at Heathrow the preparations for the handover to Air Spain were completed. It is an interesting footnote to the El Al experiences with Britannias that the aircraft which flew the last flight was the same one which flew the first scheduled flight across the North Atlantic.

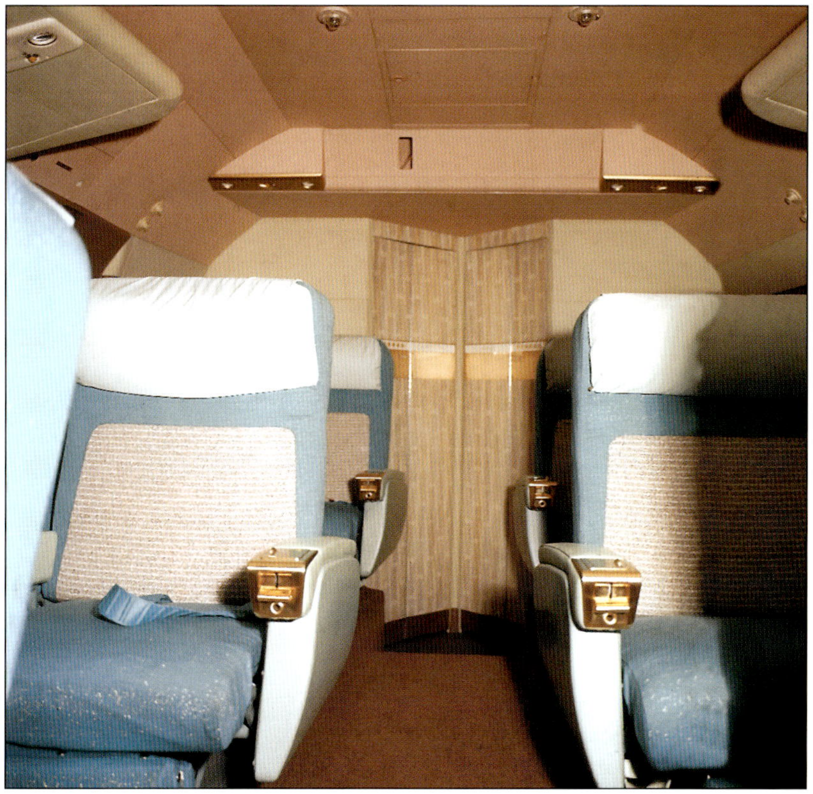

Towards the end of their life, El Al Britannias were reupholstered into this pink and blue scheme.

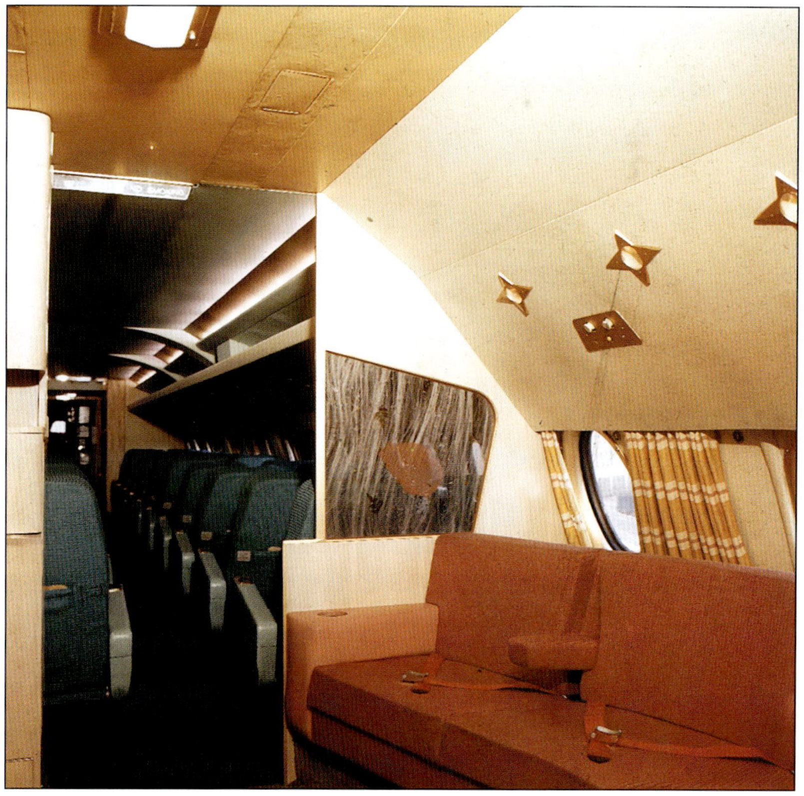

A view of the lounge area at the rear of one of El Al's Britannias.

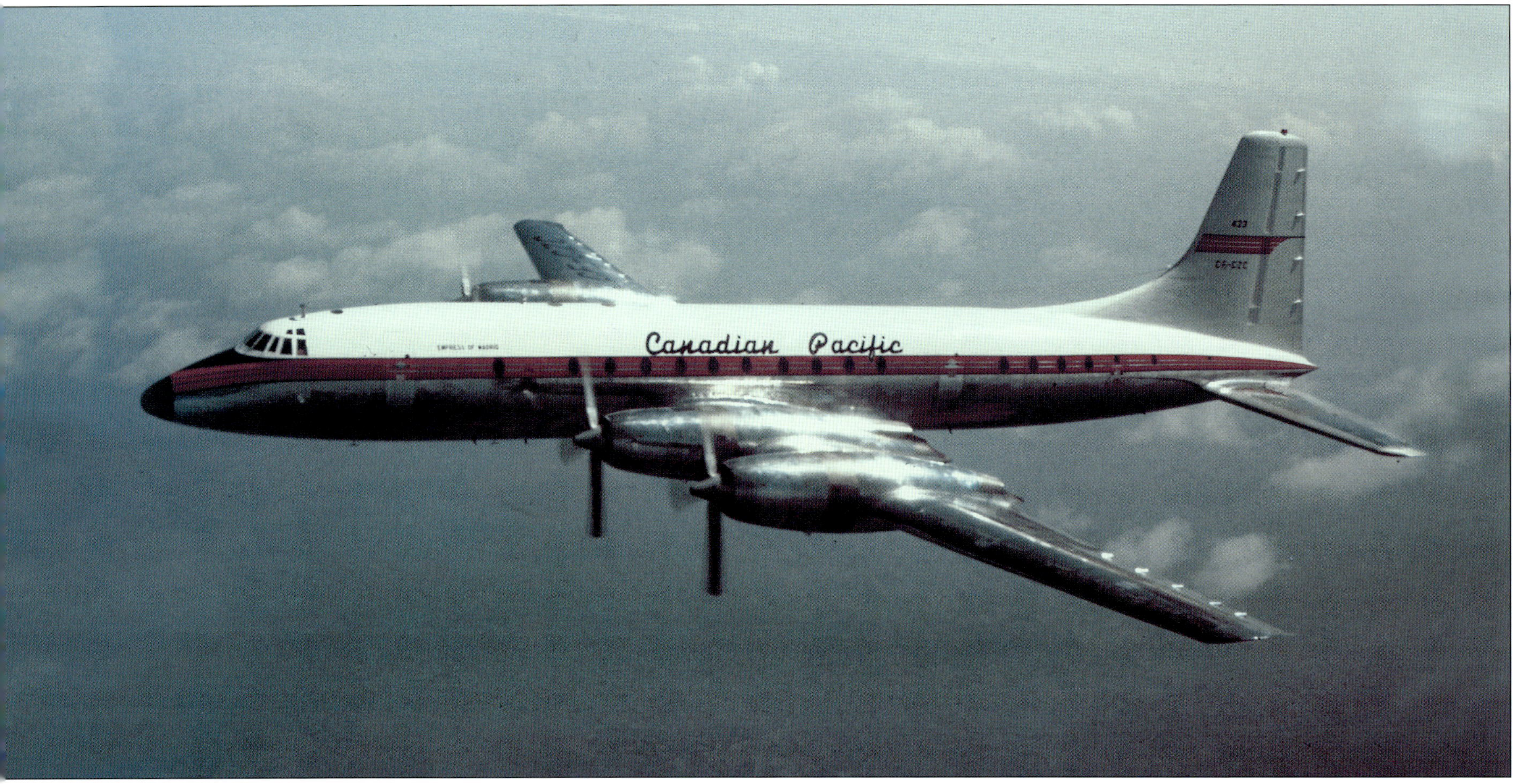

Two views of Canadian Pacific Airline's Britannia Series 314 CF-CZC, above during a test flight from Filton prior to delivery to the airline and below in company with G-ANCD, the only Britannia to carry the full livery of America's Northeast Airlines which alas was cancelled in June 1958. Later that month the aircraft, in the colours of Compañía Cubana de Aviatión, embarked on a sales tour of South America.

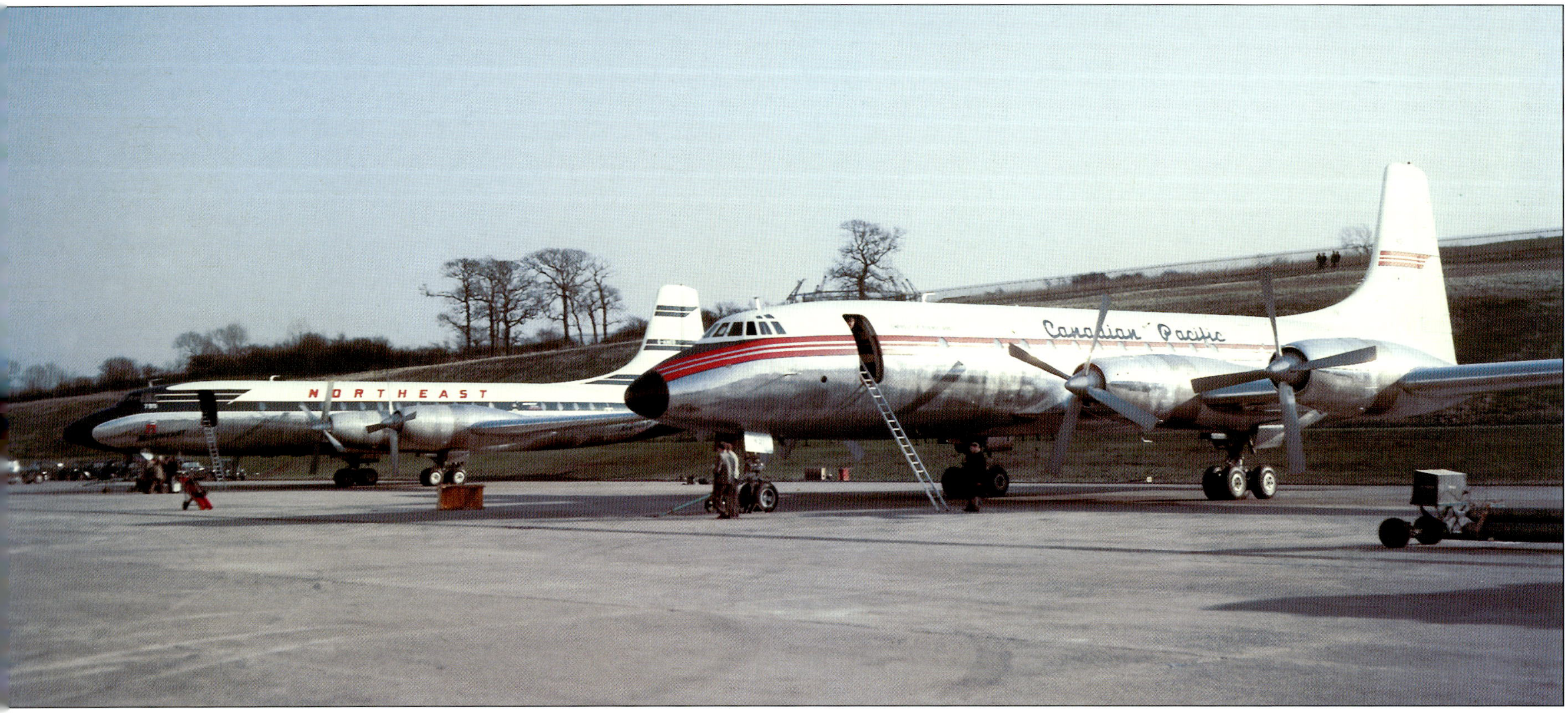

IN SERVICE WITH CANADIAN PACIFIC AIRLINES

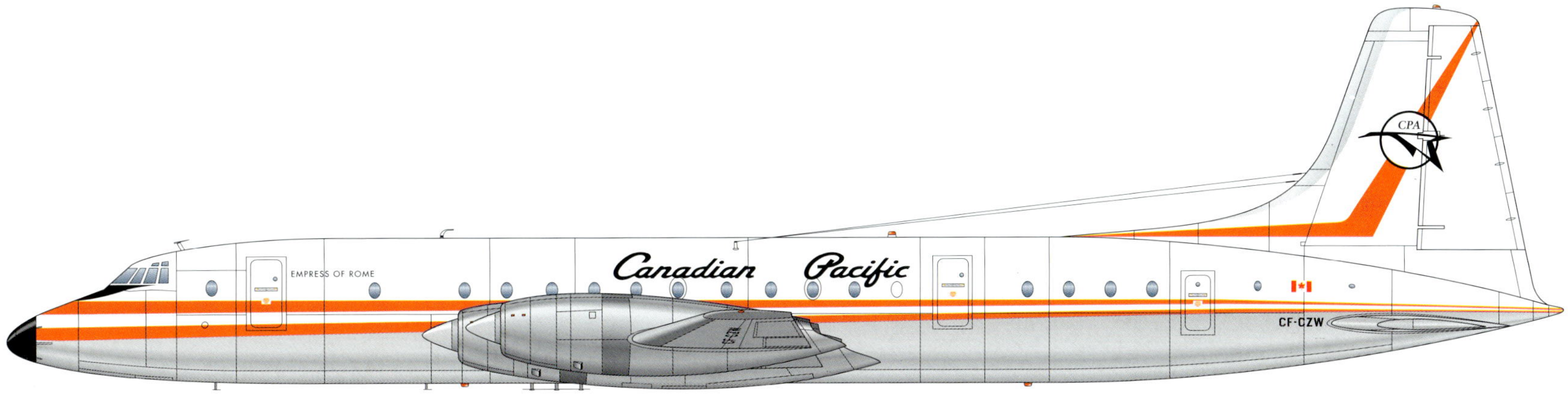

The largest overseas airline to put the Britannia into passenger service was Canadian Pacific, with headquarters in Vancouver. The airline signed a contract with the Bristol Aeroplane Company to purchase three of the long-range Britannia 310 aircraft on 3rd October 1955, and also placed an option on five further airframes.

The airline intended to put the Britannias into service in 1957, and was hoping to fly them from Vancouver to Amsterdam, Auckland, Hong Kong, Lima, Mexico City, Sydney and Tokyo. A 100-seater layout was envisaged, and the great attraction was the long range which the aircraft offered. A non-stop flight by polar route from Vancouver to Amsterdam or Tokyo was possible, which would give the airline a commercial advantage over its rival, Trans Canada Airlines.

However, problems with the Proteus engines caused delays and a Certificate of Airworthiness was only awarded to Britannia G-AOVA on 25th January 1957. On 30th January, this aircraft flew non-stop from Prestwick to Winnipeg (3,800 miles at a ground speed of 366mph), at that time the longest west-bound flight across the Atlantic by a commercial airliner.

In Winnipeg, severe weather trials began. The aircraft was left for 24hrs in the open, in the extreme cold, and the engines then started without trouble, using the on-board

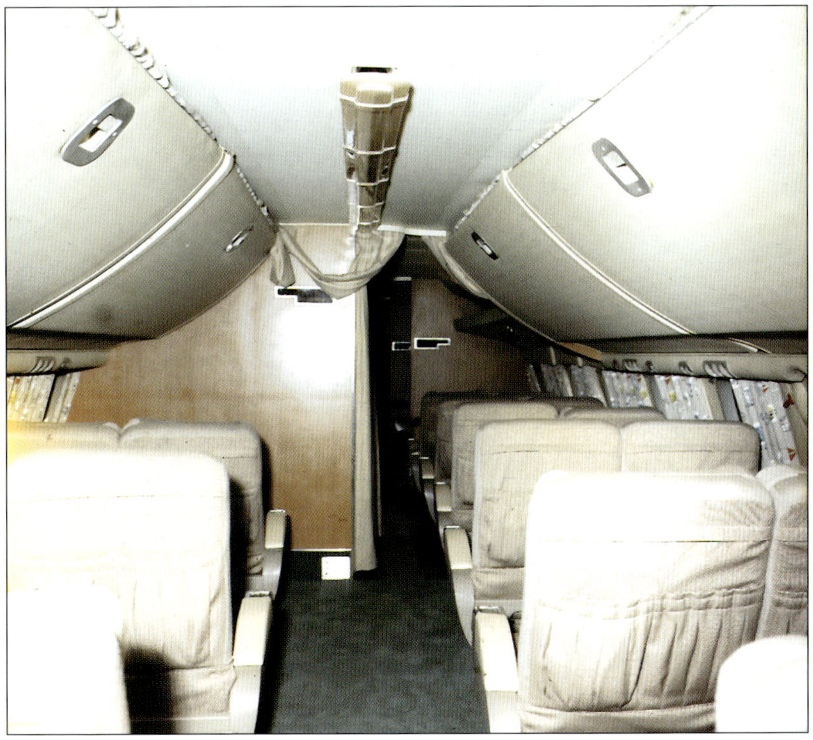

Looking forward in the First Class section towards the Economy cabin, in a Canadian Pacific Britannia.

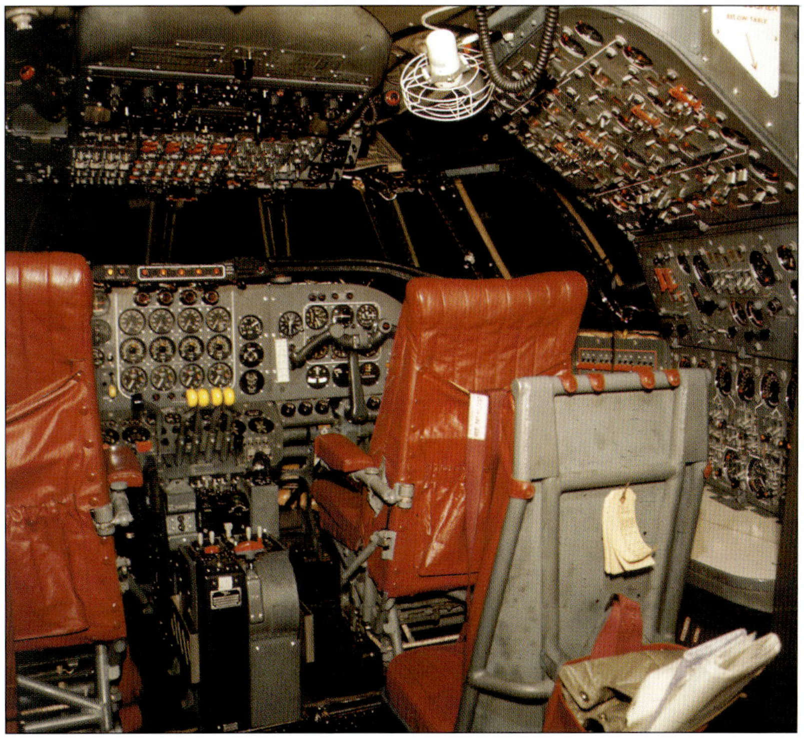

A view of the cockpit, complete with red leather seats in CF-CZA, the first Britannia delivered to Canadian Pacific.

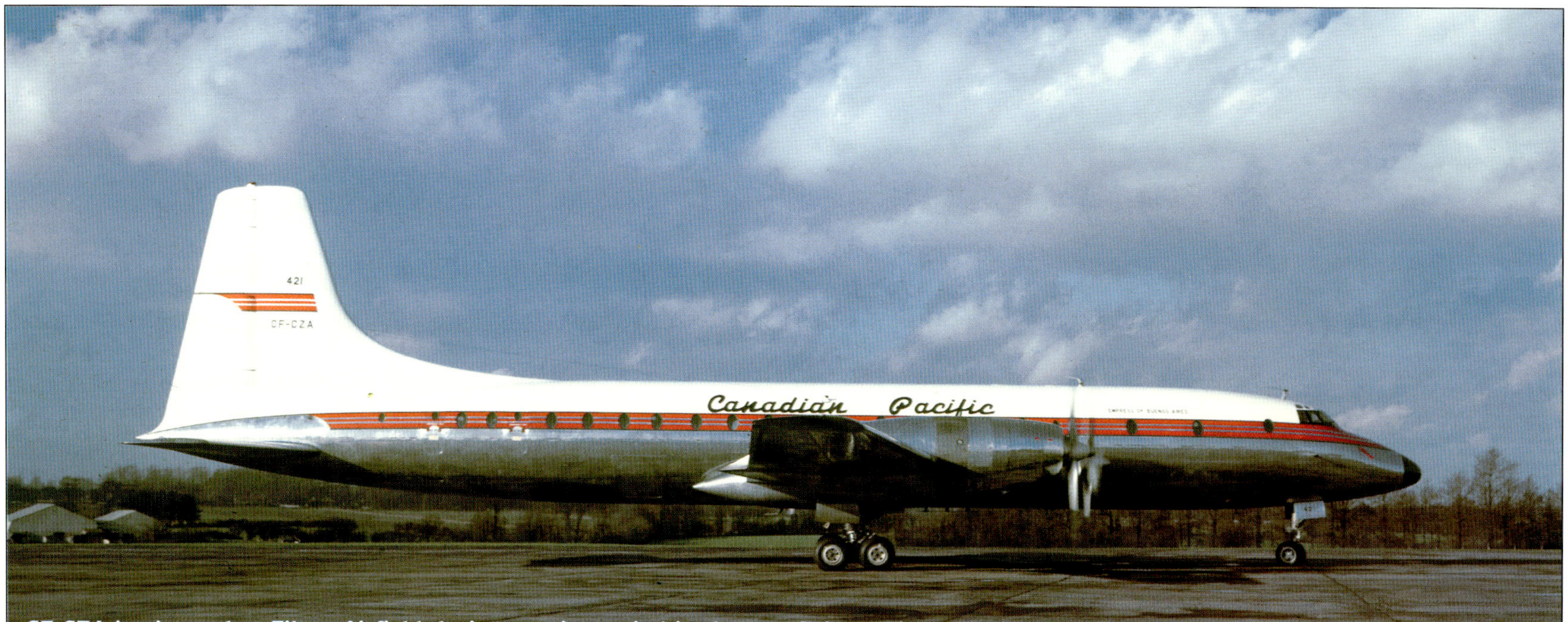

CF-CZA is pictured at Filton Airfield during a quiet period in the test flying, prior to delivery to Canadian Pacific.

batteries. All control surfaces operated normally, as did the cabin heating. The aircraft was then raised on jacks and undercarriage retraction tests were carried out, without trouble. The winter flying programme then started and there was only one hitch in an otherwise trouble-free set of tests. At one point in a flight, it was noticed that the front top panel of the spinner fairing on No. 2 propeller was loose so the engine was shut down and the aircraft returned to Winnipeg on three engines. On the ground, it was found that the fairing had not been correctly fastened and two of the fasteners had been sucked into the engine, causing slight damage to the entry vanes and the compressor blades. It was decided to replace the whole engine.

Once this was done, the winter testing continued and two take-offs and landings at Winnipeg in poor conditions, with visibility only 25 yards and a crosswind gusting to over 30 knots, were successful. The aircraft then flew to Vancouver for a final series of tests in runway-slush conditions, and some fast taxiing and accelerate-stop tests were conducted with no handling problems. This concluded the winter testing of the aircraft.

At this stage it was planned to demonstrate the long range of the Britannia with a non-stop flight from Vancouver to the UK. However it was first decided to fly from Vancouver to Honolulu, one of Canadian Pacific's sectors, but on this flight one of the engines developed an oil leak so the aircraft had to divert to San Francisco with the faulty engine shut down. Nevertheless, the aircraft's return to Europe was by another record-breaking flight when G-AOVA flew from San Francisco to Ciampino Airport, Rome via Idlewild Airport, New York. For the leg from New York into Italy on 8th March, there were 50 passengers and a take-off weight of 175,000lb. There was a gradual improvement of weather conditions over the Atlantic so that, with progressively less fuel on board, the Britannia could cruise higher, eventually levelling out at 29,000ft and finally touching down in Rome at 1040hrs on 9th March. The flight took 12hrs 20mins, averaging 382mph over the 4,700miles.

Further record-breaking flights were achieved by the long-range Britannia during 1957. On 30th June, G-AOVA flew the 5,100 miles from London to Vancouver in 14hrs 40mins. It took off from Heathrow at 0800hrs and landed in Vancouver at 1420hrs local time, achieving the fastest-ever time between the two cities and the first ever non-stop journey between the UK and the west coast of Canada.

These events were the preamble to the introduction of Britannias to the Canadian Pacific fleet. During 1957 Canadian Pacific increased its order for the long-range Britannias (Series 314) to six aircraft, registered as CF-CZA to CF-CZD, CF-CZW and CF-CZX. Five of these were built in Belfast and only one, CF-CZX, in Bristol. The first to fly was CF-CZA on 11th January 1958 and, after its maiden flight in Belfast, it transferred to Bristol for test flying. When this had been successfully completed, it flew from Filton via Montreal to Vancouver on 20th February for the opening ceremony of Canadian Pacific's new $1.4 million hangar at Vancouver, built specially for the Britannia fleet. On this flight the Captain was Bristol's Chief Test Pilot, Walter Gibb, and on board were a flight crew of nine and over 50 passengers, including representatives of Canadian Pacific and Bristol Aeroplane Company. The flight crew included three CPA captains.

The return journey was planned as another record-breaking flight, but the tail wind was a mere thirteen knots with the result that instead of a destination well into continental Europe, CF-CZA had to touch down at London, Heathrow after a flight of 13hrs 57mins. Following this return trip from Vancouver, CF-CZA returned to Belfast where Short Brothers completed the furnishing of the aircraft to CPA standards and on 1st April 1958 she was handed over to Canadian Pacific.

The second Britannia, CF-CZB, first flew on 14th April and CF-CZC on 13th May. CPA therefore had three Britannias in service by the end of May but unfortunately this represented a slip of several months from the original planned schedule for the beginning of the summer. CPA did, however, introduce Britannias on their prized route, Vancouver to Amsterdam, on 1st June 1958. (A special inaugural flight for journalists and travel agents from Amsterdam to Vancouver non-stop on the weekend of 17th/18th May was foiled by strong head winds, so that a refuelling stop had to be made at Goose Bay).

The cabin layout finally decided on was for sixteen first class and up to 72 tourist and economy class passengers. The cockpit layout was different from that adopted by BOAC as CPA did not have a separate radio operator, these duties were shared by the two pilots. There was a jump seat between the pilots for a flight engineer if required, and a separate position for the navigator as well as three bunks in a crew rest area, which were essential on long flights.

The Britannias soon proved to be popular with passengers. The Vancouver-Amsterdam route was flown in 13hrs 30mins, representing a time saving of 30% over the earlier piston-engined aircraft, even allowing for a refuelling stop at Søndre Strømfjord, Greenland. There was also a twice-weekly service introduced, Amsterdam-Søndre Strømfjord-Vancouver-Honolulu-Canton Island-Nandi-Auckland/Sydney, where the Britannias proved much more popular than the slower DC-6Bs.

With the delivery of the sixth Britannia, CF-CZW, Canadian Pacific introduced the aircraft into their Far East network. There was a proving flight from Vancouver to Tokyo on 12th August 1958 and after some demonstration flights while in Tokyo, the aircraft returned to Vancouver, covering the 4,700 miles in a record 13hrs 30mins. This was the precursor to the introduction of the scheduled Vancouver-Tokyo service on 24th August 1958 (and another record flight a few weeks later with a scheduled flight from Tokyo to Vancouver non-stop in 11hrs 44mins).

In March 1958, Canadian Pacific announced plans to compete directly with Trans Canada Airlines on the Vancouver-Winnipeg-Toronto-Montreal route, and to open routes from Vancouver to Calgary, Saskatoon, Edmonton and Regina. At the end of January 1959, the Canadian Government announced that CPA could operate a Vancouver-Montreal service, but restricted this to a once daily timetable. Britannias opened this service on 4th May.

Initially CPA used their Series 314 aircraft, with 89 seats (38 first class and 51 tourist class) and the Britannias quickly became more popular against the slower Constellations and Viscounts

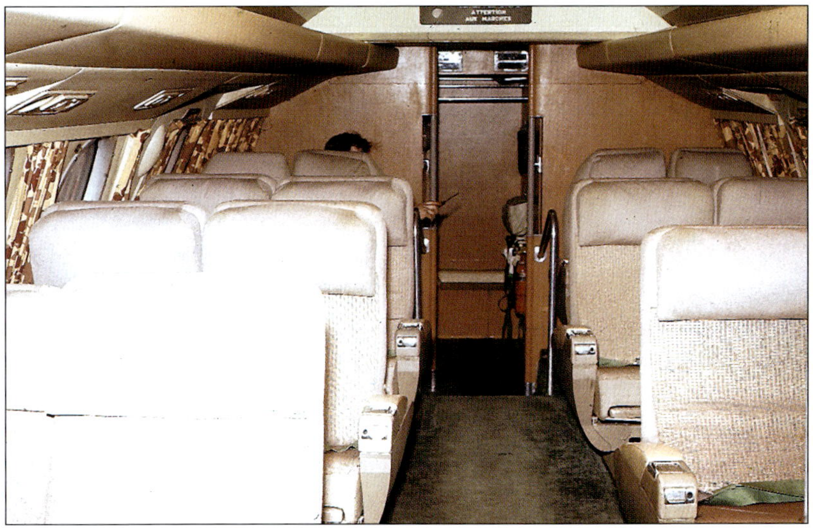

Two images of the interior of Canadian Pacific Britannias.

ABOVE: Looking toward the rear, in the First Class section, with two by two seating.
RIGHT: Also in the First Class section, a close-up of the comfortable seating units upholstered in a pink fabric.

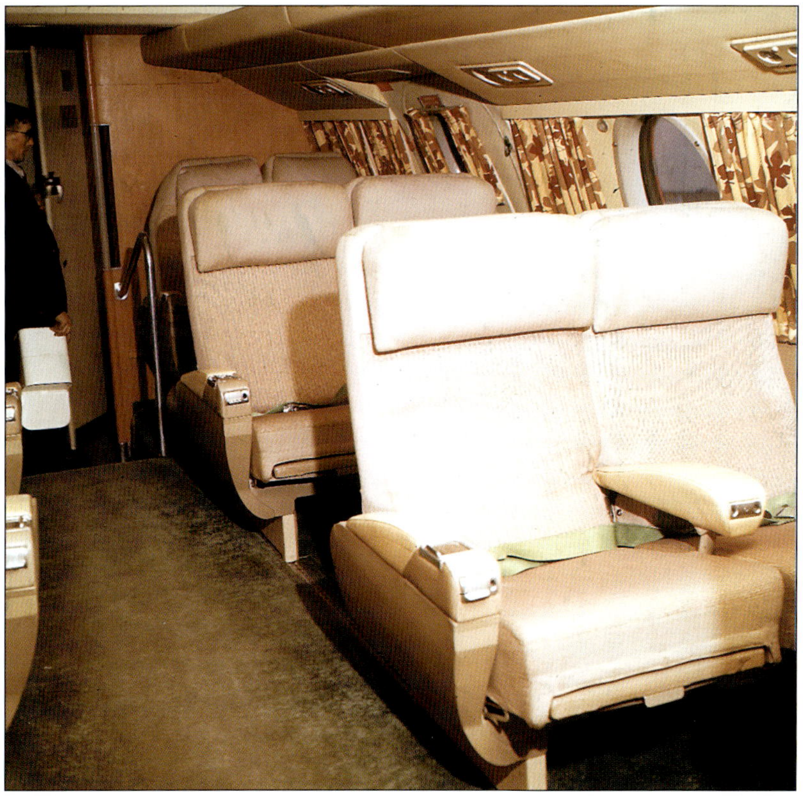

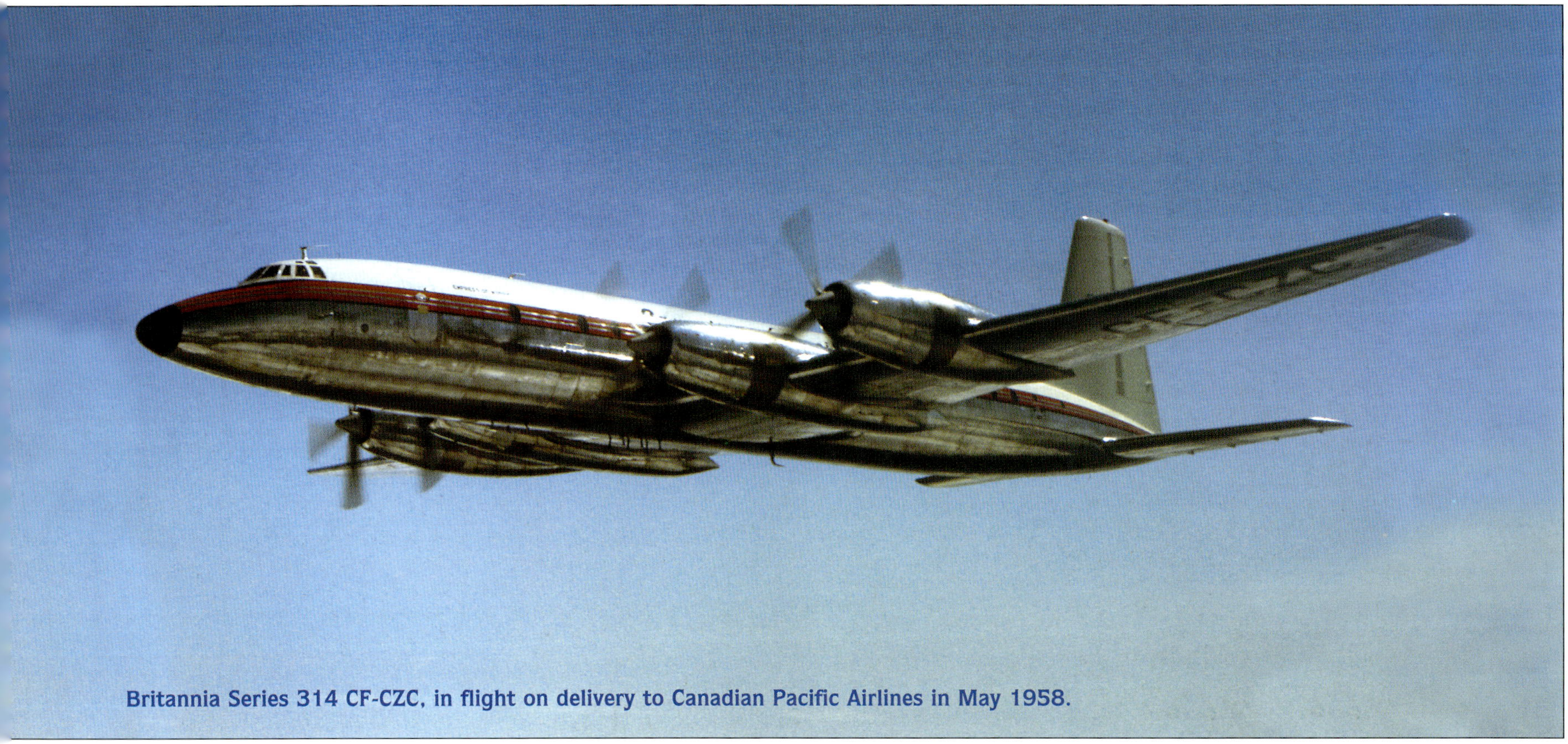

Britannia Series 314 CF-CZC, in flight on delivery to Canadian Pacific Airlines in May 1958.

operated by TCA. Within six months, Canadian Pacific claimed load factors of 84% west-bound from Winnipeg and 95% east-bound from Winnipeg. The 2462 miles between Vancouver and Montreal were flown once daily each way by Britannias and twice weekly, on Sundays and Wednesdays, the flight from Montreal continued beyond Vancouver to Tokyo and Hong Kong, returning back from Hong Kong on Mondays and Thursdays.

With these new routes proving successful, CPA needed more Britannias to meet the demand. They had ordered four Douglas DC-8s with Rolls Royce jet engines, but they would not be available until the spring of 1961 so CPA approached Bristol in order to arrange a short term lease of two Series 324 aircraft. These aircraft were certified to an all-up weight of 185,000lb and the lease agreement for the aircraft, registered as CF-CPD and CF-CPE, was announced in September 1959. The first aircraft was delivered on 17th October 1959 and the second followed four weeks later, bringing CPA's Britannia fleet to eight, the largest for any operator outside the UK.

The two Series 324 aircraft were mainly kept on the Vancouver-Winnipeg-Toronto-Montreal route, whilst the six Series 314 aircraft were allocated to the Vancouver-Tokyo-Hong Kong route, and to the Amsterdam-Søndre Strømfjord-Edmonton-Vancouver-Honolulu-Canton Island-Nandi-Auckland-Sydney route. Furthermore, by early 1960, the Britannias had replaced DC-6Bs on many of the South American routes, for example operating a twice-weekly service on the route Vancouver-Mexico City-Lima-Santiago-Buenos Aires. They also took over the route Toronto-Montreal-Lisbon-Madrid, and their long range enabled them to fly Montreal-Lisbon non-stop, omitting the refuelling stop in the Azores. On 1st March 1960 this route was further extended to Rome.

The summer of 1960 saw the peak of Britannia operations by Canadian Pacific but the following summer, the delivery of the first three of the jet-propelled DC-8s brought an end to the domination of trans-continental flying by turbo-prop aircraft. First, the DC-8s took over the Vancouver-Amsterdam schedule on 30th May 1961, then the service to Tokyo and Hong Kong on 10th October 1961. Britannias continued to operate the services to South America, Lisbon, Madrid and Rome, and also supplemented the services to Amsterdam and Hong Kong when demand required it, but the greater speed of the DC-8s made the reduction of the Britannia fleet inevitable.

The first to go were the two leased Series 324s, with CF-CPD returning to Filton on 12th February 1961 and CF-CPE on 11th April, reducing the CPA Britannia fleet to the original six aircraft. About fifteen months later there was a disaster when CF-CZB suffered an engine failure on take-off at Honolulu and crashed, killing 27 of the 40 people on board. The remaining five aircraft stayed with CPA until 1964 but were all eventually replaced by faster jet aircraft.

At the time when piston and turbo-prop aircraft were

beginning to be replaced by jet aircraft, there was a significant development of so-called charter flying in which Britannia aircraft were much used. An early example of this was a flight by CPA's CF-CZA from Vancouver to Prestwick, arriving on 17th July 1959 with 96 Canadian tourists on board who then returned by CF-CZD on 27th July. Neither flight was a scheduled flight as each aircraft had been chartered from CPA by the tour operator for a single flight.

During 1960 there was a big increase in charter flights across the North Atlantic, with Canadian flights arriving at Heathrow, Manchester and Prestwick. The first Britannia charter from Manchester seems to have been on 12th August 1960 when CF-CZX left Ringway for Goose Bay. The same aircraft was used for other charter flights from Manchester to Quebec, Montreal or Vancouver.

During the summer of 1961, a series of charter flights were made by Britannias into Heathrow, Prestwick and Belfast, with CF-CZD making a non-stop flight from Vancouver to Prestwick on 6th June to launch the programme. The flights into Belfast were popular, probably because five of the six Britannias had been built in Belfast. For this season, at least two of the aircraft had their seating re-arranged allowing up to 125 passengers and crew on board for the transatlantic charter flight.

The five Britannias remained with CPA, mainly on charter work until May 1964 but for that summer, one, CF-CZW, was leased to British Eagle returning in October. For the 1965 season, three Britannias, CF-CZD, CF-CZW and CD-CZX, were used on the transatlantic route from Canada to Europe, whilst the other two, CF-CZA and CF-CZC, were sold to Air Links in May and by August had been re-registered as G-ATGD and G-ATLE and entered into service with Transglobe Airways. The first CPA charter of the year to the UK was by CF-CZW from Vancouver to Gatwick on 7th/8th May, and during July and August this became a regular weekly flight. There were four or five flights per week from Gatwick to Canadian cities, among them Calgary, Edmonton, Montreal, Quebec, Toronto, Vancouver and Winnipeg. During the summer, thousands of Canadian tourists had crossed the Atlantic to European destinations which included Amsterdam, Athens, Budapest, Copenhagen, Frankfurt, Lisbon, Madrid, Milan, Munich, Oslo, Paris, Rome, Shannon, Stockholm, Vienna and Warsaw.

By the end of the summer season, the CPA Britannias had flown eleven charter flights to Belfast, twenty to Prestwick and 52 to Gatwick, with only occasional delays being experienced. But the age of the Britannias was beginning to show and one aircraft, CF-CZW, was particularly prone to trouble. On one occasion she was stranded at Gatwick for twelve days, arriving from Oslo on 31st May with a charter flight to Montreal and not being able to continue the flight until 12th June. On 27th June she again suffered engine trouble en-route from Amsterdam to Canada and diverted to Gatwick, where the passengers were transferred to another aircraft whilst CF-CZW was flown empty to Southend for repairs. Next day she was back on charter flights again.

On 6th September the same aircraft again experienced engine trouble and again diverted to Gatwick during a

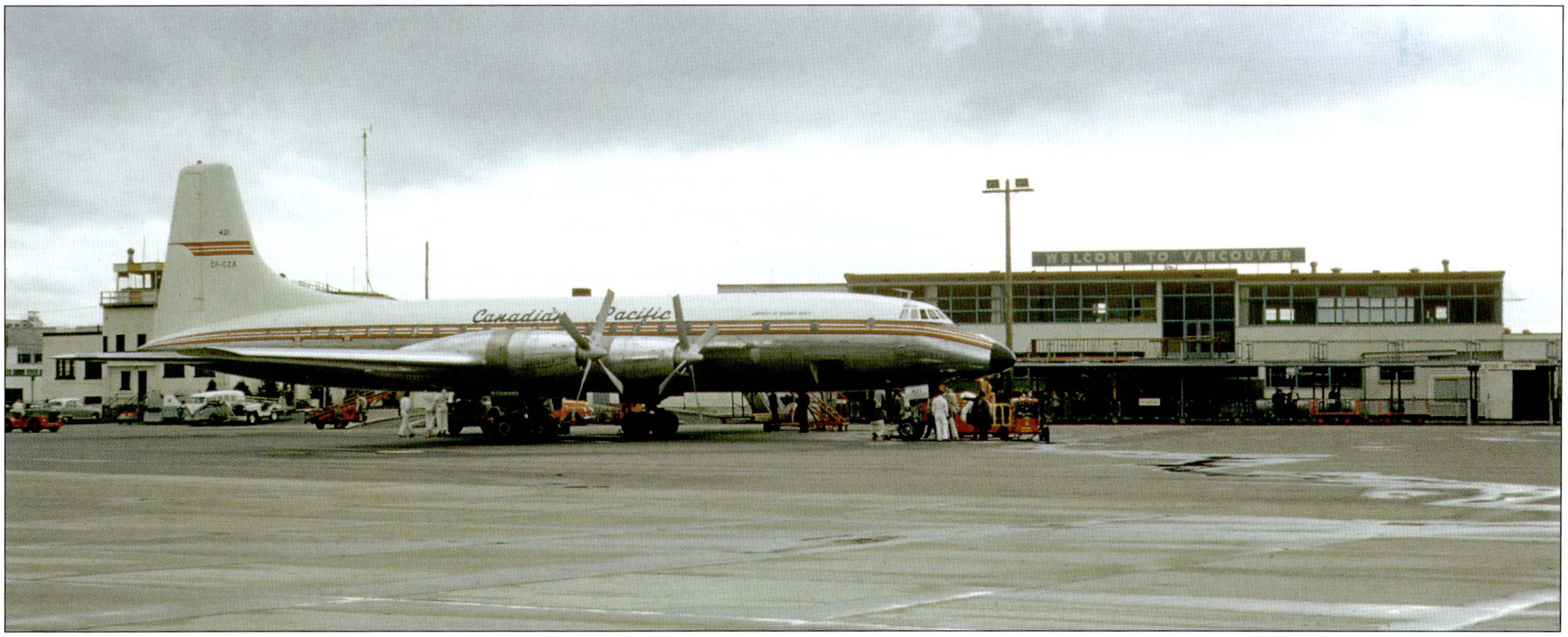

CF-CZA stands at Vancouver, after the record route-proving flight from London on 23rd February 1958. The aircraft covered the 5,100 miles in 13hrs 57 minutes, overflying the North Pole.

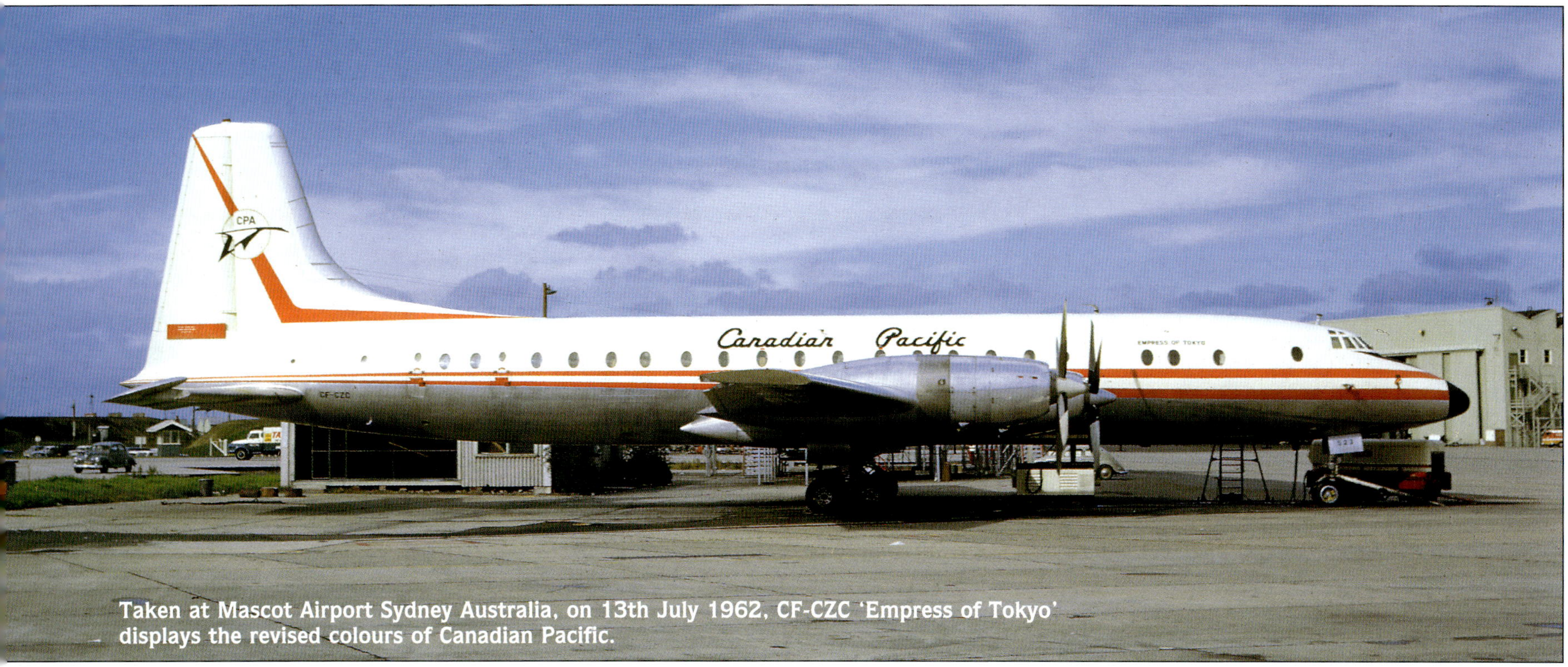

Taken at Mascot Airport Sydney Australia, on 13th July 1962, CF-CZC 'Empress of Tokyo' displays the revised colours of Canadian Pacific.

flight from Paris to Montreal. Repairs this time were carried out at Gatwick and the flight continued, but with a twelve hour delay. But these stories were unusual and the Britannias remained popular and were well remembered by passengers long after they had been replaced by the newer, faster jets.

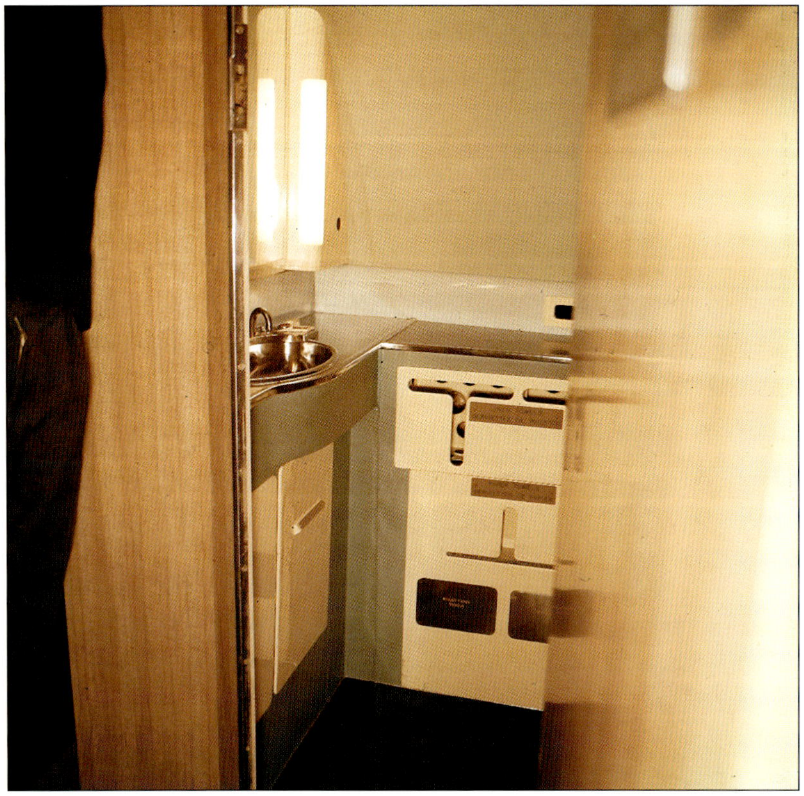

A view through the toilet door on board a Canadian Pacific Britannia.

The final Britannia charter flight from Belfast flew out on 29th August 1965. The final one from Gatwick took a party of Canadian tourists back to Vancouver on 23rd/24th October, and the final (westwards) flight through Prestwick was a Budapest-Prestwick-Vancouver service which CF-CZD flew on 28th/29th October.

All seven surviving CPA Britannias went on to be operated by independent British carriers. CF-CZA and CF-CZC entered service with Transglobe, as previously stated, and the two Series 324 aircraft, CF-CPD and CF-CPE, were acquired by Cunard Eagle Airways (later British Eagle) in 1961. The other three aircraft, CF-CZD, CF-CZW and CF-CZX, entered service with Caledonian Airways. The original plan was for them to be used on a summer charter programme in 1966, but the declaration of independence by Rhodesia in 1965 and the subsequent organisation of the oil airlift to Zambia gave them a different role. It also speeded up their transfer. CF-CZX was flown to Southend for servicing and was re-registered as G-ATMA on 28th December 1965. CF-CZD flew a final (eastward) transatlantic charter flight Vancouver-Prestwick-Amsterdam on 3rd January 1966, then went straight to Southend for conversion. It was re-registered to Caledonian Airways as G-ATNZ on 31st January 1966. CF-CZW flew direct from Vancouver to Southend on 23rd January for conversion and was re-registered to Caledonian Airways as G-ASTF on 14th February 1966. These three aircraft proceeded to contribute to the oil airlift into Zambia during the next phase of their lives.

IN SERVICE WITH BRITISH INDEPENDENT AIRLINES

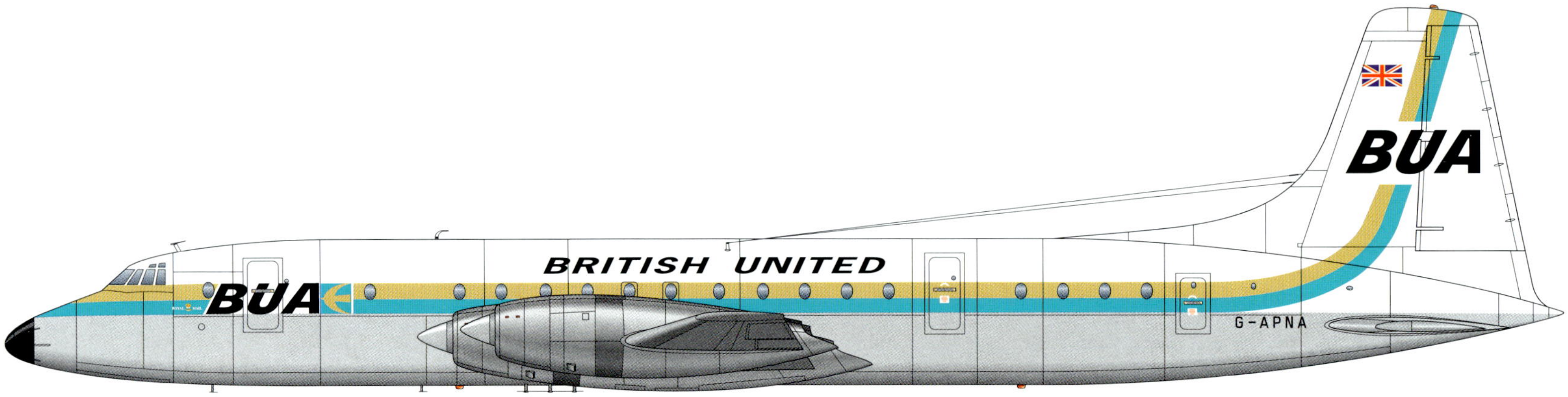

AIR CHARTER LTD

The Britannia aircraft raised the profile of British independent airlines. Until the mid-1950s, the independents had usually only managed to afford to buy second-hand aircraft sold off by the national airlines. However this changed in September 1958 when Freddie Laker's Air Charter Ltd bought a Britannia Series 300. Although 'new' it had had a somewhat checkered history during construction.

Originally ordered by BOAC as a Series 302, this option was cancelled and it was then ordered as a Series 305, together with four more of the same, by Capital Airlines. When this order was cancelled it was taken up by Northeast Airlines but this again was cancelled because of financial problems. Eventually the Britannia, registered G-ANCE, flew her maiden flight on 3rd September 1958 from Belfast to Filton in the livery of Air Charter. She was furnished to that airline's requirements, designated a Series 307 variant, and delivered to them on 17th September.

On 1st October. she flew her first charter flight of a kind that was to become very familiar, taking service personnel and technicians to Christmas Island from Stansted via Goose Bay, Vancouver and Honolulu. On Monday, 6th October, she returned to Stansted with 126 servicemen on board then, the day after her arrival, she was off again, this time with 96 passengers again bound for Christmas Island. She landed back at Stansted on 12th October with 112 service personnel and fifteen crew on board.

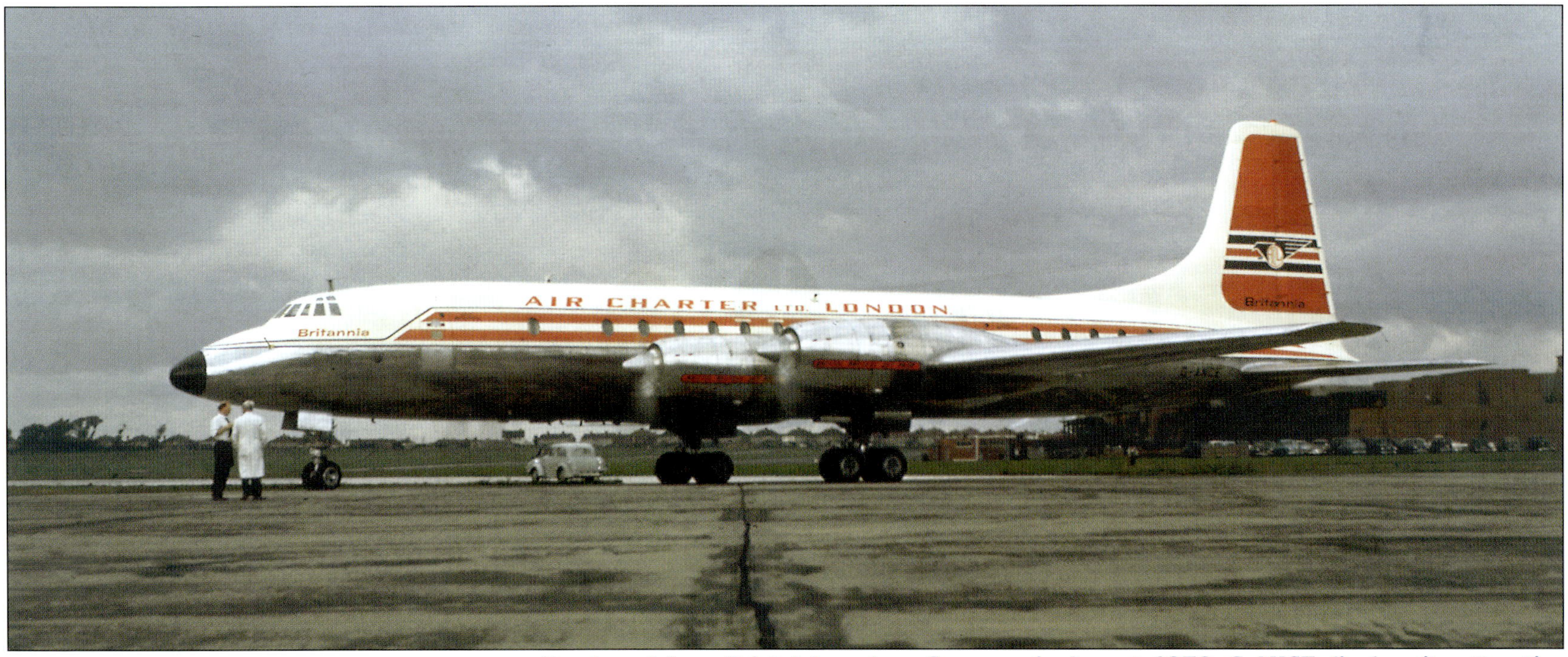

Purchased from Bristol Aeroplane Company in August 1958, G-ANCE displays its attractive Air Charter colour scheme during an engine test, prior to delivery.

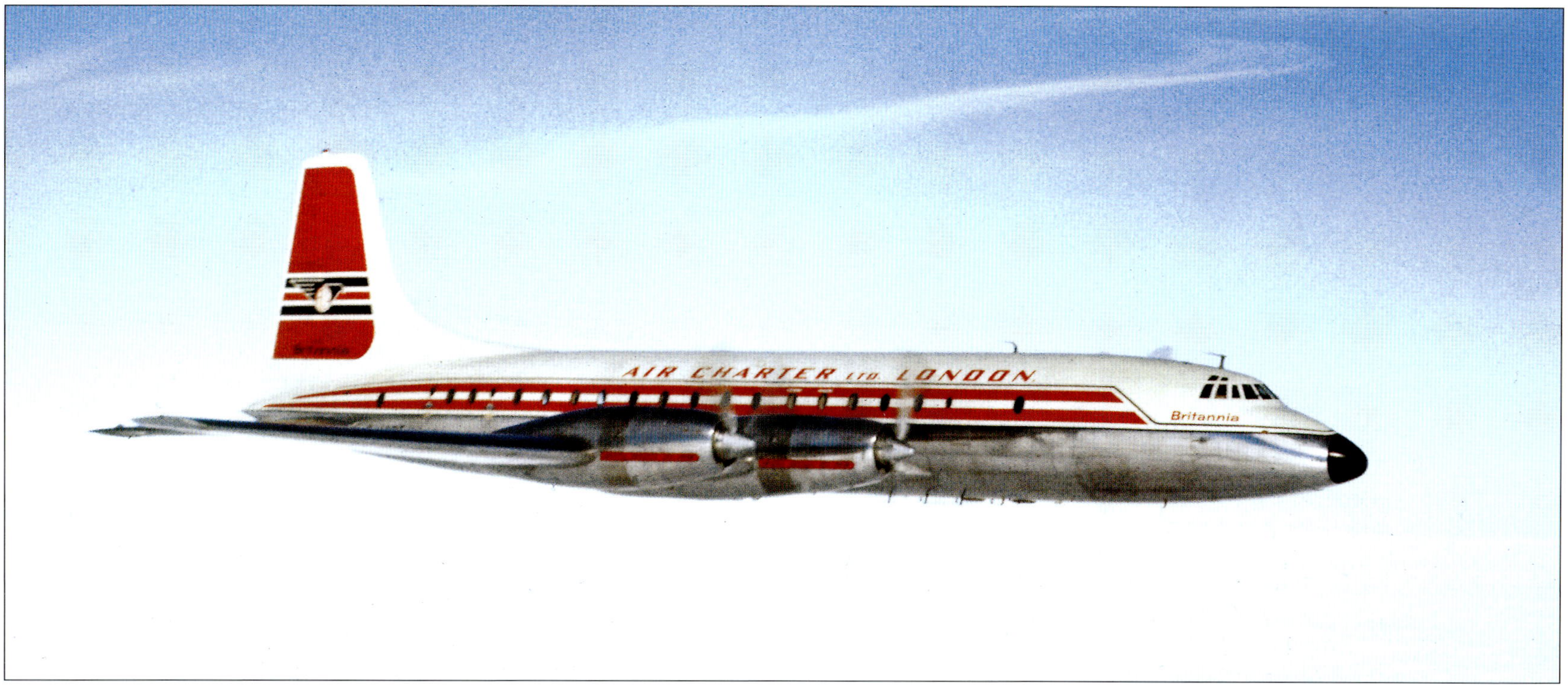

A rare air-to-air shot of Britannia Series 305 G-ANCE, on a test flight.

These flights to and from Christmas Island took about 29 hours in each direction (including re-fuelling stops). Such was the popularity of the Britannia for this purpose that more Government chartered flights followed.

On 2nd November she flew non-stop from Stansted to Bahrain and, during the next few weeks, she flew several more parties of servicemen to and from Christmas Island, with re-fuelling stops at either Gander, Goose Bay, Keflavík and Montreal. The final flight of 1958 was on 19th December, non-stop from Montreal to Stansted in ten hours.

There then followed a period of crew training so that more people were able to fly Britannias. On 21st January 1959 G–ANCE took off from Stansted, again with troops on board, this time bound for Bermuda via Canada then, on 23rd January, she flew back non-stop from Bermuda to Stansted in 10hrs 2mins. Next, on 5th February, she took off on a longer charter with 100 service personnel, bound for Adelaide and Sydney. She arrived in Australia on 8th February, after re-fuelling at Bahrain, Colombo and Singapore. From Sydney she flew on to Christmas Island to collect 112 passengers who were flown back to Stansted via San Francisco and Montreal. The last leg in the charge of Captain Hellary, one of Air Charter's original captains, from Montreal to Stansted took just 8hrs 58mins, making the whole round-the-world flight time 72hrs 30mins in just seven days with the flight ending at Stansted at 1350GMT on 12th February. On 18th February G-ANCE was off again, this time with more troop movement from Stansted to the Far East via Istanbul and Bahrain. She returned via Brindisi on 23rd February and the next day was off again for Christmas Island via Gander.

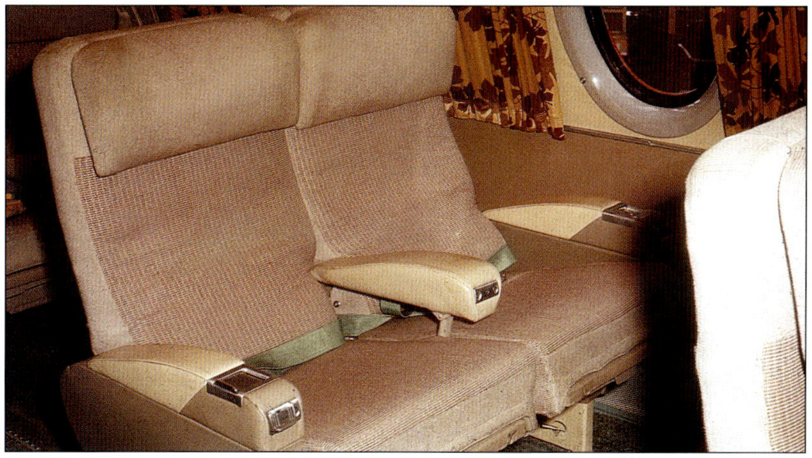

An interior view of G-ANCE taken in the First Class section, furnished in similar colours to Canadian Pacific aircraft.

With so much work available it is not surprising that Air Charter arranged to acquire a second Britannia, one with a similar initial history to G-ANCE. Having been a prospective BOAC/Capital/Northeast Series 305 order, she was the aircraft that had undertaken the sales tour of Spain, Portugal and South America during June 1958, registered as G-ANCD. She was then leased short term to El Al and on her return to the Bristol Aeroplane Company on 6th March 1959, was converted to Air Charter's requirements by Aviation Traders and handed over to Air Charter on 25th May, modified almost to Series 320 specification and with Bristol Proteus 765 engines.

G-ANCD's first revenue earning flight was on 27th May, a passenger charter from Stansted to Lisbon, followed by

another service to Lisbon the same evening. Then, on 29th May, she flew a Government charter mission to the Far East via Istanbul.

During the previous months, G-ANCE had been on Air Charter missions to many places around the world, among them Bahrain, Bombay, Brindisi, Istanbul, Singapore and Tehran. The regular charters to Christmas Island stopped on 10th March but resumed on 14th May, and both Britannias undertook a series of charters to Lisbon in the middle of June. An unusual charter by G-ANCE started on 4th July with a flight to Leopoldville in the Belgian Congo to collect Europeans who were stranded there by the war in the country. The plane returned to Brussels packed with a full load of Belgian nationals, and then flew back to Stansted on 8th July.

HUNTING-CLAN

Hunting-Clan was another independent airline, somewhat like Air Charter, which ordered two Britannias in late 1957. The actual order was in the name of the parent company, British Commonwealth and Shipping Co, and the first aircraft, ordered as a Series 310, variant 317 and registered as G-APNA, was originally in the British and Commonwealth livery. She was handed over on 11th December 1958.

Her first proving flight was on 8th January 1959 from Heathrow via Bahrain to the Far East, returning on 12th January. There then followed several charter flights involving the movement of ships' crews. (British and Commonwealth owned the Clan and the Union Castle shipping lines). G-APNA left Heathrow on 31st January and returned on 9th February, during which time it carried 170 seamen of five different nationalities in various directions, linking Britain with India and Hong Kong, and Germany with Japan. By the time of the Britannia's return to Heathrow, it had travelled about 20,000 miles over nine days.

During the next two months there was relatively little charter work available but, in mid-April, Hunting-Clan was awarded a long-term contract to transport servicemen and their families between Heathrow and Singapore. This contract replaced an earlier one using piston-engined Hermes aircraft which had taken three and a half days (with overnight stops) to cover what took a Britannia just 24 hours. The Britannia flew to Singapore with re-fuelling stops at Istanbul, Karachi and Bombay and this straight-through flight was very popular with the service personnel.

This extra work enabled Hunting-Clan to take the second Britannia it had ordered, G-APNB, which was delivered on 30th April and entered service in May. Both Britannias were fitted with 114 rearward facing seats and operated about six round trips per month to Singapore and Hong Kong. The success of this contract meant that the British Government awarded Hunting-Clan two more service contracts, one from Heathrow to Aden via Benina, Libya with a flight time of 14hrs, and the other from Heathrow to Nairobi, again re-fuelling at Benina with a flight time of 15hrs.

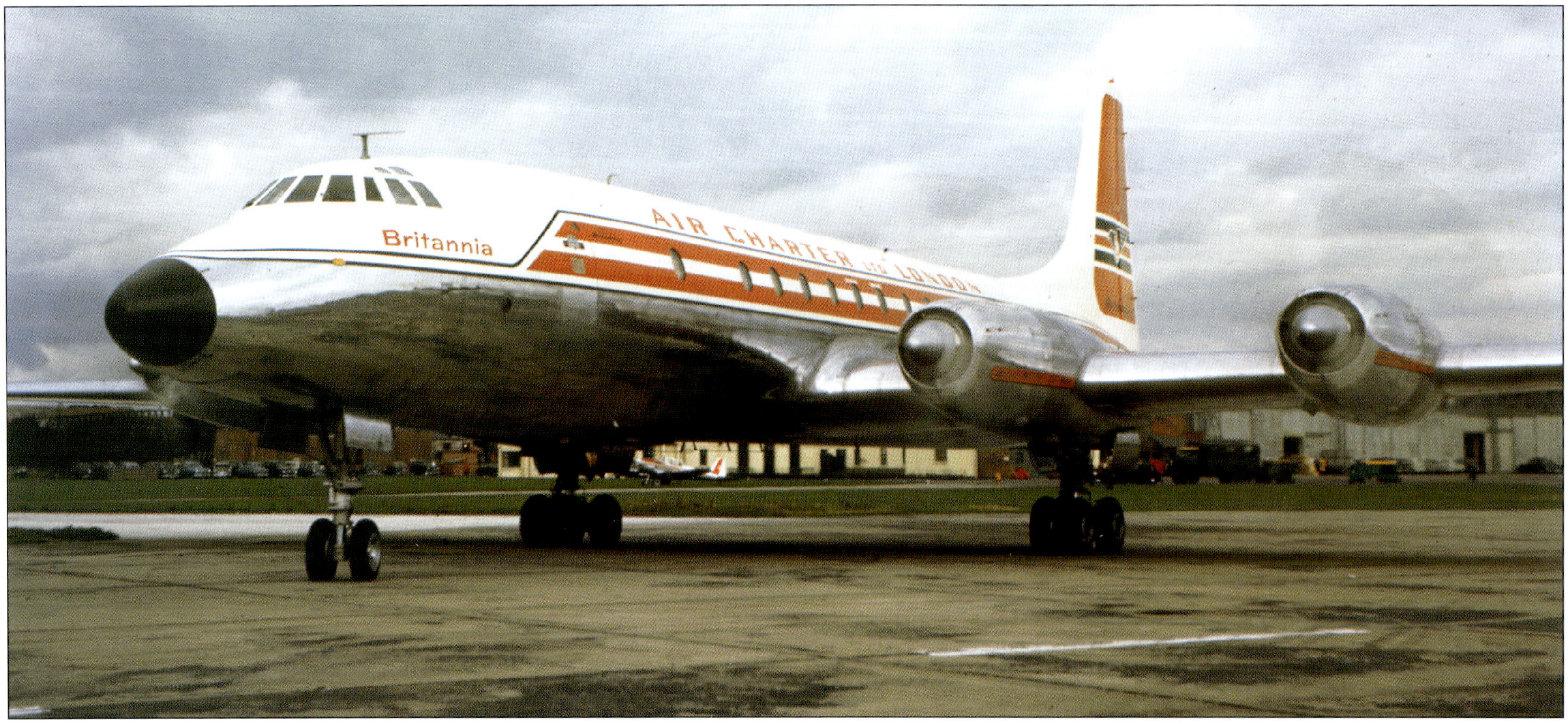

Destined to carry these colours for a short ten month period until repainting into the British United livery in July 1960, G-ANCE was to be the only Britannia to wear the Air Charter colour scheme.

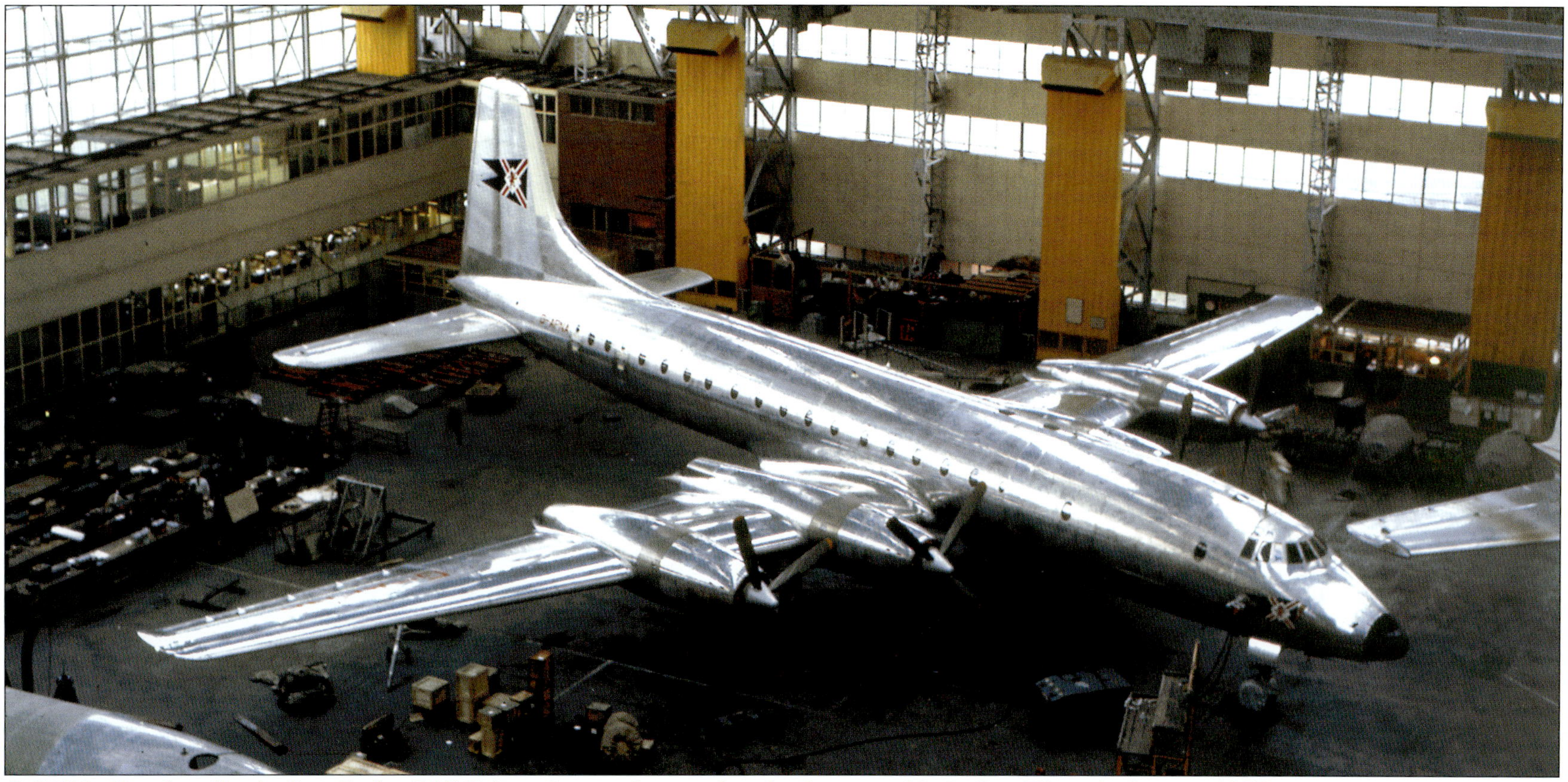

G-APNA, Hunting-Clan's first Series 317 Britannia stands complete in the assembly hall at Filton in August 1959, prior to the application of the full colours of the British and Commonwealth Shipping Company (Aviation) Ltd.

During the twelve months from the summer of 1959 to the summer of 1960, various manoeuvrings took place which led eventually to the merger of Air Charter and Hunting-Clan. By October 1959 the four Britannias (two owned by each company) were well established in the role of troop transporting, and after discussion it was decided to base all four aircraft at Heathrow from 1st November onwards. On 28th October, Air Charter's Britannia G-ANCD flew troops from Stansted to Nicosia, returning three days later to Heathrow. After crew training she operated her first troop transporting from Heathrow to Benina on 8th November but, on her return on 12th November, bad weather in the Heathrow area forced a diversion to Hurn. Because of continued bad weather, she flew from Hurn to Stansted on 13th November in order to take-off with her next planeload of troops from Stansted to Brindisi. Hunting-Clan's Britannia G-APNB also had to divert from Heathrow to Stansted when returning from Nicosia because of bad weather then, after a quick turn round, she took another troop flight to Hong Kong via Istanbul.

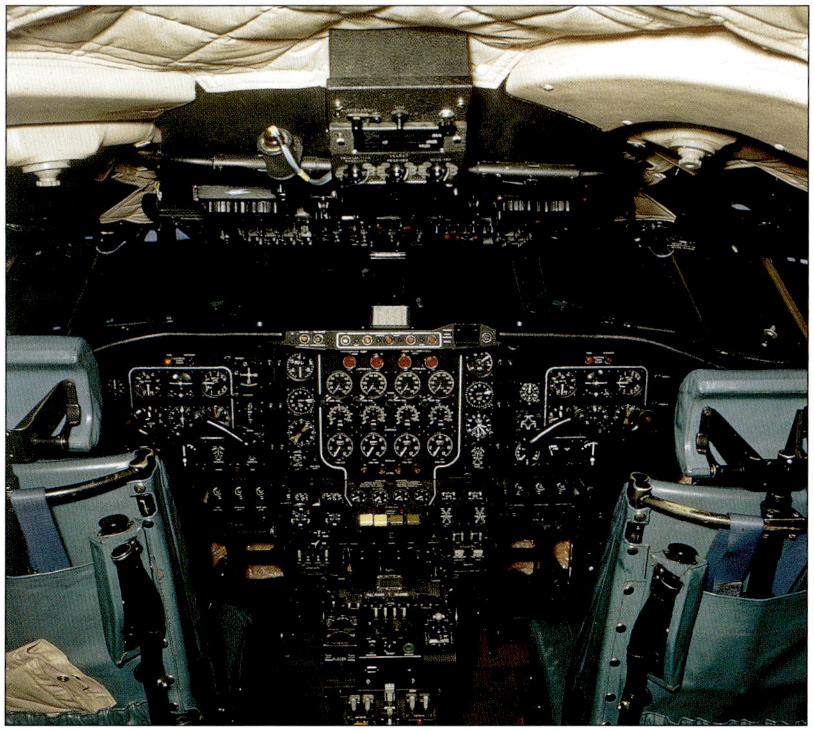

The cockpit interior of G-APNA, complete with turquoise leather seats. Note the roof padding, a similar design to the Comet.

Once the weather over Heathrow improved, all four Britannias were based there and continued with troop transporting, although this arrangement only lasted for two months. In January 1960, it was decided to leave the two Hunting-Clan Britannias at Heathrow while transferring the two Air Charter Britannias to Gatwick. This began on 18th January when G-ANCE flew back from Istanbul to Gatwick, then on 21st January she flew from Gatwick to Bombay. That same morning, G-ANCD arrived at Gatwick from Benina then set off again for Benina on 23rd January.

For some time during this period, the Hunting-Clan Britannias were chartered by East African Airways to operate

scheduled passenger services between Heathrow and Entebbe and Nairobi, via Rome and Khartoum. This arrangement stopped when the new Comet 4 jets ordered by East African Airways were delivered.

In April 1960 Air Charter's Britannia base moved again back to Stansted. G-APNB landed at Stansted on the morning of 22nd April on a flight from Istanbul and took off late that night for Benina. During the last week of April, G-ANCD arrived at Stansted from Istanbul then, on 5th May, G-ANCE arrived there and finally G-APNA arrived on 12th May from Filton after an overhaul.

BRITISH UNITED AIRWAYS

Stansted remained the base for these four Britannias for over a year and they were involved in regular troop movements to and from the places previously mentioned. Following successful merger talks Air Charter and Hunting-Clan became British United Airways on 1st July 1960 under Freddie Laker as Managing Director (until then he was Managing Director of Air Charter). Gradually the four Britannias were repainted in the colour scheme of the new airline.

All four British United Airways' (BUA) Britannias remained based at Stansted until the autumn of 1961. BUA then decided to replace its Viscounts with Britannias on its schedules to East Africa making a significant improvement to the service. The Viscounts had to make several re-fuelling stops when flying between Gatwick and Entebbe, but the Britannia 317s, fitted with Proteus 757 engines boosted by water injection, could usually manage to fly this route non-stop.

The opening of the East Africa service required a change of base to Gatwick for the two Britannia 317s, G-APNA and G-APNB. G-APNB began by flying from Gatwick to Entebbe on 2nd October 1961, arriving back on the 4th. Leaving Gatwick again on the same day, she flew via Entebbe, Ndola and Lusaka to Salisbury. The two routes, from Gatwick to Salisbury and from Gatwick through Entebbe to Nairobi, were then flown regularly once each week.

On 22nd October, G-APNA returned to Gatwick after an overhaul which enabled BUA to extend its service into Africa. On 8th November, this Britannia took off from Gatwick for Freetown, Sierra Leone, at the start of a once-weekly service to and from the capital.

The transfer of the two Britannia 317s to Gatwick meant that there were only the other two BUA Britannias (Series 307s) left at Stansted for trooping duty. BUA therefore leased two Series 312 aircraft from BOAC, the first, G-AOVI, being

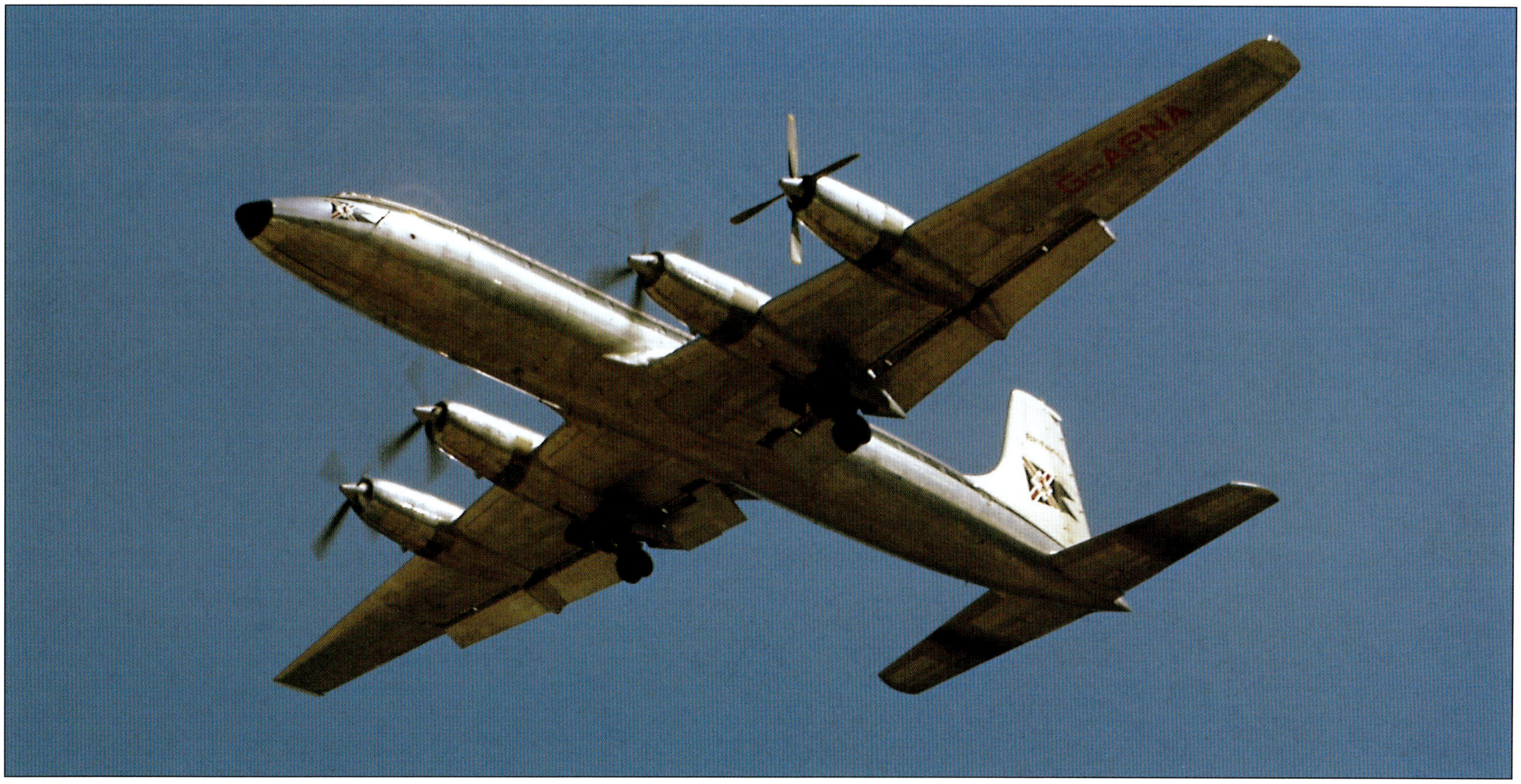

G-APNA returns from an early test flight with one engine shut down after compressor problems.

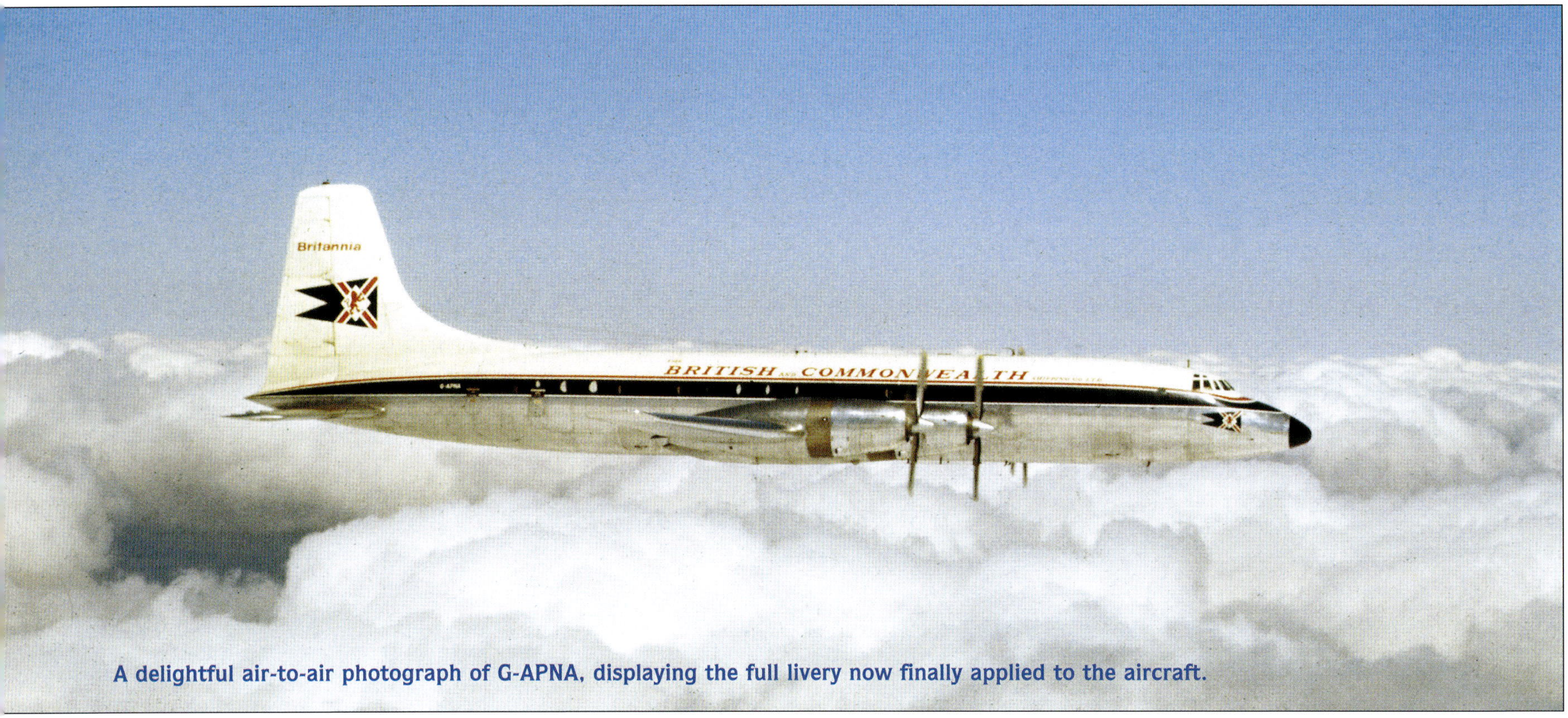

A delightful air-to-air photograph of G-APNA, displaying the full livery now finally applied to the aircraft.

delivered to Stansted on 21st September 1961 and the second, G-AOVE, delivered on 27th September. After conversion work and repainting in BUA livery, G-AOVI departed on 26th September for Nicosia and G-AOVE, after a similar conversion, took off for Nicosia on 6th October.

As troop movement work was still considerable, BUA leased two more Britannias in the New Year - two Series 313 aircraft from El Al. The first was re-registered as G-ARWZ and delivered to Stansted from Tel Aviv on 13th February 1962. (She was the Britannia which flew El Al's first transatlantic flight to New York). The second, G-ARXA, was delivered to Stansted on 14th March and, with these two additions, the BUA Britannia troop carrying fleet totalled six aircraft.

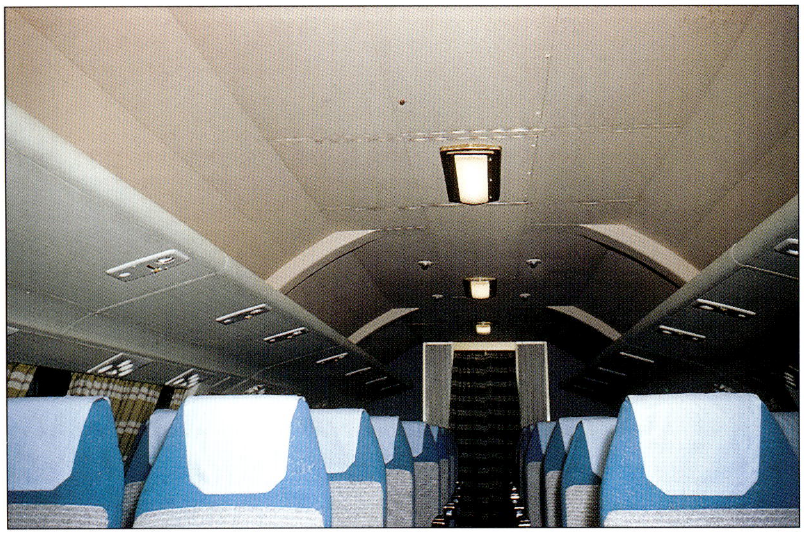

An interior view of G-APNB which demonstrates the crisp and simple design adopted for the passenger cabin.

The carrying of service personnel by BUA had by now become routine, with more than three years experience by the people involved. One very a-typical flight was by G-ARXA which took off from Stansted around midnight on 14th/15th December 1962 bound for Istanbul and Singapore. Soon after take-off, No. 2 engine caused trouble and had to be shut down, so that the fully laden Britannia diverted to Gatwick. The engine repair turned out to be more extensive than expected, so G-ANCE was flown from Stansted to Gatwick to pick up the stranded troops and resume their transfer to Singapore nearly 24 hours late. But this disruption was rare and generally there was a high level of reliability in the Britannia flights. On average about eighteen arrivals and departures took place at Stansted each week, transferring troops to Aden, Idris, Tripoli, Nicosia and Singapore. There were also other occasional charters, e.g. by G-AOVE from Stansted to Jeddah on 20th May and by G-ARXA from Stansted to New York on 13th July. The Britannias were kept busy.

During 1964, however, the fortunes of the BUA Britannias began to change. BUA lost the contract for troop movements to the Far East to the fast growing British Eagle International Airways, causing BUA to return the two leased Series 312 aircraft to BOAC in June 1964.

Earlier in the year there were still charter flights to pick up in addition to the usual troop movements. G-AOVE flew from

Stansted to Beirut on 21st April, leased for a month to Middle East Airlines as a temporary replacement for a Caravelle which had crashed at Dhahran. She was then returned by MEA to BUA and by BUA to BOAC on 5th June. The other leased BOAC Britannia, G-AOVI, worked a series of charters for Lloyd International; on 6th June from Glasgow to Palma and Rimini, on 19th June from Stansted to Gibralter, and on 21st and 26th June from Stansted to Luxembourg. On her final return from Luxembourg, G-AOVI was returned to BOAC on 1st July and the total BUA Britannia fleet was reduced to six aircraft.

During the autumn of 1964, all regular BUA troop flights came to an end and G-ARXA was returned to El Al on 3rd October. The final troop flight under the original contract seems to have been from Stansted via Istanbul to Singapore, leaving on 30th September. This was by G-ANCE, the original Air Charter Britannia 307.

The base for the five remaining Britannias now moved to Gatwick. These were G-ANCD, G-ANCE, G-APNA, G-APNB, all owned by BUA and G-ARWZ leased by BUA from El Al. From Gatwick the African work continued, to Entebbe, Freetown, Lusaka, Nairobi, Ndola and Salisbury, but the delivery of two new VC-10s resulted in the faster jets taking over much of the slower turbo-props' work. Nonetheless trooping work continued. While the VC-10s flew the Gatwick-Aden route, the Britannias, frequently G-ARWZ, flew Gatwick-Akrotiri as well as regular holiday charters to Palma and Tenerife. Throughout the winter G-ARWZ flew regularly between Gatwick and Tenerife, with up to four return flights per week. She also flew more troop charters to Aden, Akrotiri and Malta during January 1965. Her final BUA charter flight was Aden to Gatwick, arriving on 9th February, and she was then returned to El Al on 26th March.

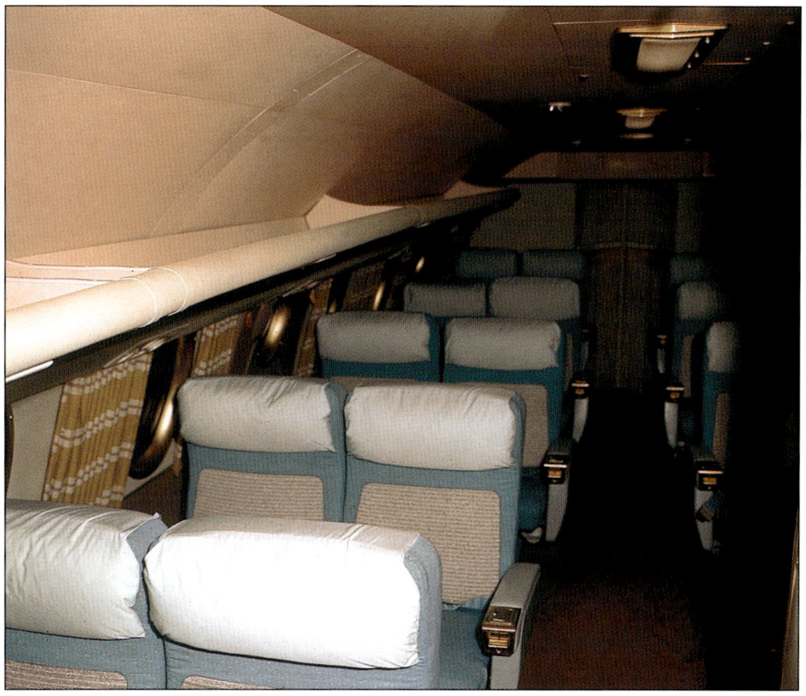

An alternative view of the First Class interior trimmed in blue and pink.

During the summer of 1965 the BUA Britannias did a great deal of work, helped by the late delivery of BAC 1-11 jets. BUA

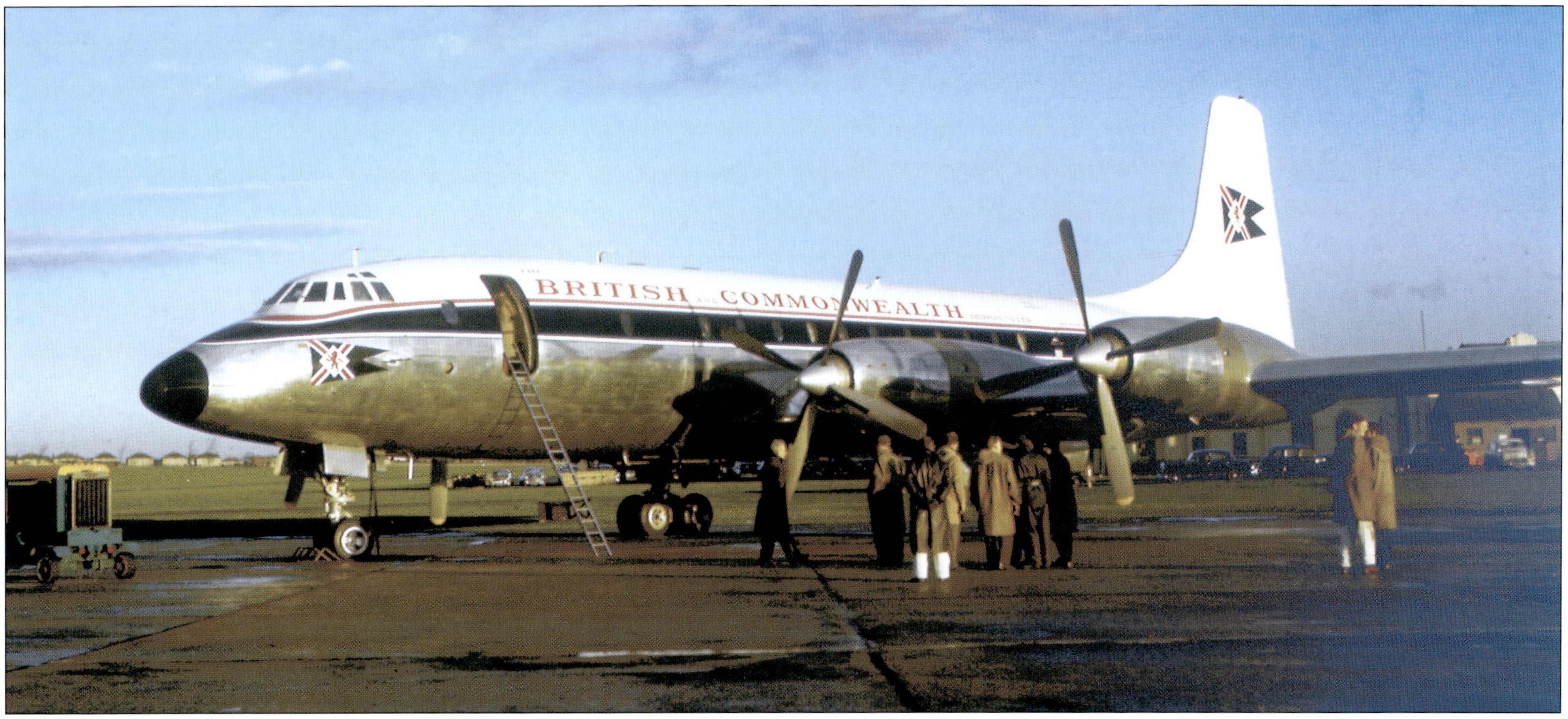

The second aircraft for British and Commonwealth is prepared for its first flight on the morning of 10th November 1958.

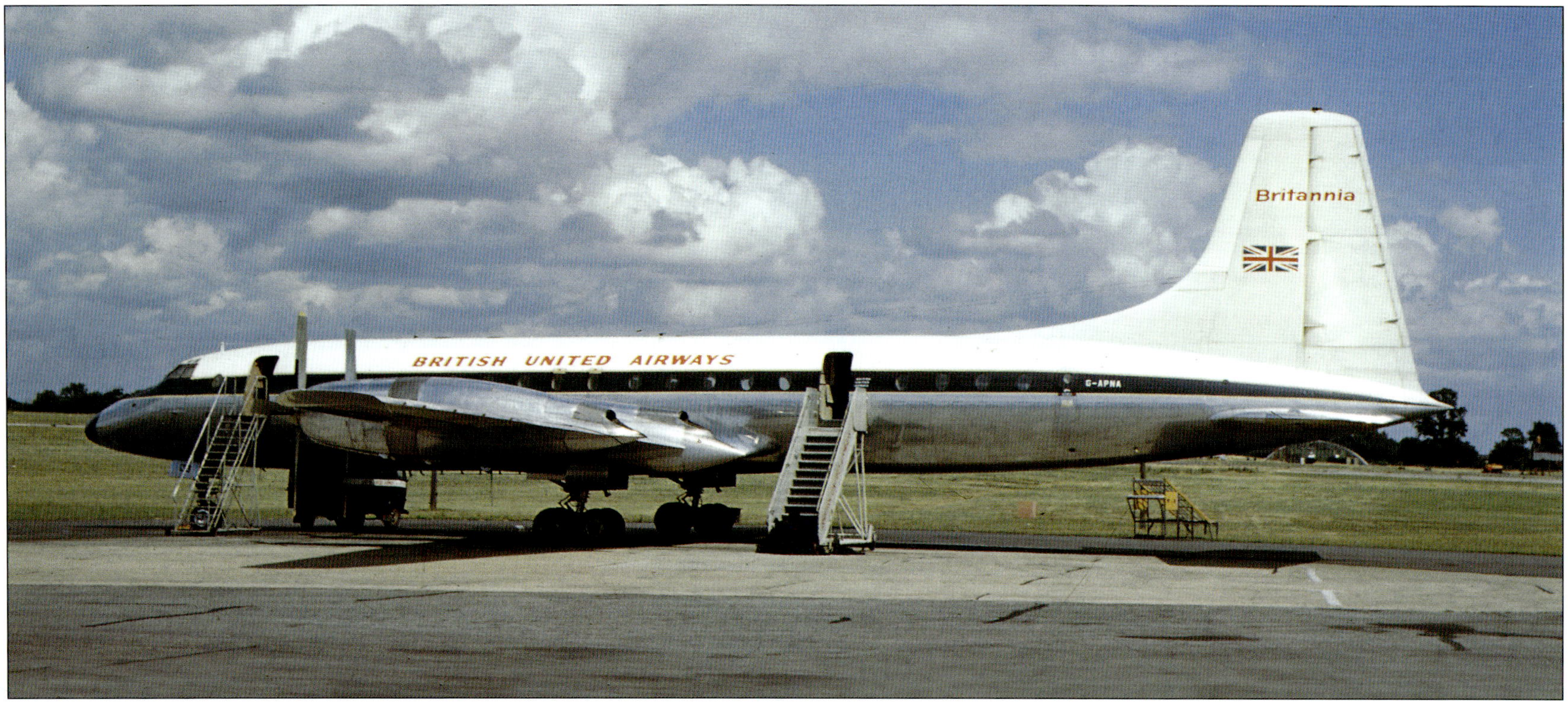

G-APNA, newly repainted in the full colours of British United Airways at Gatwick airport in June 1962.

was so short of aircraft for the summer holiday season that it leased a Series 309 Britannia, G-ANCH, from Bristol Aeroplane Company and at times other Britannias from Transglobe Airways. All these aircraft flew people from Gatwick to a variety of holiday destinations including Barcelona, Ibiza, Las Palmas, Ljubljana, Naples, Palma, Pisa, Rimini, Seville, Tangier, Tarbes, Valencia and Venice, chartered by a large number of tour operators. There were also charters to take passengers to P & O cruise liners at Genoa and Venice and to take pilgrims to Amman and Tel Aviv.

The end of the Far East troop work and the delivery of the VC-10s caused a change in work for the BUA Britannias, away from exclusively passenger carrying towards freight carrying.

A selection of views of British and Commonwealth and British United Airways Britannia passenger cabin interiors.

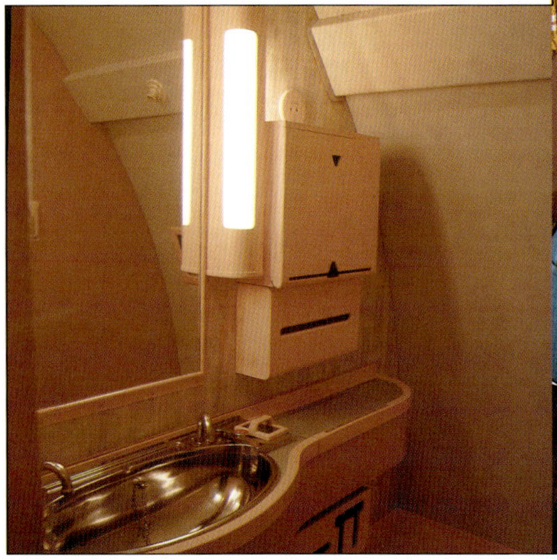

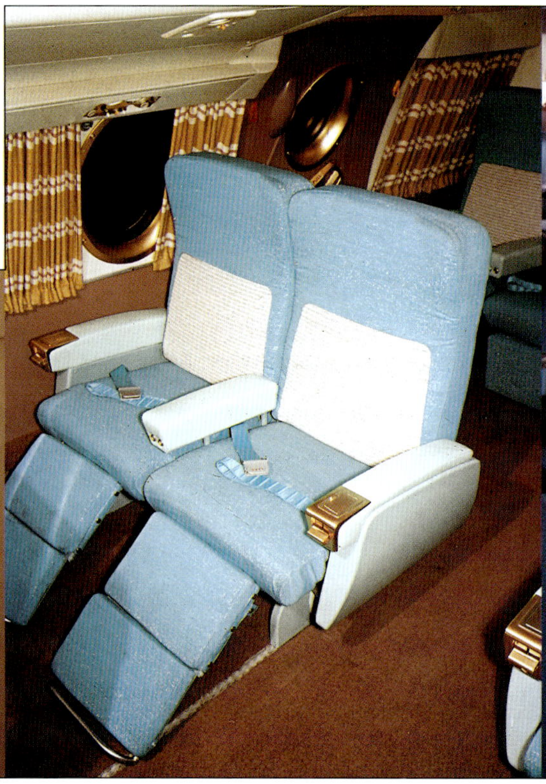

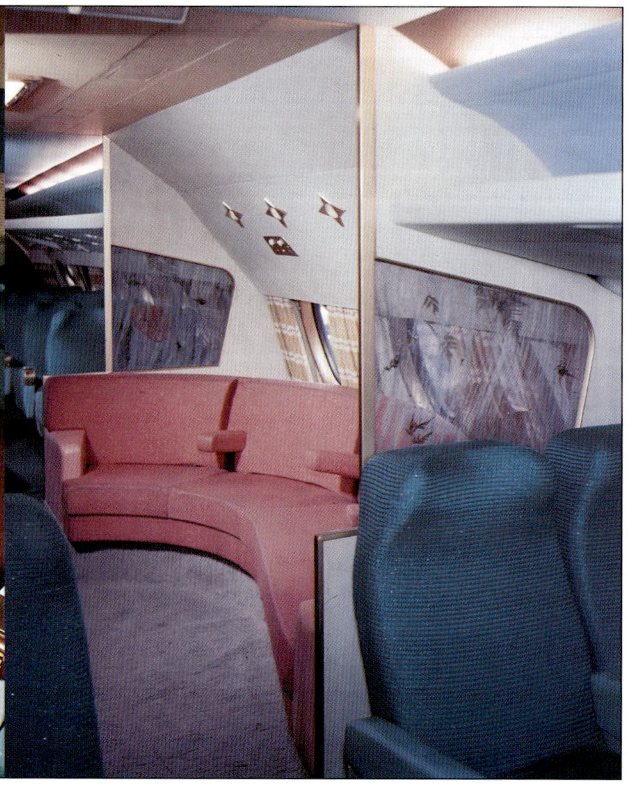

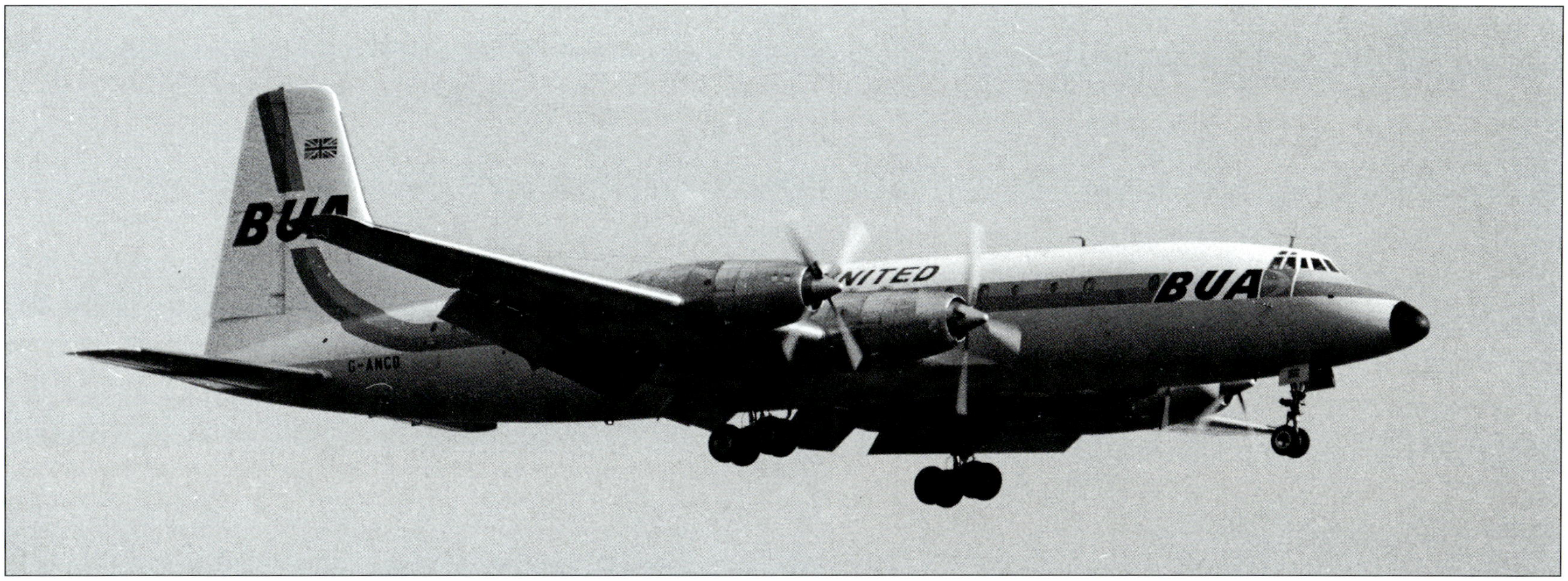

Series 307F Britannia G-ANCD, approaches Gatwick airport wearing the sandstone and blue livery of BUA.

This change required a conversion, fitting a large cargo door in place of the front port side passenger door and strengthening the cabin floor to take freight. This changed the Series 307 aircraft to be like the RAF Series 253s, but was redesignated 307F.

The first aircraft to be converted was G-ANCE, worked on by Aviation Traders at Stansted. She test flew from Stansted, then flew a Gatwick to Palma service on 18th June and, on that evening, flew the BUA 'Africargo' schedule from Heathrow to Africa. G-ANCD also experienced the same conversion and was delivered back to BUA on 6th September. From then on these two 307F Britannias shared the 'Africargo' schedule from Heathrow to Entebbe, Lusaka, Ndola and Niarobi via various staging points. Apart from decreasing the journey times taken by their predecessors, DC-6As, they raised the payload per journey from thirteen to seventeen tons. When not required for cargo work, the 307Fs were used on passenger work out of Gatwick.

During the winter of 1966 there were a series of charters; skiers from Gatwick to Geneva, holidaymakers from Gatwick to Tenerife and various troop charters from Gatwick (and sometimes Manchester) to Akrotiri, Düsseldorf, Gütersloh and Hanover. There were also some other troop charters still available. For example, on 3rd January 1967, G-APNA flew from Gatwick to Karachi (non-stop), and thence to the Far East, returning on 6th January. There were also regular charters for P & O, carrying tourists to join cruise liners in the Mediterranean. For example, on 14th and 15th December 1966, all four BUA Britannias flew cruise passengers from Gatwick to Venice in a total of eight trips. They also substituted for other BUA aircraft which became temporarily unserviceable and, on 3rd April 1967, G-APNA flew a Viscount's load of passengers from Bournemouth to Palma.

At the end of the 1967 season the decision was taken by BUA to retire the Britannias by the end of 1968. On 2nd October 1967, G-APNA was ferried from Gatwick to Stansted

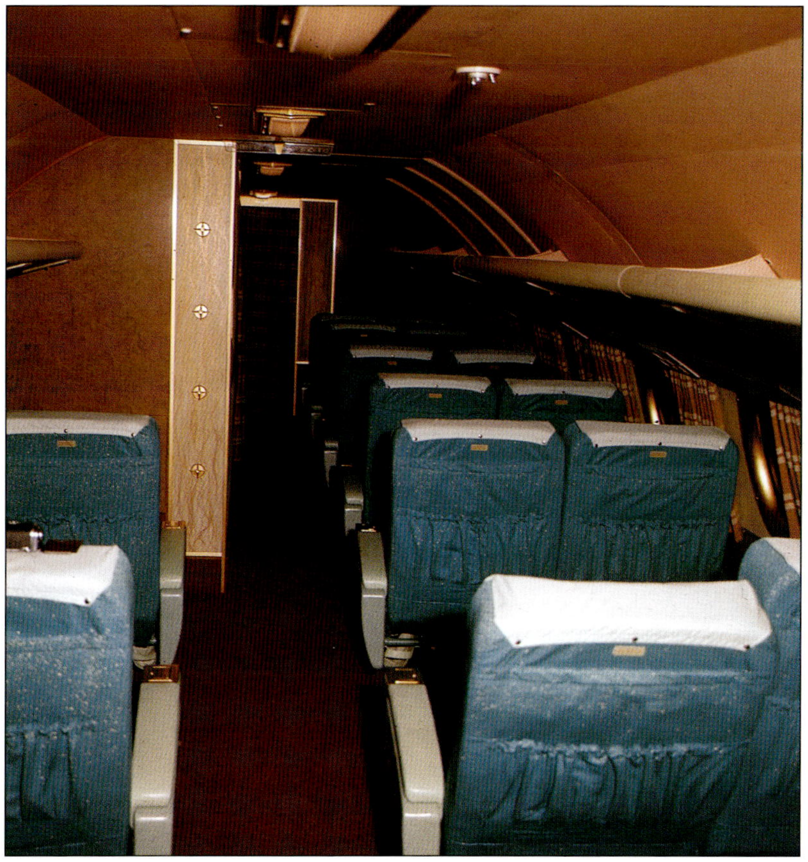

The First Class cabin in a British United Britannia.

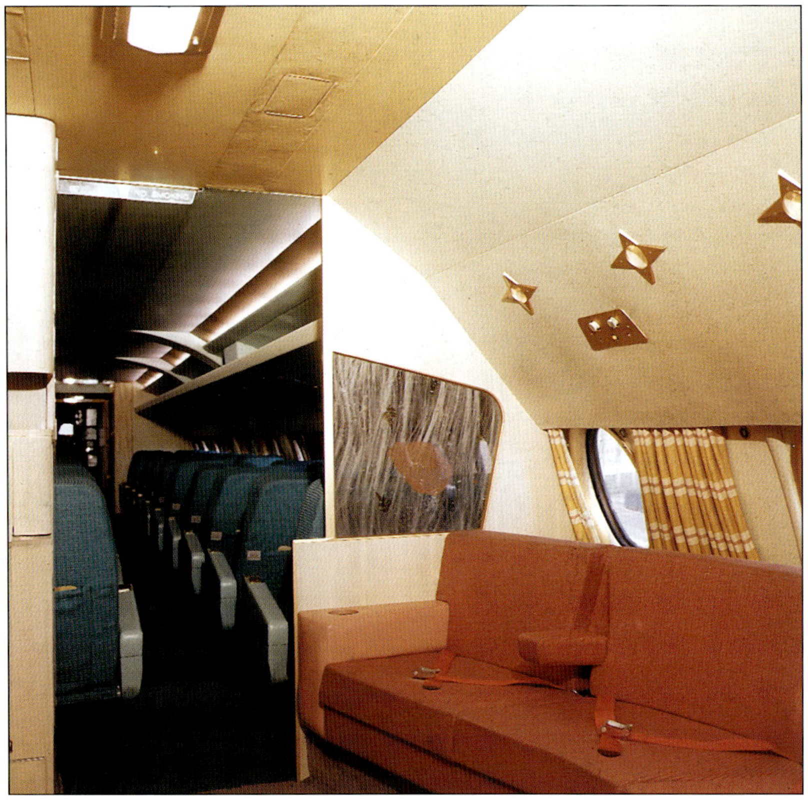

The lounge seating in the bar area at the rear of the aircraft.

having been sold to Donaldson International Airways (who immediately leased her to Lloyd International). Later, G-APNB was also sold to Donaldson but did not fly for them until April 1969. Meanwhile the BUA 'Africargo' schedule continued, now from Gatwick rather than Heathrow. There were large numbers of tour charters to the usual European destinations and there were still the occasional troop charters or charters for other operators, e.g. G-ANCD on 1st May flew from Gatwick via Prestwick to Toronto with 132 passengers and a crew of seven, on charter for Transglobe Airways.

At the end of the 1968 tourist summer traffic, the sole remaining flying for the last two BUA Britannias, both 307Fs, was on the 'Africargo' run. The final flight on this route by G-ANCD arrived back at Gatwick on 16th November 1968, and she then went into store. The last ever 'Africargo' flight flown by a BUA Britannia was by G-ANCE which touched down at Gatwick on 22nd January 1969. Thereafter this service was taken over by BUA VC-10s, also equipped with cargo doors.

So ended the association of BUA and its pre-merger companies with Britannia aircraft. During the preceding decade, BUA had owned or leased eleven Britannias and had used them in a wide variety of roles, ranging from a short flight across the English Channel to flights to Christmas Island and around the world. The reputation which the aircraft had acquired during this time was demonstrated by the ease with which BUA sold them on to new customers.

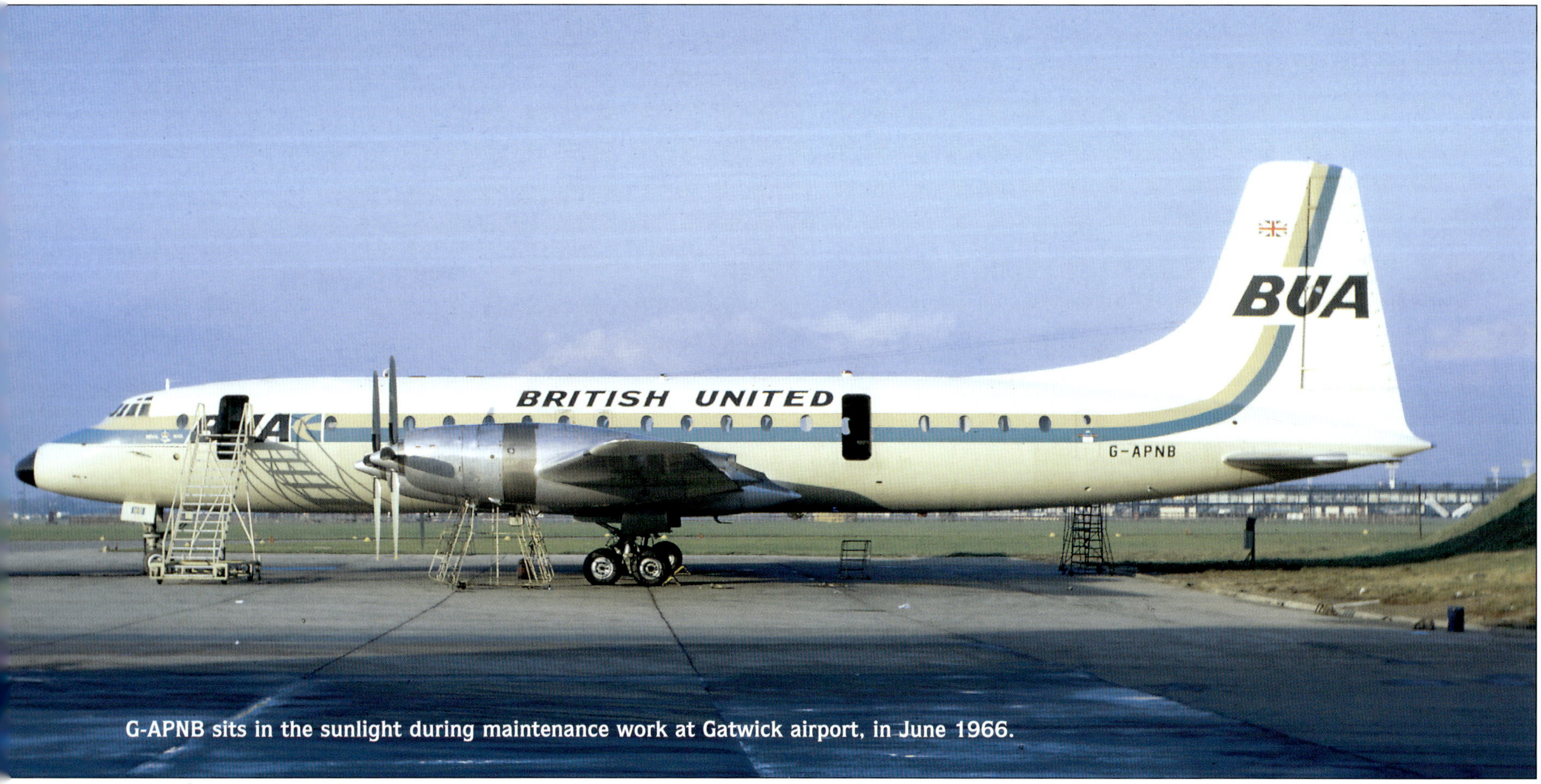

G-APNB sits in the sunlight during maintenance work at Gatwick airport, in June 1966.

IN SERVICE WITH CALEDONIAN AIRWAYS

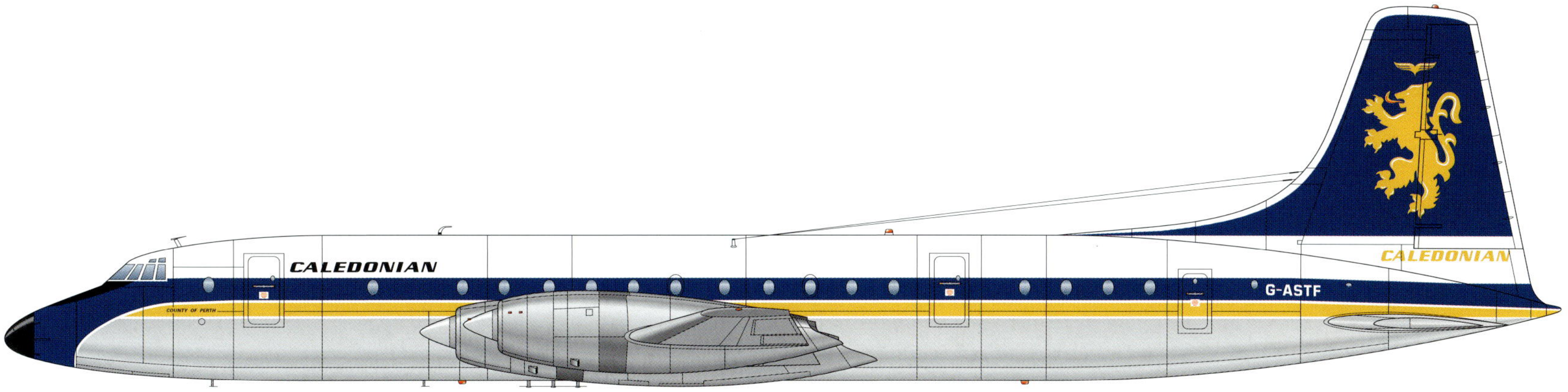

In November 1961, a fully laden DC-7C inaugurated the Caledonian Airways service and, within five years, the Airline had a fleet of six Britannias and an order for a new Boeing 707. This rapid growth came about because the US Civil Aviation Board allowed Caledonian to fly transatlantic charter flights between Europe and North America.

The DC-7Cs were the aircraft which first built up Caledonian's reputation, but by 1964 they were getting old and competitor airlines were starting to buy more modern equipment. So Caledonian agreed to buy three Series 312 Britannias from BOAC in December 1964. The first, G-AOVI, was handed over on 18th December and flown to Southend for overhaul by Aviation Traders and fitted out to Caledonian specification.

The next aircraft, G-AOVH, arrived at Southend on 7th March 1965 and a week later, after a very rapid turn-round, she was leased to Royal Air Maroc and flew from Gatwick to Rabat in order to take pilgrims to the Hadj festival at Jeddah. This type of charter work, out of the usual tourist season, became an important part of Caledonian's activities. Pilgrims were flown from Tehran and Kabul as well as Rabat to Jeddah for religious festivals.

On 14th April G-AOVI left Gatwick with a party of tourists for Venice and then a series of troop-moving flights took place between 17th and 21st April. There were flights between Ballykelly, Northern Ireland and British bases in West Germany and, towards the end of the month, more troops were moved between Hong Kong and Gibralter.

The following month, on 8th May 1965, the inaugural Caledonian transatlantic charter flight left Gatwick via Gander for New York, undertaken by G-AOVI. By the end of the month, the third Britannia, G-AOVJ, entered Caledonian service and the subsequent pattern of usage of the three aircraft was quickly established, with transatlantic charter flights, holiday tour flights to the Mediterranean and troop flights to the Middle East, Far East and the Caribbean.

The transatlantic charter flights originated in Gatwick or Prestwick and flew to Boston, New York or Toronto. If the headwinds were too strong, or if the loads were heavy, there had to be re-fuelling stops at Gander or Halifax, otherwise the flights were non-stop to the final destination. A few of the Atlantic flights began from Manchester, the first such being by G-AOVH on 7th/8th July 1965 to New York via Gander, whilst the first charter out of Prestwick was on 17th June 1965 by G-AOVI to Toronto. By early July there were regular charter flights by Britannias from Prestwick to Montreal, New York and Toronto.

A few charter flights originated in Belfast, beginning with G-AOVI on 9th July to New York via Shannon. Because of the limited runway length at Belfast (Aldergrove), it was not possible to fly a fully loaded Britannia non-stop across the North Atlantic and re-fuelling stops were made at either Shannon or Prestwick.

By the end of the summer season, the Britannias had made a total of 134 North Atlantic charter crossings to Canada and the northern United States. Of these, 96 originated or ended at Gatwick, 32 at Prestwick, 4 at Manchester and 2 at Belfast.

In addition to the North Atlantic work, other charter work was also undertaken. There was a once-weekly service from Gatwick to Palma, leaving every Saturday during the summer, and once a fortnight there was a service from Gatwick to Alghero (Italy), Constanta (Romania) and Dubrovnik (Yugoslavia). A series of Government sponsored charters went from Manchester to Idris and Tripoli. Some Chartered services went further, to Accra, Aden, Bombay, Calcutta, Lagos, Singapore and Tel Aviv, with some flights undertaken on behalf

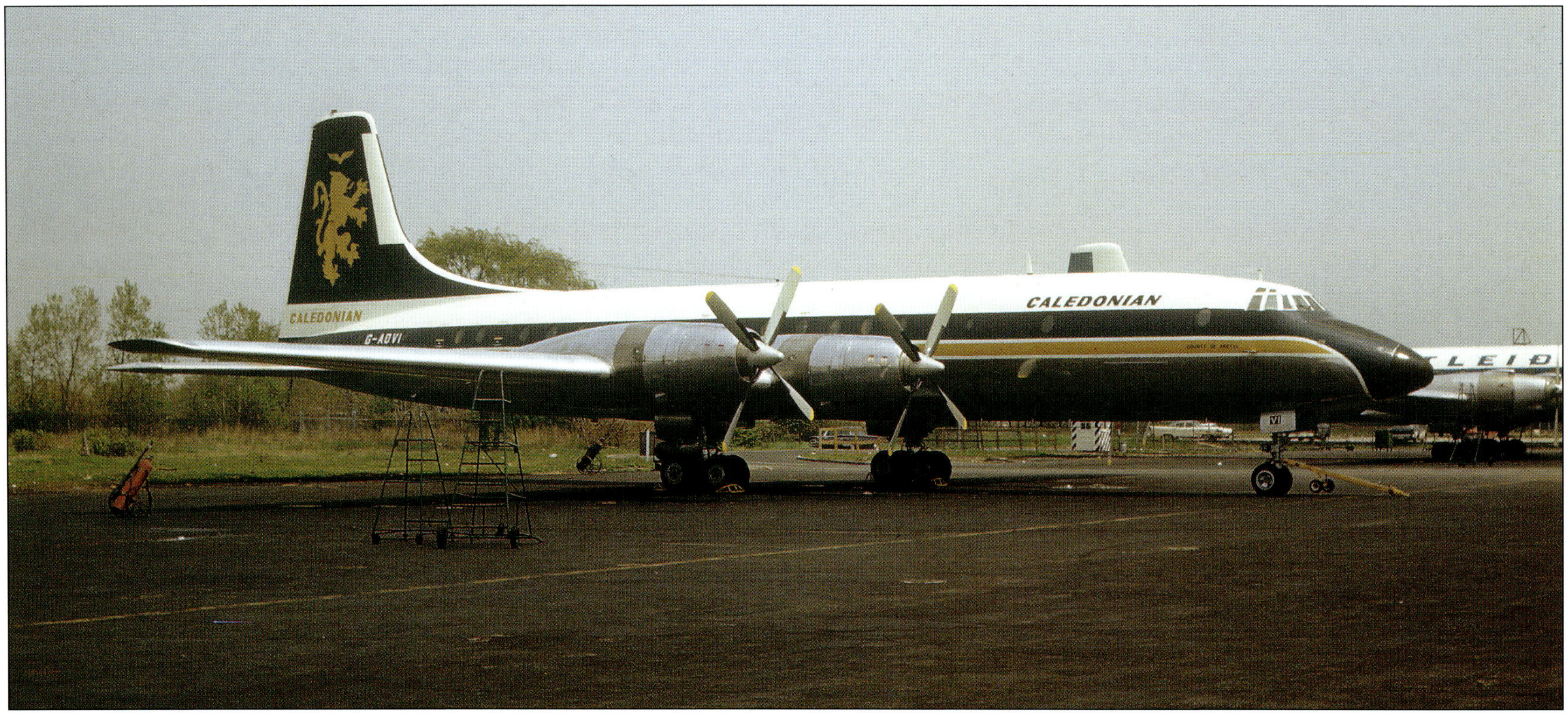

Caledonian Britannia G-AOVI 'County of Argyll' sits idle at John Fitzgerald Kennedy Airport, New York on 14th of May 1965.

of British United Airways who had problems because of delayed delivery of new BAC 1-11 aircraft.

It was a very busy season and all three Britannias were worked hard. It also looked as if 1966 would be even busier, for Caledonian successfully obtained an extension to its charter licence which enabled it to operate charter flights into the USA from nineteen European countries.

In preparation for this, Caledonian arranged to purchase three more Britannias from Canadian Pacific who were retiring them in favour of Douglas DC-8s. The plan was to have six Britannias available for the summer charter rush but things did not work out so simply. On 11th November 1965, Rhodesia declared independence and as a result oil supplies to Zambia (which normally travelled through Rhodesia) were disrupted. The British Government organised an airlift of oil from the port of Dar-es-Salaam to the Zambian cities of Lusaka and Ndola. This airlift was begun by the RAF but on 28th December the first Caledonian Britannia, G-AOVH, left Gatwick for Dar-es-Salaam via Khartoum. Being an ex-BOAC series 312 aircraft, it had neither a forward freight door nor a specially strengthened freight floor. However, it was immediately engaged in ferrying 40-gallon oil drums from Dar-es-Salaam to Lusaka and occasionally to Ndola.

Flying into Lusaka presented the aircrews with particular problems because of the weak structure of the airport runways and taxiways. The RAF had stationed a squadron of Gloster Javelin aircraft at Lusaka at the beginning of the Rhodesian problem, but they discovered that the aircraft had to be moved every day or else they started to sink into the concrete. The Britannias were much heavier and they therefore had to operate with very low tyre pressures in order to spread the aircraft weight over as wide an area of the runway as possible. The consequence of this was a very high rate of tyre wear.

Aviation Traders, who had fitted out the Britannias to Caledonian's specification, sent a team out to Dar-es-Salaam in order to maintain the aircraft during the oil airlift. One of their first tasks was to repair substantial damage to the floor of G-AOVH, caused when some oil drums shifted shortly after take-off from Dar-es-Salaam.

One of the three ex-Canadian Pacific Britannias, G-ATMA, left Gatwick on 7th January 1966 for Tanzania and joined G-AOVH on the oil airlift. The second of these ex-CPA Britannias, G-ATNZ, joined the airlift on 5th February, as a result of which G-AOVH returned to Gatwick on 14th February. Thereafter Caledonian kept the two remaining Britannias on airlift duty until the end of May.

The airlift proceeded smoothly apart from one incident involving G-ATNZ. The aircraft was attempting a battery start (using its on-board batteries) but when this failed, a ground power unit was called up which was successful. Unfortunately no chocks had been put in front of the wheels so that on start-up the aircraft rolled forward on to the power unit, thereby seriously damaging one of the engines. However Aviation Traders managed to repair the damage on site, without returning the aircraft to the UK.

By the end of their contribution to the Zambian oil airlift, the two Caledonian Britannias had transported over 4,600 tons of oil between Dar-es-Salaam and Zambia. Before being returned to normal passenger service, each had to be overhauled to remove the results of transporting oil drums. G-ATNZ flew her first after-oil passenger charter service on 21st June with a flight from Gatwick via Gander to New York, whilst G-ATMA returned to passenger service on 1st July with a flight of pilgrims from Gatwick to Tarbes (for Lourdes, France).

During the 1965 Christmas holiday period, several Britannia charters were flown by Caledonian to North America. These were usually trouble free but, as sometimes happens, all the bad luck seemed to be centred on one flight. G-AOVI took off from Gatwick with a full load on the evening of 8th December, expecting to fly for eight hours to Gander but about 20 minutes after take-off, the Captain was forced to shut down one engine and return to Gatwick. Some four hours later, the same aircraft took off again for Gander but after flying for some hours into excessive headwinds, it had to turn back to Gatwick because of shortage of fuel. After a three hour turn-round, it took off at 1100hrs on 9th December for Prestwick and Gander, which it reached late that night. Subsequently, and without further trouble, it reached Port of Spain, Trinidad and finally returned to Gatwick via the Azores on 14th December.

Early in the New Year, Britannias began operating charters to Bermuda and the Caribbean, with destinations at Nassau, Barbados and Trinidad. The last of the ex-Canadian Pacific aircraft, G-ASTF, was delivered in March and was immediately leased to Royal Air Maroc. On 5th March she flew a planeload of Hadj pilgrims from Rabat to Jeddah. G-AOVI also joined in this work shortly afterwards, as did G-AOVJ later. On 19th April G-AOVI finished work for Moroccan pilgrims but started work on a series of charter flights from Gatwick to Amman, being leased to Royal Air Maroc during this time. The other two Britannias finished their pilgrim transporting by the end of the month.

The summer of 1966 was as busy as expected and Caledonian's six Britannias were all heavily occupied. The North Atlantic charter programme was the main element, with the principal destinations being Montreal, New York and Toronto, but more European points of departure were added, as stated above, and also several new destinations.

The programme began on 29th April with G-AOVJ leaving Manchester for Montreal and Toronto. The same aircraft returned with a party of Canadians on 30th April to Prestwick and then back again with a charter flight on the night of 30th April/1st May from Prestwick to Montreal. The Gatwick to North America charters began on the evening of 1st May with a flight to New York via Gander, arriving midday on 2nd May.

During the summer, Gatwick flights went to Boston, Detroit, Montreal, New York, Ottawa, Philadelphia, Syracuse and Toronto. Manchester charters went to Boston, Montreal, New York and Toronto and, from Belfast, charters went to New York and Toronto. For the first time, some European cities outside the UK were also served by the Caledonian Britannias, including Amsterdam, Copenhagen, Dublin, Prague, Vienna and Zagreb. Hamburg and Luxembourg also had a charter flight from Ottawa.

During this summer there was also a busy programme of UK charter flights to European holiday destinations. On average, Britannias flew eleven round trips per week on these

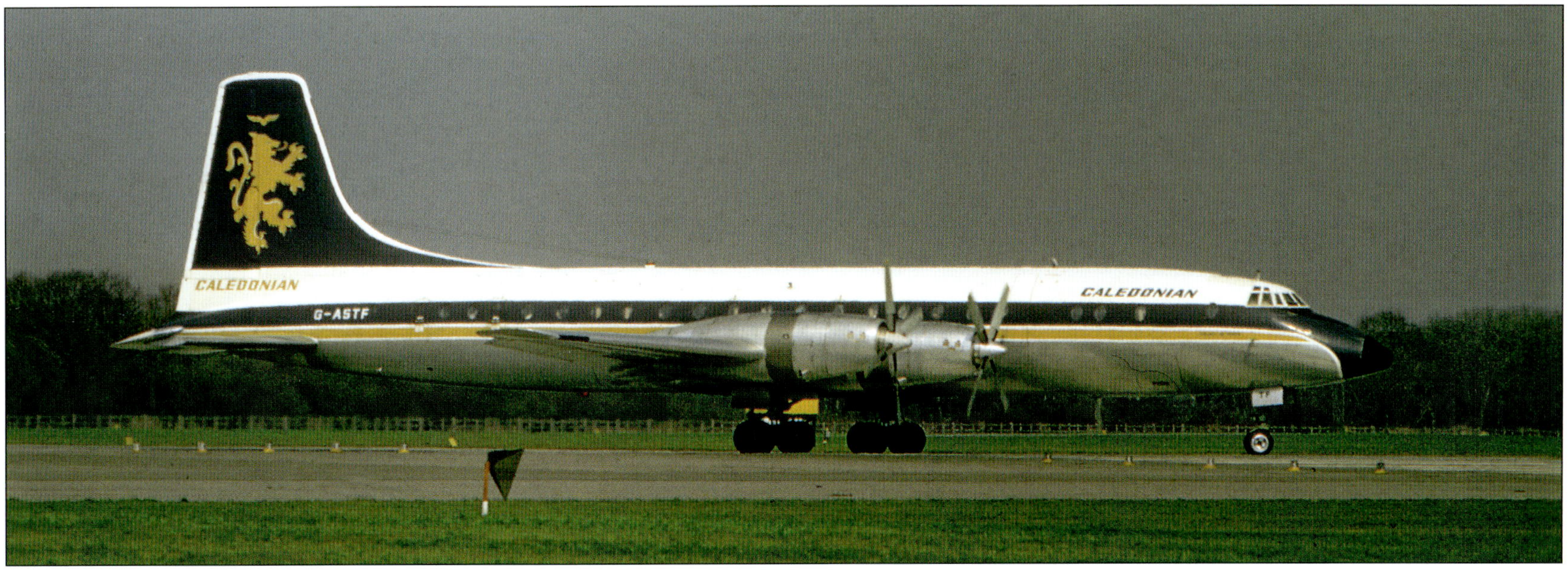

G-ASTF 'County of Perth' a Series 314 Britannia of Caledonian, turns on to the runway at Gatwick on the 6th of March 1969.

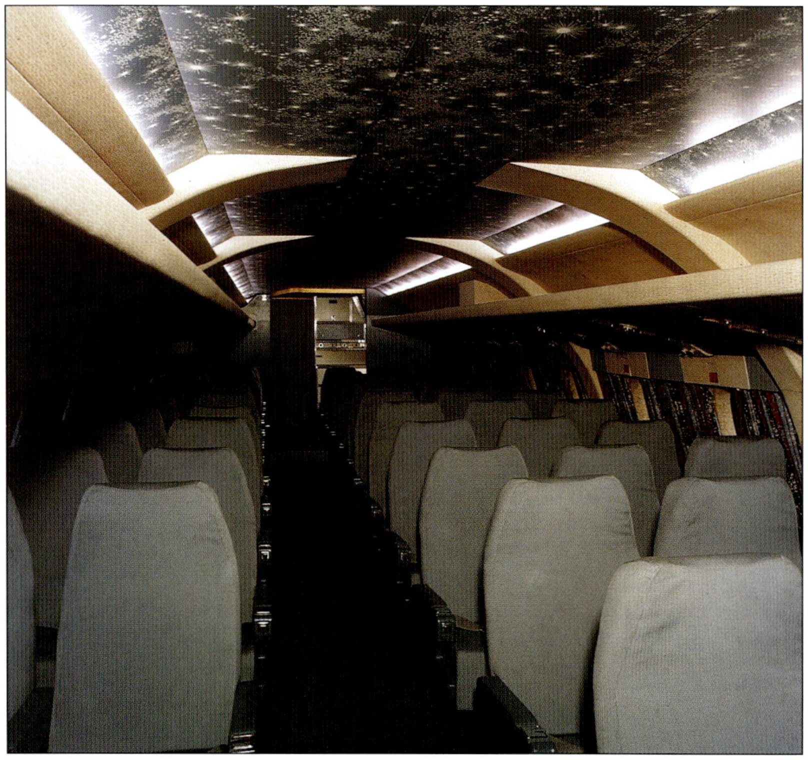

The interior of a Caledonian Britannia looking aft.

holiday routes, mainly from Gatwick and Prestwick.

The same kind of busy programme was flown by the Britannias in 1967, with the addition of troop movement charters from Gatwick to Akrotiri and from Belfast, Edinburgh, Gatwick and Manchester to West Germany. Also, in the spring, there was the traditional Hadj pilgrim charter flights to the Middle East. But changes were imminent, mainly caused by airlines which had begun to be equipped with the newer, faster jet aircraft.

When Caledonian received its first Boeing 707 early in 1968, it sold two of its six Britannias, G-AOVH and G-AOVI, to the newly formed Monarch Airlines. Surprisingly however, these two were immediately leased back by Caledonian for use with the traditional Hadj festival work. The remaining four Britannias still kept up a busy schedule with transatlantic charters from Belfast, Gatwick and Prestwick to the usual Canadian and American destinations and, for the first time, some charter flights originated in Birmingham (UK).

The Boeing 707s were becoming more common and were taking over more of the North Atlantic work, so it was expected that 1968 would be the last for the Caledonian Britannias. However the closure of British Eagle and Transglobe changed this, as Caledonian picked up several contracts from these defunct airlines. Not only did Caledonian retain its four Britannias but it leased a fifth, G-AOVA, from CCT Aircraft Leasing, who had bought it from British Eagle.

Another contract was for a Swiss charter carrier, Tellair. This company was founded in 1968 as a consortium of British Eagle and some Swiss agencies and the intention was to use two of British Eagle's Britannias and crews to operate IT charters for Tellair from Geneva and Zurich. The collapse of British Eagle enabled Caledonian to purchase two of their Britannias, G-ARKA and G-ARKB, and to get the contract to fly them for Tellair. Charter work began in March 1969, but in October 1969 the Swiss Civil Aviation Authority told Tellair that it must purchase the aircraft and operate them itself. As it was unable to find the money for this, Tellair's operation closed down and the Britannias reverted to Caledonian's control.

At the end of the 1969 season, G-ASTF was withdrawn from service and G-AOVA returned to CCT Aircraft Leasing. This left three aircraft, G-AOVJ, G-ATMA and G-ATNZ, all of which had a relatively peaceful time during 1970. There were charter trips to Amsterdam and Rotterdam for tourists to visit the bulb fields and, on 5th and 6th May, all three aircraft carried over 1100 Scottish football fans from Prestwick to Milan on nine flights. There were some charter flights bringing tomatoes from the Canary Islands to Gatwick, Liverpool and Manston, but there were idle times, with the aircraft waiting on the ground for up to ten days at a time. It was no surprise, therefore, when Caledonian sold off the last three aircraft.

The commercial flying by the Caledonian Britannia fleet came to an end on 9th March 1971 when G-ATNZ touched down at Manston with a cargo chartered from Las Palmas. G-AOVJ was sold to Donaldson International Airlines in November 1970, whilst G-ATNZ was leased to IAS Cargo Airlines in March 1971 and subsequently purchased by them. G-ATMA was also purchased by IAS Cargo Airlines in April 1971.

So ended a very successful association of Britannia aircraft with Caledonian Airways, an association still remembered with affection and which was accompanied by high reliability and a 100% safety record.

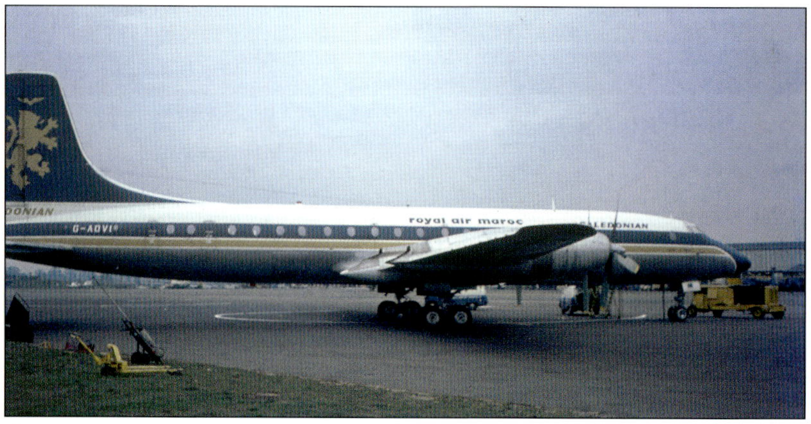

A rare shot of G-AOVI, taken at Gatwick in 1966, while on lease to Royal Air Maroc.

IN SERVICE WITH CUBANA AND AEROCARIBBEAN

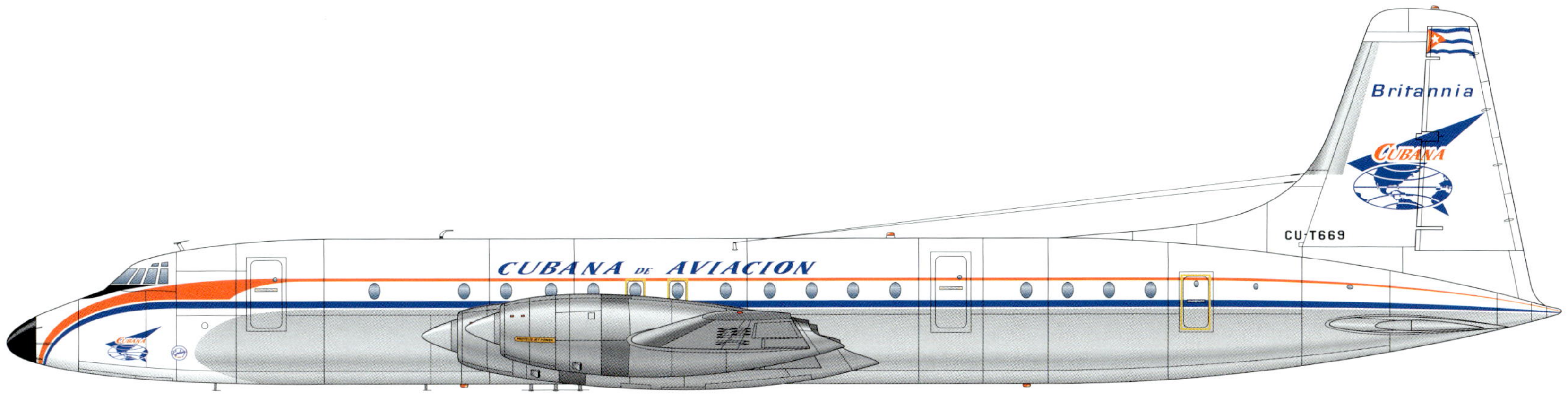

The national airline of Cuba, Compañîa Cubana de Aviación (Cubana), was founded in 1929 and by the 1950s operated an international scheduled passenger service from Cuba to the Azores, the Bahamas, Bermuda, Haiti, Mexico City, Madrid and Lisbon. It owned a Constellation, three Super Constellations, three Viscounts and some Dakotas, but the Super Constellations were ageing and in the summer of 1957 Cubana announced that it had ordered two Britannia 318s for delivery in late 1958.

As a result of this order, Bristol decided to make a sales tour of Latin America. The Britannia 305 G-ANCD, released from sale to Northeast Airlines, was painted in complete Cubana livery and flew from Filton on 7th June 1958 bound for Havana via Madrid, Lisbon and the Azores. In the next 23 days she visited fourteen cities in ten countries and by the end of the tour, which went as far south as Montevideo and Buenos Aires, as far east as Lima and north to Miami, over 1,200 passengers had been carried on twenty demonstration flights. The passengers included eight ambassadors, numerous government ministers and airline officials.

The trip was trouble-free and on return to Filton the Britannia had covered 27,000 miles in just over three weeks.

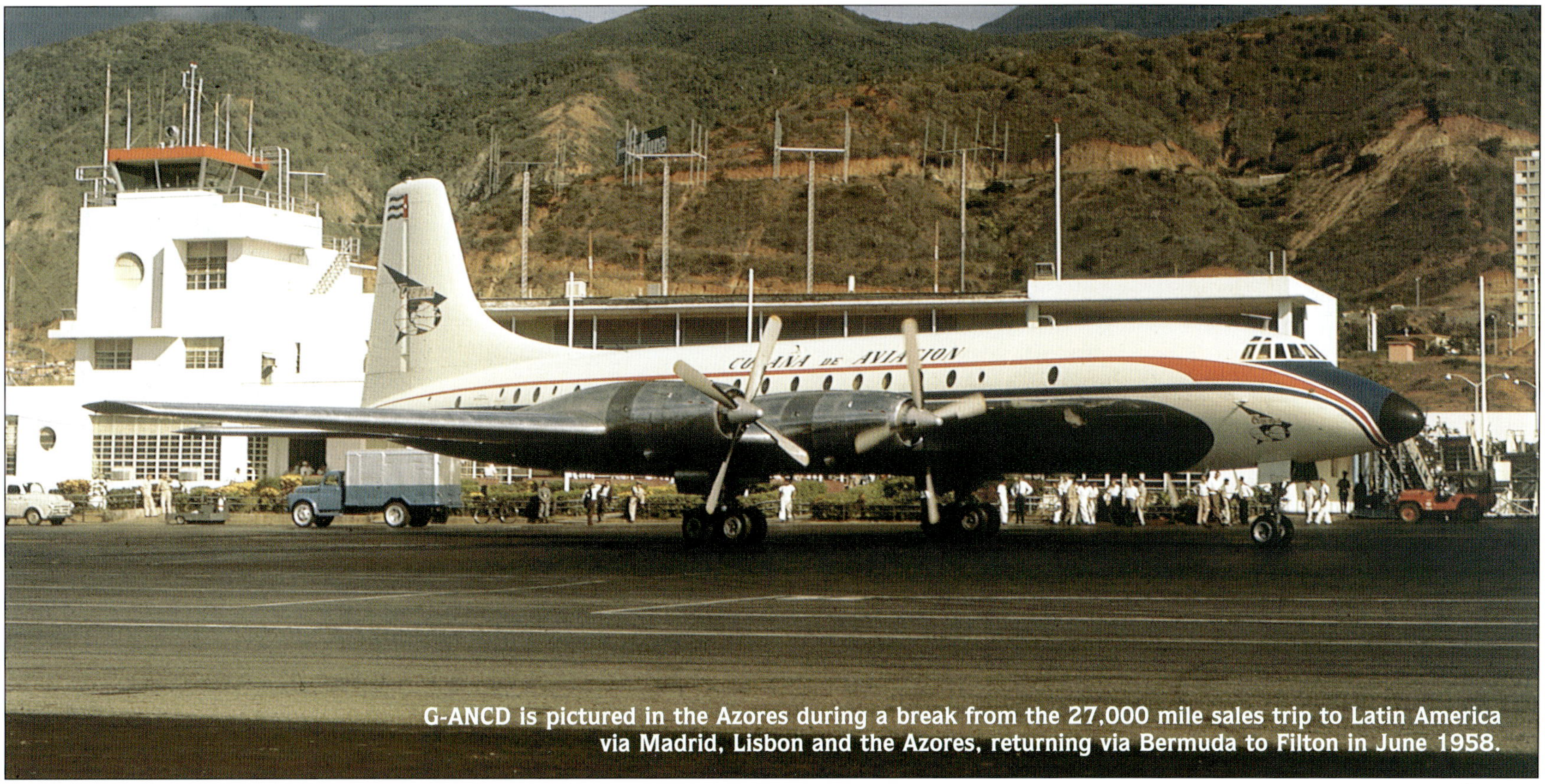

G-ANCD is pictured in the Azores during a break from the 27,000 mile sales trip to Latin America via Madrid, Lisbon and the Azores, returning via Bermuda to Filton in June 1958.

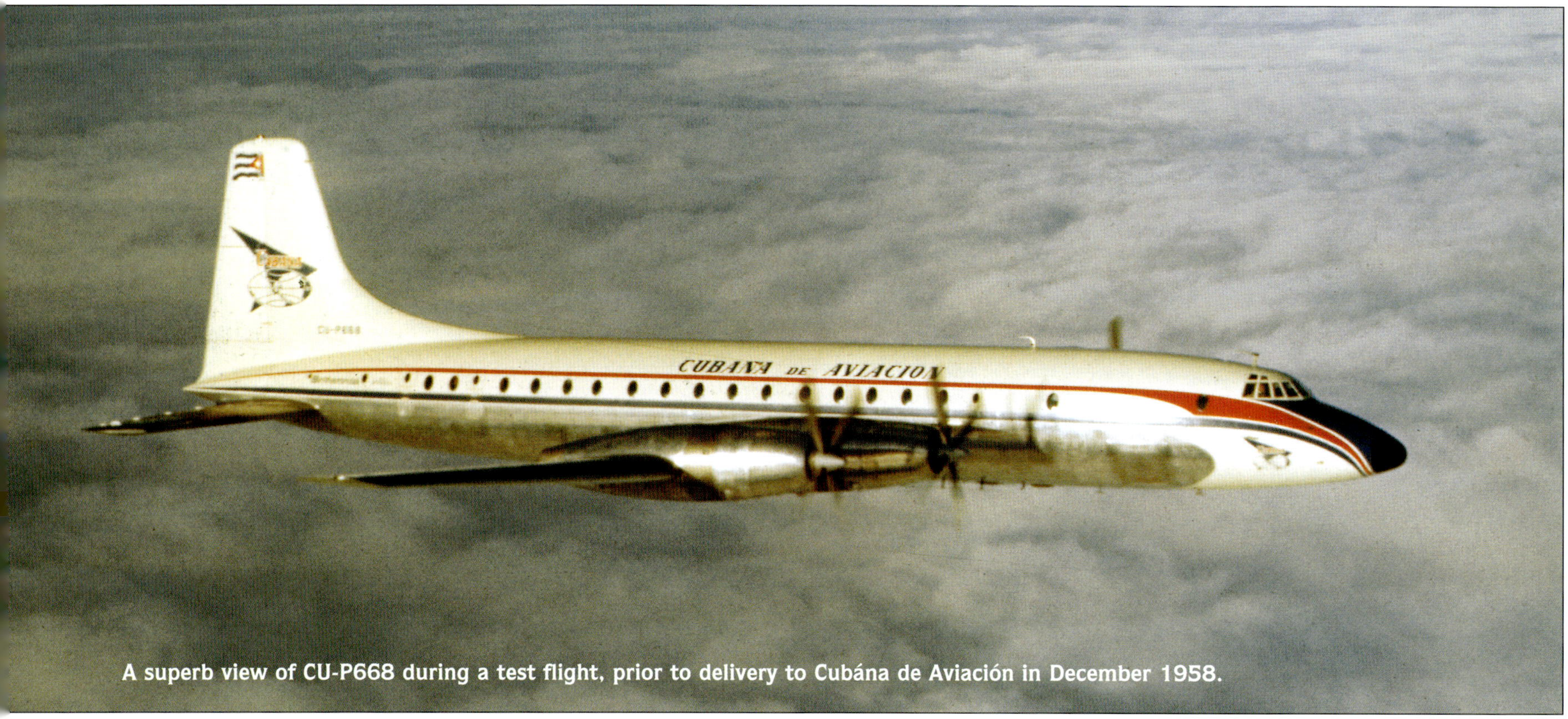

A superb view of CU-P668 during a test flight, prior to delivery to Cubána de Aviación in December 1958.

The final sector was from Bermuda non-stop to Filton in just 8hrs 50mins, arriving back on 30th June.

At the beginning of August 1958, Cubana doubled its order for Britannia 318s from two to four aircraft. The first, CU-P668, was delivered to Cubana in Havana on 18th December 1958 and within a few days was introduced on the Havana-Mexico City run, replacing the Super Constellations. The Britannia's popularity for comfort and speed built up rapidly, so that in the first ten days of January 1959 she flew six services to Mexico City and three to Miami. Then an unserviceable Super Constellation in Havana forced Cubana to substitute the Britannia on the Havana-New York run on 11th January. This was an immediate success as the Britannia was a whole hour faster on the journey than any of the competition, with very attractive levels of comfort.

The second Britannia, CU-P669, (re-registered as CU-T669 when in Cuba) was delivered to Cubana on 6th February and was quickly pressed into service. The two aircraft settled in to providing three services per week from Havana to Mexico City and three also from Havana to New York. By April, Cubana had an enviable 80% load factor on the Havana-New York run.

Early in 1959, Fidel Castro took over the rule of Cuba in a military coup which initially delayed the delivery of CU-P669 somewhat and then called in question whether Cubana would take on the other two ordered Britannias. However the airline was keen to obtain the aircraft and delivery duly took place. CU-P670 was ready for delivery in March 1959 and delivered to Cubana on 15th May once payment was received, but payment for the fourth Britannia proved more difficult.

The original plan in 1957 was for Cuba's extensive gambling empire to produce the money to pay for the Britannia fleet, but after the revolution this source of money dried up. Furthermore, during the revolution one of the airline's Viscounts was destroyed and two Dakotas were seized in mid-air. Not surprisingly this discouraged Cubans from flying, so that passenger loads and airline revenue fell.

The fourth Britannia, CU-P671 (re-registered as CU-T671), was ready for delivery on 2nd July 1959 and financial arrangements were concluded and the aircraft handed over on 26th August. But Cubana found it difficult to keep the four aircraft adequately occupied, particularly as all the routes to the US were now closed.

Because of this, Cubana offered CU-T668 for sale or lease in January 1960, the first airline to offer the second-hand or the leasing market the chance to obtain a Series 300 Britannia. She was leased by Eagle Airways (in September 1960 renamed Cunard Eagle Airways) commencing on 25th March 1960, and re-registered in Britain as G-APYY.

The other three Britannias remained in Cubana service during 1960. Their activity was particularly welcome as the Super Constellations were grounded because of an embargo on the sale of spare parts to Cuba by the United States, so that the Britannias alone were able to fly the long-haul routes.

There was a three times weekly service between Havana and Mexico City, as well as a connecting service from Havana to Bermuda and Madrid. The return flight from Madrid had a re-fuelling stop at Santa Maria in the Azores and then went on to Havana. There was also a daily service between Havana and New York but this service caused problems and, on 20th September 1960, one of the Britannias was impounded at New York because of non-payment of fees by Cubana. The aircraft was not released until November and when, early in 1961, relations between Cuba and the United States deteriorated further, Cubana suspended altogether the services from Havana to Miami and New York.

In February 1961 Cubana opened a new schedule between Havana and Prague, with re-fuelling stops at Bermuda and Santa Maria or at Gander and Shannon depending on the weather and hence the route flown. It was suspected that there was a political reason for this, for Cubana decided to buy a fleet of Ilyushin Il-14s and wanted to have them overhauled by Avia in Czechoslovakia.

The Czech airline, CSA, leased Cubana's first Britannia, CU-T668, on its return from Eagle Airways in September 1961. This Britannia, now re-registered as OK-MBA, was painted in full CSA livery and instituted a reciprocal service from Prague to Havana on 3rd February 1962.

The distance between Prague and Havana, 6040 miles, was scheduled to take 23hrs 40mins, including re-fuelling stops. Depending on Northern European weather, re-fuelling was approved at Manchester or Prestwick as well as Shannon, but there was one precautionary landing at Heathrow on 25th February when OK-MBA had flap trouble which made a ground investigation desirable.

Cubana's other three Britannias maintained the airline services to Madrid, Mexico City and Prague but a shortage of money, and hence of spare parts and lack of qualified service engineers, meant that all three Britannias were rarely serviceable at the same time. Cubana took delivery of some Ilyushin Il-18s in December 1962 for use on the Havana-Mexico City route, so the Britannias (including the leased CSA one) flew the Havana-Prague route continuously.

OK-MBA was returned by CSA to Cubana in November 1963 and replaced by another Cubana Britannia CU-T671, re-registered as OK-MBB. With this replacement, CSA was able to continue its Prague-Havana schedule until January 1969.

With the return of the leased Britannia to Cubana in 1969, the Cubana Britannia fleet was restored to four aircraft, and they continued to operate the scheduled services from Havana to Mexico City, Madrid and Prague. With Cuba's increasing

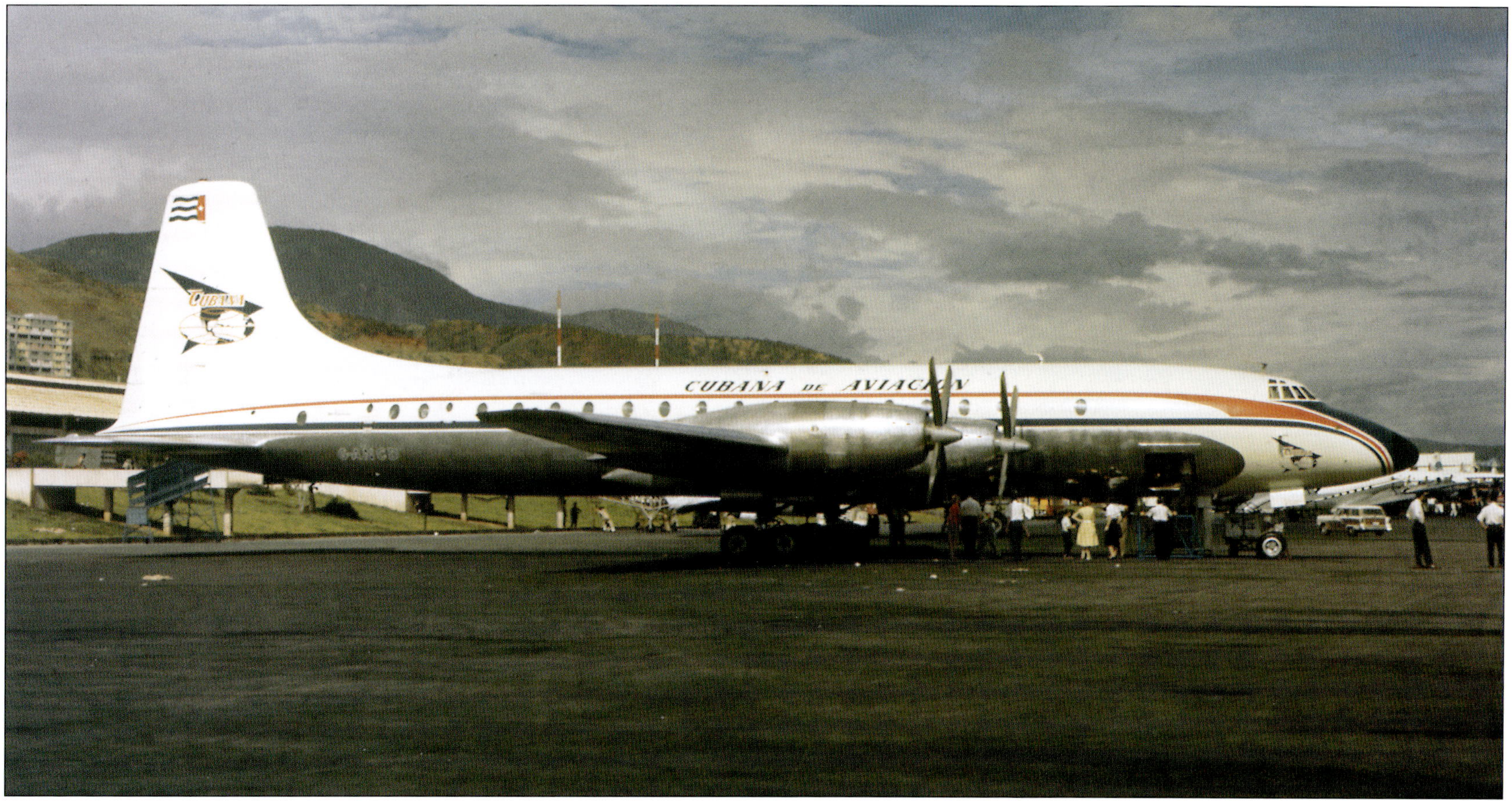

A view of G-ANCD taken in Brazil during the sales tour of South America which was undertaken by the aircraft in June 1958.

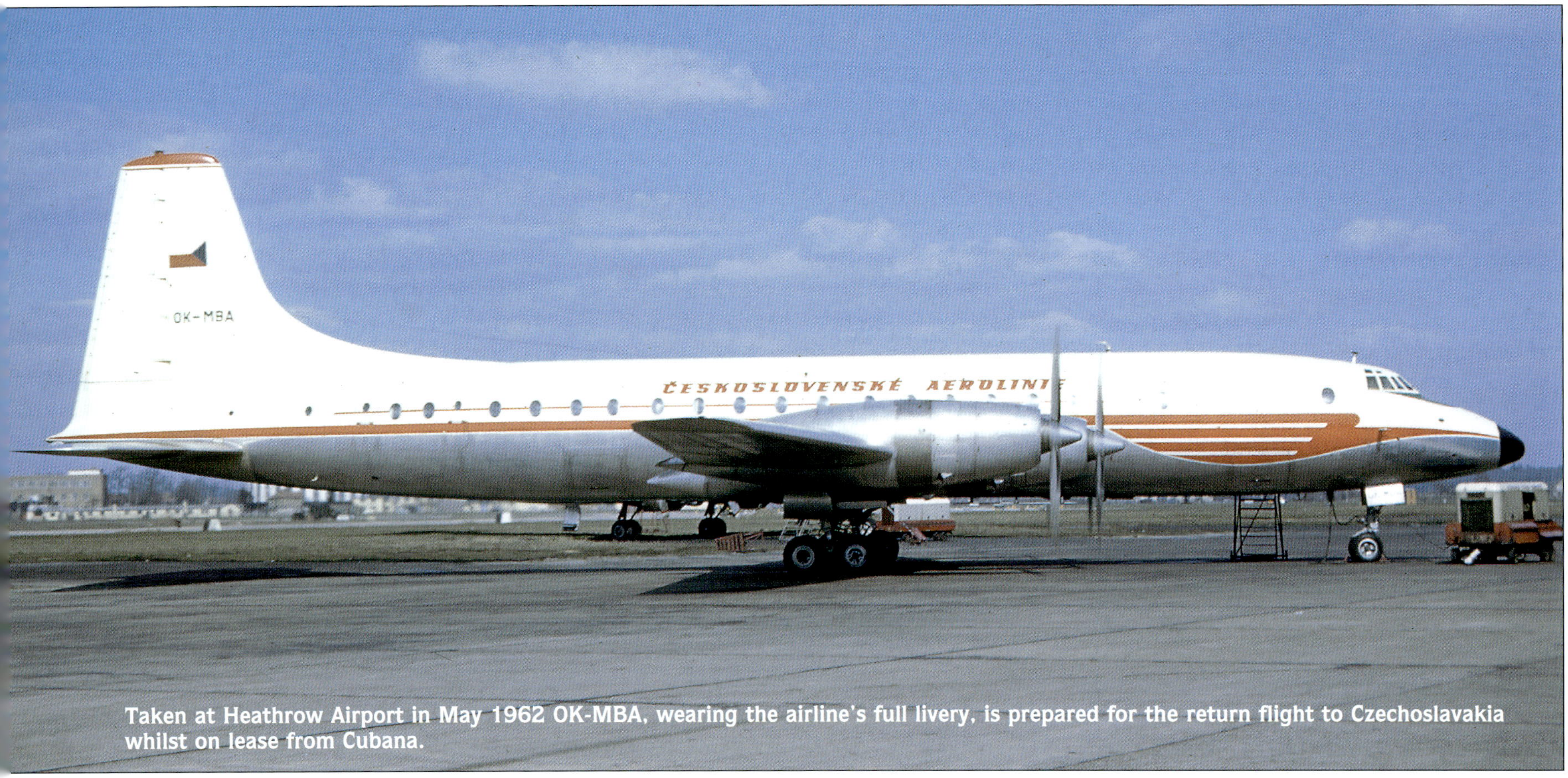

Taken at Heathrow Airport in May 1962 OK-MBA, wearing the airline's full livery, is prepared for the return flight to Czechoslavakia whilst on lease from Cubana.

military involvement in conflicts abroad, there were also an increasing number of troop movement flights. By 1973, however, Cubana started using Soviet jets for transatlantic flights and the decline in the use of Britannias began.

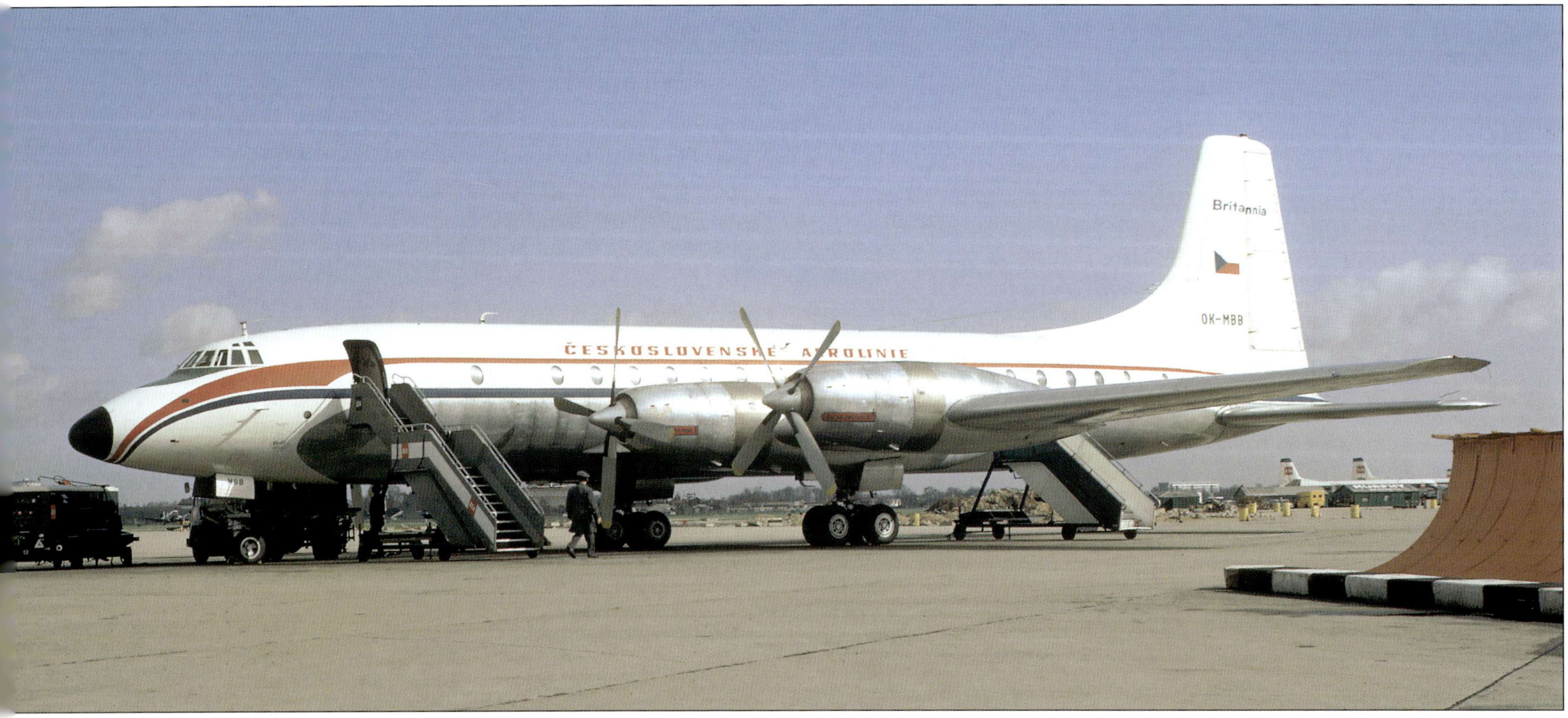

Unlike OK-MBA above, OK-MBB carried only the Cubana colours during her lease period from the Caribbean Airline. Here we see the aircraft at London's Heathrow airport in the company of two BEA Vanguards.

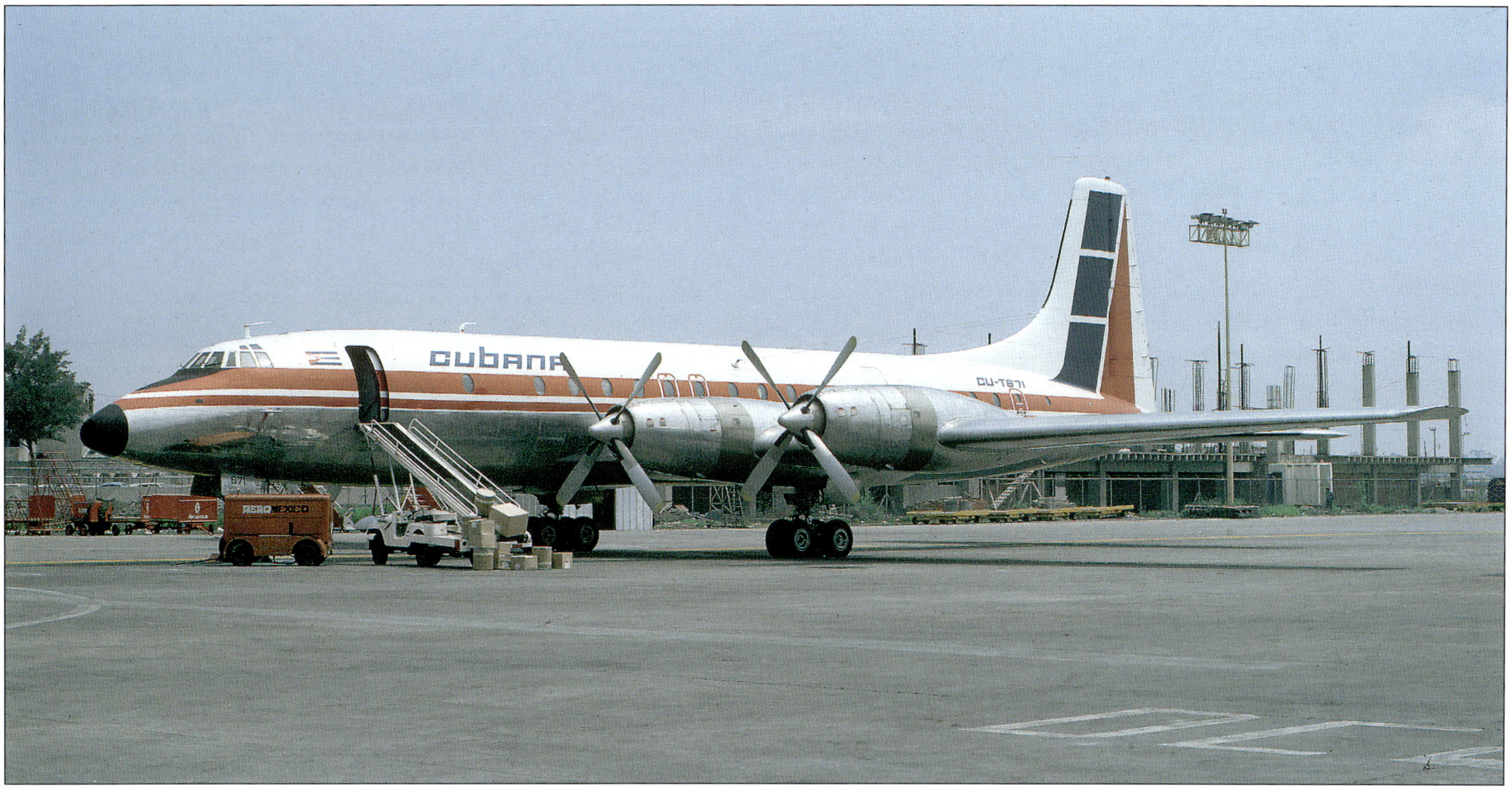

Britannia Series 318, CU-T671 wears the revised colours of Cubana at Mexico City in June 1975.

The first one to be withdrawn was CU-T670 in July 1978 whilst the others continued in operation, sometimes visiting the UK for servicing of the Proteus engines. CU-T671 paid her last (re-fuelling) visit to Shannon on 6th June 1977, whilst CU-T669 flew its final passenger flight through Shannon on 16th September 1977. Having re-fuelled, it took off but shortly afterwards developed engine trouble and had to return on three engines. Eventually it flew back empty to Havana via Keflavík, Iceland.

For the next two years, the Cubana Britannias were not seen on transatlantic duty. Then in November 1979, CU-T669 called at Shannon to re-fuel en route from Havana to Prague carrying cargo, returning two days later. Although not fitted with a large freight loading door the Cubana Britannias often performed cargo duties towards the end of their careers.

CU-T670 was withdrawn from service in July 1978, followed by the withdrawal of CU-T671 in March 1981. CU-T669 continued flying with Cubana until May 1984 when she was transferred to a new Cuban airline, Aerocaribbean. She was re-registered as CU-T114 and overhauled and re-sprayed in her new colours by Airline Engineering at Luton Airport. She began her service with Aerocaribbean on 6th July 1984, flying via Madrid to Havana. The following month, the airline's capacity was increased dramatically by the purchase of two Series 253 Britannias,G-BDUR and G-BDUP, from AFREK. These two aircraft had originally been built for the RAF and had a forward freight door and strengthened floor for freight carrying. Both were serviced and re-sprayed by Airline Engineering at Luton and flew via Shannon to Havana, the former as CU-T121 on 6th September and the latter as CU-T120 on 7th October.

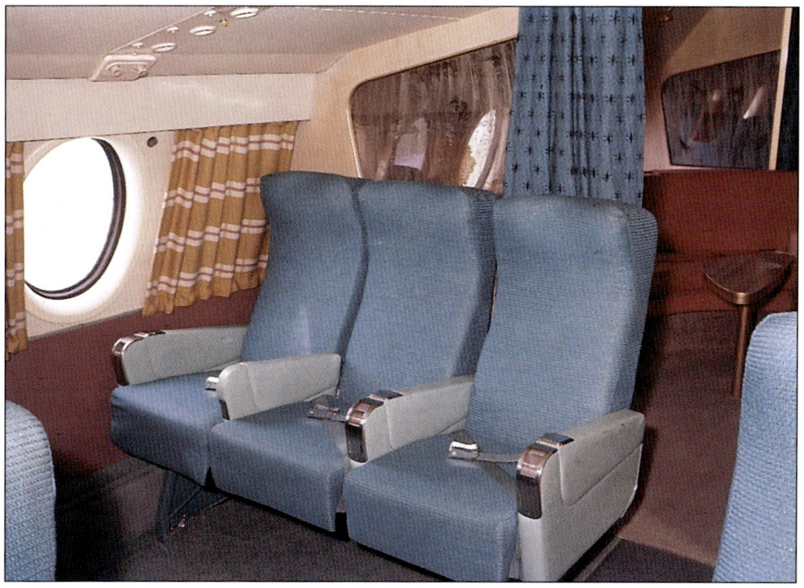

A view of the economy section of a Cubana Britannia facing the rear. Note the semi-circular lounge seating behind.

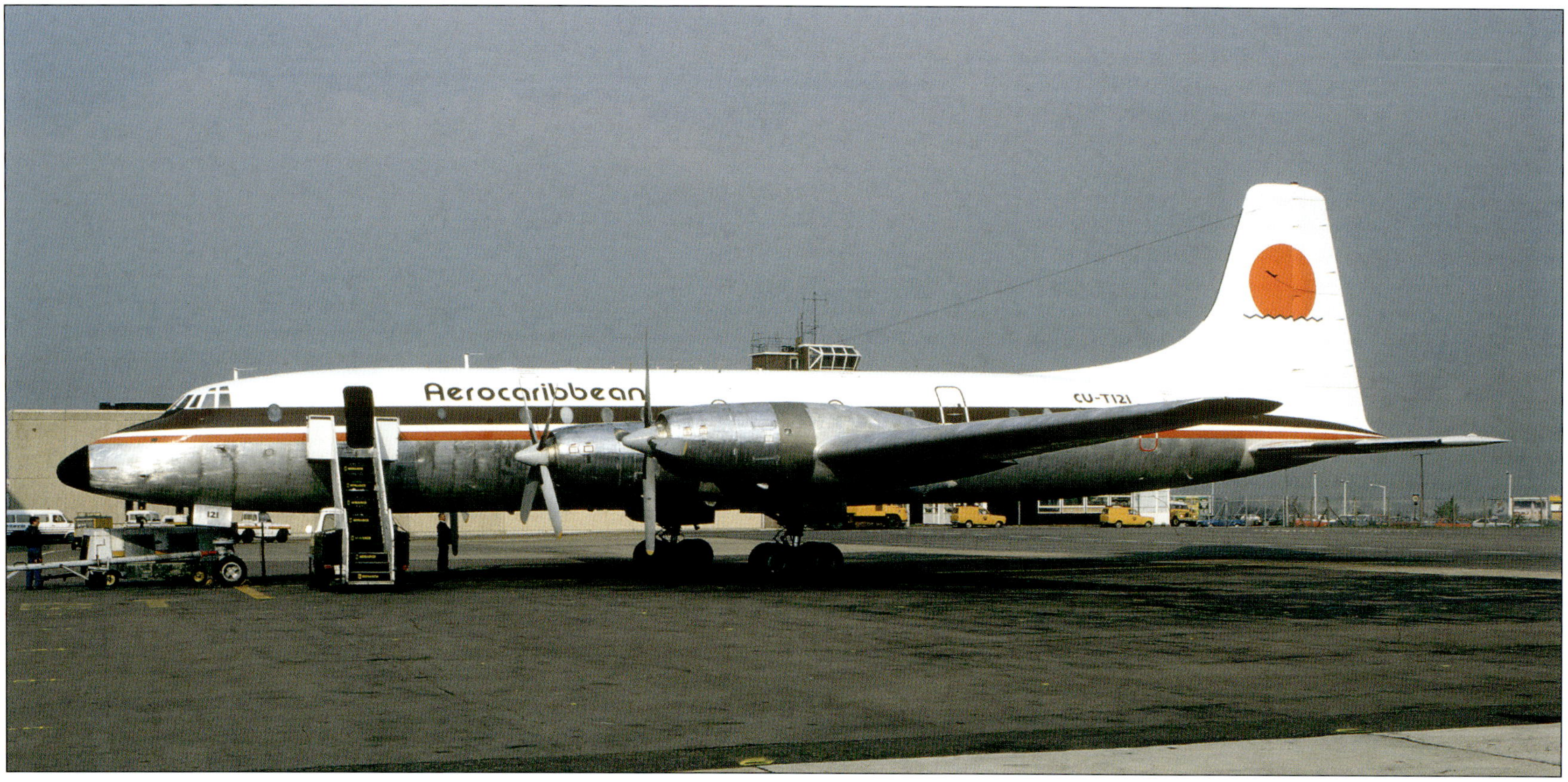

CU-T121 of Aerocaribbean, displays the recently applied company colours at Luton airport on 5th of September 1984.

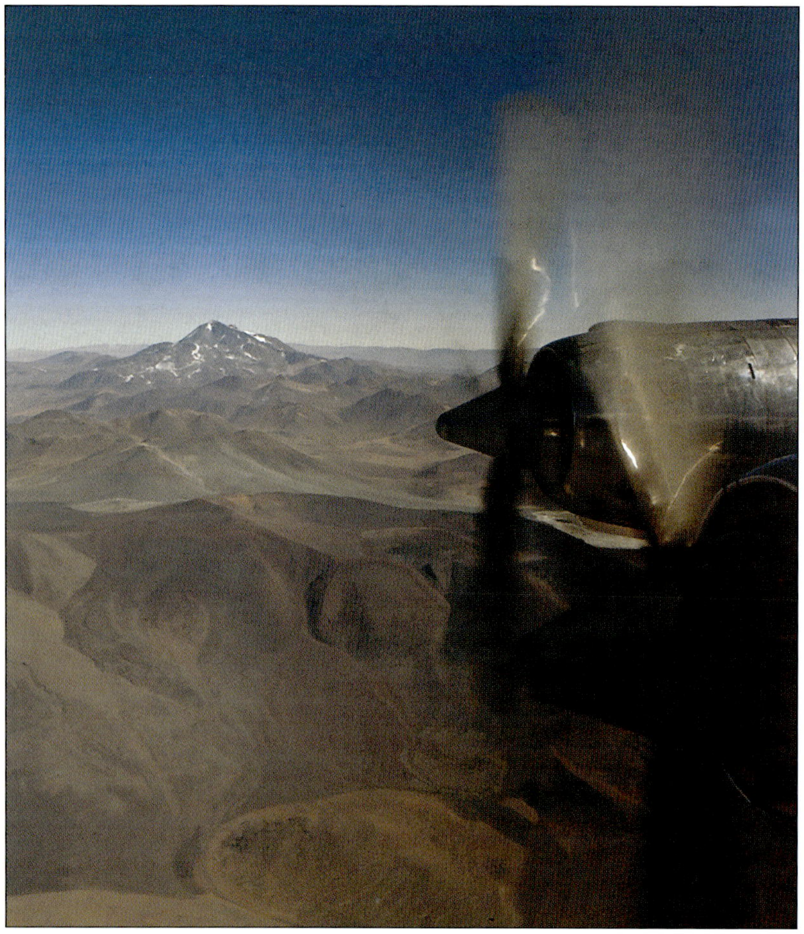

A dramatic view of the Andes mountains taken from a Cubana Britannia.

For the next few years, these three Britannias engaged mainly in freight work in the Caribbean area, with occasional passenger duty either on scheduled civilian flights or transporting military personnel. But eventually the difficulty in obtaining spares and the greater speed of the newer jet aircraft caused the Britannias to be phased out. The last Britannia flight seems to have been from Peru to Havana, with the flight by CU-T120 beginning on 21st March 1990. En route, No. 4 engine developed trouble and had to be shut down, so an emergency landing was made at Guayaquil, Ecuador. The next day she continued to Havana on three engines and on arrival was grounded for lack of spares. The same fate seems to have befallen CU-T114 and CU-T121, both grounded for lack of spares.

What is notable about this story is that Cubana was the longest operator of Britannias, an original customer still flying a Britannia 25 years later. The six Britannias which were based in the Caribbean had a 100% safety record with service spread over a variety of tasks during 30 years. It was a fine achievement.

John Byrne on behalf of Transair Cargo of Zaire, bought Britannia CU-T120 from Aerocaribbean, and restored it to flying condition for service in Africa. See story on page 151.

IN SERVICE WITH AERONAVES DE MEXICO

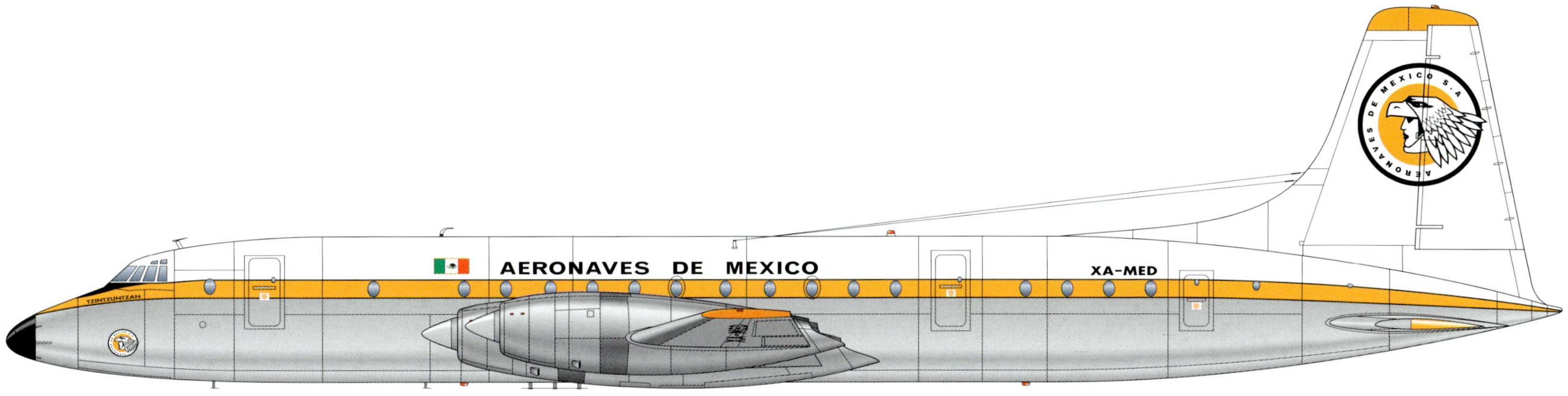

The Mexican airline, Aeronaves de Mexico, was founded in 1934 and by the 1950s had established services from Mexico City to about twenty destinations within Mexico, the longest distance being the 200 mile Mexico City-Acapulco route. At this stage they had a series of piston-engined aircraft, with the L-049 Constellations having the longest range.

In 1956, the airline applied to the American CAB for permission to operate a service from Mexico City to New York which, at 2,105 miles, was over ten times longer than any other of its routes. CAB approval was obtained on 20th June 1957.

Aeronaves de Mexico bought two Series 302 Britannias to work this new route. The pair were part of a cancelled BOAC order which Bristol were very keen to sell as, after the cancellation, the planes were waiting in Belfast without customers. So, on 21st June, the first plane made its maiden flight from Belfast to a small airfield at Weston-super-Mare, flown by Chief Test Pilot Walter Gibb, to be fitted out to Aeronaves specification. On 15th October, she was then flown to Filton for final trials before being handed over to Aeronaves de Mexico, registered as XA-MEC, on 1st November.

The second Britannia followed the same path; Belfast to Weston on 24th July, Weston to Filton on 20th November and handover to Aeronaves on 12th December, registered as XA-MED. Both of these Britannias were spaciously laid out, with seats for 28 first-class and 66 tourist-class passengers. There was a galley at the forward end of the cabin, a second galley and bar just aft of the wing and a wardrobe at the rear.

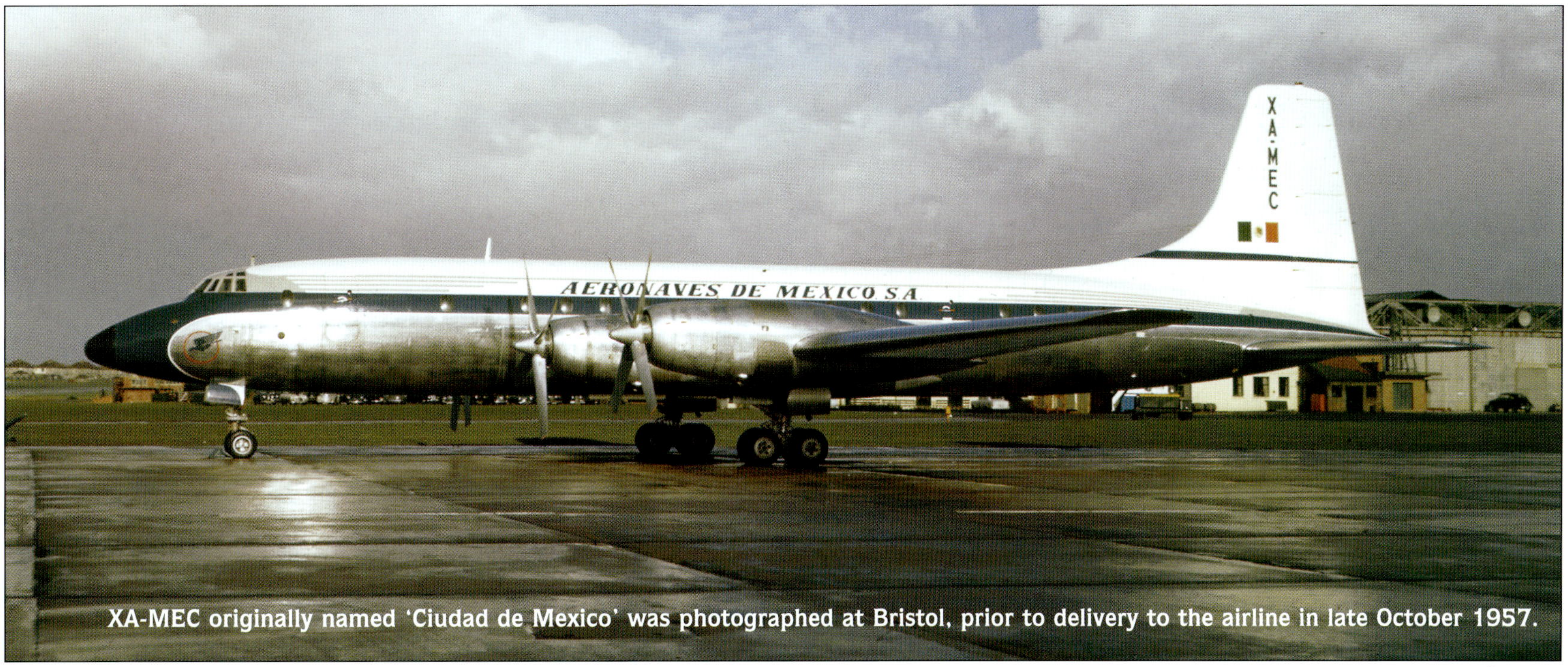

XA-MEC originally named 'Ciudad de Mexico' was photographed at Bristol, prior to delivery to the airline in late October 1957.

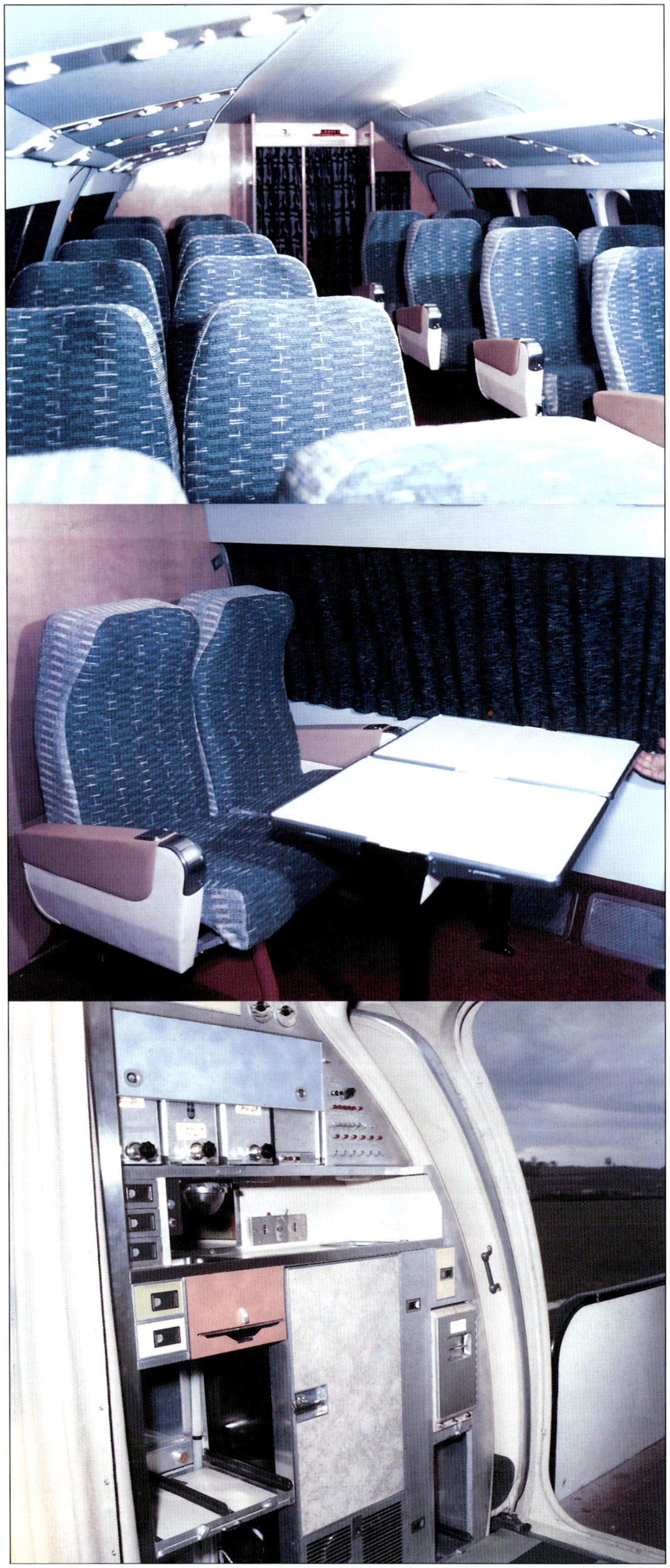

In order to service the aircraft adequately, and in particular their engines, a new company called Bristol de Mexico set up an engine overhaul and repair facility in Mexico. It serviced not only the Britannias' Proteus engines but also the Pratt and Whitney piston engines in other Aeronaves aircraft.

The Aeronaves service from Mexico City to New York began in not quite the intended manner. It was planned that the service, flown by Britannias, should begin on 16th December 1957 but while on crew training a few days earlier, XA-MEC had a minor accident and could not be repaired in time. Therefore the inaugural Mexico City-New York service, instead of being flown by a Britannia, was flown by an ageing Lockheed Constellation.

The second Aeronaves Britannia, XA-MED, arrived in Mexico City on 17th December and next day took over the scheduled service to New York which it maintained on a daily basis by itself until 7th January 1958, when XA-MEC returned to service after repair.

The 18th December was a memorable day for Britannias in New York. The Aeronaves Britannia arrived from Mexico City after a flight of 5hrs 25mins (1hr 20mins less than the scheduled time). This was also the date of the inaugural Britannia flight by BOAC from London to New York and, on the same day, an El Al Britannia took off on the first non-stop flight from New York to Tel Aviv.

Until 7th January, XA-MED's working of the Mexico City-New York route was almost faultless. Only one departure was cancelled, caused when an incorrectly fixed toilet cap flew off and damaged one of the propellers. That apart, flights were reliable and quick and the time for the northbound flight fell to a record figure of only 4hrs 57mins whilst the southbound flight time fell to only 6hrs.

Once the second Britannia arrived, the daily scheduled flight to New York was more easily covered. The schedule was later varied to give a departure time from Mexico City of 0100, so that passengers would arrive in New York at the beginning of the working day. The aircraft quickly proved very popular and Aeronaves was able to report load factors on the northbound leg of 50% and on the southbound leg of 70%.

However there was barely enough work for the two Britannias to do, so Aeronaves made use of them on some of its internal routes within Mexico. During 1958, Aeronaves de Mexico also reached an agreement with another Mexican airline, Mexicana, which allowed the latter to fly the

Left: A selection of views of the interior of Britannia XA-MED of Aeronaves de Mexico.

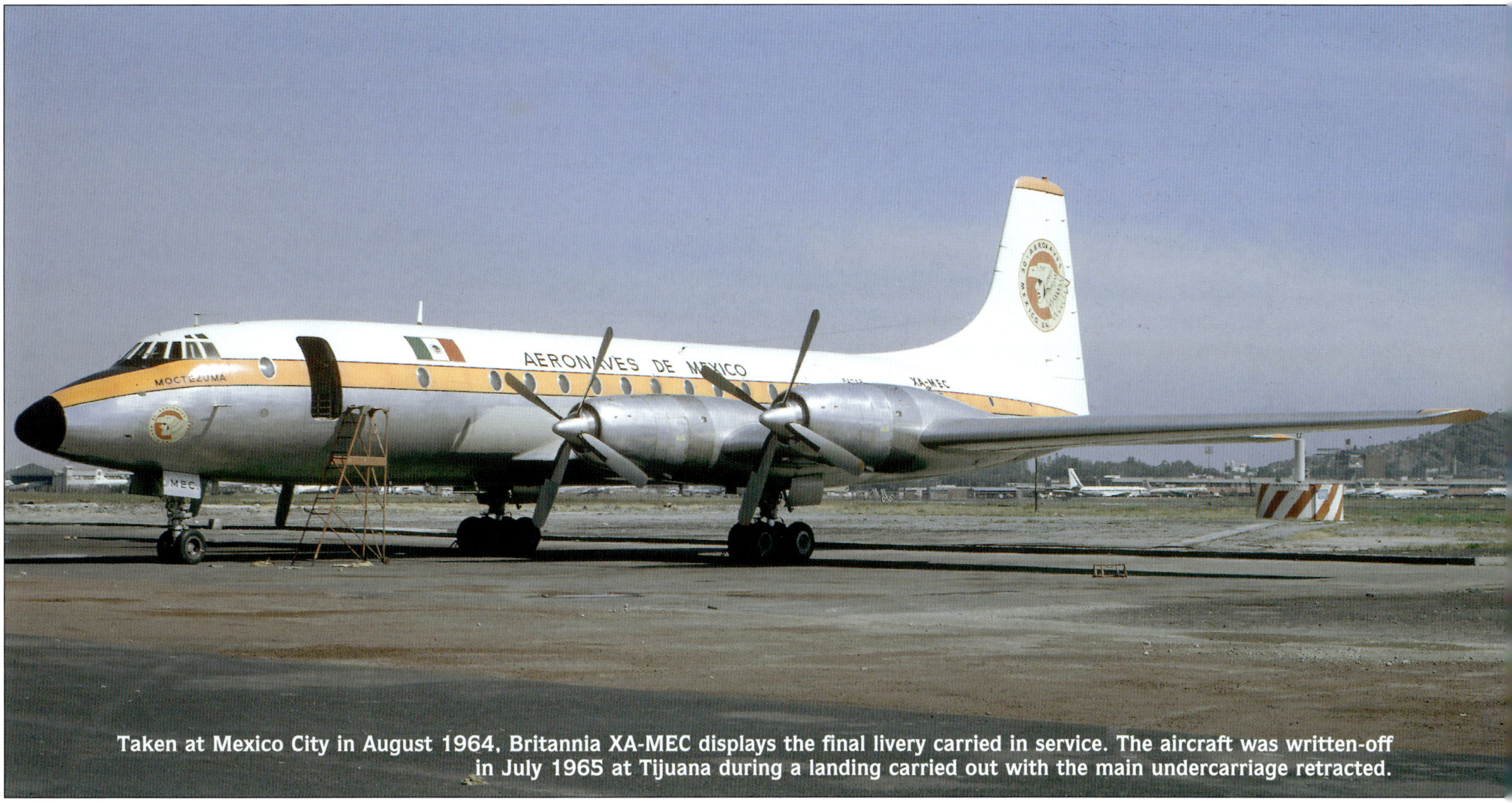

Taken at Mexico City in August 1964, Britannia XA-MEC displays the final livery carried in service. The aircraft was written-off in July 1965 at Tijuana during a landing carried out with the main undercarriage retracted.

Aeronaves Britannias between Mexico City and Los Angeles. Further financial manoeuvrings were to take place. In 1959, Aeronaves de Mexico was taken over by the Mexican Government and in 1960 the airline took over Guest Aerovias Mexico, a domestic Mexican airline. These adjustments, and the pooling arrangements which resulted, enabled services to be maintained by the sharing of aircraft and routes and gave more work to the Britannias.

However, jet aircraft were becoming available and where they were used, passengers preferred them because of the shorter journey times they made possible. Although by this time somewhat impoverished, Aeronaves bought a Douglas DC-8 which entered service on the Mexico City-New York route in November 1960, thereby relegating the Britannias to off-peak services on this route and to other routes within the Aeronaves network.

A few weeks after taking over from the Britannias, however, the DC-8 crashed on take-off at New York on 19th January 1961, so the Britannias returned to the Mexico City-New York route while the airline searched for a successor. The Britannias produced little financial help for the airline because of passengers' preference for jet aircraft which Air France and Eastern Airlines operated, attracting higher loads. The airline suffered more problems when all Aeronaves' services were halted because of a strike by flight crews on 10th November 1961. Once the strike was settled the Britannias were in action again flying to and from New York, but on 1st July 1962 another DC-8 took over and Aeronaves' Britannias never flew the route again.

The Britannias next role was operating the route from Mexico City to Tijuana which they did for the remainder of their flying time with Aeronaves. On 9th July 1965, however XA-MEC was damaged beyond economic repair. She had taken off from Tijuana but shortly afterwards experienced hydraulic trouble so that the main undercarriage would not retract completely. The crew decided to return to Tijuana and make an emergency landing. After touchdown, the aircraft ran normally for about 1,800ft; then the undercarriage collapsed completely and it slid on its belly for another 3,000ft. There were no casualties but the aircraft was considerably damaged. She never flew again and her remains were sold off as spare parts to other Britannia owners.

The sole remaining Britannia, XA-MED, continued to fly for Aeronaves de Mexico on the Mexico City-Tijuana route for several months until May 1966 when she was sold to Transglobe Airways (and re-registered as G-ANCC). Thus ended the service of the Bristol Britannias in Mexico.

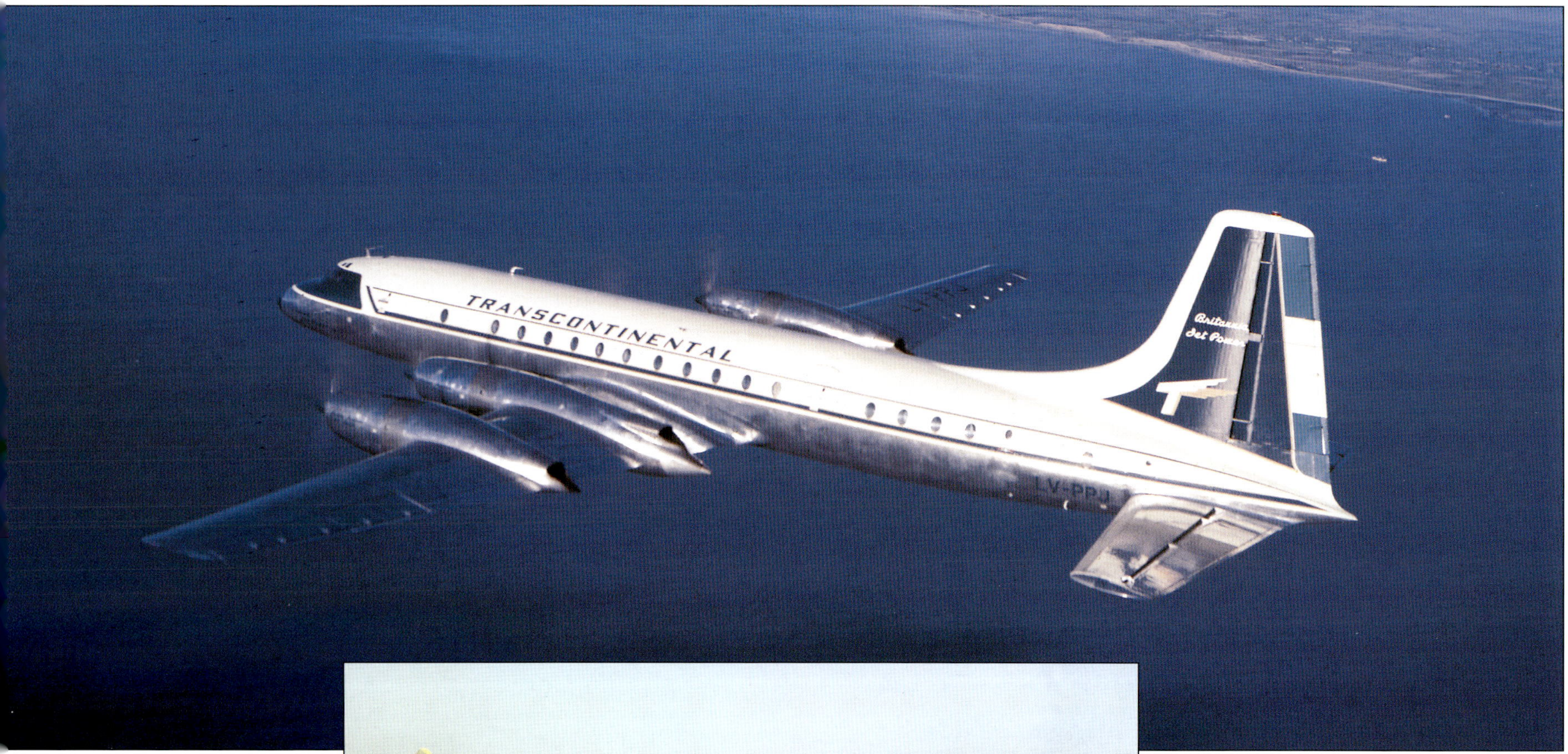

Above: A dramatic air to air portrait of LV-PPJ taken during the delivery flight to Argentina.

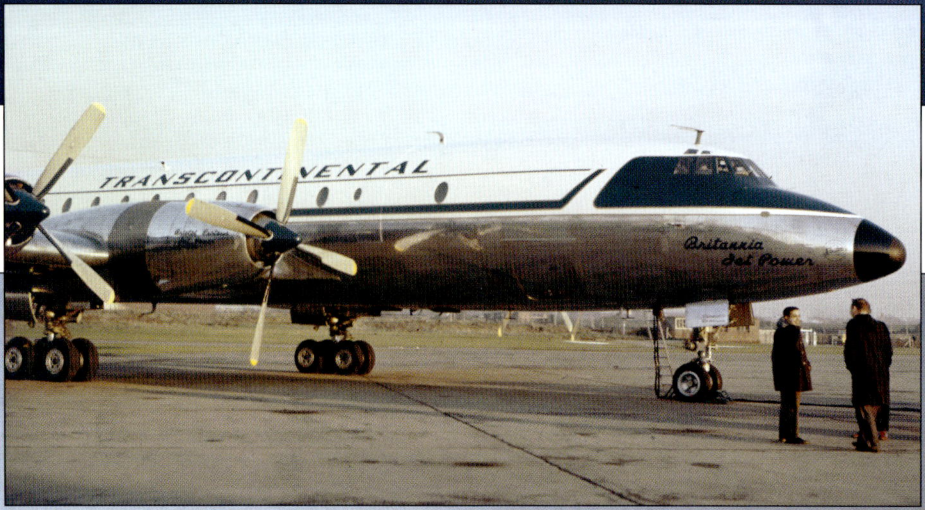

Left & Bottom: Registered to Bristol Aircraft as G-ANCF and stored at Belfast, flown to Filton as G-14-1 on 24th October 1959 and delivered to Transcontinental as LV-PPJ.

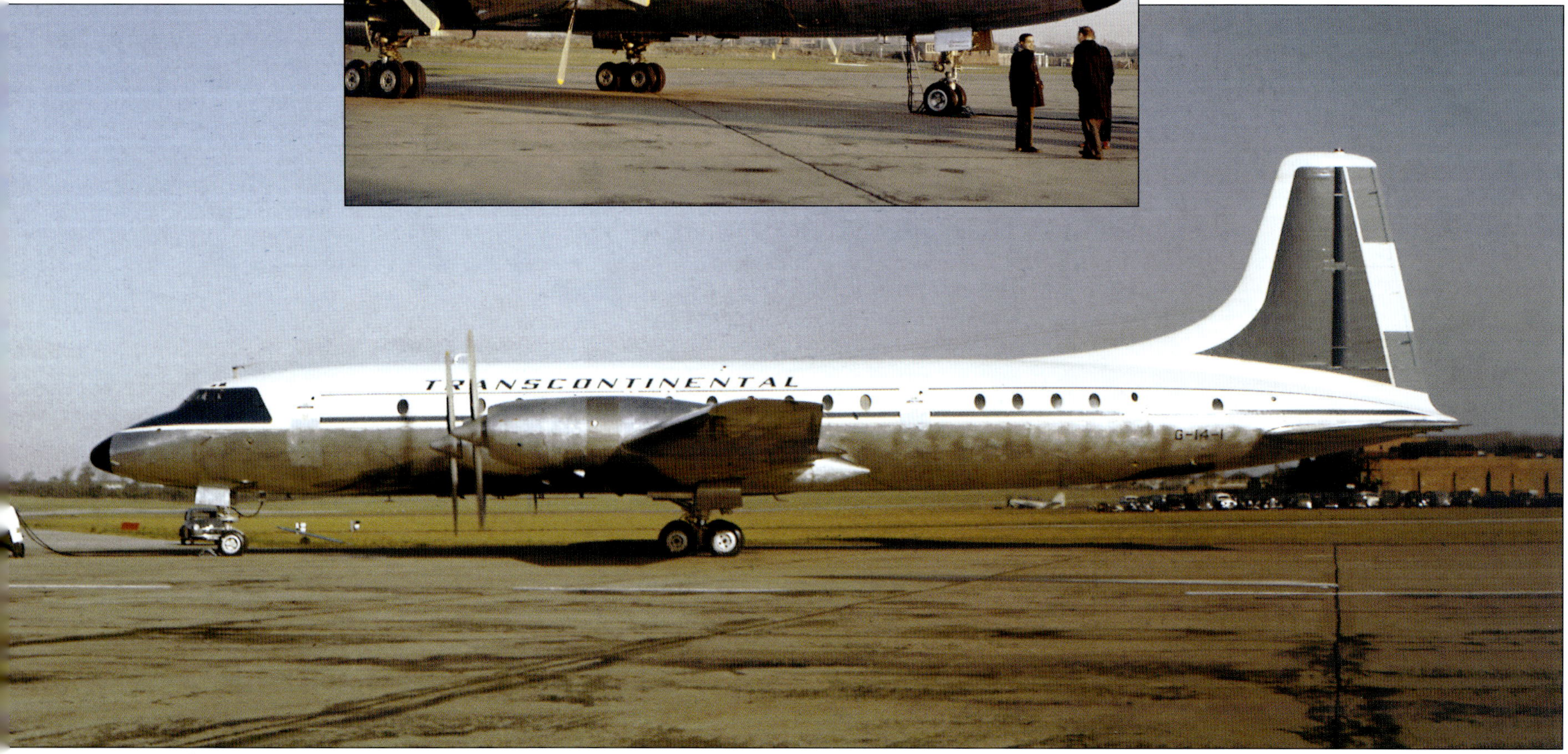

IN SERVICE WITH TRANSCONTINENTAL SA AND AEROTRANSPORTES ENTRE RIOS

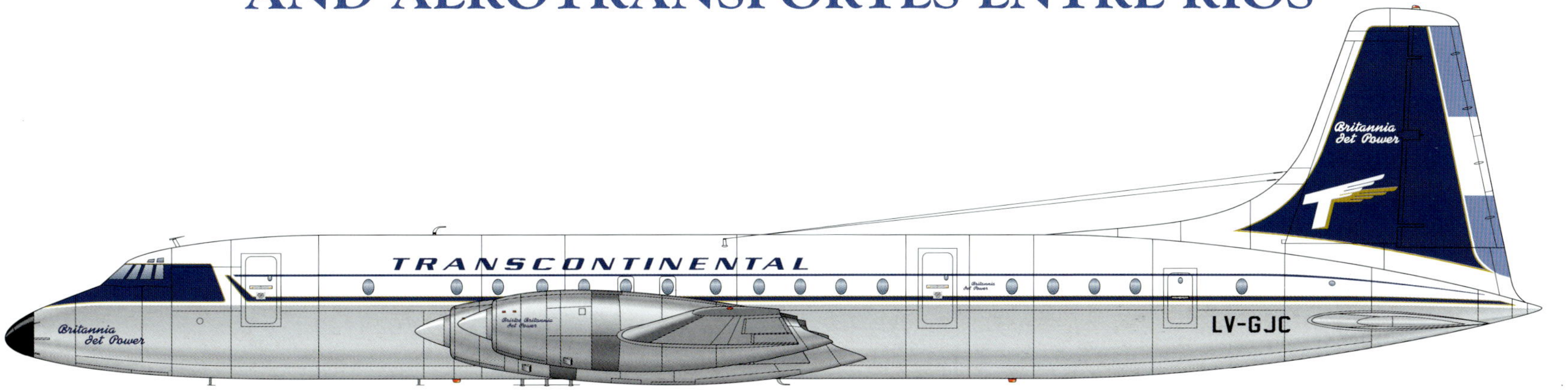

In September 1956 a new airline, Transcontinental SA, was founded with money from California Eastern Aviation and some Argentinian companies. Various passenger services began in March 1957, linking Buenos Aires with destinations in South America, using Curtiss C-46 aircraft. Within a year the airline planned a considerable expansion of service and applied for a licence to open services from Buenos Aires to Mexico City, New York and San Francisco. It purchased two Lockheed Super Constellations to operate these new routes.

The next big step was taken in September 1958 with the inauguration of the schedule from Buenos Aires via Rio de Janeiro and Caracas to New York, a total distance of 6,240 miles. The route was easily worked by the Super Constellations but Transcontinental was keen to replace these piston-driven aircraft by smoother and faster turbo-prop driven aircraft in order to compete with Pan American who, from 1959 onwards, operated Boeing 707 and Douglas DC-8 jets on the New York-Buenos Aires route.

At this stage, there were unsold Britannias from the cancelled Northeast order waiting in Belfast and in August 1959 Transcontinental signed a contract to buy two. Each aircraft was flown from Belfast to Filton for final fitting out and for the Transcontinental livery to be added. The passenger cabins were particularly impressive, with only 104 seats in a space which could accommodate up to 132 passengers, so that people were able to move about during flights, for example to visit the cocktail lounge bar. The airline was keen in its advance publicity to emphasize the merits of the Britannias, the "world's fastest, smoothest, quietest, safest turbo-jets. They are radar equipped and air conditioned", perhaps somewhat overstating the situation.

However there was some delay in releasing the finally prepared aircraft for delivery to Transcontinental while the financial details of the contract were concluded. Once concluded, the two Britannias were handed over and flew out of Heathrow for Buenos Aires on 16th and 17th December 1959, registered as LV-PPJ and LV-PPL, later becoming LV-GJB and LV-GJC respectively.

Once in Argentina they quickly set to work and a three times weekly service between Buenos Aires and New York was flown via Rio de Janeiro, Sao Paulo, Paramaribo (northbound only) and Caracas. The total journey time from New York to Buenos Aires, including stops, was 21hrs 30mins, whilst connecting flights from Buenos Aires went on to destinations within Argentina, and to Paraguay and Uruguay.

The service of the Britannias with Transcontinental seems to have been uneventful, until LV-GJC suffered rudder damage on the ground at Sao Paulo on 8th October 1960. While not grounding the aircraft, it was necessary to fly her back to Filton for repairs on 18th November. But thereafter problems mounted. There was not enough work to justify running two Britannias and within 18 months of their arrival in Argentina, Transcontinental was in serious financial difficulty. On 24th October 1961, LV-GJC was impounded at New York because of non-payment of fees and for other debts to various North American companies. Then on 8th November, all Transcontinental services stopped and the airline went into liquidation.

There was one other short-lived attempt to fly Britannias based in South America. A Series 312F, formerly G-AOVB, was purchased from the receiver of British Eagle by Aerotransportes Entre Rios (AER) of Argentina on 9th October 1969, re-registered LV-PNJ and later LV-JNL. The airline was engaged in the transport of livestock and other freight within South America and as far north as Miami and even sometimes to London. But the Britannia's contribution did not last long. On 12th July 1970, while attempting to land in thick fog at Buenos Aires (Ezeiza), Argentina, she struck a ground radar unit. She was badly damaged and written off.

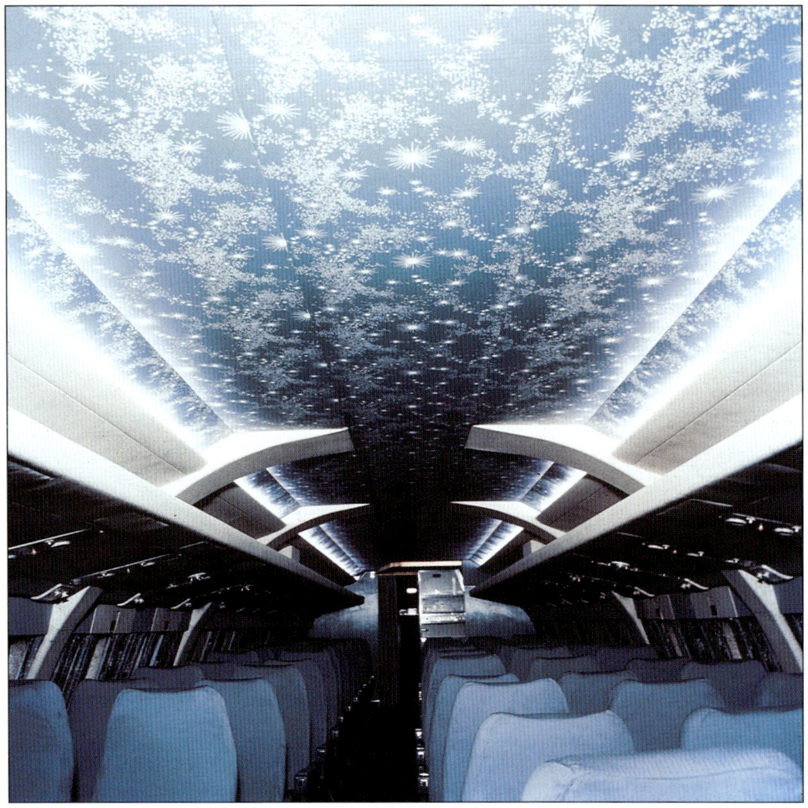

A view toward the rear of Britannia Series 305 LV-PPJ of Transcontinental S.A. displaying the unusual ceiling design based on a stylistic view of the Universe.

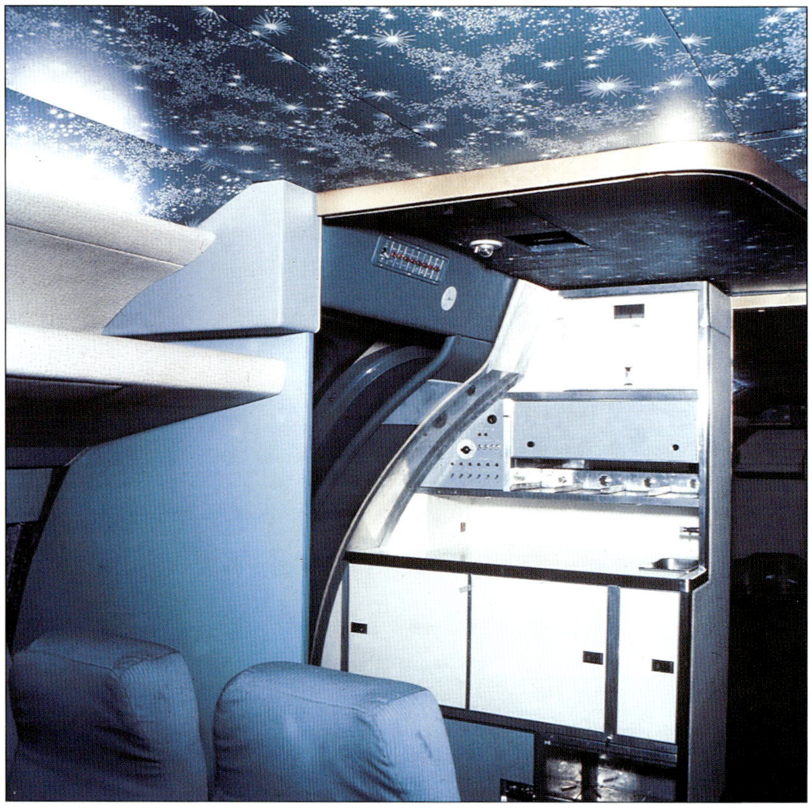

The Galley of LV-PPJ demonstrates the clean uncluttered design with plenty of space provided for the easy preparation of food for the passengers.

Converted by British Eagle to freighter configuration, G-AOVB was sold to AER of Argentina on 9th October 1969 as LV-ANJ and re-registered LV-JNL. Unfortunately the aircraft was destined to serve for a very short period with the airline for it was written-off on 12th July 1970 at Buenos Aires-Ezeiza, Argentina while landing on a foggy evening.

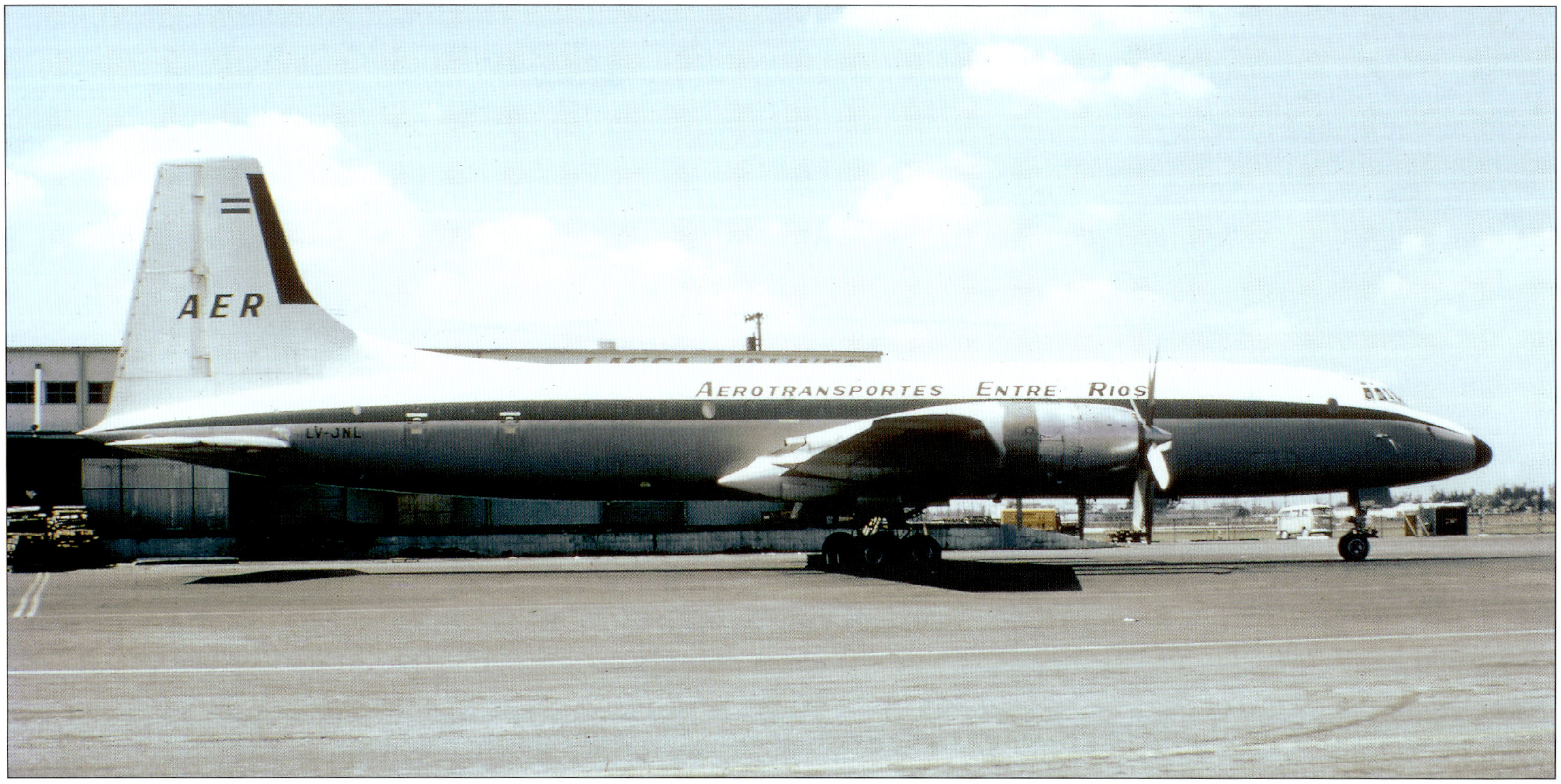

IN SERVICE WITH LAKER AIRWAYS

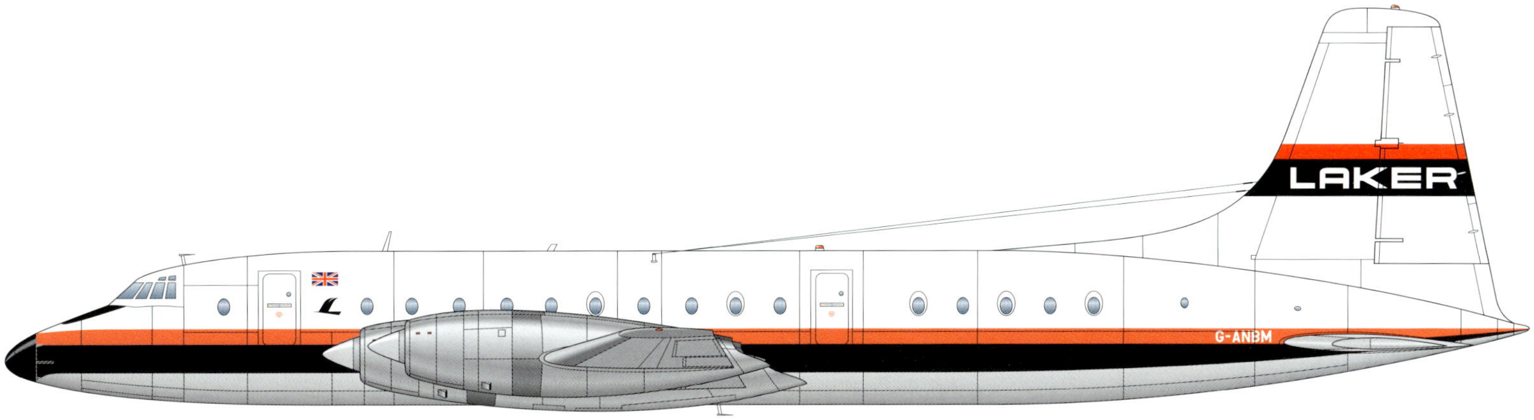

Laker Airways was founded in 1965 by Freddie Laker, former Managing Director of British United Airways. In his former role he had been familiar with Britannia aircraft and when he left BUA, several of his colleagues who had worked with Britannias left with him. These facts determined the early days of Laker Airways.

The airline was founded as a contract hire and charter operator, and three BAC 1-11 jet aircraft were ordered from the makers. However delivery could not be immediate, so Laker arranged the lease-purchase of two Britannias from BOAC's stock of stored Series 102 aircraft, G-ANBM and G-ANBN. This arrangement, concluded in February 1966, made it possible for Laker Airways to begin commercial operations during the 1966 summer tourist season.

On 4th March 1966, G-ANBM was flown from Heathrow to Prestwick for overhaul by Scottish Aviation before handover to Laker and then, on 21st April, G-ANBN was also flown to Prestwick for a similar overhaul. With this process completed, G-ANBM was test-flown for a Certificate of Airworthiness at Prestwick on 19th July and, after two further test flights, she

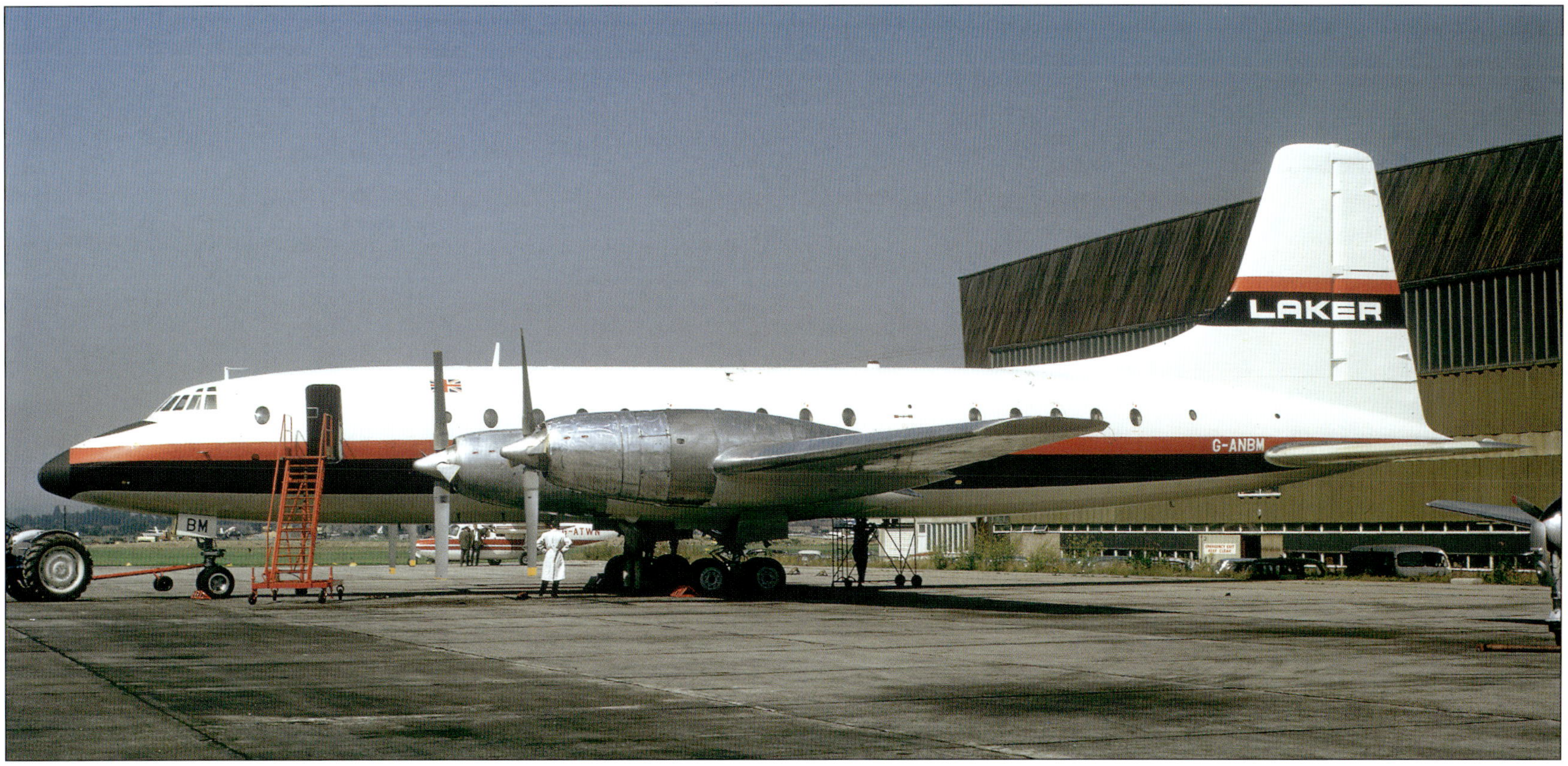

Laker Britannia Series 102 standing in the sunshine at Gatwick airport in July 1966.

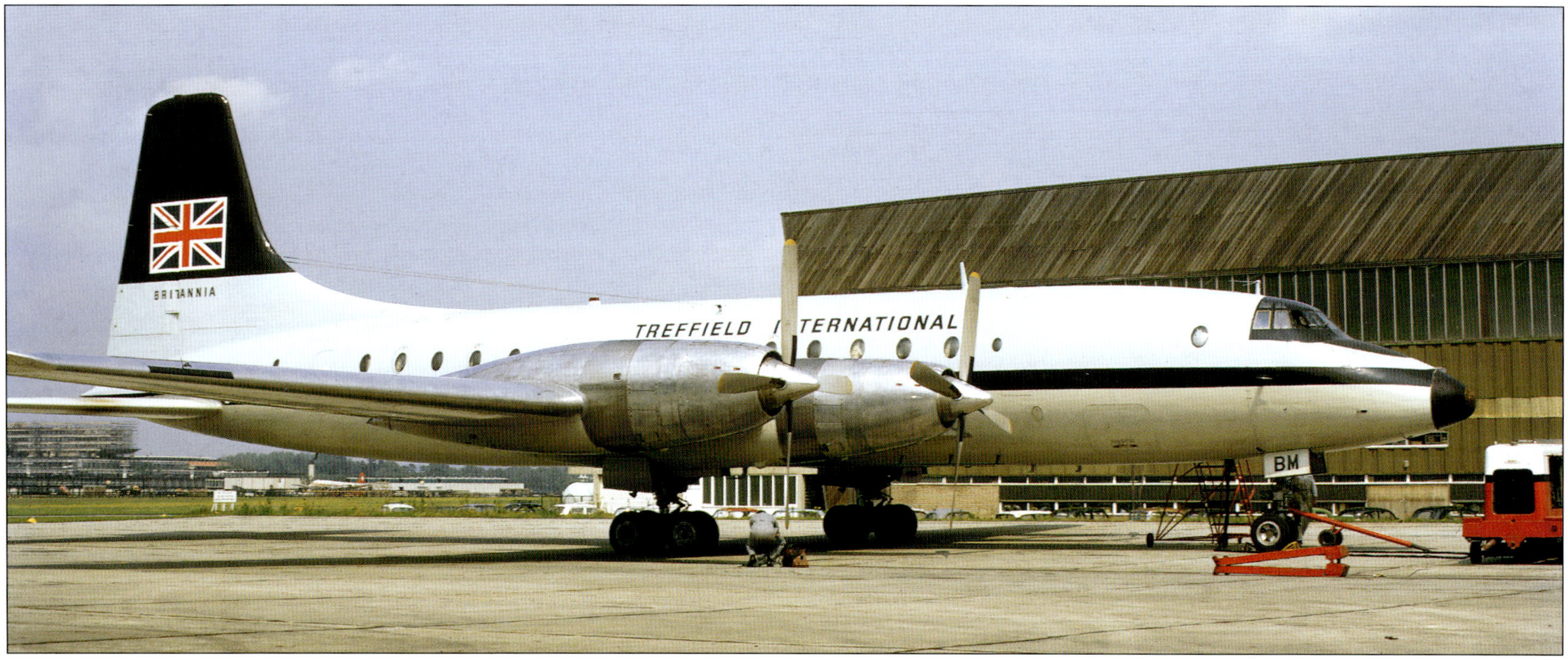

Treffield International leased G-ANBM from Laker Airways from April 1967 for six weeks. Here the aircraft is serviced at Gatwick on 31st May 1967.

was flown via Manchester to Gatwick and there delivered to Laker Airways.

After crew training, her first revenue earning work began on 29th July when she flew from Gatwick to Paris (Orly) and began a six-week lease period to Air France on passenger schedules. This ended on 6th September when she returned to Gatwick.

On 9th September she flew to Luton for a short lease to Britannia Airways (to cover for the Britannia lost at Ljubljana some days earlier), returning to Gatwick on 11th September. On 17th September, she undertook the first service for Laker Airways - a day return service from Gatwick to Cologne. Next day she reverted to leased service with Britannia Airways and before the end of September had operated to Rimini, Valencia and Venice. In addition to this, on 25th September she flew a charter from Gatwick to Venice for British United Airways.

On 26th September, G-ANBN was delivered to Laker at Gatwick after completion of her overhaul and test flight. Her first service was on 1st October, flying a party of Britannia Airways' passengers from Dubrovnik to Luton.

For the rest of the year both of the Laker Britannias had a spell of little work. On 1st October, G-ANBM flew a charter from Gatwick to Rome and two days later one to Dublin. On 9th October, she completed the sub-contracting work for Britannia Airways by flying from Valencia to Gatwick. G-ANBN flew twice across to Cherbourg on 19th and 21st October but then neither aircraft flew anywhere until G-ANBM flew from Gatwick to Athens on 12th November. On 13th November she returned on charter from Athens to Gatwick via Amsterdam and G-ANBN flew the same route in reverse on 20th November. This apart, both aircraft remained idle until mid-December.

In that month Laker arranged contract cargo work for both Britannias in Africa. One aircraft was chartered by Shell to carry drums of oil from Dar-es-Salaam (Tanzania) to Ndola (Zambia), in continuation of the oil lift operation carried out throughout 1966, mainly by RAF Transport Command Britannias. The other charter involved the transport of 'sporting ammunition' to Ndola for the local rifle club but, in the course of fulfilling these contracts, both Britannias were impounded by the authorities. G-ANBM was detained by the Ugandan authorities at Entebbe where it had to make an emergency landing en route from Dar-es-Salaam to Ndola with its cargo of ammunition. However, once the official nature of the mission was established, the aircraft was released with its cargo on 8th January 1967. G-ANBN was detained in Dar-es-Salaam until the legitimacy of the oil transporting operation was established but was then allowed to proceed, also on 8th January. She flew back to Gatwick on 9th January but returned to Tanzania to continue the oil lift to Zambia on 13th January, finally returning to Gatwick via Malta on 6th March. G-ANBM remained in Africa doing its charter work until 29th March, when it also returned to Gatwick.

The summer of 1967 saw the two Laker Britannias in a variety of charter roles. After her return from Africa, G-ANBM was prepared for a one-year lease to Treffield International and handed over to this newly formed airline on 30th April.

She flew her first charter flight for Treffield the next day, from Gatwick to Venice, but the lease only lasted for six weeks. During that time Treffield experienced operational difficulties, including the unserviceability of G-ANBM from 4th to 7th June at a critically busy period. During these few days, Treffield used the other Laker Britannia, G-ANBN, to deputise but she was otherwise mainly employed during the six weeks on holiday flights from Gatwick to Genoa, Nice, Palma and Venice and from Liverpool to Barcelona, Munich, Palma and Perpignan. The unreliability of aircraft schedules, however, together with some bad weather and the unserviceability of the Britannia G-ANBM and also of a Treffield Viscount, meant that Treffield lost a contract for holiday charter work from Cardiff. They were therefore forced to terminate the leasing contract on the Laker Britannia and G-ANBM's final Treffield service was on 11th June, Gatwick-Palma-Gatwick, at the end of which she returned to Laker Airways.

While G-ANBM was with Treffield, G-ANBN had carried out various charter flights. Passengers were flown from Gatwick to Nice (6th May), to Rotterdam (on 7th), to Basle (on 8th), to Seville (on 9th) and to Palma (on 14th), whilst football supporters were flown from Glasgow to Lisbon on 25th May, returning on 26th. On 28th May, she flew a passenger service from Liverpool to Palma on behalf of Treffield then, on 31st May, she flew a charter to Nuremberg. On 9th June she flew two trips taking tourists between Gatwick and Tunis.

On 11th June, G-ANBM returned to the Laker Britannia fleet, but neither aircraft flew again until the 17th. On that day, G-ANBM flew from Gatwick to Birmingham to operate a service to Palma, followed by a night flight from Birmingham to Barcelona. On the same day, G-ANBN operated a service to Nicosia, returning to Gatwick on 18th. G-ANBM flew Birmingham-Ibiza-Birmingham on 18th and then flew Birmingham-Valencia-Birmingham on 19th, while G-ANBN flew Gatwick to Malta. Both aircraft were back at Gatwick on 22nd June.

On 23rd June, G-ANBN flew a day charter Gatwick-Basle-Gatwick, and next day a Forces charter to Gütersloh. G-ANBM flew a charter on 24th June from Manchester to Perpignon, returning via Barcelona to Birmingham then, the next day, she flew Birmingham to Barcelona, Ibiza and Valencia. On 27th June, she flew a charter from Gatwick to Brussels while G-ANBN flew from Gatwick to Tenerife.

At this stage, however, the two Britannias had a fairly low usage, sometimes remaining idle at Gatwick for up to a week between flights. Their function as members of the Laker Airways fleet was mainly as stand-by aircraft to the BAC 1-11s in case they became unserviceable. This was a fairly rare event so that during July 1967, the peak summer season for chartering, both Britannias together only completed about twenty round trips.

From then on a pattern of usage of the Britannias continued, with ad-hoc charters to various parts of Europe and Africa, either for Laker Airways or on behalf of other operators. In August and September 1967 there were Transglobe charters to Lagos, Munich and Rimini, all from Gatwick, and one from Brussels to Lagos; for British Eagle from Liverpool to Palma and Ostend to Lagos; for Britannia Airways from Luton and for Air Ferry from Manston, all in

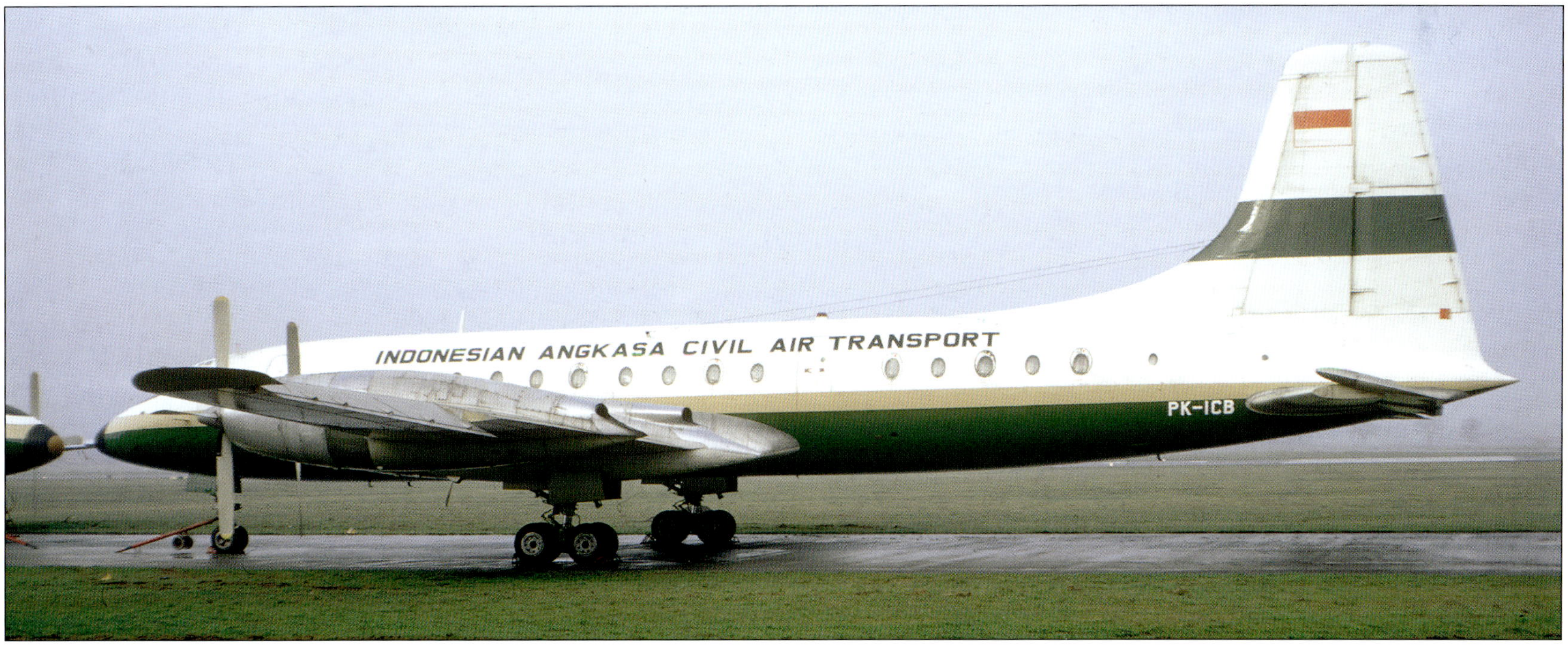

One of a pair of Laker Airways Britannia 102s sold to Indonesian Angkasa Civil Air Transport in 1969.

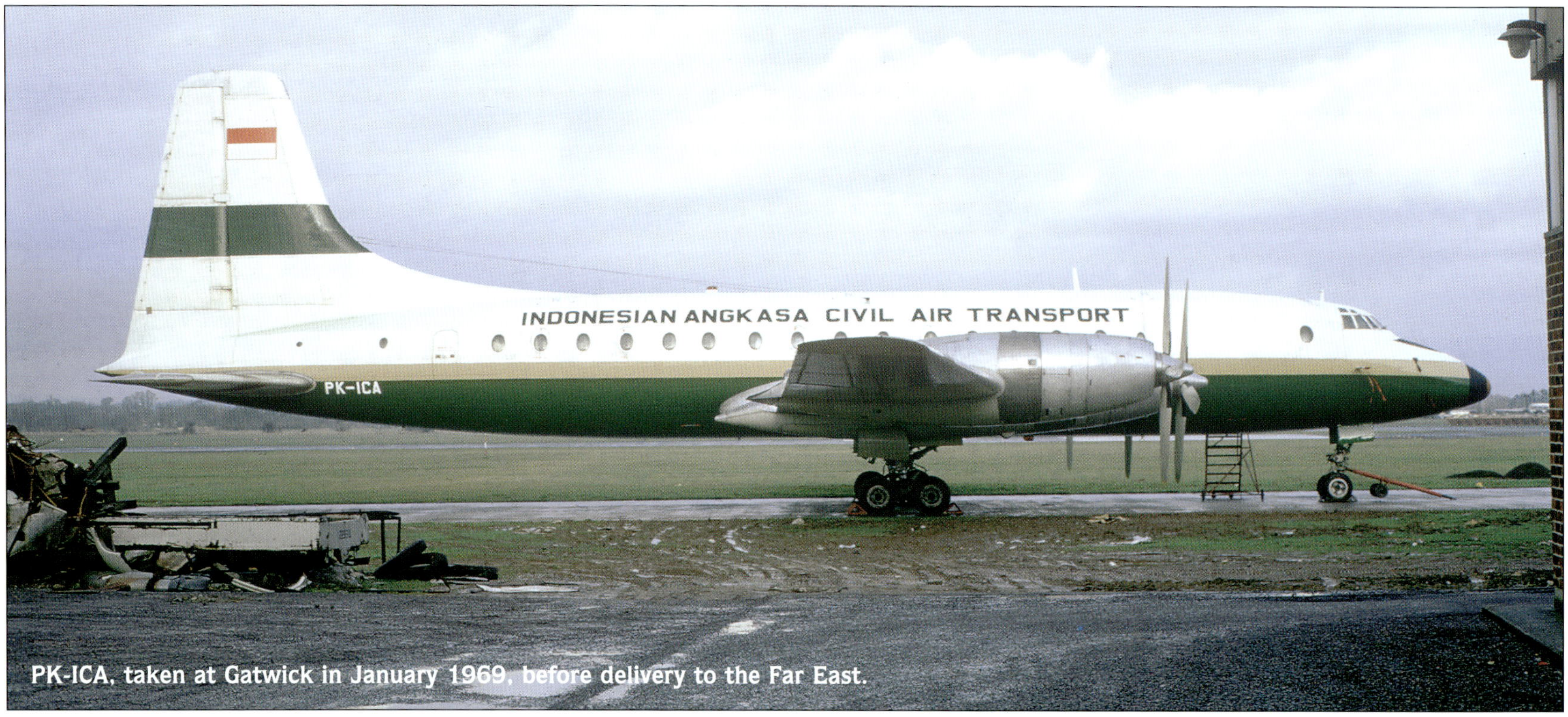

PK-ICA, taken at Gatwick in January 1969, before delivery to the Far East.

addition to Laker flights to Berlin, Lagos and Naples. Towards the end of the year, both aircraft spent time in Africa, partly because of the civil war in Nigeria, chartered by Air Carriers of Zambia, flying from Lagos, Lusaka (Zambia) or Douala (Cameroon). G-ANBM returned to Gatwick on 24th December 1967 and G-ANBN on 23rd January 1968, although both aircraft made a further trip to Africa during February. At the end of February, G-ANBM was leased to BUA to fly from Benina to Gatwick, while G-ANBN flew holiday charters to Tenerife, Palma and Nicosia. Both aircraft flew several charters to Venice during March.

In April G-ANBN was flown to Luton to begin a lease to Britannia Airways which lasted until 17th October. The reason for this was the familiar one - charter passengers preferred the shorter flight times produced by the new jet aircraft. Britannia Airways had therefore ordered Boeing 737 aircraft, but these had not yet been delivered so the Laker Britannias were leased to cover the 1968 tourist season. G-ANBN spent a busy summer, carrying thouands of holiday makers from Luton, Gatwick, Glasgow, Manchester or Newcastle to numerous destinations throughout Europe.

G-ANBM had a less busy summer. She started by flying holiday services from Gatwick and Liverpool, mainly to Benina then, on 28th May, she became the heaviest aircraft ever to land at Eastleigh Airport, Southampton, prior to a tourist flight to Genoa. On 1st June she flew to Liverpool to begin a weekly service to Palma on behalf of Arrowsmith (by then owned by Laker). Each weekend during the summer she was engaged in this transport of tourists, to Barcelona and Palma every week and to Genoa and Ibiza every fortnight. There was also some ad-hoc charter work carried out during the week, for example Gatwick-Cairo-Jeddah on 26th/27th June and Gatwick-Beirut on 15th July.

From then on through the autumn there was limited work for either aircraft. G-ANBN flew Gatwick-Palma-Kano on 7th/8th November and G-ANBM flew a Forces charter Gatwick-Berlin-Gatwick on 12th November. On 30th November both aircraft flew to Manston for freight charters to Lagos, both aircraft flying twice and then returning empty from Lagos on 13th December. G-ANBN then flew a charter from Gatwick to Dakar (Senegal) on 16th December.

Between 20th December 1968 and 5th January 1969, the two Britannias between them flew sixteen round trips between Gatwick and Palma. But this was their final act. The return of G-ANBN to Gatwick from Palma on the evening of 5th January was the last commercial flight of a Laker Britannia. Both Britannias were then replaced by Boeing 707s which Laker obtained from the grounded British Eagle fleet.

The Britannias were sold via National Aero Leasing to Indonesian Angkasa Civil Air Transport, a new Indonesian charter company. Both received new liveries and were re-registered, G-ANBM as PK-ICA and G-ANBN as PK-ICB. They left Gatwick on 11th February and never returned to England. They did some charter work based in Jakarta, but the venture was only a limited success and the airline was declared bankrupt in June 1970. The Britannias gradually deteriorated at Jakarta's Kemayoran airport and were finally scrapped in the early seventies.

IN SERVICE WITH BRITANNIA AIRWAYS

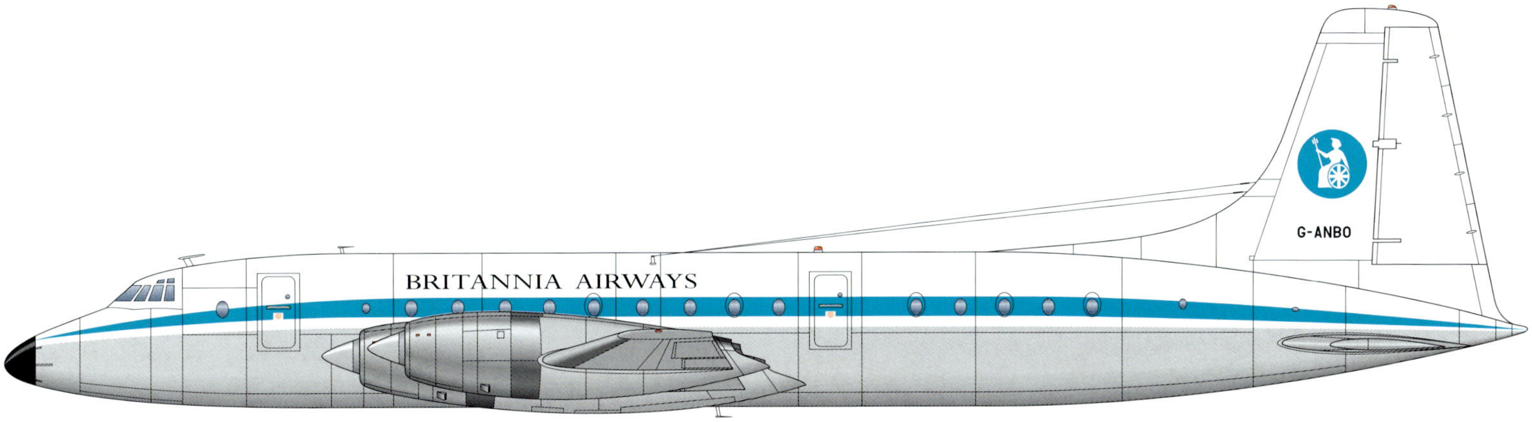

During the 1960s it became fashionable to develop inclusive holiday tours in which a single all-in payment to a tour operator paid for the return airfare to a destination on a chartered aircraft and for the accommodation at the destination. In 1962 a company called Euravia was founded to provide the air transport side of this.

In 1964 Euravia agreed to lease-purchase four ex-BOAC Britannia 102s, later increased to six, and at that stage changed its name to Britannia Airways. The acquisition of the Britannias enabled the airline to phase out its ageing Constellation 049s and 749s. The finance for the Britannia purchases came mainly from the Thomson Organisation, owners of such companies as 'The Times' newspaper, and Britannia Airways became fully owned by Thomson Industrial Holdings on 26th April 1965.

The first of the BOAC Britannias, G-ANBB, was handed over to Britannia Airways at Luton on 18th November 1964 and immediately began crew familiarisation sorties. On 6th December she made her first flight under Britannia Airways livery, taking a party of tourists and press representatives from Luton to Tenerife, returning the following day. This set the pattern for the airline's IT charter flights for the winter 1964/5 season. There were fortnightly flights from Luton to Tenerife and a few flights from Luton to Palma, but no flights from any other British Airports. However, other Britannia aircraft were being acquired and the second one, G-ANBO, was flown from Heathrow to Prestwick for overhaul by Scottish Aviation on 4th January 1965. Like all the other Britannias she was arranged in an all-tourist 112 seating configuration and re-sprayed in the new Britannia Airways' livery. She was delivered back to Luton

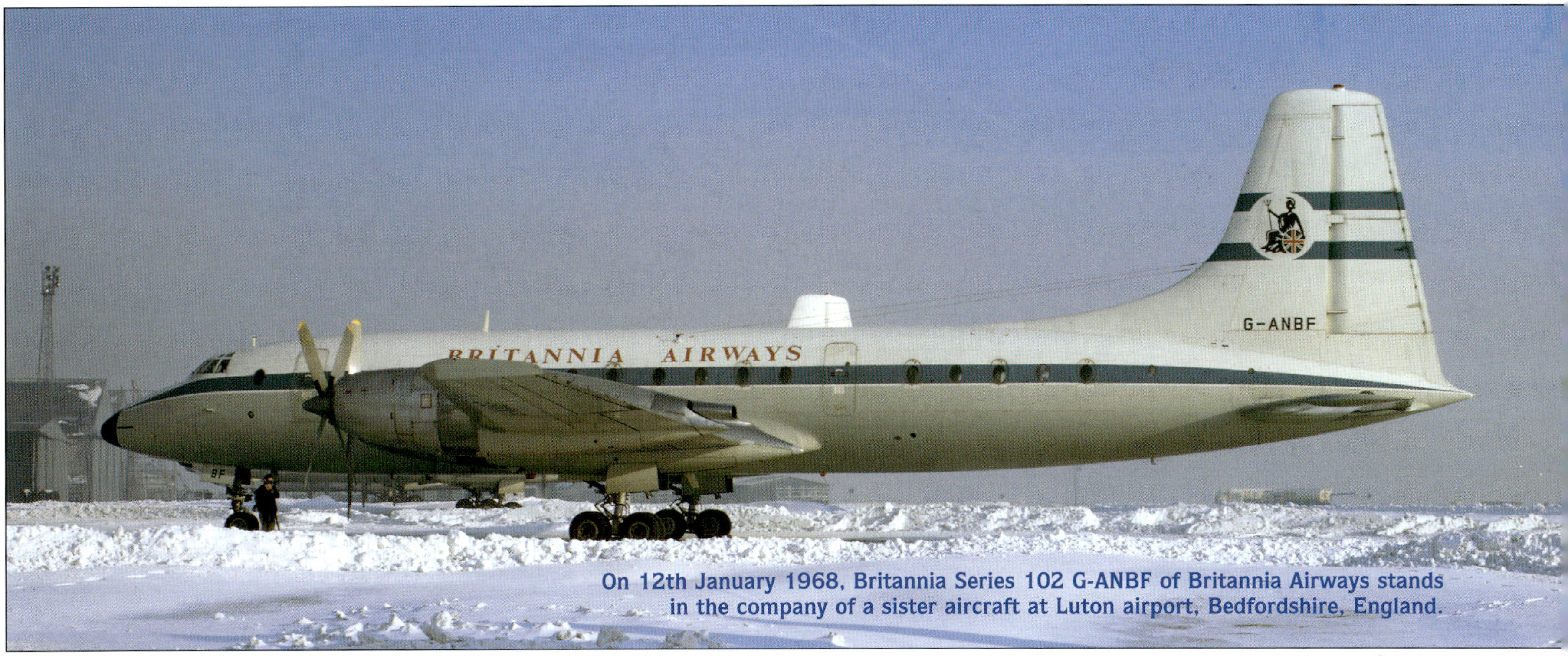

On 12th January 1968, Britannia Series 102 G-ANBF of Britannia Airways stands in the company of a sister aircraft at Luton airport, Bedfordshire, England.

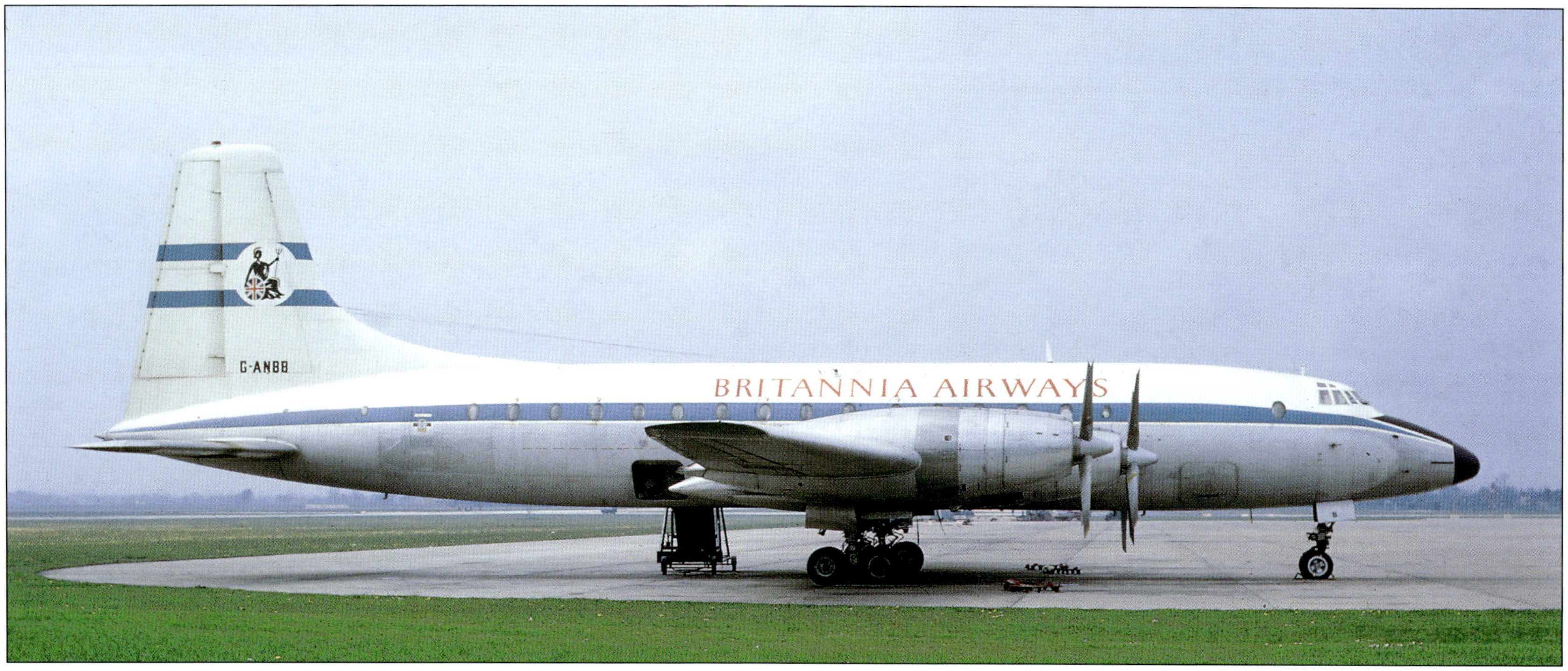

G-ANBB awaits passengers at Manchester airport on 11th May 1965. This aircraft was lost on 1st September 1966 while on approach to Ljubljana, Yugoslavia when it hit trees on high ground killing 97 of the 117 people on board.

on 10th February. Two days later, G-ANBF was flown from Heathrow to Prestwick to undergo the same overhaul and conversion, being delivered back to the airline on 10th March. On 20th March the fourth Britannia, G-ANBJ, was flown to Prestwick for overhaul/conversion, the process being completed on 16th April. At the same time the airline's first Britannia, G-ANBB, was overhauled between the 4th and 29th March, and finally G-ANBA was delivered to Luton from Heathrow on 25th March and overhauled by Scottish Aviation between 12th April and 10th May. So by May 1965, Britannia Airways had five aircraft (G-ANBA, G-ANBB, G-ANBF, G-ANBJ and G-ANBO), all overhauled, re-liveried and ready for the summer IT charter programme.

Summer 1965 was a busy time for these Britannias with UK departures from Luton, Manchester, Newcastle and Glasgow to destinations such as Barcelona, Malaga, Palma, Perpignan, Rimini, Valencia and Venice. The new Britannias were much sought after by tour operators, including Pontinental, Midland Air Tour Operators, Horizon Holidays, Sunflight, Streamline, Global Tours, World Wide and Riviera Holidays.

Most of these IT charter services were at weekends, so that ad hoc day trips could be undertaken during the week, e.g. a football supporters trip from Liverpool to Milan on 12th May, or a charter from Glasgow to Amsterdam on 16th May, both by G-ANBJ.

However there was an interruption to this busy programme on 22nd June when G-ANBF, on landing at Luton, veered off the runway and hit a mound of earth. The damage caused by this put the aircraft out of service for several weeks at a busy holiday time but luckily a replacement Britannia was quickly found. G-ANBL, another of the BOAC 102s was available so she was test-flown from Heathrow on 25th June then handed over to Britannia Airways early on 26th. She was flown immediately to Glasgow from where, on the same day, she flew a charter service to Palma and back, then the next day she flew a service to Valencia and back. After carrying out weekend IT charter journeys, she flew to Prestwick on 29th June for seat reconfiguration and painting in Britannia livery (she had been taken over in an all-white colour scheme). She returned from Scottish Aviation on 21st July and re-entered service that evening when she flew a collection of tourists from Glasgow to Rimini.

The winter of 1965/6 was generally quiet after a very successful summer charter season. There was one special mission, as a support aircraft to the Conservative Party leader, Edward Heath, during his visit to several Asian and Far Eastern countries. The Britannia flew the party, comprising several Conservative Party officials, Members of Parliament and members of the Press, leaving London just after Christmas 1965 for Pakistan, then on to Delhi on 4th January and to Labuan, East Malaysia on 7th January. Unfortunately on 8th January the Britannia developed engine trouble so could not convey Mr Heath to Saigon on the 9th, so the Malaysian Air Force flew him from Kuala Lumpur to Saigon in their new Dart Herald (a replacement Britannia was at the time stranded in Calcutta with a broken windscreen). On his return from Saigon, Mr Heath learned of the sudden death of the Indian

Prime Minister, Mr Shastri, so the itinerary was altered to allow him to attend the funeral in Delhi. After this, the Britannia carried Mr Heath and his party back to London on 14th January.

In preparation for the 1966 IT charter contracts, Britannia Airways acquired two further Britannia 102 aircraft. G-ANBI was ferried from BOAC's store in Cambridge to Scottish Aviation's Prestwick facility on 10th December 1965 and G-ANBE followed on 1st February 1966. They were delivered to Britannia Airways on 3rd February and 1st March respectively, so bringing the Airways' fleet strength up to eight Britannia 102s. With this fleet a full summer IT charter programme was carried out.

The summer season began on 28th April when G-ANBO flew a planeload of tourists from Manchester to Barcelona. At the height of the summer the destinations from Manchester were Barcelona, Genoa, Ibiza, Malaga, Palma, Perpignan, Rimini, Tarbes (for Lourdes pilgrims), Valencia and Venice. Flights from Glasgow began on 14th May as did those from Newcastle to most of the above destinations, whilst flights from Luton were even more widespread. In addition to the above destinations there were flights to Brindisi, Copenhagen, Dubrovnik, Ljubljana, Milan, Naples, Pisa and Rome.

As before, IT charter flights were usually at weekends so that other work could be undertaken in mid-week. For example there were five round-trip charters taking passengers from Luton to Belfast between 17th and 26th May, started by G-ANBO. The flights then continued on to Rome. Some scheduled BUA flights were flown by Britannia Airways' aircraft; on 13th March G-ANBJ flew from Gatwick to Las Palmas, and on 21st July G-ANBF flew from Gatwick to Bucharest. The return flight, Bucharest to Gatwick, was made by G-ANBO on 30th August. On 19th August G-ANBB flew a passenger charter from Lorient (France) to Liverpool, with the return leg flown by G-ANBF on 9th September.

Towards the end of the 1966 tourist season, in the early hours of 31st August, G-ANBB crashed on approach to Ljubljana from Luton. Of the 110 passengers and 7 crew on board, 91 passengers and 6 crew were killed. The flight had been normal until the Dolsko beacon, on the approach to Ljubljana, when the pilot radioed Air Traffic Control that he could see the runway lights and that he was making an approach to runway 31. About 2.5 miles from touchdown the pilot requested radar assistance, and the radar controller told the aircraft that it was on the approach centre line. At two miles from touchdown the pilot was told that he had drifted to the right and was given a correcting heading but nothing more was heard from the pilot. The aircraft struck the tops of some trees and crashed into a forest about one mile from touchdown and some way from the approach centre line. The official inquiry into the disaster concluded that it was due to pilot error.

The airline was not able to immediately replace this lost Britannia because, by this time, BOAC had disposed of its remaining Britannia 102s to Laker and BKS. The remaining seven aircraft therefore had a busy season in 1967. The season began on 13th March with a flight by G-ANBI from Gatwick to Basle then, on 1st April, G-ANBA began a daily charter trip from Manchester to Beauvais until 16th April, when the same aircraft began a service from Manchester to Rotterdam. Flights to these two destinations continued until 18th May, and similar flights originated in Luton.

On 13th May the main IT charter programme began from

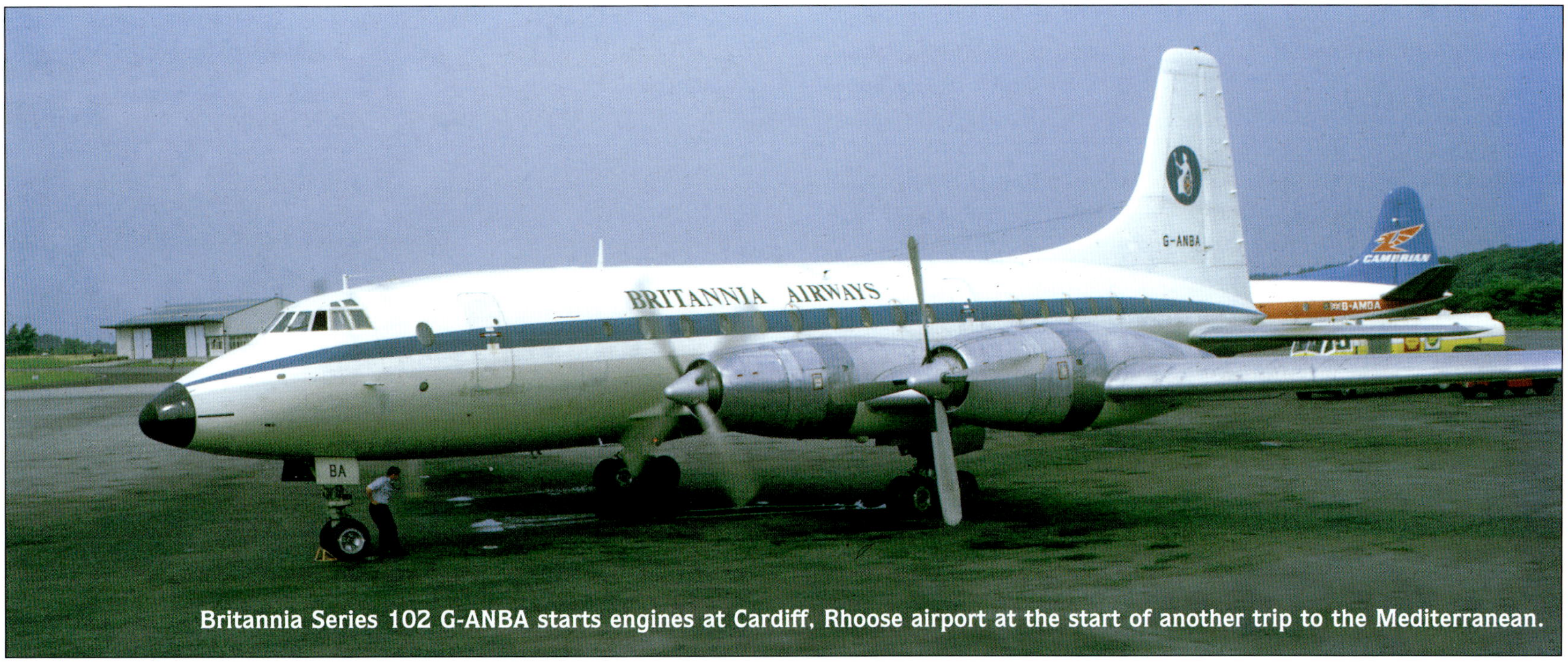

Britannia Series 102 G-ANBA starts engines at Cardiff, Rhoose airport at the start of another trip to the Mediterranean.

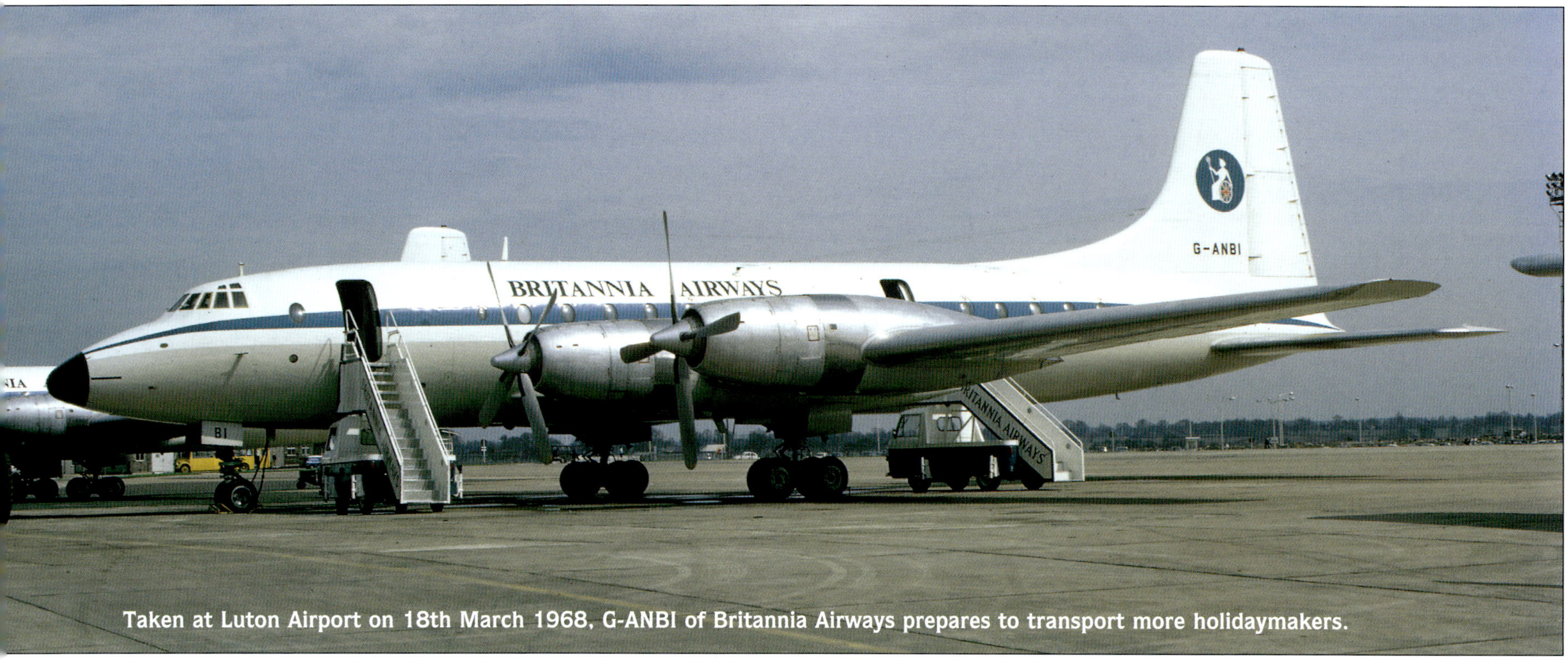

Taken at Luton Airport on 18th March 1968, G-ANBI of Britannia Airways prepares to transport more holidaymakers.

Manchester, with flights to Alicante, Barcelona, Palma and Rimini. On the same date a service from Glasgow re-opened, to Palma and from Newcastle to Barcelona. There were also a series of IT charters between Luton and Maastricht and also Gerona (Spain).

On 25th May G-ANBA joined a large fleet of aircraft ferrying football supporters from Glasgow to Lisbon, returning with them early on the morning of 26th May.

Apart from the regular IT charter commitments, there were other ad hoc assignments such as another football charter from Glasgow to Nuremberg on 31st May involving G-ANBF and G-ANBJ, and also some troop movement flights from Edinburgh and Exeter to Hanover between 3rd and 7th April involving G-ANBA, G-ANBF, G-ANBL and G-ANBO. In the same month, G-ANBL carried stranded cruise ship passengers back from Venice to Gatwick and later there was some sub-charter work for Treffield International who were running into financial difficulties. G-ANBI ferried holidaymakers from Liverpool to Munich and back on 15th June.

For the 1968 season, Britannia Airways had planned to introduce the first of its newly ordered Boeing 737s on its principal IT charter routes. But the Boeing delivery dates had slipped, so the airline was forced to lease two further Britannia 102s from BKS and Laker Airways who, at that stage, were the only other two operators of this variant in the world. The first to arrive at Luton, on 16th April 1968, was G-ANBN and with the Britannia Airways' titling above the Laker red and black cheatline, she was in service within hours of delivery. The second aircraft was G-ANBD which was ferried from Newcastle to Luton on 27th April and shortly afterwards was in service.

With the lease of the Laker Britannia, Britannia Airways took over a programme of charter flights from Gatwick which had been due to be flown by Laker Airways. On 31st March, G-ANBL opened a weekly service from Gatwick to Gerona then, on 3rd April, G-ANBO began a service from Gatwick to Palma. G-ANBE also began a short series of spring charter flights from Gatwick to Rotterdam on 15th April.

The main summer charter programme saw four weekly rotations through Gatwick, flying to Barcelona (twice a week) and to Gerona and Palma (once each per week). From Manchester the service was even busier, with regular flights to Alicante, Barcelona, Ibiza, Milan, Palma, Rimini and Tarbes. There were other charter duties to perform, some of them in order to fulfil Laker Airways' commitments, as well as services from Luton to Mahon and a new route, Luton to Bourgas.

There were also other occasional services, for example G-ANBA flew from Manchester to Kraków on 12th March, returning on the 14th from Vienna, and G-ANBF flew from Manchester to Berlin on 15th March, returning the same day. But perhaps the most impressive charter involved six Britannias (G-ANBD, G-ANBF, G-ANBJ, G-ANBL, G-ANBN and G-ANBO) when, on 14th and 15th May, they took more than 700 football supporters from Manchester to Madrid, bringing them all back on 16th May.

During 1968, IT charter programmes were run by Britannia Airways from Luton, Gatwick, Glasgow, Manchester and Newcastle, mainly to European holiday destinations but sometimes as far as Tenerife or Nicosia.

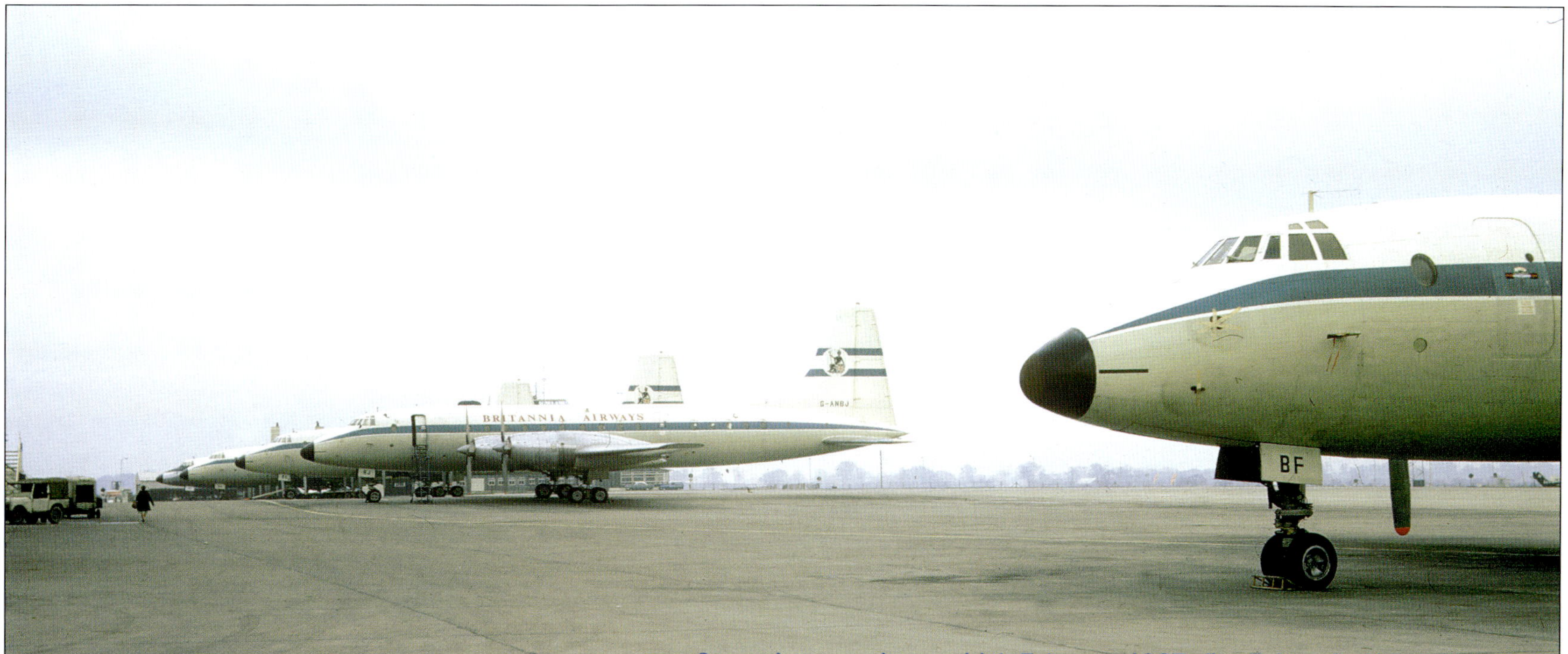

On a misty morning on 11th February 1967, five Britannia Airways' aircraft and one unidentified Britannia line the ramp at Luton Airport.

There were also some long-haul commissions. On 14th December 1967, G-ANBJ flew from Stansted via Benina to Lusaka on behalf of Lloyd International, repeating this trip again four days later, this time accompanied by G-ANBI. In the New Year there was an unusual task, ferrying 37 tons of newly printed Nigerian bank notes out to Lagos for the Nigerian Federal Government. Outgoing flights by G-ANBL (twice) and G-ANBJ began on 13th January 1968 from Luton to Lagos, with staging at Palma or once, because of poor weather, at Perpignan. The empty return flights were direct Lagos to Luton. Another Nigerian journey was on 21st February when G-ANBE flew out empty to Lagos to collect cruise ship passengers in company with a British Eagle Britannia and a Caledonian Boeing 707.

There was also more African work. On 25th June G-ANBL flew from Benghazi (Libya) via Entebbe (Uganda) to Beira (Mozambique), returning to Luton on 27th. On 17th July, G-ANBI flew a passenger charter from Luton to Entebbe. On 28th August G-ANBL flew a service Benina-Entebbe-Beira-Nairobi-Benina, returning to Luton on 30th. On 27th August, G-ANBA flew a consignment of cigarettes from Luton to Khartoum. This was a preamble to a charter by G-ANBI, stripped of passenger seats and in freighter mode, when on 19th November it flew ten tons of cigarettes from Luton via Benina to Khartoum for British American Tobacco. The same aircraft flew cargo from Manston via Benina to Lagos on 4th December and again on 4th, 11th and 18th January 1969.

On 13th December 1968, G-ANBJ was chartered to fly Luton-Benina-Entebbe, then three days later she carried a ship's crew from Benina to Durban (South Africa), returning to Luton on the 19th.

Almost all of the Britannia flights at this stage were trouble-free and therefore unremarkable, but there were occasional exceptions. On 12th February 1969 G-ANBJ was chartered to fly to Lagos. She flew empty from Luton to Gatwick on the morning of the 12th, but suffered technical problems which necessitated a return to Luton. Once repaired by the Britannia engineers she returned to Gatwick, arriving at about 1800. She loaded up and took off at 2246, touching down at Palma to refuel in the early hours of 13th February. Once refuelled, she soon took off but a new electrical snag forced her to return to Palma on three engines, having dumped fuel. She eventually took off for Lagos on 14th and then returned with no more trouble to Luton.

Some other winter charters were picked up. On 18th February, G-ANBL flew from Gatwick to Entebbe and Lusaka with a load of general cargo on behalf of Canford Aviation Services, later to become International Aviation Services. On 24th February, G-ANBJ was also chartered by Canford to carry general cargo from Luton and Rotterdam to Entebbe and Lusaka, returning via Asmara (Ethiopia) with a cargo of green peppers and chillies. The same aircraft flew similar missions on 4th, 17th and 22nd March.

During the spring of 1969, Britannia Airways was awarded an important contract by the Ministry of Defence to ferry troops and their families between the UK and West Germany. By now several Boeing 737s had been delivered to Britannia and these took most of the work, but the Britannia 102s took on some flights such as El Adem-Akrotiri-Gatwick by G-ANBF on 17th/18th December 1968, and various flights between Luton or Belfast and Berlin, Düsseldorf, Gütersloh, Hanover and Wildenrath.

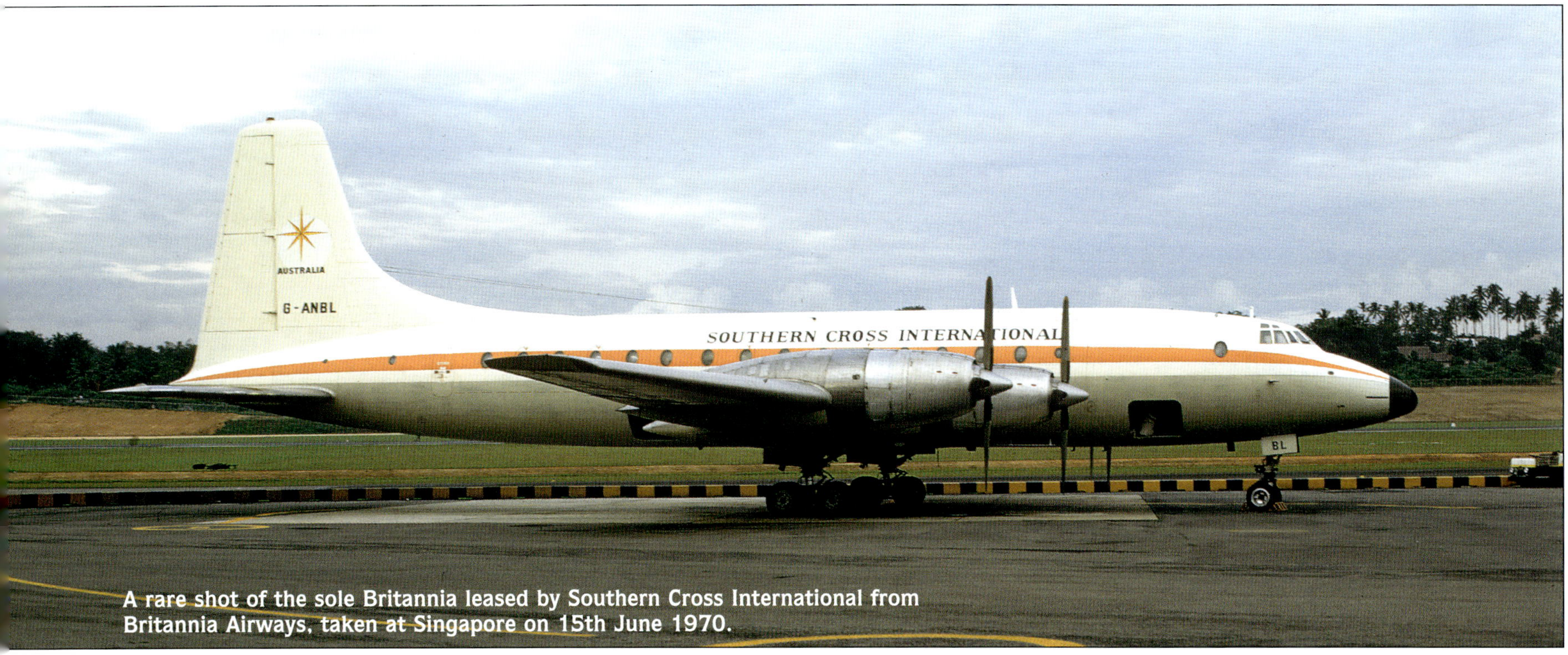

A rare shot of the sole Britannia leased by Southern Cross International from Britannia Airways, taken at Singapore on 15th June 1970.

There were also skiing charters from Luton to Munich and during the 1969 summer, these flights took holidaymakers to the Bavarian and Austrian resorts, with flights also originating in Gatwick, Glasgow, Edinburgh and Manchester. Charters to other previously serviced destinations also continued through the summer. But by now Britannia Airways was increasingly using its Boeing 737 fleet and during the autumn began withdrawing its Britannia 102 fleet. G-ANBI was withdrawn on 27th September 1969 followed by G-ANBF on 26th October and G-ANBA on 20th November. This left four Britannias (G-ANBE, G-ANBJ, G-ANBL and G-ANBO), and during the 1969/70 winter they had a fairly quiet time. There were a few of the usual charters, an MoD trooping charter from Manchester to Düsseldorf and a group of rugby supporters to take from Paris to Cardiff for the France v Wales match. A more unusual charter was by Ariana Afghan, wanting a Britannia to operate their Gatwick-Brussels-Kabul schedule after the loss of their Boeing 727. G-ANBJ and later G-ANBE took this work on between 8th February and 11th March.

The main new feature of the 1970 season was the operation of charter flights to Munich from nine different British airports, taking tourists to Bavaria for the Oberammergau festival Passion Play. Flights began on 15th May and up to three of the four Britannias remaining were engaged. Services eventually ran to Munich from Birmingham, Edinburgh, Gatwick, Glasgow, Liverpool, Luton, Manchester, Newcastle and Teesside.

While G-ANBE, G-ANBJ and G-ANBO were engaged almost exclusively on this work, G-ANBL was leased to a new company, Southern Cross International. This was the only Britannia operated by an Australian company and the venture seems to have lasted for only about a month. The Southern Cross International titling had been put on the fuselage by 20th May and by 3rd June the aircraft was seen at Bangkok, then on 15th June was reported at Singapore. At this point, however, the Australian company seems to have foundered and the Britannia returned to Luton.

For the remainder of the summer, the four Britannias took on any IT charter flights when any of the Boeing 737s were unserviceable, an increasingly rare event. G-ANBE took four trooping flights between Hanover and Glasgow on 4th and 6th August. Three of the final four flights by the Britannias were trooping flights; the final flight by G-ANBJ was a trooping flight on 13th October from Gütersloh to Luton; the final flight by G-ANBO was ferrying troops from Hanover to Luton on 15th October, and the final G-ANBE flight was also a trooping flight from Luton to Belfast on 16th November. So the last Britannia remaining in service was G-ANBL which stayed on standby duty for the next few weeks, and on 29th December 1970 operated a passenger charter from Genoa to Luton. It was the last service ever flown by a Britannia 102 for Britannia Airways.

As no buyer could be found, all seven Britannias were scrapped at Luton. During their time they had undoubtedly formed a very successful fleet, becoming a popular part of the holiday travel scene for many people during the 1960s. But greater speed and hence shorter flight times became more attractive, so they were phased out. But they filled the gap for the airline between the piston-engined era of the Constellations in the early sixties and the pure jet era of the seventies.

IN SERVICE WITH BRITISH EAGLE AIRWAYS

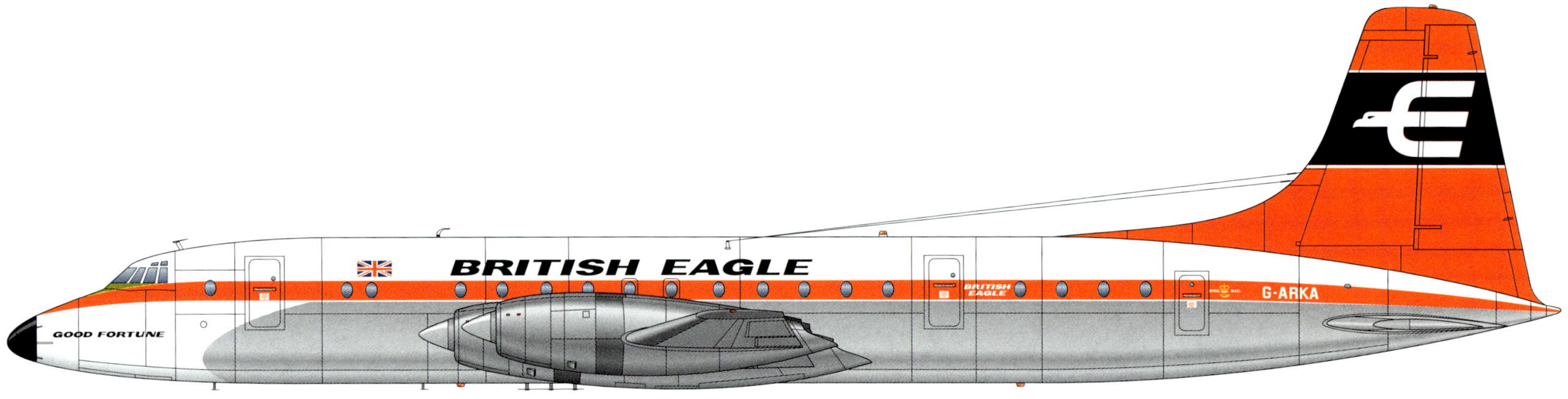

Formed in 1948 by Harold Bamberg, Eagle Aviation had become well established by 1960 as an efficient airline flying scheduled and charter services to a wide variety of destinations. By 1958 they were using Viscounts and Douglas DC-6s and, as a natural extension of their activities, were interested in introducing Britannias to the fleet.

The Britannia fleet which the airline built up eventually reached seventeen long-range aircraft, mostly the Series 312 variant. For eight years, these Britannias flew worldwide and gained a fine record for reliability and utilisation. It was regarded by many as the peak of Britannia achievement, only brought to an end by political and economic arguments which had little to do with aircraft performance.

In March 1960, it was announced that the Cunard Steamship Company had taken over the Eagle group of companies, although negotiations were not completed for another eight weeks. At the end of the negotiations, Cunard had purchased the complete share capital of the Eagle group and, as a result, the airline changed its name to Cunard Eagle Airways (still with Harold Bamberg in charge). In March, it was also announced that Eagle had arranged to lease from Cubana a Britannia 318 (CU-T668, but re-registered in the UK as G-APYY). She was serviced, rearranged internally for an initial 104 seat configuration and handed over to Eagle at Filton on 5th April 1960. She then flew to Heathrow and made her first revenue earning flight for the airline on 6th April, taking a full load of servicemen on an MoD charter to Christmas Island. From then on through the summer, she was engaged in various ad hoc charter flights, e.g. a charter for El Al from Heathrow to Tel Aviv, some MoD charters, flights from Heathrow to Bermuda, Kingston and Nassau, a charter for Trans Canada from Heathrow to Halifax via Manchester, Prestwick and Gander, returning from Halifax via Prestwick to Heathrow, and an MoD charter for troops from Heathrow to Aden.

In October 1960, Cunard Eagle opened a service on the Heathrow-Nassau route which was initially to operate every other month alternately with BOAC. Subsequently this became once a fortnight and then, from 4th March 1961, a weekly service. Permission to run these services had to be granted by the British Government and, after considerable discussion, Cunard Eagle was given permission to open a London-Bermuda-Nassau scheduled service in conjunction with BOAC. Included was a very low-fare 'Skycoach' service, single class, once a month, with a weekly service containing First Class and Economy Class seats.

Cunard Eagle was keen to extend its transatlantic operation and approached the UK and US Air Transport Licensing Boards for permission to operate scheduled services from the UK to the US East Coast, the mid-West and to Canada. This was vigorously opposed by BOAC but, in June 1961, it was announced that Cunard Eagle had been granted a licence to operate a daily service from London to New York by either Britannia or Boeing 707 aircraft, beginning on 15th August 1961 and lasting for a period of 15 years. BOAC objected and lobbied the UK Ministry of Aviation who, on 21st November, revoked the new licence so that Cunard Eagle lost the prized London-New York service.

In preparation for the hoped-for expansion, Cunard Eagle had purchased two Britannia 324s from Canadian Pacific, the first being CF-CPD which was re-registered in the UK as G-ARKA and delivered to Heathrow on 1st May 1961. So, at the beginning of the summer of 1961, Cunard Eagle had three long-range Britannias available but there was uncertainty about permission for long distance scheduled flying. It also had two Boeing 707s on order for delivery in 1962.

During the summer, the Britannias flew regular schedules between Bermuda and New York and between Nassau and Miami, as well as from Heathrow to Bermuda and Nassau.

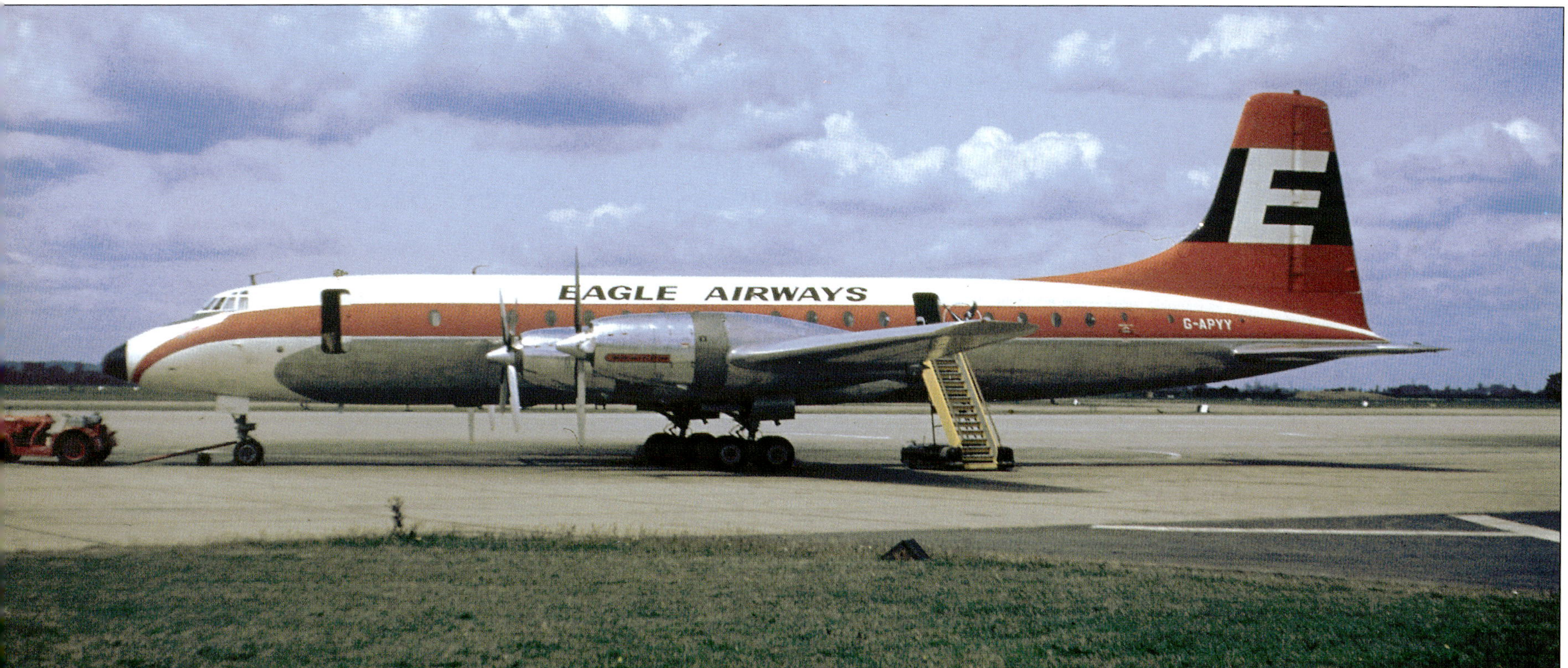

Leased from Cubana in March 1960, G-APYY wears the early livery of Eagle Airways.

Because Cunard Eagle (Bermuda) had scheduled rights on the Montreal / New York sector, it was possible to operate services through Montreal. Sixty-five flights were made through Montreal, including flights originating in Heathrow and also Belfast, Manchester and Prestwick. However, at the end of the summer 1961 season, there was more trouble for Cunard Eagle when the American CAB failed to grant the airline an 'open charter licence'. This meant that Cunard Eagle would only be able to operate less than twenty transatlantic charters in 1962, whereas the airline had expected to be able to operate more than one hundred. Consequently, the lease on G-APYY was terminated in September 1961 and the aircraft returned to Cubana.

Early in 1962, the chairman of BOAC began secret negotiations with the Board of Cunard which resulted in the formation of a new company, BOAC-Cunard, on 6th June 1962. The new company took over all the transatlantic licences held by Cunard Eagle, as well as the two Boeing 707s and several flight crews. The result was to leave Cunard Eagle in a precarious state with its profitable mid-atlantic operation gone and its fleet of Britannias, DC-6s and Viscounts having to operate mainly on charter work, largely within Europe.

1962 and 1963 were taken up with consolidating the company operations. 1962 was particularly hard, for there was still a large engineering service division at Heathrow with much less work to do now that the Boeing 707s had gone. There had to be an emphasis on charter work, in particular MoD troop movement flights. A turn round in company fortunes came on 14th February 1963 when Harold Bamberg announced that, along with a number of colleagues, he had bought back a 60% share holding in Cunard Eagle (although Cunard retained the remaining 40%). Then, in August, the name Cunard was dropped from the airline title which became British Eagle International Airlines. From then on the company fortunes rapidly improved. The basis for this remained the MoD trooping contracts, ad hoc charters and some IT charter work, but there was also an ambitious plan to operate domestic air routes within the UK from Heathrow, in direct competition with British European Airways. As can be imagined, there was objection from BEA to the loss of its monopoly. The initial application for permission to operate scheduled services from Heathrow or Gatwick to Birmingham, Edinburgh, Glasgow and Manchester had been lodged in February 1961, but it was not until August 1963 that British Eagle received approval to operate services from Heathrow to Belfast, Edinburgh and Glasgow.

The size of the Britannia fleet began to increase and the first to be added was the ex-BOAC Series 312, G-AOVT, lease-purchased in September 1963. She was handed over at Heathrow in full British Eagle livery on 13th September and after crew training, undertook her first revenue earning flight on 25th September carrying troops from Edinburgh to Malta. A second Britannia, G-AOVB, was leased from BOAC on 15th October. These two newly acquired aircraft inaugurated British Eagle's schedules from Heathrow to Belfast, Edinburgh and Glasgow and, on 4th November, G-AOVB

inaugurated the five times weekly midday schedule between London and Belfast, and G-AOVT the service between London and Edinburgh.

A further extension of British Eagle's domestic routes took place at the end of 1963 with the takeover of a Liverpool based airline, Starways, and with it a route network which included Liverpool to London, Glasgow and Cork. The domestic services in general did not prove as profitable as British Eagle had hoped, partly because of the restricted frequencies at which they were allowed to fly because of competition from BEA. The smaller capacity Viscounts were more economical, given the passenger demand, but even using these the scheduled routes were eventually suspended; Belfast-Heathrow on 19th February 1964 and Glasgow-Heathrow on 20th February, while Liverpool-Heathrow used a Britannia for one round trip per day and Viscounts on other flights.

But if scheduled domestic routes proved unsuccessful, ad hoc charters, IT work and MoD trooping tasks were increasing in volume. So the airline decided to increase its Britannias fleet and between January and June 1964 leased several more aircraft from BOAC's store. G-AOVO, an ex-BOAC Britannia 312, was leased on 17th January 1964 and flew the first flight from Heathrow to Innsbruck in February. Sadly this aircraft crashed into a mountain on approach to Innsbruck on 29th February, killing all 75 passengers and eight crew on board. The subsequent investigation suggested that the Captain was attempting a landing in too heavy a cloud cover and that while manoeuvring above the mountains near the Innsbruck VOR, the aircraft entered cloud and subsequently struck the mountain with fatal results.

Another Britannia acquired at about the same time was the unique Series 319, G-AOVA, which was leased from BAC for one month from 1st January 1964. On return to Bristol, she was leased to BUA from 12th February to 19th April and then leased to British Eagle on 25th April and later purchased by them on 29th December. She had been originally built as a prototype for the Series 310s, but she was later upgraded to full Series 320 specification and sold as the only Series 319 variant.

Two other Britannias acquired during the expansion of the airline were the two Series 308 aircraft purchased following the collapse of Transcontinental S.A. Neither aircraft had done much flying with Transcontinental and both were converted to 308F standard, which involved fitting a forward (port side) freight door and a reinforced floor so that freight could be carried. This reorganisation enabled each aircraft to carry 132 passengers, or 36,000lb of cargo, or a combination of both. The first Britannia to emerge from the conversion, re-registered as G-ANCF, flew her first contract on 2nd July 1964 from London to Adelaide. The second Britannia, re-registered as G-ANCG, was granted her Certificate of Airworthiness on 11th November, and was also used on British Eagle's MoD charter contract to Woomera, Australia via Adelaide.

Other Britannia 312s leased from the BOAC store at this time were G-AOVB, G-AOVC, G-AOVE, G-AOVF, G-AOVG, G-AOVH, G-AOVM and G-AOVN, and these aircraft were fully involved in a large amount of IT charter work during the 1964 season. British Eagle destinations from Heathrow were Alghero, Barcelona, Basle, Biarritz, Genoa, Lisbon, Naples, Nice, Palma, Perignan, Rimini, Varna and Venice. IT charters also began from Manchester on 14th May using G-ARKA and G-AOVA. In spite of all this, the most lucrative work for the airline at this stage was the MoD troop movement contracts and, in the spring of 1964, it was announced that British Eagle had been awarded a two-year contract to move troops between London and Singapore/Hong Kong. The contract, which followed on the previous one held by BUA, called for five weekly round trips, with the first flight leaving Heathrow on 10th May 1964. While the contract lasted, approximately 28,000 service personnel were transported each year. Apart from the contract to the Far East and Australia, there were also flights to Malta, Benghazi, Benina, El Adem and Akrotiri.

There were a few known mishaps in this high level of activity, fortunately with no consequential injuries. For example, on 31st July 1964, G-AOVF was on a trooping flight from Singapore to London with 111 passengers and a crew of eight on board. After landing at Karachi on a scheduled refuelling stop, she suffered a failure of the port main undercarriage although luckily, and rather surprisingly, there

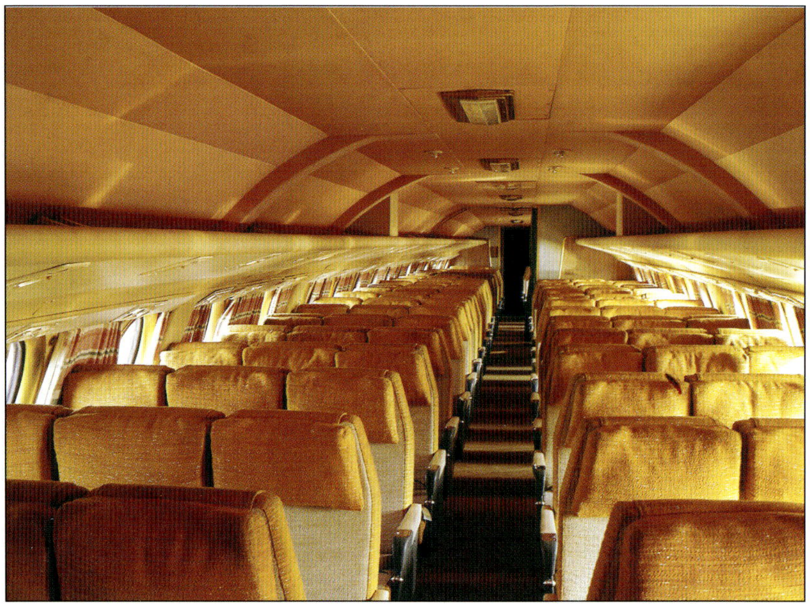

This view towards the rear of the aircraft demonstrates the golden colour trim that furnished the interior decor of British Eagle Britannias.

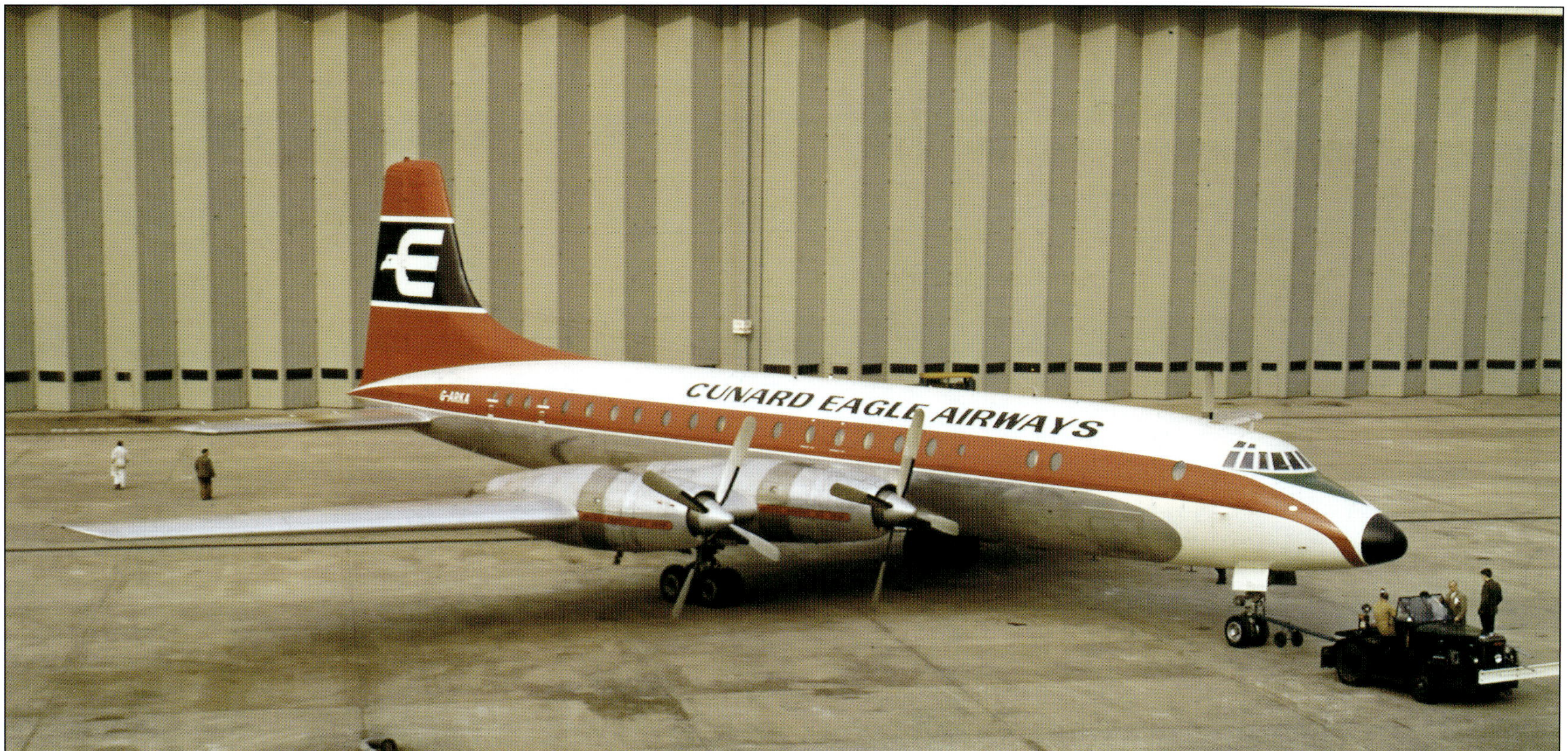

Newly painted in the livery of Cunard Eagle Airways, G-ARKA is towed in front of the Brabazon hanger at Filton airfield in March 1961.

were no casualties and little damage to the aircraft which was soon repaired and back in service.

On another trooping flight to Australia, G-AOVB was approaching Gan (in the Maldives) on 10th October 1965 with 112 passengers and a crew of eight. In daylight but poor visibility with moderate rain, the crew saw the runway approach lights one mile from touchdown at about 350ft. However, at 100ft there was very heavy rain and complete loss of forward vision, and although the pilot initiated overshoot procedure, the aircraft continued to descend, landing heavily and bouncing back into the air. As it did so, it emerged from the heavy rain and the runway in front became clearly visible, so the landing procedure was continued. The main undercarriage was undamaged by the heavy first contact, but the nose wheel assembly had been damaged and, on further contact, it collapsed completely and the Britannia came to rest with its nose on the ground. There were no injuries to anyone on board but the nose area of the Britannia was considerably damaged, so she was returned to the UK for repairs and whilst there was converted to a Series 312F variant by the installation of a cargo door.

Yet another trooping flight incident befell G-AOVM on 8th December 1966 whilst landing at Istanbul on a flight from Kuwait to London, carrying 110 passengers and a crew of nine. Landing on the airport runway in a crosswind, it veered left after touchdown and came to rest with the main undercarriage stuck in mud and the nosewheel collapsed. Again, however, there were no injuries to the occupants and only minor damage to the aircraft.

Apart from the regular trooping contract work, there were many other ad hoc duties. For example, on 3rd January 1965, a British Eagle Britannia flew a planeload of Lancashire Fusiliers to Georgetown, British Guyana because the RAF Transport Command Britannias were fully occupied at that stage flying paratroops to Kuala Lumpur, Malaysia. On 9th February, the airline began a series of trooping flights from Edinburgh to Singapore and Kuala Lumpur via Istanbul, while trooping flights were often made from Heathrow to Düsseldorf, Gütersloh, Hanover and Wildenrath in support of British Forces based in West Germany.

Whilst troop contracts continued throughout the year, there was an upsurge in IT and transatlantic charter work each summer. The 1966 season saw the Britannias flying people to the usual range of European destinations, much of the work being on behalf of the Lunn-Poly company. There were also some additional ad hoc charters, for example from Heathrow to Tarbes for pilgrims who wanted to visit Lourdes. Following these flights from Heathrow, more were arranged from other UK and Irish airports and, over the Easter weekend in March 1968, over 750 people were flown from Dublin to Tarbes and back by British Eagle Britannias.

With this amount of activity, the British Eagle Britannias achieved a high level of utilisation. Even in 1963, the

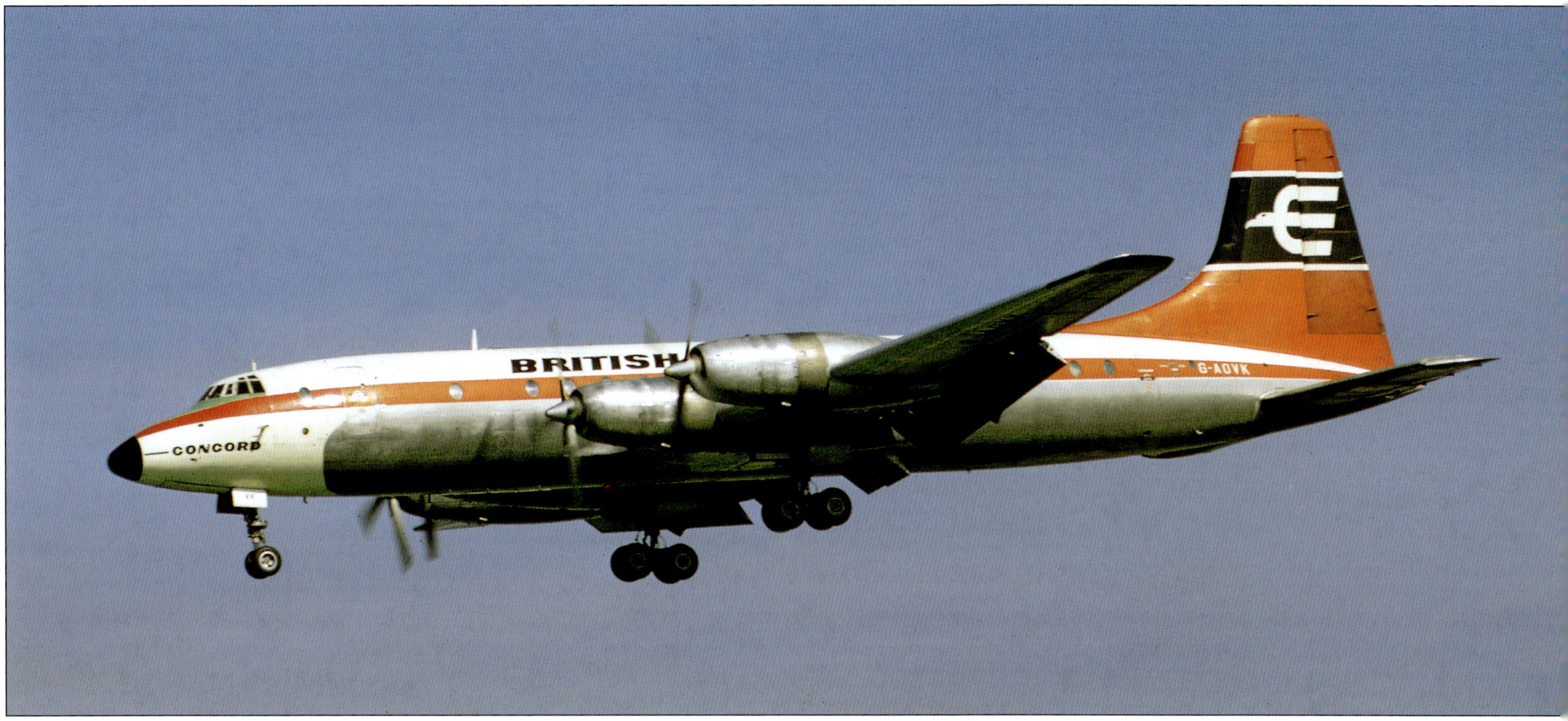

G-AOVK 'Concord' approaches Heathrow Airport in October 1966.

Britannias flew 6,162 hours, representing an average annual utilisation per aircraft of 3,102 hours. During 1966, with seventeen Britannias in service, the fleet logged up 52,308 hours and covered over 17 million aircraft miles, more than one million miles per aircraft. The average annual utilisation was 3,246 hours per aircraft with three Britannias logging over 3,500 hours each. One aircraft, G-AOVT, logged up 3,748 flying hours which was a new utilisation record for Britannias.

The transatlantic situation had, by this time, improved and from 25th March 1964, the American Civil Aeronautics Board granted British Eagle permission again to operate transatlantic passenger charter flights between any point in the UK and any point in the USA, provided that the number of charters originating in the USA did not exceed those originating in the UK by more than one-third during any calendar year. The number gradually built up but during 1965 a total of 78 charter flights was completed. Most were from Heathrow to New York or Toronto, although some were from other airports, for example on 14th July Series 319, G-AOVA, carried 119 passengers via Prestwick to New York. On 3rd June Series 324, G-ARKA, flew from Manchester to Gander and New York and, during the 1965 season, 26 transatlantic charters passed through Manchester, the majority flying via Gander to New York. The final charter flight of the season was by G-ARKB on 27th September, flying from New York to Manchester and Heathrow.

The 1966 transatlantic season was even busier, with a total of 139 flights by the Britannias. These began in earnest on 7th June when G-AOVE flew from Heathrow via Manchester and Gander to Toronto. Flights then became frequent from Heathrow via Manchester to New York, whilst services through Prestwick began on 21st June when ex-El Al Series 313, G-ARXA, flew a charter Toronto-Gander-Prestwick-Heathrow. There was also a short series of flights through Belfast beginning on 10th July when G-ARXA flew Heathrow-Belfast-Shannon-Toronto. Five other Britannias were involved in the transatlantic services besides those mentioned; G-ARKA and G-ARKB, and G-AOVB, G-AOVC and G-AOVN. The final crossing, at the end of the charter season, was on 9th November when G-ARXA flew from Toronto to Manchester.

The 1967 transatlantic season was as busy as the last with the main flights being from Heathrow, Manchester, Prestwick and Belfast to New York, Montreal or Toronto. The first such flight was by G-ARKA on 5th June from Heathrow and Manchester to New York although, on 15th May, a flight by G-AOVT conveyed tourists from Niagara Falls to Manchester. The first flight through Belfast was on 29th June, en route to Toronto, and the first in-bound service through Prestwick was on 1st July when G-ARKA landed a party of Canadian tourists. During the season, the two Series 324 aircraft, G-ARKA and G-ARKB, carried the bulk of the traffic, assisted sometimes by Series 313, G-ARXA, and

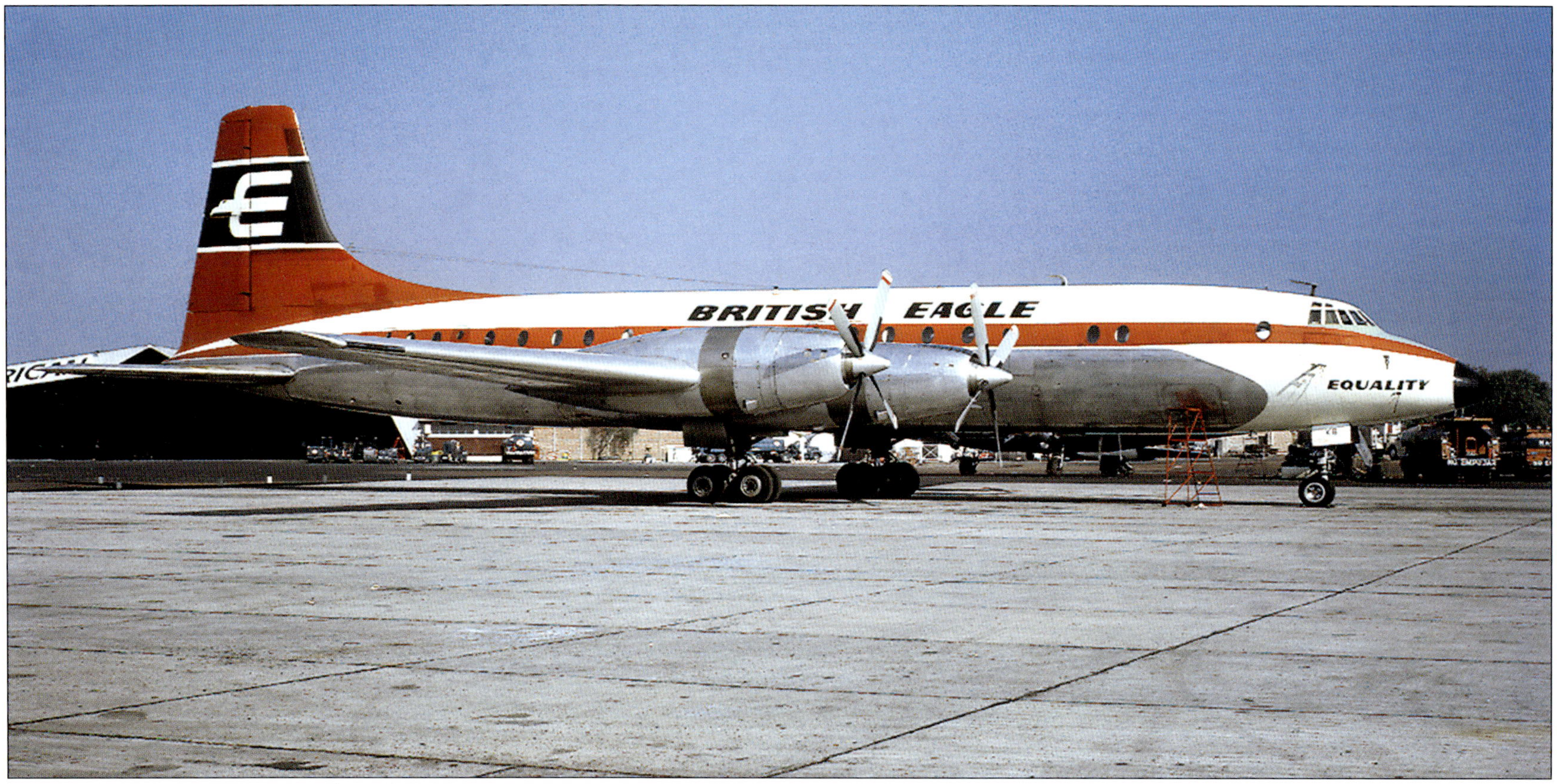

In April 1966 G-ARKB 'Equality' sits on the ramp at Mexico City after a transatlantic charter.

at peak times by Series 312, G-AOVN. During the short season, eighteen transatlantic charters passed through Manchester, nine through Prestwick and four through Belfast. The last flight of the season was by G-ARKA which, on 22nd September, flew from Manchester to Gander and New York, returning to Heathrow on 23rd September.

Other charter flights continued to occupy the British Eagle Britannias. For example, for the period from 1964 to 1968, British Eagle had permission to operate charter flights from Britain to Australia, terminating in Brisbane, Melbourne, Perth or Sydney. There was also a series of football supporters' charters within Europe, e.g. a number of daily flights from Liverpool to Istanbul beginning on 11th October 1967 with G-AOVG ending on 16th October, then a series of charter flights, Liverpool to Gütersloh, were undertaken by G-AOVG, G-ARKA and G-ARKB. Another charter was five night tourist flights from Gatwick to Rimini, flown on behalf of Transglobe between 21st July and 1st September 1967.

In 1967, another British Eagle Britannia was lost, fortunately with no injury to either passengers or crew. The event began on 19th April 1967 when Series 308F, G-ANCG, was returning to Heathrow from a routine training flight after which the crew reported two defects, a faulty propeller and a leaking valve in the port undercarriage mechanism. These faults were rectified overnight, including an undercarriage retraction test successfully carried out and the aircraft declared serviceable. So, on the morning of 20th April, the aircraft loaded with cargo, 54 passengers and eleven crew, took off en route to a refuelling stop at Kuwait, and ultimately to Adelaide. This is when the trouble started. The portside undercarriage failed to retract properly and the 'Not Locked' warning light came on, the Captain then selected 'undercarriage down' and it lowered correctly and showed 'Locked Down'. He then selected 'up' and again the 'Not Locked' light came on, and it was noticed that the undercarriage doors were not completely closed. On the third attempt to retract the undercarriage, the portside bogie which was moving sluggishly fouled the main actuator, fractured the hydraulic line and all the fluid escaped, making it impossible to lock the undercarriage down by any means. The Captain therefore decided to divert to Manston and try an emergency landing on a foam carpet on the main runway. As the Britannia landed, the undercarriage collapsed and the aircraft skidded off the foam onto the surrounding grass. Nothing caught fire and all the occupants cleared the aircraft within one minute with no injuries. The aircraft was substantially damaged, however, and it was decided that it was more economical to write it off where it was and to convert one of the Series 312 aircraft, G-AOVF, to freighter configuration. G-ANCG was therefore scrapped where she ended up, at Manston.

1968 was the final year of British Eagle's existence. There had been a gradual increase in the number of Boeing

707 jet aircraft around which meant that transatlantic charter flights (like the fortnightly London to Bermuda and Nassau and the twelve weekly flights to New York and Toronto) were now being undertaken by the Boeing aircraft.

The decrease in work which these changes represented led to British Eagle selling off two Britannia 312s, G-AOVE and G-AOVR, in the autumn of 1966 to a new Spanish charter airline called Air Spain. Then, in March 1968, a new Swiss airline, Tellair, was founded with the backing of British Eagle. The expectation was that Britannias would be used and after British Eagle's subsequent collapse, two Series 324s, G-ARKA and G-ARKB, flew in Tellair livery during the 1969 season.

For the 1968 season, British Eagle still had fourteen Britannias operational. The airline had lost its MoD Far East trooping contract in March but the Britannias were still used on other Government work, with six charters to Ascension Island. The MoD service from London to Adelaide was still flown by Britannia 308F, G-ANCF, whilst emigrants to Australia were still sometimes flown by Britannias, but the main justification for the size of British Eagle's fleet was the IT charter market. Government policy had just introduced a £50 limit on the amount of currency that travellers could take abroad which obviously affected the choice of foreign destinations, and so the airline worked hard to keep a buoyant share of the IT charter market.

The 1968 summer programme was as large as ever and there were some new routes opened, such as three services per week from Heathrow to Gerona (Spain), and services from Heathrow to Athens, Istanbul, Malta, Rhodes, Tunis, Las Palmas and Tenerife. One important new contract was to fly Germans from West Berlin to various destinations including Barcelona, Palma, Pula and Rimini, as a result of which a Britannia was based in Berlin from Monday to Friday each week between April and October.

The ad hoc charter market had always been important for the Britannias and it remained so in 1968. On 19th January, a Britannia flew 103 Chinese seamen from Hong Kong to London to join their ships in Europe. On 2nd June, Britannia 324, G-ARKB, flew the Hallé Orchestra from Manchester to Montreal at the beginning of their tour of South America, then it flew them to several countries until finally returning them via Dakar to Manchester on 13th July. The Manchester United football team was flown from Manchester to Kraków on 11th March by a British Eagle 1-11 jet, while their supporters followed in a more sedate Britannia, G-AOVN, on 12th March, with the return flights on 14th March. Another football supporters' charter on 14th and 15th May involved G-AOVA, G-AOVC, G-AOVN and G-ARXA flying to Madrid, and pilgrims were flown from Manchester to Tarbes (for Lourdes) by G-AOVT and G-ARKB on 2nd August. MoD charters involved flights by G-AOVT on 10th August, Glasgow-Edinburgh-Manchester-Brawdy (Wales); by G-AOVG on 12th September, Budapest-Manchester, and by G-ARKA on 6th October, Manchester-Le Bourget.

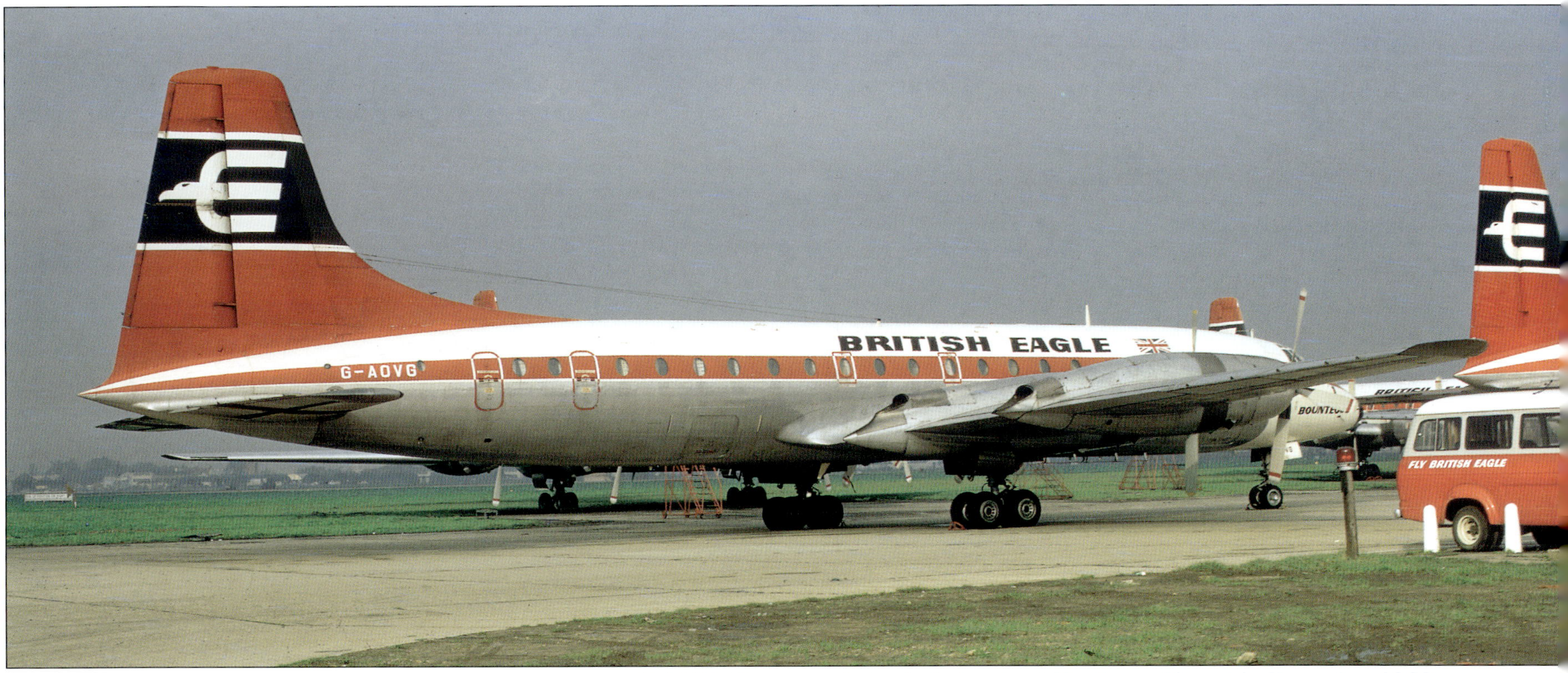

G-AOVG 'Bounteous' stands forlornly at Heathrow Airport in November 1968, in the company of other British Eagle aircraft after the demise of the airline.

But in spite of fairly healthy ad hoc charter activity, the overall commercial scene was deteriorating. The first indication of this was at the beginning of October 1968 when the company announced that its service base at Liverpool, where most of the airline maintenance took place, was to close and all work transferred to Heathrow. Another indicator was that by the end of the month, four of the Britannias (G-AOVA, G-AOVN, G-ARKA and G-ARXA) were flown to Liverpool and into storage.

Although the country's economic state suggested that the year 1968/69 would be difficult, the airline's bankers, Hambros and Kleinwort Benson, agreed on 30th October to support the operations for the next twelve months. It was then announced that the airline's IT charter licence for the London-Bermuda-Nassau route had been revoked. This meant that the banks were no longer convinced of British Eagle's ability to survive in the deteriorating cut-throat charter market so they suddenly withdrew their support. An emergency meeting of the British Eagle Board followed on 6th November and it was announced that all flying by the airline would cease from midnight that night.

The final British Eagle flight, Series 312F, G-AOVM, arrived at Heathrow on the morning of 7th November from Tel Aviv with a cargo of oranges.

It was estimated that the airline's liabilities slightly exceeded its assets, making continued trading impossible. The only way to have continued would have been to sell off some of the Britannia fleet, but no-one wanted to buy Britannias in 1968 however well maintained, as passengers wanted to fly in the faster jets. The collapse of another Britannia operator, Transglobe Airways, added to the general gloom. It was the end of one of the most prestigious chapters in British commercial aviation.

The British Eagle Board issued a statement after the company's closure, listing the reasons for the failure as "devaluation, the £50 travel restriction and the present economic situation which gave rise to a severe recession in holiday travel". Had the economic climate at the time been more favourable, the story of the British Eagle Britannias might have lasted longer than it did.

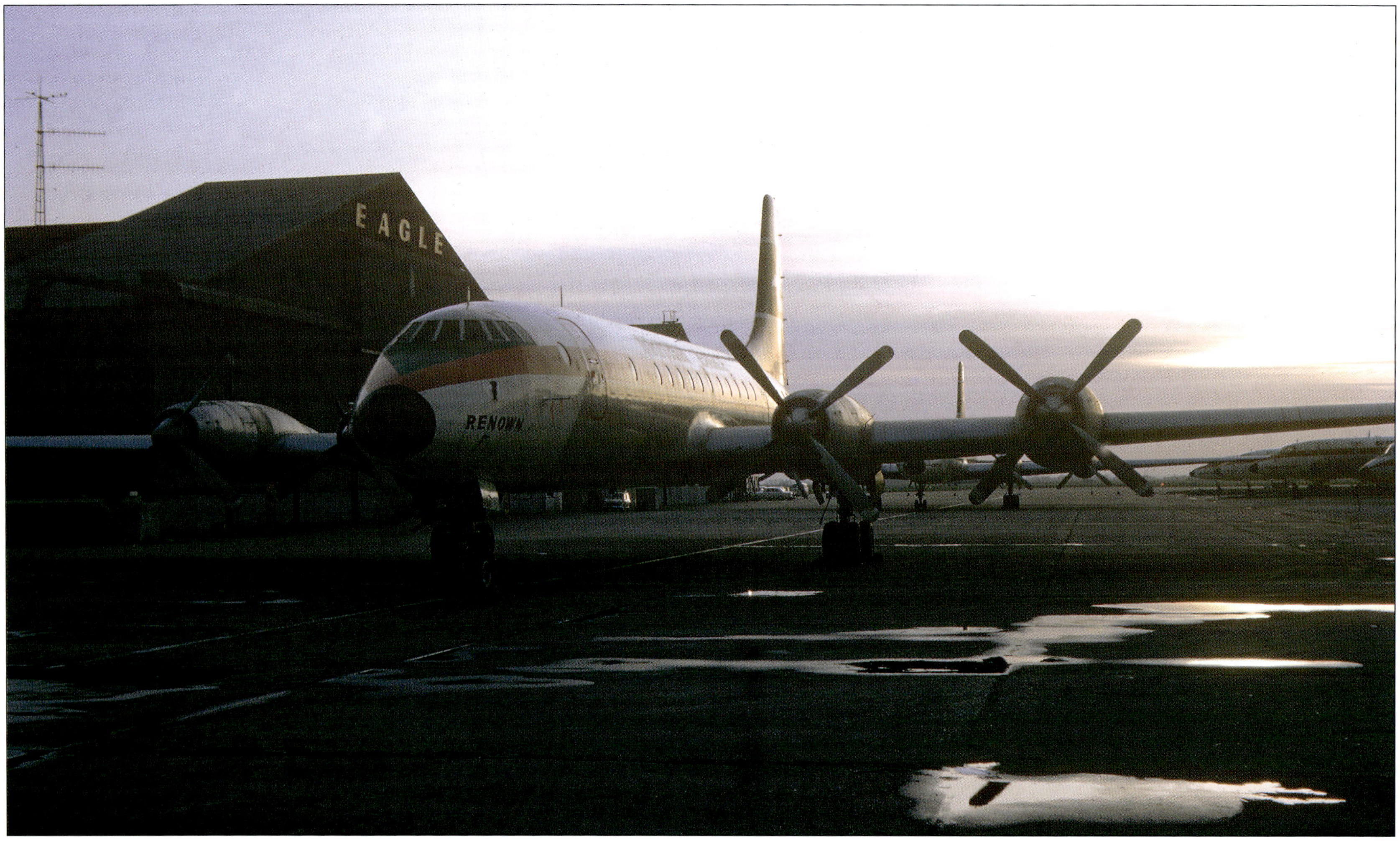

Another chapter in aviation history closed on the demise of British Eagle.
Here we see the grounded fleet at Heathrow on 23rd December 1968.

IN SERVICE WITH MONARCH AIRLINES

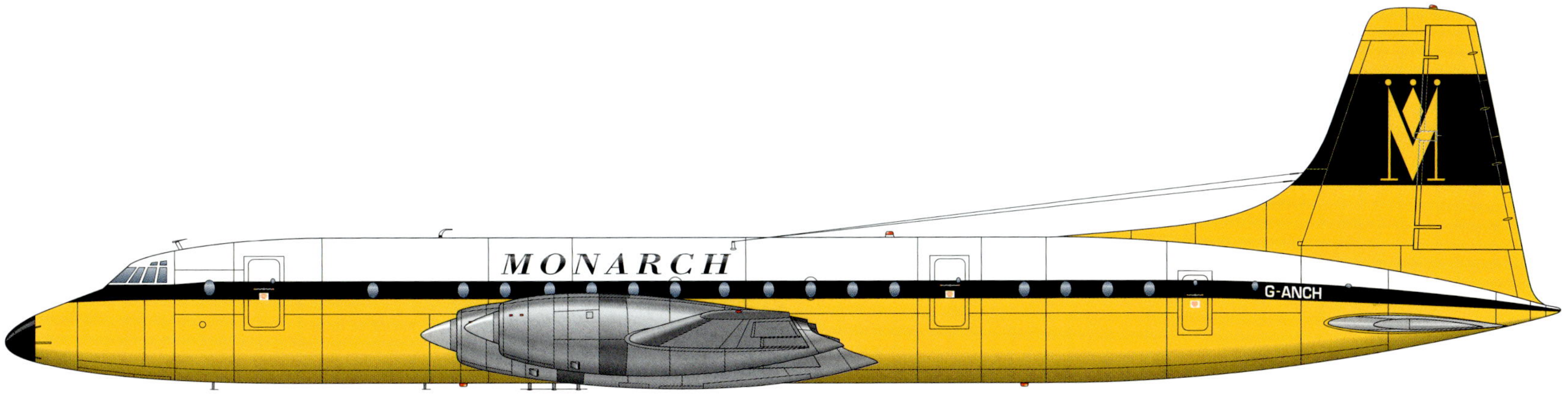

Monarch Airlines was founded in June 1967 specifically to provide IT charter transport for the British tour operator Cosmos. The founders were Don Peacock and Bill Hodgson who had left British Eagle late in 1966 to set up a maintenance organisation called Airline Engineering. Shortly after the establishment of Airline Engineering, however, Peacock and Hodgson learned that Cosmos wanted to set up its own charter holiday airline so they approached Cosmos and on 1st June 1967 Monarch Airlines was officially founded.

Don Peacock became the airline's Technical Director and Bill Hodgson the Managing Director, and the airline's base was chosen to be Luton Airport which was already a popular departure point for IT charters. The type of aircraft chosen initially for the airline was the Britannia, not surprising given the experience of the founders whilst with British Eagle.

It is somewhat ironic that Monarch Airlines' first year of operation, 1968, was British Eagle's last. Whilst British Eagle's bankers were expressing a loss of confidence in that airline with its large Britannia fleet, Monarch Airlines was starting to build up a Britannia fleet which continued to operate with Monarch for the next seven years.

At this time considerable changes were taking place in the airline industry, partly because of the increasing tendency of operators to replace turbo-prop Britannias, however immaculate, with faster flying jets such as BAC 1-11s or Boeing 707s. The result was that Britannias were coming on to the open market and Monarch bought two of these from Caledonian Airways. (Understandably, relations with British Eagle meant that their redundant Britannias were not available for Monarch to purchase). The two Britannias purchased were ex-BOAC Series 312 aircraft, G-AOVH and G-AOVI.

The first to be handed over to Monarch was G-AOVI. She was flown to Cambridge to be fitted out to Monarch's specifications and was handed over on 14th February 1968, painted in a mixture of Caledonian and Monarch livery. However she was immediately leased back to Caledonian for some three weeks of charter work ferrying Hadj pilgrims between Tehran and Jeddah. She returned from that work and arrived at Monarch's base, Luton, on 8th March where she then spent many hours in crew training as, among the eight flight crews taken on by Monarch, there was no previous experience of flying Britannias. Flight training consisted of circuits and bumps, with ILS approaches until the crews were confident about the way in which the Britannias handled in all conditions.

After this, G-AOVI returned to Caledonian to complete her Hadj contract transporting pilgrims until she finally flew back from Tehran to Gatwick on 29th March. Later that day she flew to Cambridge for her livery to be modified to the full Monarch specification. On 4th April she was collected by a Monarch air crew and flown to Luton, the first Britannia to arrive there in the full Monarch livery, fitted out with 143 passenger seats in a one-class tourist configuration.

The second Britannia, G-AOVH, was flown to Cambridge for overhaul, internal reconfiguration and re-painting on 4th April. She was delivered to Luton when finished on 20th April and then became engaged in crew training in preparation for the forthcoming summer's IT charter flights.

Monarch's revenue earning flights were therefore able to begin. In fact, on the morning of 5th April, Captain A J Berridge, Monarch's Chief Pilot, took charge of a flight from Luton to Madrid by G-AOVI with a party of Cosmos tour passengers. This was the first of many IT charter flights for Cosmos by the Britannias during the summer as well as some ad hoc charters including, on 17th April, when G-AOVI carried a planeload of passengers from Luton to Rotterdam.

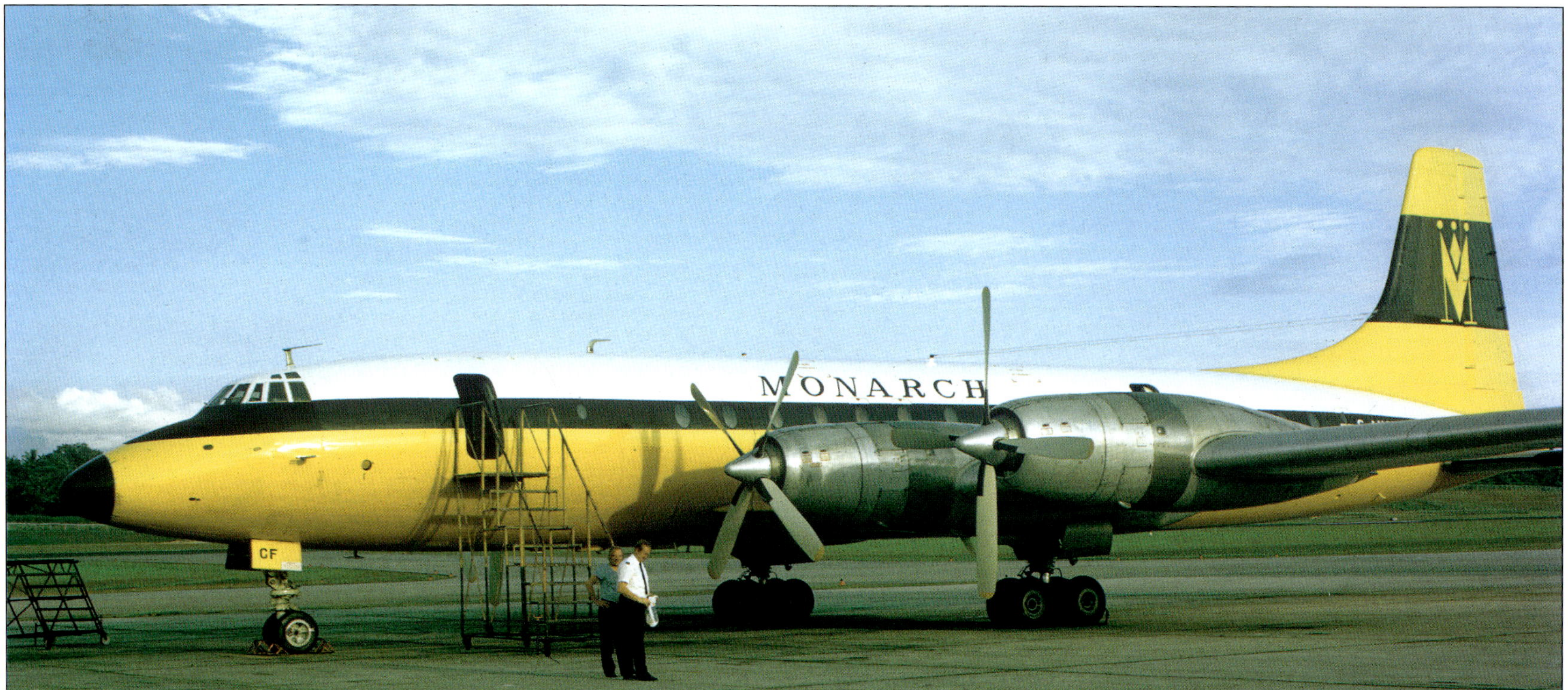

G-ANCF takes a brief rest at Singapore under the care of engineers Ginger Giblin and Wally Payne while undertaking another sector on the long journey back and forth between Adelaide (Woomera) Australia to the UK, while under contract to the Ministry of Defence.

Regular services from Luton to Basle began on 28th May with G-AOVH making the first flight. Other destinations served by the Monarch Britannias during the season included Barcelona, Bordeaux, Gerona, Ibiza, Madrid, Malaga, Milan, Palma, Perpignan, Rimini, Rome, Split, Valencia and Venice. Demand was such that several of these services were flown every week. Almost all the flights were on behalf of Cosmos and began and ended at Luton, unless the weather over Luton was bad in which case Stansted or Birmingham could be used. There were also a few ad hoc flights, with some trooping flights taking place between Luton and West German bases at Düsseldorf, Gütersloh and Hanover. On 31st May, G-AOVH flew from Gatwick to Las Palmas on behalf of BUA, and on 29th June G-AOVI flew on behalf of Channel Airways from Palma to Stansted and again on 15th October from Genoa to Stansted.

The end of summer 1968 saw an expansion of the Monarch Britannia fleet, with the first acquisition being Series 309, G-ANCH, obtained on a long-term lease from Ghana Airways. She was collected from storage in Liverpool and flown to Luton in September 1968. Serviced and re-painted in Monarch livery, she undertook her first Monarch flight on an MoD charter from Luton to Aden on 12th October.

But another factor affected the situation at this time. Although the IT charter work was diminishing with the end of the European season, some longer distance charters were becoming fashionable as people wanted to travel further in pursuit of winter sunshine. Just when Monarch was considering whether it could afford to extend its fleet came the dramatic news of the collapse of British Eagle Airways, at that stage the world's major operator of Britannia aircraft. Overnight the market was flooded with second-hand Britannias in excellent condition but at knock-down prices, not high enough to make a significant improvement to British Eagle's financial position, but low enough to represent a real bargain to Monarch with Britannia experience. Messrs Hodgson and Peacock knew the aircraft and were able to make well-judged purchases, both of functioning aircraft and as a source of spare parts.

The first of these ex-British Eagle purchases was Series 308F, G-ANCF which, having a forward freight door, was a very valuable addition to the Monarch fleet. It enabled Monarch Airlines to take over British Eagle's contract on behalf of the British Government, carrying personnel and freight out to Woomera, via Adelaide, Australia in support of rocket research being carried out there. The inaugural Monarch service began on 18th December to Darwin, via Kuwait, Bombay and Singapore. (Although this was a Monarch flight, the same aircraft had frequently flown out on the same Government mission before, in British Eagle livery!) The service was a fortnightly one, usually ending in Adelaide and G-ANCF ran it effectively for the next seven years.

The same Britannia also flew many long-range MoD journeys from Lyneham and Brize Norton to Perth and Adelaide. MoD trips were also made to Akrotiri (Cyprus), Masirah (Oman) and Gan (Maldives). The trips to Australia via the Middle East and Singapore usually ended in a return trip along the same route in reverse but, occasionally, for operational or weather reasons, the return was across the Pacific Ocean, stopping at Honolulu and then across Canada (Vancouver and Gander).

The success of this MoD work seems to have resulted in more such work being commissioned with more trooping charters starting from Edinburgh, Manchester and Teesside to British bases in West Germany, such as Berlin, Düsseldorf and Hanover and also to Gibralter.

The winter of 1968/9 saw a considerable increase in activity for Monarch. There were also new IT charter routes, to Tenerife (for sun bathers), to Munich (for skiers) and to the Far East. On Christmas Day 1968, G-AOVH was returning from a pre-Christmas charter to the Far East but unfortunately Luton Airport was indulging in Christmas festivities and was closed to incoming flights, so the Britannia had to land at Stansted instead!

In preparation for the 1969 IT charter season, Monarch purchased two more Britannia 312s from the British Eagle stock as flying aircraft, G-AOVL and G-AOVT, and another, G-AOVK, as a source of spare parts so, by early May, Monarch had six Britannias in action.

Most of the charter work for the season was for Cosmos, but there was a considerable amount of ad hoc work as well. On 15th May some 300 Italian football supporters were flown from Milan to Manchester on Monarch's Britannia G-AOVL, a Caledonian Britannia and an Itavia Dart Herald. There were also various trooping flights on 10th April, G-AOVH carried servicemen from Gütersloh to Belfast followed on 11th July when troops were carried from Gütersloh to Edinburgh. There were two trooping flights from Akrotiri to Manchester on 25th and 30th July and three flights by G-AOVL from Luton to Belfast on 23rd July, 19th and 20th August.

The 1969 summer IT season was more extensive than before and included new destinations in addition to those listed for 1968; Athens, Faro, Genoa, Mahon, Pisa, Tenerife and Tunis. With the collapse of British Eagle and the phasing out of the Caledonian Britannias, Monarch had suddenly become the world's largest operator of Britannia aircraft.

There were, as usual, charters to take pilgrims to Mecca during the Hadj festival. In addition the Britannias flew many passengers to Jeddah, from the Middle East and Africa, some of them being on behalf of Ghana Airways, originating in Accra. There were other long distance charters from Amsterdam and Rotterdam to Paramaribo in Surinam (South America) and winter charters to the Far East including at least one to Cambodia.

The level of demand for Monarch's Britannias was such that the airline purchased two more of British Eagle's 312s, G-AOVG and G-AOVN, in the autumn of 1969. There was an increasing amount of ad hoc charter work which took many different forms including, on 29th April 1970, when a ship's crew was flown from Athens to Hurn Airport, Bournemouth in order to join their ship. On 30th April and 1st May, two passenger flights went from Vienna to Manchester and on 22nd and 23rd July, while there was a dock strike, G-AOVL acted as a freighter flying goods from Belfast to Liverpool.

The 1970 summer season was increasingly busy, with all eight Britannias hard at work. While G-ANCF was heavily involved in the Government contract work to Australia, the other

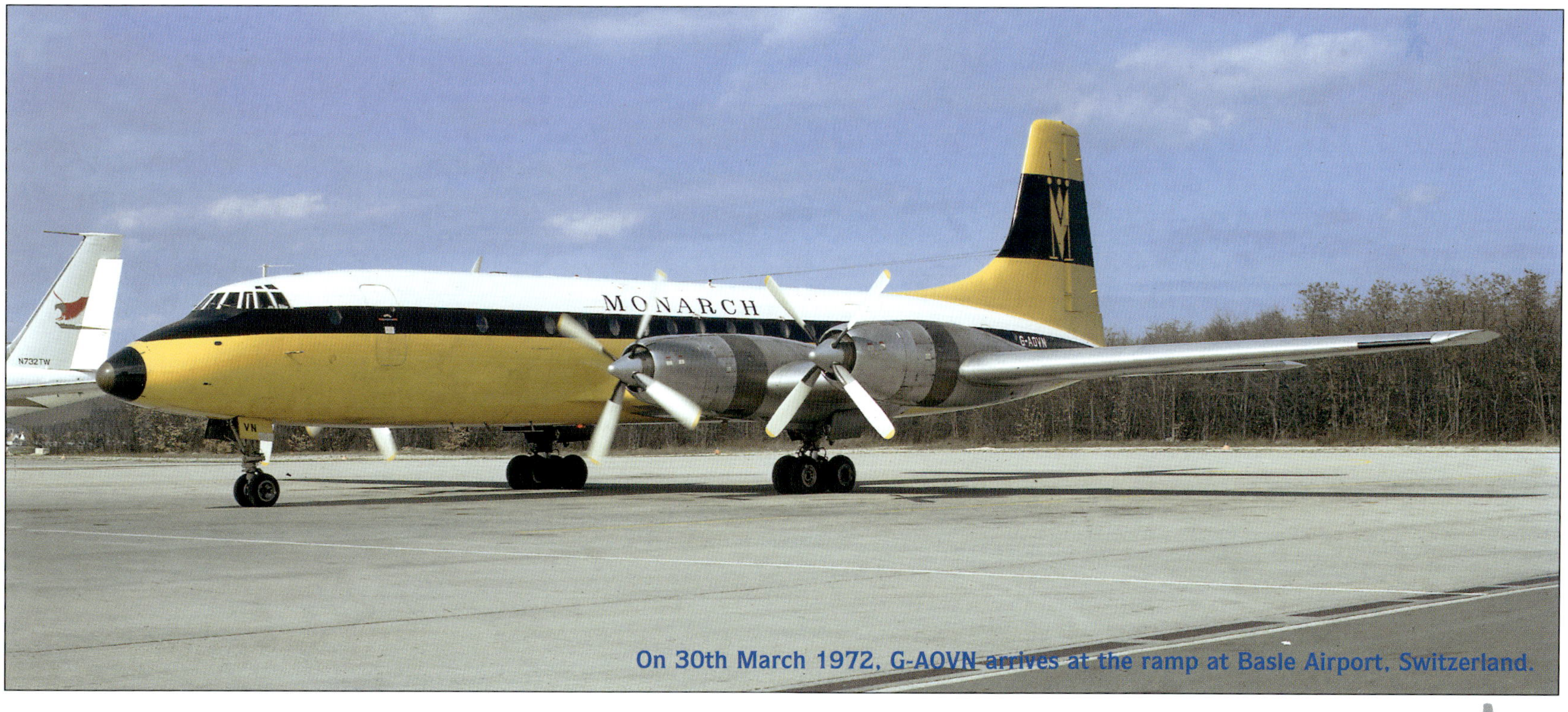

On 30th March 1972, G-AOVN arrives at the ramp at Basle Airport, Switzerland.

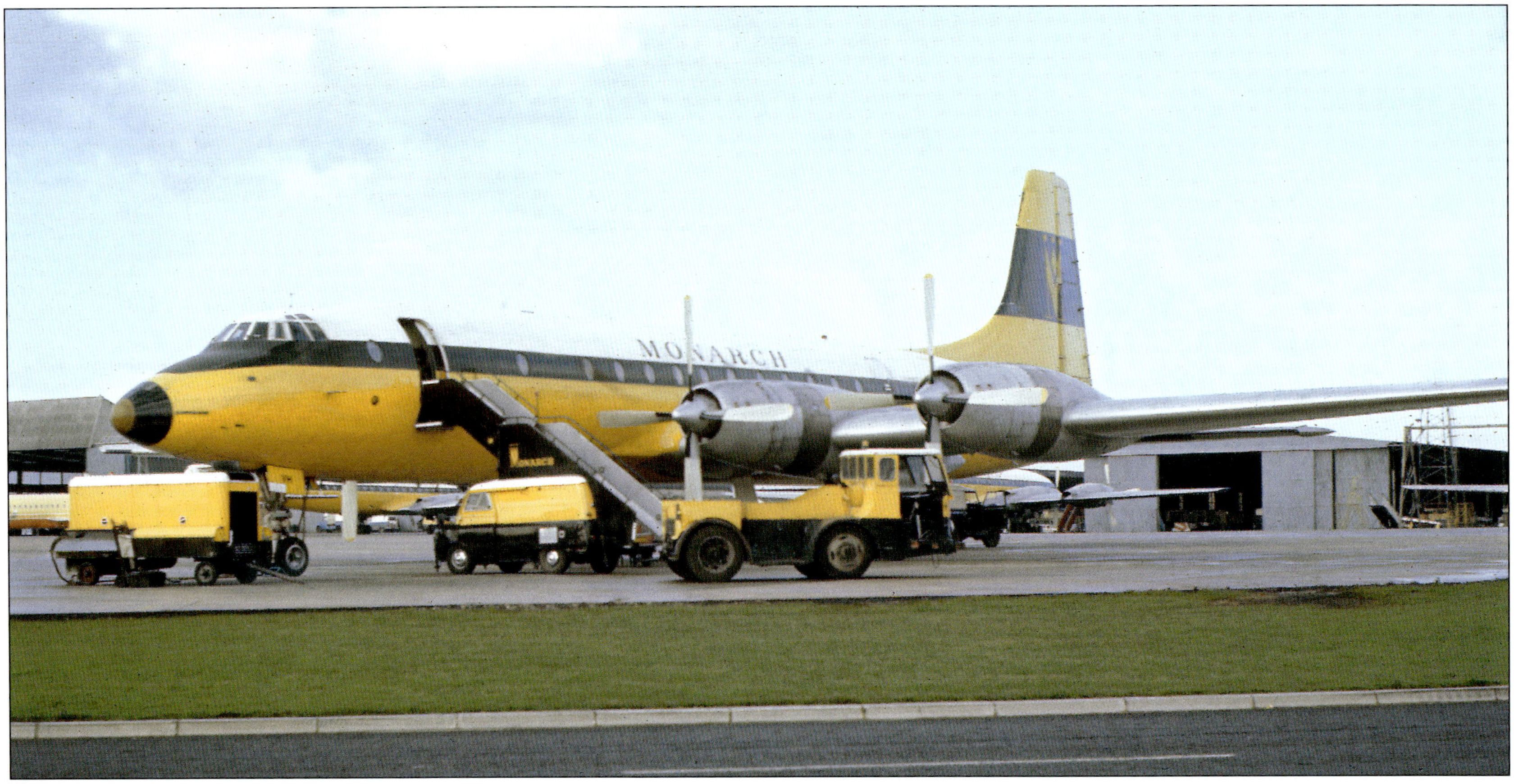

Surrounded by a variety of company vehicles, G-AOVH prepares to receive passengers for another flight to Spain.

seven Britannias carried thousands of holidaymakers on charter flights throughout Europe, the Mediterranean and North Africa.

During the 1971 season a new kind of charter contract was undertaken. Clarksons Tours, with a base in Manchester, awarded Monarch Airlines a contract to carry passengers on day-trips and short-stay trips from Manchester and Liverpool to Rotterdam (to visit the Dutch bulb fields) and to Beauvais (for three or four day visits to Paris). The first trip under this contract was on 2nd April when G-AOVH took tourists from Manchester to Beauvais, returning to Manchester that evening. Then, on 4th April, she took holidaymakers from Manchester to Palma, followed by two round trips from Manchester to Beauvais on 5th April. The first trip from Manchester to Rotterdam was flown by G-AOVH on 7th April.

Services from Liverpool began on 4th May when G-AOVH flew a day trip to Rotterdam, then the next day the first Liverpool-Beauvais flight took place. This series of flights continued until 14th May when, on that day, G-AOVI flew the final Beauvais to Manchester service and then went back to Beauvais in order to fly the final passengers, Beauvais to Liverpool for Clarksons Tours. She then returned empty to Luton. There were, however, more Clarksons Tours' passengers flown by the Monarch Britannias from Luton to Beauvais and Rotterdam during April and May. Also during the summer there were various flights from Manchester, with two to Varna (Bulgaria) on 29th May and 11th June. An MoD trooping charter on 5th June involved G-ANCH flying from Gütersloh to Manchester on 5th June and in the reverse direction on 14th August then, on 27th October, two Monarch Britannias flew pilgrims from Manchester to Tarbes for a one-night stay at the shrine at Lourdes.

1971 was the apex of activity for the Monarch Britannias. As had happened with other operators, passengers wanted faster travel so Monarch decided to re-equip with jet aircraft, choosing ex Northwest-Orient Boeing 720B-051Bs. The eight Britannias therefore were not all needed and the first to go was Series 309, G-ANCH, which had been leased from Ghana Airways. She flew her final journey for Monarch on 30th April 1972 and was then ferried to Lydd for storage. Also retired were three Series 312s, the two originals G-AOVH and G-AOVI and also G-AOVL. For the 1972 charter season, Monarch's fleet therefore comprised its remaining four Britannias, Series 308F, G-ANCF, and Series 312s, G-AOVG, G-AOVN and G-AOVT, and three newly acquired Boeing 720-051Bs. The Britannias were used on the shorter range IT charters, flying to Alicante, Barcelona, Basle, Dubrovnik, Faro, Gerona, Ibiza, Malaga, Mahon, Naples, Palma, Pisa, Pula, Rimini, Split and Venice. The 720-051Bs served the more distant destinations in North Africa and the Eastern Mediterranean.

In 1973 the same Britannia fleet received an addition when Monarch bought a Series 307F, G-ANCE, from Lloyd International. After overhaul and re-painting in Monarch livery, this aircraft entered service on 16th November. Being a freight aircraft she was used mainly on the UK-Australia service, alongside G-ANCF, until early in 1974 when she was chartered by Trans Australia Airlines to operate flood relief flights between Adelaide, Alice Springs and Darwin. Once the emergency was over, she returned to the UK and in May was purchased by the Irish airline Aer Turas.

At the end of the 1973 summer charter work, Britannia 312, G-AOVN, was withdrawn from service and her last flight was a passenger charter from Nicosia (Cyprus) to Luton on 1st November. G-AOVG continued into the New Year until her last flight from Munich to Luton on 28th January 1974, after which she was retired. This left just two Britannias in service with Monarch; Series 308F, G-ANCF (the freight aircraft involved in the UK-Australia duties) and Series 312, G-AOVT, in full passenger configuration. G-AOVT's days were also numbered because of the preference of the public for faster jets. During the 1974 season she was used mainly as a back-up aircraft to Monarch's Boeing 720Bs and BAC 1-11s but, on 9th October, she flew from Luton to Basle and returned to Luton with holidaymakers and was then retired.

However that was not the end of her story. Four days later, on 13th October, she was chartered by Northeast Airlines to take over from an unserviceable Trident at Heathrow and so she flew to Lisbon and returned that evening with a full compliment of passengers to Heathrow. The date, 13th October 1974, is the significant last date of a passenger service by a British-registered Britannia.

For most Britannias at this time, retirement was followed by scrapping, but not for G-AOVT. She was leased by Invicta International and carried out a series of freight flights to Gibralter and North Africa. Her last freight flight seems to have been in February 1975. She was then ferried first to Luton and then to Duxford where she is now owned by the Duxford Aviation Society and is on display in full Monarch livery.

The last Monarch Britannia, G-ANCF, continued with her Government contract to Australia until the end of 1975, with her final flight back from Adelaide on 18th December. She was then sold to African Safari Airways in February 1976.

So ended Monarch's experiences with Britannias. These aircraft had been responsible for building up the Airline into one of Europe's main charter companies, only made redundant by the popularity of the greater speed of jet aircraft.

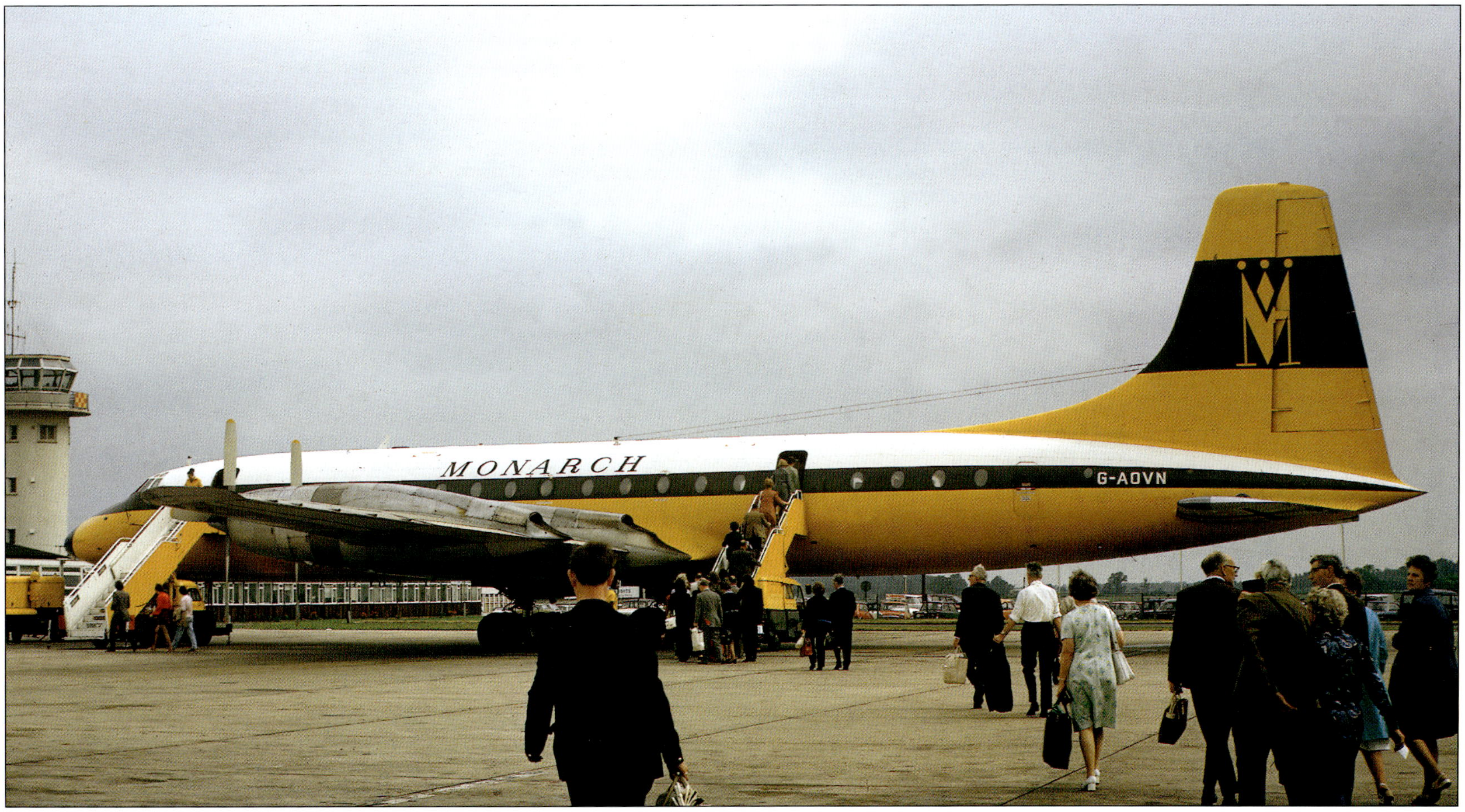

A nostalgic scene at Luton as passengers cross the tarmac to board G-AOVN for a flight to Barcelona in June 1971.

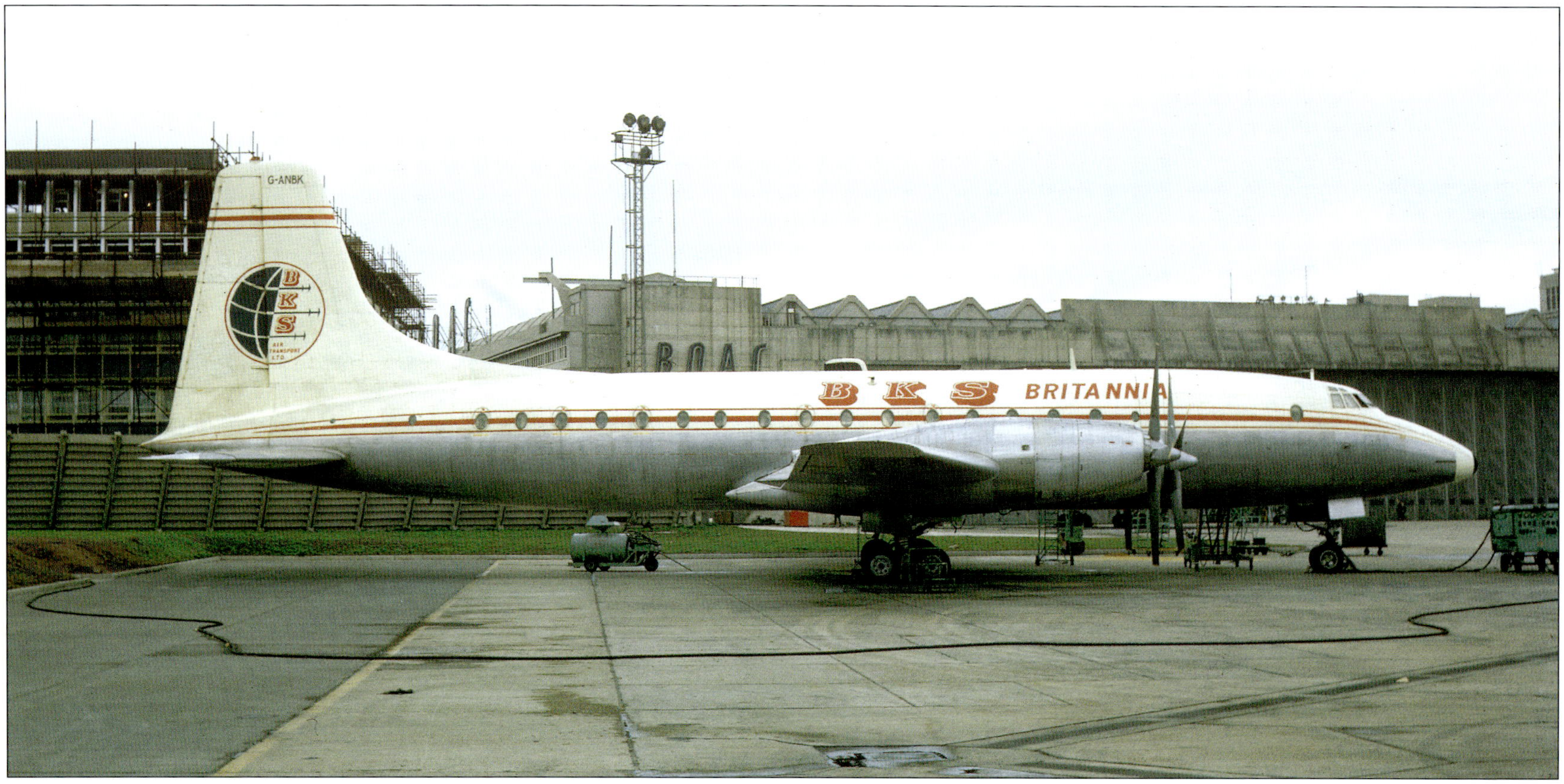

Owned by Airways Holidays and flown by BKS Air Transport on their behalf, Britannia Series 102 G-ANBK was photographed at Heathrow on 4th May 1966.

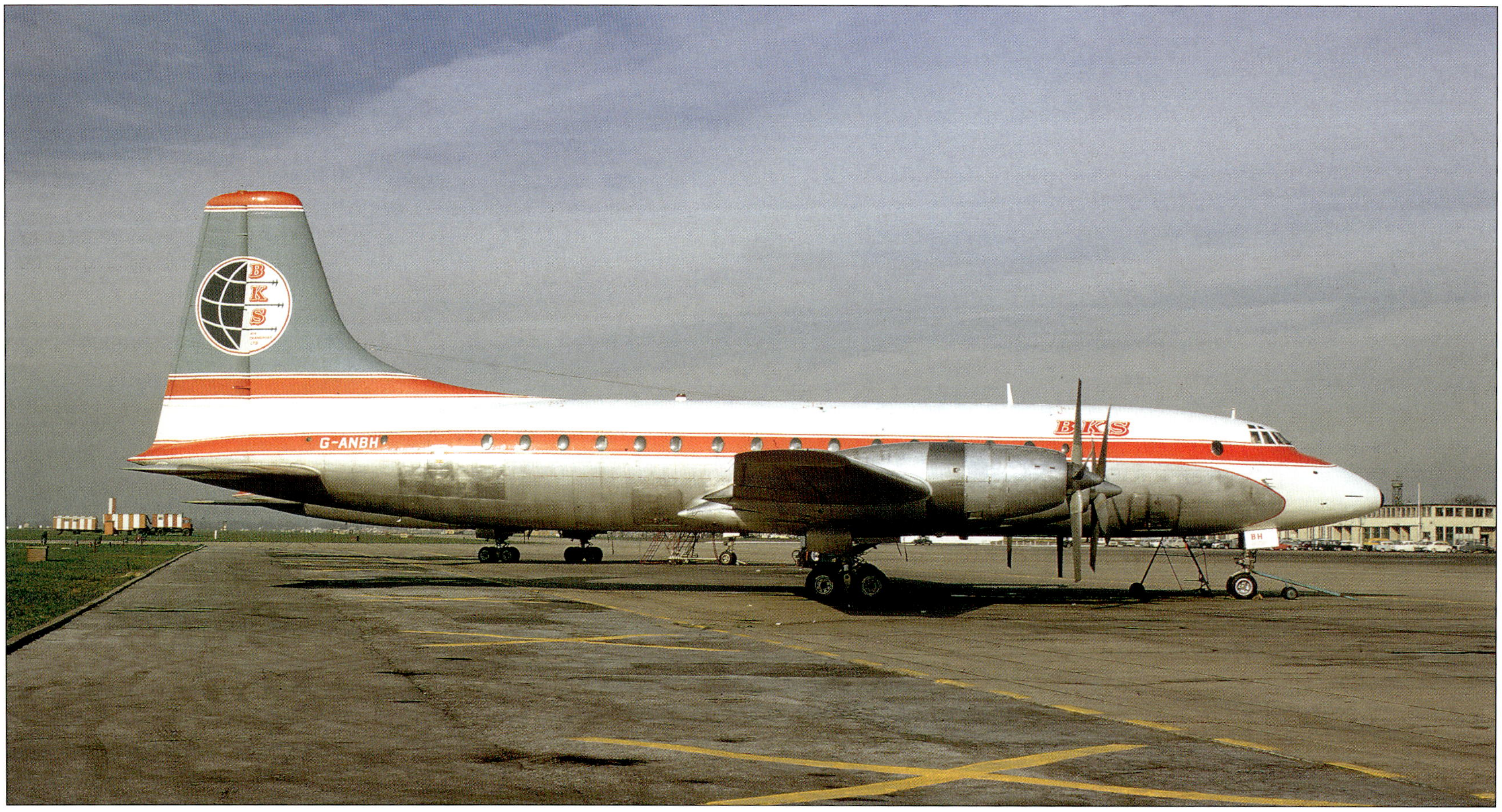

G-ANBH stands in company with sister aircraft G-ANBD on a sunny day at Heathrow Airport on 22nd March 1966.

IN SERVICE WITH B.K.S. AIR TRANSPORT LTD

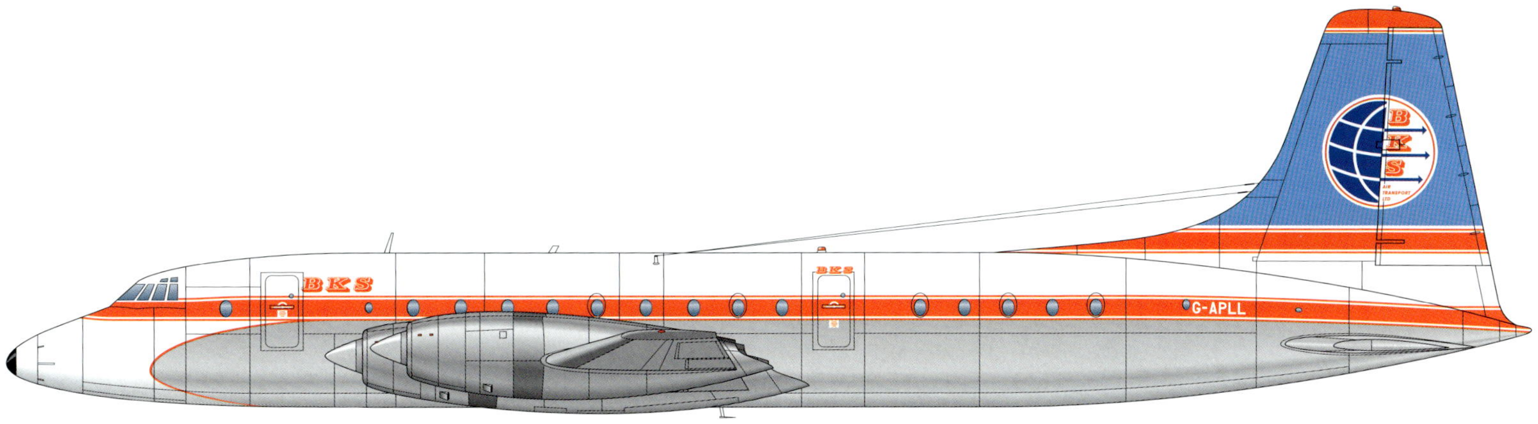

By November 1961, BOAC was attempting to sell its fleet of Britannia Series 102 aircraft even though the aircraft had seen little more than five years of service on routes to Africa and the Far East. The reason was simple and occurs throughout the Britannia's history. Competitor aircraft were becoming available, namely the Boeing 707 and the Douglas DC-8 jet aircraft and, given a straight choice, passengers preferred the faster jets. For BOAC, the Britannias therefore had to be replaced.

It was not a good time to be selling aircraft as airline profitability was at a low ebb at the end of 1961, but early in 1964 BKS arranged a lease-purchase of Series 102, G-ANBK, from BOAC. BKS Air Transport was therefore the first airline to acquire some of the ex-BOAC Britannias and after overhaul and re-painting in BKS livery, the aircraft was handed over to BKS at Heathrow on 11th April. There followed ten days of crew training (at Shannon) so that pilots, previously used to Ambassadors or Viscounts, could get used to the larger Britannia.

The first BKS Britannia service was on 24th April 1964 from the Airline's Headquarters at Newcastle to Heathrow. Subsequently the Britannia operated a service three times per day between Heathrow and Newcastle every weekday, and from early May she took over the airline's weekend services from Newcastle to Barcelona and to Rimini.

The popularity of the Britannia soon increased and the first fully laden flight from Newcastle to Heathrow was on 14th May, carrying 92 passengers and 1,858kg of freight. Both passengers and crew were enthusiastic about the new aircraft. The pattern of its use which seemed most attractive was in an all-tourist layout, accommodating up to 112 passengers, and it was in this layout that IT charters radiating out from Newcastle kept the Britannia busy during the 1964 summer season.

During the 1964/5 winter there were also other contracts. One unusual contract was a series of flights, so-called aerial cruises, to Mediterranean and North African destinations, where the Britannia and its crew would remain with the passengers throughout their holiday, visiting such places as Marrakesh, Seville and Tenerife. Such flights lasted for a week but there were other winter charters where the plane would fly passengers out to such places as Salzburg or Venice and then return to Heathrow for other business until it was time to go back and collect the previously dropped passengers.

The success of the first year of operations prompted BKS to acquire another Britannia and in March 1965 they lease-purchased another ex-BOAC Series 102, G-ANBH, delivered to Newcastle on 11th March.

During the 1965 season the BKS services expanded, with IT charter flights not only from Newcastle and Heathrow but also

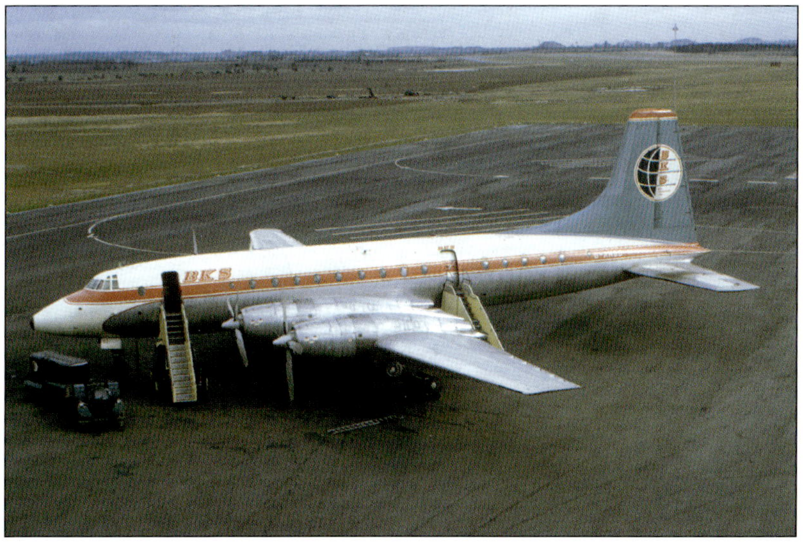

On 11th March 1968, Series 102 G-ANBD prepares to receive passengers at the aircraft's home base, Woolsington Airport, Newcastle-upon-Tyne.

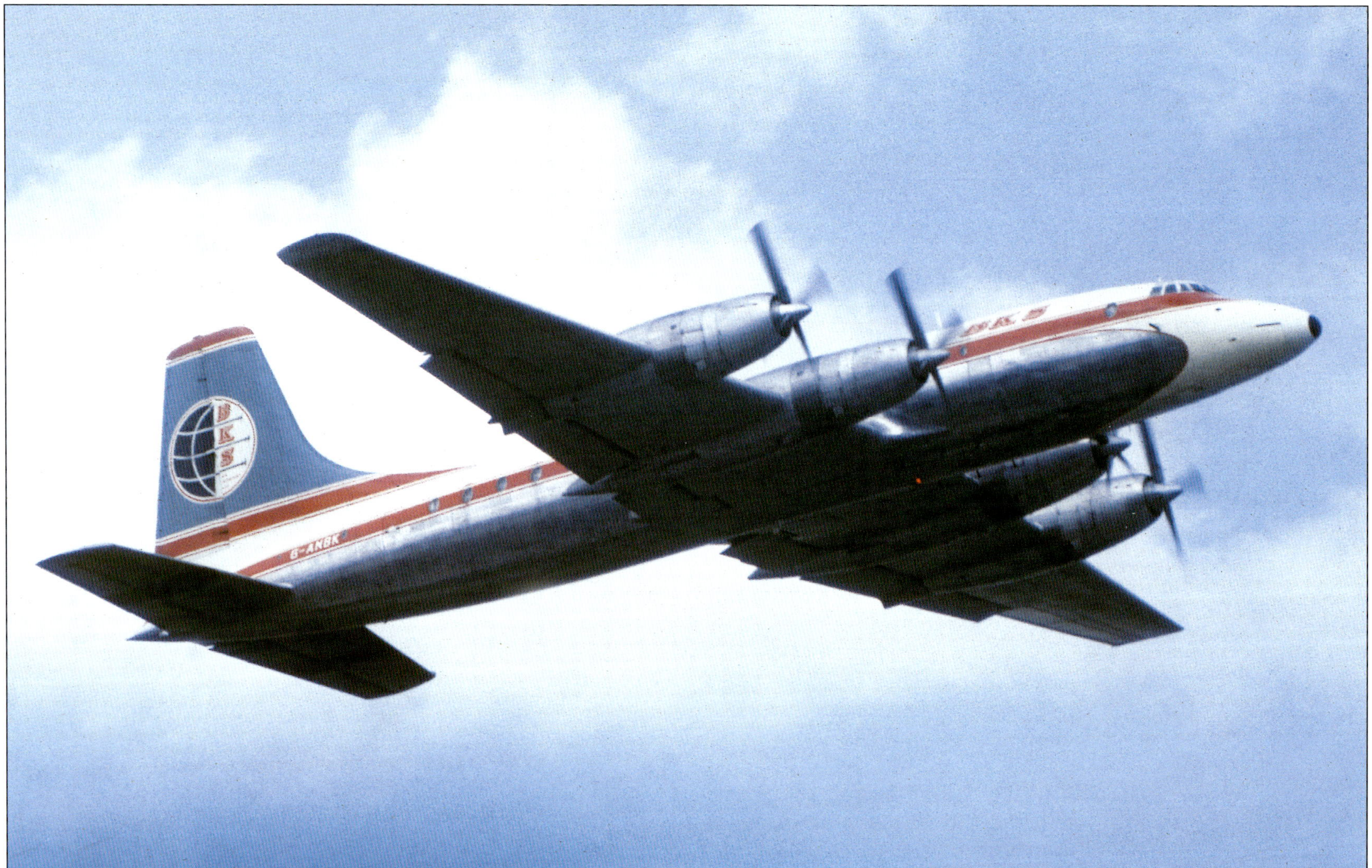

G-ANBK leaves Newcastle for another service to London Heathrow.

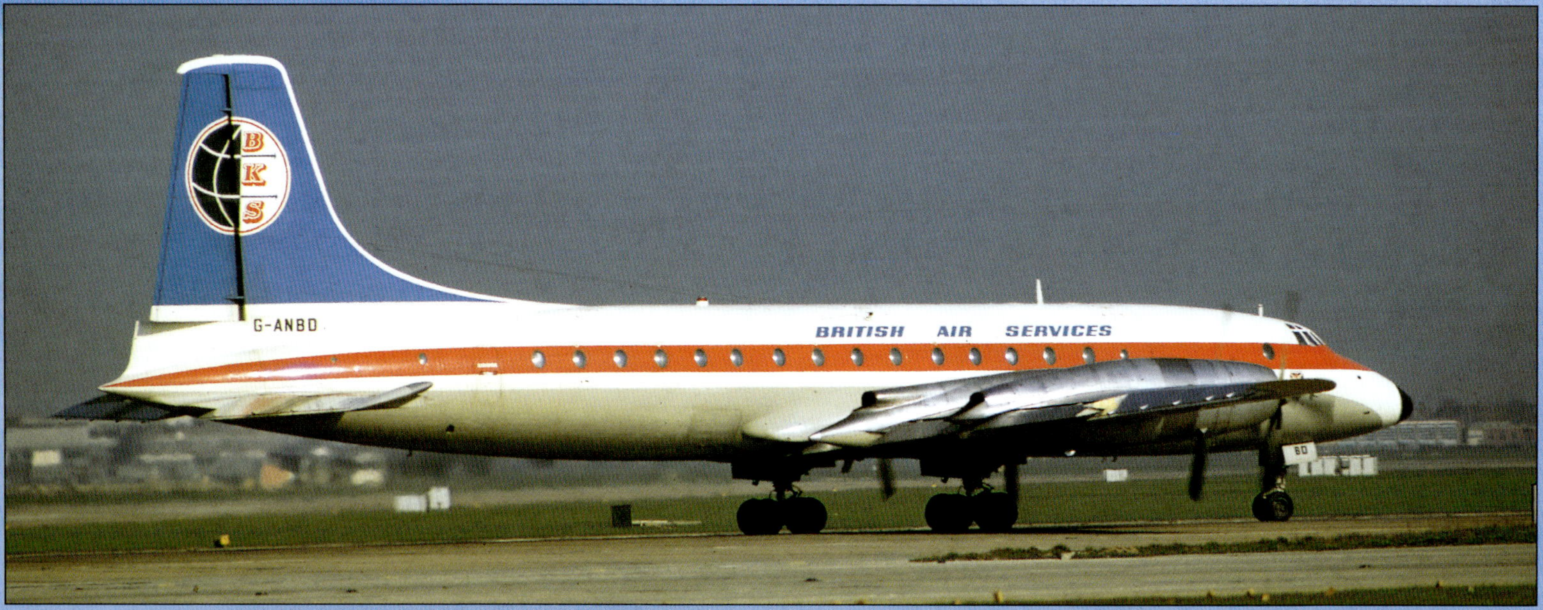

G-ANBD arrives at Heathrow sporting the latest version of the BKS livery with the British Air Services' title, on 11th February 1969.

from the newly opened Teesside. From Newcastle and Heathrow, services operated to Alicante, Dubrovnik, Genoa, Gerona, Ibiza, Ljubljana, Malaga, Pula and Salzburg whilst services linked Teesside with Barcelona, Palma and Rimini. Pilgrims flew from Newcastle to Tarbes (for Lourdes), and there was now a service five times each day between London and Newcastle, although sometimes flown by Ambassadors. A new schedule was also opened between Heathrow and Biarritz, starting on 4th June.

Another new schedule was opened between Heathrow and Teesside on 2nd November but it was only flown by Britannias when loads warranted it, usually on Monday mornings and Friday evenings. BKS would probably have closed this route at the end of 1965 but Newcastle Airport was closed to Britannias from 31st October 1965 to 1st April 1966 for runway lengthening and the building of a new passenger terminal. The Britannias therefore flew a twice-daily service between Heathrow and Teesside until the end of the year and then withdrew, leaving the service to Ambassadors and Avro HS748 aircraft.

By the end of December 1965 BKS had acquired two more of the ex-BOAC Britannia Series 102s, G-ANBD and G-APLL, by lease-purchase. G-APLL officially entered BKS service on 29th December, mainly on the Teesside-Heathrow route, and G-ANBD was given a major overhaul by Scottish Aviation Limited (S.A.L.) and then entered BKS service on 17th December. G-APLL was ferried to Prestwick for overhaul on 25th February 1966, returning on 29th March, and one of the other Britannias, G-ANBH, was also overhauled by SAL at Prestwick between mid-January and mid-February 1966. Three of the four BKS Britannias were therefore overhauled (at Prestwick) during the 1965/6 winter, during the closure of Newcastle Airport, while the only regular schedule to be kept going was the twice daily Teesside to Heathrow service and the charter work was mainly the aerial cruises.

When Newcastle Airport reopened, Britannia services from Heathrow were re-established and a new schedule, Newcastle to Jersey, was opened on 21st May 1966. Another route was also made over to Britannias when, on 1st July, Britannia G-ANBH flew from Newcastle to Belfast and from there to Edinburgh. For the rest of the summer season, Britannias flew between Belfast and Edinburgh on Mondays and Fridays because passenger loads justified it.

The BKS commitments at this time kept the four Britannias busy. The London-Newcastle route often required two aircraft each weekday, but there was also an increasing programme of IT charter work from Heathrow and Newcastle not only in the summer months but also during the winter. By the winter of 1967/8, taking tourists on skiing holidays became important, beginning on 16th December with flights from Heathrow to Turin and to Zurich, while on 17th December G-ANBK began a weekly service from Heathrow to Munich. This latter service was very popular, so much so that often on a Sunday there could be three Britannias leaving Heathrow at twenty minute intervals, taking over 300 enthusiasts to the Bavarian Alps.

The 1968 summer season for BKS required only three Britannias, so for the whole summer G-ANBD was leased to Britannia Airways beginning on 27th April and ending on 1st October. She was then ferried to Southend for storage whilst the other three Britannias maintained BKS's schedules, from Newcastle to Heathrow and Jersey and the IT charter services previously listed. There were also occasional charters for British Eagle from Heathrow and for Britannia Airways from Luton.

During 1968 however changes were afoot. In 1967 BKS became part of the British Air Services Group and in 1968 that company agreed to purchase two Trident 1E jet aircraft. These jets were faster than the Britannias, even if more noisy (nothing like the Whispering Giants!), and speed made them more popular with passengers. Two Tridents could do the work of three Britannias, so the phasing out of the Britannias became inevitable.

The next Britannia to go was G-ANBH. Her final revenue earning flight was on 25th October 1968 from Newcastle to Heathrow, and she was then ferried to Southend to join G-ANBD. This left just two Britannias, G-ANBK and G-APLL, in service until G-APLL was retired on 21st February 1969 after flying her last service from Heathrow to Newcastle.

There was, however, a temporary revival of Britannia fortunes when, on 1st February 1969, G-ANBD was returned to service, having had an overhaul and painted in British Air Services livery to match the Trident 1Es shortly to be delivered. She was put back on the London-Newcastle route but within weeks the Tridents were delivered and took over this route. They also took over most of the IT charter routes so that the two surviving Britannias were left with just off-peak schedules

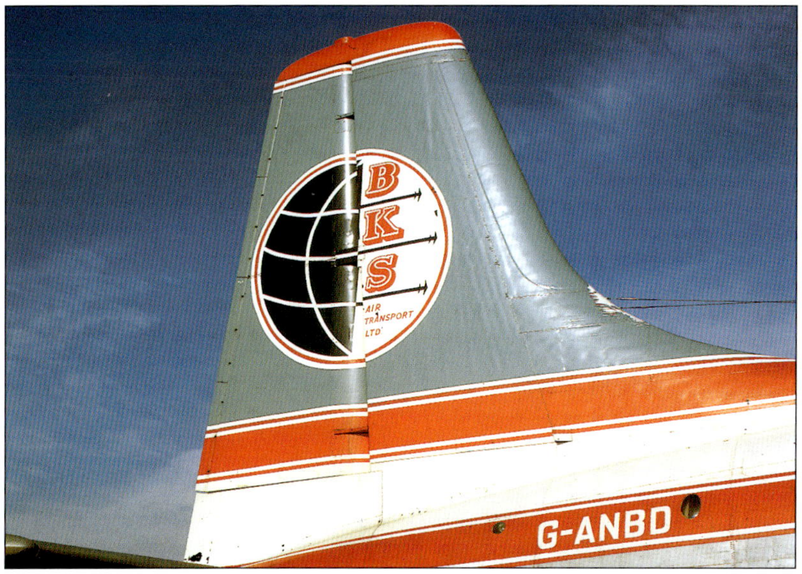

The rather stylish BKS Britannia tail logo design.

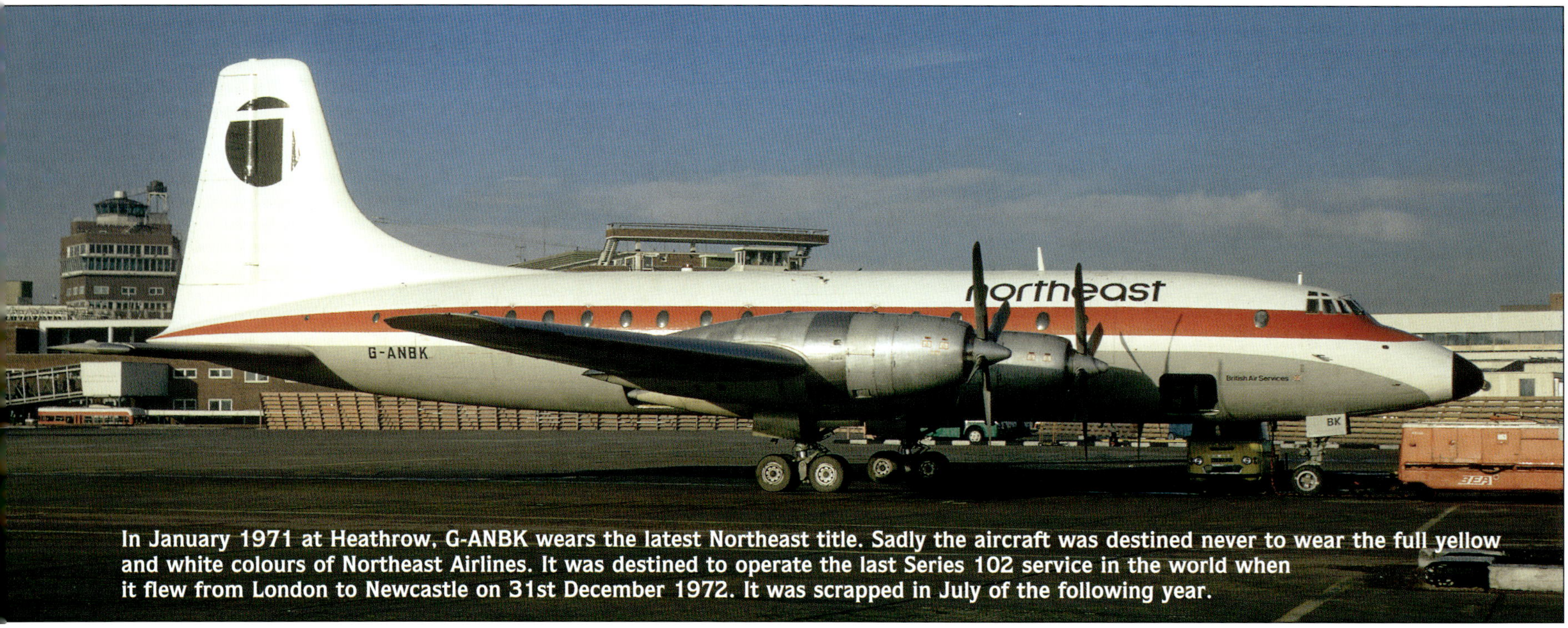

In January 1971 at Heathrow, G-ANBK wears the latest Northeast title. Sadly the aircraft was destined never to wear the full yellow and white colours of Northeast Airlines. It was destined to operate the last Series 102 service in the world when it flew from London to Newcastle on 31st December 1972. It was scrapped in July of the following year.

and less busy IT charter flights. G-ANBD continued to operate on the London-Newcastle route, with various ad hoc charters such as from Heathrow to Munich with a party of skiers until finally, on 12th January 1970, she operated the service from London to Newcastle after which she was withdrawn and scrapped.

During 1970 the last remaining Britannia, G-ANBK, was given an overhaul and re-entered service on 16th December, but with a new label and livery as, on 1st November 1970, the airline had changed its name to Northeast Airlines. G-ANBK was given a hybrid livery, somewhere between the BKS original and the new Northeast one. It was not fully the new one, it was unique.

For the following year she performed reliably, acting as a back-up to the Tridents. She was the last Britannia Series 102 in passenger service and when, on 31st December 1971, she was retired from service it was the end of an era. It ended the operational career of the Britannia 102s in world airline service. G-ANBK was subsequently offered for sale but no buyers were found and she was therefore scrapped.

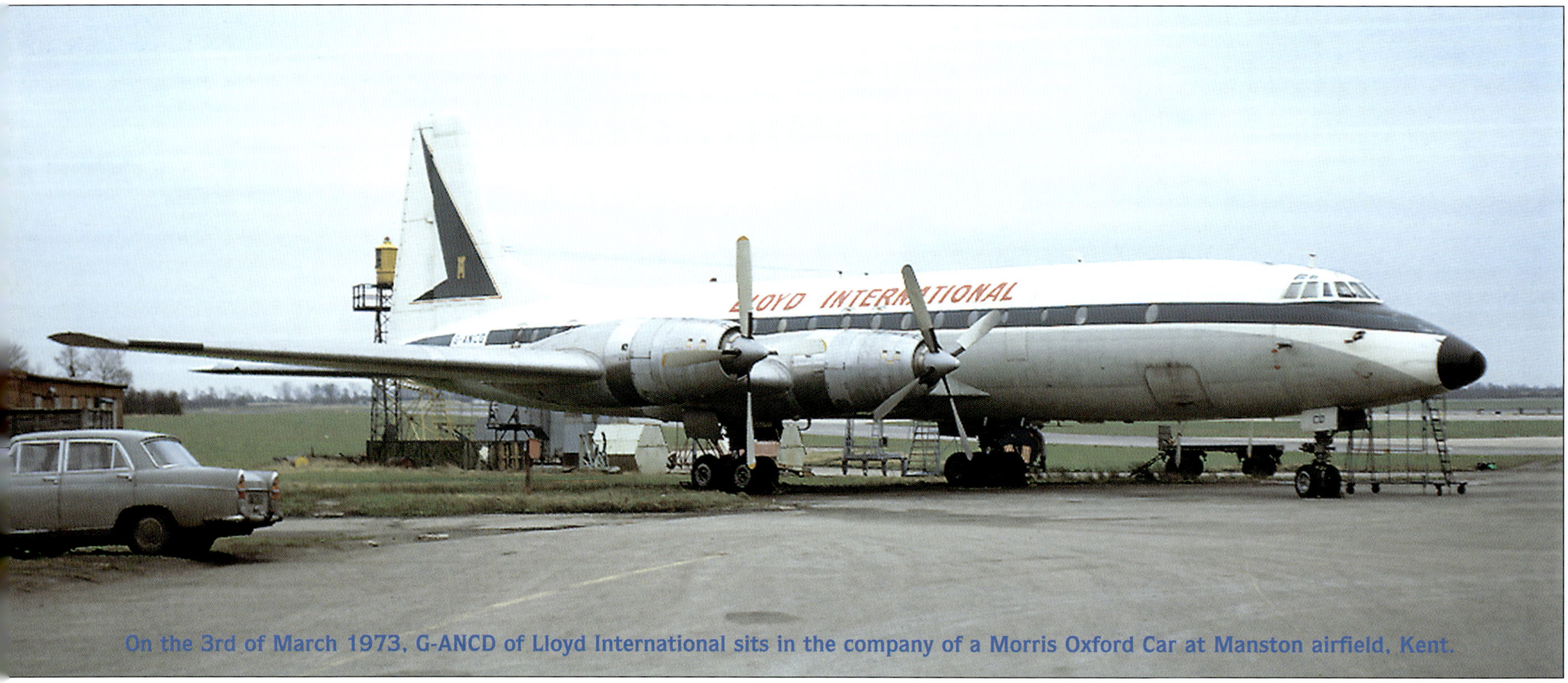

On the 3rd of March 1973, G-ANCD of Lloyd International sits in the company of a Morris Oxford Car at Manston airfield, Kent.

IN SERVICE WITH LLOYD INTERNATIONAL AIRWAYS

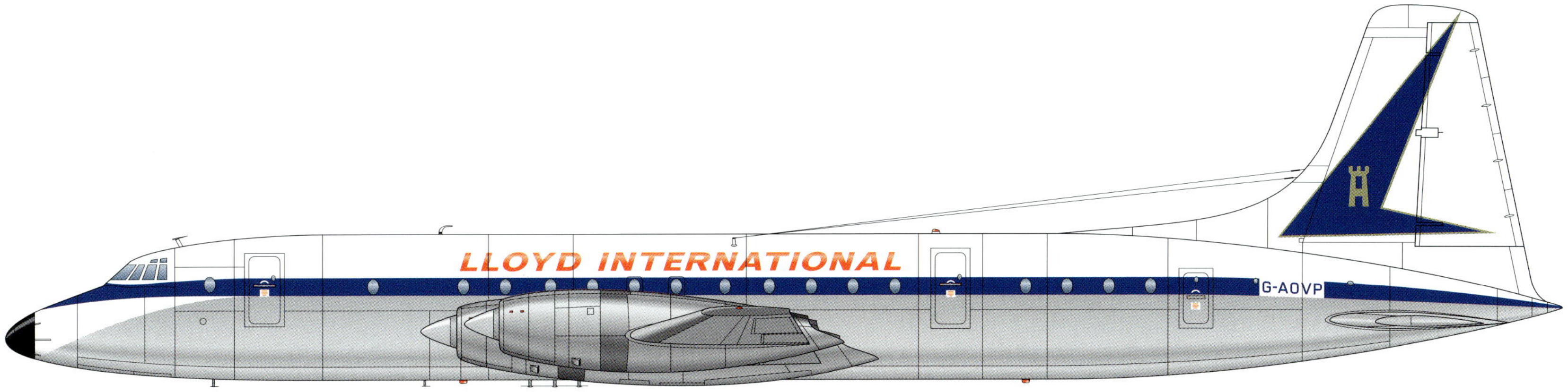

Lloyd International Airways was founded in January 1961 by two ship-broking partners, Brian Lloyd and Alastair Macleod, as a low-cost airline linking the UK with the Far East and carrying ships' crews and cargo. It developed into a busy cargo haulier, chartered by several of the world's major airlines.

Service began with the airline using a Douglas C-54 Skymaster followed by three more and a DC-6C. It soon acquired a reputation as a reliable operator, based at Gatwick, with work on long-haul services to the Far East, MoD work to various locations and some IT holiday charters to European destinations, usually from Glasgow.

The work level justified the purchase of more aircraft and in January 1965 Lloyd International lease-purchased two ex-BOAC Britannia 312s, G-AOVP and G-AOVS. The first Britannia actually delivered was G-AOVP, on 15th April. She was then handed over to Aviation Traders for overhaul, test flown on 17th June, then flown to Shannon for a spell of intensive crew training.

Her first revenue earning service began on 2nd July when she took a passenger charter flight from Stansted to Santa Maria (Azores). Where she flew on to is obscure, but it seems likely to have been Central or South America. She returned to the UK on 8th July, landing at Lloyd's base at Gatwick, then on the afternoon of 9th July she flew to Glasgow and next day began a series of IT charter flights on behalf of Mercury Air Holdings. Mercury had previously used Lloyd's DC-6 and Skymaster aircraft but during the early part of 1965, the work had been given to Britannia Airways who used their Series 102 Britannias. The arrival of G-AOVP at Glasgow meant that Lloyd got this work back. On 10th July she took off with a party of holidaymakers for Palma, then returned to Glasgow and late that night flew another party to Valencia. The following day she took more Mercury holidaymakers to Barcelona and Rimini.

This burst of activity was, however, the only work done by Lloyd in Scotland during 1965. Immediately after this, on the morning of 12th July, G-AOVP returned to Gatwick and departed that evening for the Far East, with a first re-fuelling stop at Istanbul. It was the first of many charter flights, to Bangkok, Bombay, Hong Kong, Kuala Lumpur and Singapore, and these long-distance flights involved re-fuelling stops at such places as Baghdad, Bahrain, Damascus and Karachi as well as Istanbul.

In addition there were regular sub-charters for British Eagle from Heathrow and for British United and Caledonian from Gatwick. Trek Airways also sub-chartered G-AOVP on 28th August for a flight from Luxembourg to Johannesburg.

Charters to the Far East continued, with ships' spare parts and crews frequently making up full loads as well as some strange cargoes brought westwards. In the weeks leading up to Christmas 1965, G-AOVP flew many tons of oriental dolls from Hong Kong to Gatwick, then shortly before Christmas there was suddenly a demand for work from an unusual quarter. Rhodesia, as it was then called, declared independence from Britain, with serious consequences for land-locked Zambia as indicated elsewhere. Two RAF Britannias began flying full oil drums between Dar-es-Salaam (Tanzania) and Lusaka (Zambia) and on 31st December Lloyd's G-AOVP began doing the same. When fully loaded, a Britannia could carry fifty-five 44-gallon oil drums, a cumbersome load but well within the aircraft's capacity. G-AOVP continued with this oil ferrying until 4th May 1966, when she returned to Gatwick via Benina for an overhaul before the busy summer season based in the UK.

The second of Lloyd's Britannias, G-AOVS, was delivered to Aviation Traders for overhaul in July 1965 and returned to Lloyd's at Stansted on 17th August. She was immediately leased to British Eagle with whom she remained until 1st December, when she was delivered to Aviation Traders at Stansted for conversion to Series 312F standard.

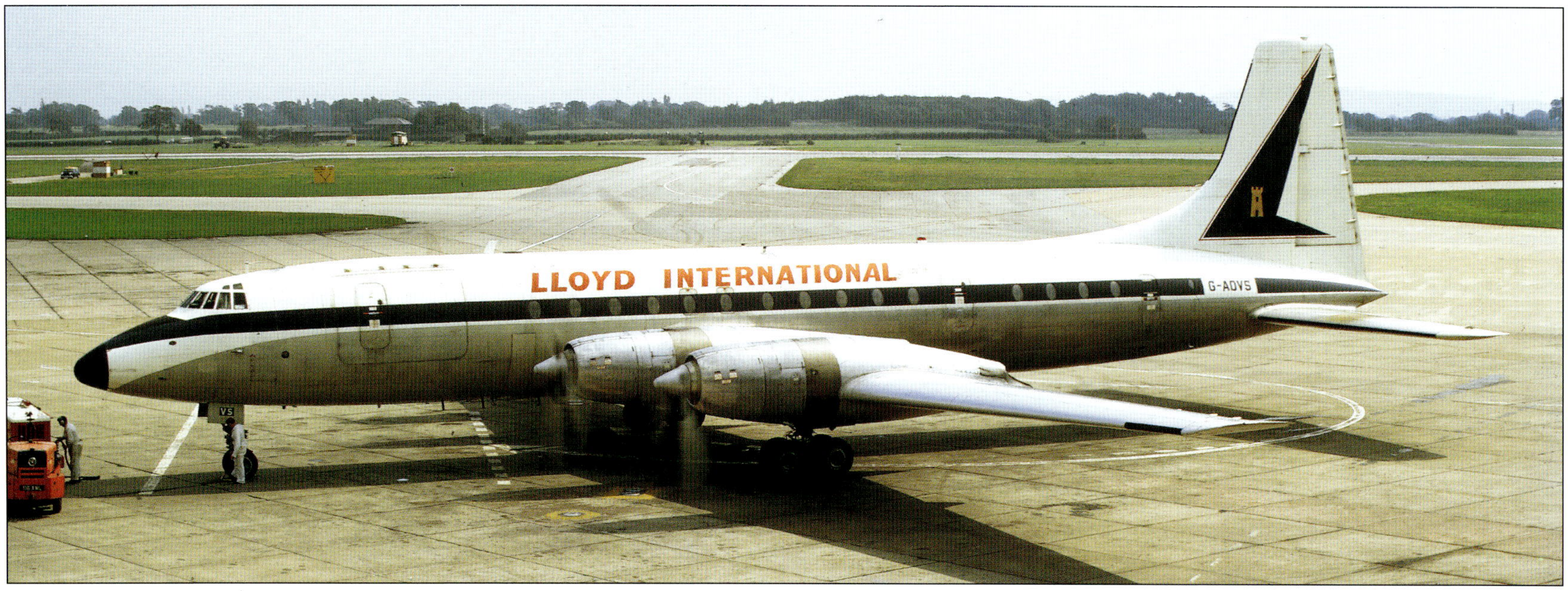

G-AOVS prepares to taxi to the runway for take-off, on the start of another holiday flight from Manchester on 8th August 1970.

This conversion was somewhat similar to that done on British United's Britannia 307, G-ANCE. A large panel on the forward port side of the fuselage was removed and replaced by a new section including an upwardly hinged door. The door used here was 79in high and 123in long (somewhat larger than the door fitted to the RAF and British Eagle converted Britannias, 72in by 88in). The cabin floor was also strengthened to take larger cargo loads. Once converted, the 312F Britannias could accommodate up to 132 passengers in a one-class tourist layout or up to eight standard freight pallets, or an appropriate combination of the two. The total payload could be eighteen tons.

The conversion of G-AOVS took somewhat longer than expected, but after flight testing she entered Lloyd service on 14th June, flying cargo from Liverpool to Belfast during a national seamen's strike. By then the 1966 season was well under way. An IT charter was flown by G-AOVP on behalf of Transglobe on 15th May, then the next day she began an extensive series of IT charter flights on behalf of a West German travel agent, from Berlin to several European and Mediterranean resorts. This charter programme required weekday flights which enabled the same aircraft to fly Scottish holidaymakers at weekends from Glasgow to Mediterranean destinations on behalf of Mercury Air Holidays. This Mercury commitment began on 21st May with a flight from Glasgow to Palma, and routes were then opened to Venice (28th May), to Rimini (4th June), Valencia (5th June) and Ostend (3rd July).

As soon as she was available G-AOVS was put to work, as the continuing seamen's strike created the need for a lot of cargo to be air-lifted. Having loaded freight in Belfast, she flew on to Glasgow and the next day (15th June) completed four trips to Belfast delivering freight each time. On 16th she flew another freight trip to Belfast and then flew on to Heathrow. During the early part of July, both Britannias made several other freight flights between Glasgow and Belfast.

There were also some long distance charters. On 9th July G-AOVS flew from Gatwick to Lagos on behalf of BUA then, on 10th July, she flew from Gatwick to Seville on behalf of Caledonian. On 14th July, G-AOVP flew from Gatwick to Lagos for BUA.

During the autumn, Lloyd International transferred its operations base from Gatwick to Stansted as this made it easier to keep contact with Aviation Traders who did all the airline's maintenance and also had a base at Stansted. By September, most of Lloyd's flying began from Stansted, although charters sometimes required passengers or freight to be picked up from Gatwick.

Lloyd's plan had been to convert G-AOVP to freighter configuration during the winter of 1966/7, but so much work was available that it was decided to fly the Britannias as they were throughout the winter and do the conversion later. One interesting task was to bring the British polo team's ponies from Argentina to the UK in December 1966, and G-AOVS left Stansted for Buenos Aires re-fuelling in the Cape Verde Islands on 9th December. The 'cargo' consisted of 26 ponies accompanied by Lord Beresford and seven grooms, and the flight back was in three stages ending with a touchdown at Gatwick on 15th December. The next day, G-AOVS flew with cargo from Stansted to the Far East via Baghdad, returning to Stansted on 19th December.

Lloyd's other Britannia, G-AOVP, was kept busy throughout the winter with charter flights, mainly with Dutch charters from Amsterdam to the Antilles (Caribbean) and Indonesia. This was important for the company because on 20th December G-AOVS suffered a nose-wheel collapse when taxiing for take-off, and the consequential damage to the aircraft took nearly two months to repair. So, for the early part of 1967, G-AOVP was the only operational Britannia which Lloyd had.

The return of the repaired G-AOVS to service sent her on a charter from Manchester to Bucharest on 1st March. Thereafter, until the end of the summer season, both Britannias were kept busy with the IT charter work mainly done by G-AOVP while the long distance charter work was given to G-AOVS, which had the freight capacity. Because of the amount of work available, Lloyd was not keen to withdraw G-AOVP from service for the cargo door conversion. Conveniently however, Mercury Air Holidays was forming its own airline, Donaldson International, and in the process it allowed Lloyd to lease its first aircraft, an ex-British United Britannia 317, G-APNA. This lease lasted for eighteen months from 2nd October, ending with the aircraft's return to Donaldson after overhaul on 5th May 1969.

G-AOVP was withdrawn from service on 21st November 1967 for freight conversion and returned on 8th April 1968. At the beginning of the 1968 summer, Lloyd therefore had three Britannias available, although between 7th April and 25th May G-APNA was overhauled in preparation for the summer IT charter work. The IT programme provided a very busy time for the trio. For example, on 14th June all three left Stansted; G-AOVS for Toronto at 0107 hours, G-APNA for Glasgow at 0334 hours and G-AOVP also for Glasgow at 0403 hours. The following day they all began in Glasgow. G-AOVS left for Helsinki just before 0900 hours(she was on a charter from Toronto to Helsinki and had made a re-fuelling stop at Glasgow), G-AOVP left for Palma at 1100 and G-APNA also left for Palma shortly after.

A pattern of activity was beginning to emerge during the 1968 summer season. Lloyd no longer continued the charter to fly German tourists from Berlin to Mediterranean resorts as this had been transferred to Channel Airways with their new Trident jets. Passengers wanted the faster jet travel, but what Lloyd could offer was the use of Britannia freighters which kept them busy, picking up charter work on scheduled services.

Airlines using them included BEA, El Al and East African Airways. In particular G-AOVS was chartered by El Al for freight work from 24th September onwards, flying regularly between Tel Aviv and Amsterdam, Frankfurt, Heathrow, New York or Paris. In fact, by the end of the year El Al became a regular client of Lloyd.

Lloyd had to hand G-APNA back to Donaldson International by May 1969 but the amount of ad hoc freight work which they could acquire made Lloyd keen to purchase more suitable aircraft. With the contraction of demand for Britannias by British United, two of their Britannias, Series 307Fs, G-ANCD and G-ANCE, were available and Lloyd quickly bought them.

G-ANCD was overhauled and entered service with Lloyd on 16th February, flying a passenger charter on behalf of Monarch Airlines from Luton to Malaga. G-ANCE, after her overhaul, flew her first flight for Lloyd on 1st March. When G-APNA had gone back to Donaldson at the beginning of May, Lloyd's fleet was therefore four Britannias, all having had the freight carrying conversion. Although there remained a little shorter range IT charter work to pick up, the majority of their work from now on was freight charter work.

Lloyd had a regular charter commitment to fly defence equipment from Hurn (Bournemouth) to Dhahran (Saudi Arabia), which began on 6th April 1969 and ended on 8th

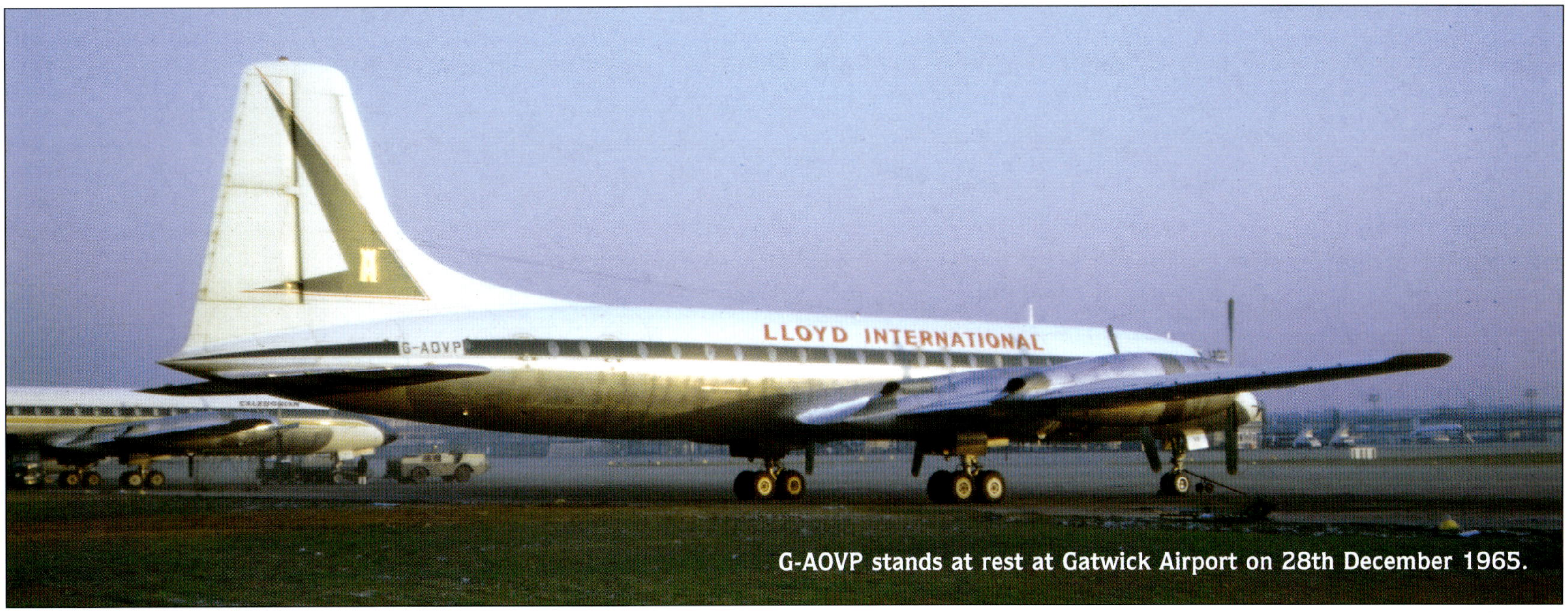

G-AOVP stands at rest at Gatwick Airport on 28th December 1965.

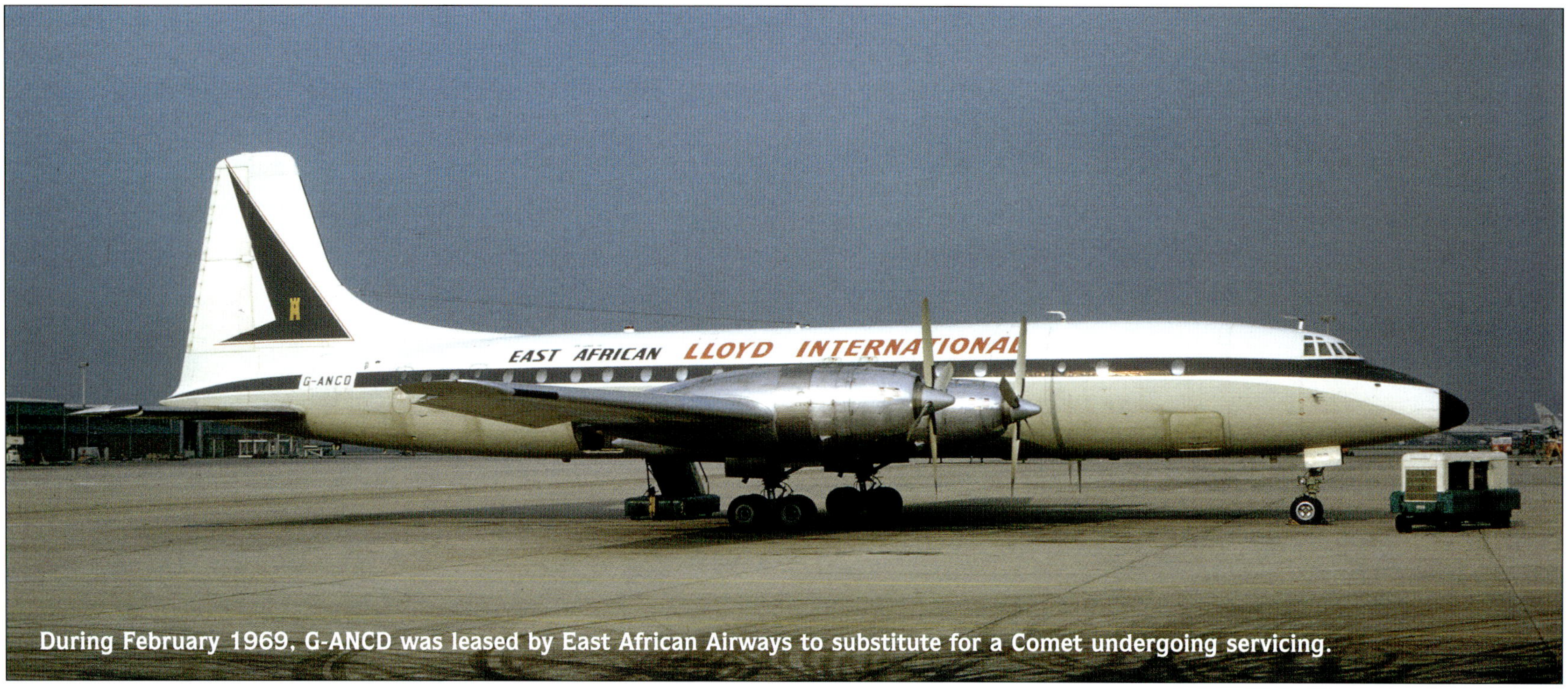

During February 1969, G-ANCD was leased by East African Airways to substitute for a Comet undergoing servicing.

November using both G-ANCD and G-AOVP. Similar cargoes, including defence equipment, industrial machinery and consumer goods, were flown from Stansted to Abadan, Abu Dhabi, Beirut, Cairo, Dhahran, Jeddah, Riyadh and Tehran. There were still other MoD charters and, on 20th July, G-AOVS flew 116 passengers from Prestwick via Gander to Cocoa (Florida), returning the next day to Stansted then immediately flying to Lyneham for a charter to Singapore.

In November 1969 Aviation Traders won a contract to convert several BEA Vanguard aircraft to a Merchantman configuration, somewhat similar to the Britannia freight conversion. While this conversion was going on, BEA leased one of the Lloyd Britannias to do some international freight work and G-ANCE began, on 8th November, with a flight from Heathrow to Frankfurt and back to Manchester before returning to Heathrow. Subsequent freight flights (in which both G-ANCE and G-AOVS took part) linked Heathrow with Amsterdam, Belfast, Frankfurt, Glasgow, Manchester, Milan, Paris and Stockholm. This work continued into the summer of 1970.

During the 1970 summer, G-ANCD was almost continuously engaged in freight service from Stansted via Rotterdam, Maastricht or Istanbul to the Far East. G-AOVS was largely used for BEA freight services whilst G-AOVP worked for El Al out of Tel Aviv. G-ANCE was elusive, but on 26th July she flew a charter from Stansted to Warsaw and on 29th August she re-fuelled at Stansted en route from New York to Turin.

Changes took place in October. G-AOVS ended a spell of work for El Al on 1st October and started a new assignment with BEA on 4th October, resuming El Al work on 30th November. G-AOVP ended a spell of work with BEA on 4th October, was overhauled and then on 3rd November took up a new assignment with El Al. In the New Year, East African Airways signed an agreement to lease a Lloyd's Britannia to operate a scheduled freight service linking Heathrow with Dar-es-Salaam, Entebbe, Lusaka and Nairobi. The service was actually inaugurated by G-ANCD on 28th January 1971, returning via Cairo to Stansted on 31st January. Thereafter Lloyd maintained a weekly service over this route.

G-AOVP's lease with El Al ended on 30th April and G-AOVS also returned to Lloyd's control on 16th May. El Al however used the services of G-ANCD out of Frankfurt on 19th May while East African Airways used G-AOVP on 20th May and G-ANCE on 27th May. BEA also continued to charter Lloyd's Britannias from time to time and by the end of the year the three freighter aircraft were still in service, G-ANCD with East African Airways, and G-AOVP and G-AOVS with El Al.

However the level of utilisation was decreasing with the Far East work much reduced. As a consequence Lloyd International's parent company, Lloyd Aviation Holdings, called in a receiver for the airline on 16th June 1972, and all its flying therefore ceased. So ended the story of the airline that pioneered the use of Britannias for cargo charter work. To some the closure of the airline seemed premature, but the increasing availability of Boeing 707s in passenger and cargo configurations meant that the Britannias were becoming less attractive and had less earning power than the Boeings. They had done a good job for Lloyd, and Lloyd Aviation Holdings felt that the time had now come to move on. It is worth noting, however, that all four Britannias were sold on to other operators for whom they worked for several more years.

IN SERVICE WITH DONALDSON INTERNATIONAL AIRWAYS

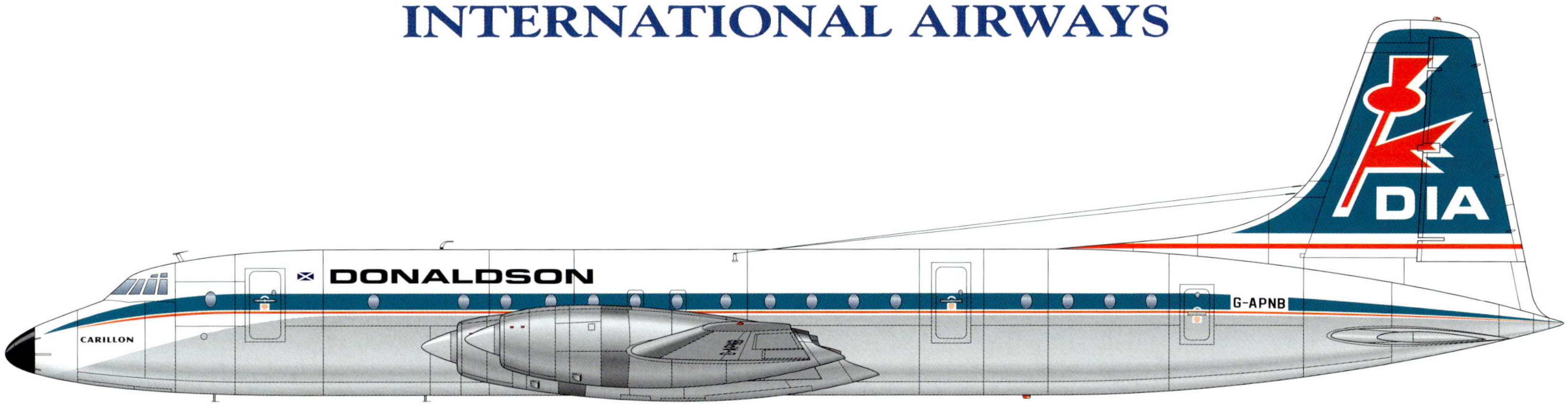

The story of Donaldson International Airways' experience with Britannias overlaps with that of Lloyd International Airways, as the earlier chapter makes clear.

Donaldson International Airways was originally founded in 1964 as a subsidiary of the Waverley Shipping Company of Glasgow, and another associate company was Mercury Air Holdings who organised summer IT charter holidays originating in Glasgow. Their flights were mainly run by Lloyd International using their DC-6s and then Britannias, so initially Donaldson had no aircraft of its own. However, in October 1967, it acquired its first aircraft, an ex-British United Britannia Series 317, G-APNA, which it immediately leased to Lloyd International who used her on their own work, including some Mercury/Donaldson assignments, for about eighteen months.

During 1968, Donaldson announced that it would launch its own Britannia operations in the spring of 1969, based at Gatwick, using two Series 317 aircraft, G-APNA returned from its Lloyd lease and G-APNB, another ex-British United aircraft which it purchased and which was delivered to Gatwick on 16th January 1969 after overhaul and painting in the new Donaldson livery.

The unexpected collapse of British Eagle in November 1968 meant that several well-maintained Britannias became available on the second-hand market and Donaldson decided to purchase one of them, a Series 312 aircraft, G-AOVC. Once overhauled and re-painted, she was delivered to Gatwick on 4th June 1969.

The first commercial operation by any Donaldson Britannia was by G-APNB. Ironically this was a sub-charter on behalf of her former owner, British United Airways, carrying a party of 'Silver Arrow' rail-air passengers from Le Touquet to Gatwick on 28th March 1969. The first fully commercial flight by Donaldson was on 25th April when G-APNB took a charter flight from Gatwick to Milan, then transferring to Zurich and returning to Gatwick on 27th April.

On 3rd May G-APNB launched the Mercury Air Holdings IT charter flights to Mediterranean destinations with a flight from Glasgow to Palma. She undertook a charter on 8th May, Rotterdam-Athens-Gatwick and on 17th May another charter, Glasgow-Palma. At this stage the next two Britannias became available, G-AOVC on 4th June and G-APNA on 16th June, so the full range of holiday IT charter flights could be implemented. G-AOVC flew a charter from Glasgow to Barcelona on 7th June, and on 8th June from Glasgow to Rimini. The Glasgow-Venice service began on 22nd June, then Glasgow-Ibiza on 6th July. The passenger demand was such that all three Donaldson Britannias were kept busy transporting Scottish tourists between Glasgow and Mediterranean resorts. The holiday charter programme meant that there were sometimes up to six flights to Barcelona and five to Palma each weekend, with other (fewer) flights to Ibiza, Ostend, Rimini and Venice.

In addition to the relatively short range IT holiday charters, there was also longer-range charter work. Flights were undertaken from Gatwick to New York, Los Angeles, Niagara Falls, Toronto and Vancouver, as well as flights in other directions, e.g. to Kingston (Jamaica), Port of Spain (Trinidad and Tobago), Hong Kong, Nairobi and Singapore. These were usually passenger charters but some were different, for example transporting ships' crews between the Far East and Europe.

The IT charter requirements remained busy until the autumn, but as they slowed down the number of passenger charters to the Far East increased. The final transatlantic flight of the season through Belfast was on 18th August, Gatwick-

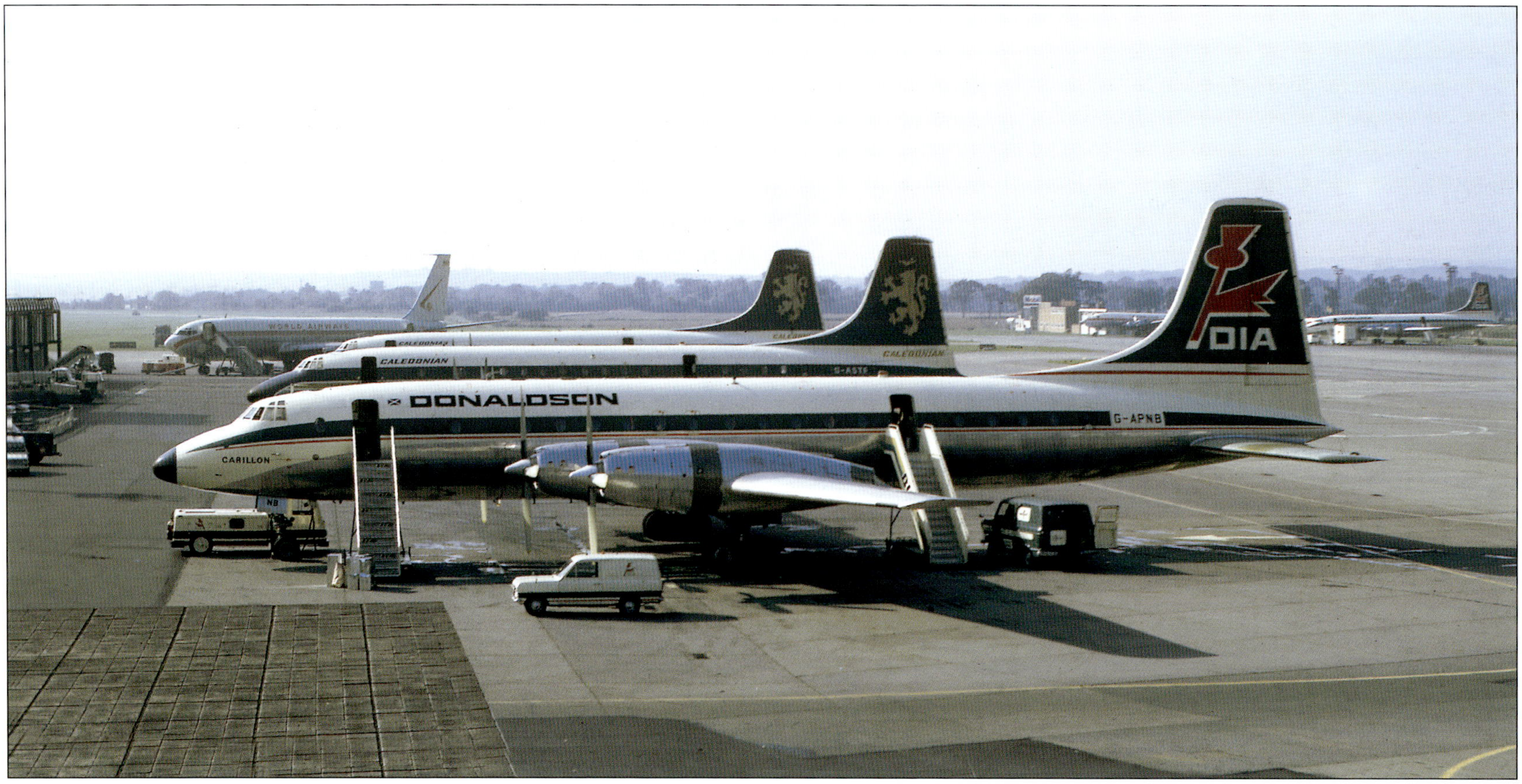

Four Britannia aircraft are in view in this nostalgic shot taken at Gatwick Airport in October 1969.

Belfast-Keflavík-Toronto, and through Prestwick the last flight was on 4th September. Direct flights from Canada, Toronto-Gatwick, ended on 17th September, Gatwick-Montreal-Gatwick was flown on 9th/10th October, whilst the final IT charter from Palma by G-APNB was on 11th October. On 14th October G-APNA was sub-chartered by Loftleidir from Glasgow to Keflavík, then back on 15th October to Glasgow before returning to base at Gatwick. On 25th November G-AOVC was chartered to take football supporters from Glasgow to Lisbon, and on 17th December a Donaldson Britannia flew a day return journey, Glasgow to Keflavík. Next day G-AOVC took a passenger charter from Glasgow via Gander to Toronto.

During the winter there were ad hoc charters to the Far East which by now produced the bulk of the airline's revenue. Charters from Gatwick and also from Amsterdam, Brussels, Frankfurt and Rotterdam went to places like Bangkok, Hong Kong, Jakarta, Kuala Lumpur and Singapore. There were also occasional cargo charters, like loads of tomatoes from the Canary Islands or fruit from Spain to Gatwick. Even so, the winter level of work remained low, with all the Britannias idle for days at a time.

Aircraft usage began to pick up in the New Year of 1970. First there were charters to take pilgrims from Accra to Jeddah on the Hadj pilgrimage, with G-AOVC taking this flight on 20th January and then the other Britannias became involved. G-APNA took more pilgrims on 18th February. On 20th February G-APNB flew a Gatwick to Berlin charter and on 28th, G-APNA flew a Gatwick to Gibraltar charter. On 11th/12th March G-AOVC flew a freight charter, Teesside to Lagos then, on 13th March, G-APNB flew the first transatlantic charter of the season from Gatwick to Gander. There were other charters; G-AOVC Gatwick to Karachi on 6th April; G-APNA Gatwick to Aden on 16th April; G-AOVC Istanbul to Glasgow on 21st April; G-APNB Gatwick to Karachi on 22nd April. On 25th April a day trip charter saw G-AOVC take aviation enthusiasts to Hanover, and on 29th April G-APNA took football supporters from Manchester to Vienna.

The 1970 summer IT season, with the usual link for Donaldson with Mercury Air Holdings' programme, began on 2nd May. G-APNA flew the first tourists from Glasgow to Palma and thereafter flew this service once a week until the end of the month. The route Glasgow-Rimini was re-opened by G-APNB on 29th May, then Glasgow-Barcelona on 30th May. On 21st June, flights to Ibiza and Ostend began, again by G-APNB, and during the summer, flights to these Mediterranean resorts were maintained by the three Britannias each weekend.

Transatlantic charters were also flown, with G-APNA flying the first one on 1st June, Gatwick-Gander-Toronto, followed the same evening by G-APNB. Donaldson's Britannias were, however, beginning to feel the competition from the newer jets. American airlines were beginning to use DC-8s or 707s and British competitors were using 707s or VC-10s. In comparison the Britannias were now ageing and even if well maintained were slower.

The somewhat bleak situation was improved for the airline by a national dock strike in the UK which stranded goods at ports around the country and which led to a demand for charter aircraft to move these goods. The three Britannias owned by Donaldson at the beginning of the year had not undergone the freight conversion, but in May Donaldson purchased an ex-British Eagle Britannia Series 312F, G-AOVF, which gave the airline a freight moving capacity. After overhaul and re-painting, she was delivered to Belfast on 15th July and three hours after delivery flew to Liverpool to begin her revenue earning operations. Donaldson had begun freight charter work to Belfast with G-AOVC on 12th July, then the next day she had flown Belfast-Rotterdam twice, and once on 14th. She then flew freight charters to Stansted, Liverpool and Castle Donnington on 15th and 16th July. G-AOVF then arrived and G-AOVC reverted to her normal type of charter work at Gatwick. G-AOVF concentrated on the freight movement work until her final trip of this kind on 2nd August, by which time she had completed 34 round trips. She was withdrawn by Donaldson and sold to IAS on 31st October 1972.

There were still charter flights to be had and Donaldson managed to secure a proportion of these although the competition made this harder. The airline therefore decided that it had to get some jet aircraft and announced, in the autumn, that it had acquired two ex-Pan American Boeing 707s and had decided to phase out its Britannias.

The consequence of this was the retirement of two of the Britannias over the 1970/1 winter. G-AOVC flew her last mission, a round trip passenger charter between Gatwick and Stockholm, on 27th September. She was subsequently presented to the Stansted Fire Training School and never flew again. G-APNB flew her last commercial service as a charter from Gatwick to Constantine (Algeria) on 5th March 1971 and the next day she flew to Luton and was subsequently sold to Airline Engineering and broken up for spares.

The remaining two Donaldson Britannias, G-AOVF and G-APNA, had a fairly busy summer season in 1971. The longer-range charters were usually taken by the newly acquired Boeing 707s, but the Britannias kept responsibility for IT charter services from Glasgow as well as occasional longer trips. On 13th June G-APNA flew from Glasgow to Montreal to take a tourist party to Helsinki, returning from Helsinki on 26th July and from Montreal via Keflavík to Gatwick on 28th July. There was a series of flights from Gatwick to Karachi, starting on 6th September with G-AOVF who also flew from Gatwick to Cairo on 23rd October, returning via Abu Dhabi to Gatwick on 25th October. G-APNA flew to the West Indies via Santa Maria on 12th October, to Bodo (Norway) on 15th October and to Kano (Nigeria) on 4th November. On 19th November she replaced a grounded Dan-Air Comet 4 on a Gatwick to Athens service, taking a second round trip to Athens the next day.

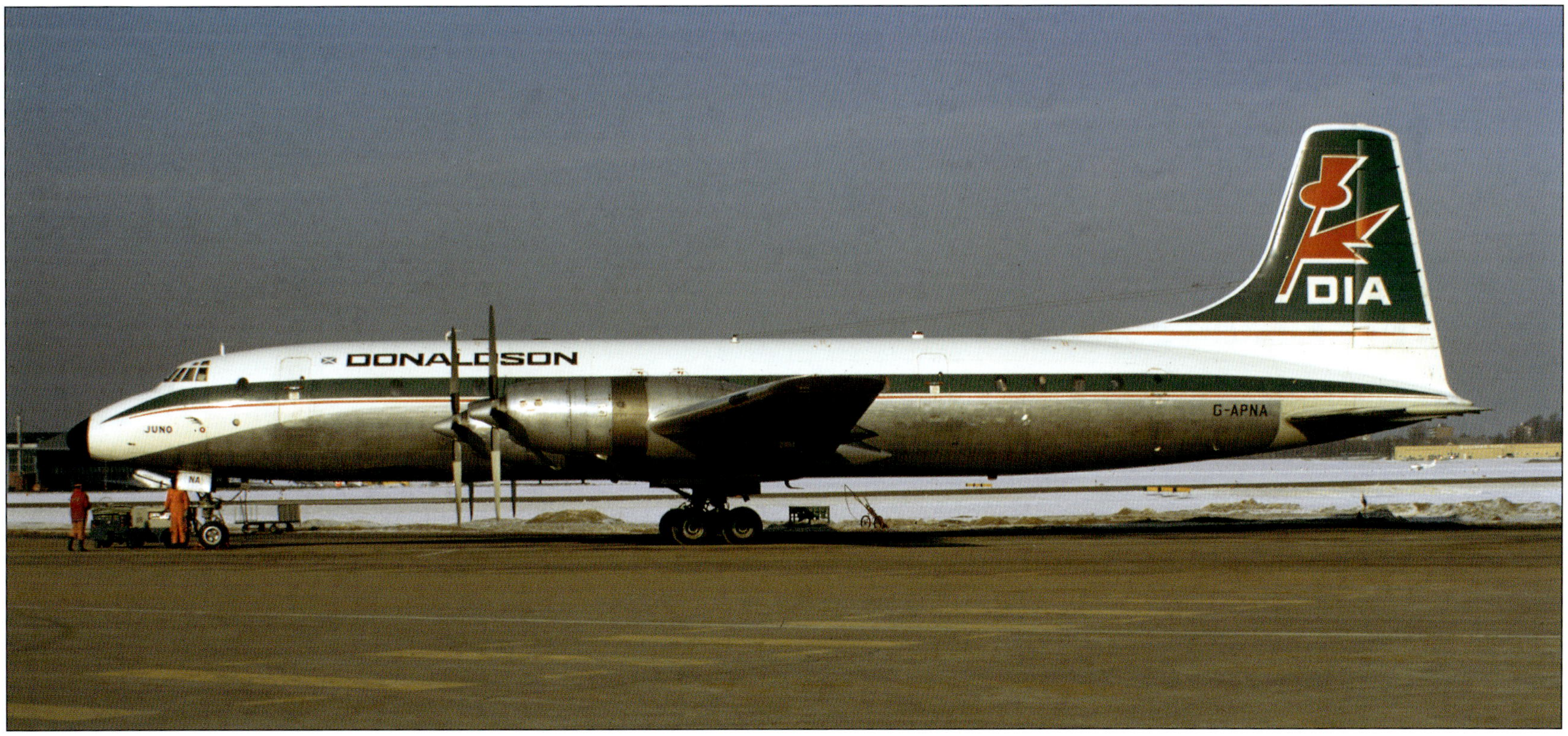

G-APNA 'Juno' is caught in the process of being connected to an aircraft ground power unit, on a cold morning in February 1970.

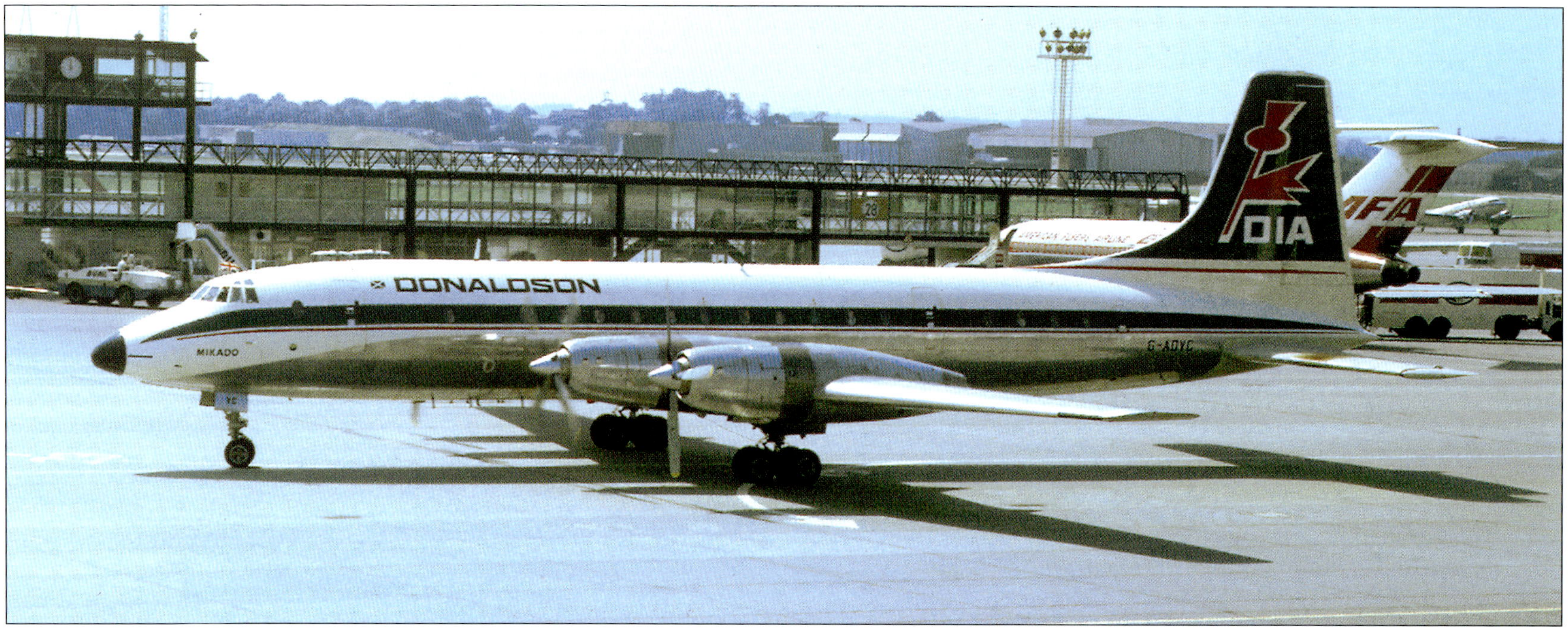

G-AOVC 'Mikado' taxies to the stand at Gatwick on return from the Mediterranean on 29th August 1970, less than a month before she was withdrawn from service.

The arrival of more Boeing 707s prompted the withdrawal of another Britannia in May 1972. G-APNA was withdrawn on 31st May, but as she had not had the freight door conversion, she did not attract a buyer. She was eventually sold to International Aviation Services and broken up for spares in October 1972.

G-AOVF, the only Series 312F which Donaldson had, did not last much longer for she could not compete with the earning power of the Boeing 707s. In July 1972 she was withdrawn and sold to International Aviation Services in October 1972. She went back into service, flying with cargo between Gatwick, the Middle East and Africa until eventually she was preserved in the RAF Museum, Cosford, in the livery of her first owner, BOAC.

Donaldson International continued with a fleet of four Boeing 707s once the Britannias had gone, but various operating problems caused the end of all flying by Donaldson on 8th August 1974. The Britannias had been the airline's first aircraft and had performed well for them but, as in other instances, they were phased out because of the greater speed which the newer jets could achieve.

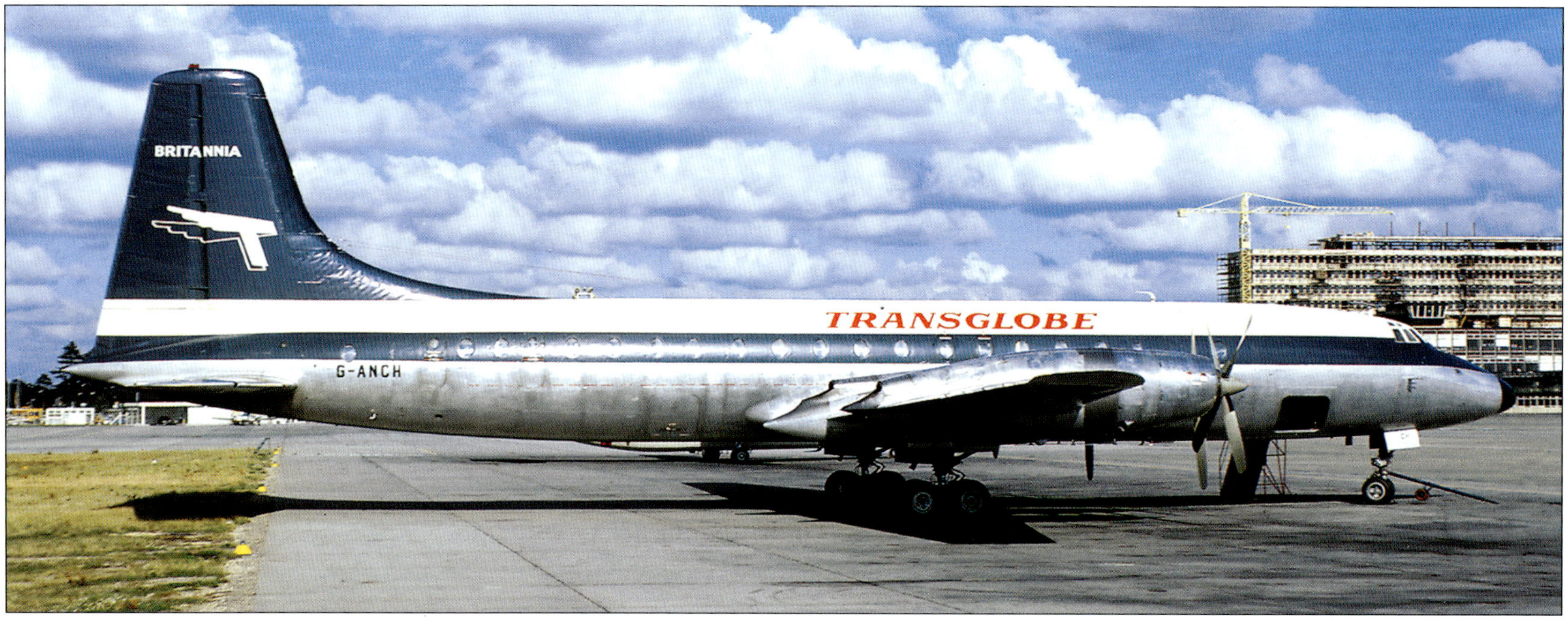

Ex Ghana Airways, Series 309 G-ANCH stands idle at Gatwick in late September 1967.

IN SERVICE WITH TRANSGLOBE AIRWAYS

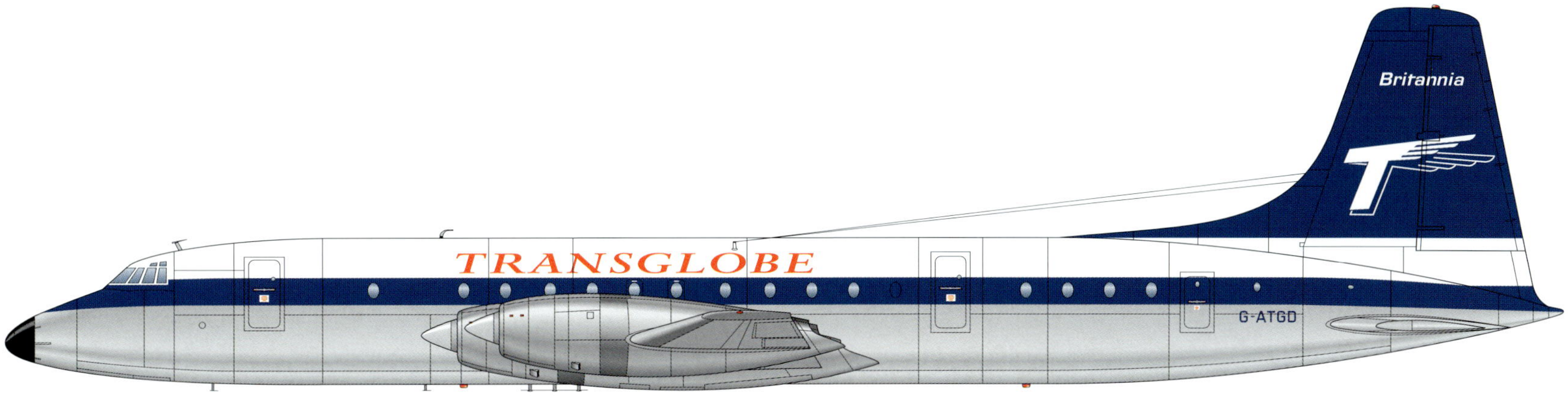

In 1958 an airline called Air Links was founded at Gatwick owning just one aircraft, a Dakota. In 1965 this airline changed its name to Transglobe Airways and retired its current fleet of Canadair Argonaut aircraft in favour of two ex-Canadian Pacific Britannia Series 314 aircraft.

The reason for the switch of aircraft was the somewhat more cut-throat nature of the holiday charter business which was developing. Passengers were opting in favour of more modern aircraft, turbo-prop driven like Viscounts and Britannias and away from older, noisier piston-driven aircraft like Argonauts. The acquisition of Britannias certainly boosted Transglobe's image.

The first Britannia to arrive at Southend, prior to an overhaul by Aviation Traders, was Canadian registered CF-CZA. She was converted to a 125-seat all-tourist configuration and it was originally intended that she should be leased directly to British United Airways. She was delivered from Southend to Gatwick on 8th July 1965 in full BUA livery but, three hours after arrival and without operating any service for BUA, she was returned to Southend. She was re-registered on the British list as G-ATGD and flown back to Gatwick on 30th July in Transglobe livery. For the next two months she was sub-chartered by BUA and Caledonian, but also flew some ad hoc charter flights for Transglobe.

The general pattern of flying over the three years of Transglobe's existence contained the same elements, i.e. lease contracts to other carriers, ad hoc charters and IT flights in the name of Transglobe, but in differing proportions.

The second Britannia which Transglobe leased, CF-CZC, arrived in Southend for overhaul on 17th June. She was eventually re-registered as G-ATLE and delivered to Gatwick on 12th December and her first revenue earning service, after some hours of crew training, was on 18th December flying from Gatwick to Khartoum. On 19th December, G-ATGD flew a charter across the Atlantic, to New York via Gander, followed on the 20th when G-ATLE flew the same journey. G-ATGD flew back to Gatwick non-stop, arriving on 21st December, whilst G-ATLE returned via the Azores, arriving at Gatwick on 23rd.

During the winter of 1965/6, international developments changed the scene for Transglobe and some other airlines. Rhodesia declared independence from Britain, with serious consequences for Zambia, as previously stated.

An oil airlift from Dar-es-Salaam to Lusaka was organised and Transglobe, along with other carriers, became involved in this. Transglobe's G-ATGD was allocated to assist, beginning on 1st January 1966 but not without incident.

The oil airlift task required the transporting of fifty-five 44-gallon oil drums from Dar-es-Salaam to either Lusaka or Ndola on each trip, a load of around ten tons. The task would have been much easier if G-ATGD had had the freight conversion but even so, the crews got the loading and unloading process well organised, with a turn round time of about 35 minutes, so that two round trips per day were possible.

Early in the airlift, the Britannia was slightly damaged by a fork-lift truck but this was soon adequately repaired. However a more serious incident occurred at the beginning of February when, on a return flight from Lusaka to Dar-es-Salaam, there was an electrical fire in No. 3 Proteus engine. This resulted in a successful emergency landing at Dar-es-Salaam, but the aircraft had to be withdrawn from service for extensive repairs prior to making a return to Southend in the UK for Aviation Traders to make permanent repairs. While grounded in Tanzania, G-ATGD made another contribution to the airlift. It loaned its three serviceable Proteus engines to other Britannia operators until they could get replacements flown out from Bristol. Eventually G-ATGD flew back for its

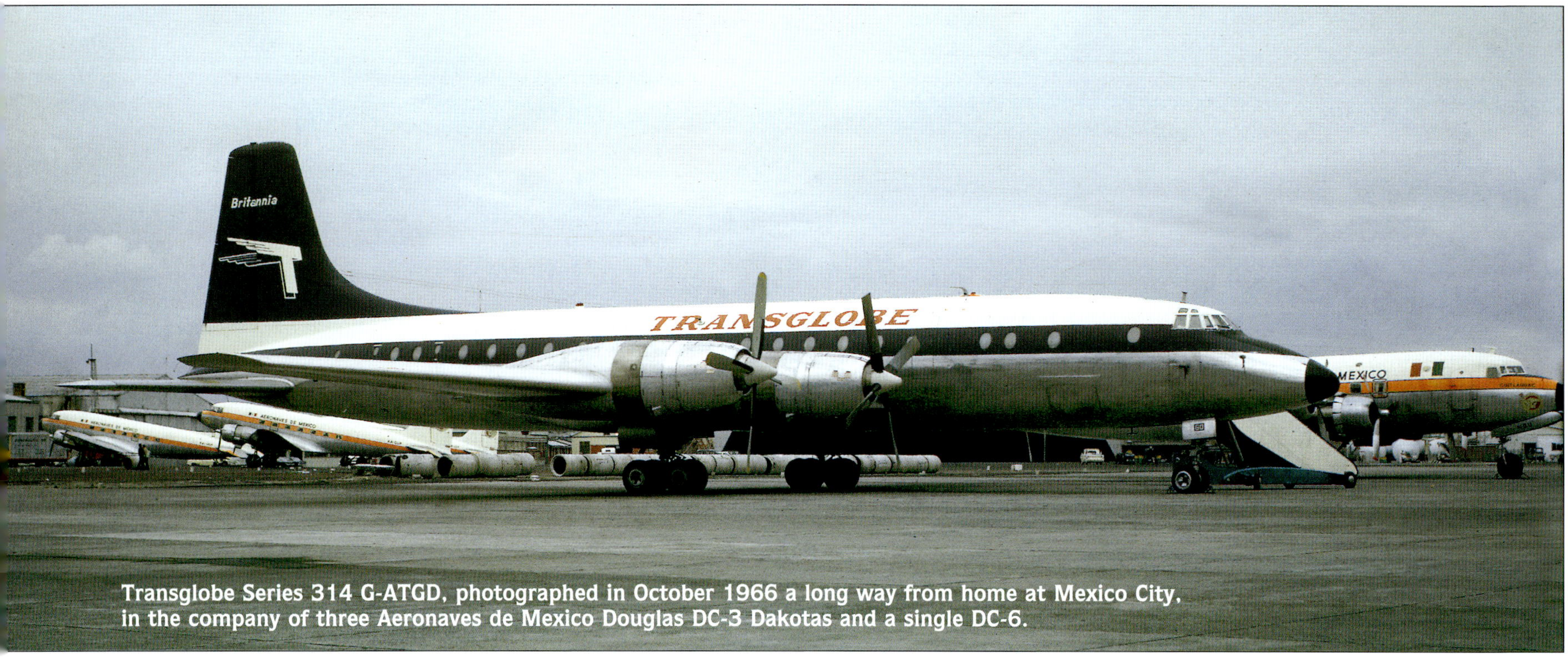

Transglobe Series 314 G-ATGD, photographed in October 1966 a long way from home at Mexico City, in the company of three Aeronaves de Mexico Douglas DC-3 Dakotas and a single DC-6.

own major repairs in mid-March, but it took no further part in the oil airlift.

During the winter the other Britannia, G-ATLE, was heavily engaged in charters to the Middle East and Africa (Khartoum, Bahrain and Nairobi), and a transatlantic service to New York via Gander on 12th and 14th January. On 11th February, she flew Istanbul to Belfast then, on 24th February she flew an MoD charter from Gatwick to Akrotiri (Cyprus). Other IT charters in March were to Athens, Bahrain, Düsseldorf, Istanbul and Malaga as well as a longer African charter, Gatwick-Idris-Kinshasa (Zaire), on 24th, returning on 26th March.

Because of the growth of charter work, Transglobe purchased the sole remaining Britannia Series 302, XA-MED, from Aeronaves de Mexico, which was delivered to Gatwick after overhaul and re-registered as G-ANCC on 12th July 1966. Also purchased were the remains at Tijuana of the other Aeronaves Britannia, which had landed with a collapsed undercarriage in July 1965. Transglobe had originally considered re-building the remains but eventually recovered the serviceable parts for spares which they brought back to Gatwick, leaving the remnants in Mexico.

The majority of work undertaken by the Transglobe Britannias during the 1966 summer season consisted of IT holiday charter flights from Gatwick to Mediterranean resorts; to Catania, Dubrovnik, Ljubljana, Malaga, Perpignan, Palma, Pisa, Rhodes, Tunis and Valencia. These flights were on average about three hours long, but the ex-Canadian Pacific Britannia Series 314s were capable of much longer flights, having been originally designed for transatlantic flying such as from Vancouver to Amsterdam. So while IT holiday flights occupied the aircraft at weekends, they were also available for longer flights during the week.

On 20th/21st June G-ATGD flew Canadian tourists from Toronto to Vienna. On 27th June, G-ATLE flew British tourists from Gatwick to Toronto, then more Canadians from Toronto to Vienna, then more British from Gatwick and Belfast via Gander to New York on 29th/30th June. On 4th July G-ATLE flew from Gatwick to Toronto then, on 5th July, transatlantic flights from Prestwick to Toronto began. The third Britannia, G-ANCC, also did some transatlantic missions, for example Vienna to Toronto on 9th August, Toronto via Gander to Gatwick on 10th August.

The final transatlantic service of the season into Scotland was on 23rd September by G-ATLE, Toronto-Prestwick, whilst the final services into England were on 14th October, by G-ATGD, New York-Gatwick and by G-ANCC, Toronto via Gander to Gatwick. Up to the end of 1966 various other long-range charters were flown, e.g. on 27th October by G-ATLE, Gatwick-Asmara (Eritrea); on 6th November by G-ATGD, Gatwick-Tunis; on 14th November by G-ATGD, Gatwick-Far East (via Bahrain) returning on 20th November; and on 27th November by both G-ATGD and G-ATLE via Santa Maria, Azores to the Caribbean.

It was evident that long-haul operations could be expanded so Transglobe looked to increase its fleet. First they tried to lease-purchase two Canadair CL-44D aircraft, but the American CAB placed an embargo on this sale, and Transglobe were forced to go elsewhere. Eventually, in November 1966, they leased a Britannia Series 309, G-ANCH, which was owned by the British Aircraft Corporation. She was jointly leased to Transglobe and Ghana Airways until May 1967 then solely to Transglobe thereafter. She flew her first Transglobe mission, Gatwick to Benina, on 16th December 1966.

The winter 1966/7 was quite quiet. There was a small supply of work but each aircraft had periods of idleness so time was used for crew training and aircraft maintenance.

In 1967 Transglobe made a move to increase its share of transatlantic charter work, and therefore to depend less on IT charter work. The transatlantic flights more often began or ended at Gatwick but now Belfast, Manchester or Prestwick were used as well. Birmingham was also used for the first time on 16th July, but was only used twice throughout 1967. Destinations in North America were Toronto (by far the most popular), Montreal, New York, Ottawa and Vancouver while more ambitious charters were Brussels-Toronto, Toronto-Gatwick-Belgrade and Frankfurt-Vancouver via Søndre Strømfjord. This volume of work meant that occasionally all four Transglobe Britannias were airborne over the Atlantic at the same time.

In addition there were other IT charter commitments. Some flights began at Manchester but most began at Gatwick and the destinations included Barcelona, Genoa, Ibiza, Las Palmas, Lisbon, Ljubljana, Malaga, Munich, Palma, Rimini, Split, Tenerife, Valencia and Venice. From time to time some services were flown on behalf of BUA or Caledonian.

On 4th October 1967, leased Britannia G-ANCH was returned to the British Aircraft Corporation at Wymeswold on completion of the lease. By then Transglobe had arranged with Seaboard World Airlines to take delivery of the first of six Canadair CL-44D aircraft in April 1968. These were derivatives of the Britannia built by the Canadians, designed for freight carrying and with a special swing tail, hinged at one side to accommodate large long loads.

Transglobe's first CL-44D, G-AWDK, was delivered to Gatwick on 5th April 1968 and flew much of the transatlantic work in 1968. Meanwhile several Britannia flights to East and South Africa were sub-charter flights on behalf of African Safari Airways and Trek Airways. During the summer there was an extensive amount of transatlantic charter flying and IT charter flights, and as the autumn came there was more ad hoc contract work.

But behind all this activity a serious financial situation for Transglobe was developing. On 28th November 1968, the company announced that it was ceasing all flying because it could not raise any more capital to keep the airline solvent. The reasons it gave were its continued use of obsolete turbo-prop aircraft on its transatlantic service and its agreement to the purchase of the six Canadair CL-44D aircraft at an 'excessive' price of £6.5 million.

Whatever the reasons, the collapse of Transglobe came just three weeks after the collapse of British Eagle. So in this short time almost a quarter of the world's Britannias appeared on the second-hand market. Two of Transglobe's Britannias, G-ANCC and G-ATLE, were at Gatwick at the time of the collapse and saw no more airline service. The third, G-ATGD, was stored at an unknown location until it was eventually sold to African Safari Airways. Transglobe's CL-44s did fly again when the airline was revived by some of its employees as Tradewinds Airways, and they flew for many years on cargo charter work before eventually being replaced by Boeing 707s.

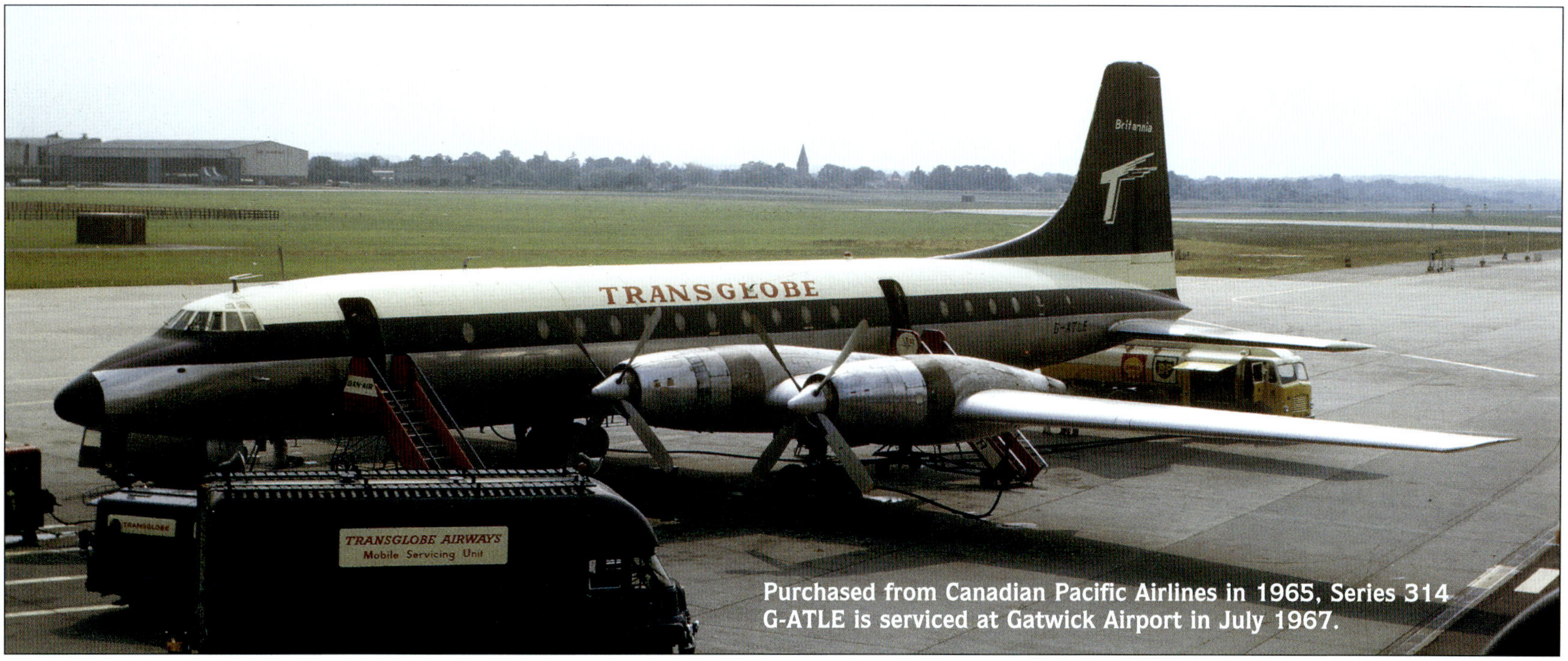

Purchased from Canadian Pacific Airlines in 1965, Series 314 G-ATLE is serviced at Gatwick Airport in July 1967.

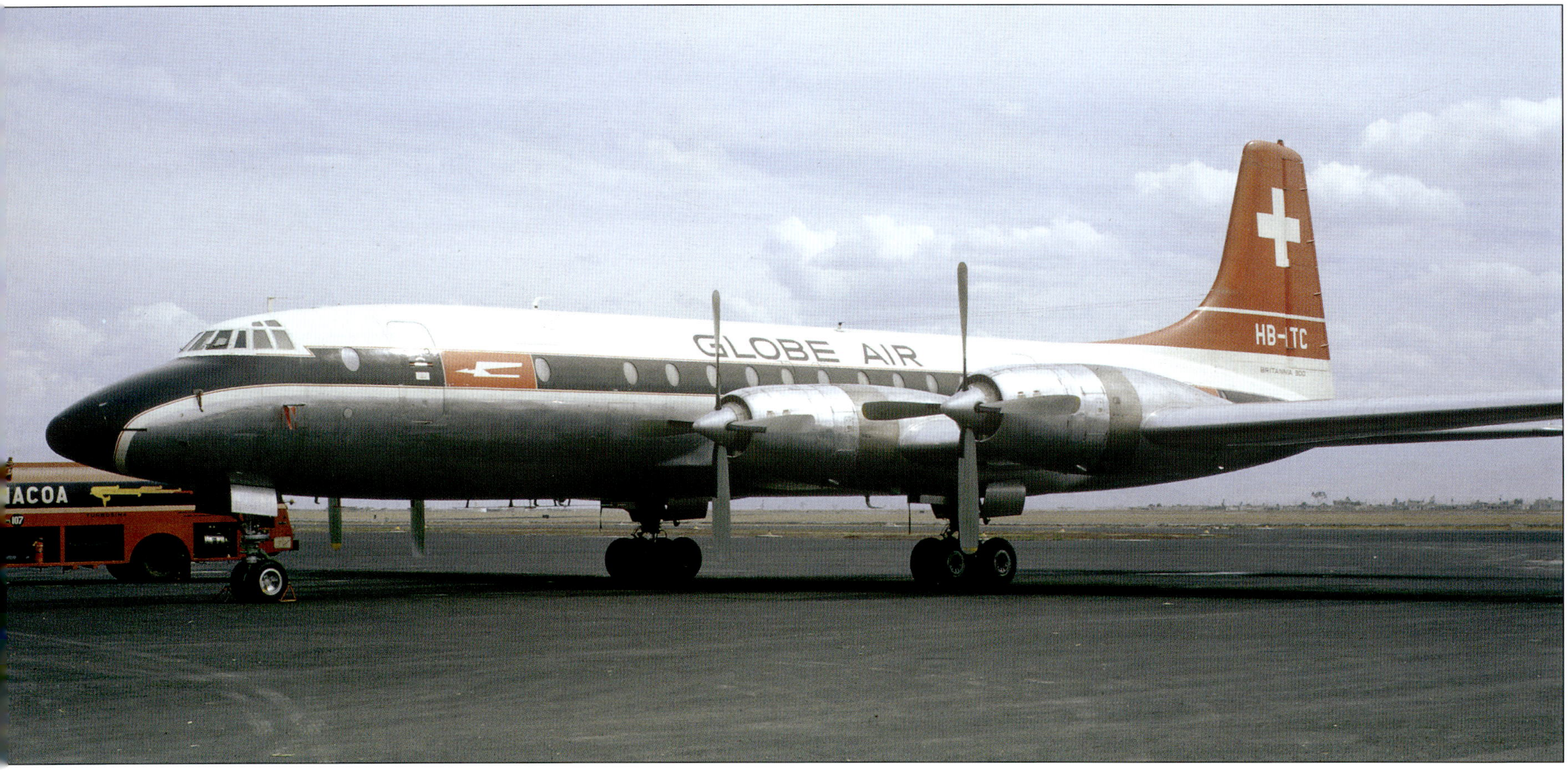

ABOVE: Britannia Series 313 HB-ITC of Globe Air of Switzerland, was photographed just after arrival at Mexico City on a transatlantic charter flight, in January 1966.

BELOW: G-ARKA, a Britannia Series 314 , sports the newly applied livery of Tellair at London Luton Airport in March 1969, while under lease from CCT Aircraft Leasing Limited.

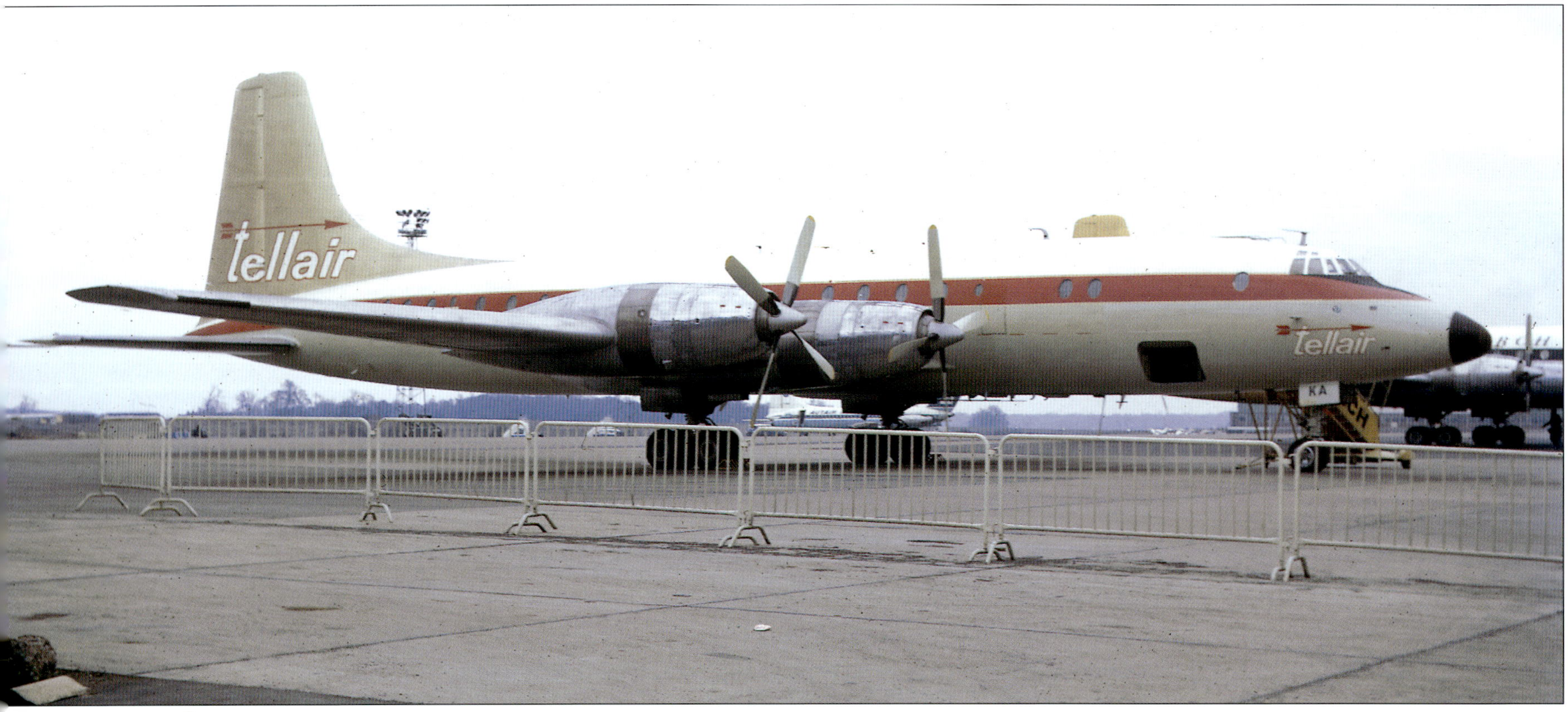

IN SERVICE WITH EUROPEAN CHARTER AIRLINES

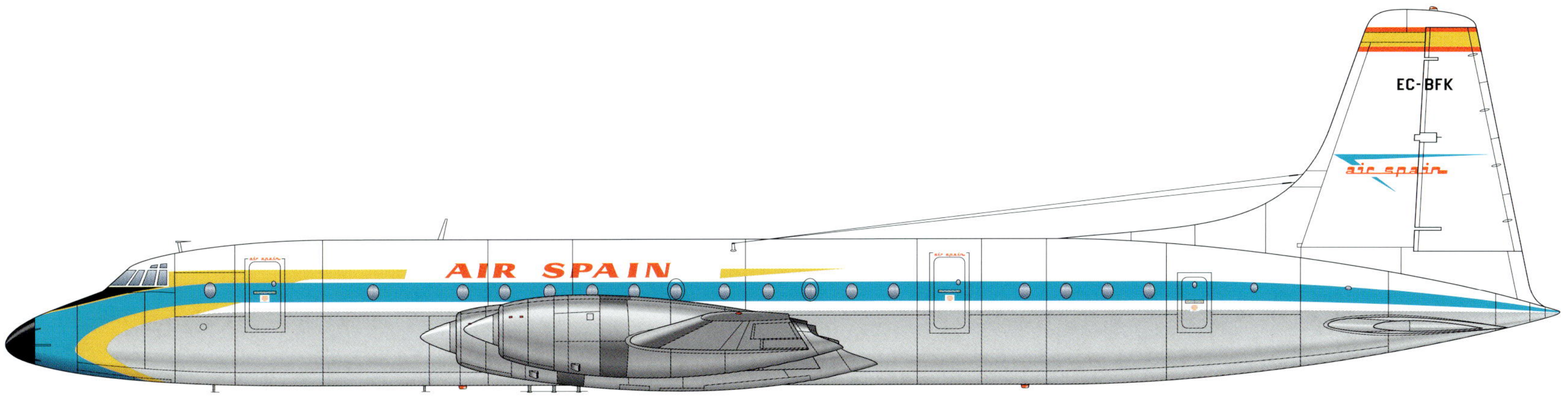

GLOBE AIR

Globe Air was founded in 1957 with the intention of challenging the monopoly of Swissair and Balair in operating scheduled and charter flights from Switzerland. Under its managing director, Karl Rudin, it steadily built up a network of IT charter flights from its base, Basle, to many European holiday destinations.

These flights began in 1961 using ex-BEA Ambassadors, assisted in 1963 by a new Dart Herald. As the reputation of Globe Air grew, however, so did the demand for longer distance flights. This made the purchase of a Britannia sensible and ex-El Al Series 313, 4X-AGA (re-registered as HB-ITB) was bought by Globe Air, overhauled and delivered to Basle on 2nd April 1964.

Her first service flight was two days later, and she began to establish regular flights to Athens, Cairo, Entebbe, Las Palmas, Nairobi and Palma. In addition, ad hoc charters went further, to Bangkok, Colombo, Hong Kong, Johannesburg and Tokyo. There was a particular emphasis on wildlife safaris and Globe Air set up an associate company, Globe Air East Africa, to carry tourists to Central Africa for this purpose.

The demand for services became so great that Globe Air decided to purchase a second Britannia, also an ex-El Al Series 313. 4X-AGD (re-registered as HB-ITC) was delivered to Basle on 8th March 1965 and entered service six days later, flying a planeload of tourists from Basle to Nairobi.

The airline continued to operate successfully during 1965/66, but in April 1967 there was a disaster. HB-ITB was operating a charter flight from Bangkok to Basle via Bombay and Cairo but, whilst flying towards Cairo, bad weather forced a diversion to Nicosia (Cyprus). The weather there was also poor and the Captain made two abortive attempts to land during a severe thunderstorm. On his third attempt the plane crashed into a hillside about three miles from the runway. Of the 130 passengers and crew on board, all but four were killed.

This accident, halving the Britannia fleet, had a devastating affect on the company. Passenger confidence, even if unjustified, fell and in order to fulfil its commitments, Globe Air had to sub-charter other Britannias at extra expense. Then, in June 1967, the Swiss Government ordered the airline to re-organise its management. The final blow came after the summer season of activity when the managing director, Karl Rudin, was arrested in connection with a charge of embezzlement. On 12th October 1967, the airline declared itself bankrupt.

AFRICAN SAFARI AIRWAYS

Karl Rudin, however, survived and the following month formed a new airline, African Safari Airways. He bought the surviving Globe Air Britannia, HB-ITC, which was re-registered with a Ugandan mark, 5X-UVH, and delivered to Zurich on 30th December 1967. Several ex-Globe Air personnel joined the new airline, which continued as Globe Air had done to provide transport out to East Africa for tourists going on safari holidays. In due course, the new airline aquired two Britannia Series 314s; G-ATGD was purchased from Transglobe and re-registered 5X-UVT, later 5Y-AYP, and was delivered on 26th April 1970. G-ATMA was leased from Caledonian and re-registered 5Y-ANS at the end of 1969. However the airline did not last much longer and, in April 1971, 5Y-ANS was sold to IAS Cargo Airlines. 5Y-ALP was withdrawn from service at the same time and stored at Biggin Hill, but scrapped at the end of the year. This left 5Y-ALT which seems to have remained in Africa at least until 1973. But African Safari Airways suspended operations at the end of 1971.

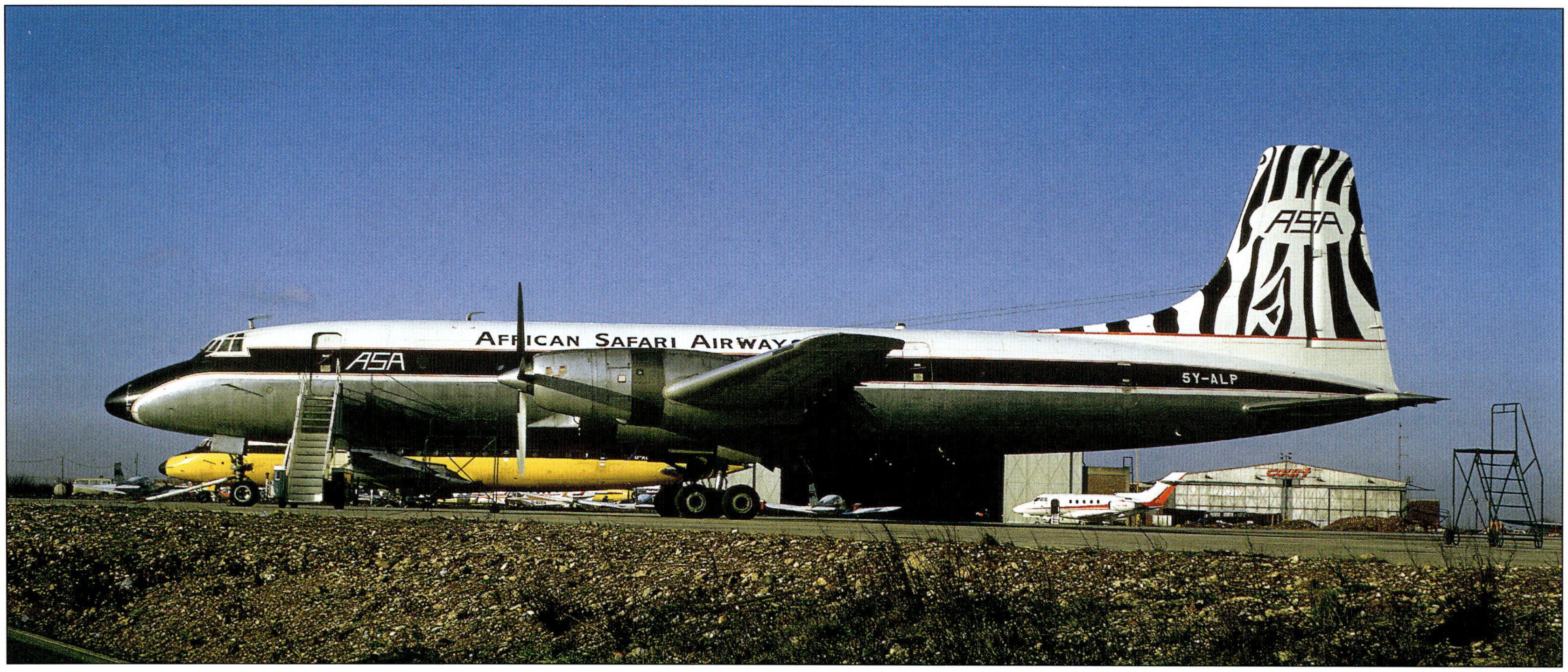

Britannia Series 314 5Y-ALP, wearing the distinctive African Safari Zebra livery, sits in the sunlight in December 1970 at Luton Airport, during a maintenance visit to overhaul its port inner engine.

AIR SPAIN

By the mid-1960s, Europeans had become used to travelling to sunny regions for their holidays and IT charter contracts were becoming increasingly popular. With this in mind a new airline, Air Spain, was formed in April 1966 with the aim of providing charter holidays into Spain. It was founded by Jose Rivero de Aguilar who became Managing Director and the headquarters were set up in Madrid, although most flying was from Palma.

The airline began by purchasing two Series 312 Britannias from British Eagle. The first G-AOVR after overhaul and repainting in its new livery, was handed over at Heathrow on 20th October 1966, first registered as EC-WFJ and then re-registered as EC-BFJ. The second, originally G-AOVE, was delivered to Air Spain as EC-WFK on 29th December 1966 and re-registered as EC-BFK. A third Britannia was also bought from El Al, a Series 313, 4X-AGB. After overhaul at Heathrow by British Eagle, it was delivered to Air Spain as EC-WFL on 5th May 1967 and re-registered

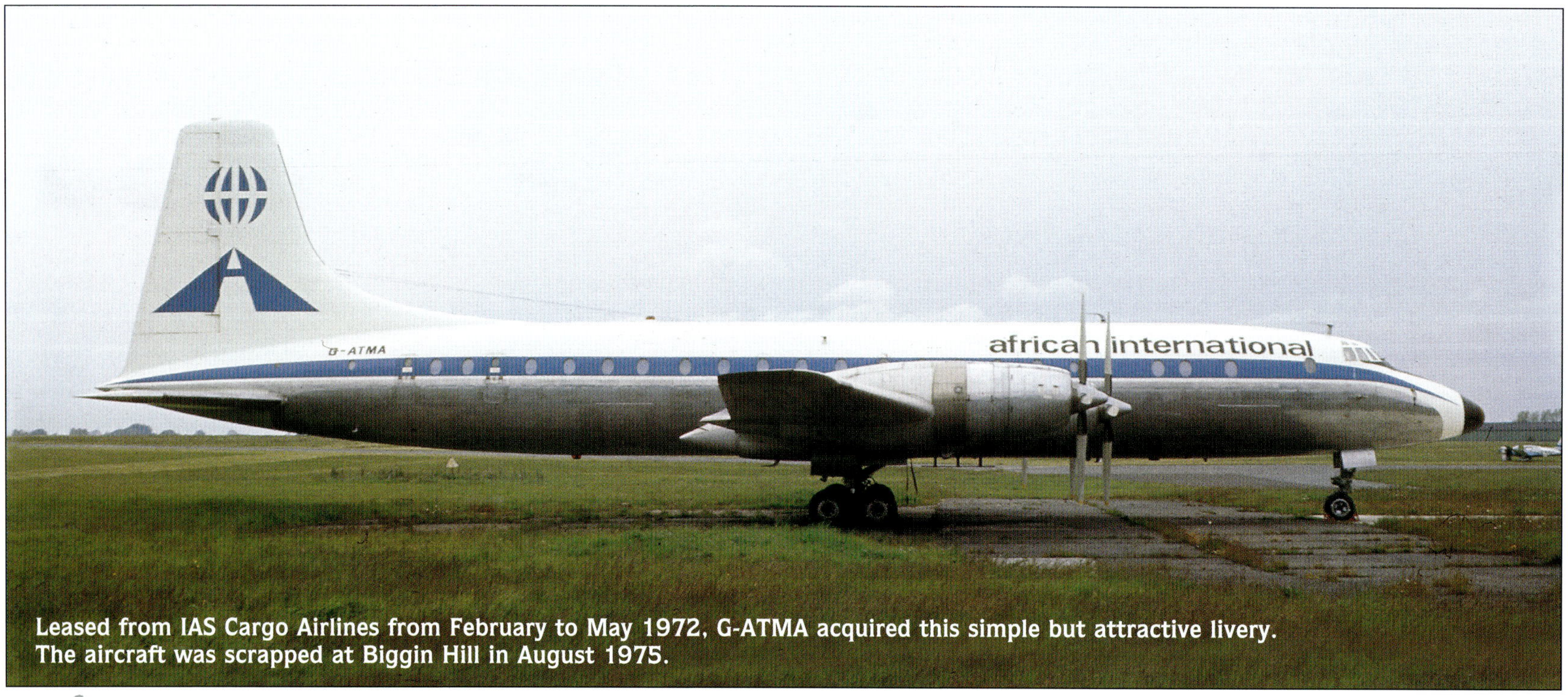

Leased from IAS Cargo Airlines from February to May 1972, G-ATMA acquired this simple but attractive livery. The aircraft was scrapped at Biggin Hill in August 1975.

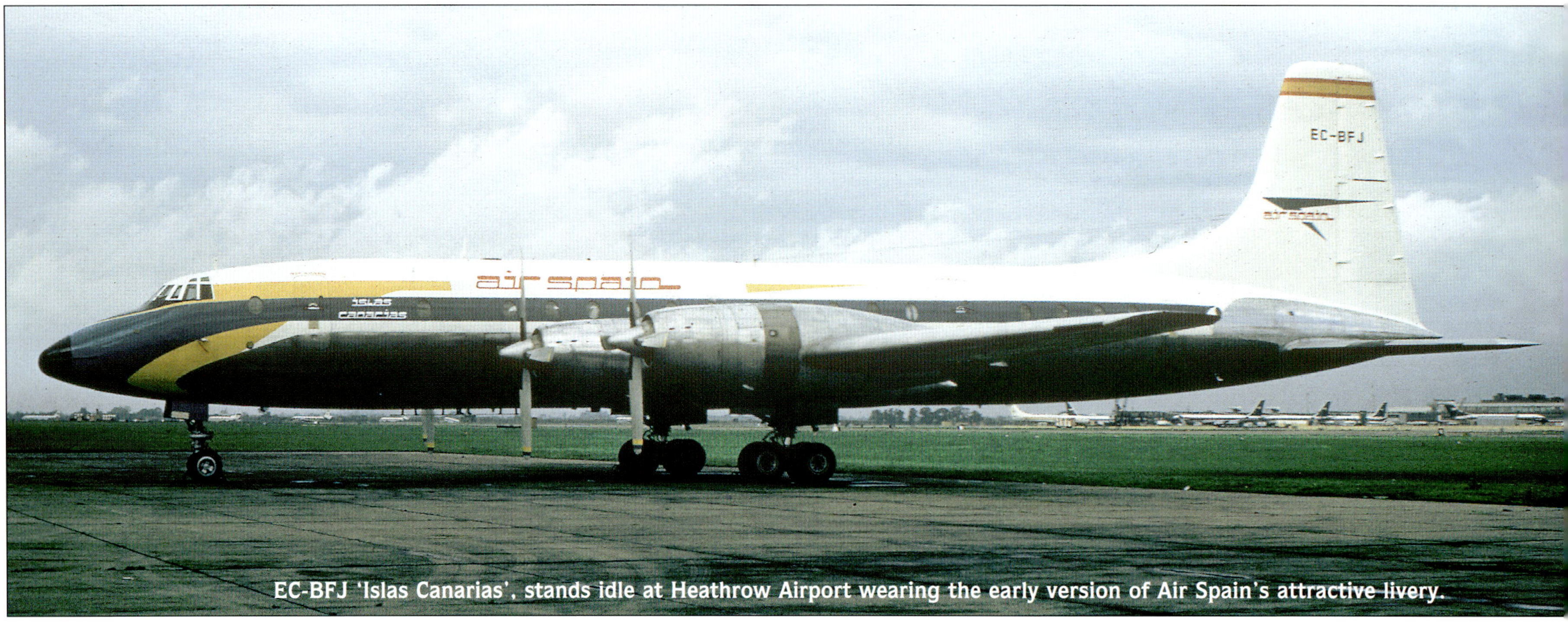

EC-BFJ 'Islas Canarias', stands idle at Heathrow Airport wearing the early version of Air Spain's attractive livery.

as EC-BFL. The airline was therefore ready to launch a considerable IT charter service for holidaymakers wishing to go to Spain.

The service began on 26th March 1967 when EC-BFJ flew holidaymakers from Birmingham to Palma. It built up to quite a sizeable operation with services from Birmingham weekly to Palma, Ibiza and Barcelona. There were also services from Gatwick to Madrid, Palma, Barcelona and sometimes Ibiza, whilst flights into Spanish destinations were also taken from Basle, Düsseldorf, Geneva, Helsinki and Rotterdam.

During the winter months when IT charter services closed down, the airline took on ad hoc charters, in particular the carrying of tomatoes from Spain and the Canary Islands to West Germany and England. In the summer of 1968, the demand for Air Spain's services began to change and IT charter programmes from British airports were drastically reduced, although services from other European airports continued to be popular. There was also a series of flights from Basle to Caribbean destinations including Cuba. Then in the autumn, as before, there was a series of cargo charters, flying Spanish tomatoes to Northern Europe, particularly the UK.

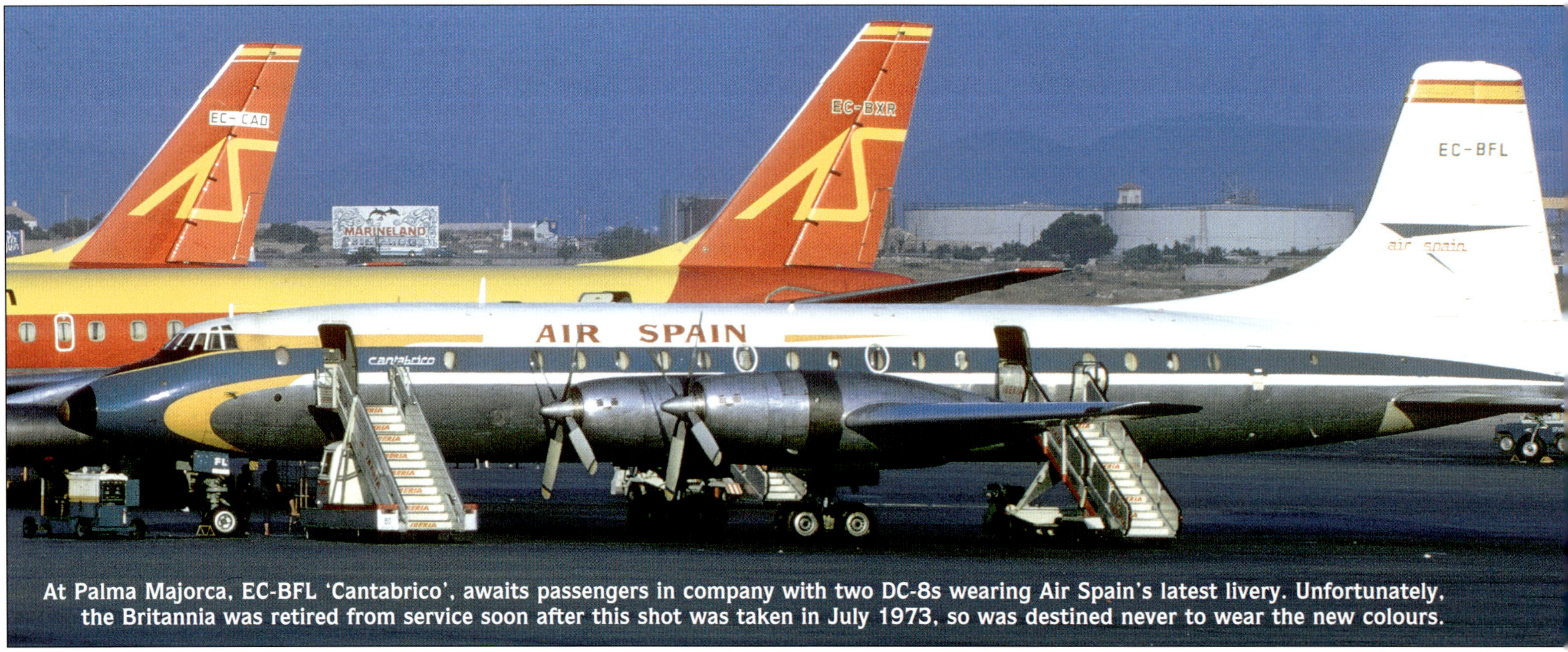

At Palma Majorca, EC-BFL 'Cantabrico', awaits passengers in company with two DC-8s wearing Air Spain's latest livery. Unfortunately, the Britannia was retired from service soon after this shot was taken in July 1973, so was destined never to wear the new colours.

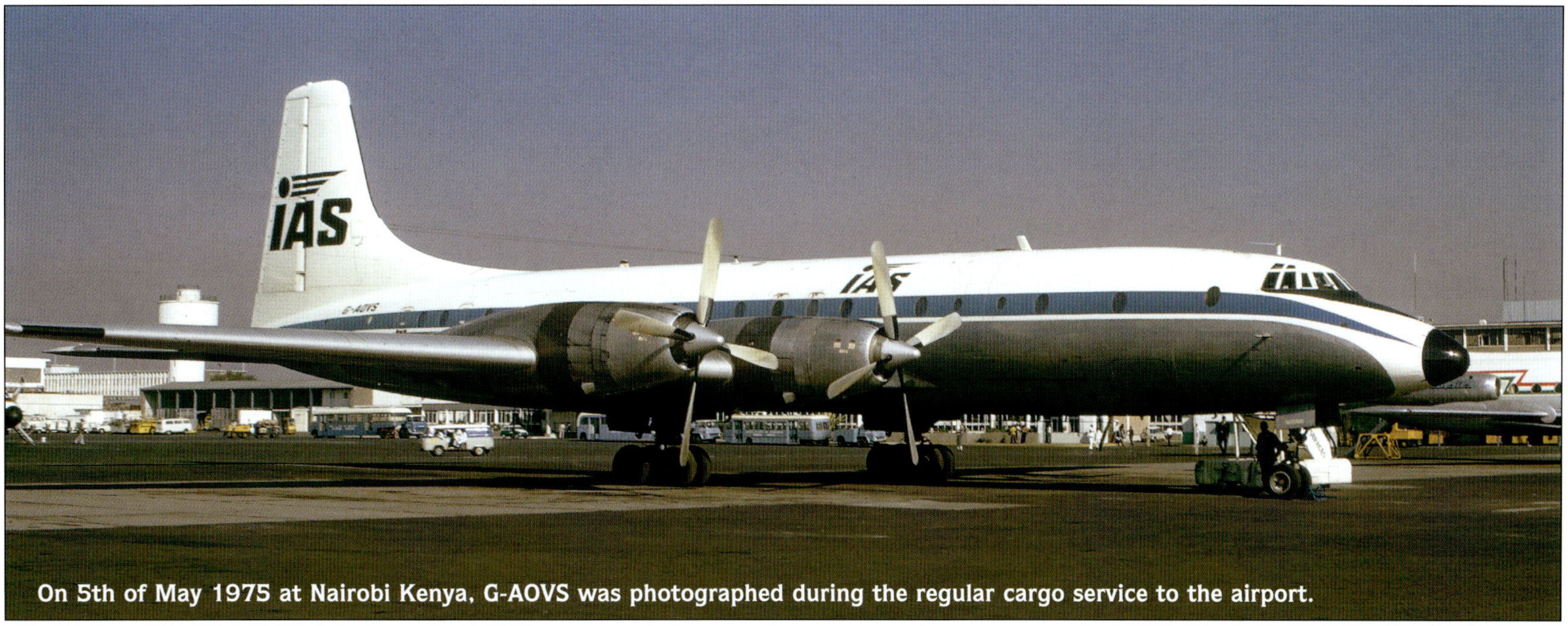

On 5th of May 1975 at Nairobi Kenya, G-AOVS was photographed during the regular cargo service to the airport.

In the autumn of 1969, Air Spain purchased a fourth Britannia, Series 312F, G-AOVM, from the receiver of the bankrupt British Eagle. She was overhauled at Luton and delivered to Air Spain and re-registered as EC-BSY on 2nd December 1969. For the next two seasons, the same pattern of work continued with passenger charters mainly from Northern European airports outside the UK to Spain and the Canary Islands, and with ad hoc charter work, mainly taking tomatoes the other way. For example, during the winter of 1969/70, 49 round trips were flown between Alicante, Las Palmas and Tenerife into Liverpool.

During the early 1970s the aircraft situation was changing. Jet aircraft were becoming more available, even on the second-hand market and their greater speed over that of the turbo-props gave them preferential passenger appeal. Recognising this, Air Spain began to re-equip with jets, choosing Douglas DC-8s, and to sell off their Britannias. EC-BSY was sold to the Royal Aircraft Establishment, Boscombe Down, in November 1971. Her time with Air Spain had lasted less than two years but, serialised as XX 367, she remained airworthy and flew for many subsequent years.

EC-BFJ was withdrawn and sold to International Aviation Services in April 1973, but she was cannibalised for spares after being flown to Biggin Hill. EC-BFK and EC-BFL were withdrawn from use during 1972 at Palma, and also sold to International Aviation Services. They were both broken up there and the reusable parts taken back to the UK.

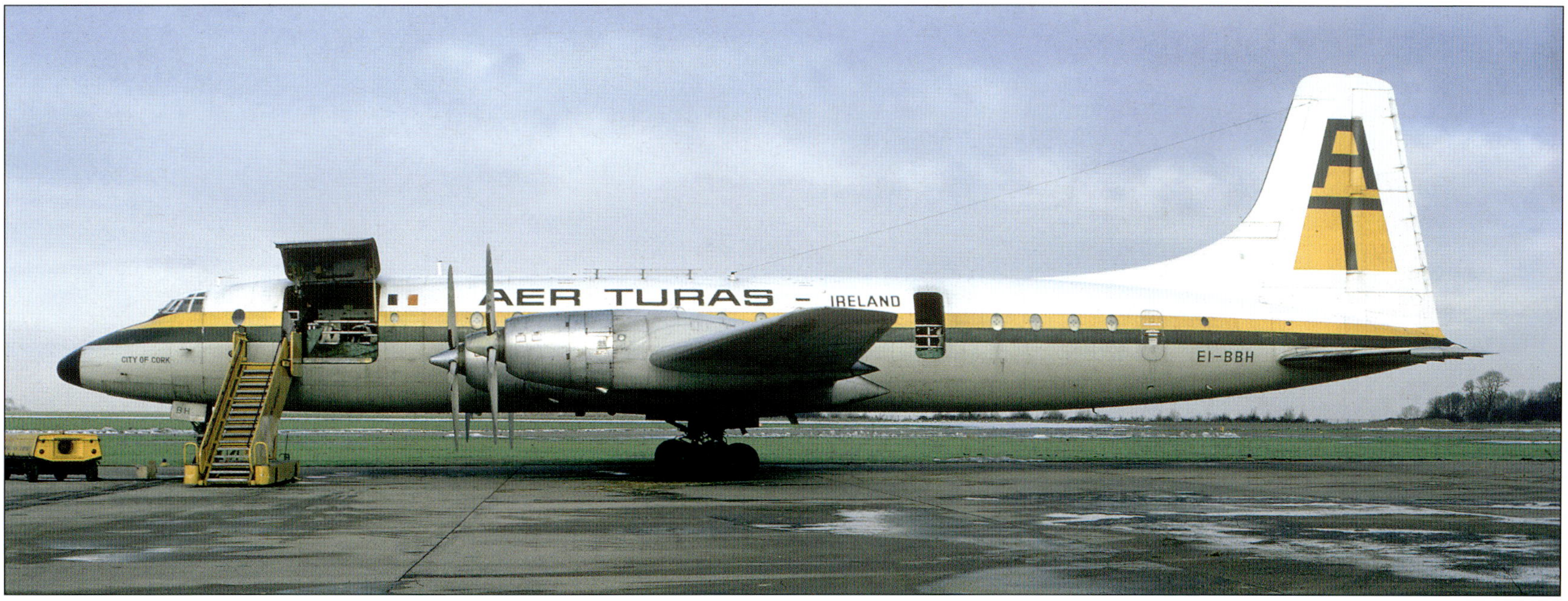

At East Midlands Airport in February 1979 EI-BBH 'City of Cork', prepares to off-load her cargo.

ADDITIONAL BRITANNIA OPERATORS

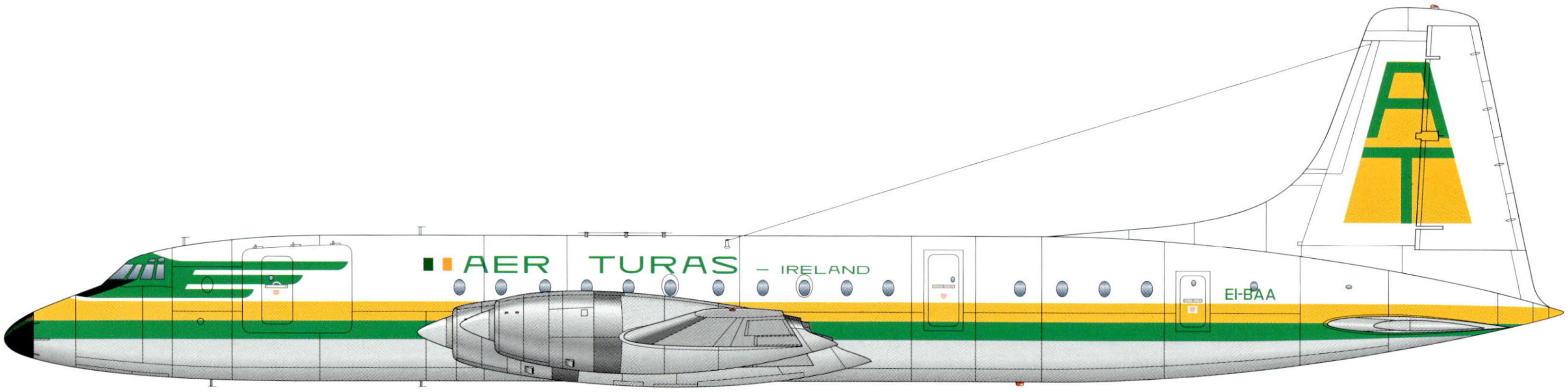

By the early 1970s, if an airline was interested in purchasing a Britannia aircraft it was possible to find one on offer which had already had one or perhaps two previous owners. It was a decade when there were a lot of offers available. For example, 22 RAF Britannias were decommissioned and offered for sale in 1975 and 1976 and several airlines bought them. The great majority of these were small operators with a fleet of only one or two Britannias, but the exceptions to this were IAS Cargo Airlines, Aer Turas, Young Cargo Services and Katale Aero Transport, all four of which had fleets of five or more Britannias. These four airlines are dealt with next.

IAS CARGO AIRLINES

International Air Services (IAS) was formed in 1971 and on 5th April that year purchased one Britannia from African Safari Airways, a Series 314 aircraft which, at that stage, was registered as CF-CZX from her Canadian Pacific days, but now reverted to G-ATMA which she had when previously owned by Caledonian Airways (1965-9). The aircraft was leased from IAS by a Nigerian company, African International Airways, from February to May 1972 and used to take cargo between Nigeria and Europe. In June 1972, IAS took back the aircraft and operated its own cargo service using her between Gatwick and Africa.

The demand for this cargo service was sufficient enough for IAS to buy five more Britannias and to set up a base in Nairobi to handle the African end of the charters. By this date, spares for the Britannias were becoming difficult to obtain and the airline's policy was to use some of the aircraft as a supply of spare parts which were cannibalised as necessary, in order to keep the other planes airworthy.

The first two aircraft were Series 307F, G-ANCD, leased from Aivex Holdings and Shackleton Aviation on 22nd September 1973 and Series 309, G-ANCH, bought from Ghana Airways in December 1972. The other three were all Series 312F aircraft; G-AOVF was purchased from Donaldson International on 31st October 1972, G-AOVP was purchased from Lloyd International on 10th July 1973, and G-AOVS was leased from Lloyd International on 18th January 1973.

The details of the operation of these aircraft are not clear, but some of them flew a cargo service regularly between Gatwick and East Africa for some years. Eventually, however, the airline began to purchase some jet-powered freighters (DC-8s and 707s) and, as a result, the Britannia fleet was gradually withdrawn.

G-ATMA was the first to go, being withdrawn from service in June 1973. G-ANCH's history seems uncertain. She may not have flown for IAS after April 1973, but what is clear is that she was finally withdrawn and scrapped in August 1973 at Biggin Hill.

G-AOVP was flown continuously by IAS from purchase until being withdrawn in August 1975, although she was not broken up until June 1977, also at Biggin Hill.

G-ANCD was leased by African Cargo Airways in May 1975. She flew on for several other airlines before being withdrawn in October 1982 at Hurn.

G-AOVF remained with IAS, apart from a short lease to African Cargo Airways, until April 1976 when she went to Invicta International. She continued flying until May 1984 when she was flown to RAF Cosford, where she is now preserved in their Museum in the livery of her first owner, BOAC.

G-AOVS, their last Britannia, was operated by IAS until December 1975 when she was leased to Invicta on 1st January

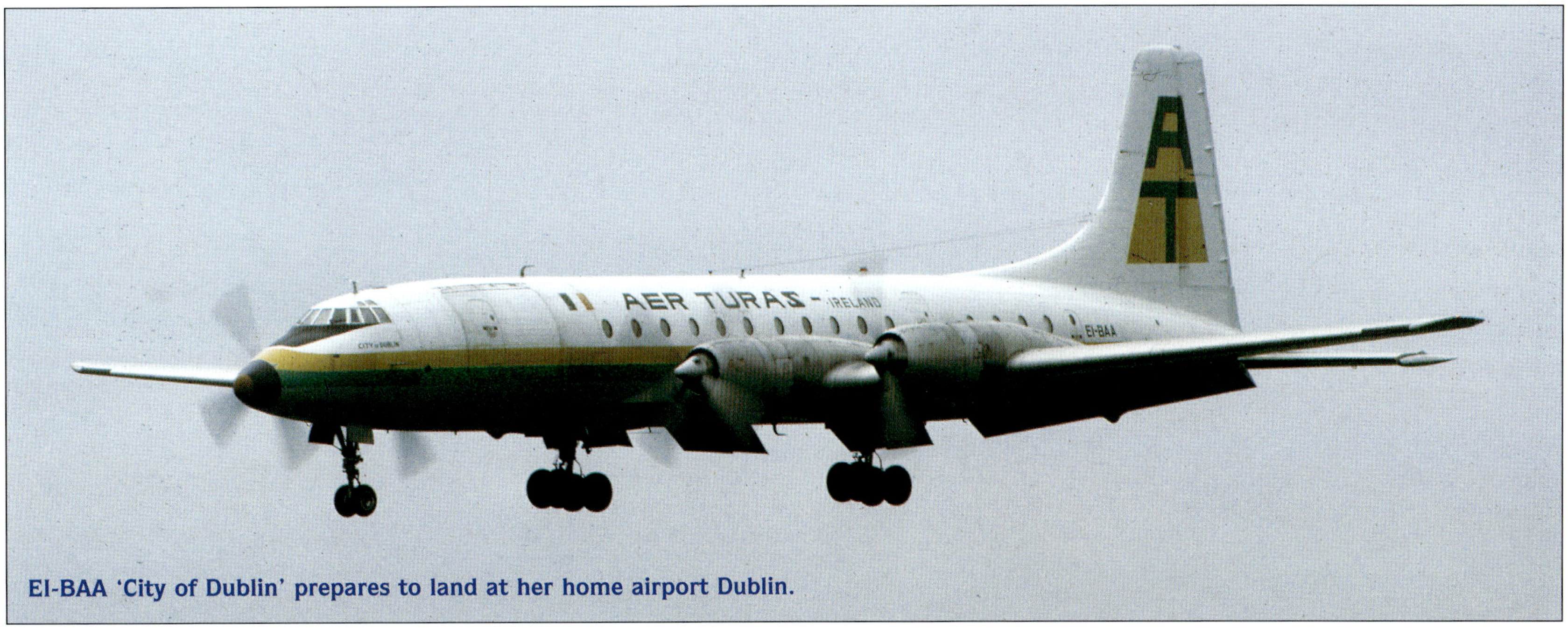

EI-BAA 'City of Dublin' prepares to land at her home airport Dublin.

1976 for six months. The following year, she was leased to Redcoat Air Cargo from May and finally sold to them in April 1979.

AER TURAS

The Irish independent airline, Aer Turas, had for some years been engaged in carrying racehorses between Eire and race courses in the UK and on the Continent. By 1970 it had an ageing fleet of DC-4 and DC-7 aircraft and it was decided to replace them with Britannias. As a first step it arranged the lease/purchase of an ex-Monarch Airlines Series 307F, G-ANCE, in May 1974.

In order to facilitate the transport of horses it was convenient to have the large front port-side cargo door, which of course the 307F variant already had. Further modifications were carried out and most passenger fittings were removed to provide space for horseboxes and points of attachments of these to the fuselage. The aft end of the fuselage was partitioned off to produce a galley and toilet access for the grooms and other attendants.

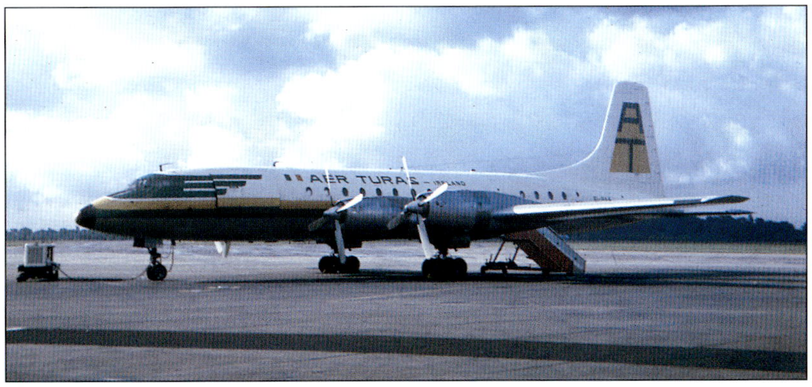

Aer Turas Britannia EI-BAA at Manchester in June 1974 wearing a rather (retro) livery with a stylised wing on the forward fuselage worn during the early months of ownership.

With the reconfiguration completed, the aircraft was given the Irish registration EI-BAA and delivered to Dublin on 24th May. She was immediately put to work transporting racehorses from Dublin, regularly flying to Cambridge, Deauville, Le Bourget and Luton but sometimes going much further afield e.g. to Milan, North Africa, New York and Punta Arenas (Southern Chile). In November 1974 she picked up a rather different ad hoc charter to operate for two months in Saudi Arabia for Pauline Construction (Middle East) Ltd, ferrying building materials to the site of a new airport. With 138 round trips, 2000 tonnes of cargo were carried. Once this was over, EI-BAA returned to Dublin after an overhaul, to resume her more usual work.

Aer Turas found the Britannias very useful for transporting racehorses so they decided to enlarge the fleet, just at the moment when the RAF was offering its entire fleet of 22 Britannias for sale. In September 1975 they purchased an ex-RAF Series 253F, XM 491, which they refurbished, repainted and re-registered as EI-BBH.

The nature of the racehorse ferrying work was very seasonal, at times very intense and at other times very slack. So while at times it was possible to keep two or more Britannias fully occupied, for others there was little for them to do and so they were leased out to other airlines. EI-BBH was leased to Cyprus Airways from September 1976 to April 1988 and to Gemini Air Transport from March to May 1979.

At the same time, Aer Turas began to be concerned

about the difficulty of obtaining spares for Britannias so, in association with Airline Engineering who had serviced Monarch Airline's Britannias, Aer Turas acquired two more ex-RAF aircraft. One of these, Series 252F, XN 392, was purchased in December 1975 and after the removal of usable spares the remains were scrapped in May 1976. The other one was also a Series 253F, XL 640, re-registered to Aer Turas as EI-BCI. The airline's intention seems to have been to reconfigure the cabin layout for commercial passenger use so as to seek contract work, but the history of the aircraft with Aer Turas is not very clear. It seems that Aer Turas wanted to purchase the aircraft in September 1976, but this sale failed to go through.

In February 1977 she was sold to a new Portuguese operator, Eurafric, and flown out of Luton in her new livery bound for Dublin (to do some crew training) and then Lisbon. Soon after take-off, however, the crew received a warning of trouble with the undercarriage which necessitated a return to Luton. While the aircraft was parked awaiting attention, the nose wheel suddenly retracted with the main gear remaining down. The result was that the fuselage tilted and the nose came down heavily on to a tractor and was considerably damaged. Temporary repairs were carried out at Luton, followed by more extensive repairs at Bristol.

In fact EI-BCI seems never to have operated for Eurafric. She was in service with Aer Turas in early 1978 while EI-BAA was being overhauled, operating livestock and shorthaul bloodstock charters. (This was a new growing market, transporting cattle and other live animals, not just racehorses). Later that year she was again back in service with Aer Turas because of the high demand for livestock and bloodstock transport work. Then, as part of the Aer Turas policy of re-equipping with newer replacements for the ageing Britannias, she was offered for sale and was finally bought by Redcoat Air Cargo in August 1979.

There was one other Britannia flown by Aer Turas, ex-RAF Series 253F, XL 639, leased in June 1977 and registered as EI-BDC. She immediately operated two livestock charters from Cork, one to Milan and the other to Le Havre. She was then sub-leased to Cyprus Airways for two spells; 19th June to 5th July and 17th September to 7th November 1977. For Aer Turas she operated a series of livestock flights from Dublin, Shannon and Cork and was finally sold to Eurafric in January 1978.

By 1981 Aer Turas' fleet of Britannias had all been sold or scrapped. What is interesting is the aircraft which replaced them. In the case of most airlines which flew Britannias, the successors were Boeing 707s or Douglas DC-8s, principally on the grounds of their greater speed. Aer Turas rejected that alternative on the grounds of relative fuel inefficiency of the jets, uncertainty about noise restrictions in the future and the high cost of maintenance of jets. Instead they went for the Canadian derivative of the Britannia, the CL-44.

During the time of Aer Turas' use of the Britannias, another Irish organisation also bought a Britannia. Interconair, a division of the (Irish) Intercontinental Meat Company, bought a Britannia, Series 253F XL 658, which was re-registered in Ireland as EI-BBY in August 1976. She was used to transport cattle from Ireland to the UK and continental Europe but on 30th September 1977, after just over one year of service, she

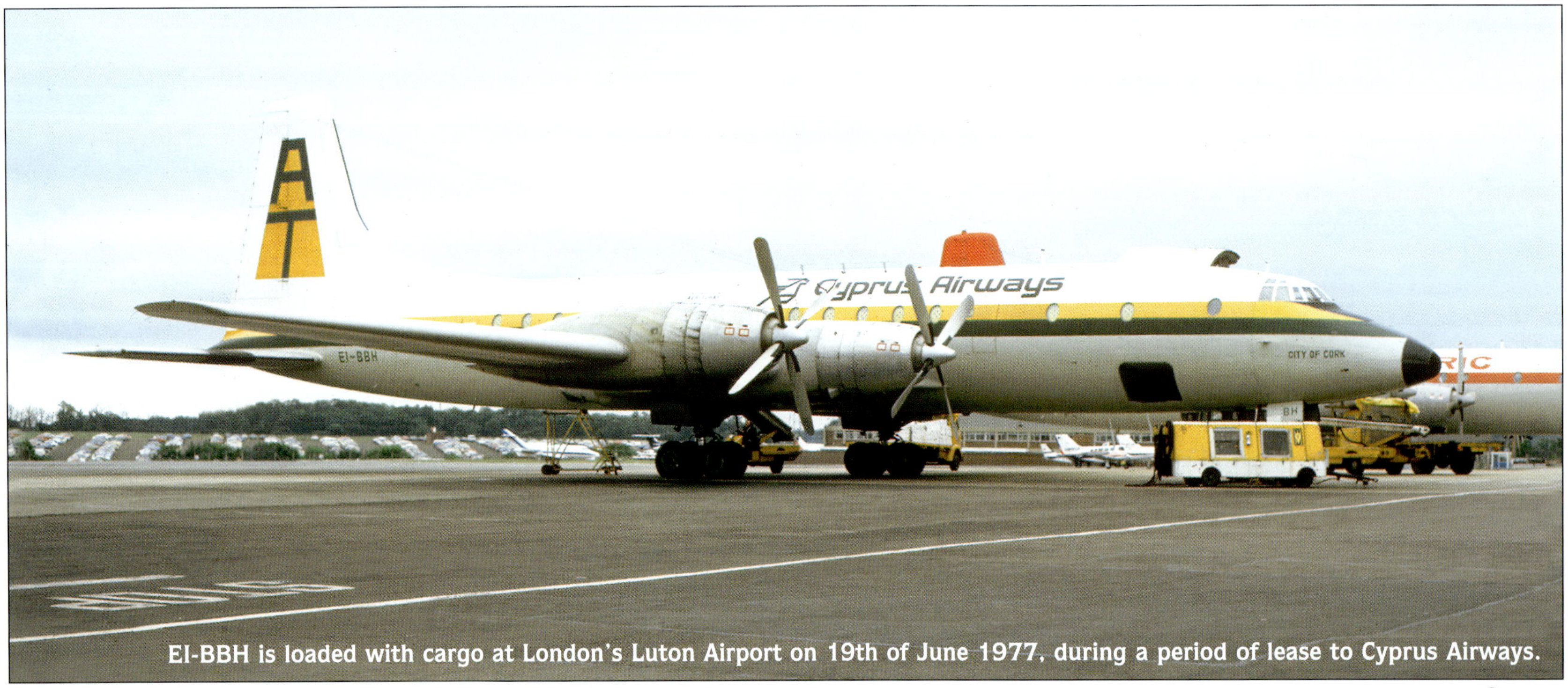

EI-BBH is loaded with cargo at London's Luton Airport on 19th of June 1977, during a period of lease to Cyprus Airways.

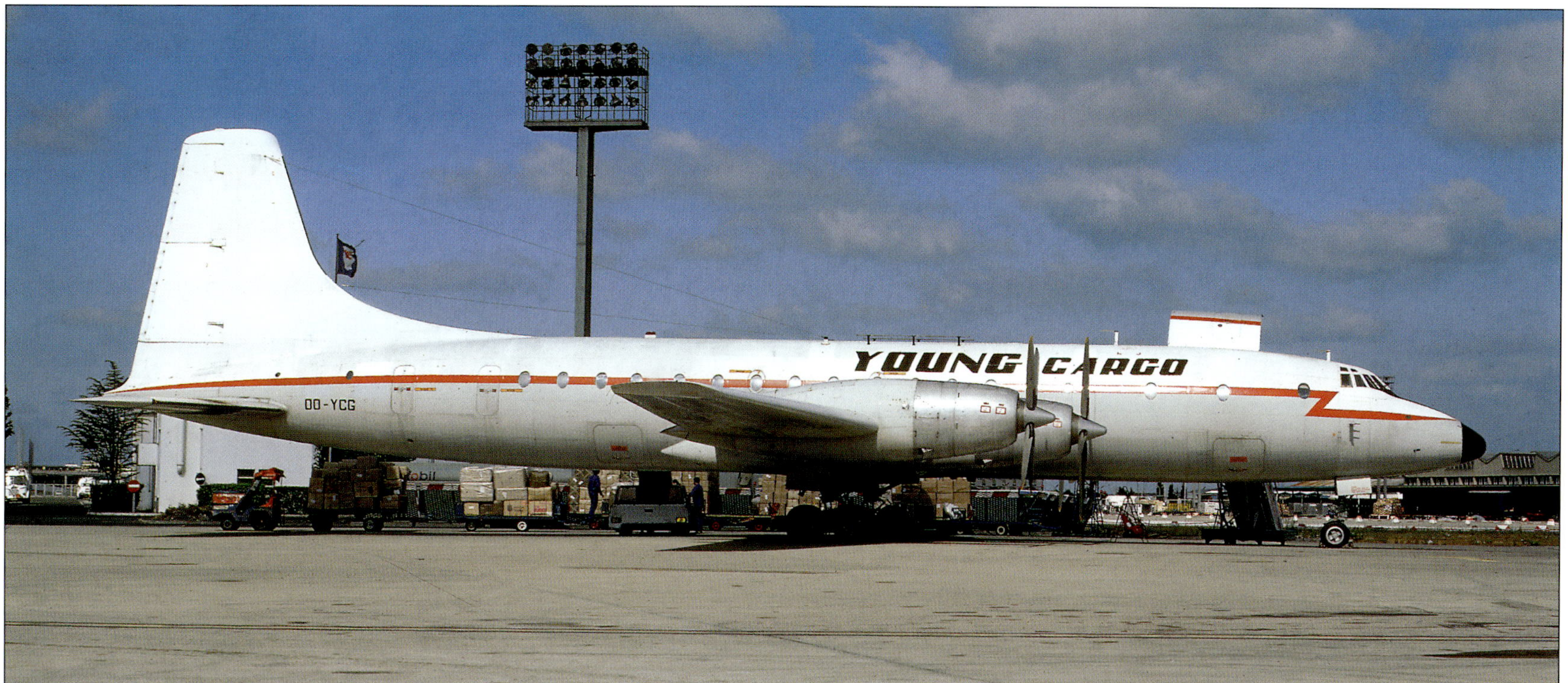

In June 1976, OO-YCG of Young Cargo is loaded with freight at Ostend Airport Belgium.

crash-landed and caught fire just short of the runway at Shannon Airport. All on board escaped without injury but the aircraft was declared a write-off and so that airline ceased operating.

YOUNG CARGO SERVICES (YOUNG AIR CARGO)

In the mid-1970s Young Cargo Services, a Belgian airline based in Gosselies and Brussels, already operated a Canadian CL-44, the Britannia derivative. It then took a bold decision to buy eight ex-RAF Britannias. Its intention was to operate four of these and to use the other four as a source of spare parts, which were otherwise becoming hard to obtain. But whatever the intention, the actuality did not quite match it.

All the Britannias bought were the RAF Series 253F variants, with the forward portside freight loading door and a strengthened forward fuselage floor, and so were particularly suited to cargo work. The first two purchased by Young Air Cargo on 5th September 1975 were XL 635 and XL 659 and both were given Belgian registrations, OO-YCA and OO-YCB respectively. The former aircraft seems to have been quickly put to work on cargo charter work between Belgium and destinations in Africa, the latter aircraft being used as a source of spares.

During 1976, five more Britannias were bought by Young Air Cargo. On 10th February, XM 489 was bought and re-registered as OO-YCC although it was not operated by Young Air Cargo but used as a source of spares. Similarly on 4th March, XM 518 was bought, registered as OO-YCD, and also used as a source of spares then, on 23rd April, XM 497 was purchased as OO-YCF (although this registration mark was never painted on the fuselage) and left at Stansted as a source of spares. Next, on 6th May, XL 636 was purchased, re-registered as OO-YCE and delivered at Brussels but she only had a short service with Young Air Cargo before being withdrawn from service and stored at Ostend. The fifth arrival on 11th June 1976 was XM 498. Registered as OO-YCG, she was delivered to Brussels but within a month she was back at Stansted for re-painting in the livery of Liberia World Airways to which she was leased. She was not used again by Young Air Cargo.

So, by the end of 1977, Young Air Cargo had two Britannias operational and under its command, OO-YCA and OO-YCE, and a healthy supply of spare parts available from OO-YCB, OO-YCC, OO-YCD and OO-YCF.

In August 1977 Young Air Cargo bought XL 637 which was registered as OO-YCH. Apart from a short lease to Liberia World Airways in September 1977, she operated for Young Air Cargo until December 1978 when she was withdrawn from service, but subsequently purchased by Domaine de Katale (later named Katale Aero Transport).

During 1977 Young Air Cargo decided to modernise its fleet by leasing two Boeing 707s and it gradually withdrew its Britannias. OO-YCA was leased to Liberia World Airways but never delivered. The aircraft was withdrawn by Young Air Cargo in September 1977 and purchased by Domaine de Katale in April 1979.

Young Air Cargo operated with its leased Boeing 707s for several months, but its operations ceased during 1979.

KATALE AERO TRANSPORT (DOMAINE DE KATALE)

Katale Aero Transport, a company based in Goma (Zaire), was the world's last operator of a sizeable fleet of Britannia aircraft. Over the years from 1977 onwards, the fleet numbered up to seven aircraft although not all were airworthy and some were used as a source of spares, as was the case with other airlines at the time. Also Katale did not usually repaint its Britannias but usually kept the livery of the previous owner, just adding Katale titling.

There had been links between Britannias and Zaire since 1975, involving the airlines Agence et Messagers Aérienne du Zaire (AMAZ), Zaire Aero Service, IAC Airlines and Lukum Air Services. Each of these owned just one Britannia, by comparison with which the involvement of Katale was much bigger and lasted longer.

The first Britannia that Katale purchased came from Zaire Aero Service. She was an ex-RAF Series 252F aircraft, registered in Zaire as 9Q-CPX. She had been with Zaire Aero Service since February 1977 but was leased to Katale in November 1977 and later purchased by them. By 1991 Katale had withdrawn the aircraft by January 1991 and she was scrapped in Goma, Zaire.

Katale's activities were almost entirely internal to Zaire. From the base in Goma the task for aircraft was to fly cargoes of coffee, fruit and other agricultural produce from Goma to destinations within Zaire. There was also a need to transport consumer goods, machinery etc. around the country where the roads were often poor and the distances large. (Goma to Mbuji-Mayi 500 miles; Mbuji-Mayi to Kinshasa 600 miles, each by direct flight). People who could afford it also valued the quickness of flying, for example Kinshasa to Mbuji-Mayi took around two hours.

Katale's initial experience with the first Britannia must have been favourable for negotiations soon began to buy more. OO-YCH, an ex-RAF Series 253F which had been owned and then stored by Young Air Cargo since December 1978, was purchased by Katale in April 1979 and re-registered as 9Q-CBT. It seems to have been stored again and presumably used as a source of spares. OO-YCG, also an ex-RAF Series 253F and also owned by Young Air Cargo, was purchased by Katale in May 1979 and re-registered as 9Q-CDT. She was eventually sold on to Business Cash Flow Aviation in July 1988.

The next two purchases were in 1982. In April 1982, the airline purchased a Britannia ex-RAF Series 253F, registered G-BHAU, from Swordvale Aviation Ltd. She was re-registered as 9Q-CHU and flown to Zaire. After about four years she was withdrawn from service, stored at Kinshasa and broken up for scrap in 1986. Katale also purchased another ex-RAF Series 253F variant from Swordvale Aviation Ltd. This was purchased

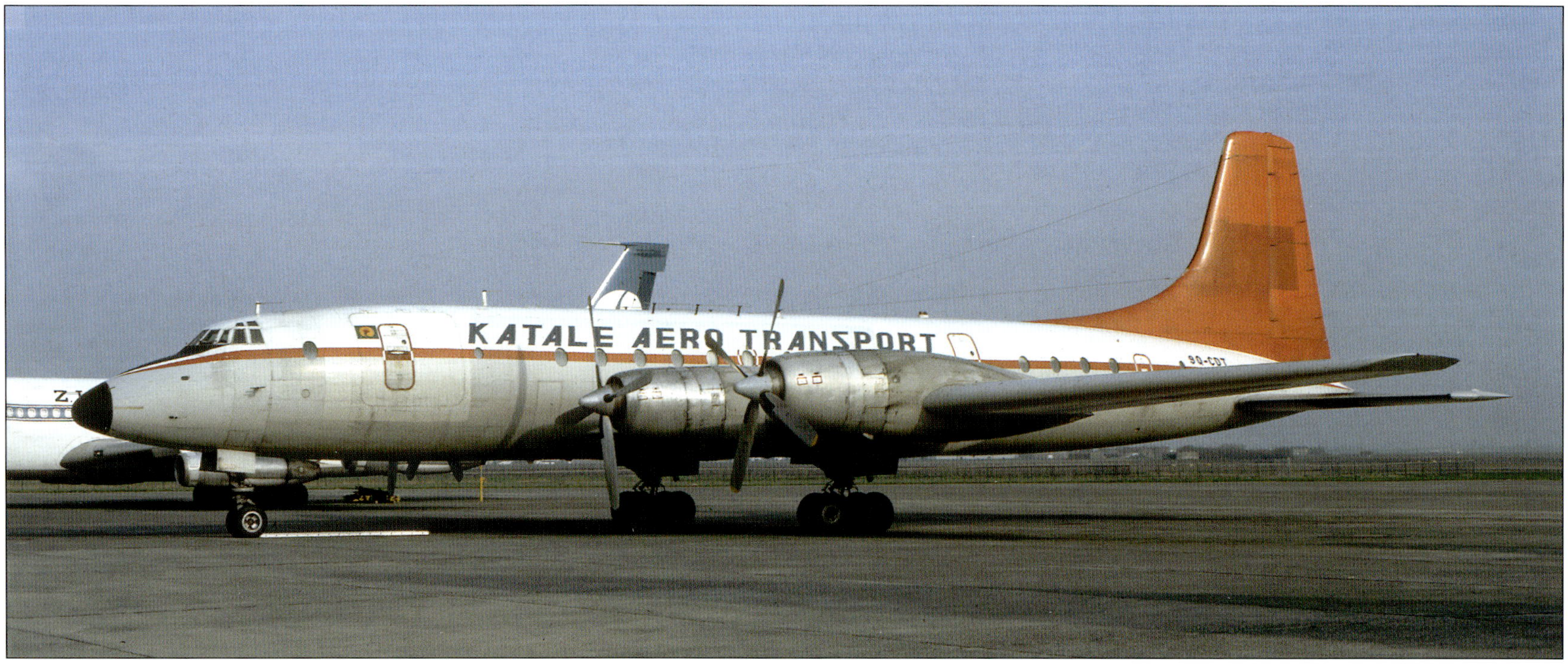

On 24th March 1980, 9Q-CDT sits idle at Ostend Airport Belgium.

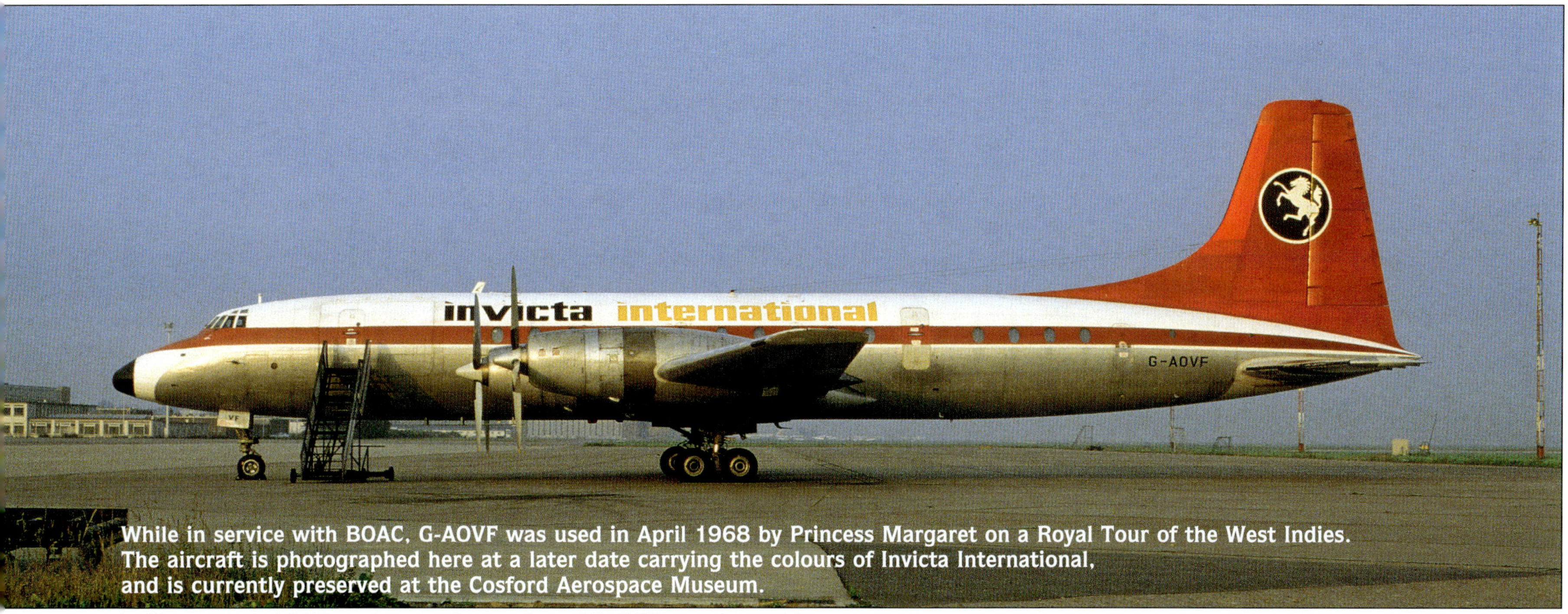

While in service with BOAC, G-AOVF was used in April 1968 by Princess Margaret on a Royal Tour of the West Indies. The aircraft is photographed here at a later date carrying the colours of Invicta International, and is currently preserved at the Cosford Aerospace Museum.

in November 1982 and re-registered as 9Q-CGP, serving with Katale for some years until eventually being withdrawn and broken up at an uncertain date but definitely by 1992.

There were two final purchases. In March 1984, Katale bought a Series 312F variant, owned at that time by the MoD and based at Boscombe Down. She was re-registered as 9Q-CHY and soon ferried to Zaire to begin service for her new owners. She did this until April 1989 when she was sold to Business Cash Flow Aviation.

9Q-CUM, the last to be purchased, was sold to Katale by Lukum Air Services in July 1986. She never flew for Katale, but was used as a source of spares.

The reason for the withdrawal of the Britannias is the familiar one. Late in 1988 Katale decided to retire its Britannias in favour of more modern (and faster) Boeing 707s and DC-8s. Also, by this time, the Britannias were beginning to show the wear and tear of age, so that their reliability was becoming suspect. The success of the fleet for Katale is a tribute to the skill of the maintenance teams.

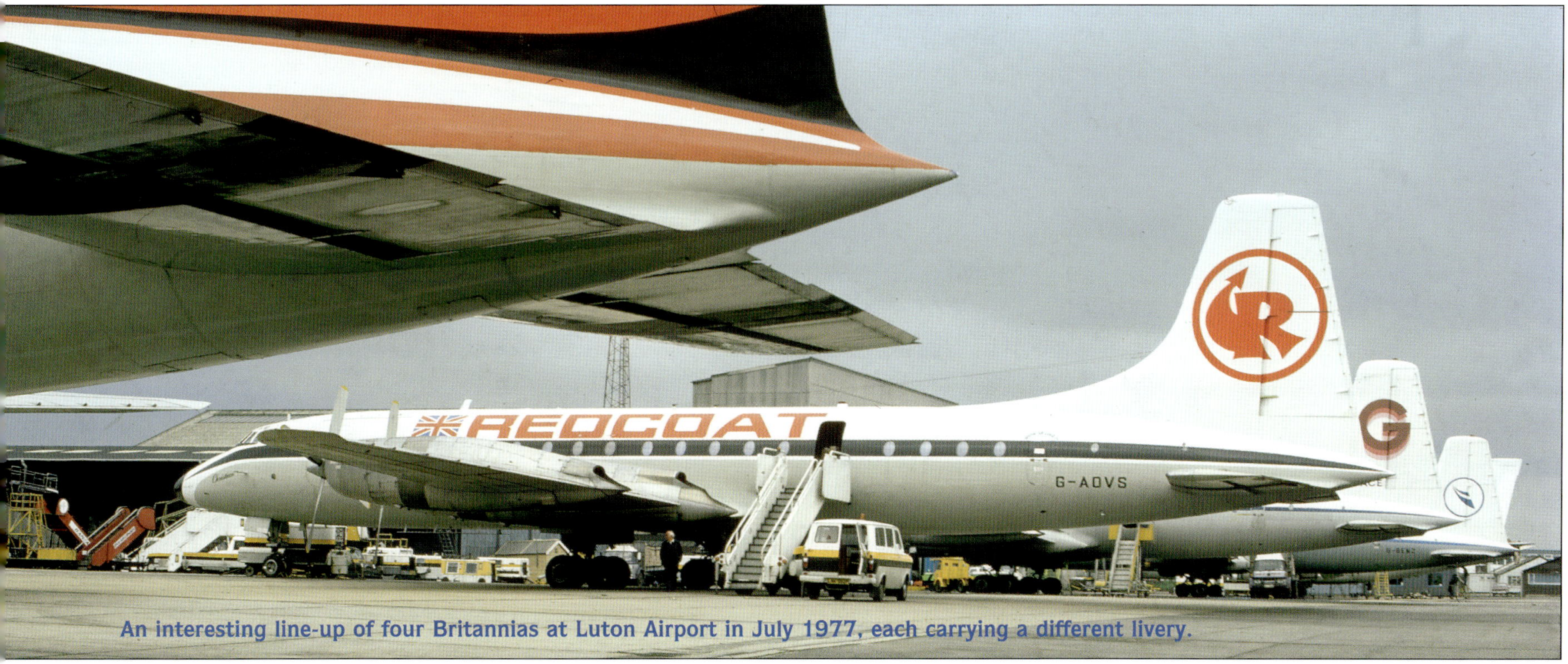

An interesting line-up of four Britannias at Luton Airport in July 1977, each carrying a different livery.

IN SERVICE WITH INVICTA AND REDCOAT AIR CARGO

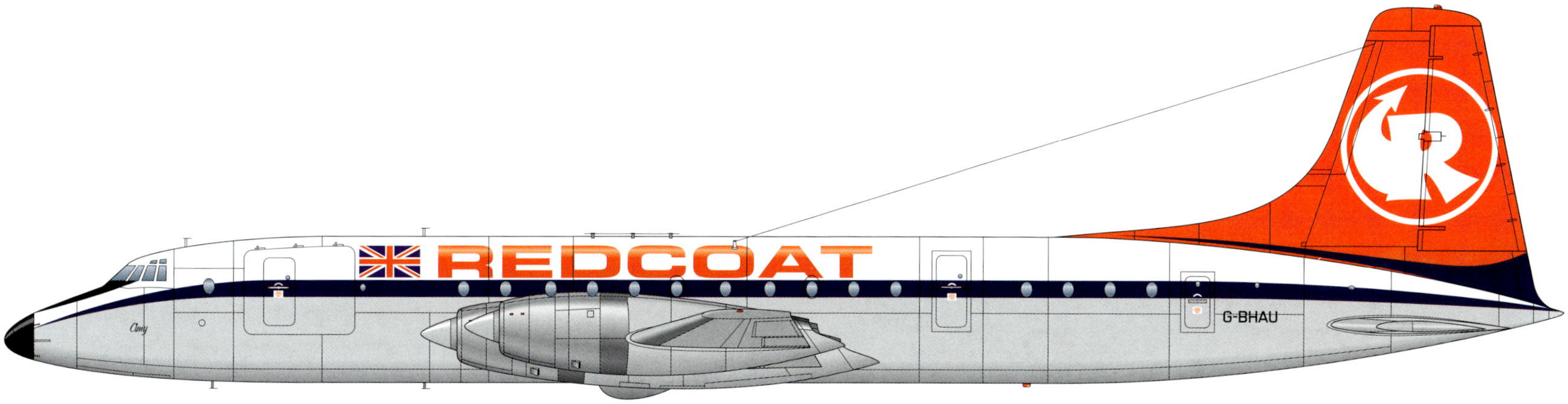

Both of these airlines were based in Britain and each ran a small-scale operation, with never more than three Britannias each.

INVICTA

Invicta had operated for a number of years with various types of aircraft (not Britannias) but because of financial difficulty had ceased operations and sold off the aircraft in October 1975. However operations began again in December 1975 and the airline acquired two Britannias in 1976.

The airline had previously had brief experience of the Britannia when it leased Series 312, G-AOVT, from Monarch Airlines from 13th December 1974 to 10th March 1975. This was long enough to appreciate the merits of a Britannia and perhaps to see the attraction of the freighter modification, with the large cargo door at the front of the fuselage. All of the Britannias which it subsequently used were freighter modifications.

The first Britannia which was acquired after resumed operations was leased from Westwings Aviation. It was Series 312F, G-AOVS, leased on 1st January 1976, which had the distinction of flying the first commercial cargo for the new airline. Three months later Invicta leased another Britannia of the same variant, G-AOVF, from IAS Cargo Airlines in April 1976. (Later, on 8th November 1978 Invicta bought her from IAS Cargo). These two Britannias undertook a wide range of cargo charters, including carrying racehorses and cattle, operating mainly throughout the UK and mainland Europe. A third Britannia 308F, G-ANCF, was leased by Invicta from Monarch Airlines on 14th June 1976 until 7th January 1977 when Invicta bought her.

The airline continued with these aircraft for a few years without exactly flourishing. G-AOVS was returned at the end of the lease in June 1976, whilst G-ANCF flew her last service for Invicta on 30th October 1980 and was then sent for a major overhaul. This left only G-AOVF operating for Invicta. She was leased out to IAC Cargo Airlines but Invicta, as a separate Airline, ceased to exist in 1981.

REDCOAT AIR CARGO

Redcoat Air Cargo was formed in 1976 and began by leasing an ex-RAF Britannia, Series 253F, 9G-ACE, from its owner Gemini Air Transport. The lease ran from 7th May 1976 for one year.

The airline immediately began running a weekly cargo service from Luton (its UK base) to Accra (Ghana). This was successful enough for the aircraft owner, Gemini, to want to use the aircraft for the same purpose itself once the lease ran out. This was the cause of some friction between the companies, for Redcoat had already made plans to purchase a Britannia of its own in order to continue the service which it had built up using the Gemini leased aircraft.

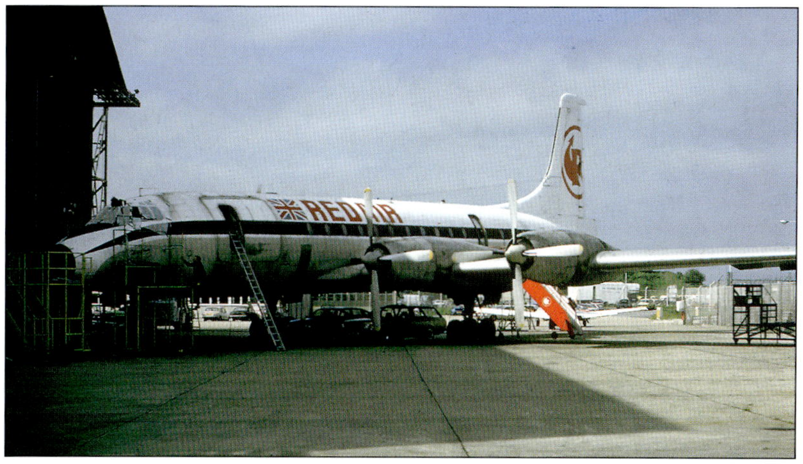

G-AOVS of Redcoat, carrying the spurious registration G-BRAC and the titles of Redair, for its starring role in the BBC TV series 'Buccaneer'.

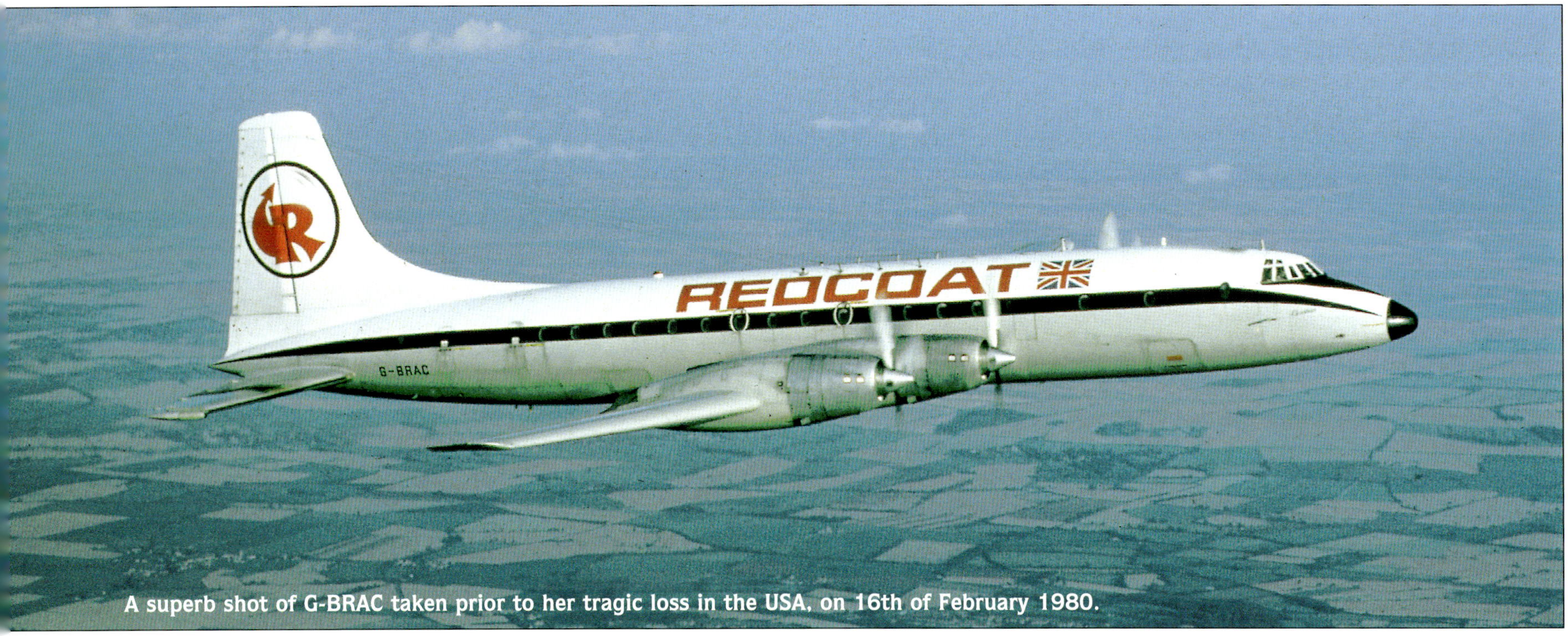

A superb shot of G-BRAC taken prior to her tragic loss in the USA, on 16th of February 1980.

Matters came to a head when G-AOVS, with a load of cargo for Accra on board, was refused permission by the Ghanaian authorities to land at Accra. The aircraft had to divert to Sal (Cape Verde Islands) to re-fuel and then return to Luton with the Accra load still on board. There followed some high level discussion, to the extent of suggesting that if Redcoat was not allowed to fly into Ghana then Gemini, as a Ghanaian company, might not be allowed to fly into the UK. Matters were finally resolved and Redcoat was allowed to fly into Ghana, and on 27th May 1977 G-AOVS landed at Accra with 17.5 tonnes of cargo on board.

The cargo service which Redcoat established was a weekly one from Luton to Accra. It took split freight charters (minimum 1 tonne) to places in West Africa like Accra, Abidjan, Bamako, Banjul, Bissau, Lomé, Monrovia, Dakar, Cape Verde Islands, Conakry, Freetown, Niamey and Nouakchott (Mauritania). Goods carried out included building equipment, machinery, mining equipment and oil related cargo, whilst returned cargo included fruit from Accra, Abidjan and Dakar and furniture from Ghana.

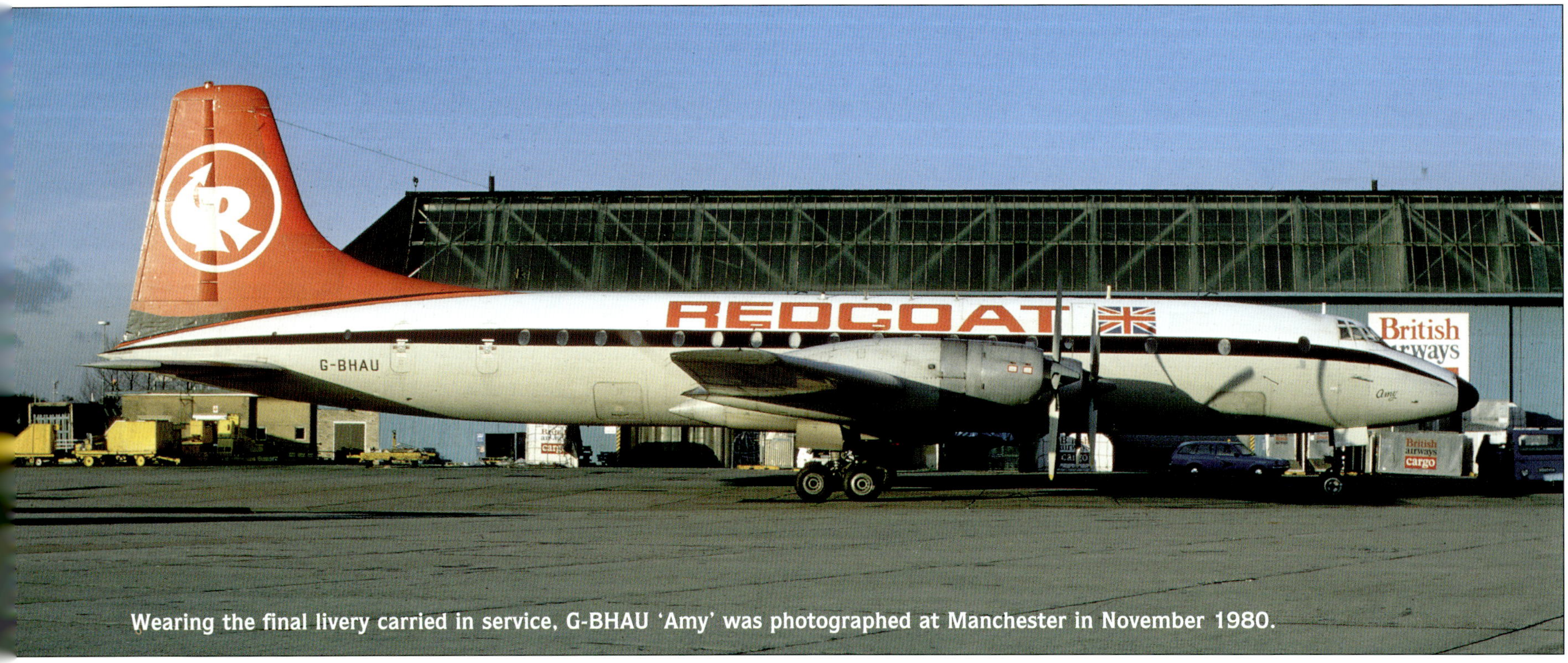

Wearing the final livery carried in service, G-BHAU 'Amy' was photographed at Manchester in November 1980.

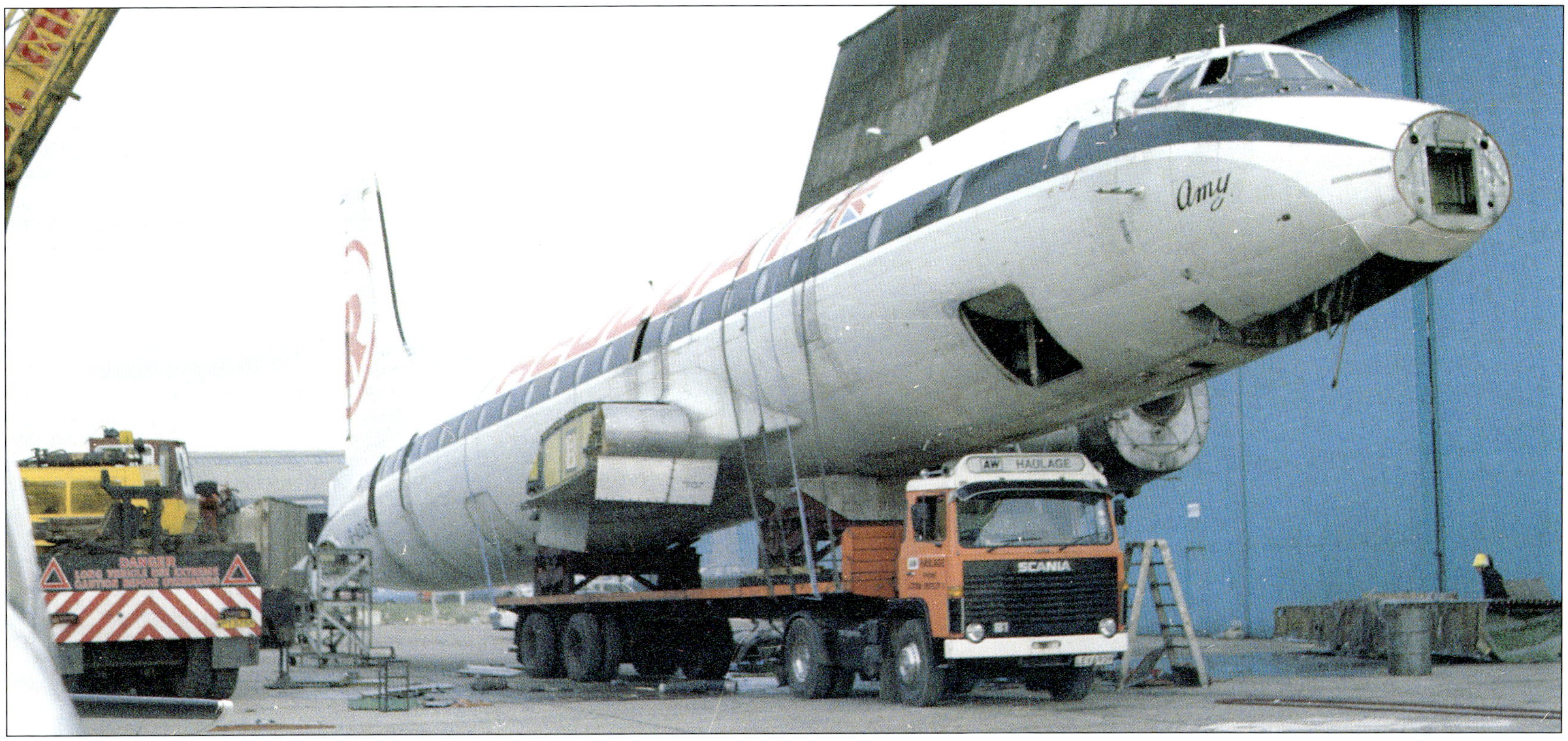

In July 1979, G-AOVS is prepared for transport to the fire dump ot Luton Airport.

The first months of its operations had been sufficiently encouraging for Redcoat to want to expand its Britannia fleet. The first addition was an ex-BOAC Series 312F, G-AOVS, mentioned above. After passing through various owners it was leased by Redcoat from Aivex Holdings on 5th May 1977 (and subsequently purchased by Redcoat in April 1979). The next addition was a purchase from Eurafric of another Britannia, this time an ex-RAF Series 253F, registered as G-BRAC. She changed ownership on 4th June, was overhauled and re-painted, then flew her first service for Redcoat on 5th July 1978, taking over 12 tonnes of Ford motor components from Luton to Cologne.

The airline had developed into a general cargo transporting facility. Cattle were carried from Stansted or Manston to destinations in Italy; a replacement 108ft mast with rigging and sails for the yacht 'Condor', a contender in the Whitbread round the world yacht race, was flown out to Liberia; 16 tonnes of Gerry Cottle's circus equipment (excluding animals!) were transported from Keflavík (Iceland) to Luton; one typical split freight cargo, on one of the airline's regular weekly runs to West Africa, comprised car spares, Ghana postage stamps and general construction equipment making up a total load of 16 tonnes being shipped by 20 different exporters.

During the autumn of 1979, G-AOVS and G-BRAC were used as part of the equipment for the BBC TV drama series 'Buccaneer'. However, in spite of optimistic statements about the future being made by Redcoat during 1978/9, events turned out less favourably. In July 1979 G-AOVS was withdrawn from service and then, in February 1980, G-BRAC was lost shortly after take-off from Boston with a cargo load en route via Shannon to Luton. The weather was poor and wing icing seems to have been the cause of the accident, with the aircraft being unable to gain height after leaving the runway. The crash wrote off the aircraft and killed seven people, the crew and some people on the ground.

So within a few months Redcoat's fleet was reduced to one Britannia, G-BHAU. This aircraft had been leased from Eurafric

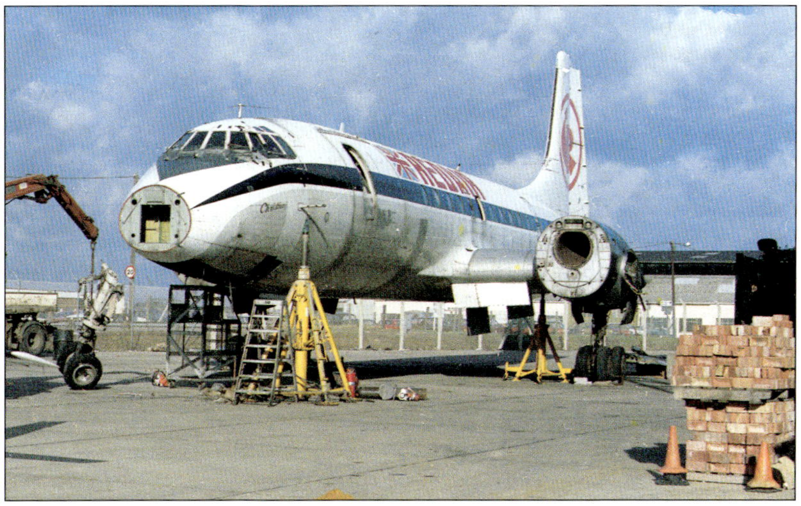

'Christine' is seen being dismantled at Luton. (Note that the aircraft carried 'Christine' and 'Amy' on opposite sides of the nose).

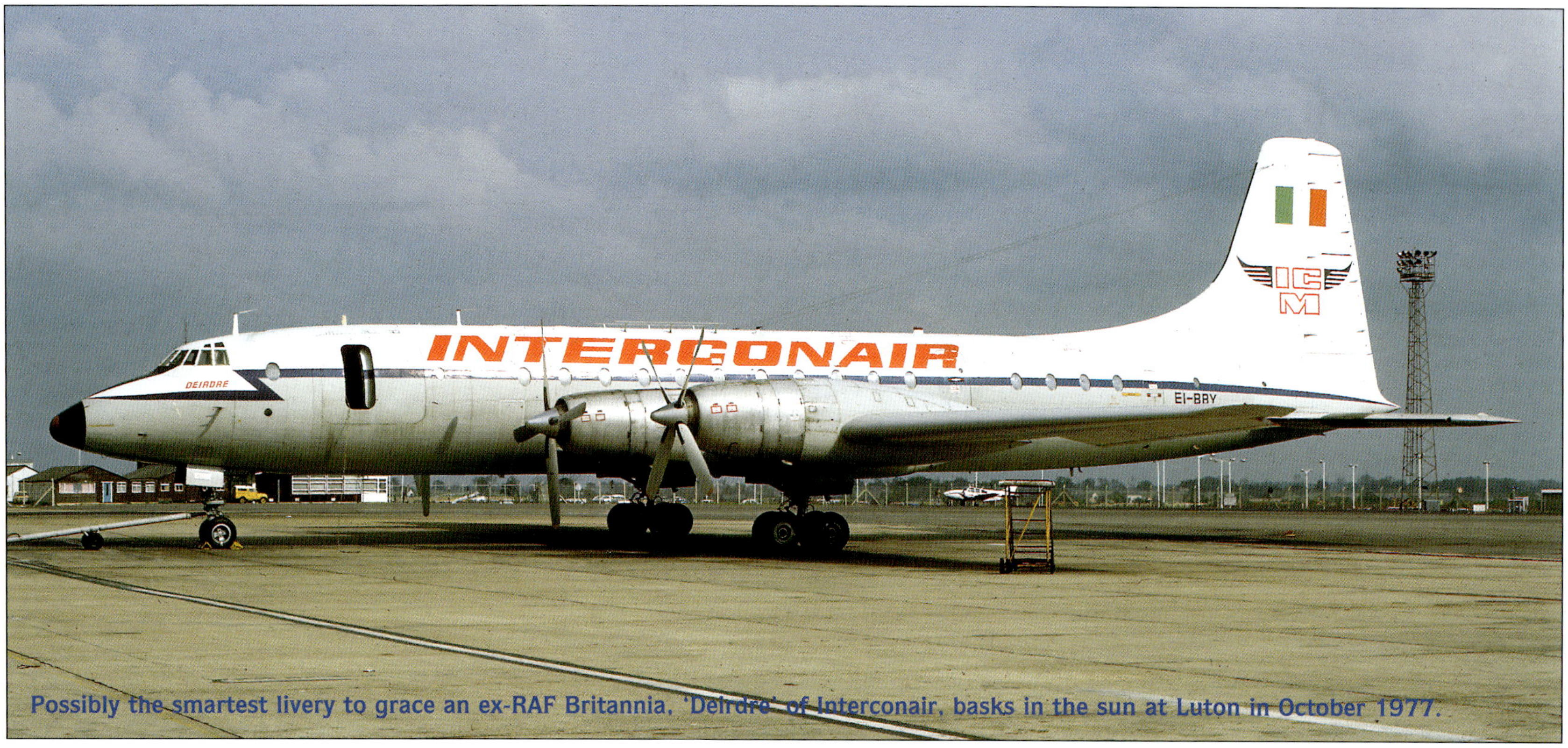

Possibly the smartest livery to grace an ex-RAF Britannia, 'Deirdre' of Interconair, basks in the sun at Luton in October 1977.

on 13th August 1979 to replace G-AOVS, but after the loss of G-BRAC it was the only Britannia remaining with the airline after February 1980. She carried on actively, mainly ferrying cattle from Forli (Italy) to Nigeria.

There was also some ad hoc cargo charter work to be had, enough for Redcoat to lease another Britannia, Series 253F, G-BEMZ, from Black Arrow Leasing via Gaylan Air Cargo on 22nd September 1981.

By December 1981, however, it was clear that the airline was no longer economic and Redcoat ceased operations. G-BEMZ was returned to Black Arrow Leasing and G-BHAU was sold on to Swordvale Aviation.

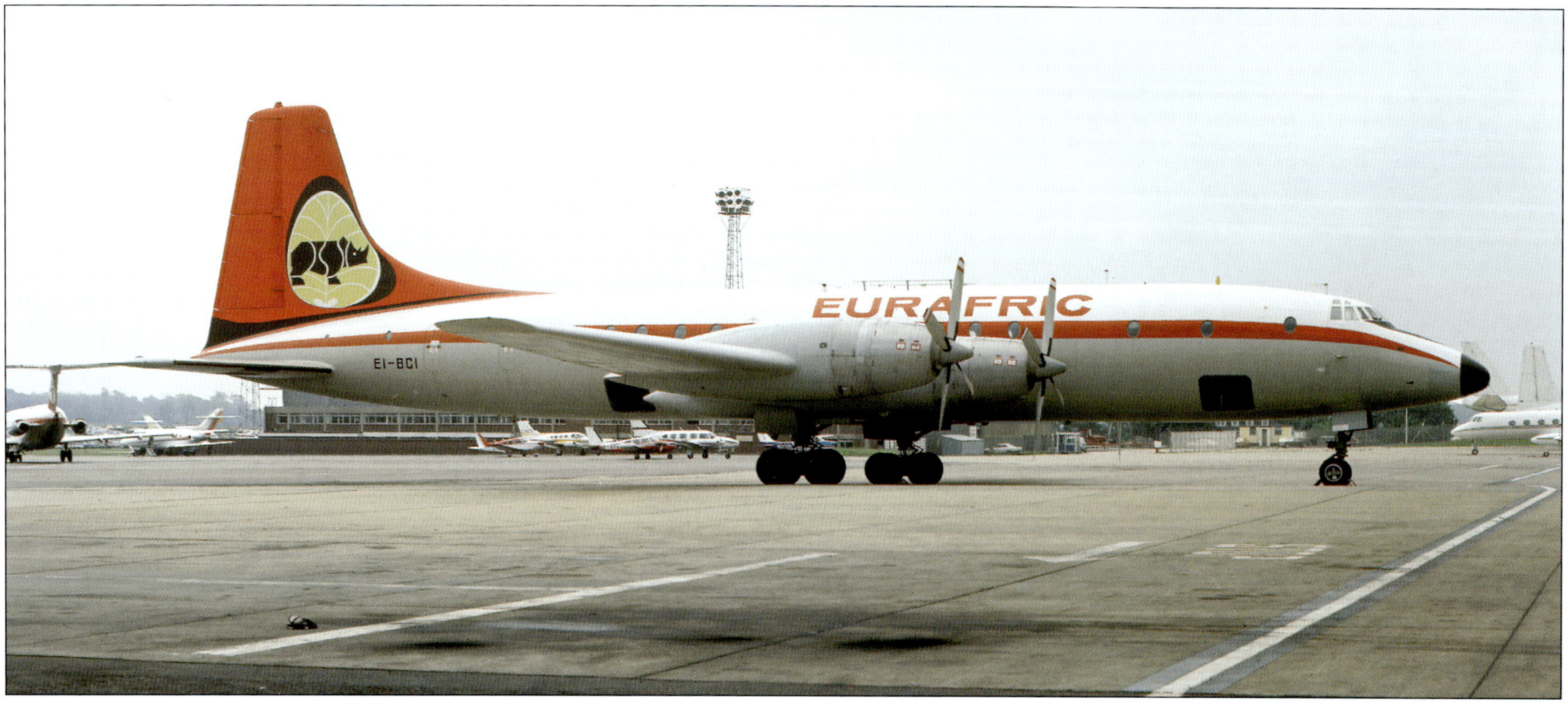

Ex-RAF Series 253 CMk 1 EI-BCI, wears the attractive livery of Eurafric at Luton in July 1977.

IN SERVICE WITH INTERCONAIR, EURAFRIC AND AFREK

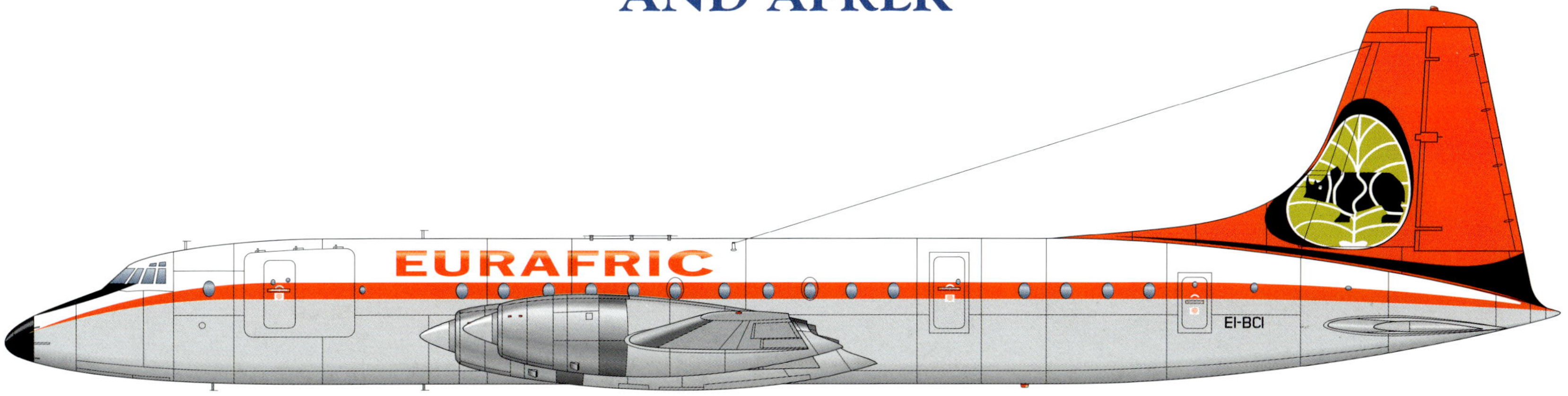

These three airlines are the only European airlines not yet dealt with. Each had only a small-scale Britannia operation involving one, or at the most, two aircraft.

INTERCONAIR

The operation of this airline was short and ended in a crash and write-off, as described in the section on Aer Turas. The airline was formed in 1976 as a division of the Irish based Intercontinental Meat Company. It acquired, via Airline Engineering, an ex-RAF Britannia Series 253F, registered in Ireland as EI-BBY. The handover was on 10th August 1976 and the Britannia commenced work on cattle charter flights. However, just over a year later on 30th September 1977, it was badly damaged when landing at Shannon and the damage was severe enough for the aircraft to be deemed irreparable. This was not only the end of the aircraft but also caused the collapse of the airline itself.

EURAFRIC

This small airline had a very eye-catching livery, with the tailfin painting incorporating a rhino. Details of airline operations are scarce but what is known for certain is that the airline was based in Lisbon.

In September 1976 ex-RAF Britannia Series 253F, XL 640, was due to be sold by its current owner Monarch Airlines to Aer Turas. This sale failed to go through and the aircraft was subsequently bought in March 1977 by Eurafric and registered in Ireland as EI-BCI. It was promptly leased by Eurafric to Aer Turas and apparently never operated any commercial flight for Eurafric. What is clear is that having finished the Aer Turas contracts it remained on the ground at Luton until purchased by Redcoat Air Cargo in August 1979.

Eurafric also purchased another ex-RAF Britannia, Series 253F, XL639, also registered in Ireland as EI-BDC. The purchase was made from Airline Engineering in January 1978 but by June the aircraft had been sold on to Redcoat Air Cargo. In the intervening six months, however, it seems that it did carry out some cargo service for Eurafric, presumably between Europe and Africa.

AFREK

Afrek, a Greek airline based in Athens, purchased two ex-RAF Britannia Series 253F aircraft in 1976. XM 496, now registered in the UK as G-BDUP, was purchased from its current owners, Monarch Airlines Engineering, in May 1976. XM519, registered in the UK as G-BDUR, was purchased from Airline Engineering in July 1976. The airline was part of a Greek construction company, Edok Eter, and was used to ferry personnel, company cargo and supplies under contract to places in the Middle East and West Africa.

Initially the level of work kept both Britannias busy, supplying construction sites in Douala (Cameroon) and in Kano and Maiduguri (Nigeria). There were also some charter cargo flights, for example flying fresh fruit from Thessalonica (northern Greece) to Tripoli. But as Edok Eter finished its construction work in Douala and Kano, the only remaining work for the airline was to Maiduguri and that flight was only required about once a month.

During January 1983 G-BDUR had a routine service at Luton (by Monarch Aircraft Engineering) and its flight back to Athens on 18th January was the company's final operation. On 1st February the Afrek Managing Director announced that the Nigerian Government's embargo on imports had made the airline operation into Nigeria impossible. Furthermore the Nigerians owed Edok Eter a great deal of money for work already completed.

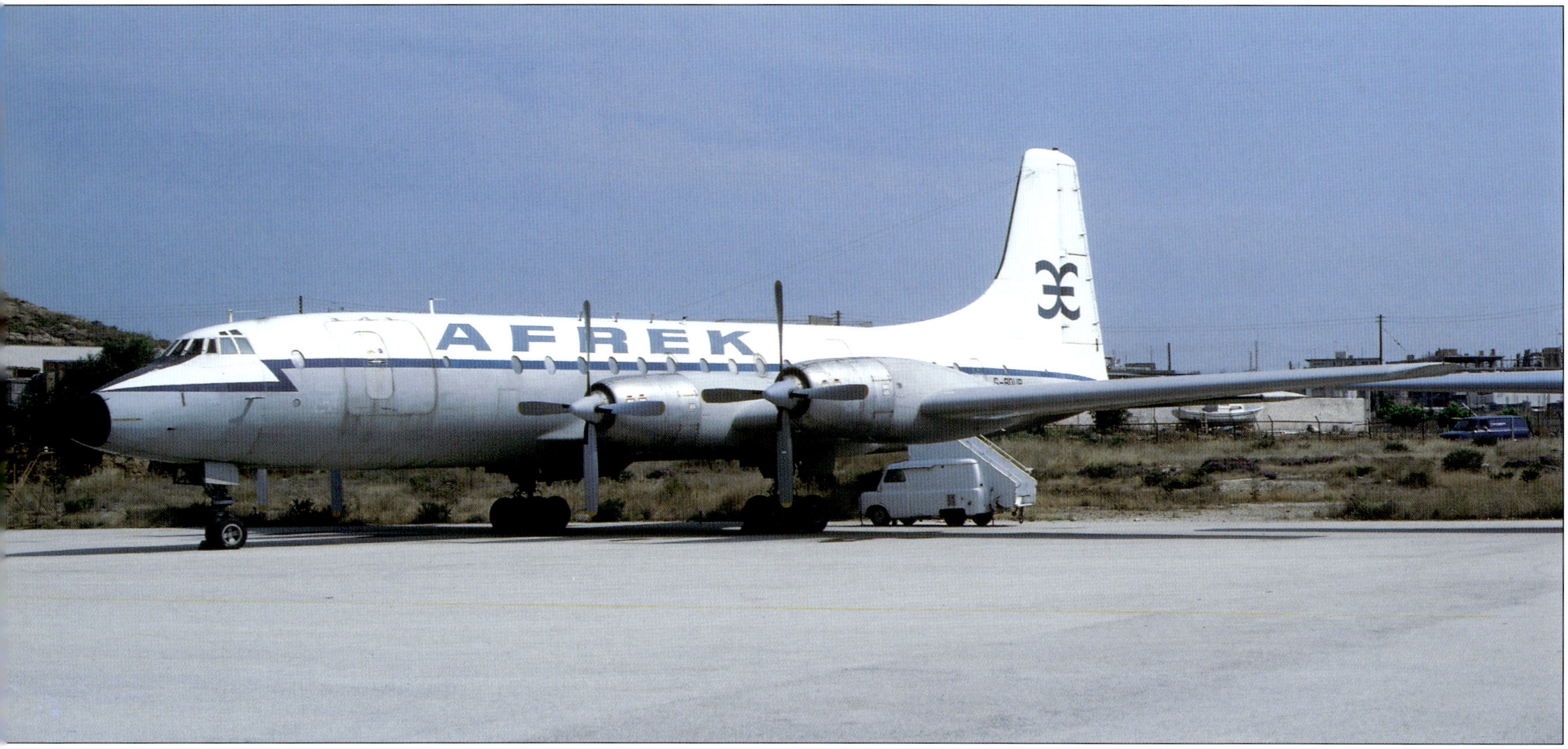

Photographed during storage at Athens Greece in June 1979, G-BDUR looks the worst for wear. The aircraft was resurrected to serve with Aerocaribbean from late in 1984.

Both Britannias therefore remained grounded in Athens, although regularly maintained by a dedicated engineer, Tom Lowe. Once it was clear that Afrek would not fly again, the aircraft were offered for sale and, after overhaul, both G-BDUP and G-BDUR went to Aerocaribbean in August 1984 for several more years of service.

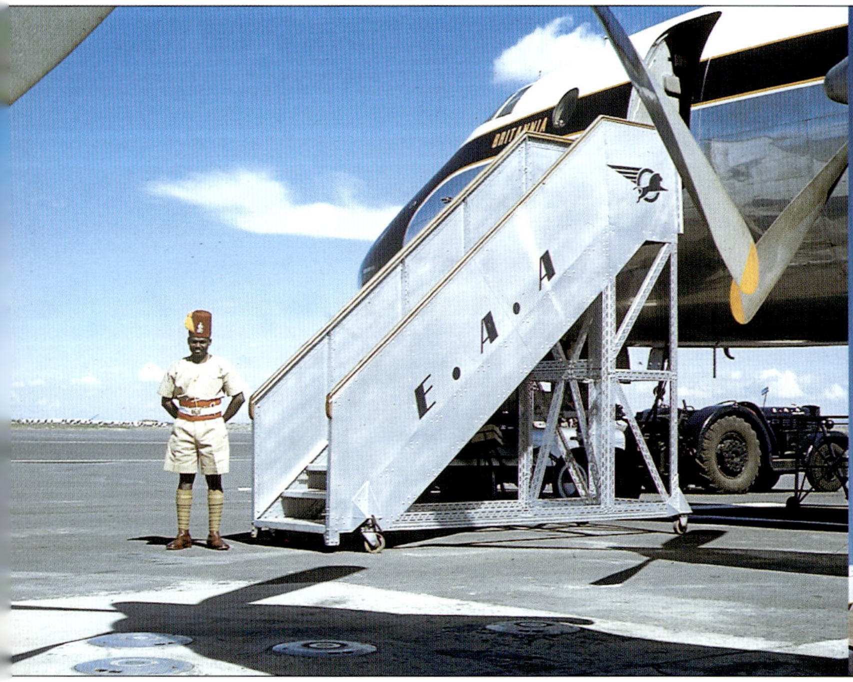

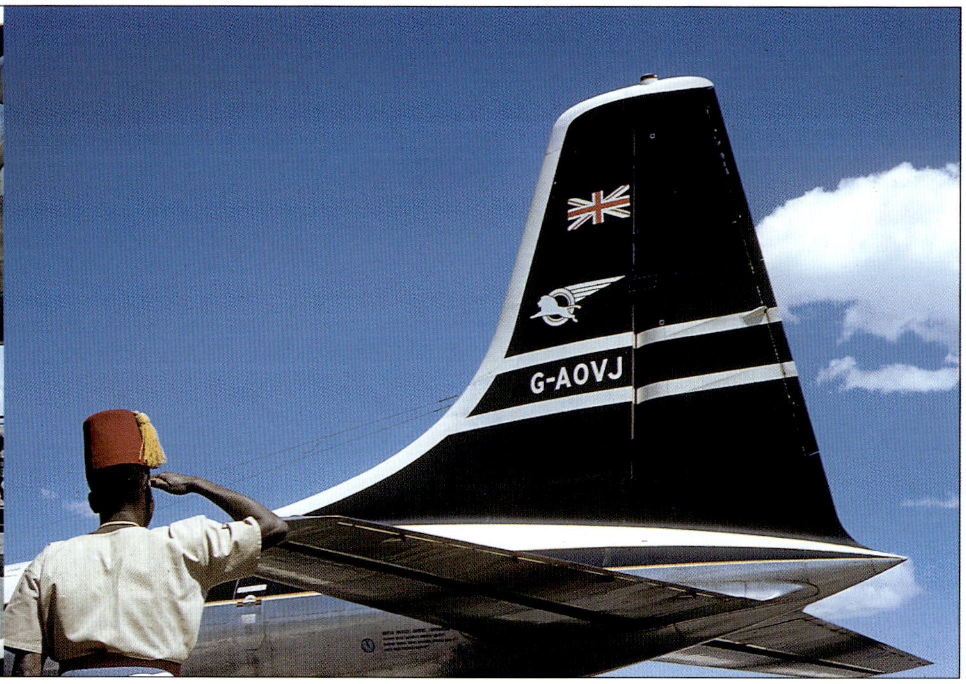

Two nostalgic views of G-AOVJ at Nairobi Kenya, while under lease to East African Airways from BOAC in the early 1960s.

IN SERVICE WITH AFRICAN CARRIERS

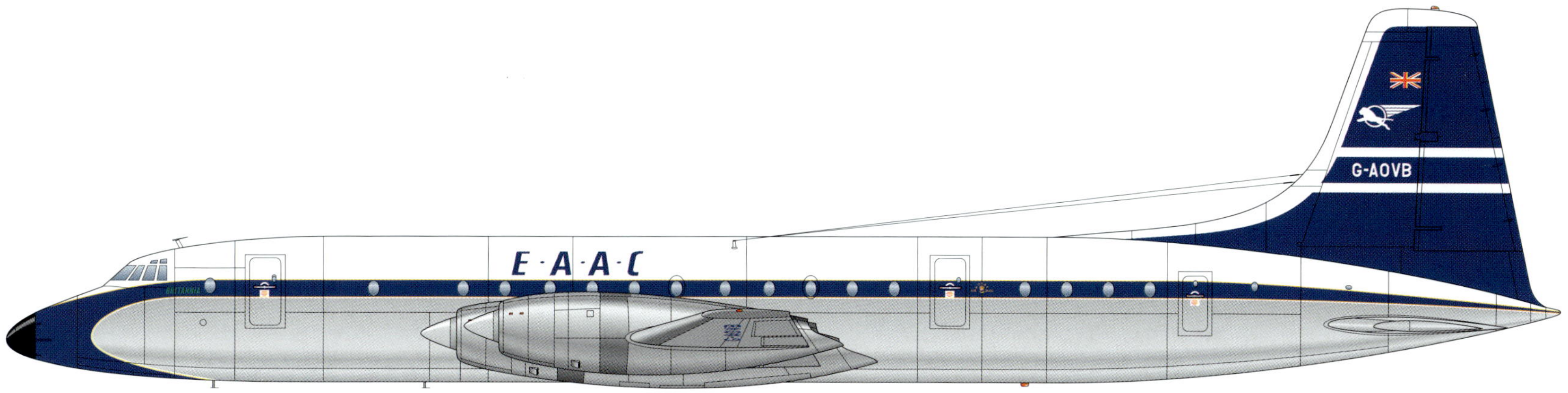

EAST AFRICAN AIRWAYS CORPORATION (EAAC)

EAAC was an airline jointly owned by Kenya, Tanganyika, (now called Tanzania), and Uganda. Between 1958 and 1973 it leased nine different Britannias, mostly for periods of less than a year each and with never more than two at any one time. As the aircraft were leased and not bought, they retained their British registrations.

In sequence the aircraft were: BOAC Series 102, G-ANBN for a time 'in 1958'; BOAC Series 312, G-AOVB from 5th November to 3rd December 1958; BOAC Series 312, G-AOVO from 'late 1958' to 'early 1959'; BOAC Series 312, G-AOVT 'during 1959'; Hunting Clan Series 317, G-APNA and G-APNB 'during 1960-61'; BOAC Series 102, G-ANBO 'during late 1961'; Lloyd International Series 312F, G-AOVP 'during 1968'; Air Charter Series 307F, G-ANCD, February 1969.

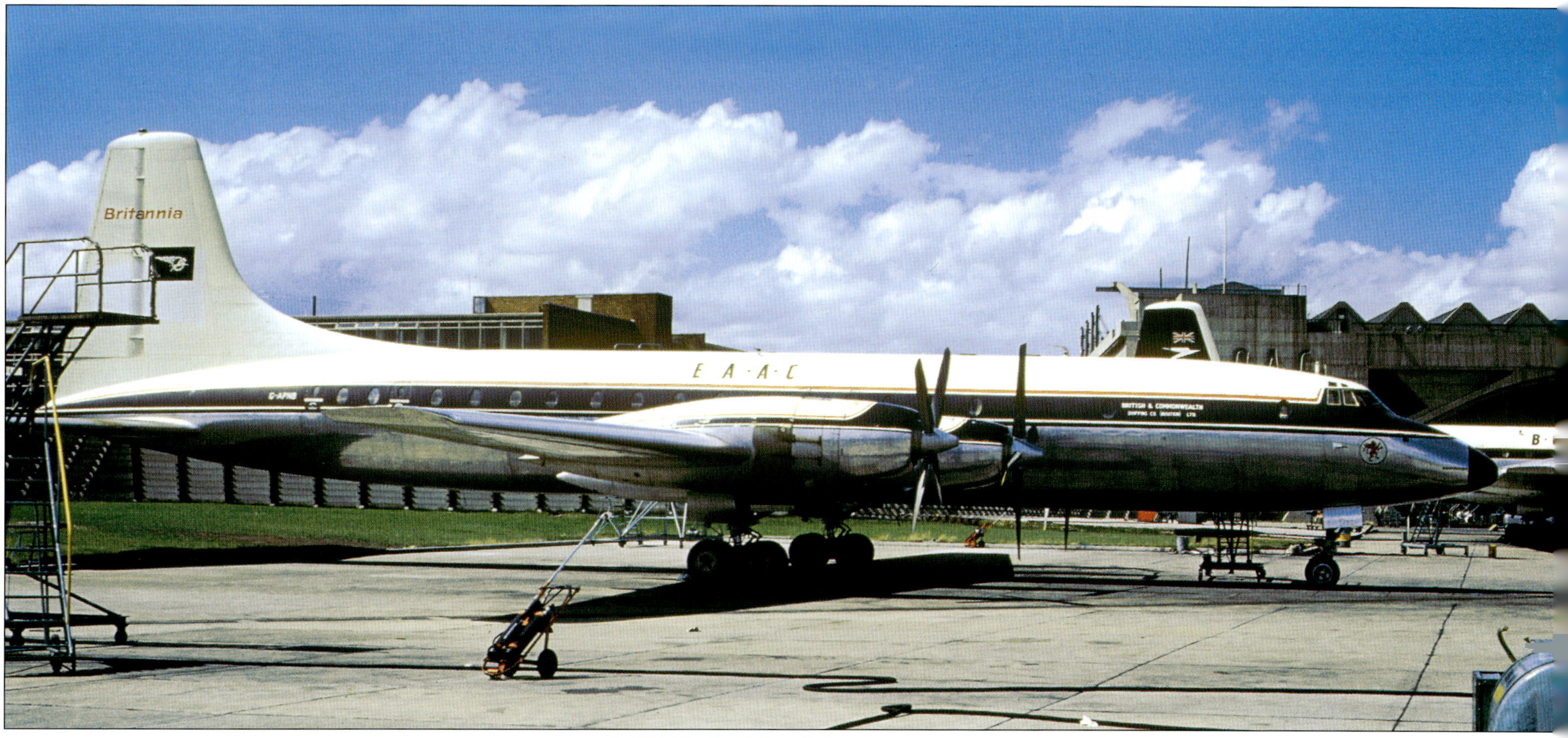

G-APNB of British & Commonwealth sits on the BOAC ramp at Heathrow Airport while under lease to East African Airways in August 1960.

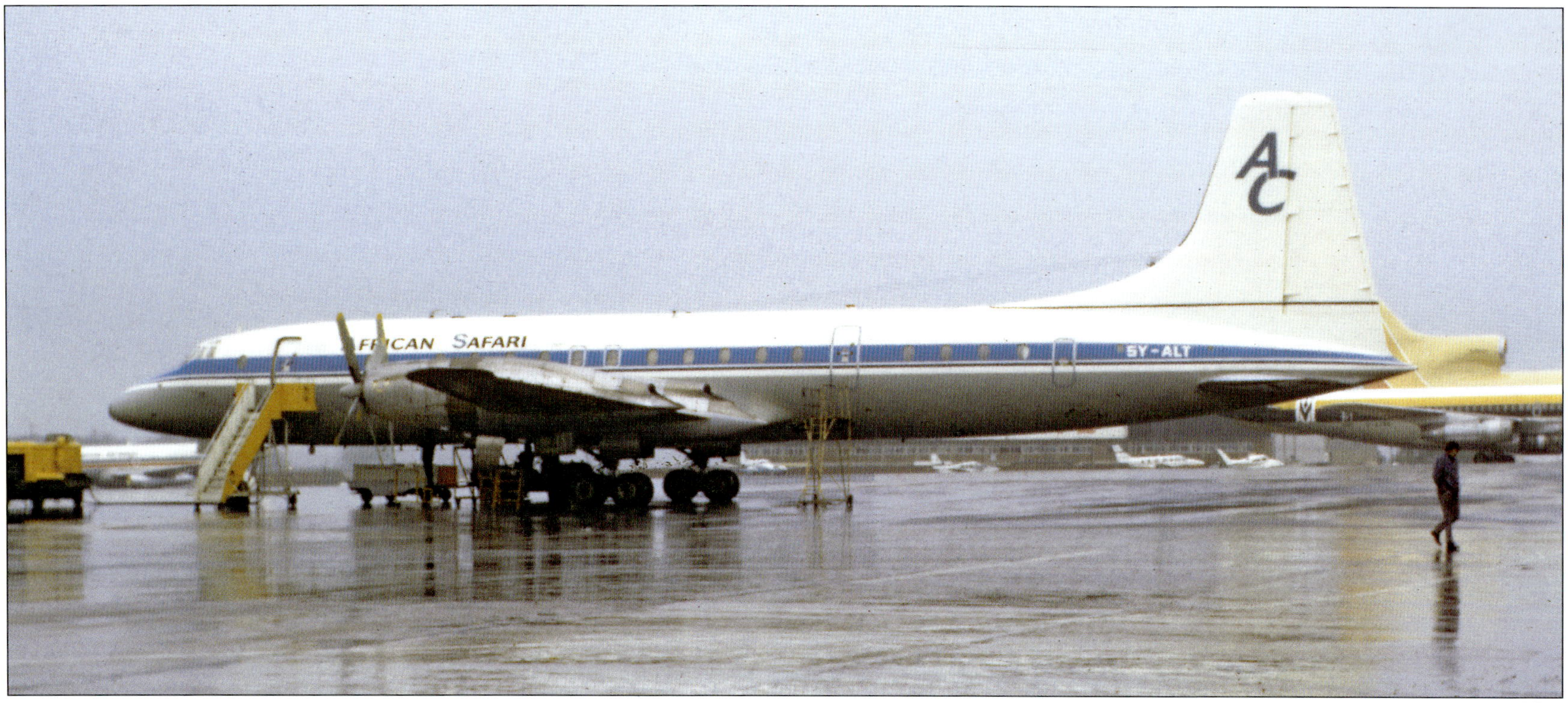

5Y-ALT is seen at Luton in November 1974 after the aircraft was transferred from African Safari to African Cargo Airways.

These aircraft were used on passenger flights within East Africa and from there into Europe, particularly the UK. With the last two leased Britannias having had the freight conversion, they had the added ability to carry cargo. The airline ceased operating the Britannia in 1973 and the last Britannia was returned to her owners and continued to fly on various leases for the next six years.

AFRICAN CARGO AIRWAYS

African Cargo Airways acquired a Britannia in 1973. She was a Series 313 aircraft originally owned by El Al and sold to African Cargo by African Safari

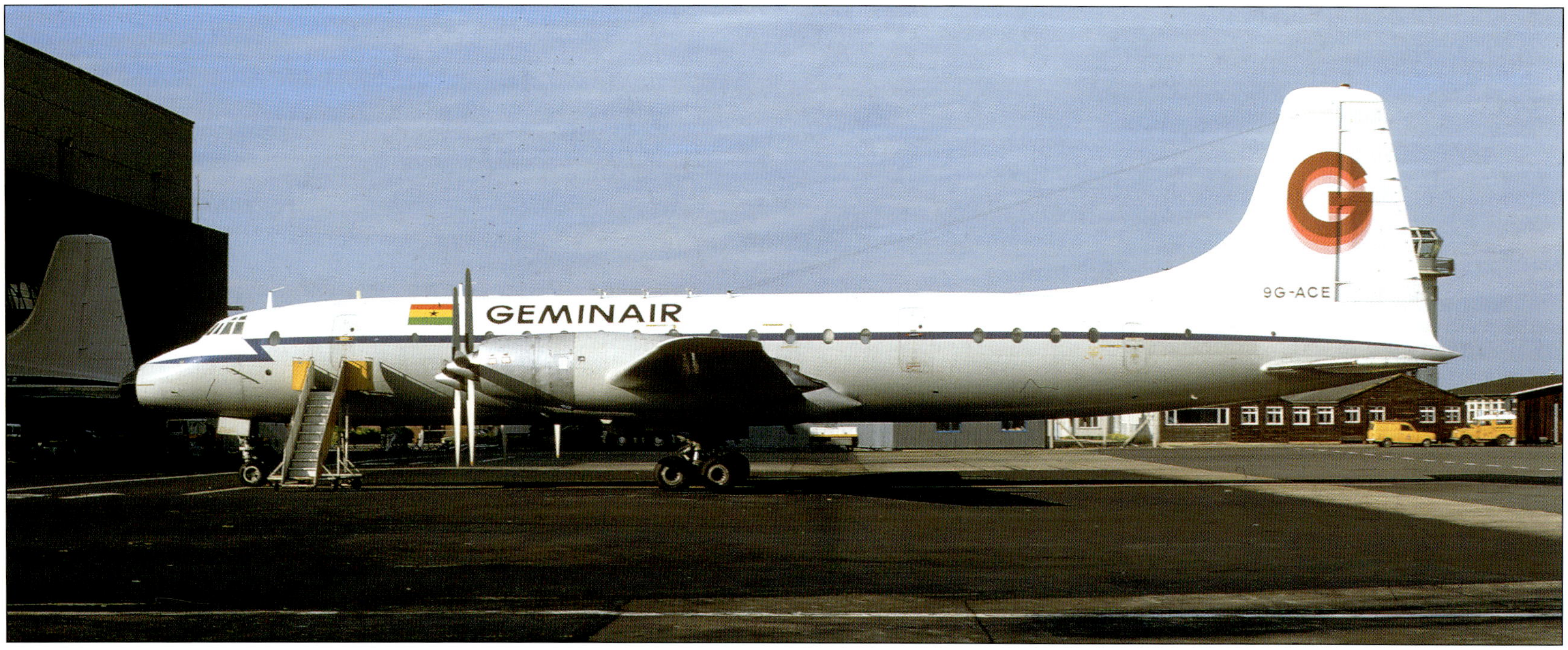

9G-ACE sits in the sunlight in immaculate condition, at Luton in June 1976.

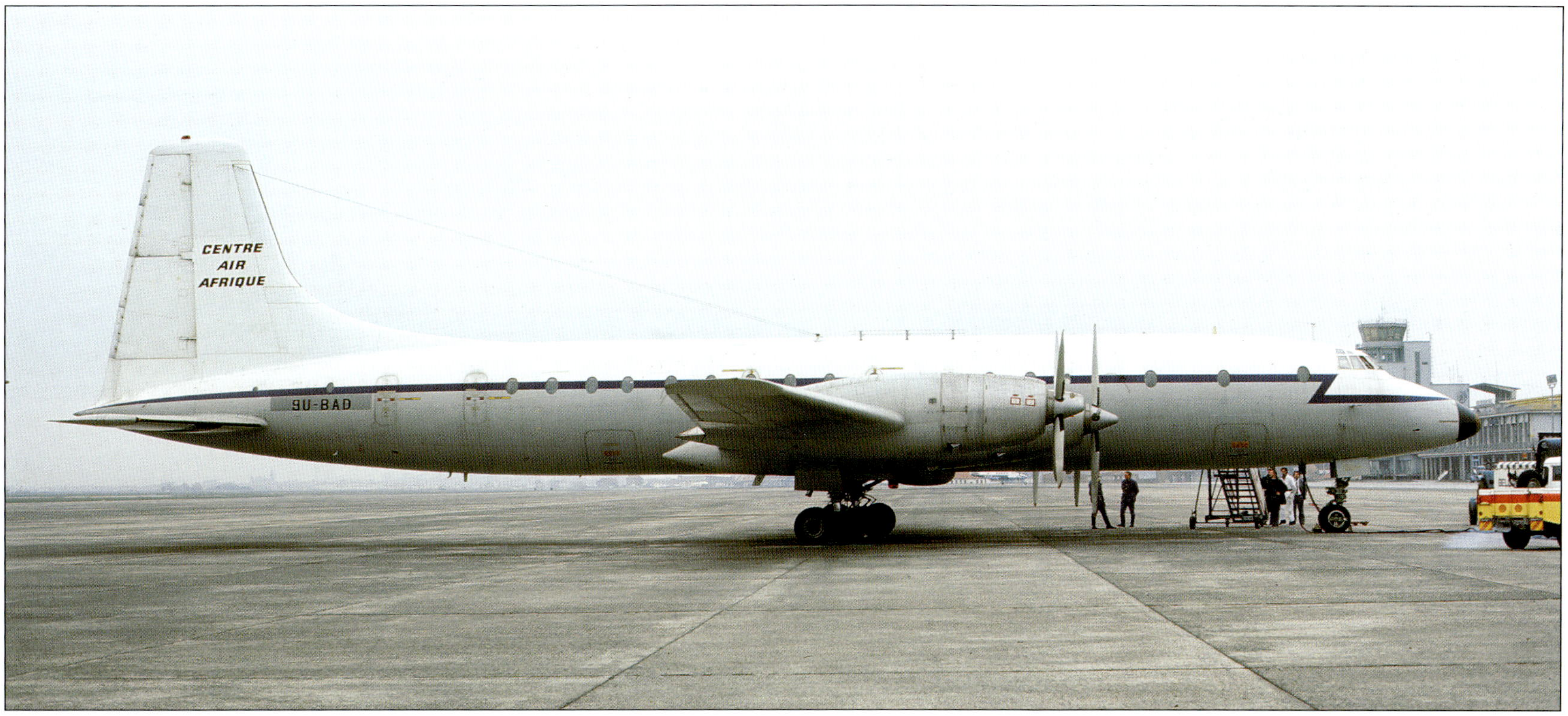

9U-BAD was destined to serve barely a year for Centre Air Afrique before being impounded for non-payment of overdue debts at Charleroi Belgium. Here we see the aircraft in happier times at Ostend on 10th of March 1976.

Airways and registered as 5Y-ALT. Two other Britannias were leased to African Cargo. One was a Series 307F owned by Shackleton Airways and leased from 13th May 1975, re-registered as 5Y-AYR. Another was a Series 308F owned by Monarch Airways and registered as G-ANCF which was leased by African Cargo on 1st February 1976, re-registered as 5Y-AZP.

The three Britannias were operated on ad hoc and regular cargo charters. Journeys were mainly within East Africa but sometimes journeys to Europe were undertaken. Servicing and more fundamental overhauls took place in the UK, usually in Luton or Manston.

The company had only limited success, and it went out of

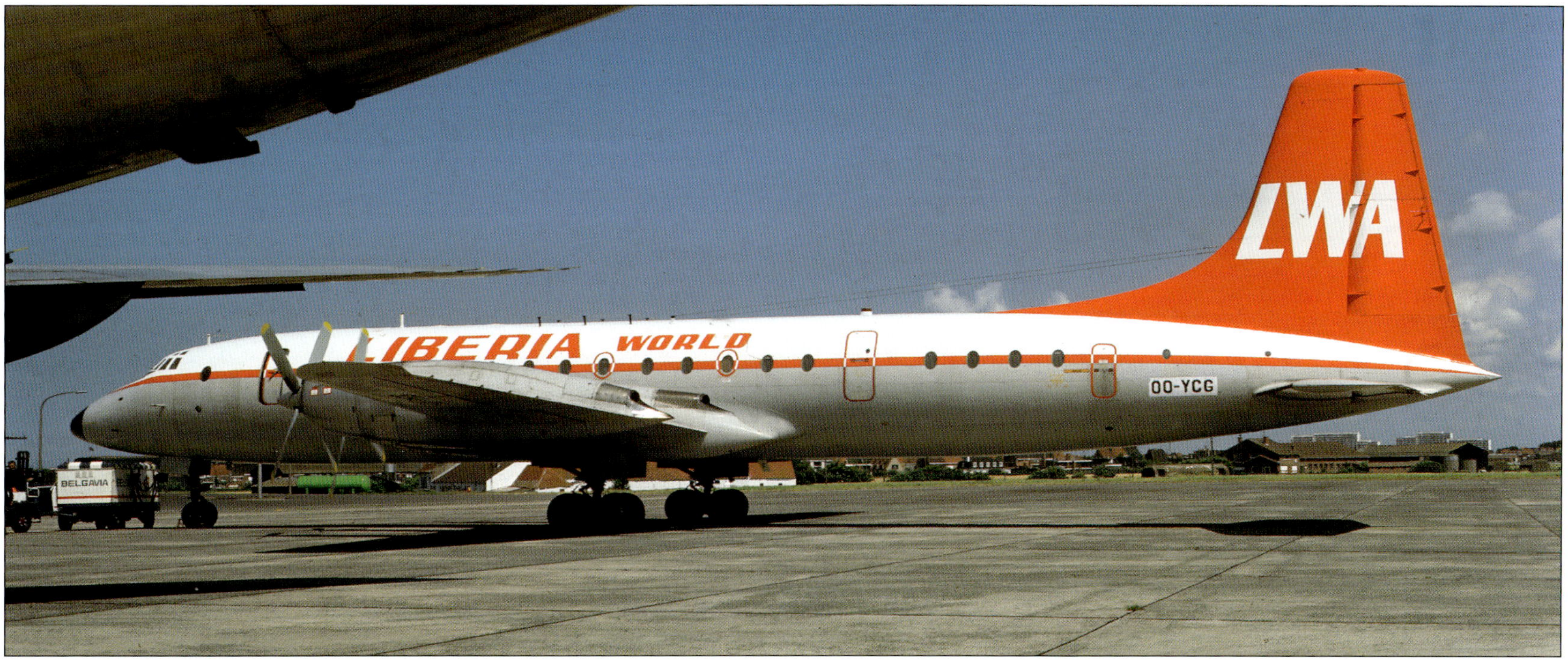

OO-YCG of Liberia World is seen at Ostend on 20th of July 1977.

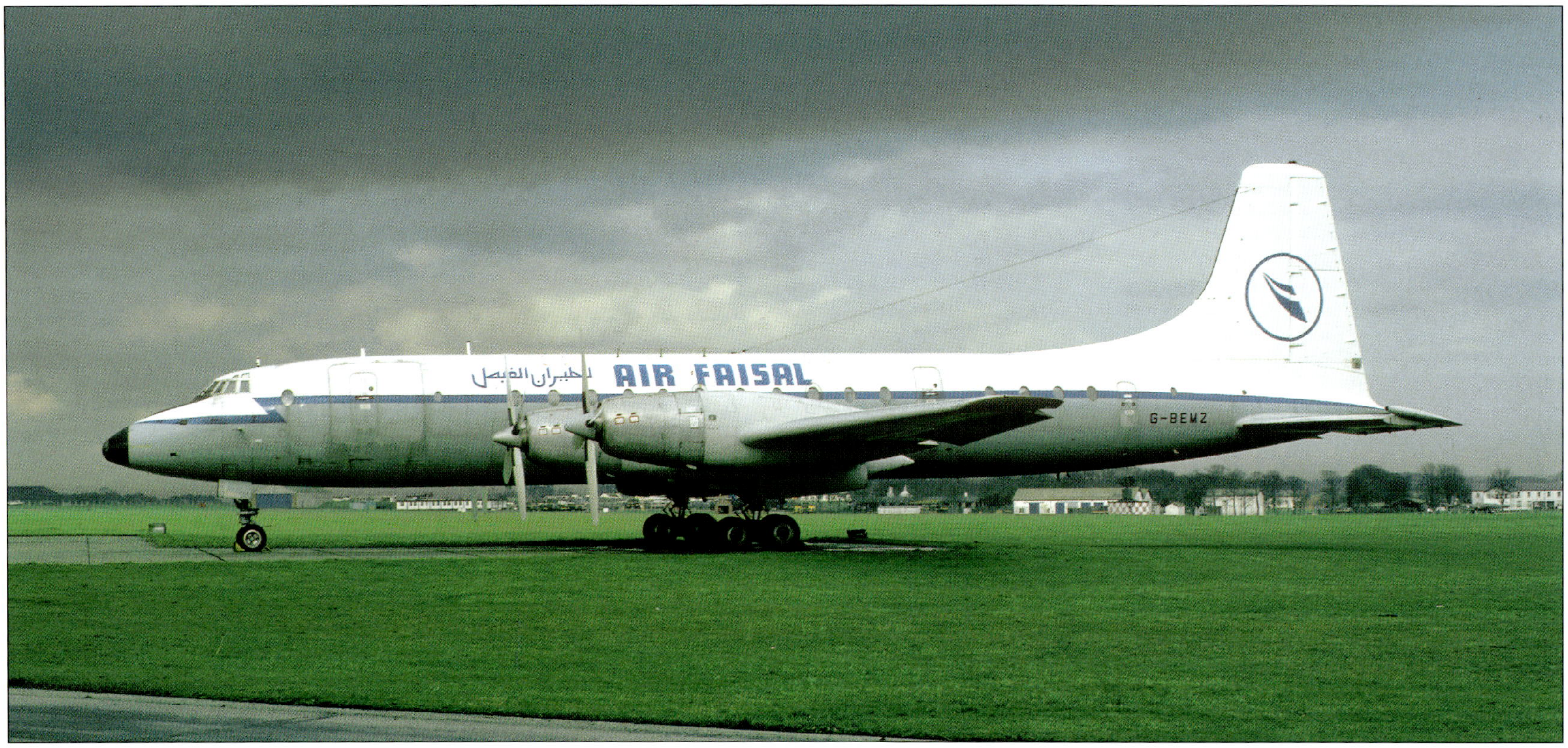

Normally used on services between Bombay and Dubai, G-BEMZ was pictured in April 1979 during a rare visit to England.

business early in 1977.

GEMINAIR

In the 1960s there had been some experience of Britannia aircraft by Ghana Airways, with one bought and four others leased at various times. It was not therefore very surprising when a new cargo carrier, Geminair, was founded in 1975 in Ghana. The company bought a Britannia Series 253F, XM 520, from the RAF on 16th September 1975, which was registered as 9G-ACE. During the next six years it was busy with cargo charters in West Africa and between West Africa and Europe. For just two months early in 1979 the company leased another Britannia, EI-BBH, from Aer Turas.

The company's Britannia operations ceased in 1981 and 9G-ACE was sold on to Lukum Air Services as 9Q-CUM in September.

CENTRE AIR AFRIQUE

For a short time a Britannia was based in Rwanda. An ex-RAF Series 253F aircraft, XL 657, was purchased by Centre Air Afrique from Monarch Airlines, re-registered as 9U-BAD and flown to Kigali (Rwanda) on 10th March 1976, presumably to begin flying within and from Central Africa. However, in February 1977, the Britannia was impounded in Ostend Belgium for the non-payment of landing fees and other bills, as a result of which the airline went bankrupt. 9U-BAD was later scrapped there.

LIBERIA WORLD AIRWAYS

A somewhat more successful venture was set up by Liberia World Airways which planned to lease two Britannias and start a cargo service based in Liberia. It arranged to lease two ex-RAF Britannias, both Series 253F variants, from Young Cargo Services.

The first of these, OO-YCG, was re-registered as EL-LWG, repainted in Liberia World colours and delivered in July 1977 to begin work. The second, OO-YCH, was similarly re-registered as EL-LWH and repainted in Liberia World colours in August 1977, but never delivered. The aircraft was sold to Katale in April 1979, flown to Zaire in LWA colours and eventually broken up for spares in 1992.

EL-LWG continued to operate with Liberia World Airways until being withdrawn in September 1978. She was then stored at Manston until purchased by Katale in May 1979.

IN SERVICE WITH SMALL MIDDLE EASTERN CARRIERS

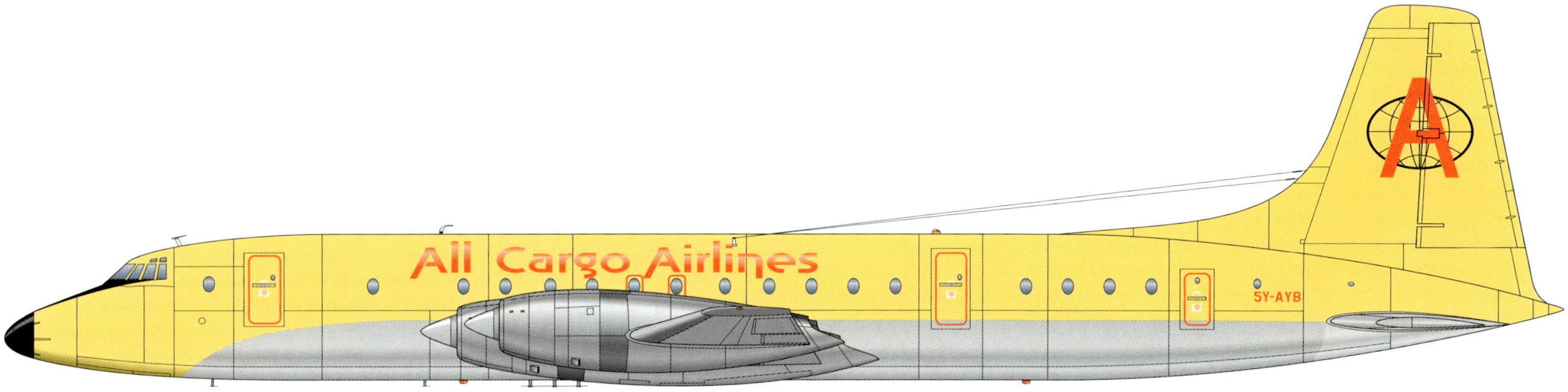

Outside of Europe there was no significant holiday charter business but, by the mid-1970s, even as jet aircraft were becoming available to convey passengers around at higher speeds than before, there was still a lot of cargo which could be transported satisfactorily at lower speeds. For this purpose the freight carrying Britannias were suitable and popular.

AIR FAISAL

The principal Middle Eastern airline in this business was Air Faisal based in Dubai. It first purchased an ex-RAF Series 253F Britannia, XM 490, in November 1975, registering her as G-BDLZ. She was delivered to the company at Luton and the Air Faisal livery was applied around the old RAF livery. The aircraft was set to work in service mainly between Dubai and Bombay.

Air Faisal intended to buy another Britannia, ex-RAF Series 252, XN 404, in 1976 but the sale was never completed. In November of that year the aircraft was broken up and scrapped at Luton, presumably to provide a source of spares for Air Faisal.

On 14th May 1976 the company did acquire another Britannia, also an ex-RAF Series 253F, XL 660. Initially she seemed likely to work for Trans Gulf Air Cargo and was painted in their livery, but this deal was never completed. That titling was removed and on 11th February 1977 she was registered by Air Faisal as G-BEMZ and joined G-BDLZ on flights between Dubai and Bombay.

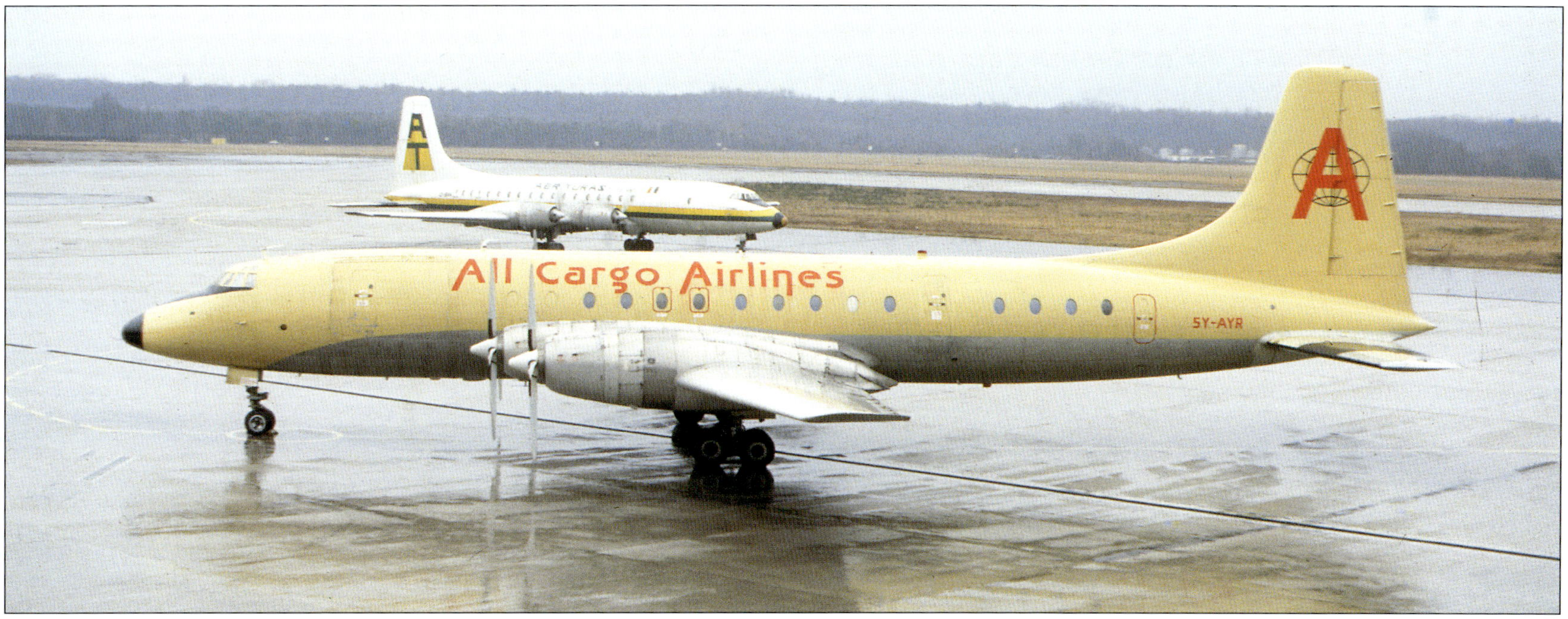

In February 1979, All Cargo Airlines' sole Britannia, 5Y-AYR, sits on the ramp at Milan while Aer Turas EI-BAA 'City of Dublin' taxies by.

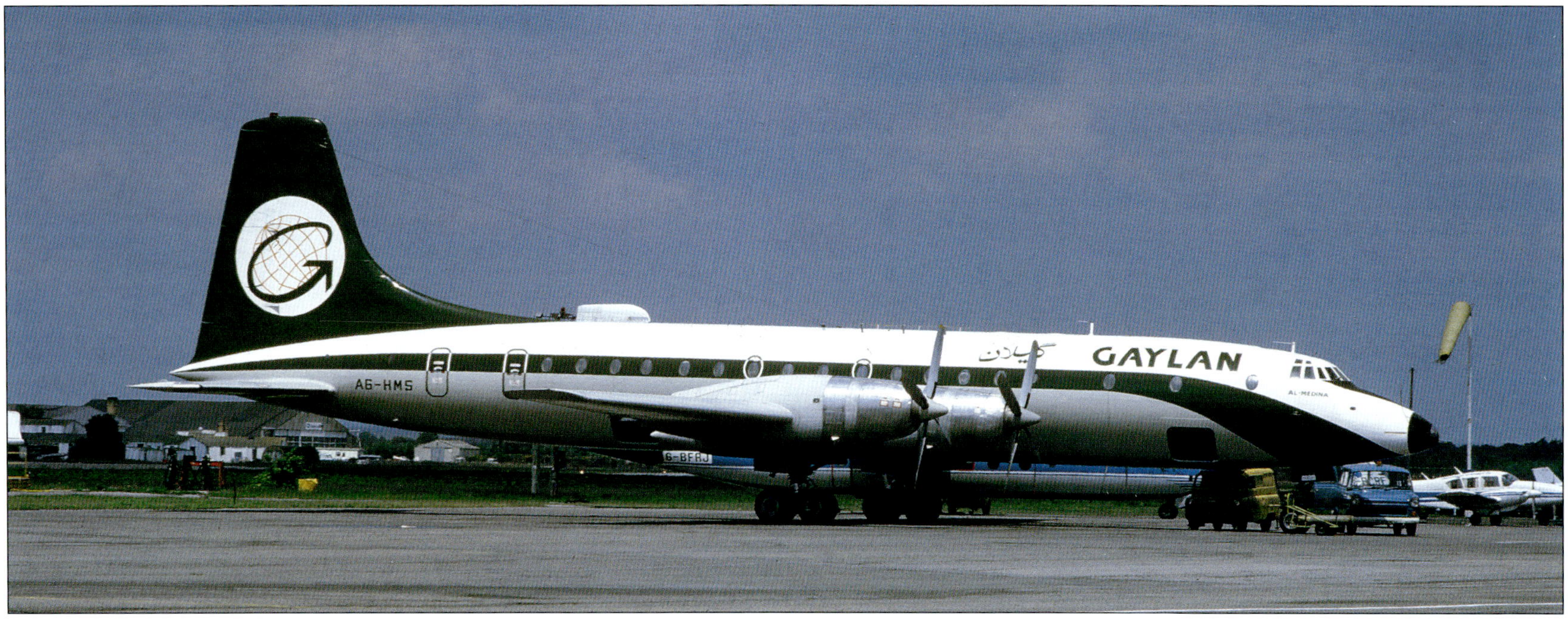

At Manston on 29th May 1980, A6-HMS of Gaylan, is prepared for another journey.

For the period between December 1976 and September 1977, G-BDLZ was leased to Air Works, India, which suggests that there may have been some financial link between the two airlines.

What is clear is that the popularity of the Britannia service was so great that Air Faisal leased another Britannia, Series 307F from Westwings Aviation Services via Trans Gulf Air Cargo, operating with the registration 5Y-AYR, during part of 1978.

Both the Britannias owned by Air Faisal were grounded in August 1978 for suspected drug smuggling. G-BDLZ was withdrawn from use in May 1979 and broken up in September of that year, whilst the Certificate of Airworthiness for G-BEMZ expired during her grounding. She was sold by HM Customs and Excise to T F Richter and Co. Ltd in September 1979, trading as Gaylan Air Cargo, for whom she subsequently worked.

TRANS GULF AIR CARGO

As indicated above, the history of Trans Gulf Air Cargo overlaps with that of Air Faisal. Trans Gulf leased Britannia Series 307F, G-ANCD re-registered as 5Y-AYR, from Westwings Aviation Services in November 1977. Sub-leasing the aircraft to Air Faisal produced some income for Trans Gulf but once the lease ended and the aircraft returned to Westwings, by the end of 1978, Trans Gulf seems to have ceased further operations.

ALL CARGO AIRLINES

Another airline with a short life and limited success was All Cargo Airlines. This airline leased 5Y-AYR from Westwings in December 1978. She was painted in the All Cargo Airlines' livery, but how much commercial activity she then performed is not clear. What is clear is that after three months, no leasing payment had been made so Westwings re-possessed the aircraft and All Cargo Airlines' Britannia operations ended.

GAYLAN AIR CARGO

Gaylan Air Cargo, like Air Faisal, was based in the Gulf region and, as stated above, they obtained the use of G-BEMZ via a purchase from HM Customs and Excise. She had been financed by Black Arrow Leasing Ltd from February 1980 onwards and Gaylan Air Cargo leased her from Black Arrow. She was re-registered in the United Arab Emirates as A6-HMS and painted in the Gaylan livery. 5Y-AYR, still owned by Westwings, was also leased to Gaylan from August 1979.

On 3rd April 1981, A6-HMS reverted to her UK registration G-BEMZ but this change produced no success. By the middle of 1981 Gaylan Air Cargo had ceased trading so 5Y-AYR was returned to Westwings and G-BEMZ was returned to Black Arrow Leasing who owned her. She went on to fly profitably for several more years, for Redcoat Air Cargo and then Katale Aero Transport.

IN SERVICE WITH NIGERIA, GHANA AND MALAYAN AIRWAYS

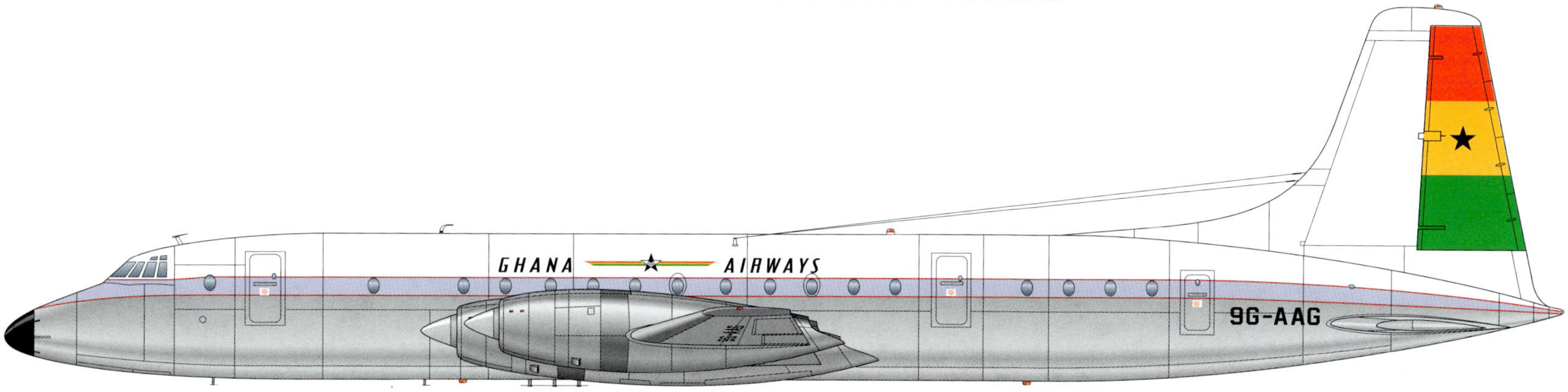

By around 1960, when BOAC decided that it would start to phase out its Britannia fleet and re-equip with jet aircraft, it began to release several Series 102 aircraft on to the market. This enabled some airlines to adopt a pattern of fairly short term leasing.

NIGERIA AIRWAYS

Nigeria Airways leased a Britannia, G-ANBH, for a period of a few months in 1958 and then leased another, G-ANBE, in April 1958 which it returned in 1960. Over the period from 1959 to 1963, it leased a total of eight more Britannias; G-ANBA for about twelve months beginning April 1959; G-ANBB for about eight months from June 1959; G-APLL for about six months starting 'early in 1959'; G-ANBM for about three months from November 1959; G-ANBN for about six months beginning in October 1960; G-ANBK for about nine months starting 'early in 1961' and G-ANBF for twelve months from November 1961. All these were BOAC-owned Series 102 aircraft. There was one more, G-AOVT, a BOAC Series 312 aircraft leased by Nigeria Airways from 1963, until she was lease-purchased by British Eagle in 1963.

All these aircraft were used on the main BOAC scheduled services between London and Lagos three times per week.

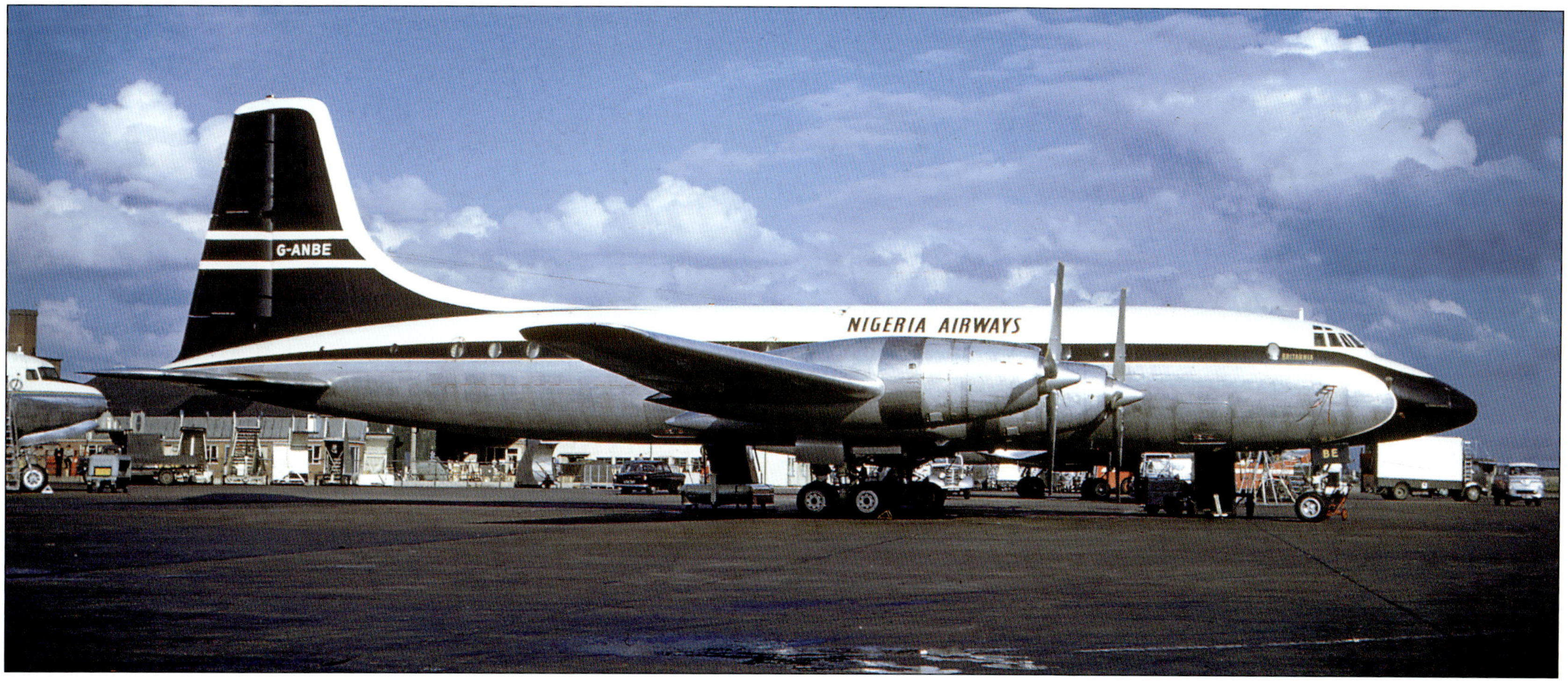

On 18th June 1960, Britannia Series 102 G-ANBE on lease to Nigeria Airways from BOAC, awaits passengers at London Heathrow.

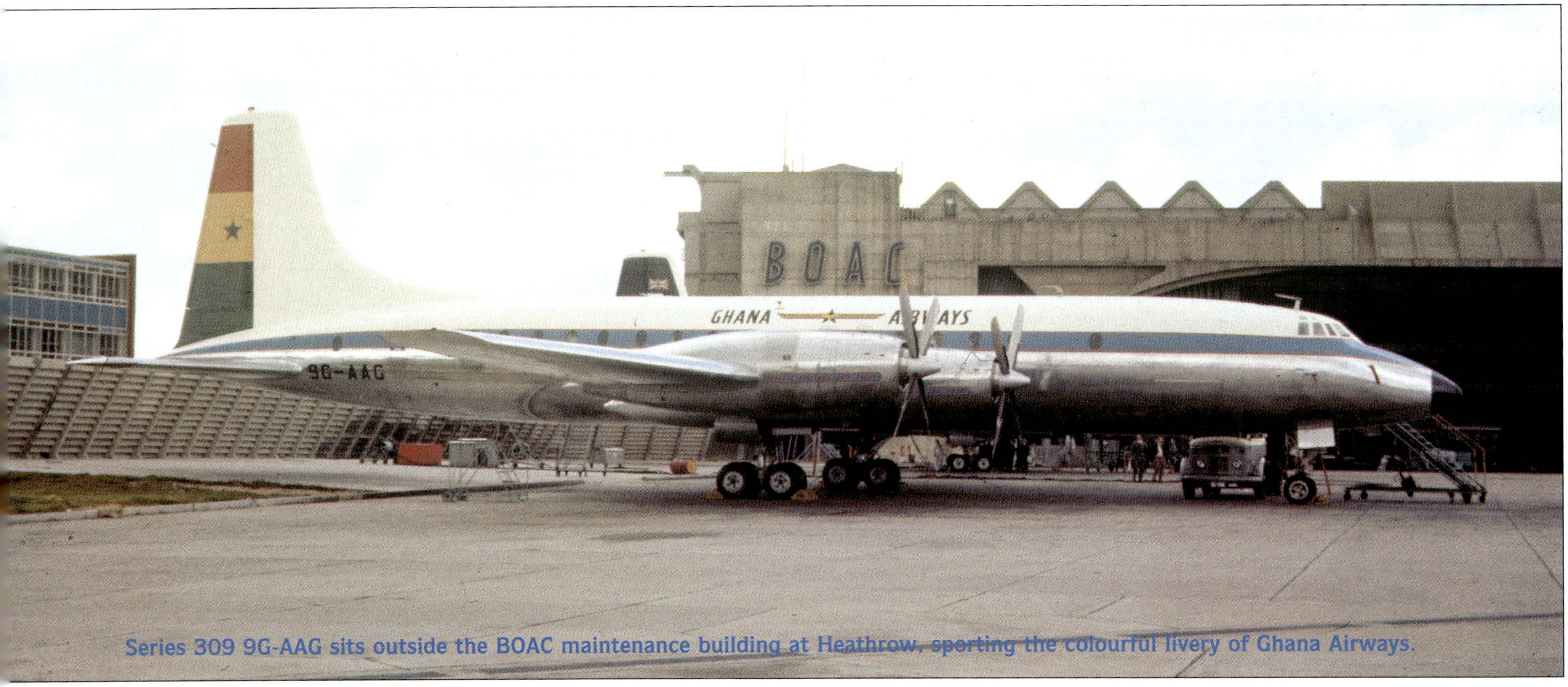

Series 309 9G-AAG sits outside the BOAC maintenance building at Heathrow, sporting the colourful livery of Ghana Airways.

GHANA AIRWAYS

Ghana Airways had a more continuous involvement with Britannias than did Nigeria Airways.

The airline was formed on 5th July 1958 in Accra by the Ghanian Government (60%) capital and BOAC Associated Companies with (40%) capital. Two Herons were bought for national routes and a seven year agreement was signed with BOAC to operate the Accra-London service, initially with a

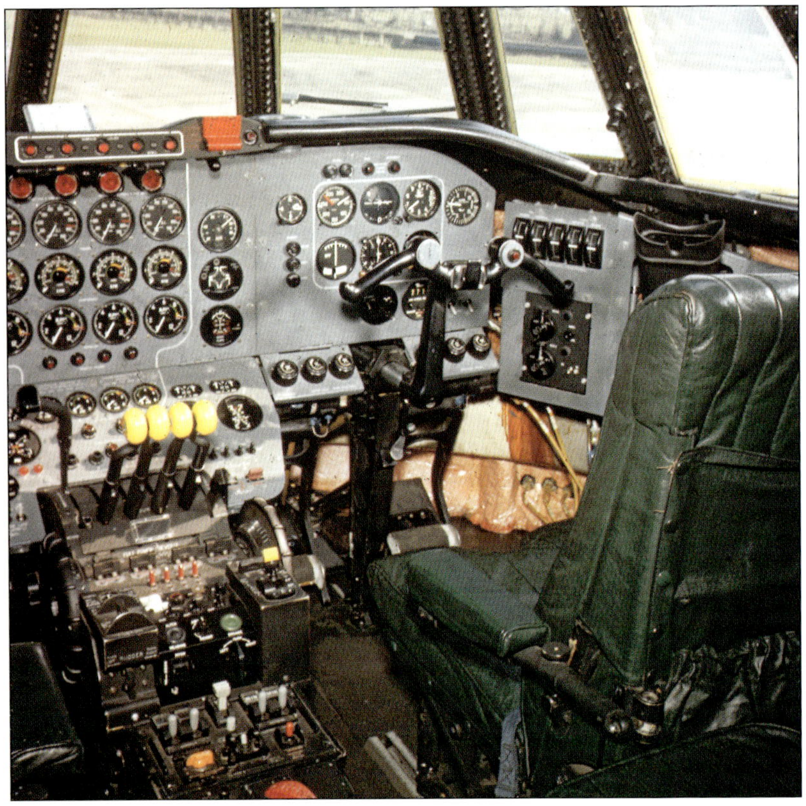
The interior of the cockpit of 9G-AAG, displaying the unusual green leather seating.

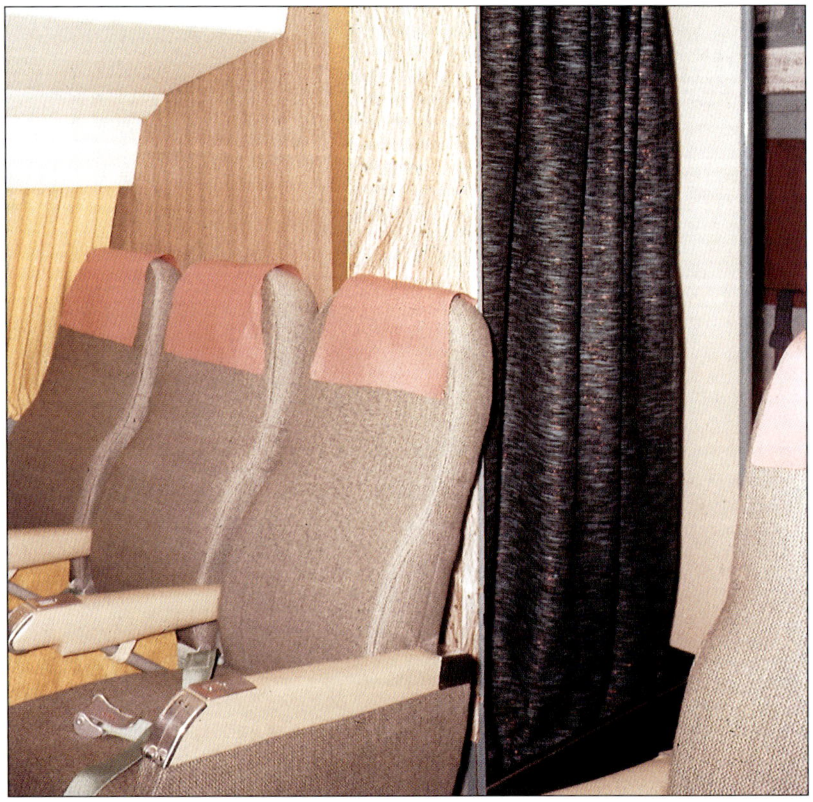
A view of the interior of the economy class seating of a Ghana Airways' Britannia.

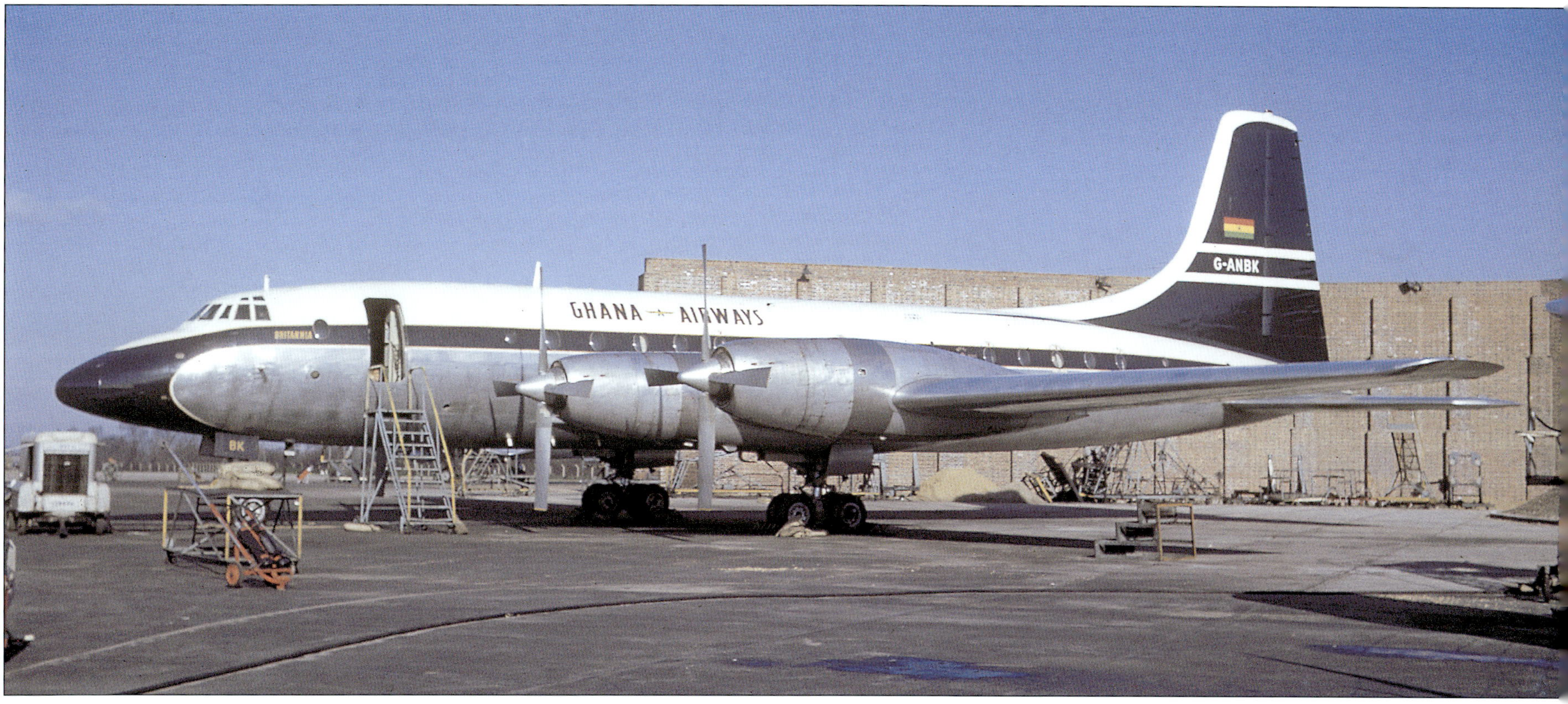

At Heathrow in June 1960, Britannia Series 102 G-ANBK wears the livery of Ghana Airways, whilst under charter from BOAC.

Boeing Stratocruiser from 16th July 1958. A Britannia Series 102 G-ANBK was introduced on 14th April 1959 and the Stratocruiser phased out on the 30th May.

Other BOAC Britannias chartered were G-ANBC, G-ANBE and G-ANBI. These aircraft performed well and Ghana Airways ordered two Series 300 aircraft from the manufacturer. The first, G-ANCH, a Series 309 was re-registered 9G-AAG and delivered on 27th July 1960, and was immediately used for crew training at Filton.

The second G-AOVA a Series 319 was re-registered 9G-AAH and named 'Osagyefo' and handed over at Filton on 8th November 1960. It was quickly put into service on the 2nd December 1960 operating the Accra-London service replacing the BOAC Britannias. This aircraft was operated by Ghana Airways until 31 December 1963, when it was returned to the Bristol Aeroplane Company.

Apart from the twice weekly Accra-London service, 9G-AAG also operated the annual Hadj pilgrimage from Accra-Jeddah. By June 1965 Ghana were operating two Vickers VC-10s on international routes and the Britannia became surplus to requirements. After a period of leasing to British United Airways, Transglobe, British Eagle and Monarch Airlines, the aircraft was finally sold to IAS in December 1972 for spares.

MALAYAN AIRWAYS

Malayan Airways leased no fewer than nine Britannias in the period between September 1961 and April 1963. All were Series 102 BOAC aircraft but they were leased for only a short time, often for only a month. The aircraft were; G-ANBA, G-ANBE, G-ANBF, G-ANBI, G-ANBJ, G-ANBM, G-ANBN, G-ANBO and G-APLL.

Although the BOAC Series 102 services ended in November 1962, G-ANBE continued to fly for Malayan Airways on the Kuala Lumpur-London route until March 1963.

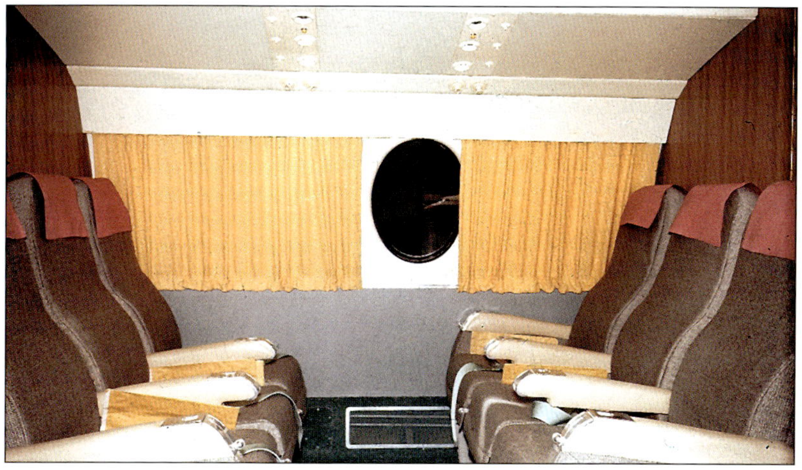

Face-to-face seating in the economy section of 9G-AAG.

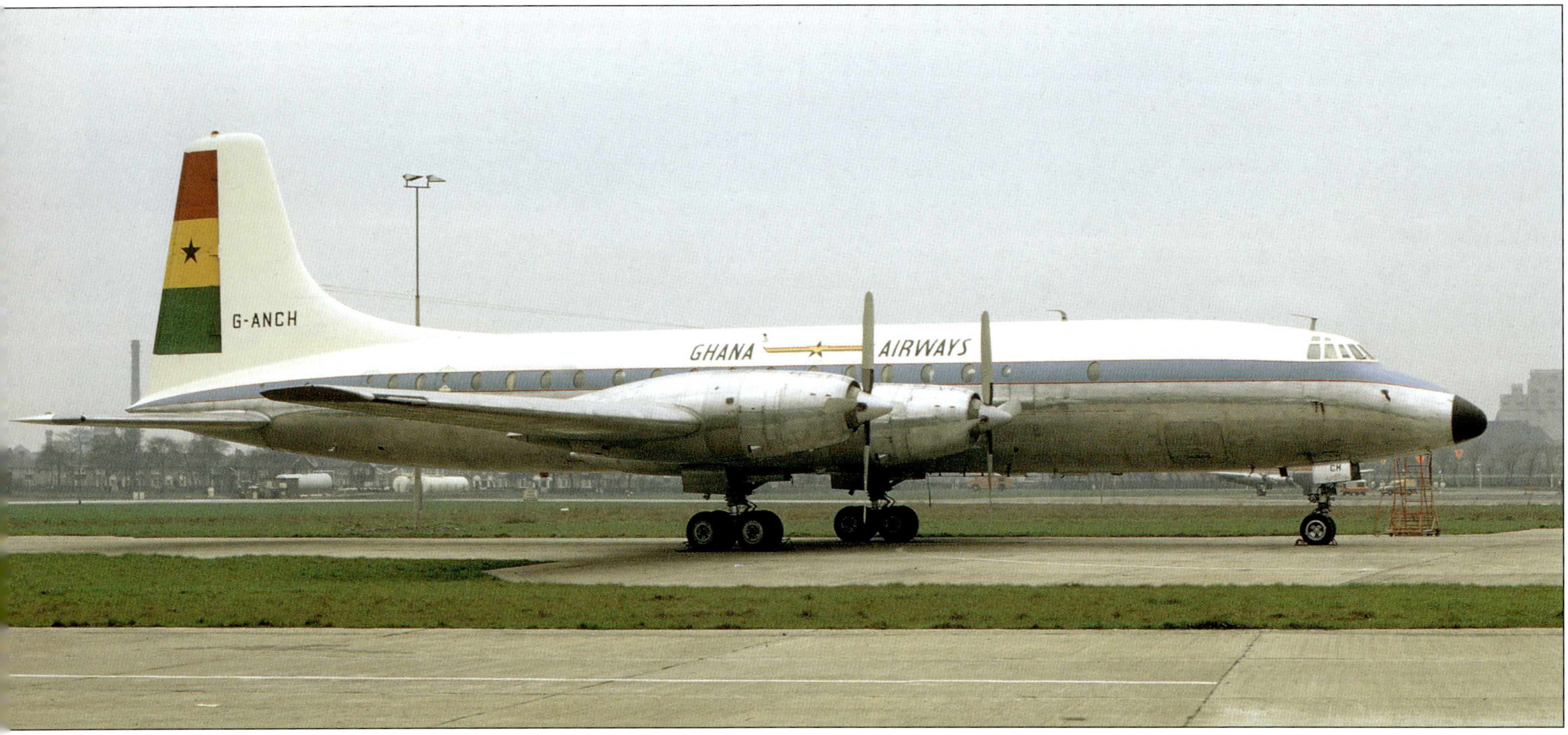

Above: While owned by the Bristol Aircraft Company, G-ANCH was leased by Ghana Airways for a period of seven months in 1968. Here we see the aircraft in the airline's full colours at Liverpool Airport on 23rd March 1968.

Below: G-AOVJ was leased to BWIA for a few months early in 1961. At the BOAC maintenance base at Heathrow Airport the aircraft wears the British West Indian Airways' stickers during this lease.

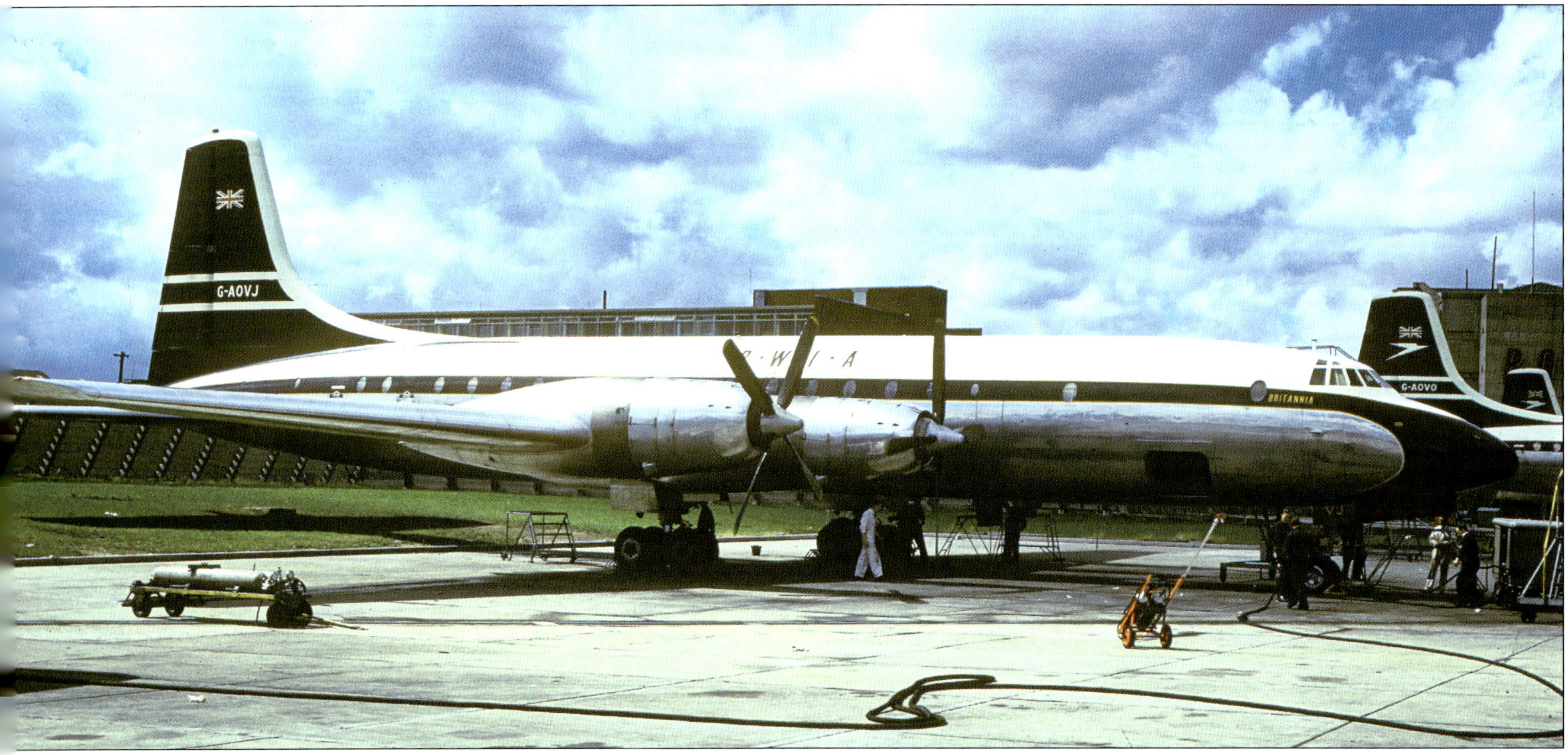

BRITANNIA OPERATIONS IN ZAIRE

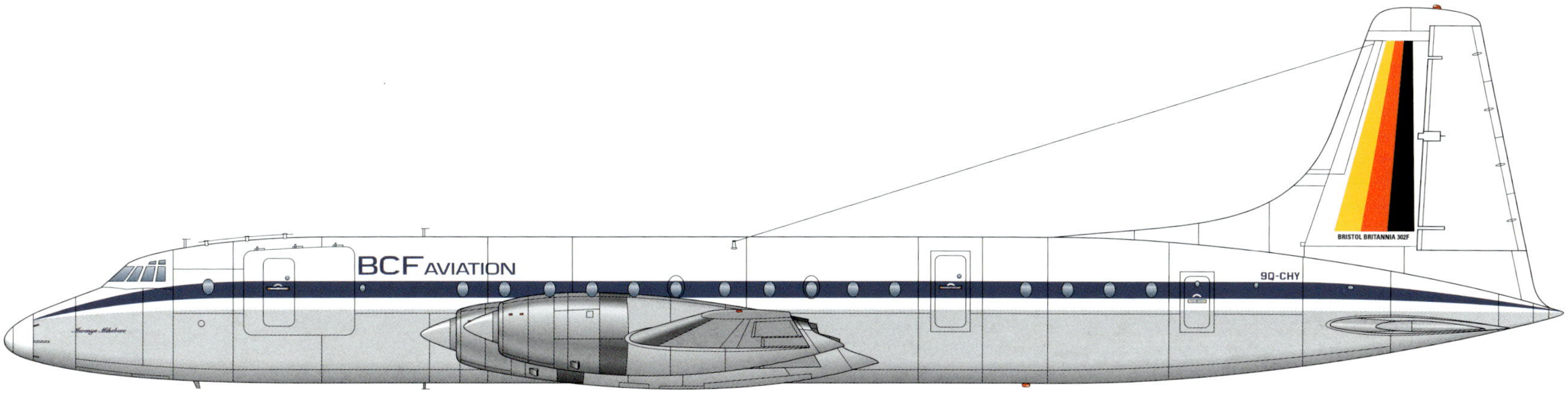

AMAZ

In 1976 an airline based in Kinshasa, Zaire, named Agence et Messagers Aérienne du Zaire (AMAZ for short) purchased an ex-RAF Britannia 253F from Monarch Airlines. She was re-registered in Zaire as 9Q-CAJ, but in fact never reached there. She was ferried from Luton, where she had been stored, to Brussels on 15th November 1976 with the intention of flying on, but the sale fell through and she was returned to Luton. On 14th April 1977, she was bought by Airline Engineering (re-registered as G-BEPX) who used her for ground testing of Proteus engines in curious circumstances. The outer parts of each wing, beyond the inner nacelles, were removed as was the fuselage aft of the wing roots. This truncated part-aeroplane was seen to 'taxi' on a runway from time to time, testing overhauled engines. When the amount of work on overhauling Proteus engines declined, she was scrapped in April 1980.

ZAIRE AERO SERVICES

The next attempt to set up Britannia services in Zaire was somewhat more successful. Zaire Aero Services purchased an ex-RAF Britannia 252F, one of the three original 252 series, in February 1977. It was re-registered in Zaire as 9Q-CPX and was immediately leased to and worked for Katale Aero Transport. The exact financial and operational connection between ZAS and KAT

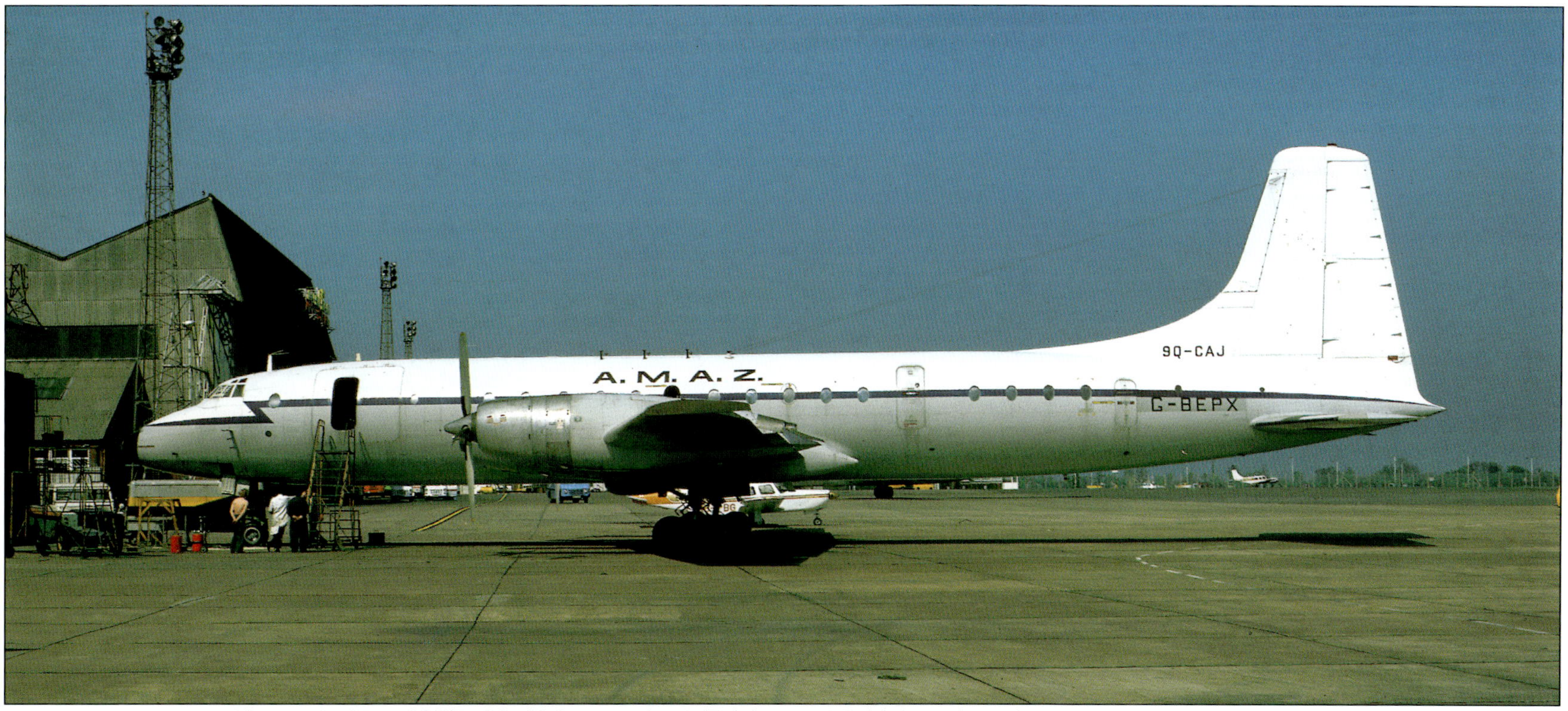

At London Luton Airport in May 1977, 9Q-CAJ wears both Zairian and British registrations after purchase by Airline Engineering Ltd. The aircraft was destined to end her life as a Proteus test rig devoid of her outer wings and rear fuselage.

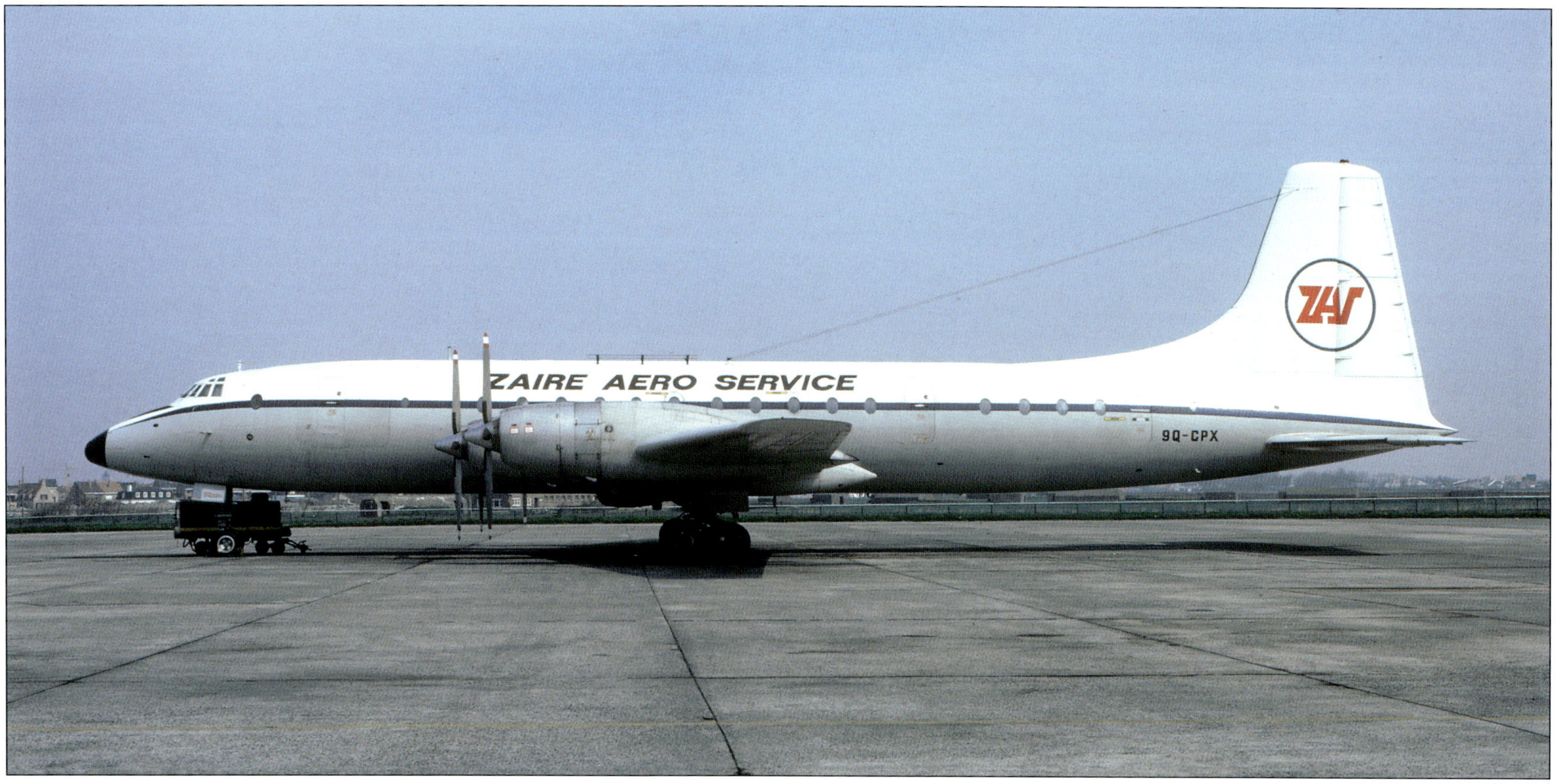

Top: Ex-RAF 9Q-CPX of Zaire Aero Services stands idle at Ostend in April 1978.
Top Right: Destined to end her days at Kinshasa, Zaire in July 1986, 9Q-CUM is seen on 9th of October 1982 wearing the colours of Lukum Air Services at Ostend, the favourite destination of ex-RAF Britannias in Europe.
Bottom: Again at Ostend, 9Q-CAZ of International Cargo Airlines awaits another task. This aircraft is preserved at RAF Cosford Museum in the UK wearing the colours of her first owner, BOAC.

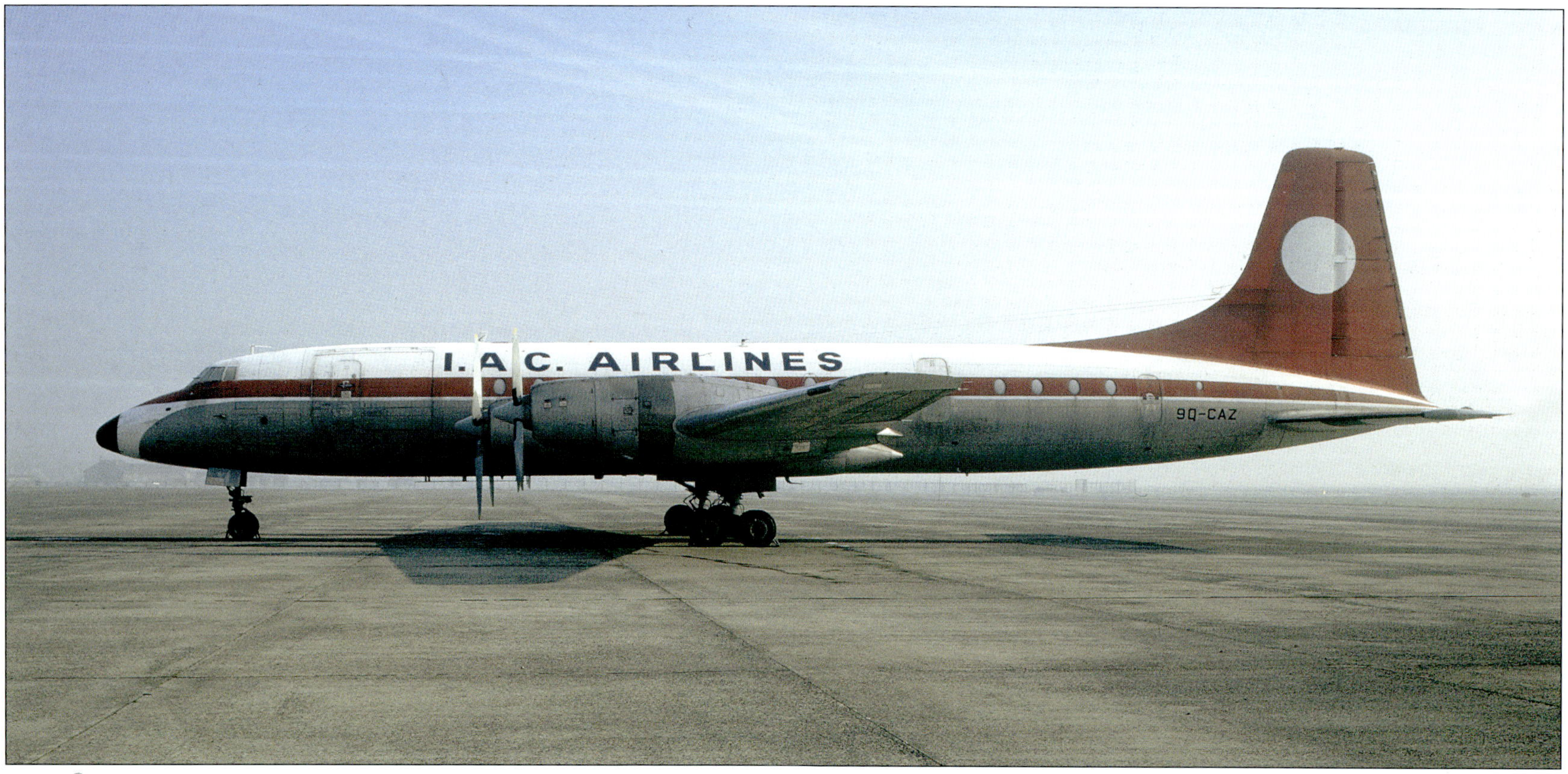

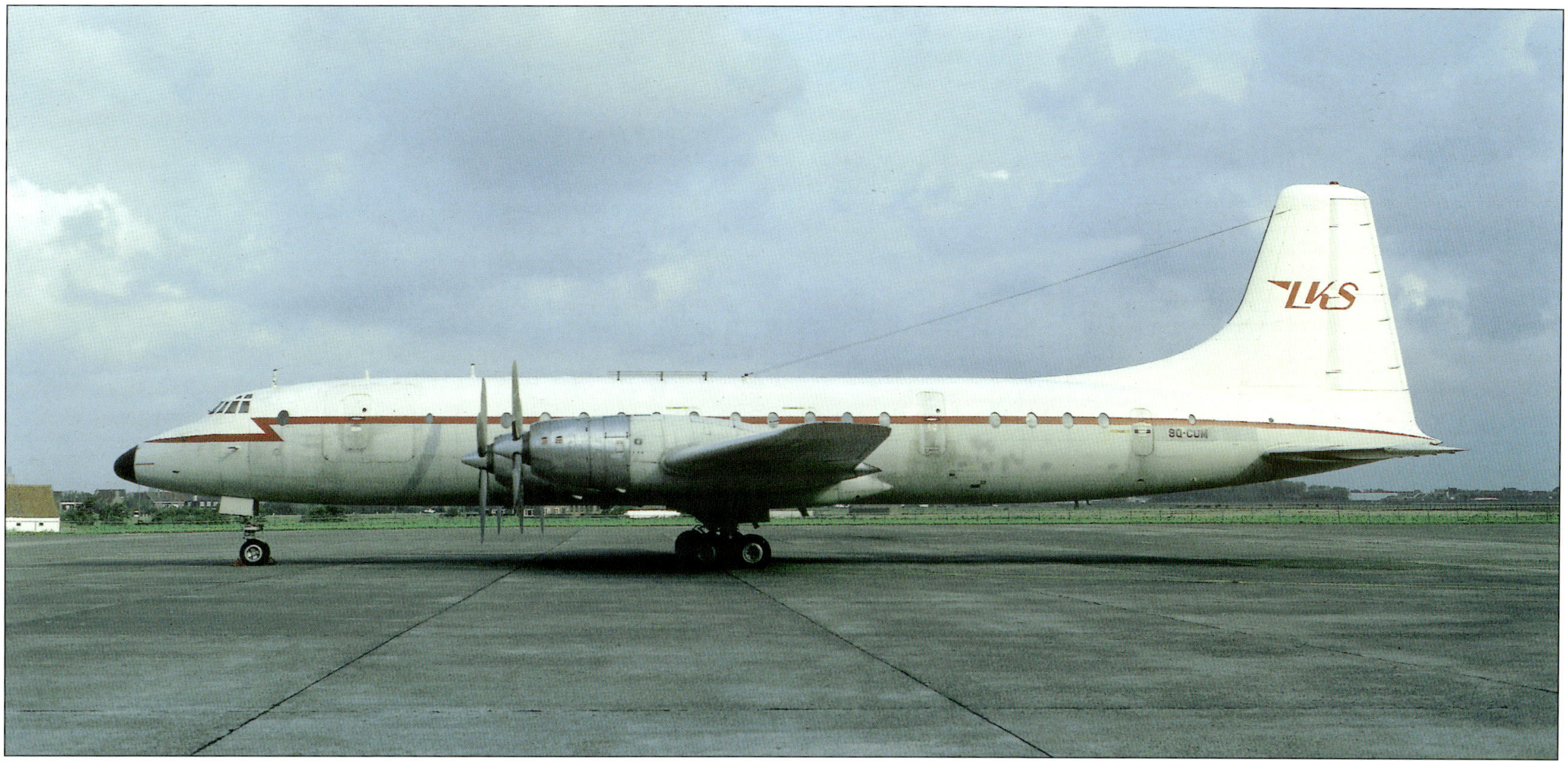

is not clear, but what is clear is that 9Q-CPX operated for a number of years until 1981 and was eventually scrapped at Goma, Zaire.

IAC AIRLINES

Another operator of just one Britannia was Zaire based IAC Airlines. Between January and June 1981 IAC leased 9Q-CAZ, originally a BOAC Series 312 aircraft, from Invicta International. She presumably carried out general cargo charter duties in those six months but there are no details available.

What is known is that after the return of the aircraft to Invicta, and after the collapse of Invicta itself, 9Q-CAZ was flown back to the UK in 1984 and is now preserved at RAF Cosford in the livery of her first owner, BOAC, and with her original registration, G-AOVF.

LUKUM AIR SERVICES

A rather different story is that of Lukum Air Services, another small airline which bought a Britannia 253F from Geminair in 1981. Registered as 9Q-CUM, this aircraft operated cargo charters very successfully for a number of years and was retired only when Lukum purchased a Douglas DC-8 freighter in 1986. Lukum then sold the Britannia to Katale Aero Transport, who broke her up to become a source of spares.

BCF AVIATION

Yet another small-scale operator of Britannias in Zaire was Business Cash Flow (BCF) Aviation. BCF had been in existence since 1985, transporting perishable food and other household items between populated centres in Zaire. In that country the large rain forests make road or rail travel difficult and unreliable, so air transport is popular. A service had been built up by Katale Aero Transport using Britannias, but in 1988 Katale decided to phase out its Britannias and replace them with Boeing 707 and Douglas DC-9 aircraft. Dr Mayani, who had already been chartering space on Katale's Britannias for freight transport operating as BCF, decided to set up his own airline. He bought two Britannias from Katale, Series 253F, 9Q-CDT, and Series 312F, 9Q-CHY, together with all of Katale's remaining Britannia spares, and with these he founded BCF Aviation.

The intention was only to operate one of the aircraft, 9Q-CHY, principally on the route between Kinshasa and Mbuji-Mayi, but sometimes with ad hoc charters to other places like Gbadolite and Goma. Quite often on a flight to a distant city from Kinshasa, passengers had a large amount of cargo whilst on the return journey to Kinshasa there would be very little luggage. So the passenger seating arrangement was somewhat unusual, a maximum of seventeen seats, with the rest of the fuselage space available for luggage and cargo.

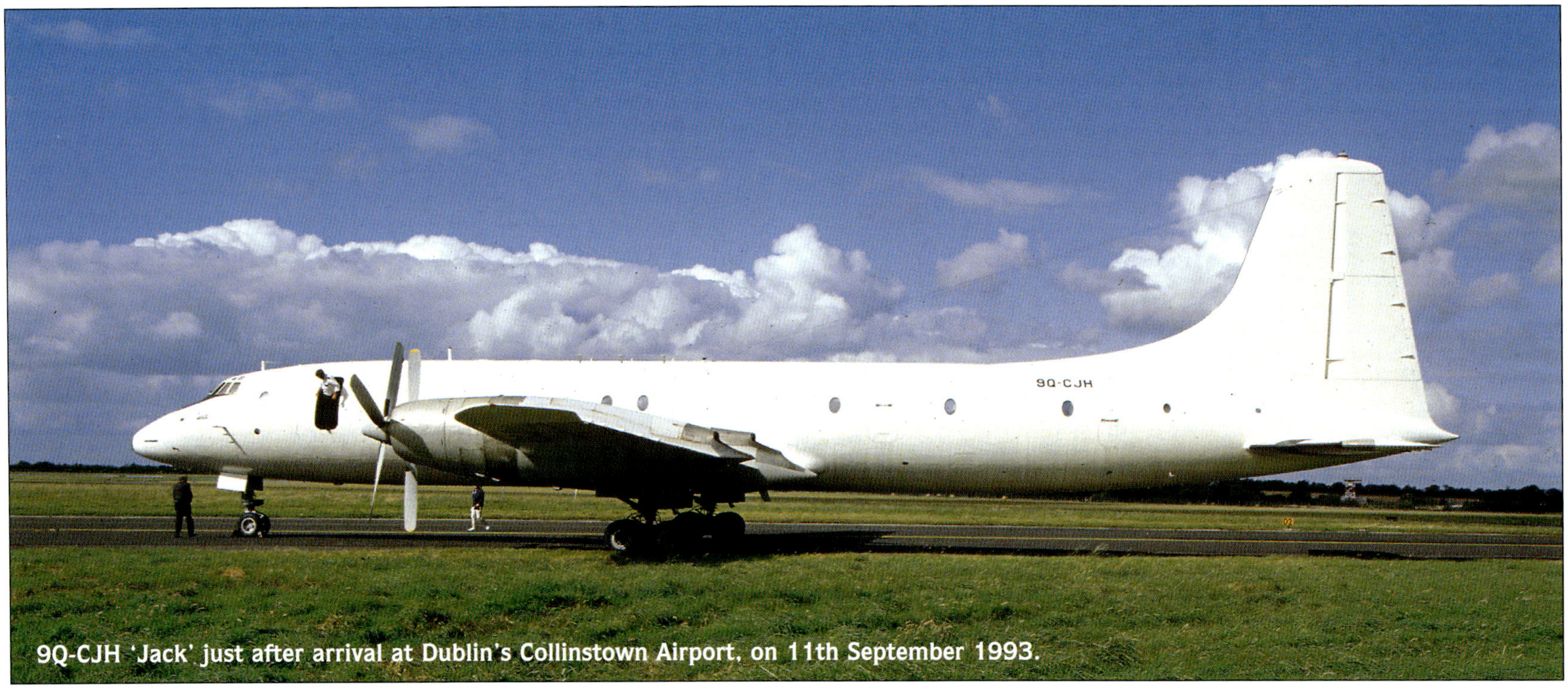

9Q-CJH 'Jack' just after arrival at Dublin's Collinstown Airport, on 11th September 1993.

BCF established a daily service between Kinshasa and Mbuji-Mayi and ran a well-used facility. The airline changed its livery and repainted 9Q-CHY in the new colours in 1990, but the age of the Britannia aircraft was beginning to tell and equipment failure and hence flight delays were becoming more frequent. The situation is made clear by a flight by 9Q-CHY on 5th July 1991 from Kinshasa to Mbuji-Mayi. While in the air there was a loss of oil pressure on one engine, so this engine had to be shut down and the aircraft returned to Kinshasa. Next day, after the trouble had apparently been repaired, the journey was resumed but on this flight an oil leak developed in another engine. This time however it was decided to continue the flight to Mbuji-Mayi. While there, the oil reservoirs were filled up to their maximum and the flight back to Kinshasa began but en route there were serious problems with oil supply to all four engines. The final part of the journey into Kinshasa was completed safely, but not without a very anxious time on the flight deck.

After investigations, Dr Mayani decided that he did not want to spend any more money on trying to keep the old Britannia airworthy and he put it up for sale.

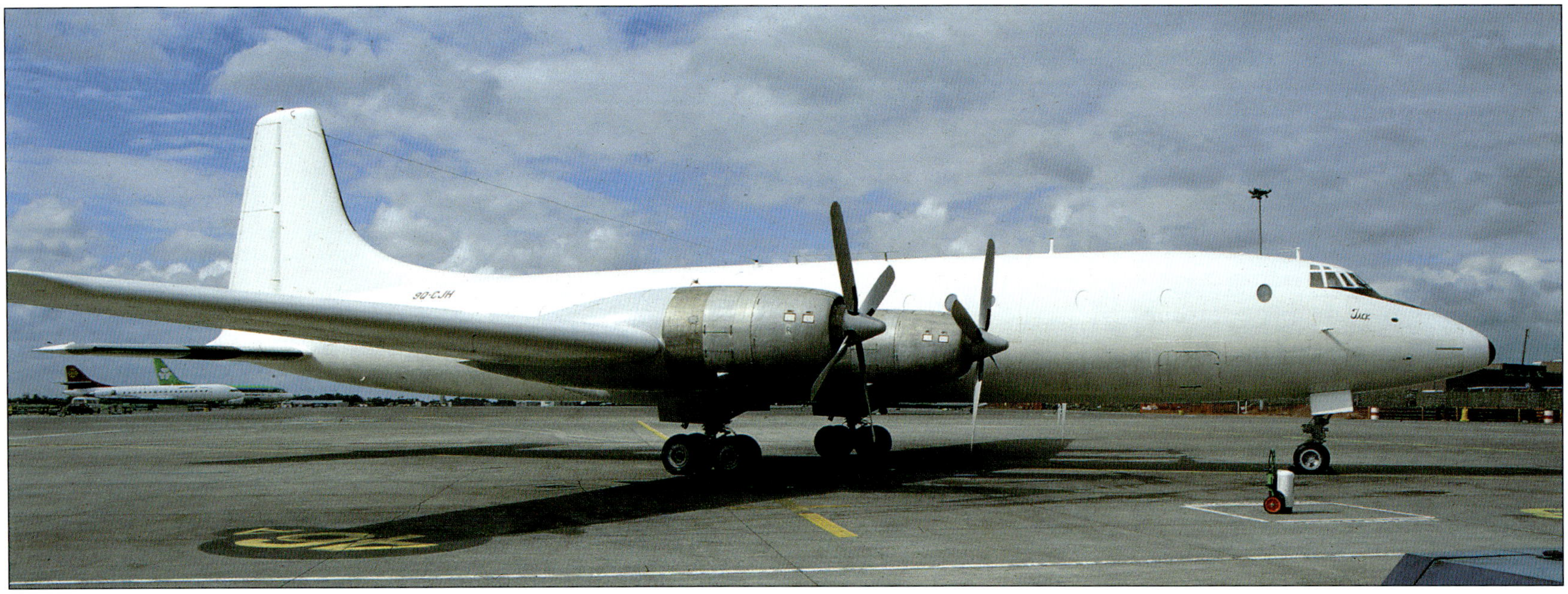

After six days on the ground at Dublin in which a hydraulic leak was rectified, 9Q-CJH sits ready for the short flight to Filton, on Thursday 16th September 1993.

THE RESCUE OF 9Q-CJH FOR TRANSAIR CARGO — FROM CUBA TO ZAIRE

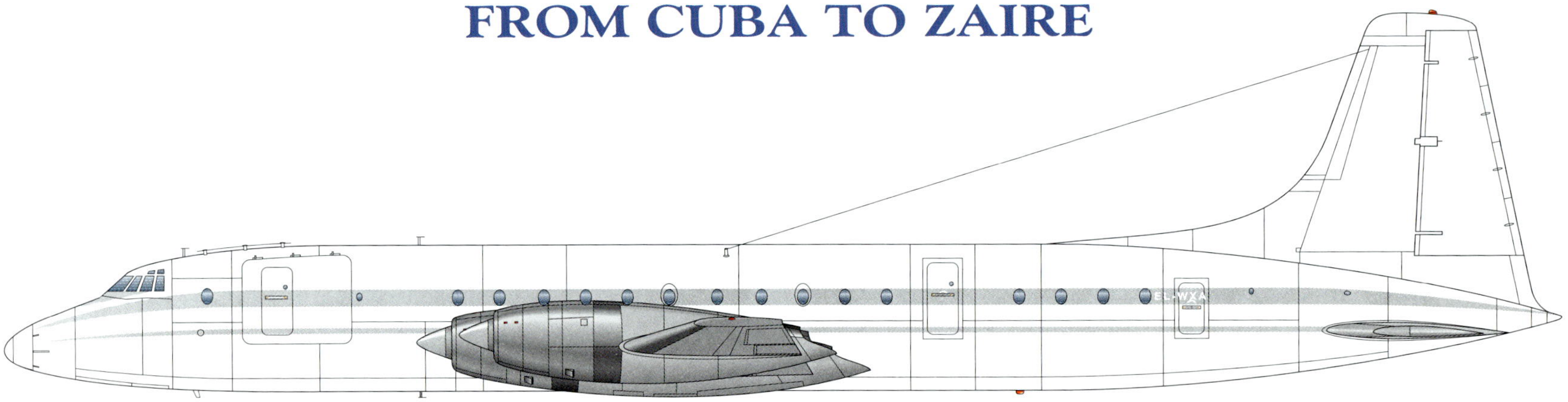

The final flight by a Britannia in Cuba, with Aerocaribbean, in March 1990 and the grounding of the last BCF Aviation Britannia in Zaire in July 1991 made it seem likely that the Whispering Giant had finally been silenced. But this was not the case and the reason centres largely around one man, John Byrne, who had been Technical Director of BCF Aviation and an erstwhile Britannia flight engineer.

He was determined to see Britannias flying again and he planned to use them in a small new service, Transair Cargo, based in Zaire. This story highlights the difficulties in keeping an increasingly old aircraft airworthy and the persistence which is needed.

John Byrne faced two initial problems; where to find and buy airworthy aircraft and where to obtain a supply of spare parts. The most recently grounded Britannia, 9Q-CHY owned by BCF, was not available as BCF understandably would not sell her to someone who would restore her and then compete with their ongoing operations. There were, however, some Britannias on offer in Cuba which were said to be in a pretty good condition and so John Byrne visited Havana with a view to purchasing CU-T120 and CU-T121 as flying machines and also the remains of CU-T114 and CU-T671 as a source of spares.

CU-T120 was in the best condition and it was decided to get her to an airworthy state. The main problem was that the No. 2 engine was unserviceable and was found to need a replacement turbine. The problems with CU-T121 were greater as she needed four replacement engines, and the cockpit had been vandalised and needed a great deal of work done to it. John Byrne, on behalf of Transair Cargo, made an offer for all

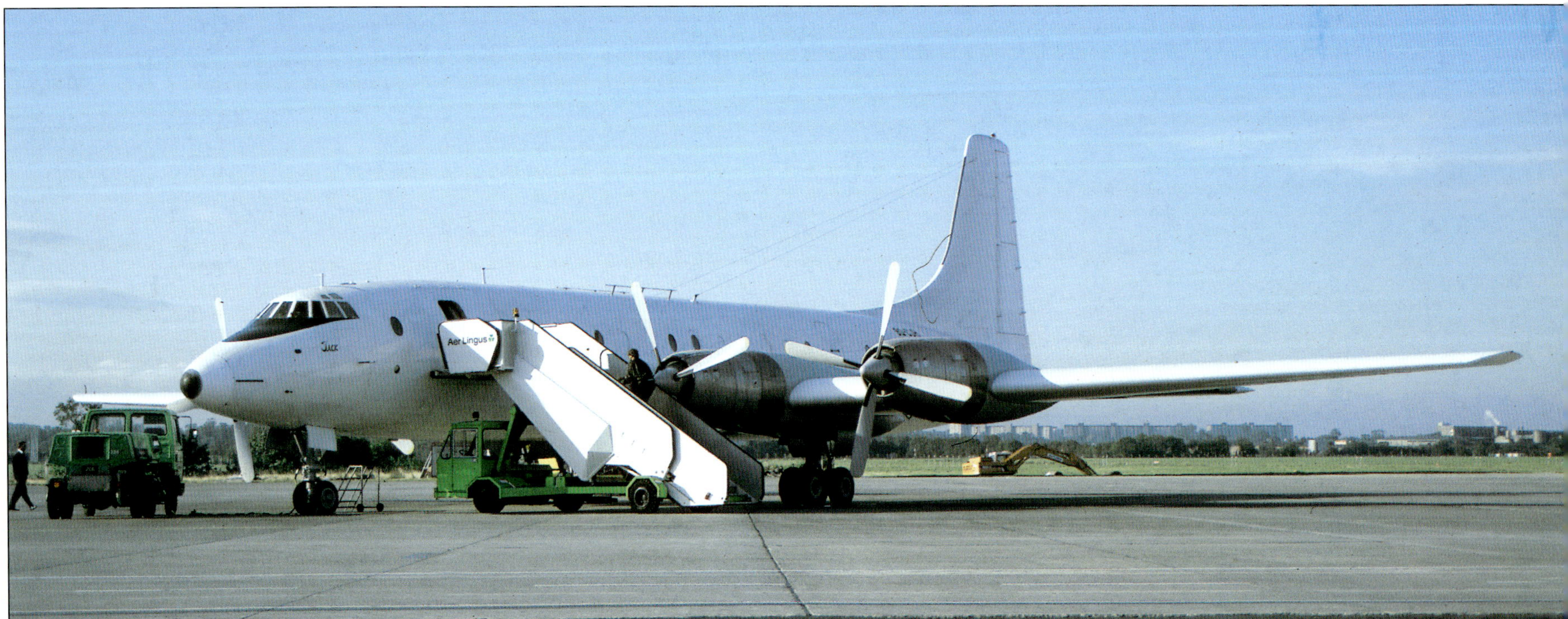

Fifteen minutes before engine start, 'Jack' is prepared for departure from Dublin on Thursday 16th September 1993.

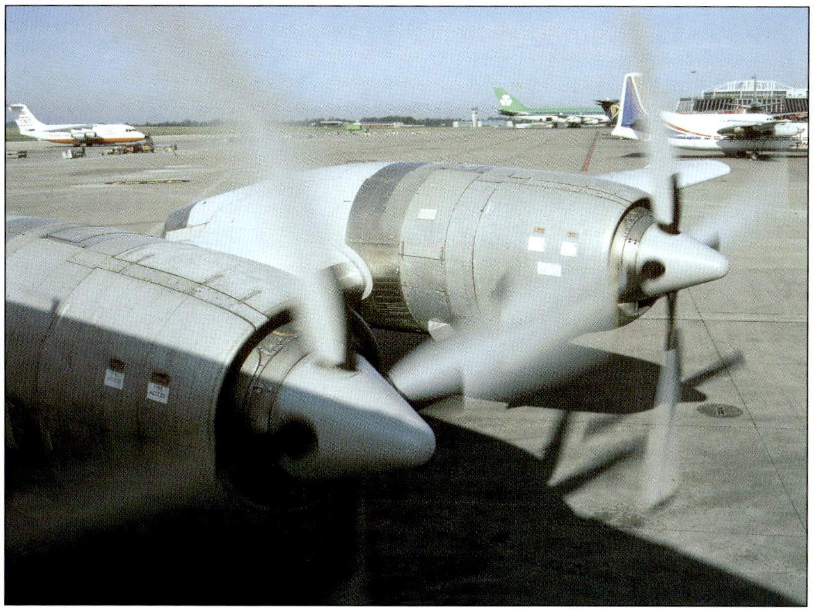

Engines were started at 09.56 onThursday 16th September 1993.

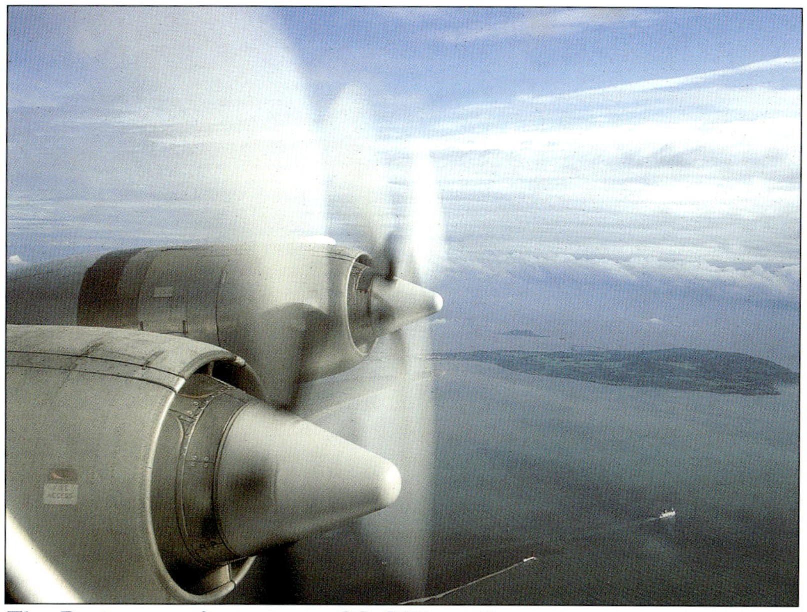

The Proteus engines power 9Q-CJH on the 58 minute flight to Filton.

four aircraft, CU-T120 and CU-T121 and the cannibalised remains of CU-T114 and CU-T671, in October 1992.

Once the deal had been accepted in principle, a replacement turbine for CU-T120's No. 2 engine was acquired in the UK and arrangements made for it to be shipped out to Cuba, although protracted negotiations meant that it did not arrive until mid-April 1993. Meanwhile new radio equipment and radar were installed, replacing heavy Soviet equipment, and a satellite based GPS navigation system was also fitted on the flight deck.

When the turbine eventually arrived, it was fitted to No. 2 engine and testing of all the engines began. This went well until a compressor on No. 3 engine failed, thereby reducing the power plant to just three serviceable engines again. An inspection of the spare parts in Havana made the engineers think that they could build one good engine from the available parts, and this they did. But the newly constructed engine soon failed. It was now the end of June and Transair Cargo was getting restive. There was even an idea of flying the Britannia on three engines only, from Havana to the UK, and to pick up a serviceable Proteus engine located at Coventry. Luckily wiser ideas prevailed, as to attempt a long flight in an aircraft which had not flown for three years and with only three of the four engines functional would have been very risky.

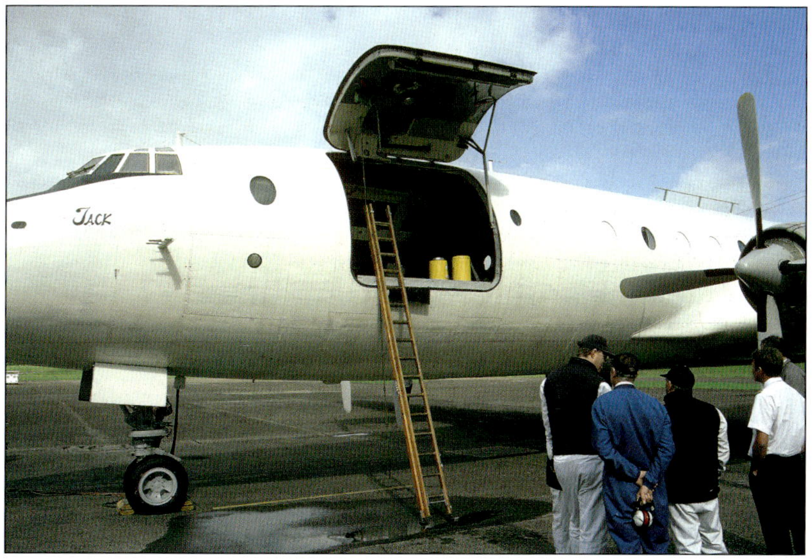

Access to the Transair Cargo aircraft was only for the sure footed, by way of a step ladder.

So the spare engine was shipped from the UK to Cuba, arriving in mid-August. It was quickly installed and ground tests then confirmed that the aircraft was ready to conduct a test flight. The aircraft had her Cuban registration, CU-T120, replaced by the Zairean registration 9Q-CJH. The last two letters were in memory of a flight engineer, Jack Horan, who had worked extensively with Britannias and had taught John Byrne much when they were both at Katale Aero Transport. In preparation for the long flight via the UK into Africa, it was decided to respray the aircraft, paint on the new registration letters and apply the name 'Jack' on the fuselage below the flight deck windows.

The only test flight which 9Q-CJH undertook was on 25th August, taking off and landing back at Havana after 1hr 17mins. All went well until the last few minutes, when the undercarriage failed to lower. It had to be wound down and locked down manually, after which there was a safe landing.

There then followed a busy few days during which all the Britannia spares, including major Proteus engine components which Transair Cargo had bought, were fitted into the 9Q-CJH fuselage and firmly tied down. Eventually all were properly stowed and the aircraft was ready on 10th September.

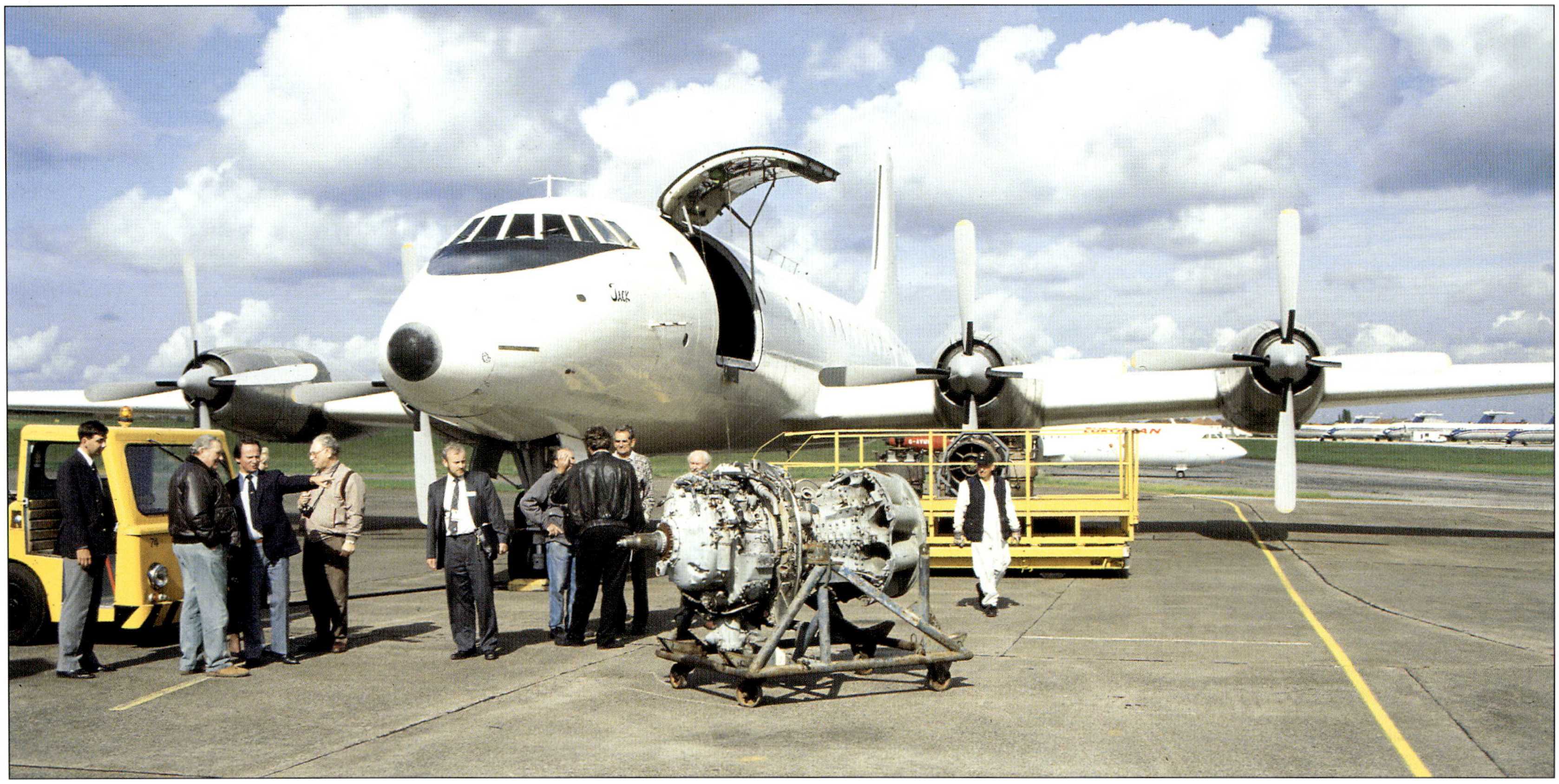

Following arrival at Filton, the Britannia unloaded engines and spare parts for overhaul at a Midlands' workshop.

The crew for this flight comprised; Captain Vervaeke, a veteran Belgian with many hours of experience flying Britannias in Zaire; Captain Marc Adriaansens, also a Belgian, and one of the Transair executives; then as extra adviser and interpreter Captain Romilio Oms Hildago; finally Tony de Bruyn as auxiliary crew member and 'Propliner' reporter.

Departure was scheduled for 1300 local time so that it would be possible to reach Filton before noon on the following day (Saturday) as Filton would only be open until noon on that day. However, in the final checks before departure, an inverter malfunctioned and had to be replaced. This took two hours and meant that the time slot into Filton was lost.

The actual take-off time was 1537 local time. This second flight after the years of idleness showed up only two significant faults, a non-functioning indicator for the starboard gear-up position and an unserviceable galley. But neither was any handicap to the flight itself.

The flight to Gander took 7hrs 20mins. The end was marked by a rather curved approach to the runway and finally a heavy landing because of some wayward readings from the cockpit instruments. But the final bump on touchdown had a beneficial result. The galley was shaken into life!

Refuelling, oil and other checks were completed within one hour of landing and, as a direct flight to Filton was impossible because of the delayed departure from Havana, a new flight plan was filed to Dublin. The crew took a quick snack in the airport and were ready to take-off again, but at that moment a radio signal told the crew that there was a delay of one hour because of clearance restrictions en-route to Ireland. Eventually the engines were started at 0408 local time but in the run up to full power, the rate of revolution in engine No. 4 fluctuated haphazardly. Luckily John Byrne correctly identified the cause as a faulty inverter and by some internal switching

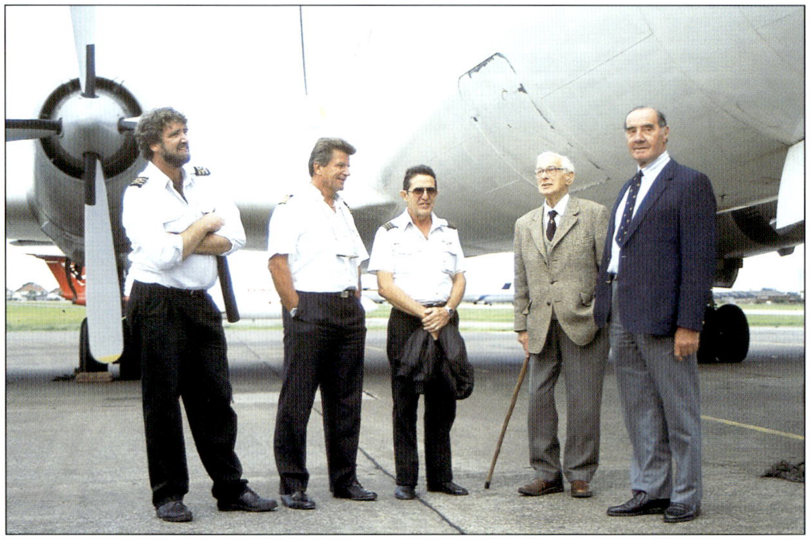

Sir Archibald Russell, head of the Britannia design team and Walter Gibb, the Chief Test Pilot of the Bristol Aircraft Company, meet the crew of 9Q-CJH at Filton.

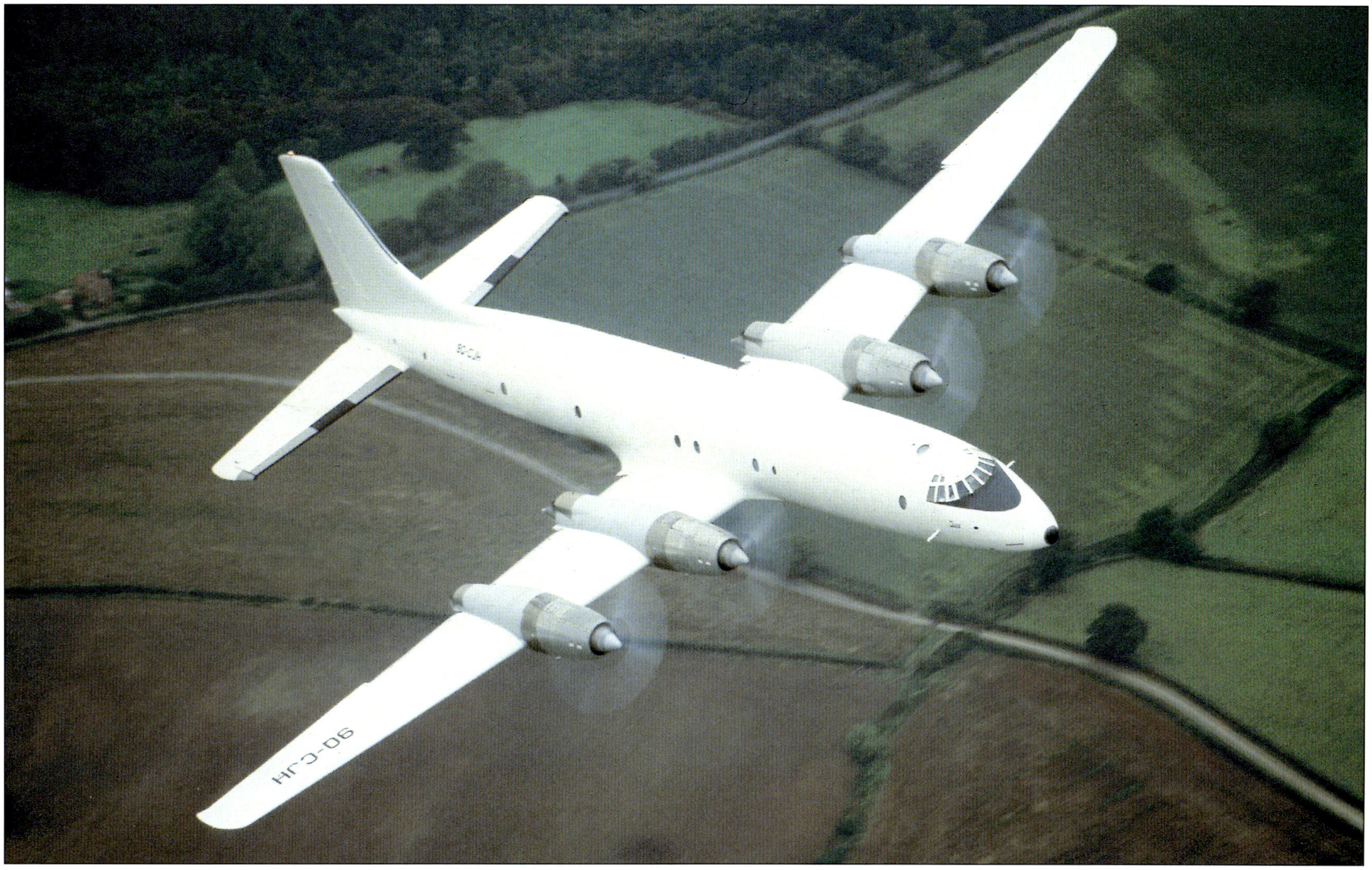

After departure from Filton, the aircraft was flown in the Bristol area for approximately fifteen minutes, for an air-to-air photographic session.

overcame the problem. So the take-off was not delayed and took place at 0421 local time.

The North Atlantic crossing began at a cruise altitude of 18,000ft with a later clearance to 23,000ft. At this altitude the Britannia found some very favourable west winds of up to 70 knots, increasing the ground speed to 370 knots. The crossing was therefore faster than expected, with the sector Gander to Dublin taking just 6hrs 24mins.

Dublin had been chosen because Aer Turas, with its Britannia experience, had offered free handling while 9Q-CJH was there. It was decided to stay there for two days as Filton was closed on Sunday and would not re-open until Monday, 13th September. Furthermore a hydraulic leak had developed during the transatlantic sector and this had to be investigated.

Everything was finally ready for the next flight leg, Dublin to Filton on 15th September. However No. 1 engine refused to light, probably because the cold and damp Irish weather had got in amongst the ageing Britannia. The problem was not rectified until late afternoon, so the departure was delayed until the next day (16th), inconveniencing the reception committee of officials and enthusiasts waiting at Filton.

Next day, Thursday 16th September, was a better day and all four engines started up and at 1016 9Q-CJH took off. At the request of many locals she made a high speed low level pass along the runway before setting a course across the Irish Sea to West Wales and then Filton. She did a low pass over the Filton runway and finally touched down at 1113.

There was a large group of people as a welcoming party, the event being hosted by the Rolls-Royce Heritage Trust, the successor to Bristol Aero Engines. Two notable celebrities present were Sir Archibald Russell, head of the Britannia design team and Walter Gibb, the Chief Test Pilot for the Britannia.

While mingling took place near the aircraft, the load of engines and spare parts brought from Cuba by the Britannia were off-loaded for delivery to the UK overhaul shop. By 1600

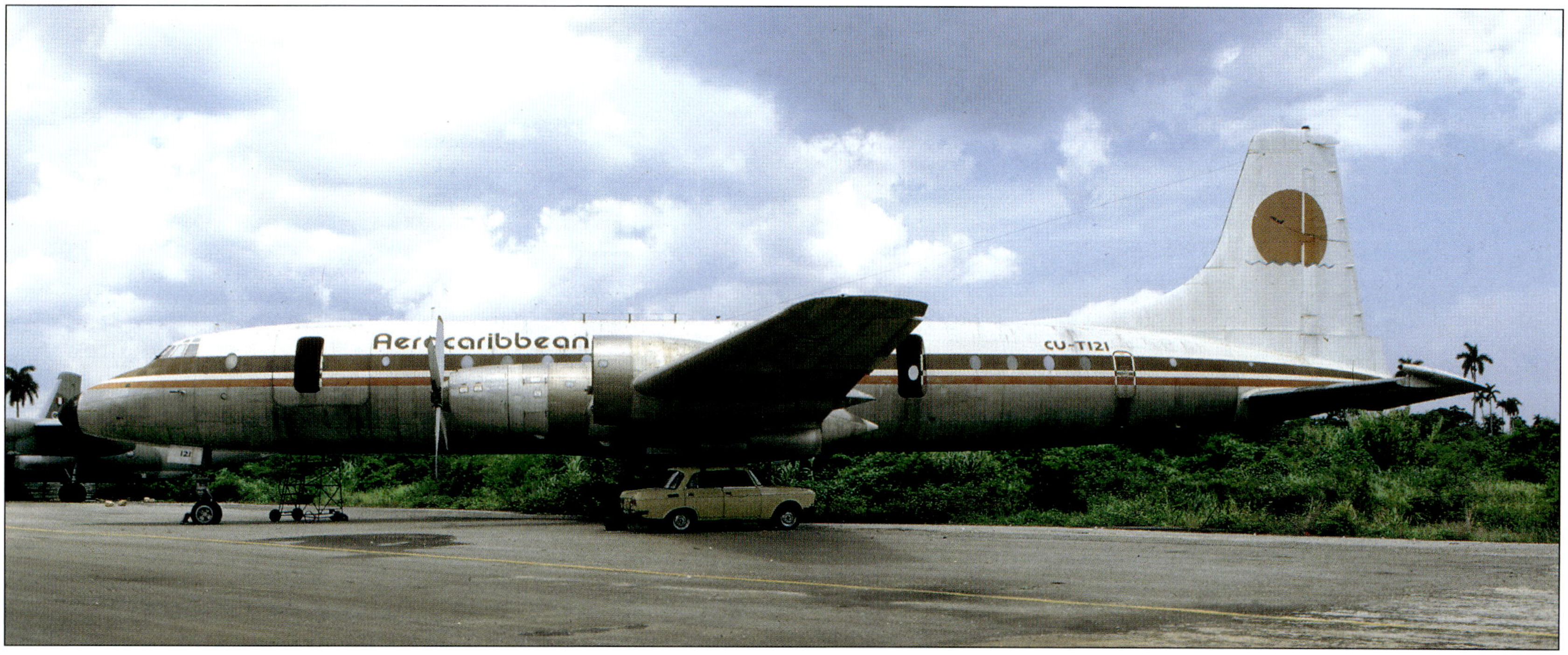

The sister aircraft of 9Q-CJH, CU-T121, remained at Havana after the rescue of the Transair Cargo Britannia in September 1993. After unsuccessful negotiations to purchase the aircraft, it was eventually broken-up in November 1995.

hours the aircraft was re-fuelled and ready for departure to Ostend, and at 1625 the engines were started and minutes later she took off. She did one low-level pass along the runway, a short air-to-air photographic session over the Severn Estuary and then set course for Ostend.

However another snag had occurred when, during the photographic session, the Britannia's flaps were set at 15° and subsequently they could only be retracted by means of the emergency system. That apart, the flight to Ostend was uneventful and lasted just 1hr 12mins.

The stay at Ostend was planned to last some days, to enable snags that had appeared so far to be rectified and to get the Britannia in better shape to tackle the longer legs ahead. By the afternoon of Thursday, 23rd September she was loaded and ready to go and, at 1900 in the evening, the four Proteus engines were wound up and take-off was at 1913, bound for Cairo.

The flight was uneventful except for a strong headwind across the Mediterranean, and the aircraft touched down at Cairo after 7hrs 39mins. Once on the ground, there was an amusing incident at the apron when the Egyptian marshaller wanted the Britannia to turn through 360°, a startlingly unusual manoeuvre. The crew obeyed, but having done this it became

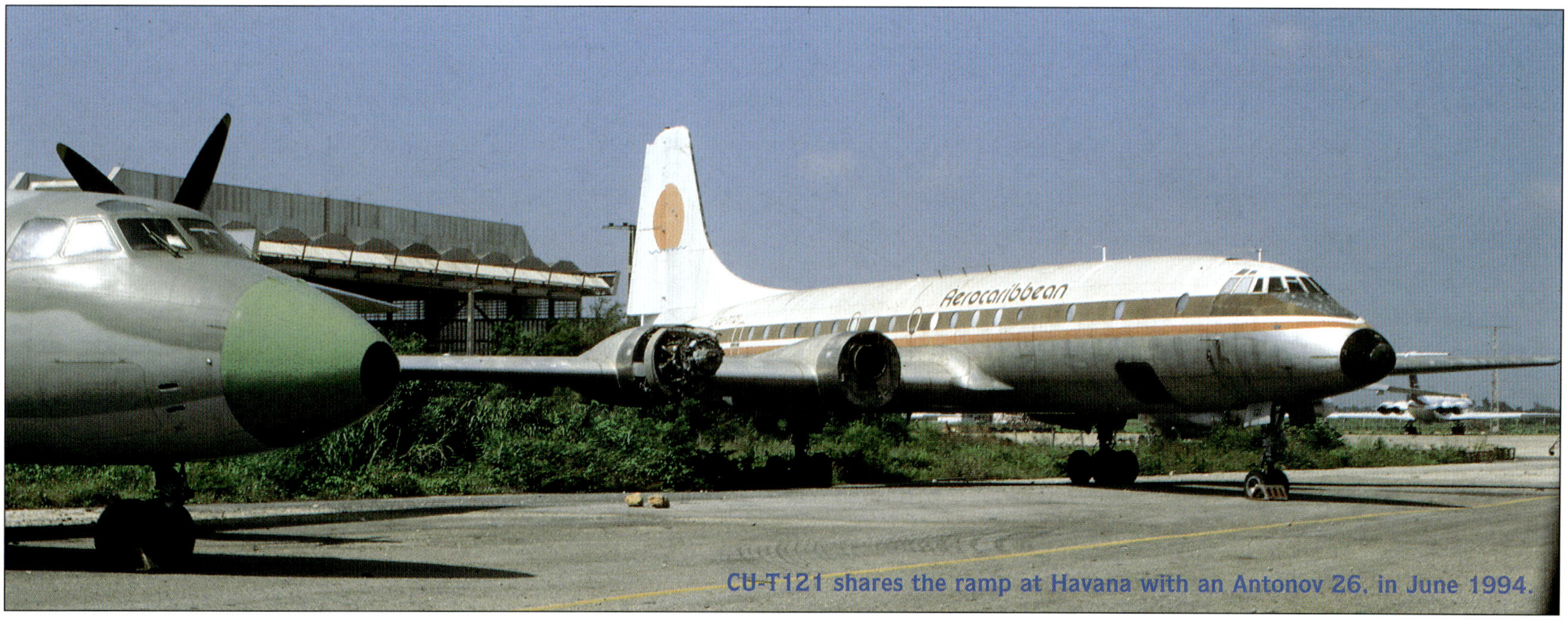

CU-T121 shares the ramp at Havana with an Antonov 26, in June 1994.

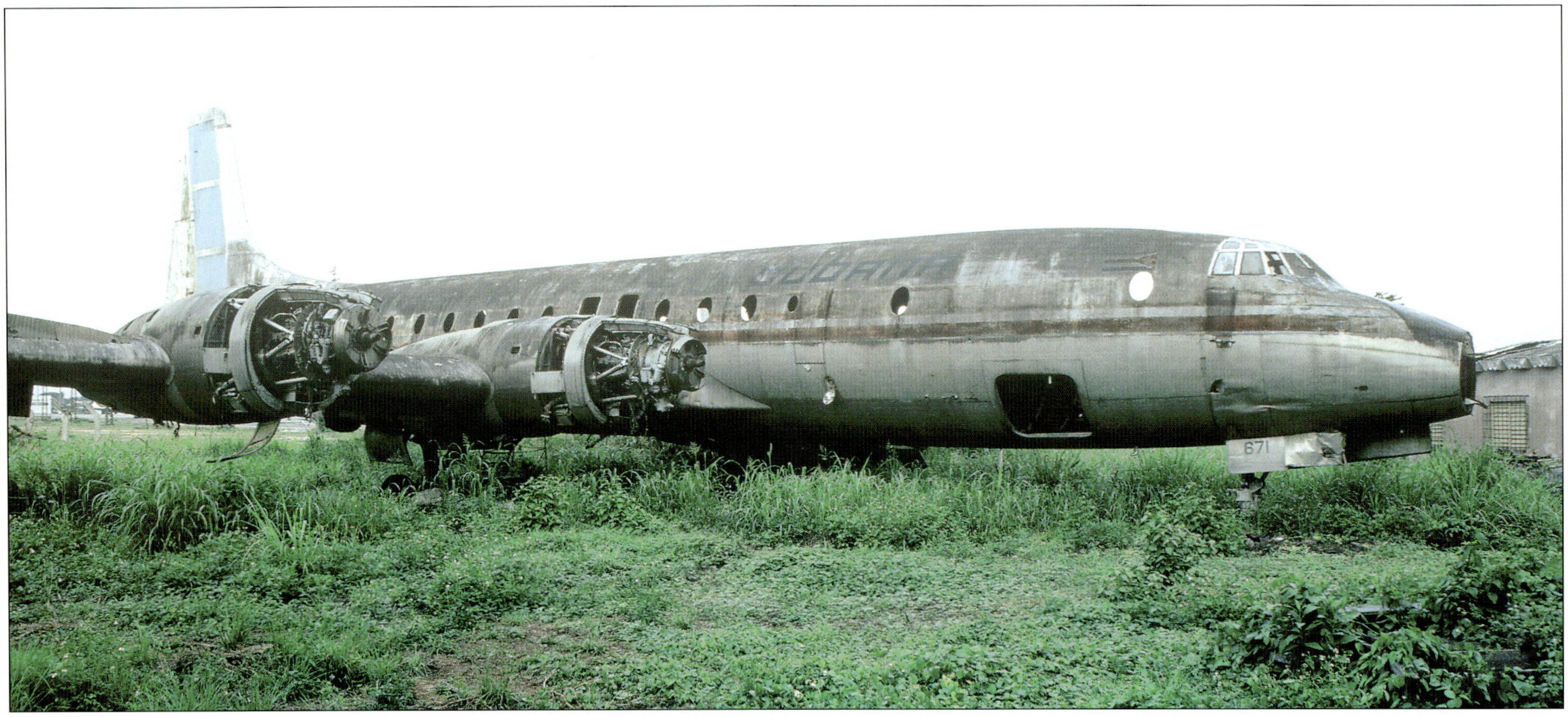

Britannia CU-P671 slowly decays on the perimeter of Havana's José Marti Airport, in June 1994. The aircraft has since been broken-up.

clear that he wanted the aircraft nearer to one of the hydrant refuelling points. Once this was clear, the pilots put the propellers into reverse pitch and the problem was easily solved, in a manner that the marshaller had obviously not considered.

With an efficient turn round of just two hours, the engines were restarted at 0606 on 24th September. Take-off was at 0628 and the next leg, to Goma, took 7hrs 27mins. This leg took the Britannia into the region where the Proteus engines had first experienced trouble with icing in their intakes nearly 40 years earlier. On this flight there were three occasions of flame-out on No. 3 engine while flying through high cloud over Uganda, but the relighting plugs (installed after the earlier malfunctioning) caused only momentary trouble and the flight continued as planned.

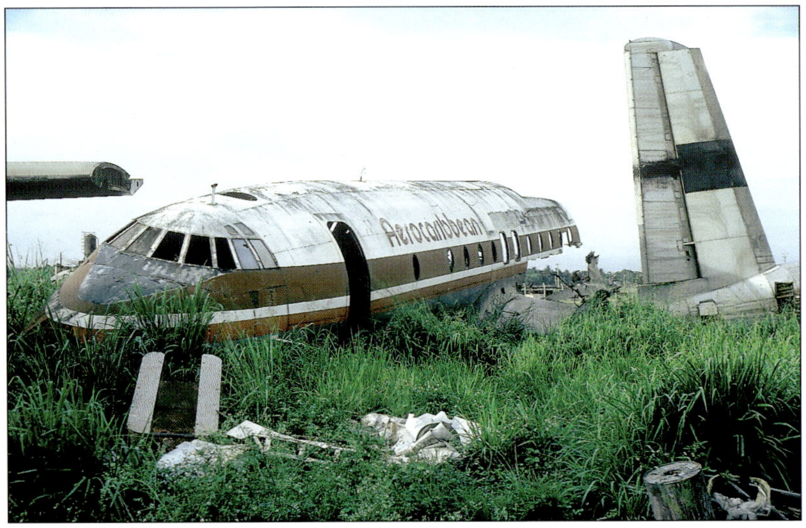

The remains of an unidentified Aerocaribbean Britannia, taken in June 1994 at Havana.

On the ground at Goma, the Britannia and her crew were warmly welcomed by the entire Transair Cargo management who had flown over from Kinshasa for the occasion.

Two days later, on 26th September 1993, after immigration and importation papers had been processed, the Britannia was allowed to fly the last leg of her journey to her new base at Kinshasa. She touched down at 1125 local time after a flight of 2hrs 29mins. Her arrival was a remarkable personal triumph for John Byrne, for without him it is doubtful if the event would ever have taken place.

A few days later, on 4th October, her first commercial service for Transair Cargo began to justify the whole venture, when she flew a full load of margarine from Kinshasa to Mbuji-Mayi.

About a month later there was a near disaster when 9Q-CJH landed at Kinshasa with the main undercarriage down but with the nose wheel retracted. There was consequently considerable damage to the propellers and the forward part of the fuselage. After temporary repairs she was flown to Johannesburg for comprehensive repair work to be carried out. She eventually returned to Kinshasa to work for Transair Cargo alongside their other cargo aircraft, a Douglas DC-4 and a DC-8.

THE FINAL FLIGHT OF THE BRITANNIA — OCTOBER 1997

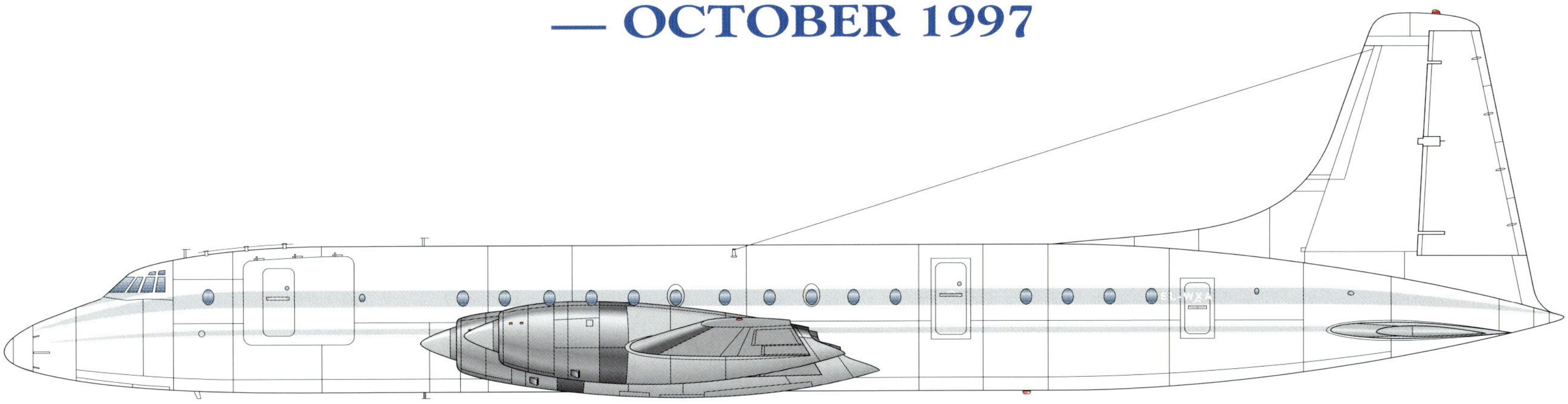

The last airworthy Britannia in the world was the one whose rescue from Cuba is described in the previous chapter. A survivor of the RAF Series 253F, registered in Zaire as 9Q-CJH, it was still flying for Transair Cargo on charters in Zaire from Kinshasa in 1996.

By this time spare parts were becoming very difficult to obtain. Furthermore a new Government in Zaire in 1997 looked with little favour on the old Britannia and so it was decided to ferry 9Q-CJH back to the UK for preservation.

However there was a problem with this plan as one of the four Proteus engines in the aircraft was out of action and needed to be replaced. Only when that had been done was the five thousand mile journey back to the UK feasible.

The journey began with a three-engined ferry flight from Kinshasa to Lanseria (South Africa) on 4th May 1997. During her time in Lanseria, the new authorities in Zaire (now renamed the Democratic Republic of Congo) struck the Britannia off their airworthiness register, so she had to be re-registered in Liberia as EL-WXA during August. Meanwhile the aircraft was being prepared for her last long journey and a replacement Proteus engine had been bought in the UK and flown out to South Africa. It was fitted into the aircraft as were various other replacements for non-functional parts.

The crew for this final flight consisted of Captain Bob

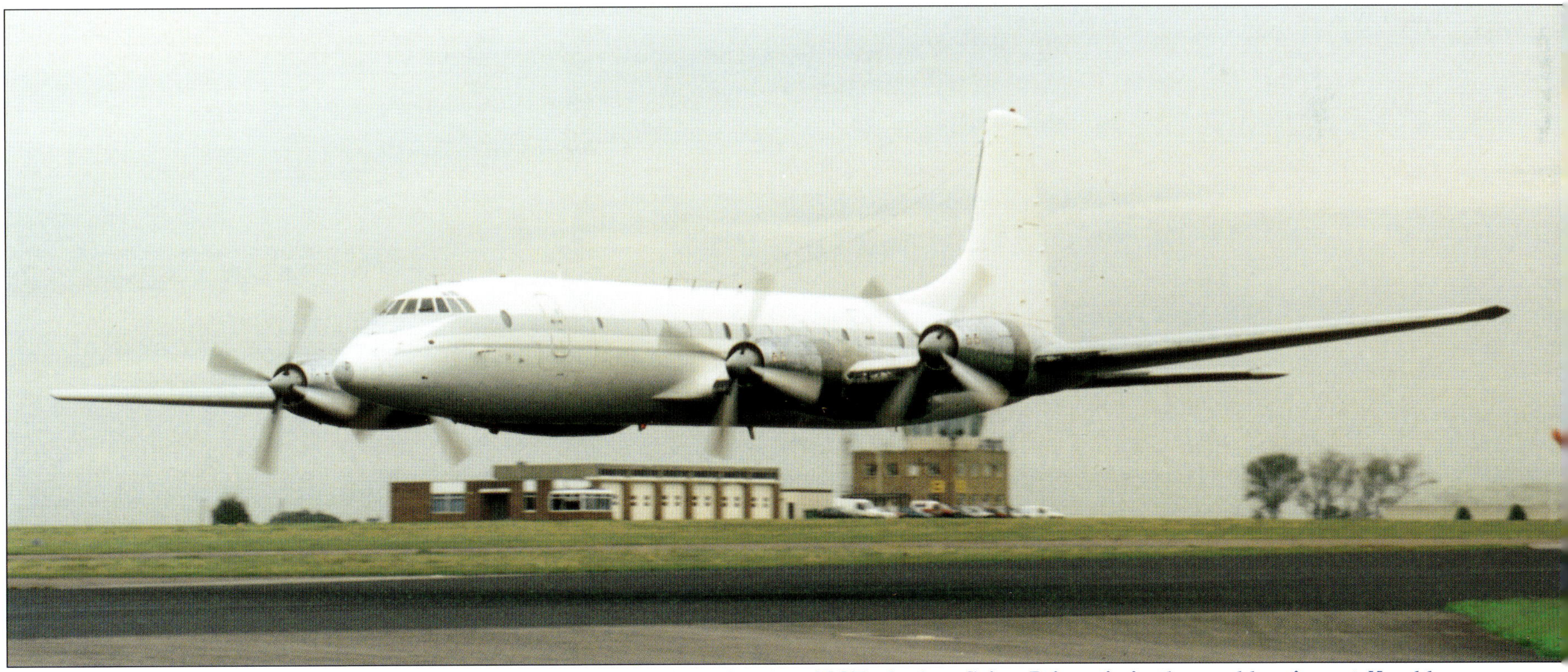

On Tuesday 14th October 1997, the last flying Britannia in the world arrives at Kemble in style, wearing the Liberian registration EL-WXA.

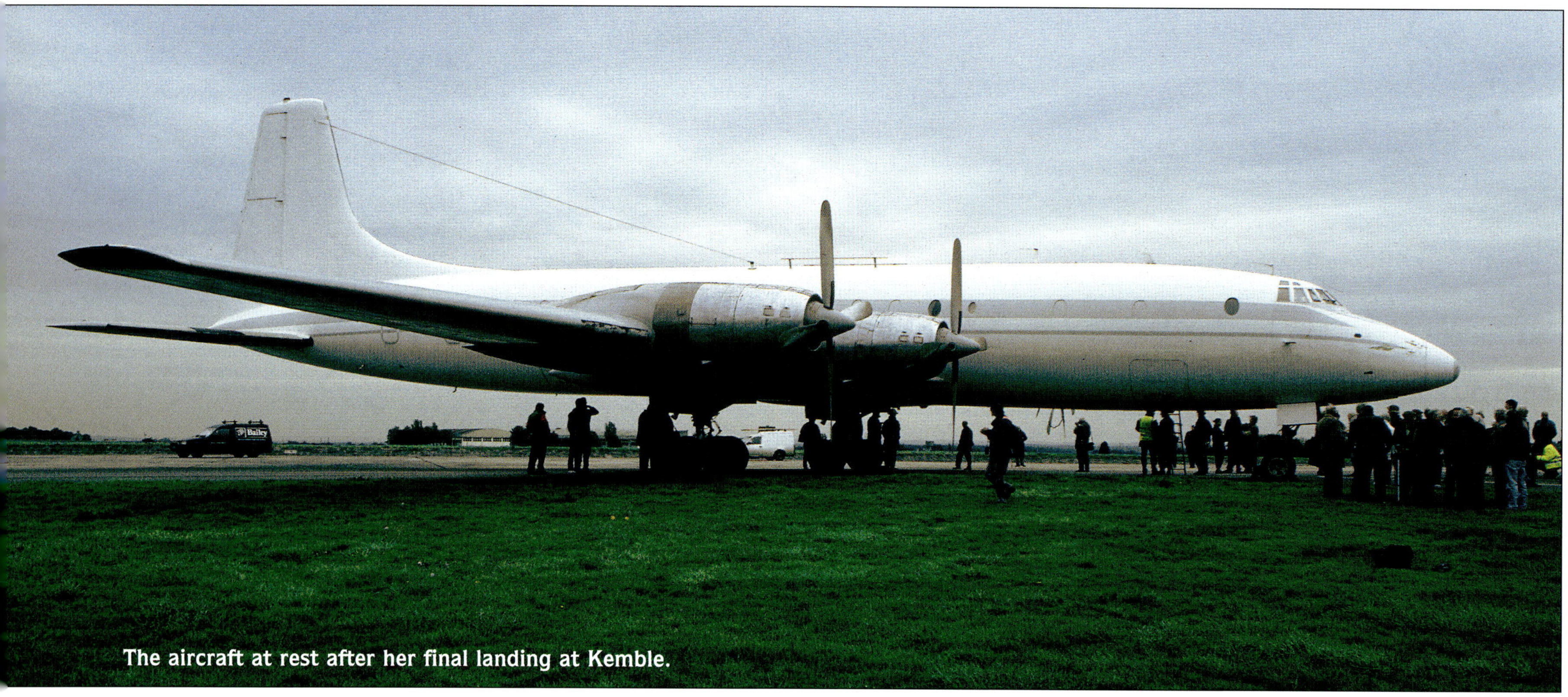

The aircraft at rest after her final landing at Kemble.

Sobek, Captain Christian Vervaeke who had been in charge of the rescue flight from Cuba into Africa in 1993, and as Flight Engineer John Byrne, the Britannia enthusiast previously mentioned, who had been largely responsible for keeping the Britannia flying in Zaire (Congo) and other parts of Africa.

The flight began from Lanseria at 0558 GMT on Sunday, 12th October 1997. There was an overnight stop on 12th/13th October at Douala (Cameroon) then, on 13th October, she flew from Douala to Palma (Majorca). There was a certain piquancy in this stop as in an earlier guise with Monarch Airlines she would have called in to Palma with loads of holidaymakers, as had other Britannias with liveries from British Eagle, Caledonian, Donaldson etc. This time the Britannia was just in the pale grey and white livery of Transair, her most recent owner.

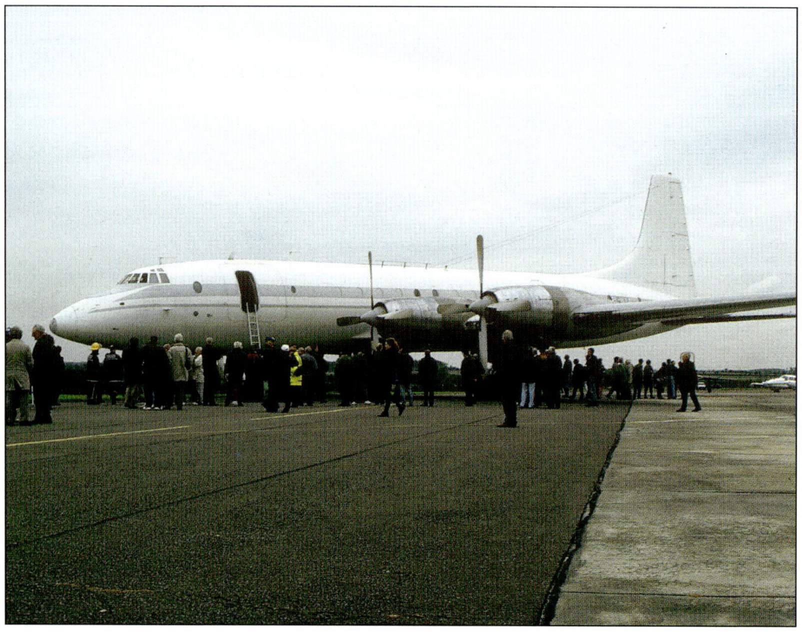

A crowd of admirers gather around EL-WXA at Kemble.

For this final historic flight, the call sign used was the original one which the Britannia used when she first entered service with the RAF as XM496 on 19th September 1960. On 14th October 1997 she took off for the last time from Palma at about 1000 bound for England.

It had previously been arranged that she would make a low altitude fly past at various airports. She performed these at Bristol, Lulsgrove (the commercial airport), then Filton (over the runway first constructed for the Brabazon), then Cardiff, then RAF Kemble, then RAF Brize Norton and finally back to Kemble for a fly past in the company of a Hawker Hunter. After a second fly past at very low level along the runway, 9Q-CJH landed for the final time and taxied to her final display ramp, thus bringing to an end Britannia operations.

And there she remains, one of the three complete Britannias preserved in this country and looked after by the Britannia Aircraft Preservation Trust. Uniquely she has Proteus engines 'in working order' which are run from time to time. At the time of writing she is still in Transair Cargo livery, but eventually it is planned to re-paint her in the RAF Transport Command livery which she had for her first owners.

VARIATIONS ON A THEME

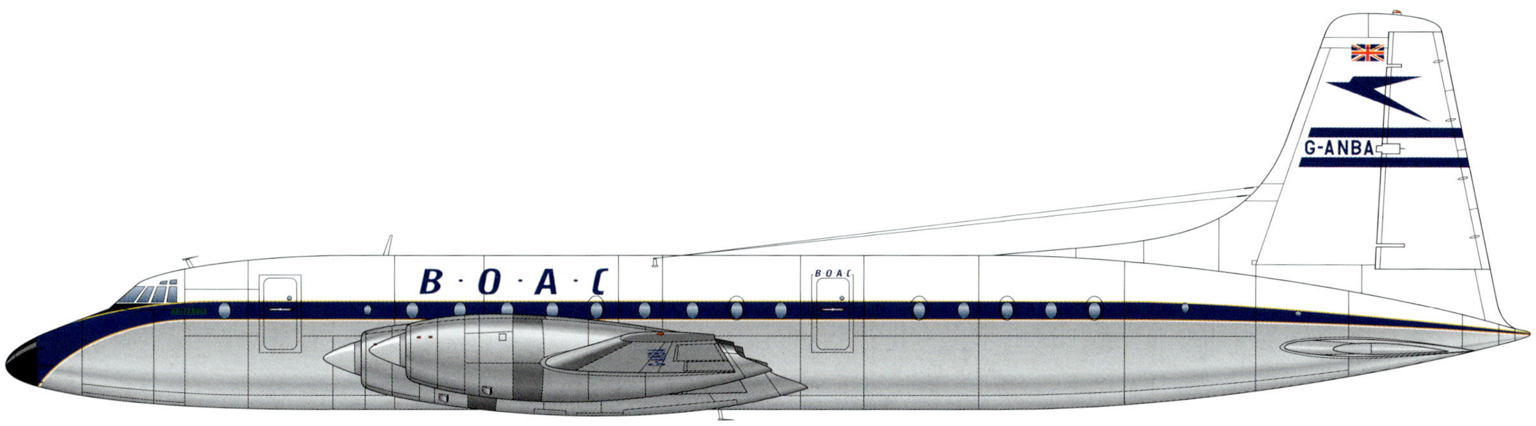

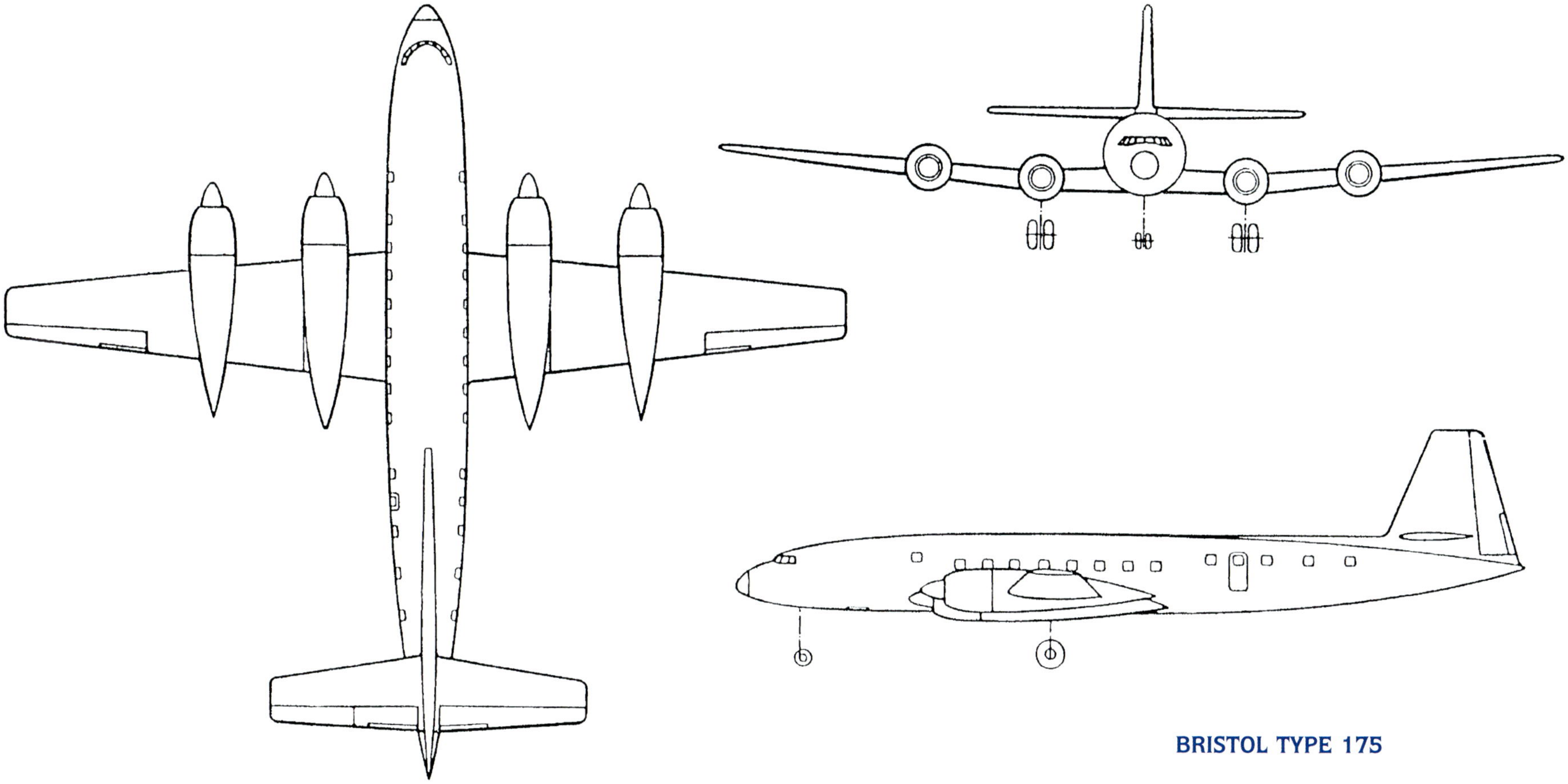

BRISTOL TYPE 175

The Bristol Type 175 as it appeared in the first brochure submitted to B.O.A.C. powered by four Bristol Centaurus piston engines and had a 120 ft wingspan.

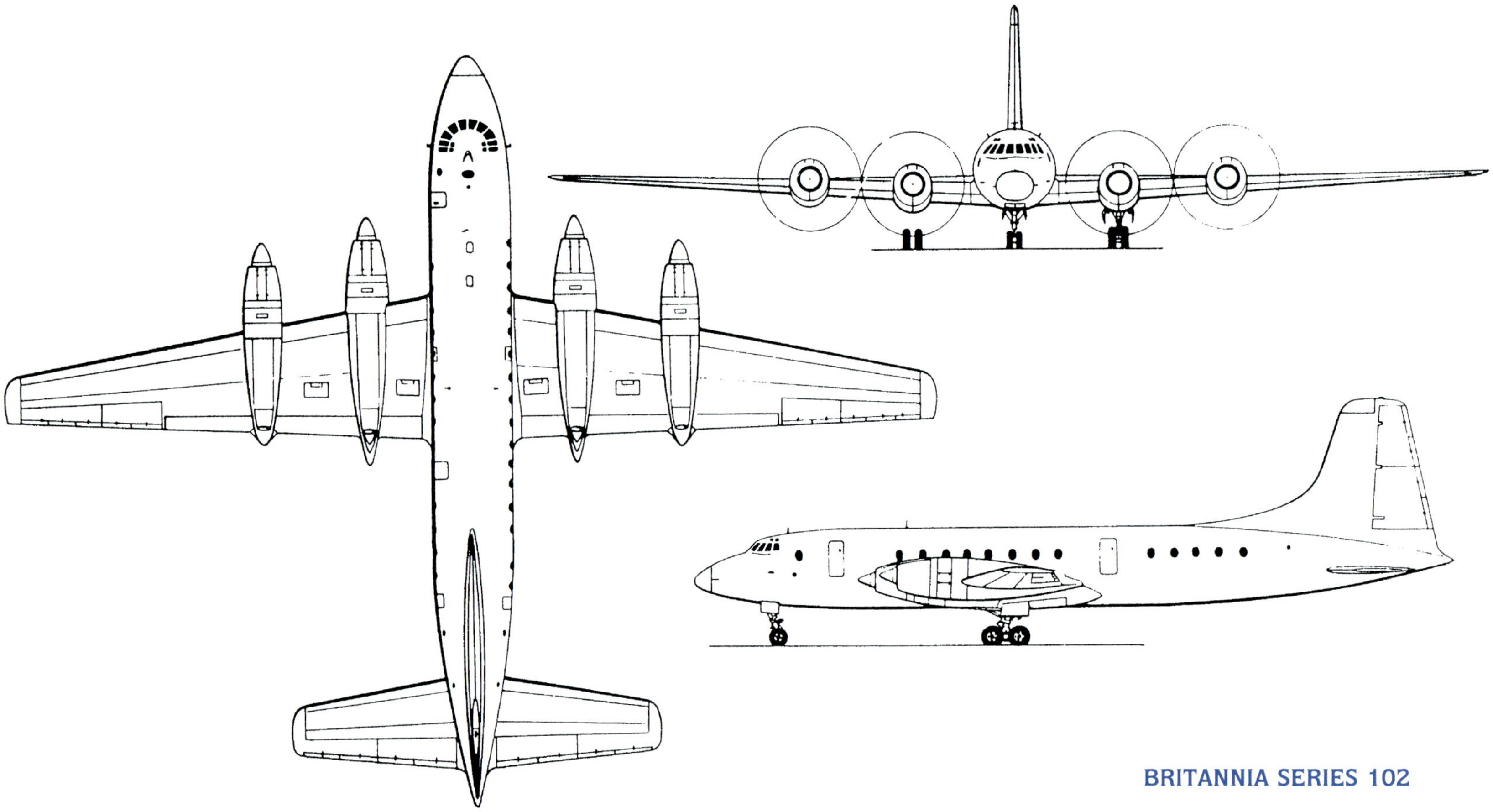

BRITANNIA SERIES 102

BRITANNIA SERIES 310

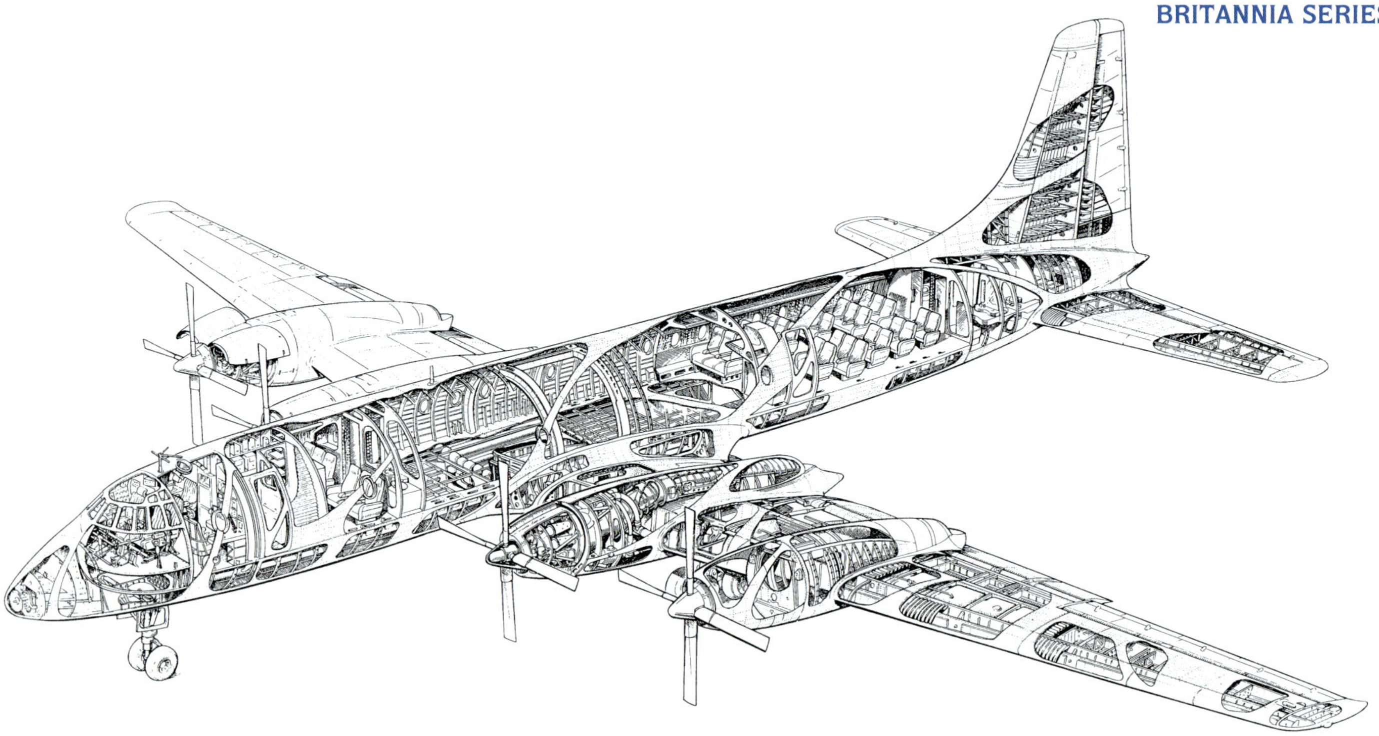

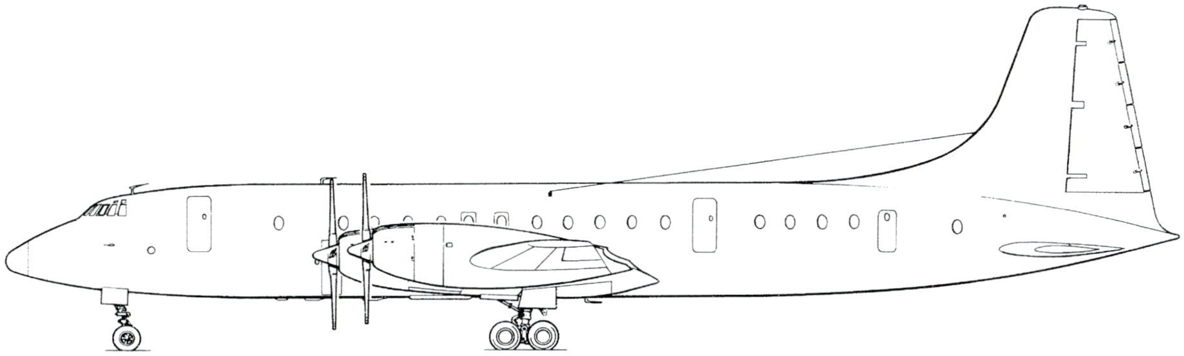

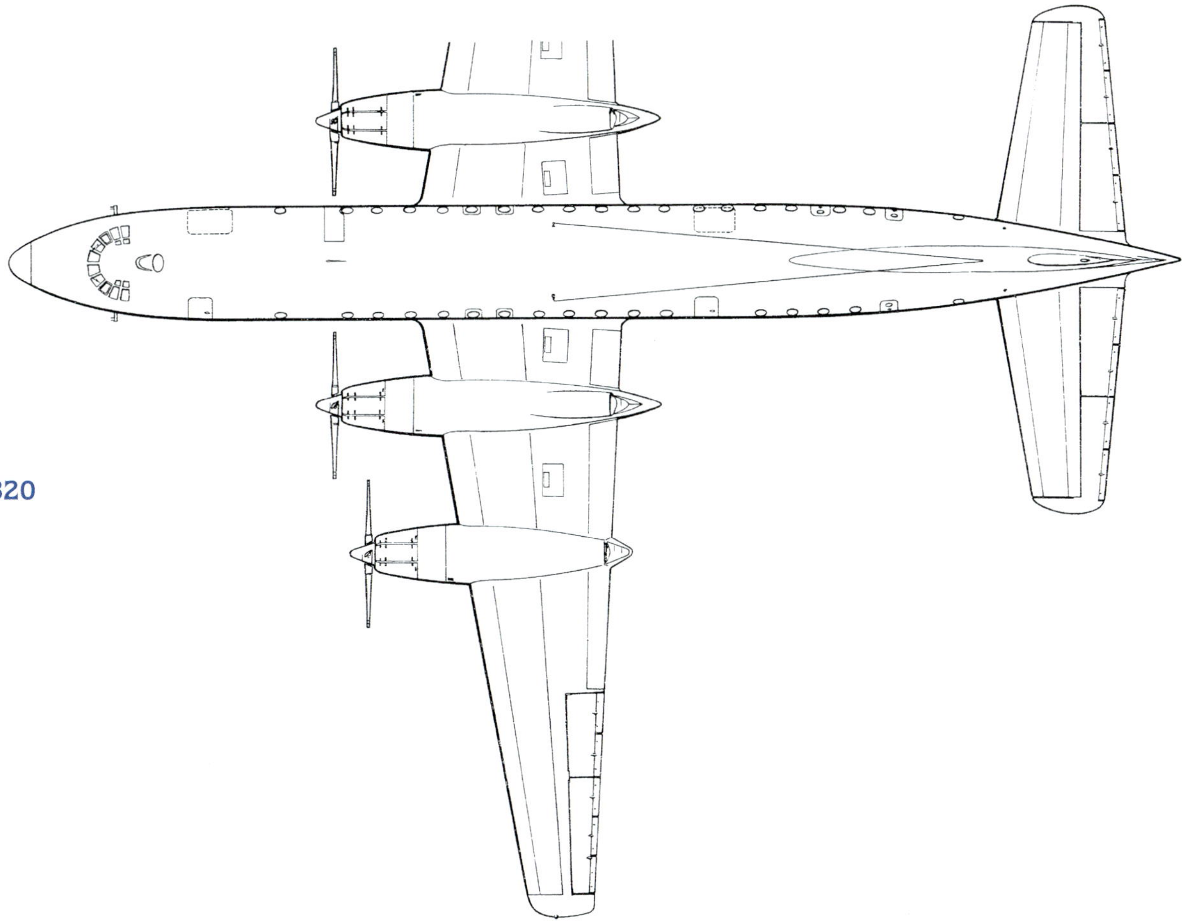

BRITANNIA SERIES 320

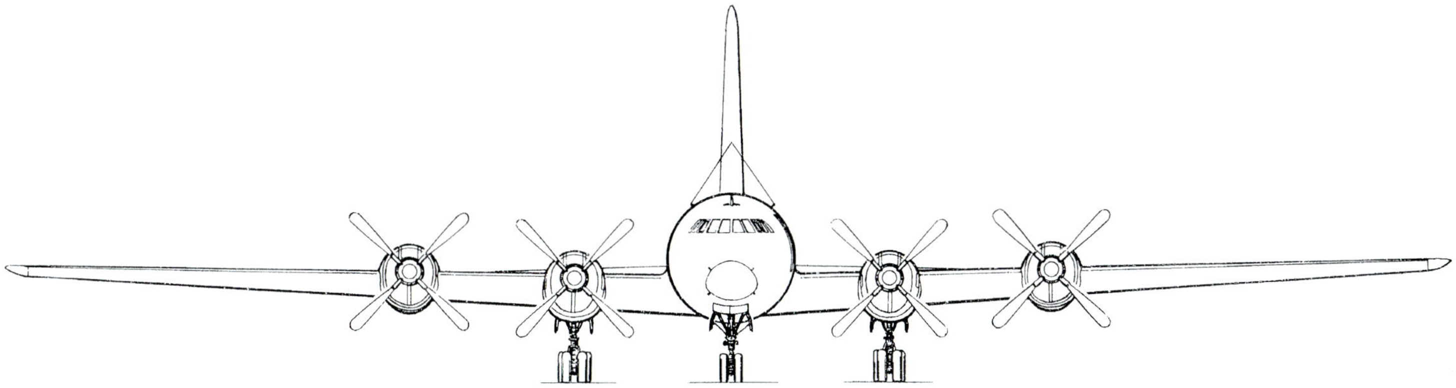

IN RETROSPECT

My talks to various people who worked with Britannias has reinforced my previous opinion that the aircraft was very popular with those who knew it.

It existed, for the world's major airlines, in the time gap between the availability of the propeller-driven, piston-engined planes and the pure jets. Had its availability after the maiden flight in 1952 been immediate and in considerable numbers, the history of turbo-prop civil airliners in general, and of the Britannia in particular, would have been rather different.

The use of the Proteus engine, with its convoluted air intake, was disastrous. It is understandable that as it 'lay on the shelf', albeit designed for the different Brabazon and Princess aircraft, it might have seemed sensible to adopt the Proteus for the Britannia. But the engine icing problem then showed up, unexpected and perhaps unpredictable for meteorologists at the time. And the time taken to understand the problem and reduce its effect to minimal significance meant that the turbo-prop Britannia was soon competing against the first generation of pure jets which travelled faster. Then the new Bristol engine, the Orion, with a straight-through air flow, lost Government support and was cancelled in 1958. It never got beyond the basic test flying stage.

And there was another factor which worked against the Britannia. Like any turbo-prop airliner of comparable size, the Britannia used less fuel per passenger mile flown than jets such as the 707 or DC-8. It therefore cost less for a Britannia to fly a planeload of passengers across, say, the North Atlantic. So BOAC wanted to offer a lower fare across the North Atlantic for a Britannia flight than for a pure-jet flight; 'it takes longer but you pay less'. However the fare structure was imposed in those days by the International Air Transport Association, and they would not allow any such differential fares. Had these been allowed, it seems likely that the Britannia would have been a serious competitor for the economy class passenger market.

It is too easy to be wise after events. All branches of engineering have situations which, with the benefit of hindsight, could have been different. But without that, it is clear that the Britannia gained the affection of airline staff, many air crew and passengers. The attitude of the manufacturers is summed up by Sir Stanley Hooker who wrote that the Britannia built up "a reputation of being the fastest, smoothest, quietest and safest propeller aircraft in the world which gave many years of service to BOAC, the RAF and other operators". The air crews' attitude is summed up by Air Chief Marshal Sir Thomas Kennedy who wrote "for the sheer fun of flying, the Britannia took a lot of beating". And the speed with which second-hand Britannias were bought, once BOAC had decided to re-equip with jets, shows the enthusiasm within the airline industry for the aircraft, particularly in the charter business. Even with its chequered history between maiden flight and the granting of its Certificate of Airworthiness, the Britannia developed into a remarkable aircraft and has a justifiably important place in aviation history, described by Phil Lo Bao as "perhaps the all time classic (turbo-prop airliner)".

Frank McKim

PRODUCTION LIST

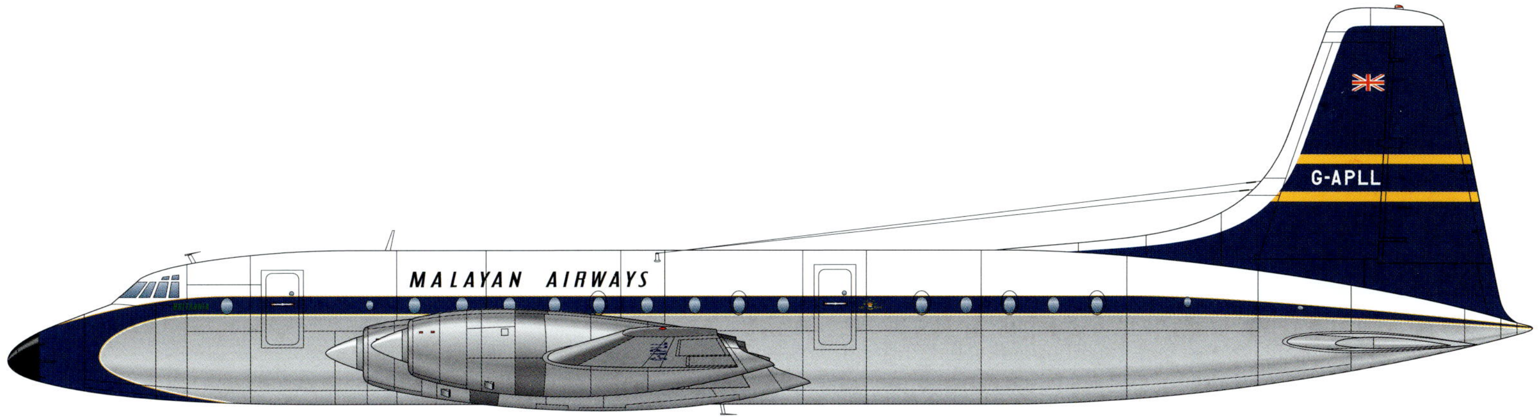

BRISTOL BRITANNIA PRODUCTION

12873

Series 100. Built at Filton. Allocated VX 442, then WB 470 for Ministry of Supply, but not taken up. Registered G-ALBO for BAC. Flew maiden flight for Britannia, 16.8.52, and flight testing thereafter including dramatic flap failure incident, 5.54. To RAF as 7708M, 30.10.60, where it was used for ground-based instruction. Broken up at St. Athan Wales 12.6.68.

12874

Series 101. Built at Filton. Allocated VX 447, then WB 473, then registered G-ALRX for Ministry of Supply. 23.12.53 (ff), thereafter test flying. Written off in River Severn Estuary after crash landing due to engine fire, 4.2.54. Forward fuselage used by manufacturer for ground instruction. In 1976 moved to Boscombe Down for safety training. At present remains housed at RAF Kemble.

12875

Allocated serial VX454 - used as systems test rig.

12902

Series 102. Built at Filton. Registered G-ANBA for BOAC. 5.9.54 (ff). 22.8.57 (del). Leased to Nigeria Airways for some months, '59, and to Malayan Airways for one month, '61/2. Sold by BOAC to Britannia Airways, 26.3.65. Withdrawn 20.11.69, and broken up at Luton, 6.70.

12903

Series 102. Built at Filton. Registered G-ANBB for BOAC. 18.1.55 (ff). 18.6.57 (del). Leased to Nigeria Airways 1959/60 and to Cathay Pacific Airways for a fortnight '61. Leased to Britannia Airways, 18.11.64. Written off after crashing on approach to Ljubljana, Yugoslavia, 1.9.66.

12904

Series 102. Built at Filton. Registered G-ANBC for BOAC. 29.6.55 (ff). 30.12.55 (del). Leased to Ghana Airways, 1960. Written off at Khartoum, 11.11.60. (Undercarriage failed to lock on approach to airport, so emergency landing, when undercarriage collapsed. Damage uneconomic to repair.)

12905

Series 102. Built at Filton. Registered G-ANBD for BOAC. 14.11.55 (ff). 30.12.55 (del). Withdrawn from use and stored at Cambridge from Jan. 63. Leased to BKS Air Transport, 11.65. Sub-leased to Britannia Airways, 27.4 to 1.10.68. Retired 1.70. Broken up at Newcastle, 5.70.

12906

Series 102. Built at Filton. Registered G-ANBE for BOAC. 17.1.56 (ff). 2.3.56 (del). Leased to Nigeria Airways, 1958, to Ghana Airways, 1960, to Malayan Airways, 1963. Returned to BOAC and stored at Cambridge April 1963. Leased to Britannia Airways, 1966, and sold to them, 3.70. Withdrawn by Britannia Airways, 12.70 and broken up at Luton, 7.72.

12907

Series 102. Built at Filton. Registered G-ANBF for BOAC. 23.2.56 (ff). 14.3.56 (del). Flew first royal flight, 7.57, of Queen Elizabeth the Queen Mother to then-called Salisbury, Rhodesia and back. Leased to Malayan Airways for a few weeks, 1961, to Nigeria Airways for a few weeks also 1961, then again to Malayan Airways for three weeks, 1962. Returned to BOAC and operated their last 102 service on 22.11.62. To Cambridge for storage 26.1.63. Leased to Britannia Airways, 2.65 and eventually sold to them. Withdrawn by Britannia Airways, 26.10.69, and broken up at Luton, 5.70.

12908

Series 102. Built at Filton. Registered G-ANBG for BOAC. 29.3.56 (ff). 8.5.56 (del). Re-registered G-APLL, 19.3.58. Leased to Nigeria Airways, 58, to Malayan Airways, 1962. Returned to BOAC, wfu at Cambridge, Jan 63. Sold to BKS Air Transport, 16.11.65. Withdrawn by BKS, 21.2.69, and broken up at Newcastle, 9.69.

12909

Series 102. Built at Filton. Registered G-ANBH for BOAC. 9.5.56 (ff). 24.7.57 (del). Leased to Nigeria Airways, 1958. Returned to BOAC and stored at Cambridge from 11.11.62. Leased (10.3.65) and then sold (30.9.65) to BKS Air Transport. Withdrawn by BKS, 25.10.68, and broken up at Southend, 1969.

12910

Series 102. Built at Filton. Registered G-ANBI for BOAC. 24.5.56 (ff). 29.6.56 (del). Operated BOAC's first Britannia schedule, London to Johannesburg, 1.2.57. Leased to Ghana Airways, '60; to Malayan Airways, '62. Returned May 62, to storage at Cambridge Jan 63. Leased (3.2.66) and then sold (29.4.66) to Britannia Airways. Withdrawn by Britannia Airways, 27.9.69 and broken up at Luton, 2.70.

12911

Series 102. Built at Filton. Registered G-ANBJ for BOAC. 5.8.56 (ff). 22.11.56 (del). Leased to Malayan Airways, 1962. Wfu at Cambridge Nov 62. returned to Heathrow for sale to Paraense Transportes Aeros which fell through, wfu again 9. 63 Leased to Britannia Airways, 5.5.65 and sold to them July 1970. Withdrawn by Britannia Airways, 13.10.70, and broken up at Luton, 3.71.

12912

Series 102. Built at Filton. Registered G-ANBK for BOAC. 14.9.56 (ff). 12.2.57 (del). Leased to Nigeria Airways, 1961. Wfu Cambridge Dec 62. Leased (11.4.64) and then sold (3.70) to BKS Air Transport. She was the last Britannia Series 102 in passenger service and flew the last ever 102 service, London to Newcastle, 31.12.71. Withdrawn by BKS (then renamed Northeast Airlines), and broken up, 3.72, at Newcastle.

12913

Series 102. Built at Filton. Registered G-ANBL for BOAC. 24.2.57 (ff). 2.3.57 (del). Leased to Cathay Pacific Airways for six weeks, 1960/61. Wfu at Cambridge Nov 62. returned to Heathrow for sale to Paraense Transportes Aeros which fell through, wfu again. Leased to Britannia Airways, 26.6.65. Sold to them 29.7.70. Sub-leased to Southern Cross International for one month, 5.70. Flew the last ever Britannia commercial service for Britannia Airways, 29.12.70. Withdrawn by Britannia Airways and broken up at Luton, 7.72.

12914

Series 102. Built at Filton. Registered G-ANBM for BOAC. 6.3.57 (ff). 11.3.57 (del). Leased to Nigeria Airways, 1959/60; to Malayan Airways, 1961/2; Wfu Dec. 62. To Laker Airways, 4.66 to 6.67, during which period there were two short sub-leases to Air France and Treffield International. Sold to Aero Leasing 19.1.69, for onward sale to Indonesian Angkasa Air Transport, 2.69, re-registered PK-ICA. Withdrawn by Angkasa Civil Air Transport, 6.70, and broken up at Jakarta, 12.71.

12915

Series 102. Built at Filton. Registered G-ANBN for BOAC. 11.4.57 (ff). 4.5.57 (del). Leased to EAAC, 1958; to Nigeria Airways, '60/1; to Malayan Airways, 1962; Wfu Cambridge Jan. 63. To Laker Airways, 21.4.66 to 21.1.69, during which period there were sub-leases to Air Carriers of Zambia, to Monarch Airlines and to Britannia Airways. Returned to Laker Nov. 68. Sold to Aero Leasing (21.1.69) for onward sale to Indonesian Angkasa Civil Air Transport, 2.69. and registered PK-ICB. Withdrawn by Angkasa Civil Air Transport, 6.70, and broken up at Jakarta, 12.71.

12916

Series 102. Built at Filton. Registered G-ANBO for BOAC. 17.5.57 (ff). 31.5.57 (del). Leased to Cathay Pacific Airways, 1960/1; to Malayan Airways, 1961 and again 1962; to EAAC, 1961. Wfu Cambridge, Dec. 62 . Leased (4.1.65) and then sold (16.3.70) to Britannia Airways. Withdrawn by Britannia Airways, 15.10.70, and broken up at Luton, 5.71.

12917

Series 301. Built at Filton. Registered G-ANCA for Bristol Aeroplane Company on 11.3.55. Registered to MOS on 26.5.56 and rolled out in Capital Airlines colours for two days before first flight on 31.7.56. Used on sales tour to the U.S.A. & later to South America for tropical trials. Prototype Series 300 aircraft used for development flying, organised partly by Ministry of Supply, partly by Bristol. Crashed at Downend, Bristol, 6.11.57, when on a test flight, the reason for which was never established, but control appeared to have been lost on the final turn to landing, perhaps because of an autopilot fault. Written off.

12918

Series 302. Built at Belfast. Flown as G-18-1 on 21.6.57. Delivered to Weston-Super-Mare for reconfiguration. Registered G-ANCB for BOAC, but order cancelled. Sold by Bristol Aircraft Ltd to Aeronaves de Mexico, (del) 1.11.57, re-registered XA-MEC. She was named 'Ciudad de Mexico', then 'Tenochtitlan' and finally 'Acapulco'. Retired after accident (main undercarriage collapse on landing) at Tijuana, Mexico, 9.7.65. Broken up for spares at Tijuana.

12919

Series 302. Built at Belfast. Flown as G-18-2 on 27.7.57. Delivered to Weston-Super-Mare for reconfiguration Registered G-ANCC for BOAC, but order cancelled. Sold by Bristol Aircraft Ltd to Aeronaves de Mexico, (del) 15.12.57, re-registered XA-MED and named 'Mexico City' later 'Tzintzuntan'. Sold to Transglobe Airways, 12.5.66, reverted to original UK registration G-ANCC. Grounded when Transglobe went bankrupt, 11.68. Sold to IAS Cargo Airlines as a source of spares in the same month. Broken up at Biggin Hill, Kent, during 8.70.

12920

Series 305. Built at Belfast. Originally ordered for BOAC (order cancelled), then by Capital, USA (order cancelled), then Northeast Airlines USA. First flown as G-18-3 on 1.6.57 and delivered to Filton. Modified to F.A.A. conditions and registered to Bristol Aircraft Limited as G-ANCD on 3.1.58. Painted in Northeast colours with US registration N6595C. On 29.1.58, flown in Northeast colours but with British marks as G-ANCD. The C of A was issued on 25.3.58 but the Britannia was not delivered to Northeast as they cancelled their order. It was repainted in full Cubana colours for a sales tour starting 8.6.58 to Cuba and South America via Spain and the Azores returning on 30.6.58. It was then leased to El Al as a series 306 in their colours and registered 4X-AGE from 17.7.58 to 6.3.59. Leased to Air Charter, later merged into British United Airways, 24.3.59, during which time she was converted by Aviation Traders to a Series 307 variant. Leased to Lloyd International 17.2.69, during which she was converted to a freighter, 307F variant. Sub-leased to East African Airways, 2.69. In 1973 ownership of the aircraft passed to Shackleton Airways. Leased to IAS Cargo, 9.73. Leased to African Cargo Airways, 13.5.75, re-registered 5Y-AYR. When African Cargo went out of business, 1977, operated by Westwings Aviation and leased to Transgulf Air and sub-leased to Air Faisal, 1978. Leased for a short time in 1979 to All Cargo Airlines, leased to Gaylan Air Cargo for some months before Gaylan went bankrupt. Withdrawn at Hurn, Bournemouth, 10.82. Later broken up.

12921

Series 305. Built at Belfast. First flown as G-18-4 on 3.9.58 (ff). Originally ordered by BOAC (order cancelled), then by Capital Airlines, USA (order cancelled), then by Northeast Airlines, USA allocated N6596C (order cancelled). Registered for Bristol Aircraft Ltd G-ANCE and converted to Series 307. Sold to Air Charter, later merged into British United Airways, 12.9.58. In 1966 converted to freighter, Series 307F. Sold to Lloyd International, 26.2.69. Stored at Stansted in June 1972 on collapse of Lloyd. Sold to Monarch Airlines, 22.6.73. Leased to IAS Cargo for two weeks, 1.74. Sold to Aer Turas, 5.74, re-registered EI-BAA and named 'City of Dublin'. Leased for two months to Pauling Construction, 11.74 to 1.75. Retired at Dublin, 4.79. Used for spares and the remains broken up, 5.81.

12922

Series 305. Built at Belfast. First flown as G-18-4 on 19.11.58 (ff). Originally ordered by BOAC (order cancelled), then by Capital Airlines, USA (order cancelled), then by Northeast Airlines, USA Registration N6597C allocated but not used, (order cancelled). Registered for Bristol Aircraft Ltd G-ANCF and converted to Series 308. Eventually sold to Transcontinental SA, 24.8.59, Flown from Belfast to Filton as G-14-1 on 24.10.59. Painted in their colours and registered LV-PPJ, delivered via Heathrow on 16.12.59. Later changed to LV-GJB. Sold to British Eagle, 16.1.64, reverting to her UK registration, G-ANCF, converted to 308F freighter named 'New Frontier', later 'Resolution'. Sold to Monarch Airlines, 6.12.68. Leased to IAS Cargo for one month, 12.73 to 1.74. Leased to African Cargo Airways, 2.76, re-registered 5Y-AZP and sub-leased to Invicta. After African Cargo went out of business, bought by Invicta, 7.1.77, reverting to her UK registration G-ANCF. Retired 30.10.80. Preserved. Now owned by Britannia Aircraft Preservation Trust at RAF Kemble who plan to restore her in British Eagle livery for display.

12923

Series 305. Built at Belfast. 20.11.59 (ff). Originally ordered by BOAC (order cancelled), then by Capital Airlines, USA (order cancelled), then by Northeast Airlines, USA allocated N6598C (order cancelled). Registered G-ANCG to Bristol Aircraft Limited. Sold to Transcontinental S.A. on 24.8.59. First flight 20.11.59 and flown to Filton the next day as LV-PPL for Modification to 308 Series. Delivered via Heathrow on 17.12.59. Later changed to LV-GJC. Stored at New York from Oct. 1961-Feb 1964. Sold to British Eagle, 23.2.64, re-registered G-ANCG. Converted to freighter, Series 308F, 4.64. Named "Enterprise" later "Trojan". Damaged beyond repair after an emergency landing with wheels up on a foamed runway at Manston, Kent, 20.4.67. Broken up there.

12924

Series 305. Built at Belfast. 19.2.60 (ff). Originally ordered by BOAC (order cancelled), then by Capital Airlines, USA allocated N6599C (order cancelled), then by Northeast Airlines, USA (order cancelled). Converted by Bristol Aircraft Ltd to Series 309 and registered G-ANCH. Leased to Ghana Airways, 27.7.60, re-registered 9G-AAG, then re-leased to BUA, 6.65, again as G-ANCH, until 7.10.66; re-leased to Transglobe Airways, 6.12.66 to 30.9.67; to Monarch Airways, 25.9.68 to 5.72; otherwise operated by Ghana Airways. Sold to IAS Air Cargo, 12.72 as a source of spares. Flown to Biggin Hill and broken up Aug. 1973.

12925

Series 312. Built at Filton. 29.1.58 (ff). Registered G-AOVH for BOAC. 11.2.58 (del). Flew BOAC's final Britannia transatlantic service on 1.3.64. Leased to British Eagle, 6.11.64, named 'Crusader'. Leased to Caledonian Airways, 7.3.65, named 'County of Angus'. Leased to Royal Air Maroc, 3.65, for the two months of the Hadj festival. Sold to Monarch Airlines, 1.4.68. Retired from commercial flying, 11.71, at Luton, then used for cabin staff training. Broken up at Luton, 6.72.

12926

Series 312. Built at Filton. 15.2.58 (ff). Registered G-AOVI for BOAC. 10.4.58 (del). Leased to BUA, 22.9.61. Leased (18.12.64) and then sold (4.65) to Caledonian Airways, named 'County of Argyll'. Leased to Royal Air Maroc, 4.66, for Hadj festival work. Sold to Monarch Airlines, 14.2.68, but leased back to Caledonian Airways for one month in 1968. Retired and stored at Luton, 1.72. Broken up at Luton, 4.72.

13207

Series 200 registered 25th Feb. 1952 as G-AMYK to the Bristol Aircraft Limited. Registration cancelled March 1955. Converted to Series 311 and used to develop the series 312 for BOAC. Now registered G-AOVA. First flight 31.12.56 at Filton. Used for engine and long-range trials, departed 30.1.57 for cold weather testing in Canada, Honululu-San Francisco in February, London-Vancouver in June and Singapore in November. The aircraft was rejected by BOAC and converted to a Series 319 and sold to Ghana Airways. September 1960, re-registered 9G-AAH and named 'Osagyefo'. Returned to Bristol Aircraft Limited in December 1963 back to G-AOVA. Leased to British Eagle (one month) and BUA (two months) in '64. Later leased (25.4.64) and then sold (29.12.67), to British Eagle, named 'Justice'. Sold to CCT Aircraft Leasing, 25.3.69, and promptly leased to Caledonian Airways, named 'County of Fife'. Returned to CCT, 2.70, who sold her to Airline Engineering as a source of spares. Flown to Coventry and broken up 10.71.

13208

Series 200 registered as G-AMYL to Bristol Aeroplane Co. on 25.2.53. The aircraft was not built and the registration was cancelled on 11.3.55.

13230

Series 312. Built at Filton. Registered G-AOVB this was the first of eighteen long-range Britannias for BOAC. First flight on 5.7.57, delivered by Chief Test Pilot W F Gibb to BOAC at Heathrow on 10.9.57, by the end of the month operating test flights to the USA and the Caribbean. Leased to EAAC (for about one month, 1958), leased to BWIA to fly in conjunction with BOAC on scheduled routes, 1960. Sold to British Eagle, 15.10.63, named 'Resolution' and then 'Endeavour'. Converted to freighter (Series 312F). Sold to AER, Argentina, 9.10.69, re-registered LV-PNJ, later LV-JNL. Written off attempting to land in fog near Ezeiza Airport, Buenos Aires, Argentina, 12.7.70.

13231

Series 312. Built at Filton. Registered G-AOVC for BOAC. 22.10.57 (ff). 15.11.57 (del). Operated BOAC's first scheduled turbo-prop Transatlantic service on 19.12.57. Leased to British Eagle, 15.5.64, named 'Sovereign'. Sold to Donaldson International, 20.5.69, named 'Mikado'. Withdrawn 27.9.70 and then presented to Stansted Fire Training school. Destroyed by fire and the remains broken up, late '70.

13232

Series 313. Built at Filton. 28.7.57 (ff). Registered 4X-AGA for El Al. 5.9.57 (del). Leased to BUA, re-registered G-ASFV, for two weeks in 1963, when she operated on behalf of El Al during a strike by El Al's staff. Sold to Globe Air, 2.4.64,re-registered HB-ITB. Crashed Nicosia, Cyprus, 19.4.67, when trying to land in a severe storm. Written off there.

13233

Series 313. Built at Filton. 2.9.57 (ff). Registered 4X-AGB for El Al. 19.10.57 (del). Leased to BUA, 14.2.62, re-registered G-ARWZ. Returned to El Al, 26.3.65, with original registration. Sold to Air Spain, 3.67, re-registered EC-WFL and later EC-BFL, named 'Cantabrico'. Withdrawn from use at Palma 7.73. Sold to IAS Cargo, 9.73, as a source of spares at Palma. Broken up at Palma during 74, reusable parts being taken back to UK.

13234 (1st use of serial number) Series 250 registered to the Bristol Aircraft Limited. on 23.11.53. Cancelled 11.3.55. This aircraft not completed. (2nd use of serial number) Series 313. Built at Filton. 4.10.57 (ff). Registered 4X-AGC for El Al. 28.11.57 (del). Made two record-breaking runs with El Al; New York to London in 8hr 3min, 3.12.57, and New York to Tel Aviv in 14hr 56min, 19.12.57. Leased to BUA, 14.3.62, re-registered G-ARXA. Leased to British Eagle 22.4.66. Named 'Talisman', later 'Liberty' and finally 'Renown'. Returned to El Al 8.11.68 and stored at Liverpool with three other British Eagle Britannias. Sold to Monarch Airlines, 11.70, at Luton, as a source of spares. Broken up at Luton, 11.70.

13235

Series 312. Built at Filton. 13.11.57 (ff). Registered as G-AOVD for BOAC. 6.12.57 (del). On Certificate of Airworthiness flight, crashed in fog near Bournemouth, possibly due to mis-reading of altimeter, 24.12.57, and was completely destroyed.

13236

Series 312. Built at Filton. 8.12.57 (ff). for BOAC, registered G-AOVE. 21.12.57 (del). Leased to BUA, 27.9.61. Sub-leased to MEA, 21.4.64. Returned to BOAC via BUA, 5.6.64. Leased (6.6.64) and then sold (30.11.66) to British Eagle, named 'Adventurer', later 'Perseverance', then 'Talisman' and finally 'Renown'. Sold to Air Spain, 11.66, re-registered EC-WFK and subsequently EC-BFK, named 'Mediterraneo', later 'Islas Canarias'. Retired at Palma, 1972. Sold to IAS Cargo for spares. Broken up at Palma, 1974.

13237

Series 312. Built at Filton. 18.12.57 (ff) for BOAC, registered G-AOVF. 2.1.58 (del). Leased to British Eagle, 4.3.64 to 27.11.68, named 'Friendship' and converted to Series 312F. Sold (by BOAC) to Monarch Airlines, 22.1.70. Leased (21.4.70) and later sold (24.7.72) to Donaldson International, named 'Nike'. Sold to IAS (UK) Ltd, 31.10.72, named 'African Queen'. Leased to African Safari Airlines, 1.11.72, for six weeks. Leased by IAS to Invicta (1976) Ltd, 4.76. Returned to IAS who later sold her to Invicta, 8.11.78. Leased to Redcoat Cargo, 3.8.79, for two months. Leased to IAS Cargo Airlines, 6.1.81 and re-registered 9Q-CAZ. Sold to Proteus Aero Services, 5.84. Flown, 31.5.84, to RAF Cosford for preservation. Now at the Aerospace Museum, Cosford, painted in the colours of her original owners, BOAC.

13238

Series 312. Built at Filton. 10.1.58. (ff). for BOAC, registered G-AOVG. 19.3.58 (del). Short lease to BEA, April to May 61. Then leased to British Eagle, 3.4.64, named 'Bounteous'. Repossessed by BOAC on the collapse of British Eagle in late 1968. Sold to Monarch Airlines, 10.10.69. Retired from commercial flying, 28.1.74, at Luton and then used for cabin staff training. Broken up at Luton, 8.74.

13393

Series 314. Built at Belfast. 11.1.58 (ff). Registered CF-CZA for Canadian Pacific Airlines. 9.4.58 (del). Named 'Empress of Buenos Aires', later 'Empress of Hong Kong'. Sold to Air Links/Transglobe, 5.65, and leased to BUA, 7.65, re-registered G-ATGD, returning to Transglobe, 9.8.65. Sold to African Safari Airways, 16.9.69, re-registered 5X-UVT, later 5Y-ALP. Withdrawn at Biggin Hill, 4.71 and broken up there, 12.71.

13394

Series 314. Built at Belfast. 14.4.58 (ff). Registered CF-CZB for Canadian Pacific Airlines. 29.4.58 (del). Named 'Empress of Vancouver' and later 'Empress of Lima'. Crashed at Hickham Field, Honolulu, Hawaii, 22.7.62, on attempted overshoot. Written off.

13395

Series 314. Built at Belfast. 13.5.58 (ff). Registered CF-CZC for Canadian Pacific Airlines. 20.5.58 (del), named 'Empress of Madrid', later 'Empress of Tokyo'. Sold to Air Links/Transglobe, 6.65, re-registered G-ATLE. Leased to Trek Airways, 6.68, until the collapse of Transglobe in 11.68. Sold to IAS Cargo, 30.12.69, as a source of spares. Remains used for fire training by ground staff at Gatwick. Finally broken up at Gatwick, 3.84.

13396

Series 314. Built at Belfast. 13.6.58 (ff). Registered CF-CZD for Canadian Pacific Airlines. 27.6.58 (del), named 'Empress of Santiago', later 'Empress of Buenos Aires' then 'Empress of Winnipeg'. Sold to Caledonian Airways, 31.1.66, re-registered G-ATNZ, named 'County of Inverness'. Leased, 10.3.71, and then sold, 20.4.71, to IAS Cargo for spares. Stored at Biggin Hill and broken up there, 6.72.

13397

Series 253 RAF C.Mk.1 (civilian 253F). Built at Belfast. Serialised XL-635 for RAF 99 Sqn at Lyneham 29.12.59 (ff). 30.1.60 (del), named 'Bellatrix'. Sold to Young Air Cargo, 5.9.75, registered OO-YCA. Broken up at Stansted, 7.77.

13398

Series 253 RAF C.Mk.1 (civilian 253F). Built at Belfast. Serialised XL 636 for RAF 99 Sqn at Lyneham 23.4.59 (ff). 4.6.59 (del), named 'Argo'. Sold to Young Air Cargo, 6.5.76, re-registered OO-YCE. Withdrawn by Young Air Cargo, 12.77 and broken up at Ostend, 8.80.

13399

Series 253 RAF C.Mk.1 (civilian 253F). Built at Belfast. Serialised XL 637 for RAF 99 Sqn at Lyneham 12.5.59 (ff). 28.6.59 (del), named 'Vecia'. Sold to Young Air Cargo, 8.76, registered OO-YCH. Leased to Liberia World Airways, re-liveried and re-registered EL-LWH but never delivered. Sold by Young Air Cargo to Katale Aero Transport, 27.4.79. Allocated registration 9Q-CKG but not used. She was ferried to Goma as EL-LWH in Liberia World livery, where she seems to have been used as a source of spares. Broken up at Goma by 1.92.

13400

Series 253. RAF C.Mk.1 Built at Belfast. Serialised XL 638 for RAF 99 Sqn at Lyneham 22.6.59 (ff). 5.8.59 (del), named 'Sirius'. Written off at Khormaksar, Aden, 12.10.76. (She ran off the end of the runway on landing, was fairly badly damaged but had her tail fin blown off so that the runway could continue to be used. She was broken up where she lay.)

13418

Series 312. Built at Filton. 27.2.58 (ff). Registered G-AOVJ for BOAC. 23.4.58 (del). Leased to BWIA, 1961, for some months. Leased (28.4.65) and then sold (12.11.69) to Caledonian Airways, named 'County of Aberdeen'. Sold to Donaldson International, 11.70, as a source of spares. Withdrawn at Stansted, 12.70, then used by fire school for airport training until completely destroyed.

13419

Series 312. Built at Filton. 18.3.58 (ff). Registered G-AOVK for BOAC. 11.5.58 (del). Leased (31.5.65) and then sold

(1.12.67) to British Eagle, named 'Concord'. Sold to CCT Aircraft, 11.4.69. Sold to Airline Engineering, 25.5.69, as a source of spares. Broken up at Luton, 2.70.

13420
Series 312. Built at Filton. 9.4.58 (ff). Registered G-AOVL for BOAC. 20.5.58 (del). Leased to BWIA, 1958, for some months. Leased (30.4.65) and then sold (18.4.68) to British Eagle, named 'Enterprise', later 'Resolution'. Leased (17.2.69) and then sold (31.7.69) to Monarch Airlines. Retired, 4.71. Broken up at Luton, 7.71.

13421
Series 312. Built at Filton. 29.4.58 (ff). Registered G-AOVM for BOAC. 10.6.58 (del). Leased (28.3.64) and later sold (12.67) to British Eagle, named 'Team Spirit'. Converted to freighter, Series 312F. Sold to Air Spain, 6.3.69, re-registered EC-BSY. Sold to (UK) Ministry of Defence, 11.71, serialised XX 367, based at Boscombe Down. Sold to Katale Aero Transport, 3.84, re-registered 9Q-CHY named 'Hubert'. Sold to Business Cash Flow, 4.89. Retired, 6.7.91 and stored at Kinshasa. Said to have been used for spares. Probably broken up at Kinshasa, but uncertain.

13422
Series 312. Built at Filton. 16.5.58 (ff). Registered G-AOVN for BOAC. 4.7.58 (del). Sold to British Eagle, 2.6.64, named 'Prospect'. Converted to freighter, Series 312F. Sold to Monarch Airlines, 6.3.69. Leased to African Safari Airways for one month, 1972. Retired at Luton, 11.73. Broken up at Luton, 2.74. Nose section of fuselage was used for cabin staff training for Laker Airways and then Orion Airways at East Midlands Airport.

13423
Series 312. Built at Filton. 3.7.58 (ff). Registered G-AOVO for BOAC. 4.9.58 (del). Leased to EAAC, 1958/9. Leased to British Eagle, 17.1.64, named 'Bonaventure'. Crashed into a mountain on approach to Innsbruck in low cloud, 29.2.64, and was written off.

13424
Series 312. Built at Filton. 22.7.58 (ff). Registered G-AOVP for BOAC. 15.9.58 (del). Leased to BEA April & May 1961. Leased to Lloyd International, 15.4.65, and converted to freighter, Series 312F. Sub-leased to EAAC during 1968. Sold to Lloyd International, 17.1.69. Sold to IAS Cargo, 10.7.73. Retired and stored at Biggin Hill, 8.75. Broken up at Biggin Hill, 6.77.

13425
Series 317. Built at Filton. 10.10.58 (ff). Registered G-APNA for Clanair (which later became part of BUA). 11.12.58 (del) to British & Commonwealth Shipping Company, which merged into BUA, 1.7.60. During 1960-'61, leased for periods to BOAC, EAAC and BEA. Sold to Donaldson International, 2.10.67, named 'Juno'. Leased to Lloyd International, 10.67 to 5.69. Retired at Baginton, Coventry, 5.72. Sold to IAS Cargo, 10.72, as a source of spares. Broken up at Coventry, 7.73.

13426
Series 317. Built at Filton. 10.11.58 (ff). Registered G-APNB for Clanair (which later became part of BUA). 30.4.59 (del) to British & Commonwealth Shipping Company, which merged into BUA, 1.7.60. After the merger, G-APNB was painted in BUA livery. During 1959-61, leased for periods to BOAC, EAAC and BEA. Sold to Donaldson International, 10.67; in the same month she was leased to Lloyd International, being returned to Donaldson, 1.69. At that stage she acquired the name 'Carillon'. Retired, 3.71, and stored at Luton. Sold to Airline Engineering, 6.10.71 as a source of spares. Broken up at Luton, 11.71.

13427
Series 312. Built at Filton. 17.12.58 (ff). Registered G-AOVT for BOAC. 1.1.59 (del). Leased to EAAC, 1959; to BEA, 1961; to Nigerian Airways, 1961. Sold to British Eagle, 13.9.63, named 'Enterprise', later 'Ajax'. Sold to Monarch Airlines, 18.8.68. Leased to Invicta for three months, 1974/5. Retired, 3.75. Donated by Monarch to Duxford Aviation Society for preservation. Flown to Duxford, 29.6.75, and now on display there in Monarch Airways livery.

13428
Series 314. Built at Filton. 19.6.58 (ff). Registered CF-CZX for Canadian Pacific Airlines. 3.7.58 (del), named 'Empress of Santa Maria', later 'Empress of Montreal'. Sold to Caledonian Airways, 28.12.65, re-registered G-ATMA and renamed 'County of Midlothian'. Sold back to Canadian Pacific, 31.10.69, reverting to original registration (CF-CZX). Leased to African Safari Airways, 12.69, re-registered 5Y-ANS. Sold to IAS Cargo Airlines, 5.4.71, with earlier UK registration (G-ATMA). Leased to African International, 9.4.71 to 18.5.72, registered firstly as 5Y-ANS and then G-ATMA. Returned to and operated by IAS Cargo from 5.72 until withdrawn and stored at Biggin Hill, 6.73. Broken up at Biggin Hill, 8.74.

13429
Series 312. Built at Filton. 4.8.58 (ff). Registered G-AOVR for BOAC. 3.10.58 (del). Sold to British Eagle, 22.2.65, named 'Talisman'. Sold to Air Spain, 20.10.66, re-registered EC-WFJ, later changed to EC-BFJ, named 'Atlantico' then 'Islas Canarias'. Sold to IAS Cargo Airlines, 4.73, as a source of spares. Broken up at Biggin Hill, 8.75. Many of the internal cabin fittings were used in restoration of G-AOVT at Duxford.

13430
Series 312. Built at Filton. 5.9.58 (ff). Registered G-AOVS for BOAC. 29.10.58 (del). Leased to Lloyd International, 4.7.65. Sub-leased to British Eagle, 7.65, for six months. On return to Lloyd International, converted to freighter, Series 312F. Leased to El Al, 12.70, for six months. Sold to IAS Cargo, 18.1.73. Sold to Aivex Holdings, 28.12.73, and promptly leased back to IAS Cargo. Leased to Invicta (1976) Ltd, 1.1.76. Leased, 5.77, and then sold, 4.79, to Redcoat Air Cargo, named 'Christian'. Retired at Luton, 10.79. Used as part of TV series 'Buccaneer', for which it was given the registration G-BRAC (after the crash of the real G-BRAC, 2.80) and the imaginary titling 'Redair '. Withdrawn at Luton, broken up and the fuselage used for ground fire training.

13431
Series 313. Built at Filton. 21.2.59 (ff). Registered 4X-AGD for El Al. 7.3.59 (del). Leased to BUA for two weeks 18.3.63, re-registered G-ASFU, when she operated on behalf of El Al during a strike by El Al's staff. Sold to Globe Air, 8.3.65, re-registered HB-ITC. Sold to African Safari Airways, 26 12.67, re-registered 5X-UVH and later (1970) 5Y-ALT. Sold to African Cargo Airways, 11.73, named 'Intraco Pionair'. Withdrawn at Stansted, 5.75, as a source of spares. Broken up at Stansted, 6.77. Remains used by Airport Fire Service for training.

13432
Series 318. Built at Filton. 24.11.58 (ff). Registered CU-P668 for Cubana. 16.12.58 (del), re-registered

CU-T668, named 'Libertad'. Leased to Eagle Airways, 25.3.60, with UK registration G-APYY, renamed 'Liberated'. (Eagle Airways became Cunard Eagle Airways on 1.9.60). She returned to Cuba on 19.9.61, was repainted in Cubana's new livery and then leased to Ceskoslovenské Stétni Aerolinie (CSA), 10.61 to 5.64, re-registered OK-MBA. Back in Cuba as CU-T668. W/o in 1984, broken up in 1995.

13433
Series 318. Built at Filton. 19.1.59 (ff). Registered CU-P669 for Cubana. 6.2.59 (del), re-registered CU-T669. Transferred to Aerocaribbean, 6.7.84, re-registered CU-T114. Retired and stored at Havana, 1990. In 10.92 sold to John Byrne for Transair Cargo, Zaire. Broken up for spares which were transported to Zaire. Remains scrapped at Havana, 1995.

13434
Series 253 RAF C.Mk.1 (civilian 253F). Built at Belfast. Serialised XM 489 for 99/511 Sqn RAF. 7.4.60 (ff). 5.5.60 (del), named 'Denebola'. Sold to Young Air Cargo, 10.2.76, registered OO-YCC. Used only for spares. Broken up at Gosselles, Belgium, 1978.

13435
Series 253 RAF C.Mk.1 (civilian 253F). Built at Belfast. Serialised XM 490 for 99/511 Sqn RAF. 16.5.60 (ff). 9.6.60 (del), named 'Aldebaran'. Sold to Euroworld, 29.10.75. Sold to Air Faisal, 17.11.75, registered G-BDLZ and renamed 'Al Mubarak'. Leased to Air Works, India, 12.76 to 9.77. Immobilised because of suspected drug smuggling, 8.78. Withdrawn, 5.79 and broken up at Luton, 9.79.

13436
Series 253 RAF C.Mk.1(civilian 253F). Built at Belfast. Serialised XM 491 for 99/511 Sqn RAF. 16.6.60 (ff). 7.7.60 (del), named 'Procyon'. Sold to Aer Turas, 8.9.75, re-registered EI-BBH and renamed 'City of Cork'. Leased to Cyprus Airways, 9.76 to 4.78 and to Gemini Air Transport for two months in 1979. Sold to Katale Aero Transport, 11.81, re-registered 9Q-CMO in the name of Transair Cargo. Withdrawn and broken up in Zaire by 1.92.

13437
Series 318. Built at Filton. 2.4.59 (ff). Registered CU-P670 for Cubana. 15.5.59 (del), re-registered CU-T670. Leased to CSA, 1963. Retired by Cubana and stored at Havana, 1978. Broken up at Havana, 1995.

13448
Series 253 RAF C.Mk.1 (civilian 253F). Built at Belfast. Serialised XL 639 for RAF 99 Sqn at Lyneham 28.8.59 (ff). 8.10.59 (del), named 'Atria'. Sold to Guiness Peat Aviation, 10.2.76, registered EI-BDC. Sold to Airline Engineering, 10.2 77. Leased to Aer Turas and to Cyprus Airways for various periods during 1977. Sold to Eurafric, 20.1.78. Sold to Redcoat Air Cargo, 4.6.78, re-registered G-BRAC. Written off by crashing in bad weather after take off from Logan airport near Boston, Mass. 16.2.80, probably due to a combination of wing icing and air turbulence.

13449
Series 253 RAF C.Mk.1 (civilian 253F). Built at Belfast. Serialised XL 640 for RAF 99 Sqn at Lyneham 8.10.59 (ff). 2.11.59 (del), named 'Altares'. Sold to Monarch Airlines 13.1.76. Sold to Eurafric, 3.77. Leased to Aer Turas during '77 and '78, being then registered EI-BCI. Leased to Redcoat Air Cargo, 13.8.79, re-registered G-BHAU. Sold to Swordvale Aviation, 2.12.81 and then to Katale Aero Transport, 4.82, re-registered 9Q-CHU. Withdrawn by Katale and broken up at Kinshasa, 1986.

13450
Series 252 RAF C.Mk.2 (civilian 252F). Built at Belfast. Registered G-APPE for Ministry of Supply. 13.10.58 (ff). Serialised XN 392 and sent to A&AEE Boscombe Down, 3.59. Delivered to RAF 99 Sqn at Lyneham 18.9.59, named 'Acrux'. Sold to Aer Turas, 18.12.75, as a source of spares. Withdrawn by Aer Turas, never flown, and broken up at Coventry, 5.76.

13451
Series 252 RAF C.Mk.2 (civilian 252F). Built at Belfast. Registered G-APPF for Ministry of Supply. 7.12.58 (ff). Serialised XN 398 for RAF 99 Sqn at Lyneham 19.3.59 (del), named 'Altair'. Sold to Euroworld, 11.9.75. Sold to Zaire Aero Service, 1.2.77, re-registered 9Q-CPX. Leased (11.77) and later sold to Domaine de Katale (Katale Aero Transport). Withdrawn by Katale in the mid-1980s and later broken up at Goma (Zaire).

13452
Series 252 RAF C.Mk.2 (civilian 252F). Built at Belfast. Registered G-APPG for Ministry of Supply. 3.3.59 (ff). Serialised XN 404 for RAF 99 Sqn at Lyneham 6.4.59 (del), named 'Canopus'. Sold to Shackleton Aviation, 11.12.75. Sale to Air Faisal in 1976 negotiated but not completed. Withdrawn by Shackleton, 1976, and broken up at Luton (with spares to Air Faisal?), 11.76.

13453
Series 314. Built at Belfast. 22.7.58 (ff). Registered CF-CZW for Canadian Pacific Airlines. 7.8.58 (del), named 'Empress of Edmonton', later 'Empress of Toronto'. Leased to British Eagle, 20.5.64, re-registered G-ASTF and named 'Concord'. Returned to Canadian Pacific, 15.10.64, with original registration and now named 'Empress of Rome'. Leased to Caledonian Airways, 27.1.66, with the same UK registration (G-ASTF) and named 'Flagship Bonnie Scotland', later 'County of Perth'. Retired, 11.69, and stored at Gatwick. Broken up at Gatwick, 10.70.

13454
Series 253 RAF C.Mk.1 (civilian 253F). Built at Belfast. Serialised XL 657 for RAF 99 Sqn at Lyneham 23.11.59 (ff). 23.12.59 (del), named 'Rigel'. Sold to Monarch Airlines, 31.12.75. Sold to Centre Air Afrique, 10.3.76, re-registered 9U-BAD. Impounded in Belgium, 2.77, for non-payment of bills by airline which went bankrupt. Broken up at Ostend, 2.77.

13455
Series 253 RAF C.Mk.1 (civilian 253F). Built at Belfast. Serialised XL 658 for 511 Sqn RAF. 3.12.59 (ff). 5.2.60 (del), named 'Adhara'. Sold to Airline Engineering, 26.5.76, for onward sale to Intercontinental Meat Company, 24.6.76, registered EI-BBY and renamed 'Deirdre'. Crash-landed at Shannon, 30.9.77, and written off.

13456
Series 253 RAF C.Mk.1 (civilian 253F). Built at Belfast. Serialised XL 659 for 511 Sqn RAF. 1.2.60 (ff). 4.3.60 (del), named 'Polaris'. Sold to Young Air Cargo, 5.9.75, registered OO-YCB. Used for spares and finally broken up at Ostend, Belgium, 12.77.

13457
Series 253 RAF C.Mk.1 (civilian 253F). Built at Belfast. Serialised XL660 for 99 Sqn RAF. 4.3.60 (ff). 23.4.60 (del), named 'Alphard'. Sold to Air Faisal, 14.5.76, registered G-BEMZ leased to Trans Gulf Air Cargo, returned Feb 77. Sold

via T F Richter & Co to Black Arrow Leasing, 14.2.80. Leased to Gaylan Air Cargo, 9.4.80, re-registered A6-HMS. Reverted to her UK registration, G-BEMZ, 3.4.81. Leased to Redcoat Air Cargo, 22.9.81. Sold via Swordvale Aviation to Katale Aero Transport, 11.82, re-registered 9Q-CGP, named 'Mandefu'. Withdrawn and broken up by 1.92.

13508

Series 253 RAF C.Mk.1 (civilian 253F). Built at Belfast. Serialised XM 496 for 99/511 Sqn RAF. 24.8.60 (ff). 19.9.60 (del), named 'Regulus'. Sold to Monarch Airlines Engineering, 6.1.76, registered G-BDUP, and sold on to Afrek, 21.5.76. Wfu at Athens. Sold to Aerocaribbean, 8.84, via Monarch Airlines Engineering, re-registered CU-T120. Grounded at Havana due to lack of spares, 3.90. Sold to John Byrne for Transair Cargo, 10.92, re-registered 9Q-CJH and renamed 'Jack', but repairs meant that flight to Zaire was not completed until 9.93. Transair decided to cease operations in 1997, 9Q-CJH was registered EL-WXA and ferried to UK for preservation. She arrived 14.10.97, and is now preserved at RAF Kemble.

13509

Series 253 RAF C.Mk.1 (civilian 253F). Built at Belfast. Serialised XM 497 for RAF. 17.11.60 (ff). 5.12.60 (del), named 'Schedar'. Sold to Young Air Cargo, 23.4.76, registered OO-YCF and left at Stansted as a source of spares. Broken up at Stansted, 7.77, but remains used by BAA Fire School until 5.81.

13510

Series 253 RAF C.Mk.1 (civilian 253F). Built at Filton. Serialised XM 498 for 99/511 Sqn RAF. 30.9.59 (ff). 19.10 59 (del), named 'Hadar'. Sold to Young Air Cargo, 11.6.76, registered OO-YCG. Leased to Liberia World Airways, 11.7.77, re-registered EL-LWG. Retired 9.78 and stored at Manston. Sold to Katale Aero Transport, 8.5.79, re-registered 9Q-CDT. Sold to Business Cash Flow Aviation, 7.88, and used as a source of spares at Kinshasa. Remains broken up at Kinshasa by 1.92.

13511

Series 253 RAF C.Mk.1 (civilian 253F). Built at Filton. Serialised XM 517 for 99/511 Sqn RAF. 24.11.59 (ff). 3.12.59 (del), named 'Avior'. Sold to Monarch Airlines, 21. 10.75, for onward sale to AMAZ, 8.76, re-registered 9Q-CAJ, but the deal fell through. Sold to Airline Engineering, 14.4.77, re-registered G-BEPX. She was used as a non-flying engine test bed for Proteus engines at Luton. Broken up at Luton, 4.80.

13512

Series 253 RAF C.Mk.1 (civilian 253F). Built at Filton. Serialised XM 518 for RAF. 18.12.59 (ff). 30.12.59 (del), named 'Spica'. Sold to Young Air Cargo, 4.3.76, registered OO-YCD. Used as a source of spares and finally broken up at Gosselles, Belgium, 1978.

13513

Series 253 (civilian 253F). Built at Filton. Serialised XM 519 for 99/511 Sqn RAF. 28.1.60 (ff). 8.2.60 (del), named 'Capella'. Sold via Airline Engineering to Afrek, 2.7.76, registered G-BDUR. Grounded at Athens, 2.83, because of unpaid debts by Nigeria to the airline. Bought by Monarch 30.7.84. Sold to Aerocaribbean, 8.84, re-registered CU-T121. Stored at Havana, Cuba, 10.90. Sold to John Byrne for Transair Cargo, 10.92, but used as a source of spares for 'Jack' 9Q-CJH. Broken up at Havana, 11.95.

13514

Series 253 (civilian 253F). Built at Filton, the last Britannia to be built there. Serialised XM 520 for 99 Sqn RAF Lyneham. 9.3.60 (ff). 21 3.60 (del), named 'Arcturus'. Sold to Gemini Air Transport, 16 9.75, re-registered 9G-ACE. Leased to Redcoat Air Cargo for one year 1976/7. Sold to Lukum Air Services, 9.81, re-registered 9Q-CUM. Sold to Katale Aero Services, 7.86, as a source of spares. Broken up at Kinshasa, Zaire, 9.86.

13515

Series 318. Built at Filton. 29.4.59 (ff). Registered CU-P671 for Cubana. 22.8.59 (del), re-registered CU-T671. Leased to CSA, re-registered OK-MBB, 11.63 to 1.69. Then returned to Cubana and previous registration (CU-T671). Retired in 1979 and stored at Havana. In 10.92 sold to John Byrne for Transair Cargo, Zaire. Broken up for spares which were transported to Zaire. Remains scrapped in 1995.

13516

Series 324. Built at Filton. 9.10.59 (ff). Registered G-18-8 for Bristol Aeroplane Company. Leased to Canadian Pacific Airlines, 16.10.59 to 12.2.61, re-registered CF-CPD, named 'Empress of Amsterdam'. Leased to Cunard Eagle (which became British Eagle), 9.3.61, re-registered G-ARKA and named 'Good Fortune'. Sold to British Eagle, 1.12.67. Sold to CCT Aircraft Leasing, 21.3.69. Leased to Tellair, Switzerland, re-registered HB-ITF (but apparently never carried). Operated for Tellair by Caledonian Airways, 3. 69. to 10.69. Sold to Airline Engineering, 6.71, as a source of spares. Broken up at Coventry, 10.71.

13517

Series 324. Built at Filton. 4.11.59 (ff). Registered CF-CPE for Canadian Pacific Airlines. Leased by Bristol Aircraft Ltd to Canadian Pacific, 13.11.59 to 11.4.61, named 'Empress of Mexico City'. Leased to Cunard Eagle (which became British Eagle), 1.5.61, re-registered G-ARKB and named 'Endeavour', later 'Resolution'. Sold to CCT Aircraft Leasing, 11.4.69. Leased to Tellair, Switzerland, re-registered HB-ITG (but apparently never carried). Operated for Tellair by Caledonian Airways, 4. 69. to 11.69. Sold to Airline Engineering, 6.71, as a source of spares. Broken up at Coventry, 10.71.

In addition to these 85 production aircraft, there were four others built for special purposes. Two were Series 100 aircraft; two were Series 312 aircraft.

Of the two Series 100 aircraft, one was used at Filton as a 'Functional Mock-up', testing all aspects of internal layout in the fuselage. The other one was used at RAE, Farnborough, in a water tank test, to establish how long the fuselage could withstand pressure cycles (due to a pressure difference between the inside and outside of the fuselage, equivalent to an aircraft taking off, climbing to high altitude and then returning to ground level again), without any metal failure. This test became mandatory after the identification of the reason for the early Comet I crashes.

The two Series 312 aircraft were used for exactly the same purpose, the only difference being the water tank test for the Series 312 aircraft was carried out at Filton rather than at Farnborough.

SPECIFICATION OF BRITANNIA 102 & 253 SERIES

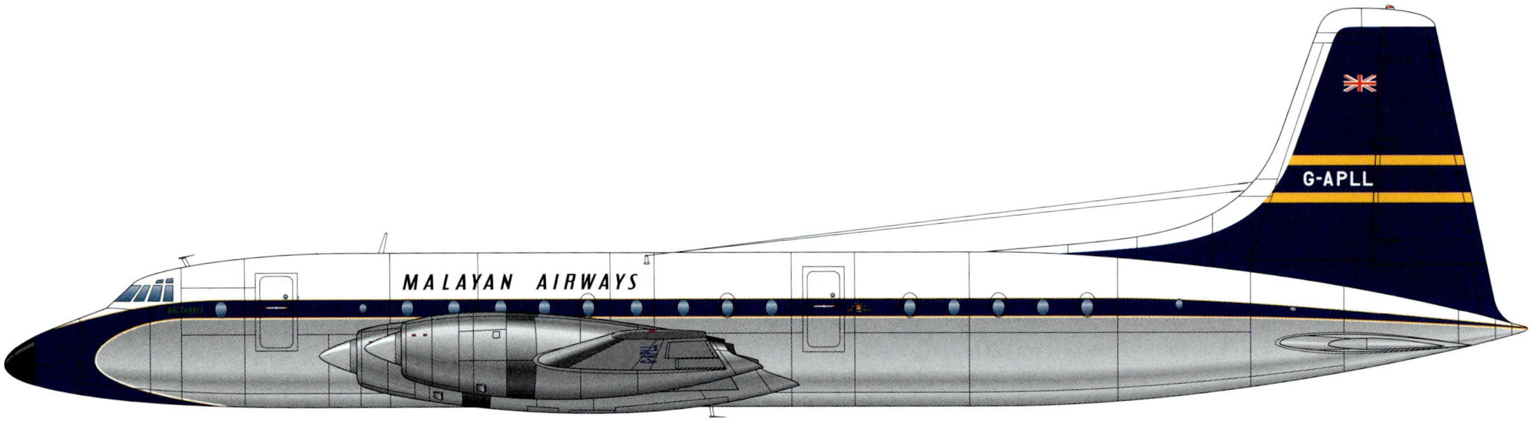

BRISTOL BRITANNIA 102 SERIES

Length: .... 114' 0" (34.75m)

Wing Span: .... 142' 3.5" (43.38m)

Height: .... 36' 9" (11.20m)

Wing area: .... 2,075 sq ft (192.7sq mtrs)

Tailplane span: .... 55' 0" (16.76m)

Wheel track: .... 31' 0" (9.45m)

Wheelbase: .... 35' 3" (9.45m)

MTOW: 160,000lb (70,300kg)

Fuel capacity: .... 6,690 Imp. gallons - 30,327 Litres

Engines: ....4 Proteus 705 turboprops rated at 3,900 e.h.p. driving 16ft (4.87m) de Havilland hydromatic four blade hollow steel or duralumin propellers

Max. Cruising speed: 361mph (580km/h)

Range with Max Payload: .... 3,450 miles (5,552 km)

Passenger accommodation: .... 75 - 115 seats

Cargo space .... 665 cu ft

BRISTOL BRITANNIA 253 SERIES

Length: .... 124' 3" (37.89m)

Wing Span: .... 142' 3.5" (43.38m)

Height: .... 37' 6" (11.43m)

Wing area: .... 2,075 sq ft (192.7sq mtrs)

Tailplane span: .... 55'.0" (16.76m)

Wheel track: .... 31'0" (9.45m)

Wheelbase: .... 42' 1.4" (12.8m)

MTOW: 180,000lb (81,646kg)

Fuel capacity: .... 8,580 Imp. gallons - 39,000 Litres

Engines: ....4 Proteus 255 turboprops rated at 4,455 e.h.p. driving 16ft (4.87m) de Havilland hydromatic four blade hollow steel or duralumin propellers

Max. Cruising speed: 403mph (648km/h)

Range with Max Payload: .... 4,480 miles (7,200 km)

Passenger accommodation: .... 59 - 115 seats

Cargo space .... Srs 253 - 6,120 cu ft

.... Srs 252 - 5,850 cu ft

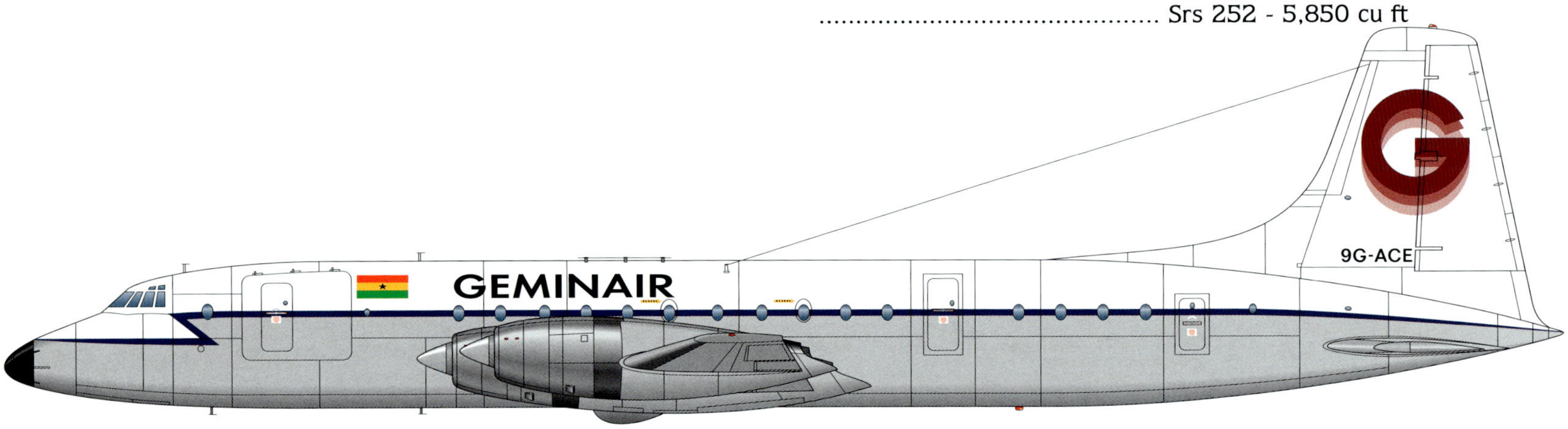

SPECIFICATION OF BRITANNIA 310 & 320

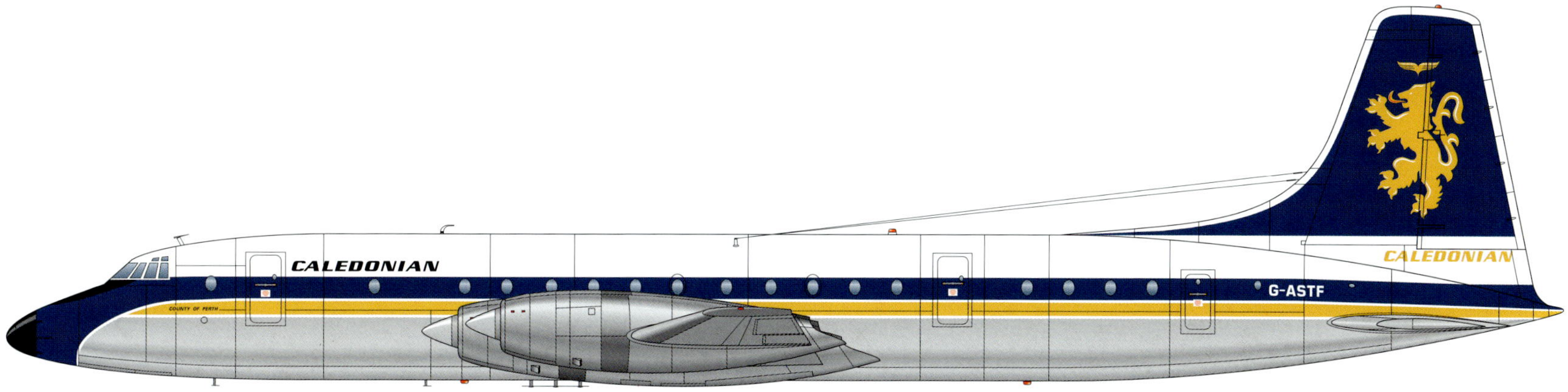

BRISTOL BRITANNIA 310 SERIES

Length: .... 124' 3" (37.89m)

Wing Span: .... 142' 3.5" (43.38m)

Height: .... 37' 6" (11.43m)

Wing area: .... 2,075 sq ft (192.7sq mtrs)

Tailplane span: .... 55'.0" (16.76m)

Wheel track: .... 31'0" (9.45 m)

Wheelbase: .... 42' 1.4" (12.8m)

MTOW: 185,000lb (83,914kg)

Fuel capacity: .... 8,580 Imp. gallons - 39,000 Litres

Engines: ....4 Proteus 755 turboprops rated at 4,120 e.h.p. later Proteus 761, also 765, 766 rated 4,450 e.p.h.driving 16ft (4.87m)de Havilland hydromatic four blade hollow steel or duralumin propellers

Max. Cruising speed: 403mph (580km/h)

Range with Max Payload: .... 4,680 miles (7,532 km)

Passenger accommodation: .... 81 - 139 seats

Cargo space .... Srs 312 - 900 cu ft

.... Srs 312F - 5,850 cu ft

BRISTOL BRITANNIA 320 SERIES

Length: .... 124' 3" (37.89m)

Wing Span: .... 142' 3.5" (43.38m)

Height: .... 37' 6" (11.43m)

Wing area: .... 2,075 sq ft (192.7sq mtrs)

Tailplane span: .... 55'.0" (16.76m)

Wheel track: .... 31'0" (9.45m)

Wheelbase: .... 42' 1.4" (12.8m)

MTOW: 180,000lb (81,646kg)

Fuel capacity: .... 8,580 Imp. gallons - 39,000 Litres

Engines: ....4 Proteus 766 turboprops rated at 4,450 e.h.p. driving 16ft (4.87m) de Havilland hydromatic four blade hollow steel or duralumin propellers

Max. Cruising speed: 403mph (648km/h)

Range with Max Payload: .... 3,850 miles (6,195 km)

Passenger accommodation: .... 110 - 139 seats

Cargo space .... 900 cu ft

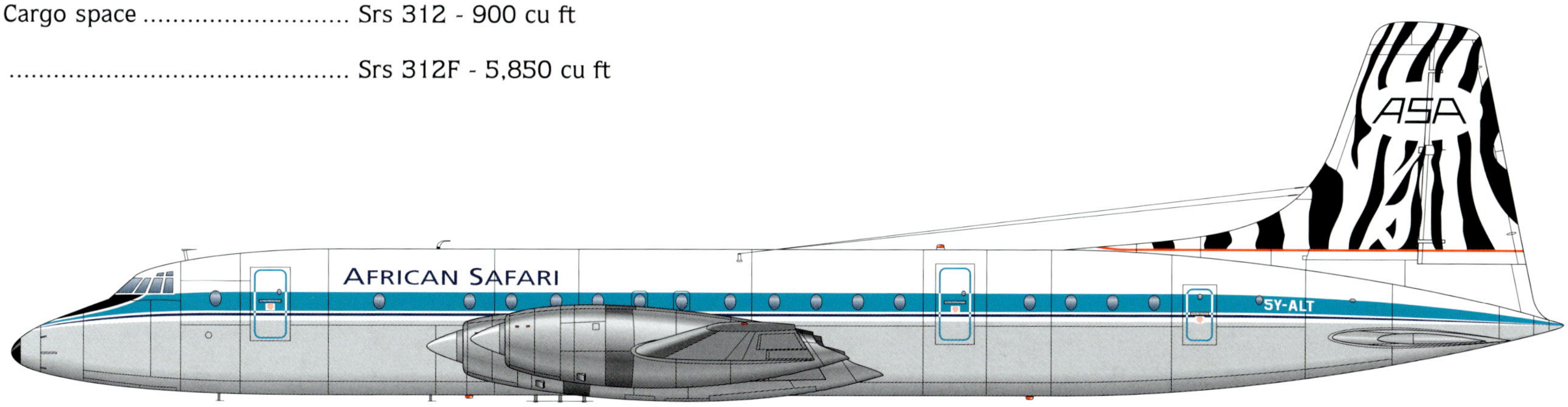

CLOSE-UP DETAIL SECTION

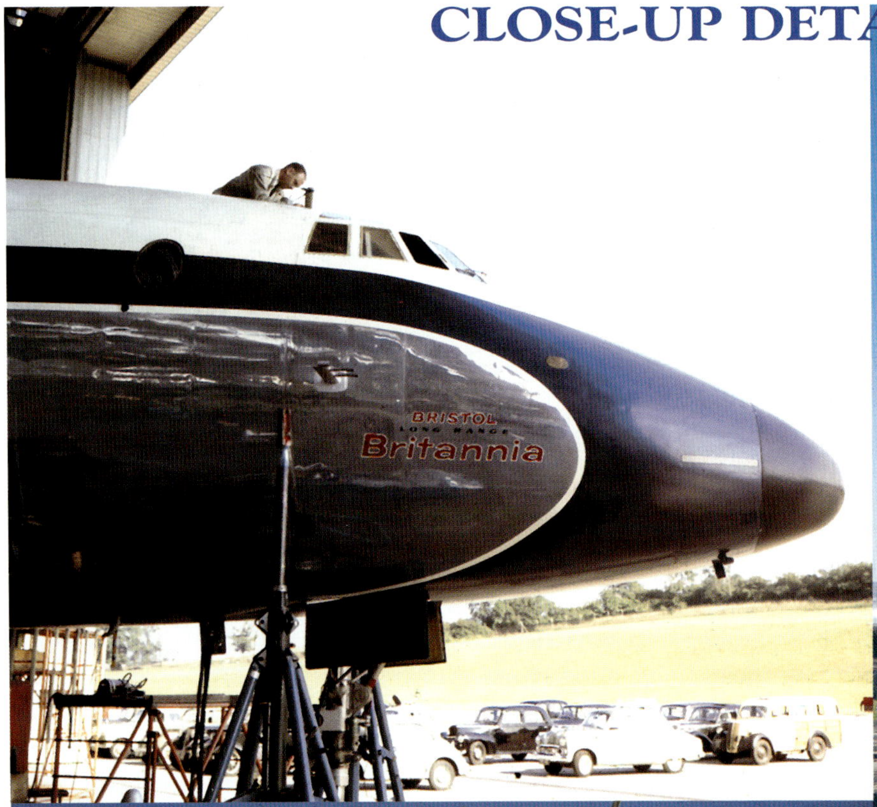

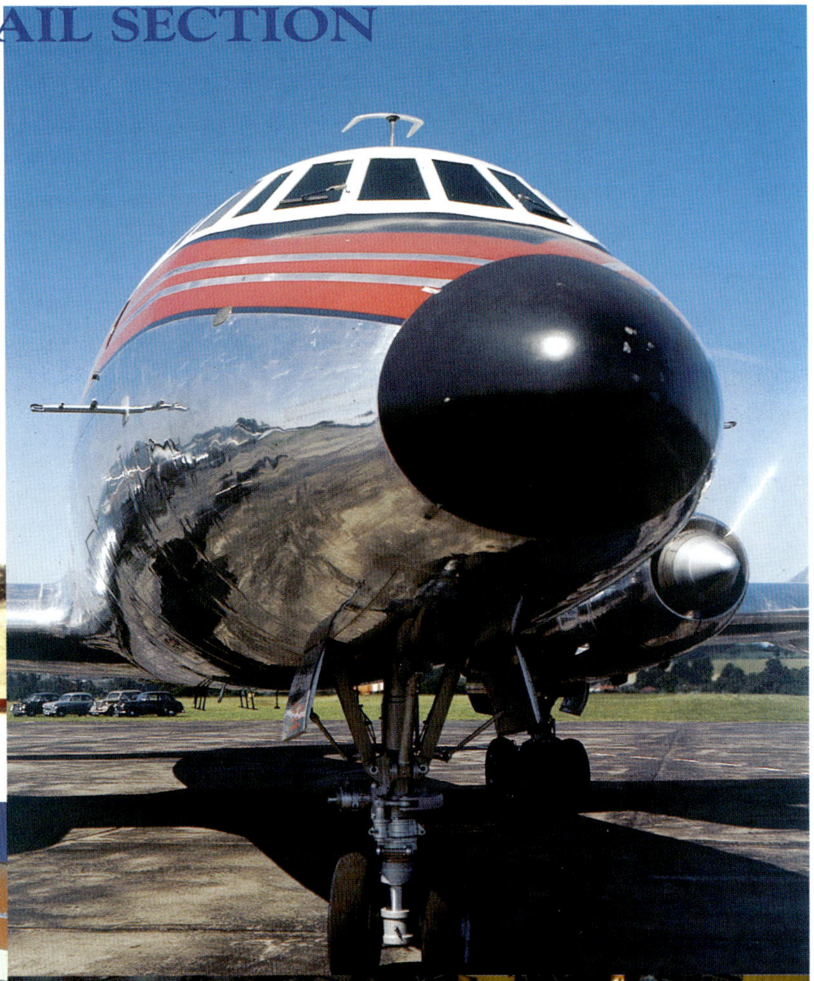

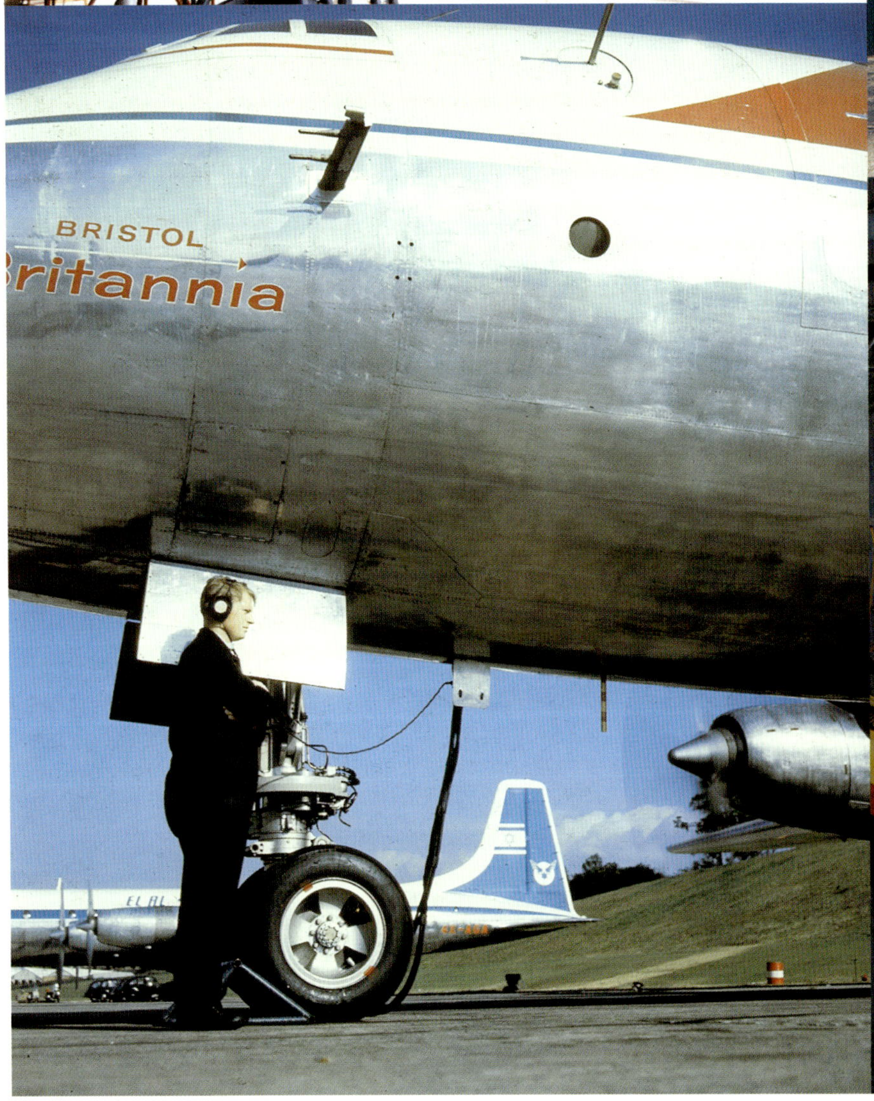

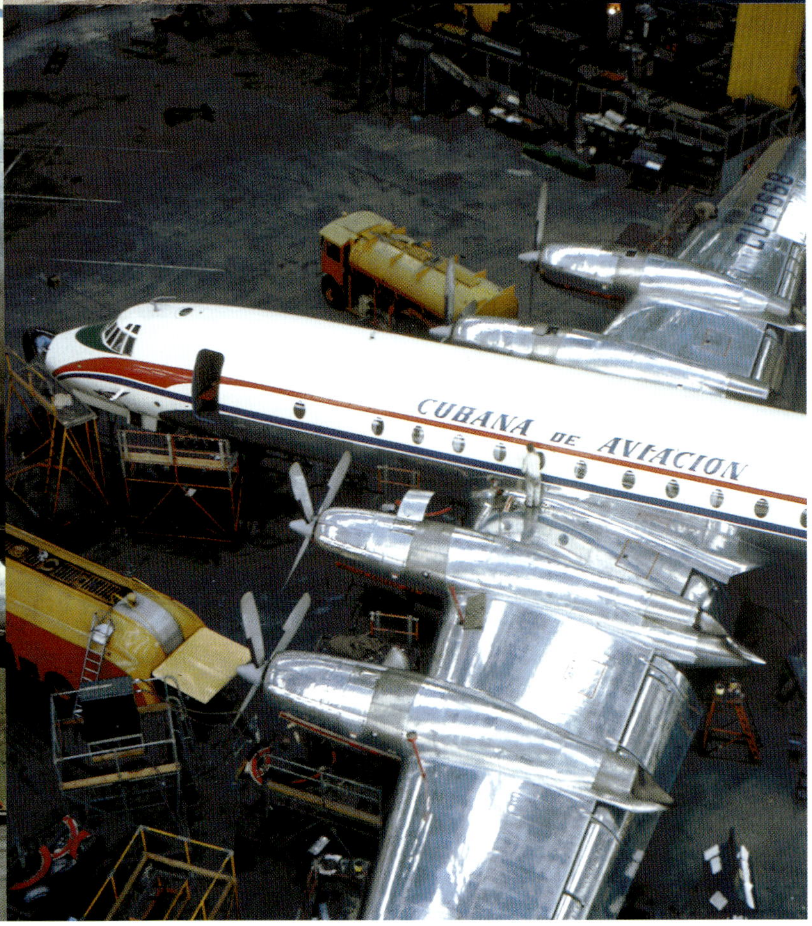

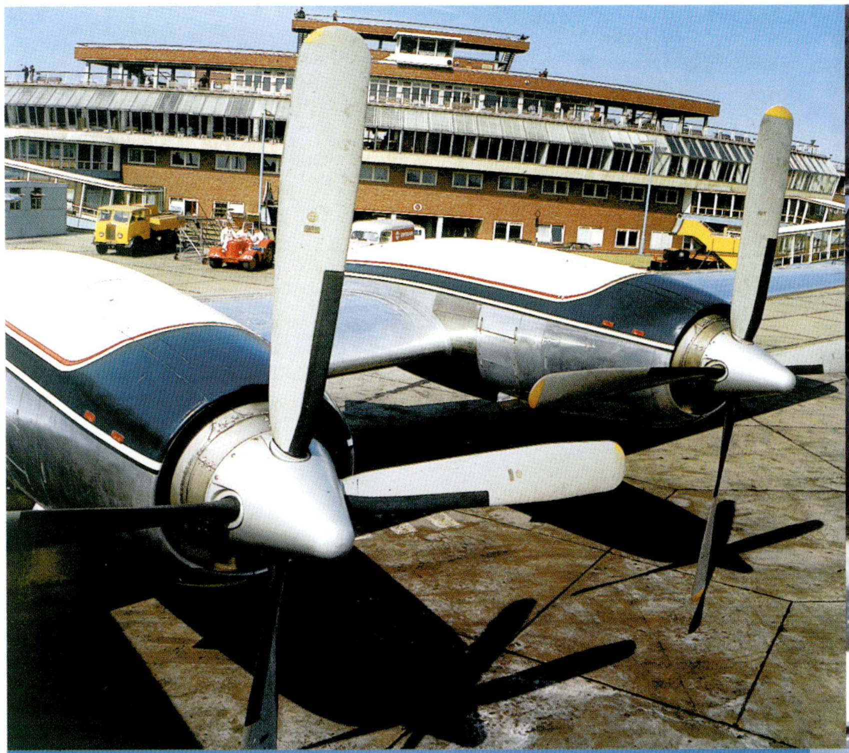

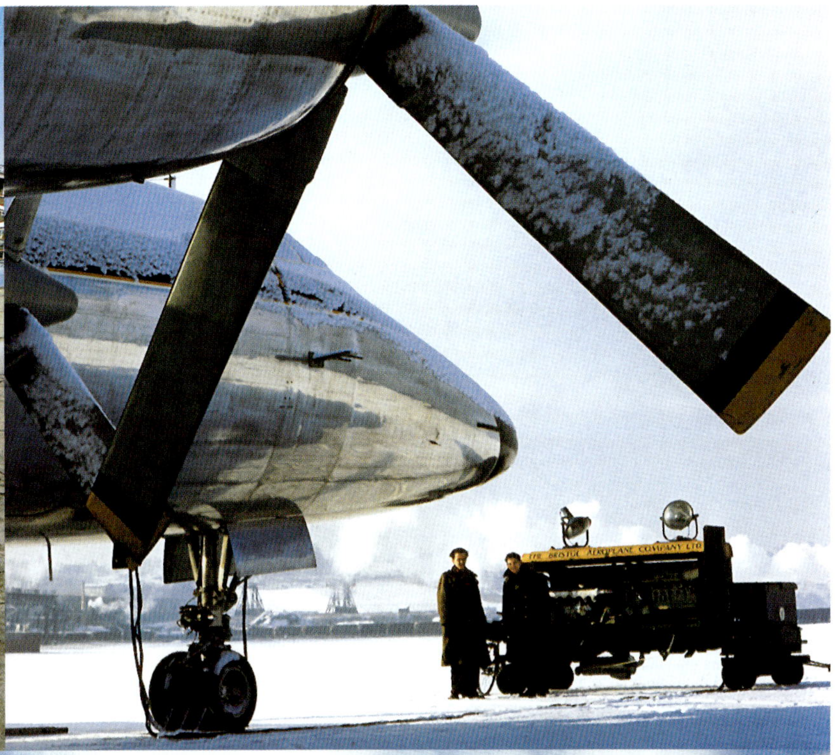

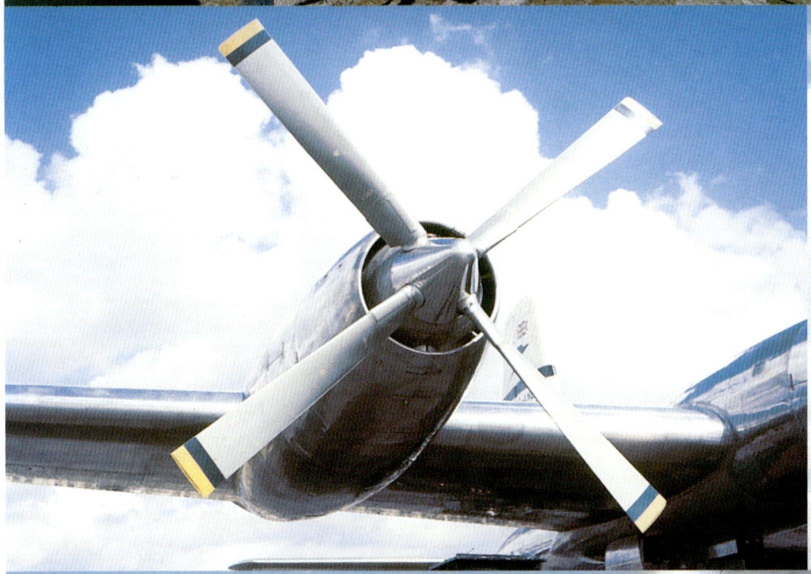

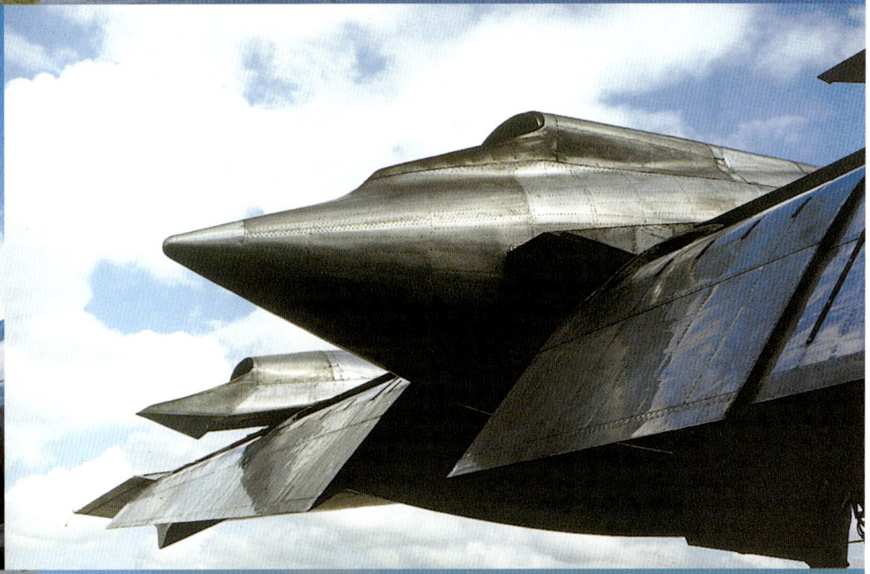

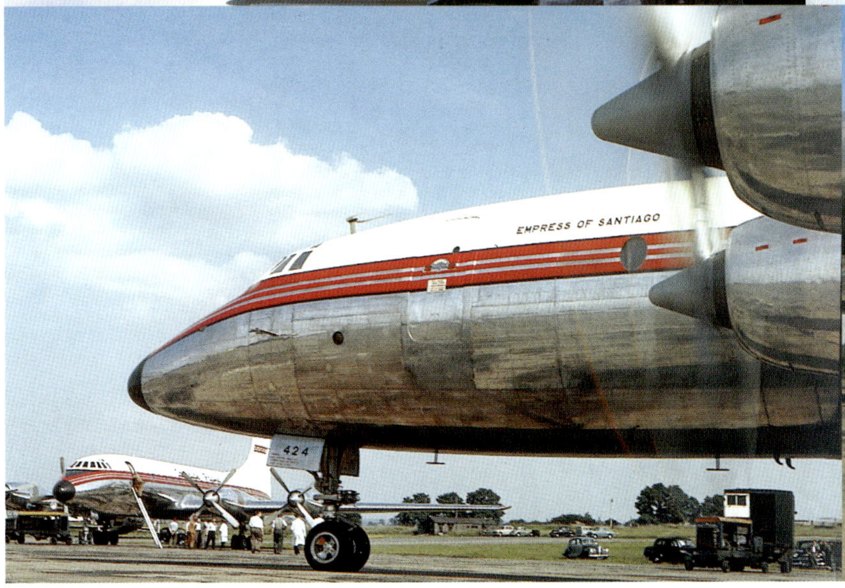
EMPRESS OF SANTIAGO
424

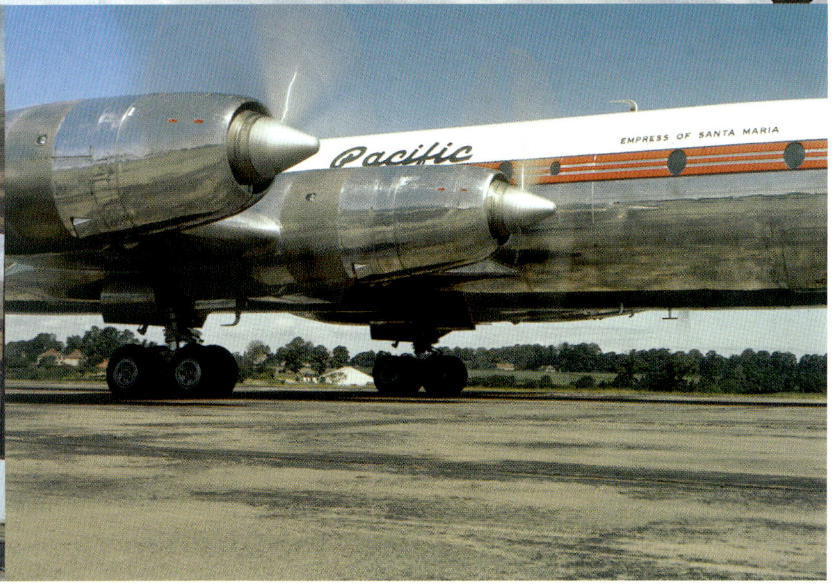
Pacific
EMPRESS OF SANTA MARIA

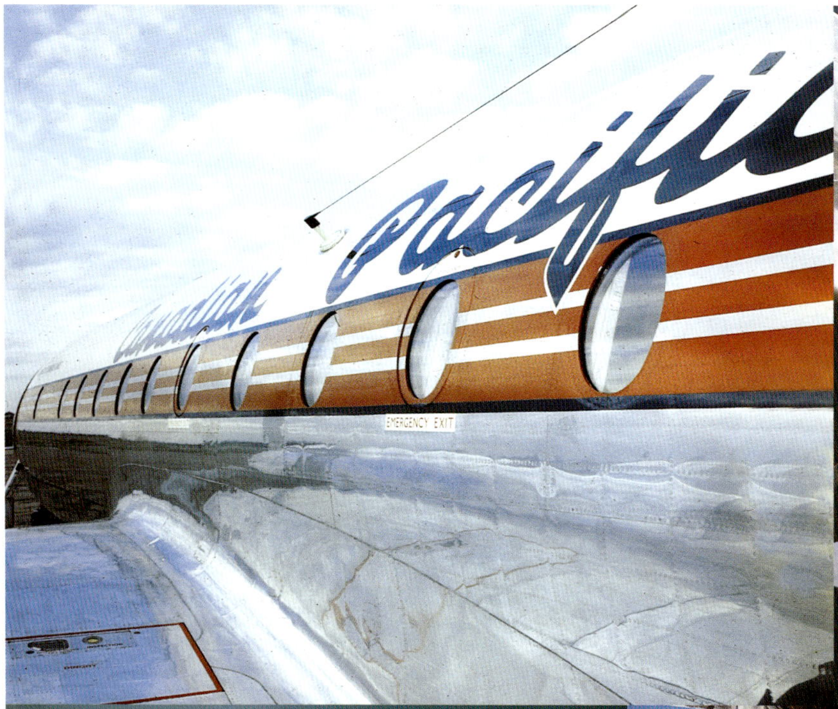
EMERGENCY EXIT

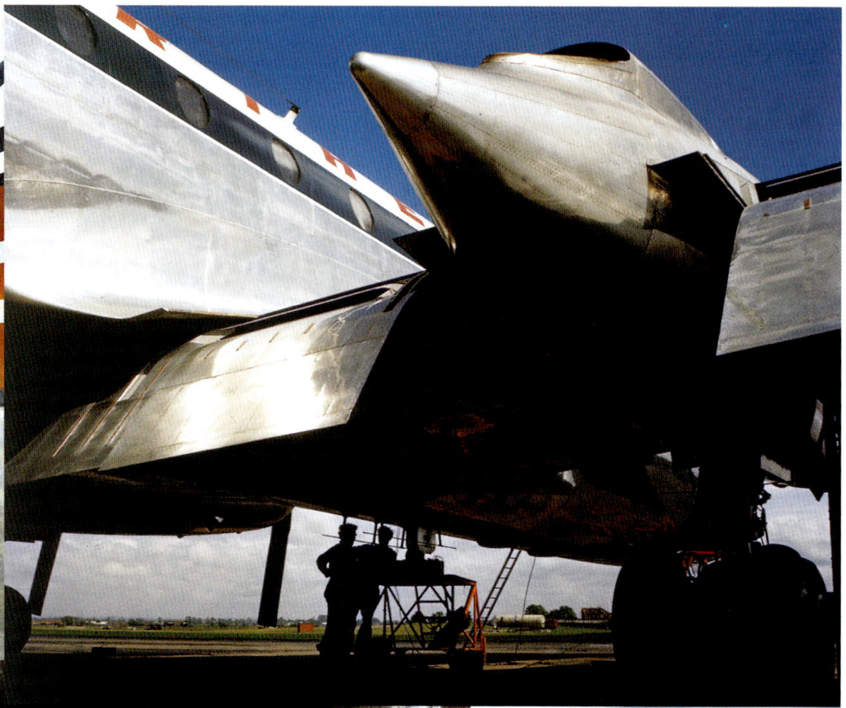

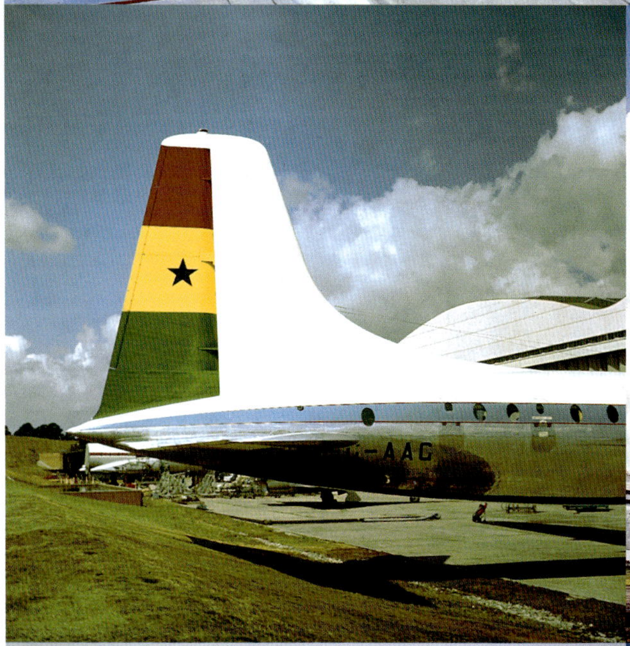

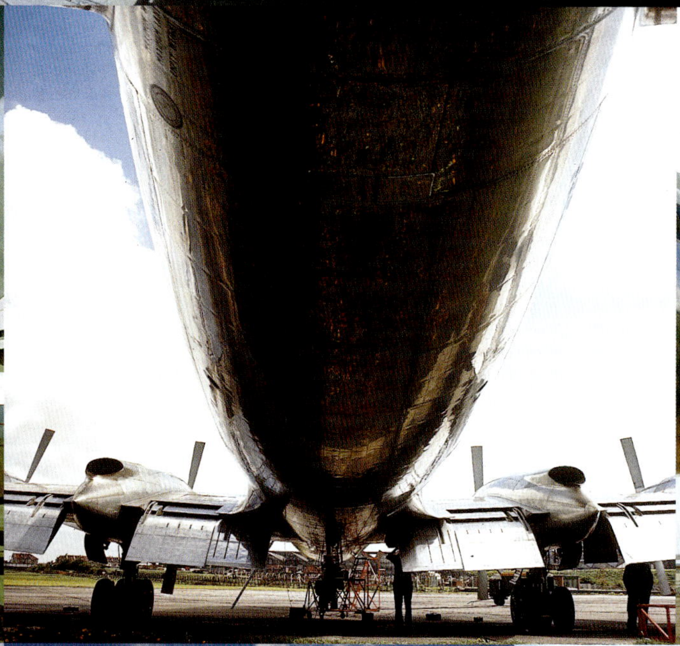

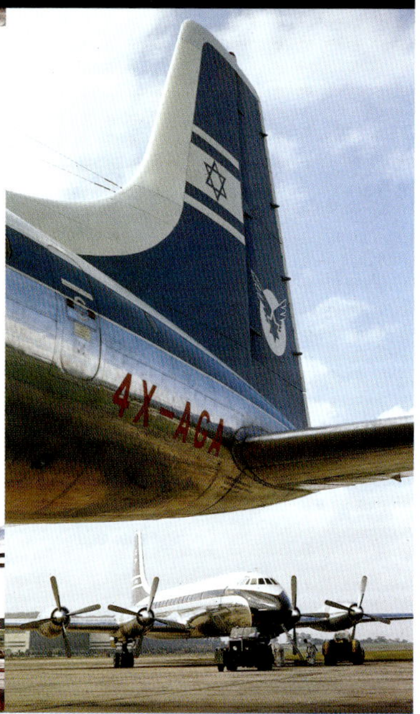
4X-AGA

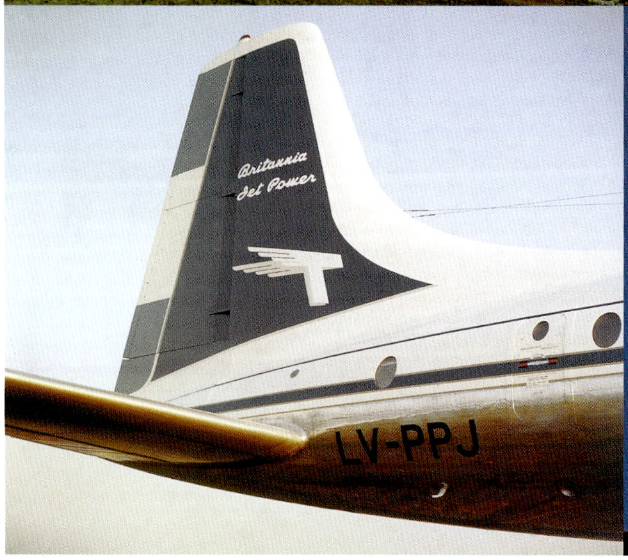
Britannia
Jet Power
LV-PPJ

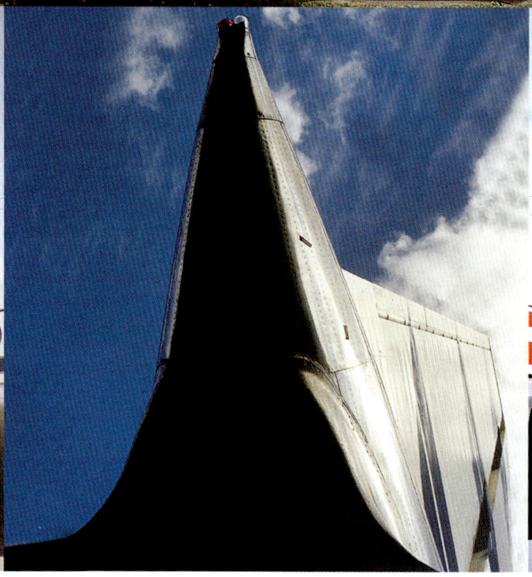

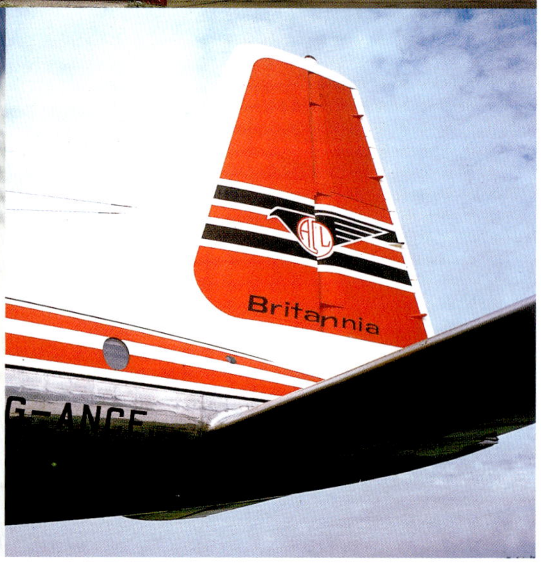
Britannia

DERIVATIVES

There were further developments which used aspects of the Britannia design, but with substantial alterations to meet different specific needs. As such they are more correctly termed derivatives rather than variants.

CANADAIR CL-28 (CP-107 ARGUS)

In 1953 the Canadian Department of Defence chose the Bristol Britannia as the basis for a long-range maritime patrol aircraft to be used by the Royal Canadian Air Force. There was detailed discussion between Bristol Aircraft and the Canadair Division of the General Dynamics Corporation as a result of which a production line was set up to manufacture these Britannia derivatives.

The wing, tail surfaces and undercarriage were the standard ones as used on the Britannia, except for changes to North American materials, but the fuselage was completely redesigned and unpressurized because of the low altitude flying which the aircraft would experience when in service.

A large weapon bay was installed in the fuselage, able to carry torpedoes, bombs, depth charges etc. The fuselage also had a transparent nose cone. There were also two obvious additions to the fuselage. Underneath the cockpit was a bubble shaped radome, housing a search radar, and at the rear of the fuselage was a large extension housing the so-called Magnetic Airborne Detector.

Anti-submarine detection and general maritime reconnaissance required a lot of electronic equipment and the normal crew included six operators to monitor the output from the various pieces of equipment on board. The engines used were 3,700 hp Wright R-3370 TC981 EA-1 piston engines, designed to give high power at low altitudes with low fuel consumption.This gave the aircraft an endurance of approximately 26.5 hours and a maximum range of about 4,420 nautical miles (8,190km). The aircraft was designated the CL-28 Argus and was built by Canadair under licence from the Bristol Aeroplane Company.

Thirty-three Argus aircraft were supplied to the RCAF between September 1957 and July 1960. These aircraft gave

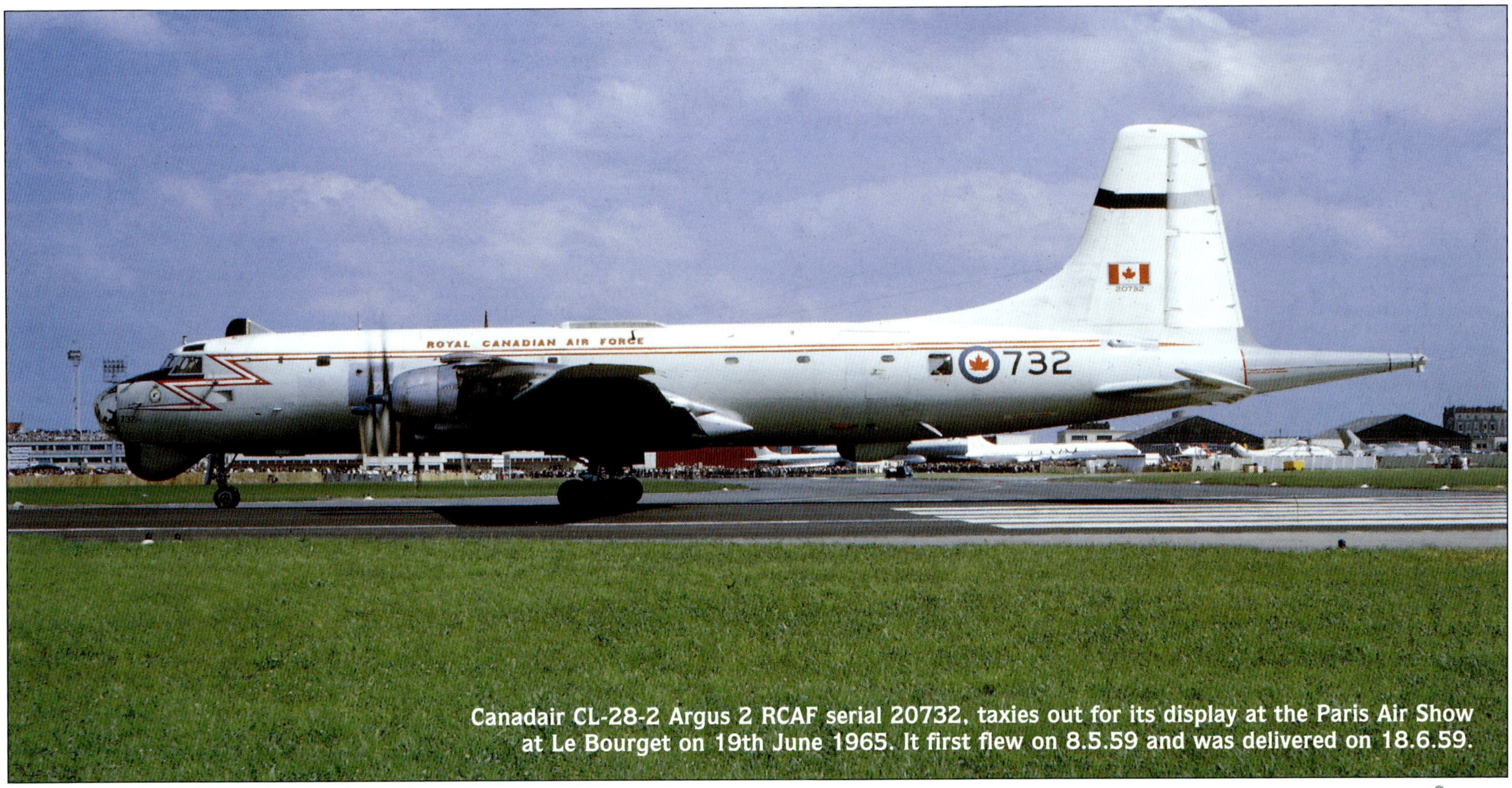

Canadair CL-28-2 Argus 2 RCAF serial 20732, taxies out for its display at the Paris Air Show at Le Bourget on 19th June 1965. It first flew on 8.5.59 and was delivered on 18.6.59.

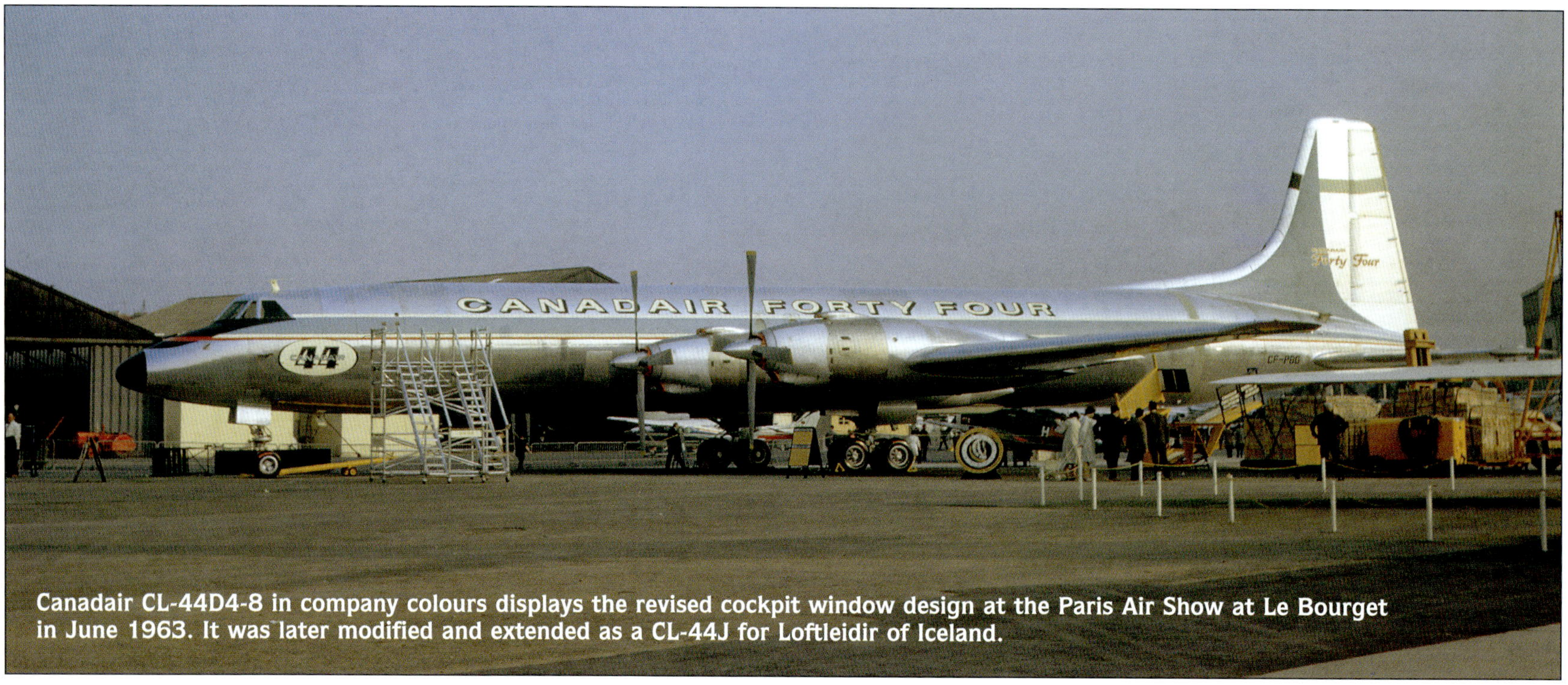

Canadair CL-44D4-8 in company colours displays the revised cockpit window design at the Paris Air Show at Le Bourget in June 1963. It was later modified and extended as a CL-44J for Loftleidir of Iceland.

good service in an anti-submarine role for many years, with the last operational flight taking place in November 1980.

CANADAIR CL-44, (CC-106 YUKON)

A further derivative was the CL-44, named Yukon by the RCAF. Early in 1957 the RCAF asked Canadair to develop an enlarged transport version of the CL-28, including a rear-loading cargo door. This new aircraft, the CL-44, used the same wing, tail surfaces and undercarriage as the Britannia (and the CL-28) but with local strengthening because of the increased weight. The fuselage was lengthened by 12ft 4in (3.76m) to 136ft 10in (41.88m) and unlike the CL-28 was pressurized.

The original intention was to power the aircraft by Orion engines, but when the development of these engines was stopped, Rolls-Royce Tyne turbo-props were fitted instead.

The CL-44 had two large doors on the port side of the

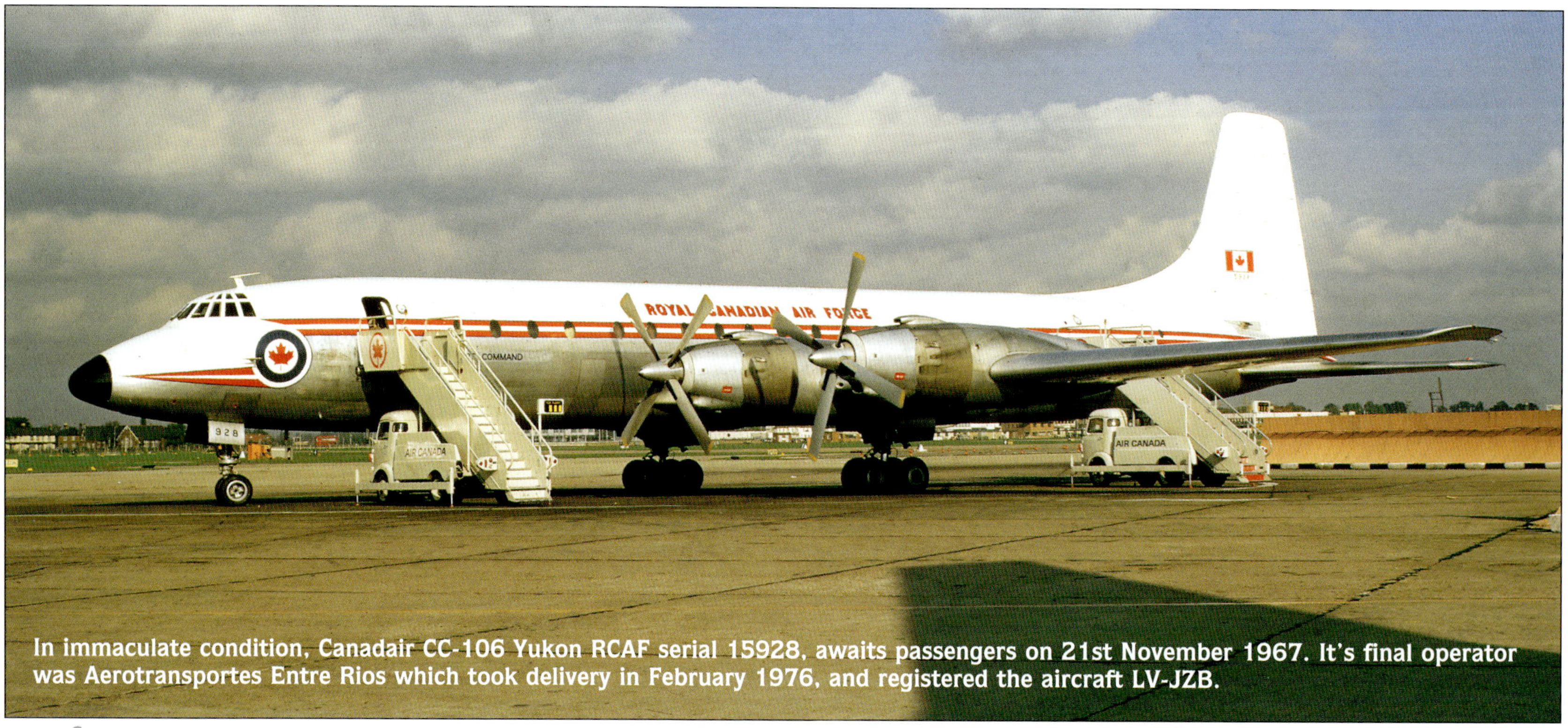

In immaculate condition, Canadair CC-106 Yukon RCAF serial 15928, awaits passengers on 21st November 1967. It's final operator was Aerotransportes Entre Rios which took delivery in February 1976, and registered the aircraft LV-JZB.

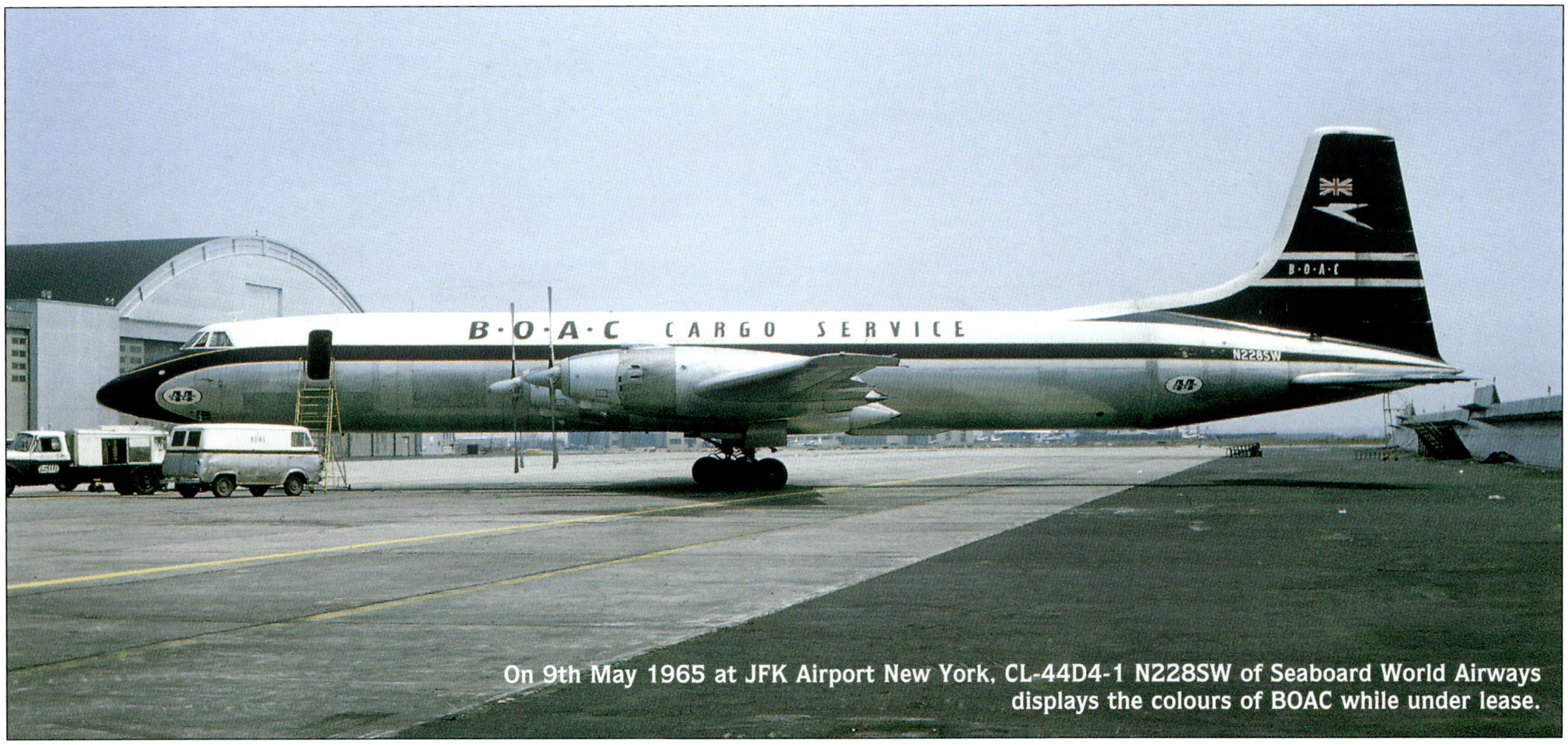

On 9th May 1965 at JFK Airport New York, CL-44D4-1 N228SW of Seaboard World Airways displays the colours of BOAC while under lease.

fuselage, before and aft of the wing, for cargo loading and could carry 134 passengers and a crew of nine. The prototype's maiden flight was on 15th November 1959 and the last of this derivative was delivered in 1961. Twelve of these aircraft were supplied to RCAF.

A similar civilian derivative also built by Canadair was the CL-44D-4, also designed for freight carrying and with the distinctive feature of a swing tail (hinged at one side), to accommodate the loading of long and large freight objects.

The large rear side door was omitted in this version. The swing-tail was operated hydraulically by two actuators in the dorsal fin of the fuselage. Eight locks fixed the tail in the closed position and an inflatable seal around the joint kept the cabin pressure fixed, no matter what the outside pressure was. It also kept out the rain. The flying controls were arranged so

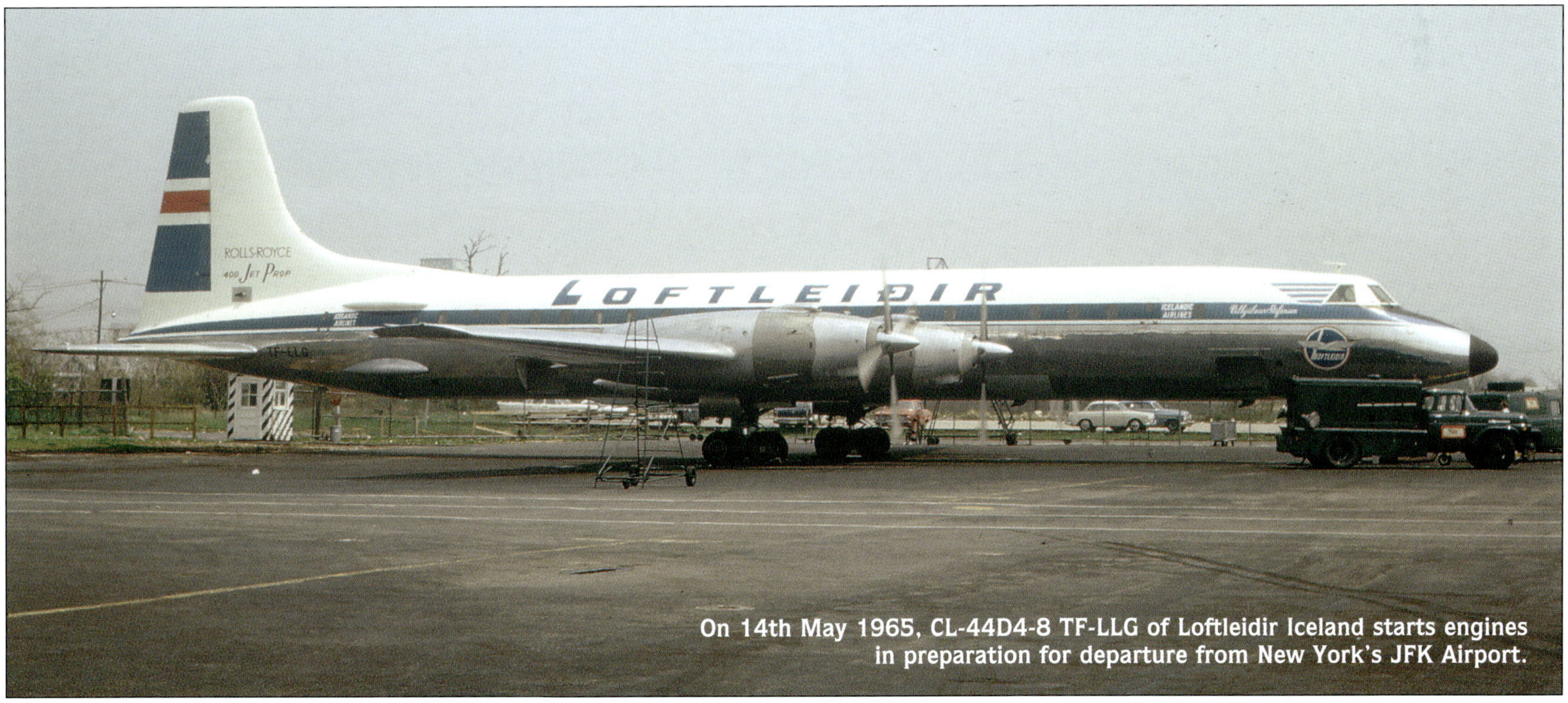

On 14th May 1965, CL-44D4-8 TF-LLG of Loftleidir Iceland starts engines in preparation for departure from New York's JFK Airport.

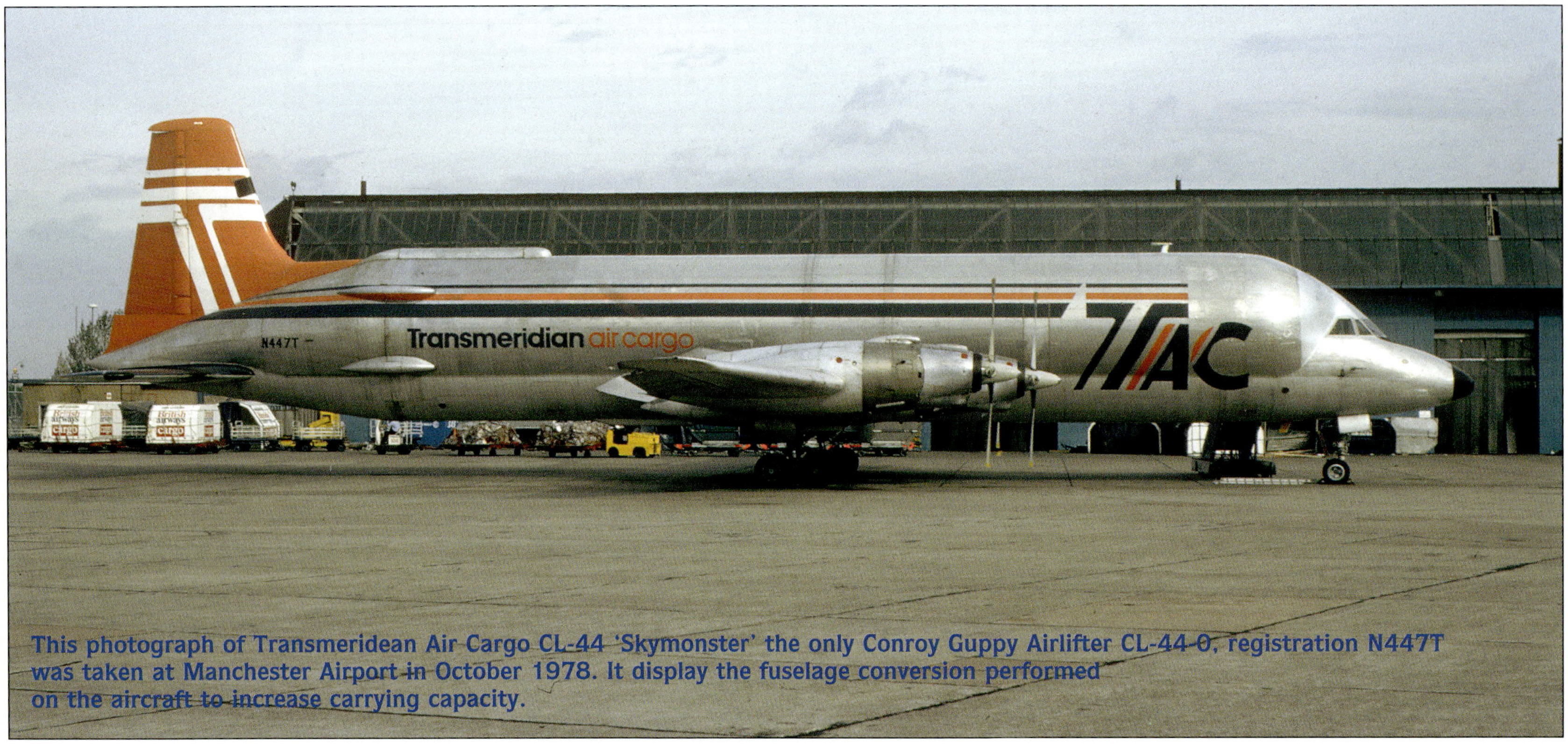

This photograph of Transmeridean Air Cargo CL-44 'Skymonster' the only Conroy Guppy Airlifter CL-44-0, registration N447T was taken at Manchester Airport in October 1978. It display the fuselage conversion performed on the aircraft to increase carrying capacity.

that connection between the flight deck and the tail surfaces was not affected by movement of the tail.

The maiden flight of this aircraft was on 16th November 1960. A total of seven entered service with Seaboard World Airlines, followed by twelve for the Flying Tiger Line and four

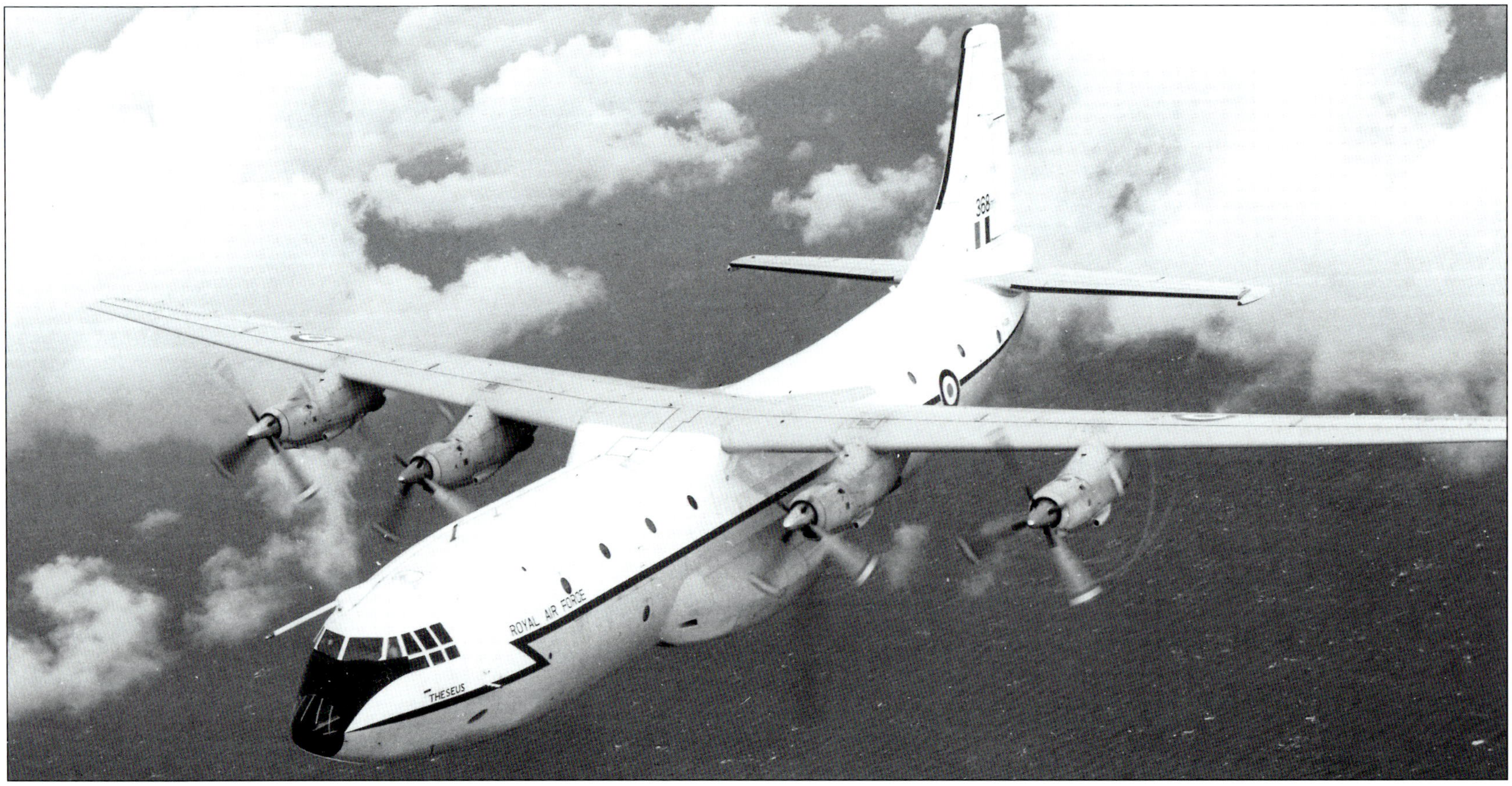

A superb shot of RAF Belfast C.1 XR 368 'Theseus' of the Royal Air Force, displaying the wing and tail assembly design borrowed from the Bristol Britannia. It was sold to HeavyLift Cargo Airlines as G-BEPS.

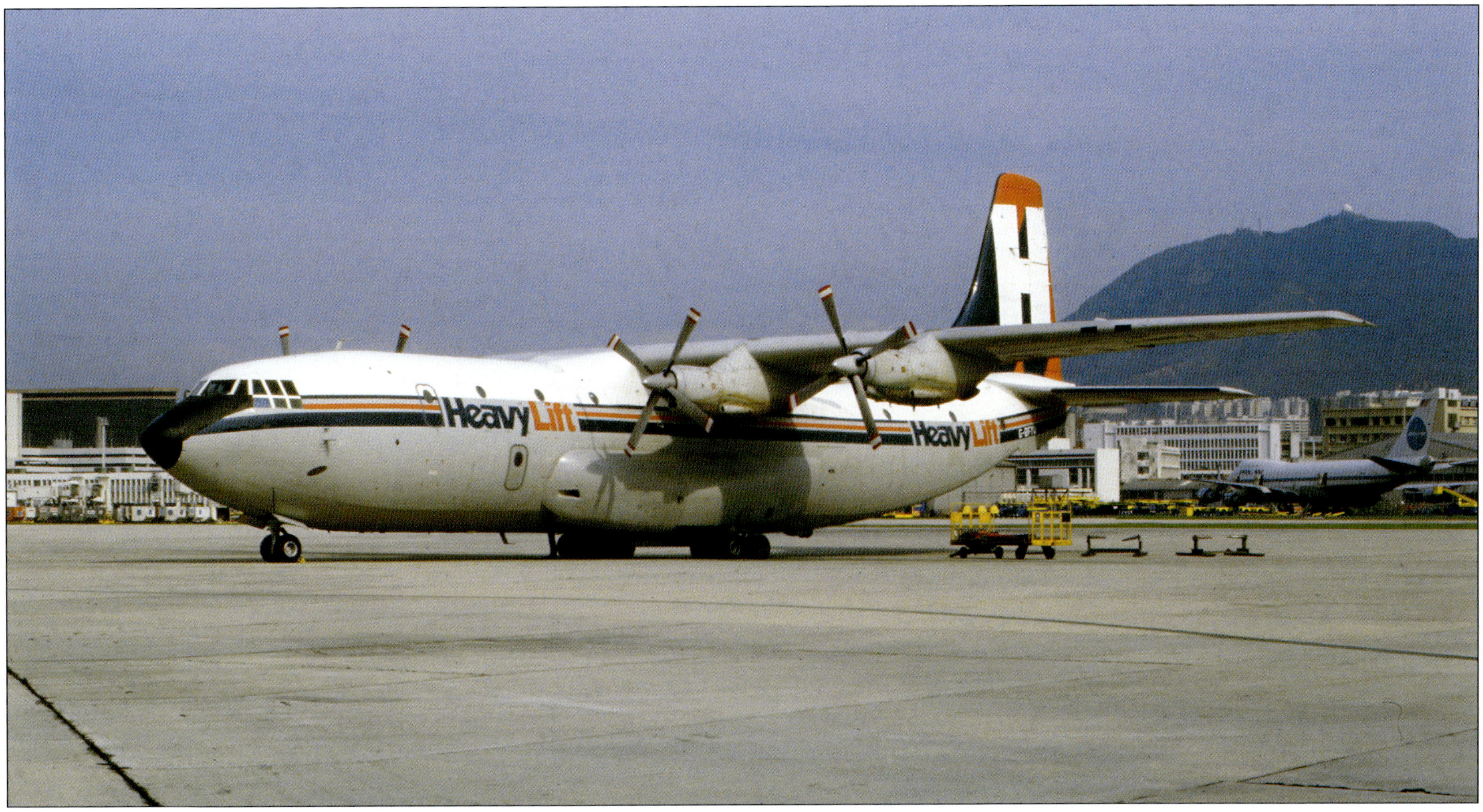

At Kai Tak Airport, Hong Kong in June 1984, ex-RAF Belfast C.1 registered G-BFYU, sports the colours of HeavyLift, the company who were responsible for civil registration of the type and the only other long term operator.

for Slick Airways, production continuing into 1964.

Another variant of this aircraft, the CL-44J, had the swing tail deleted and the fuselage lengthened to 151ft 10in, (46.27m) providing accommodation for 189 passengers. Four of these aircraft were sold to the Icelandic airline Loftleidir.

Yet another variant was the CL-44-0, with effectively a tube added to the top of the usual CL-44 fuselage so that extra large cargo loads could be carried. This aircraft was originally developed to enable it to carry Rolls-Royce RB211 engines. In total 39 CL-44s were built in all the variants and continued to have useful roles well into the 1980s.

THE SHORT BELFAST

In 1954 the Bristol Aeroplane Company became a shareholder in Short Brothers and Harland Ltd, which enabled a second production line for Britannias to be set up. Shorts assumed responsibility for the large cargo door and the heavy duty metal floor required by Transport Command for the 252/253 Britannia variants.

Soon both Shorts and Bristol began considering building a new, larger freighter based on the Britannia wings and engines, but with a high wing and either nose or tail loading. The prototype became known as the Belfast.

Detailed design caused various changes. The standard Britannia wing was split into two halves, each bolted to a centre section built into the top of the fuselage. The fuselage structure, 17ft 7in (5.36m) in diameter, was similar in detail to the Britannias. The Belfast's control systems were based on those in the Britannia and were identical in many places.

The first Belfast (initially registered as G-ASKE, XR362) had its maiden flight on 5th January 1964. Ten of these aircraft were ordered for the RAF, the last to be built, XR371, being delivered to No.53 Squadron on 3rd July 1957. But the last to be delivered was XR364, on 5th November 1971, after undergoing autoland trials at Bedford.

Belfasts were the largest aircraft ever to enter RAF service up to that point, able to carry loads of up to 77,000lb (34.926kg) and volume 11,000 cu. ft. (312cu.m). They were also the largest aircraft in the world to be equipped with a fully operational automatic landing system. They served with the RAF until No.53 Squadron was disbanded on 14th September 1976.

BIBLIOGRAPHY

BOOKS

Barnes, C H, Bristol Aircraft since 1910, (Putnam 1994)

Berry, David, Tales from the Crewroom, (Osprey 1990)

Berry, David, The Whispering Giant In Uniform, (Keyham Books 1996)

Hooker, Sir Stanley, Not much of an engineer, (Airlife 1991)

Jackson, A S, Both Feet In The Air, (T.Dalton 1977)

Littlefield, David, A History of the Bristol Britannia, (Halsgrove Press 1992)

Lo Bao, Phil (Ed.) Airlines & Airliners, Bristol Britannia (Aviation Data Centre 1996)

Pegg, Bill, Sent Flying, (Macdonald 1959)

Russell, Sir Archibald, A Span of Wings, (Airlife 1992)

ARTICLES

Anon, The free turbine, Bristol Quarterly, Autumn, 53

Anon, Britannia, Long Range Airliner, BAC, (9/54)

Anon, The Britannia at Idris, Bristol Quarterly, Winter 54

Anon, Tank testing, Bristol Quarterly, Spring 55

Anon, Britannia in Africa, Bristol Quarterly, Summer 55

Anon, Britannia Production in Belfast, Bristol Quarterly, Spring 56

Anon, Britannia Economics on Shorthauls, Bristol Quarterly, Summer 56

Anon, Operation Clockwork, Bristol Quarterly, Autumn 56

Anon, Britannias in Service, Bristol Quarterly, Spring 57, Summer 58

Anon, Proteus de-icing development, BAC, January 58

Anon, Proteus progress, Flight, (11/7/58)

Anon, The accident to G-AOVD, Flight, (1/7/60)

Anon, Eagle's Britannia conversion, Flight International (9/7/64)

Anon, The Redcoats Are Coming, Propliner, January 79

Anon, Record breaking Britannias (with El Al), Propliner, Spring 81

Anon, The last flight of G-BRAC, Propliner, December 81

Anon, Afrek grounded, Propliner, Autumn 83

Anon, Return to Filton (of XX367), Propliner, Autumn 83

Anon, Trend setting Britannias, Propliner, Autumn 86

Anon, Independent Britannias, Propliner, Autumn 87

Anon, Central and South American Britannias, Propliner, Autumn 88

Carvell, Roger, Disaster at Downend, Propliner, Summer 95

de Bruyn, Tony, Return of the Whispering Giant, Propliner, Autumn 93

Hargreaves, Roger, Britannia cargo background, Air Britain (8/77)

Houston, Captain W B, Britannia prelude, Flight (1/2/57)

Lee, Captain Lincoln, Britannia Anniversary, Flight (31/1/58)

Masefield, Peter G, The Britannia story, The Aeroplane (1/2/57)

Merton Jones, Tony, The Dragon Bites Back, Propliner, September 80

Caledonian's Pride of Britannias, Propliner 84

A brace of Britannias, Propliner, Spring 89

Transglobe's busy Britannias, Propliner, Autumn 89

European charter Britannias, Propliner, Spring 90

Supertramp Britannias, Propliner, Autumn 90

Regal Britannias, Propliner, Spring 91

Sunshine seekers, Propliner, Autumn 91

Bamberg's beautiful Britannias, Propliner, Spring 92

Thistle-tailed Britannias, Propliner, Autumn 92

Woolsington's Whispering Giants, Propliner, Spring 93

Power, Eamon, The Irish Britannias, Air-Britain Digest, February 78

Bristol's Whispering Giant, Propliner, Autumn 85

The Britannia in BOAC service, Propliner, Spring 86

Power, Eamon & Merton Jones, Tony,

Revolutionary Britannias, Propliner, Spring 88

Ramsden, J M, Vancouver-return by CPAL Britannia, Flight, (7/3/58)

6000 miles in an El Al Britannia, Flight, (3/1/58)

Rendall, Captain A S M, Proving the Britannia, Flight , (30/3/56)

Taylor, H A, Britannia to the Far East, The Aeroplane,

(26/7/57)

LIST OF ILLUSTRATIONS

GLOSSARY & ABBREVIATIONS

A. & A.E.E. — Aeroplane & Armament Experimental Establishment, Boscombe Down, 11 kms north of Salisbury, Wiltshire, England.

Airspeed Ambassador — High-wing medium range airliner with three fins, powered by two Bristol Centaurus piston engines driving 16 ft / 4.87m de Havilland propellers. Maiden flight by George Errington 10th July 1947 from Christchurch Airport near Bournemouth, Hampshire, England.

Aviation Traders (Engineering) Ltd. — Design and manufacturer of aircraft, aircraft ground equipment and aircraft maintenance at Southend and Stansted.

Argonaut — The class name given by B.O.A.C. to its 22 Canadair C-4 airliners, powered by four Merlin engines. Entered service on the 25th February 1949.

Ballykelly Airfield — Close to Lough Folye, three miles west of Limavady, Londonderry, Northern Ireland.

B.E.A. — British European Airways.

B.O.A.C. — British Overseas Airways Corporation.

Britannia Aircraft Preservation Trust — The Trust's function is to assist with the preservation and restoration of Britannias in the UK. Their aircraft are based at RAF Kemble, Cirencester.

C.P.A. — Canadian Pacific Airlines.

Changi Airfield — On Singapore's east coast, it was expanded onto reclaimed land and when completed in the early 1980's replaced Paya Lebar as the new Singapore International Airport.

Christmas Island — Discovered by Captain Cook in 1777, a large atoll in the Line Islands group just above the equator in the middle of the Pacific Ocean, now called Kiritimati.

de Havilland Comet — Four-engined jetliner. The first flight by John Cunningham was from Hatfield on 25th September 1949.

Dhahran Airbase — Airport also known as Az Zahran on the Persian Gulf, Saudi Arabia.

El Adem — Airfield near the Mediterranean coast 330kms east of Benghazi, Libya.

Gibb. Walter Frame, — Wing Commander DSO, DFC. Born March 26th 1919. Joined Bristol Aeroplane Co. in 1937 as an apprentice. During the war from 1940-1946 he was commanding Officer of No.239 Squadron. After the war he returned to Bristol and as a test pilot flew the Brabazon and later the Britannia. He was Assistant Chief Test Pilot from 1953-56. During 1953 flying a Bristol Olympus powered Canberra, he reached a world record height of 63,668ft and two years later a height of 65,890ft. He became Chief Test Pilot from 1957-60. He moved on to become the Sales and Service Manager 1960-66 and then Product Support Manager.

Filton Airfield — Airfield eight kilometres north of central Bristol. The headquarters and main production facilities of the Bristol Aeroplane Co.

Ghayaquil — Airport near the Pacific coast 250 kms south west of Quito, Ecuador.

Hooker, Sir Stanley G. OBE — Chief Engineer for Rolls Royce at their Gas-turbine Development Division at Barnoldswick Lancashire 1938-48. He moved to Bristol and became the Chief Engineer of the Engine Division of the Bristol Aeroplane Co. Ltd. and finally the Technical Director (Aero) of the renamed Bristol Siddeley Engines Ltd.

Hurn Airfield — Bournemouth where Vickers-Armstrongs had an aircraft production plant.

Idris Airfield — Previously called Castel Benito Airfield, Tripoli, Libya.

Izmir — The third largest city in Turkey formerly called Smyra, founded by the Greeks around 1000BC. A port situated on an inlet of the Aegean Sea in western Turkey 330 kms from Istanbul..

Lyneham — R.A.F. airfield seventeen kilometres south west of Swindon, England.

Orion — A twin-spool turbo-prop engine built by Bristol Aero-Engines as successor to the Proteus. First run in 1955. Fitted to the port outer nacelle on the Britannia prototype G-ALBO in August 1957. Cancelled after withdrawal of Government support in 1958.

Paramaribo — The capital of Surinam on the North Atlantic coast of South America.

Pegg, Arthur John OBE. — Born on 5th June 1906. In 1921 he joined the R.A.F. and learnt to fly in 1925. He became an instructor with No 43 Squadron and in 1930 moved to the A.& A.E.E. at Martlesham Heath as a test pilot. In 1935 he joined the Bristol Aeroplane Co. as Assistant Chief Test Pilot, becoming the Chief Test Pilot from 1947-56 after which he became the General Service Manager.

Rolls-Royce Heritage Trust — A voluntary organisation formed in 1981 to preserve the heritage of the parent company, together with the other companies which now form Rolls-Royce plc.

S.B.A.C. — Society of British Aircraft Constructors Ltd.

Tyne engine — A Rolls-Royce turbo-prop engine which powered the Canadair CL-44, Vickers Vanguard and Breguet Atlantic etc.

Scottish Aviation Ltd. — Aircraft manufacturer and aeronautical engineers for repair, overhaul and modifications, based at Prestwick Airport, Ayrshire, Scotland.

Søndre Strømfjord — Airfield on the west coast of Greenland just above the arctic circle at the head of the Søndre Strømfjord, originally called the Søndrestrom Air Base (U.S. Airbase Blue West 8 founded in October 1941). In September 1992 the U.S. base was closed and control came under the Greenland Home Rule who renamed it Kangerlussuaq, which means the big fjord.

Tarbes — Airport in southern France, fifteen kilometres north of the pilgrimage site at Lourdes.

Tellair — This was a Swiss-based airline which lasted from March to October 1969.

Wymeswold — Airfield seven kilometres north east of Loughborough, Leicestershire.

INDEX